T0137004

Communications
in Computer and Information Science

895

Commenced Publication in 2007
Founding and Former Series Editors:
Phoebe Chen, Alfredo Cuzzocrea, Xiaoyong Du, Orhun Kara, Ting Liu,
Dominik Ślęzak, and Xiaokang Yang

More information about this series at http://www.springer.com/series/7899

Miguel Botto-Tobar · Guillermo Pizarro
Miguel Zúñiga-Prieto · Mayra D'Armas
Miguel Zúñiga Sánchez (Eds.)

Technology Trends

4th International Conference, CITT 2018
Babahoyo, Ecuador, August 29–31, 2018
Revised Selected Papers

 Springer

Editors
Miguel Botto-Tobar (iD)
Eindhoven University of Technology
Eindhoven, Noord-Brabant, The Netherlands

Guillermo Pizarro (iD)
Computer Science
Politecnica Salesiana University
Cuenca, Ecuador

Miguel Zúñiga-Prieto (iD)
Facultad de Ingenieria
University of Cuenca
Cuenca, Ecuador

Mayra D'Armas
Universidad Estatal de Milagro
San Francisco de Milagro, Ecuador

Miguel Zúñiga Sánchez
Universidad Técnica de Babahoyo
Babahoyo, Ecuador

ISSN 1865-0929   ISSN 1865-0937   (electronic)
Communications in Computer and Information Science
ISBN 978-3-030-05531-8   ISBN 978-3-030-05532-5   (eBook)
https://doi.org/10.1007/978-3-030-05532-5

Library of Congress Control Number: 2018963822

This Springer imprint is published by the registered company Springer Nature Switzerland AG
The registered company address is: Gewerbestrasse 11, 6330 Cham, Switzerland

Preface

The 4th International Conference on Technology Trends (CITT 2018) was held on the main campus of Universidad Técnica de Babahoyo (UTB), Ecuador, during August 29–31, 2018, and it was jointly organized and supported by three recognized Ecuadorian institutions: Universidad Técnica de Babahoyo, Universidad Politécnica Salesiana, and Universidad de Cuenca. The CITT series of conferences aim to become the premier venue for research on technology trends. It brings together top researchers and practitioners working in different domains in the field of computer science and information systems to exchange their expertise and to discuss the perspectives of development and collaboration in these areas. The purpose of CITT is to facilitate technology and knowledge exchange among researchers, academics, and industry so as to benefit from the advances in computing technologies. The content of this volume is related to the following subjects:

- Communications
  - Internet of Things
  - Networks
  - Cloud Computing
- Security and Privacy
- Computer and Software Engineering
  - Human–Computer Interaction
  - Software Engineering
  - Information Systems
- Computational Intelligence
  - Data Engineering and Data Science
  - Artificial Intelligence
  - Applied Computing
- e-Government and e-Participation

CITT 2018 received 204 submissions in English from 269 authors coming from 17 different countries. All these papers were peer-reviewed by the CITT 2018 Program Committee consisting of 214 high-quality researchers coming from 24 different countries. To assure a thorough review process, we assigned at least three reviewers to each paper. Based on the results of the peer reviews, 53 full papers were accepted, resulting in a 26% acceptance rate, which was within our goal of less than 40%.

We would like to express our sincere gratitude to the invited speakers for their inspirational talks, to the authors for submitting their works to this conference, and the reviewers for sharing their experience during the selection process.

August 2018   Miguel Botto-Tobar
                                                               Guillermo Pizarro
                                                               Miguel Zúñiga-Prieto
                                                               Mayra D'Armas
                                                               Miguel Zúñiga Sánchez

Organization

Honorary Committee

Rafael Falconí Montalván	Universidad Técnica de Babahoyo, Ecuador
Adelita Pinto Yerovi	Universidad Técnica de Babahoyo, Ecuador
José Sandoya Villafuerte	Universidad Técnica de Babahoyo, Ecuador
Javier Herrán	Universidad Politécnica Salesiana, Ecuador
Juan Pablo Salgado Guerrero	Universidad Politécnica Salesiana, Ecuador
Andrés Bayolo	Universidad Politécnica Salesiana, Ecuador
Javier Ortíz	Universidad Politécnica Salesiana, Ecuador
Pablo Fernando Vanegas Peralta	Universidad de Cuenca, Ecuador
Jorge Mauricio Espinoza Mejía	Universidad de Cuenca, Ecuador
Lizandro Damian Solano Quinde	Universidad de Cuenca, Ecuador
Lorena Catalina Sigüenza Guzmán	Universidad de Cuenca, Ecuador
Luis Otto Parra González	Universidad de Cuenca, Ecuador

Organizing Committee

General Chair

Miguel Botto Tobar	Eindhoven University of Technology, The Netherlands

General Co-chairs

Guillermo Pizarro Vásquez	Universidad Politécnica Salesiana, Ecuador
Miguel Zúñiga Prieto	Universidad de Cuenca, Ecuador
Mayra D'Armas	Universidad Estatal de Milagro, Ecuador
Miguel Zúñiga Sánchez	Universidad Técnica de Babahoyo, Ecuador

Program Chairs

Communications

Miguel Zúñiga Sánchez	Universidad Técnica de Babahoyo, Ecuador
Willian Zamora Mero	Universidad Laica Eloy Alfaro de Manabí, Ecuador

Security and Privacy

Luis Urquiza-Aguiar	Escuela Superior Politécnica Nacional, Ecuador
Joffre León Acurio	Universidad Técnica de Babahoyo, Ecuador

Computer and Software Engineering

Miguel Botto-Tobar	Eindhoven University of Technology, The Netherlands
Miguel Zúñiga Prieto	Universidad de Cuenca, Ecuador
Angel Cuenca Ortega	Universitat Politècnica de València, Spain

Computational Intelligence

Gustavo Andrade Miranda	Universidad de Guayaquil, Ecuador
Guillermo Pizarro Vásquez	Universidad Politécnica Salesiana, Ecuador
Lorenzo J. Cevallos-Torres	Universidad de Guayaquil, Ecuador

e-Government and e-Participation

Alex Santamaría Philco	Universidad Laica Eloy Alfaro de Manabí, Ecuador

Tutorial's Chair

Rodrigo Saraguro Bravo	Escuela Superior Politécnica del Litoral (ESPOL), Ecuador

Program Committee

Abdón Carrera Rivera	University of Melbourne, Australia
Adrián Cevallos Navarrete	Griffith University, Australia
Alba Morales Tirado	University of Greenwich, UK
Alejandro Ramos Nolazco	Instituto Tecnológico y de Estudios Superiores Monterrey, Mexico
Alex Cazañas Gordon	Queensland University of Technology, Australia
Alex Santamaría Philco	Universitat Politècnica de València, Spain/Universidad Laica Eloy Alfaro de Manabí, Ecuador
Alexandra Elizabeth Bermeo Arpi	Universidad de Cuenca, Ecuador
Alexandra Velasco Arévalo	Universität Stuttgart, Germany
Alfonso Guijarro Rodríguez	Universidad de Guayaquil, Ecuador
Alfredo Núñez	New York University, USA
Allan Avendaño Sudario	Università degli Studi di Roma La Sapienza, Italy
Almílcar Puris Cáceres	Universidad Técnica Estatal de Quevedo, Ecuador
Ana Chacón Luna	Universidad Estatal de Milagro, Ecuador
Ana Guerrero Alemán	University of Adelaide, Australia
Ana Núñez Ávila	Universitat Politècnica de València, Spain
Ana Santos Delgado	Universidade Federal de Santa Catarina, Brazil
Andrea Mory Alvarado	Universidad Católica de Cuenca, Ecuador
Andrés Avilés Noles	Universidad Estatal de Milagro, Ecuador
Andrés Barnuevo Loaiza	Universidad de Santiago de Chile, Chile
Andrés Calle Bustos	Universitat Politècnica de València, Spain
Andrés Chango Macas	Universidad Politécnica de Madrid, Spain

Andrés Cueva Costales	University of Melbourne, Australia
Andrés Jadan Montero	Universidad de Buenos Aires, Argentina
Andrés Molina Ortega	Universidad de Chile, Chile
Andrés Parra Sánchez	University of Melbourne, Australia
Andrés Robles Durazno	Edinburgh Napier University, UK
Andrés Tello Guerrero	Universidad de Cuenca, Ecuador
Andrés Vargas González	Syracuse University, USA
Andrés Vazquez Rodas	Universidad de Cuenca, Ecuador
Angel Cuenca Ortega	Universitat Politècnica de València, Spain
Ángel Plaza Vargas	Universidad de Guayaquil, Ecuador
Angel Vazquez Pazmiño	Université Catholique de Louvain, Belgium
Ángela Díaz Cadena	Universitat de València, Spain
Angelo Vera Rivera	George Mason University, USA
Antonio Villavicencio Garzón	Universitat Politècnica de Catalunya, Spain
Audrey Romero Pelaez	Universidad Politécnica de Madrid, Spain
Bolívar Chiriboga Ramón	University of Melbourne, Australia
Byron Acuna Acurio	Flinders University, Australia
Carla Melaños Salazar	Universidad Politécnica de Madrid, Spain
Carlos Barriga Abril	University of Nottingham, UK
Carlos Valarezo Loiza	Manchester University, UK
César Ayabaca Sarria	Escuela Politécnica Nacional (EPN), Ecuador
Cesar Mayorga Abril	Universidad Técnica de Ambato, Ecuador
Christian Báez Jácome	Wageningen University and Research, The Netherlands
Cintya Aguirre Brito	University of Portsmouth, UK
Cristhy Jiménez Granizo	Universidad Nacional de Chimborazo, Ecuador/Pontificia Universidad Católica de Valparaíso, Chile
Cristian Montero Mariño	University of Melbourne, Australia
Cristian Zambrano Vega	Universidad Técnica Estatal de Quevedo, Ecuador/Universidad de Málaga, Spain
Daniel Armijos Conde	Queensland University of Technology, Australia
Daniel Magües Martínez	Universidad Autónoma de Madrid, Spain
Daniel Silva Palacios	Universitat Politècnica de València, Spain
Danilo Jaramillo Hurtado	Universidad Politécnica de Madrid, Spain
David Benavides Cuevas	Universidad de Sevilla, Spain
David Rivera Espín	University of Melbourne, Australia
Diana Morillo Fueltala	Brunel University London, UK
Diego Vallejo Huanga	Universitat Politècnica de València, Spain
Doris Suquilanda	Universidad de Cuenca, Ecuador
Edwin Guamán Quinche	Universidad del País Vasco, Spain
Efrén Reinoso Mendoza	Universitat Politècnica de València, Spain
Elena Jerves	Universidad de Cuenca, Ecuador
Elsa Vera Burgos	Universitat Politècnica de València, Spain
Eric Moyano Luna	University of Southampton, UK
Erick Cuenca Pauta	Université de Montpellier, France

Ernesto Serrano Guevara	Université de Neuchâtel, Switzerland
Estefania Yánez Cardoso	University of Southampton, UK
Esther Parra Mora	University of Queensland, Australia
Fabián Astudillo Salinas	Universidad de Cuenca, Ecuador
Fabián Corral Carrera	Universidad Carlos III de Madrid, Spain
Felipe Ebert	Universidade Federal de Pernambuco (UFPE), Brazil
Fernando Borja Moretta	University of Edinburgh, UK
Franklin Parrales Bravo	Universidad Complutense de Madrid, Spain
Freddy Tejada Escobar	Universidad Tecnológica Ecotec, Ecuador/Universidad Técnica Federico Santa María, Chile
Gabriel López Fonseca	Sheffield Hallam University, UK
Gema Rodriguez-Perez	LibreSoft/Universidad Rey Juan Carlos, Spain
Georges Flament Jordán	University of York, UK
Germania Rodríguez Morales	Universidad Politécnica de Madrid, Spain
Ginger Saltos Bernal	University of Portsmouth, UK
Gissela Uribe Nogales	Australian National University, Australia
Glenda Vera Mora	Universidad Técnica de Babahoyo, Ecuador
Guilherme Avelino	Universidade Federal do Piauí (UFP), Brazil
Guillermo Pizarro Vásquez	Universidad Politécnica Salesiana, Ecuador
Gustavo Andrade Miranda	Universidad Politécnica de Madrid, Spain
Héctor Dulcey Pérez	Swinburne University of Technology, Australia
Henry Morocho Minchala	Moscow Automobile And Road Construction State Technical University (Madi), Rusia
Holger Ortega Martínez	University College London, UK
Irene Cedillo Orellana	Universitat Politècnica de València, Spain/Universitat Politècnica de València, Spain
Israel Pineda Arias	Chonbuk National University, South Korea
Iván Valarezo Lozano	University of Melbourne, Australia
Jacqueline Mejia Luna	Universidad de Granada, Spain
Jaime Jarrin Valencia	Universidad Politécnica de Madrid, Spain
Jaime Meza	Universiteit Van Fribourg, Switzerland
Janio Jadan Guerrero	Universidad Nacional de Costa Rica, Costa Rica
Janneth Chicaiza Espinosa	Universidad Politécnica de Madrid, Spain
Jefferson Ribadeneira Ramírez	Escuela Superior Politécnica de Chimborazo, Ecuador
Jeffrey Naranjo Cedeño	Universidad de Valencia, Spain
Jesennia Cárdenas Cobo	Universidad Estatal de Milagro, Ecuador
Jofre León Acurio	Universidad Técnica de Babahoyo, Ecuador
Jorge Cárdenas Monar	Australian National University, Australia
Jorge Charco Aguirre	Universitat Politècnica de València, Spain
Jorge Illescas Pena	Edinburgh Napier University, UK
Jorge Lascano	University of Utah, USA
Jorge Luis Bermeo Conto	Universidad de Cuenca, Ecuador
Jorge Maldonado Mahauad	Universidad Nacional de La Plata, Argentina
Jorge Quimí Espinosa	Universitat Politècnica de Catalunya, Spain

Jorge Rivadeneira Muñoz	University of Southampton, UK
Jorge Rodas Silva	Universidad Estatal de Milagro, Ecuador
José Carrera Villacres	Université de Neuchâtel, Switzerland
José Galindo	Inria, France
José Quevedo Guerrero	Universidad Politécnica de Madrid, Spain
Josue Flores de Valgas	Universitat Politécnica de València, Spain
Juan Balarezo Serrano	Monash University, Australia
Juan Barros Gavilanes	INP Toulouse, France
Juan Jiménez Lozano	Universidad de Palermo, Argentina
Juan Lasso Encalada	Universitat Politècnica de Catalunya, Spain
Juan Maestre Ávila	Iowa State University, USA
Juan Miguel Espinoza Soto	Universitat de València, Spain
Juan Pablo Carvallo	Universidad del Azuay, Ecuador
Juan Romero Arguello	University of Manchester, UK
Juan Zaldumbide Proaño	University of Melbourne, Australia
Juliana Cotto Pulecio	Universidad de Palermo, Argentina
Julio Albuja Sánchez	James Cook University, Australia
Julio Balarezo	Universidad Técnica de Ambato, Ecuador
Julio Barzola Monteses	Università degli Studi di Roma La Sapienza, Italy/Universidad de Guayaquil, Ecuador
Julio Proaño Orellana	Universidad de Castilla La Mancha, Spain
Karla Abad Sacoto	Universidad Autónoma de Barcelona, Spain
Leopoldo Pauta Ayabaca	Universidad Católica de Cuenca, Ecuador
Lohana Lema Moreta	Universidad de Especialidades Espíritu Santo, Ecuador
Lorena Guachi Guachi	Università della Calabria, Italy
Lorena Sigüenza Guzman	Universidad de Cuenca, Ecuador
Lorenzo Cevallos Torres	Universidad de Guayaquil, Ecuador
Lourdes Illescas Peña	Universidad de Cuenca, Ecuador
Lucia Rivadeneira Barreiro	Nanyang Technological University, Singapore
Luis Benavides	Universidad de Especialidades Espíritu Santo, Ecuador
Luis Carranco Medina	Kansas State University, USA
Luis Parra González	Universidad Politécnica de Madrid, Spain
Luis Pérez Iturralde	Universidad de Sevilla, Spain
Luis Torres Gallegos	Universitat Politècnica de València, Spain
Luis Urquiza Aguiar	Universitat Politècnica de Catalunya, Spain
Manuel Beltrán Prado	University of Queensland, Australia
Manuel Sucunuta España	Universidad Politécnica de Madrid, Spain
Marcelo Zambrano	Universitat Politècnica de València, Spain
Marcia Bayas Sampedro	Vinnitsa National University, Ukraine
Marco Falconi Noriega	Universidad de Sevilla, Spain
Marco Molina Bustamante	Universidad Politécnica de Madrid, Spain
Marco Santórum Gaibor	Escuela Politécnica Nacional, Ecuador/Université Catholique de Louvain, Belgium
Maria Dueñas Romero	RMIT University, Australia
María Escalante Guevara	University of Michigan, USA
María Granda Juca	Universitat Politècnica de València, Spain

María Miranda Garcés	University of Leeds, UK
María Molina Miranda	Universidad Politécnica de Madrid, Spain
María Montoya Freire	Aalto University, Finland
María Ormaza Castro	University of Southampton, UK
Mariela Barzallo León	University of Edinburgh, UK
Mario González	Universidad de las Américas, Ecuador
Mariuxi Vinueza Morales	Universidad Estatal de Milagro, Ecuador
Marlon Navia Mendoza	Universitat Politècnica de València, Spain/Escuela Superior Politécnica Agropecuaria de Manabí, Ecuador
Martha Paredes Paredes	Universidad Carlos III de Madrid, Spain
Mauricio Espinoza	Universidad de Cuenca, Ecuador
Mauricio Verano Merino	Eindhoven University of Technology, The Netherlands
Maykel Leiva Vázquez	Universidad de Guayaquil, Ecuador
Miguel Arcos Argudo	Universidad Politécnica de Madrid, Spain
Miguel Botto Tobar	Eindhoven University of Technology, The Netherlands
Miguel Zúñiga Prieto	Universitat Politècnica de València, Spain/Universidad de Cuenca, Ecuador
Mónica Baquerizo Anastacio	Universidad Complutense de Madrid, Spain
Mónica Villavicencio Cabezas	Université du Quebec À Montréal, Canada
Nayeth Solórzano Alcívar	Escuela Superior Politécnica del Litoral (ESPOL), Ecuador/Griffith University, Autralia
Omar S. Gómez	Escuela Superior Politécnica del Chimborazo (ESPOCH), Ecuador
Orlando Erazo Moreta	Universidad de Chile, Chile/Universidad Técnica Estatal de Quevedo, Ecuador
Pablo León Paliz	Université de Neuchâtel, Switzerland
Pablo Ordoñez Ordoñez	Universidad Politécnica de Madrid, Spain
Pablo Palacios Jativa	Universidad de Chile, Chile
Pablo Saá Portilla	University of Melbourne, Australia
Patricia Ludeña González	Politecnico di Milano, Italy
Patricia Quiroz Palma	Universidad Laica Eloy Alfaro de Manabí, Ecuador
Patricio Reinoso Mendoza	Universidad Politecnica Salesiana, Ecuador
Paulina Morillo Alcívar	Universitat Politècnica de València, Spain
Paulo Guerra Figuereido	University of Illinois at Chicago, USA
Paulo Guerra Terán	Universidad de las Américas, Ecuador
Pavel Novoa Hernández	Universidad Técnica Estatal de Quevedo, Ecuador
Rafael Campuzano Ayala	Grenoble Institute of Technology, France
Rafael Jiménez	Escuela Politécnica del Litoral (ESPOL), Ecuador
Ramiro Santacruz Ochoa	Universidad Nacional de La Plata, Argentina
Richard Ramírez-Anormaliza	Universidad Estatal de Milagro, Ecuador/Universitat Politècnica de Catalunya, Spain
Roberto Larrea Luzuriaga	Universitat Politècnica de València, Spain
Roberto Sánchez Albán	Université de Lausanne, Switzerland

Rodolfo Bojorque Chasi — Universidad Politécnica de Madrid, Spain
Rodrigo Cueva Rueda — Universitat Politècnica de Catalunya, Spain
Rodrigo Saraguro Bravo — Escuela Superior Politécnica del Litoral (ESPOL), Ecuador
Rodrigo Tufiño Cárdenas — Universidad Politécnica Salesiana, Ecuador/Universidad Politécnica de Madrid, Spain
Ronald Barriga Díaz — Universidad de Guayaquil, Ecuador
Rubén Rumipamba-Zambrano — Universitat Politècnica de Catalunya, Spain
Samanta Cueva Carrión — Universidad Politécnica de Madrid, Spain
Sergio Montes León — Universidad de las Fuerzas Armadas (ESPE), Ecuador
Shirley Coque Villegas — Universidad Politécnica Salesiana, Ecuador
Tania Palacios Crespo — University College London, UK
Tony Flores Pulgar — Université de Lyon, France
Vanessa Echeverría Barzola — Université Catholique de Louvain, Belgium
Vanessa Jurado Vite — Universidad Politécnica Salesiana, Ecuador
Verónica Mendoza Moran — Universidad Politécnica de Madrid, Spain
Verónica Yépez Reyes — South Danish University, Denmark
Victor Hugo Rea Sánchez — Universidad Estatal de Milagro, Ecuador
Vladimir Robles Bykbaev — Universitat Politècnica de València, Spain/Universidad Politécnica Salesiana, Ecuador
Voltaire Bazurto Blacio — University of Victoria, Canada
Washington Velásquez Vargas — Universidad Politécnica de Madrid, Spain
Wayner Bustamante Granda — Universidad de Palermo, Argentina
Wellington Cabrera Arévalo — University of Houston, USA
Wendy Yánez Pazmiño — University of Birmingham, UK
William Venegas Toro — Escuela Politécnica Nacional (EPN), Ecuador
Willian Zamora Mero — Universidad Laica Eloy Alfaro de Manabí, Ecuador
Xavier Merino Miño — Instituto Tecnológico y de Estudios Superiores Monterrey, Mexico
Yan Pacheco Mafla — Royal Institute of Technology, Sweden
Yessenia Cabrera Maldonado — Pontificia Universidad Católica de Chile, Chile
Yuliana Jiménez Gaona — Università di Bologna, Italy

Sponsoring Institutions

Universidad Técnica de Babahoyo
http://www.utb.edu.ec

Universidad Politécnica Salesiana
http://www.ups.edu.ec/

UNIVERSIDAD DE CUENCA
DEPARTAMENTO DE CIENCIAS
DE LA COMPUTACIÓN
FACULTAD DE INGENIERÍA

Universidad de Cuenca
https://www.ucuenca.edu.ec/

Vicerrectorado de Investigación y Postgrado de la Universidad Técnica de Babahoyo
http://vip.utb.edu.ec/

Secretaria de Educación Superior, Ciencia, Tecnología e Innovación
https://www.educacionsuperior.gob.ec/

Contents

Computer and Software Engineering

Computational Intelligence

e-Government and e-Participation

Communications

Coalition Game Theory in Cognitive Mobile Radio Networks

Pablo Palacios[1](✉) and Carlos Saavedra[2](✉)

[1] Departamento de Redes y Telecomunicaciones, Universidad De Las Américas,
Quito, Ecuador
pablo.palacios@udla.edu.ec
[2] Department of Electronics and Radio Engineering, Kyung Hee University,
Yongin 446-701, South Korea
carlossaavedra@khu.ac.kr

Abstract. In this work, the impact and performance of the Coalition Game Theory applied directly to the detection and decision stages of a Cognitive Radio (CR) system is evaluated. The performance of the Coalitional Game was analyzed in terms of the Probability of detection (P_d) and Probability of false alarm (P_{fa}) versus number of secondary users (SUs). In addition, the detection accuracy and simulation time versus SU were analyzed in a structured network adapted for WiFi and LTE technologies with cognitive parameters. The results were compared using simulation scenarios to obtain data using the theoretical Non-cooperative decision method and the theoretical Centralized decision method. The evaluated system outperformed the other methods in terms of P_d, P_{fa}, detection accuracy and simulation time.

Keywords: Cognitive mobile radio networks
Probability of detection (P_d) · Probability of false alarm (P_{fa})
Coalition game theory · Spectrum decision · Spectrum sensing

1 Introduction

The Cognitive Radio (CR) technology has attracted more interest in recent years because it provides efficient use of the electromagnetic spectrum [1], jumping between different frequencies and different wireless protocols, demonstrating the potential to meet the spectrum requirements for 5G [2]. In essence, is a radio that adapts its transmission parameters according to the characteristics of the environment in which it operates, detecting and exploiting the available holes in the spectrum. In the medium term, this is the most likely solution for high data rates and mobility that requires the use of higher frequencies. However, one of the most crucial challenges for the practical implementation of CR systems is to constantly identify the presence of primary users (PU) in a wide range of spectrum in a particular time and specific geographic location, in addition to checking that there is no interference between SU (without a license) and PU [3].

© Springer Nature Switzerland AG 2019
M. Botto-Tobar et al. (Eds.): CITT 2018, CCIS 895, pp. 3–15, 2019.
https://doi.org/10.1007/978-3-030-05532-5_1

A fundamental characteristic offered by CR is that it allows total spectrum management through a process called cognitive cycle, which consists of four steps: spectrum detection, spectrum decision, spectrum sharing and mobility [4]. Within the aforementioned cognitive process, studies and research are emphasized in the first two steps, the detection and decision of the spectrum and of licensed users. Therefore, several methods have been proposed, for this work we will focus attention on methods and decision algorithms specifically studied in Game Theory and applied to CR systems, such as Coalition formation through merge and split [5], Evolutionary game [6], Cournot game model [7], among others.

The Game Theory is established as an analytical mathematical tool. The challenges of wireless networks, of an autonomous and dynamic nature, require a decentralized and diverse understanding, as well as design tools to make them more efficient. Cooperative game theory, particularly coalition game theory, is emerging as an appropriate mechanism for flexible and efficient distribution.

The existing literature has studied the performance of Coalition Game in CR networks. This is based on the detection bits of the SUs that share their sensory decisions towards an SU called "head of the coalition" that combines the detection bits of each SU using some rule for the fusion of data. A similar approach is used in [8] using different decision-combination methods. These soft decisions improve performance compared to hard decisions, such as the non-cooperative games or the individual detection and decision of each [9].

The main contribution of this work is to analyze and evaluate the performance and efficiency of the Coalition Game decision method applied, adapted and configured to a mobile radio network with cognitive characteristics, specifically for LTE and WiFi technologies through modules created for Network Simulator 3 (NS-3.23) [10]. The performance of the Coalition Game decision method is analyzed under the next parameters: detection probability (P_d), false alarm probability (P_{fa}), detection accuracy and simulation time versus number of secondary users (SUs) using simulation scenarios with numerical values and compared with the theoretical non-cooperative decision method and the theoretical centralized decision method.

2   System Model

In this article, we evaluate the decision of the spectrum using the Coalition Game decision method in a mobile network implemented specifically for LTE and WiFi with cognitive characteristics, which are state-of-the-art technologies and also basic techniques and algorithms in heterogeneous networks [11–14]. We consider the scenario like a area covered by Cognitive Mobile Radio network composed of m independent source-destination pairs of PU's. The set of primary transmitters is represented as $P_t = (P_{1t}, \ldots P_{mt})$ while the set of corresponding receivers is represented as $P_r = (P_{1r}, \ldots P_{mr})$. We assume the coexistence of n secondary transmitters in set $S_t = (S_{1t}, \ldots S_{nt})$ and their corresponding receivers in set $S_r = (S_{1r}, \ldots S_{nr})$. Here, a "primary channel" refers to a licensed spectrum band currently being utilized by a PU. This scenario is shown in Fig. 1.

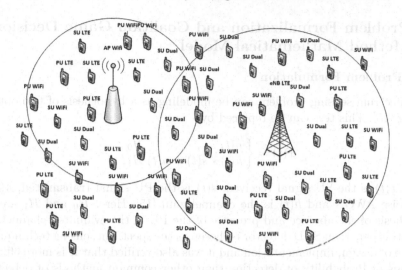

Fig. 1. Proposed system model. This is a network topology that illustrates the system model. It consists of PU (WiFi and LTE) and SU (WiFi, LTE and dual) users that share the same spectral environment, in an area covered by the AP for WiFi technology and the eNB (for LTE technology).

It is assumed that each PU complies with a fixed rate requirement of R_p bps during the entire time interval $[0, T]$ where T is expressed in seconds and that the rate requirement is less than or equal to the maximum capacity of the link between the base station (eNB or AP) and the PU. As well, it is assumed that PUs are assigned orthogonal frequency channels (OFDM), in the frequency of WiFi and LTE technology. The channels between any pair of nodes are modeled as a slow Rayleigh fading being all independent channels. It is assumed that the additive white Gaussian variance noise N_0 is present in each user, both PU and SU.

Following the general assumptions on cooperative spectrum detection, each SU can operate on any of the subchannels that have been licensed for the PUs following the cooperation rules. The decision is made by the head of the coalition by a majority of votes of the members to whom the decision is transmitted and executed immediately. Hence, we can define coalition Ω composed by the set C_Ω of SU. Also, the time interval $[0, T]$ it is divided into two main stages:

1. The *cooperation phase*: In the first fraction α_P of T, the SU in set C_Ω assist the coalition decision. This is done by the head of the coalition based on an election of the majority of the members of the coalition through some pre-established function and is transmitted to all members of the same coalition.
2. The SU *transmission phase*: In the time fraction $(1 - \alpha_P)$ of T, the SU in set C_Ω will share the licensed channel for the PUs and will be able to carry out their transmissions.

3 Problem Formalization and Coalition Game Decision Method Mathematical Model

3.1 Problem Formulation

The spectrum sensing problem can be modeling as a hypothesis of two options testing [15]. This test can be replaced by

$$x(t) = \begin{cases} n(t) & H_0 \\ h(t) * s(t) + n(t) & H_1, \end{cases} \tag{1}$$

where $x(t)$ is the SU signal received, $s(t)$ is the PU signal transmitted, $n(t)$ is the Noise AWGN and $h(t)$ is the channel gain [15]. Here, H_0 and H_1 are the hypothesis of the absence and presence of the PU in the evaluated channel.

In this paper, an SVD detector is chosen as the spectrum sensing technique for its ease of design, implementation and it was also verified that it is more efficient in terms of Probability of detection than other common methods of detection. According to [16], the received signal $x(t)$ will be factorized into a singular values R output by the SVD detector. Then, R is compared with a detection threshold λ to decide on whether the PU is present or not. More information on threshold determination can be found in [16].

The performance of spectrum detection can be primarily described by two basic metrics: Probability of detection (P_d) denoting the probability that a PU is reported to be present when the spectrum is indeed occupied by the PU and Probability of false alarm (P_{fa}) denoting the probability that a PU is declared to be present when the spectrum is actually free.

The cooperative selection and scheduling problem (Detection stage) was formulated as an Coalition game, $G = (N, u)$ where $N = S_1 \cup S_2 \ldots \cup S_n$, and $|N| = n$, and u is the payoff function that converts a user contribution into its profit. The method is structured in two stages, The *cooperation phase* and The SU *transmission phase*.

3.2 The *Cooperation Phase*

To better analyze the performance of Coalition Game Method, we start with the local (individual) SVD detection. In an environment where Rayleigh fading predominates, the P_d and P_{fa} of SU i detecting the status of PU/channel j are, respectively, given by $P_{d,i,j}$ and $P_{f,i,j}$ as follows [17]:

$$P_{d,i,j} = [PY_{i,j} > \lambda | H_1] = e^{-\frac{\lambda}{2}} \sum_{n=0}^{w-2} \frac{1}{n!} \left(\frac{\lambda}{2}\right)^n + \left(\frac{1 + \gamma_{i,j}}{\gamma_{i,j}}\right)^{w-1}$$

$$* \left[e^{-\frac{\lambda}{2(1+\gamma_{i,j})}} - e^{-\frac{\lambda}{2}} \sum_{n=0}^{w-2} \frac{1}{n!} \left(\frac{\lambda * \gamma_{i,j}}{2(1 + \gamma_{i,j})}\right)^n \right] \tag{2}$$

$$P_{fa,i,j} = [PY_{i,j} > \lambda | H_0] = \frac{\Gamma\left(w, \frac{\lambda}{2}\right)}{\Gamma(w)} \tag{3}$$

where λ is the detection threshold for PU j, w is the time-bandwidth product, $Y_{i,j}$ is the normalized output of SU i sensing the status of PU j, and $\gamma_{i,j}$ denotes the average SNR of the received signal from the PU to the SU, which is defined as $\gamma_{i,j} = P_j \, h_{j,i}/\sigma^2$, with P_j being the transmit power of PU j, σ^2 being the Gaussian noise variance and $h_{j,i} = k/d_{j,i}^v$ being the path loss between PU j and SU i; here, k is the path-loss constant, v is the path-loss exponent, and $d_{j,i}$ is the distance between PU j and SU i. $\Gamma(.,.)$ is the *incomplete gamma function*, and $\Gamma(.)$ is the gamma function. Notice that the non-cooperative P_{fa} expression $P_{fa,i,j}$ depends only on the detection threshold λ and doesn't depend on the SU's location.

An important metric is the missing probability P_m for a SU i, which is defined as the probability of not detecting a PU even though it is found and given by

$$P_{m,i,} = 1 - P_{d,i,j} \tag{4}$$

The reduction and increase in efficiency of the missing probability is directly related to the increase in the P_d and, therefore, the interference decrease in the PUs. To diminish the missing probability, the SU will relate to each other under certain parameters to form SU coalitions that collaborate with each other. Within each Ω coalition, an SU, selected as *coalition head*, collects all the SU detection bits that make up the coalition and acts as a merger center in order to make a decision for the whole coalition based on the principle of presence or absence of the PU. This can be seen as having a centralized collaborative detection class of [21,22] applied in the level of each coalition with the head of the coalition being the fusion center to which all members of the coalition inform. For the head of the coalition to make an accurate decision, logical rules such as AND or OR can be used.

In order to obtain a distributed class algorithm that allows maximize the P_d per SU, we refer to cooperative game theory [11] that provides a set of mathematical analysis tools suitable for such algorithms. Thus, the proposed collaborative problem can be structured as a (C_Ω, v) coalitional game [14] where C_Ω is the set of players (the SU's) and v is the utility function or value of a coalition. The value $v(\Omega)$ of a coalition $\Omega \subset C_\Omega$ must capture the trade off between the P_d and the P_{fa}. For this purpose, $v(\Omega)$ must be an increasing function of the P_d. By collaborative sensing, the missing probability and P_{fa} of each coalition Ω having coalition head k are, respectively, given by:

$$Q_{m,\Omega} = \prod_{i \in \Omega} [P_{m,i} * (1 - P_{e,i,k}) + (1 - P_{m,i}) * P_{e,i,k}], \tag{5}$$

$$Q_{m,\Omega} = 1 - \prod_{i \in \Omega} [(1 - P_{fa}) * (1 - P_{e,i,k}) + P_{fa} * P_{e,i,k}], \tag{6}$$

where P_{fa} , $P_{m,i}$ and $P_{e,i,k}$ are respectively given by [23] for a SU i $\in \Omega$ and coalition head $k \in \Omega$.

A suitable utility function is given by

$$v(\Omega) = Q_{d,\Omega} - C(Q_{f,\Omega}) = (1 - Q_{m,\Omega}) - C(Q_{f,\Omega}), \tag{7}$$

where $(Q_{m,\Omega})$ is the missing probability of coalition Ω and $C(Q_{f,\Omega})$ is a cost function of the false alarm probability within coalition Ω given by:

$$C(Q_{f,\Omega}) = \begin{cases} -\alpha^2.log(1 - \left(\left(\frac{Q_{f,\Omega}}{\epsilon}\right)^2\right) & if \ Q_{f,\Omega} < \epsilon \\ +\infty & if \ Q_{f,\Omega} \geq \alpha, \end{cases} \tag{8}$$

where log is the natural logarithm and ϵ is a false alarm constraint per coalition (per SU). It is important to bear in mind that the proposed cost function depends solely on the distance and the number of SUs in the coalition, through the use in its expression of the $Q_{f,\Omega}$ (the distance lies within the probability of error). Hence, the cost for collaboration increases with the number of SU's in the coalition as well as when the distance between the coalition's SU's increases. Any coalition structure resulting will have coalitions limited in number of users to a maximum of the next expression:

$$M_{max} = \frac{log\,(1 - \epsilon)}{log\,(1 - P_{fa})} \tag{9}$$

3.3   The SU Transmition Phase

TDMA is assumed, and the transmission is divided in time, based on the SUs contributions in Ω. Therefore, the time allotted for SU is given by $(1 - \alpha_P)*t_i^{\Omega}$. Its gain is directly proportional to the amount of energy spent by the SU to assist the coalition head k in the cooperation phase.

3.4   Coalition Formation Algorithm

The proposed algorithm is shown below:

1. **PHASE 1:** Local detection, where each individual SU will obtain its PU signal detection bit, using SVD detection method.
2. **PHASE 2:** Formation of adaptive coalitions, during the formation of the adaptive coalition it is assumed that any SU can randomly start the union process. Coalitions are formed based on the merge and split algorithm indicated below:
   - **Merge:** the coalition decides to merge by following the steps below:
     (a) It is decided to merge any set of coalitions if the utility function of the merge is better compared to each coalition by individual, in addition if the set of coalitions covers all the users of the partition, and by Pareto, it is preferable, given its utility function, compared to uncooled partitions.
     (b) The comparison is realized depending on the following utility function of each CR, shown in Eq. 7.
     (c) In the proposed collaboration detection game, the utility of a coalition S is equal to the utility of each CR user in the coalition.

(d) The probability of detection losses of a PU and the probability of false alert of any CR user that belongs to the coalition are given by the above mentioned probabilities, but of the coalition.
- **Split:** It is decided to separate a set of coalitions if the utility function of each coalition of the set per individual is better than the union of the coalitions.
3. **PHASE 3:** Detection of the coalition, each CR user reports his detection bit to each head of the coalition. The head of each coalition makes a final decision about the presence or absence of a primary user using an OR rule.

4 Detection Accuracy Calculation

In game theory methods, payoff is used to have an estimate tradeoff between reward and penalty. In this research, reward refers to the transmission rate by SU (in case of correct detection indicating that the PU is inactive). Penalty is the loss in the transmission rate due to interference to PU (in case of missing detection). Sensing accuracy is given by A.

$$A = P_d * (T - \delta) - P_{m,i} D_0 (T - \delta) \tag{10}$$

where $(T - \delta)$ is the data transmission duration and iδ is the sensing duration. A network structure example is shown in Fig. 2.

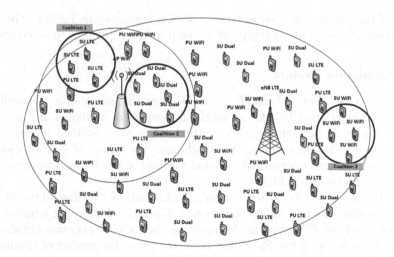

Fig. 2. An illustrative example of coalition formation for collaborative spectrum detection among SU's

5   Simulation Evaluation

5.1   Simulation Setup

A module in Network Simulator 3 (NS-3.23) that contains the four basic stages of a CR system is developed. In our simulation study, we consider a network topology with the following characteristics:

- The propagation models and mobility models are specific to NS-3. The propagation model is the Range Propagation Loss, is a model that depends only on the variable distance (range) between the Tx and the Rx, for our work adapted to the PU and SU with their respective eNB and AP. The single MaxRange attribute (units of meters) determines path loss.
- The mobility model is the Random Waypoint Model.
- Nodes are PU WiFi and PU LTE without cognitive ability (primary UE).
- The LTE and WiFi carrier frequencies are set to 729 MHz and 2400 MHz, respectively.
- The number of SU LTE and WiFi, and the number of dual SUs are variable and the values are between $0, 1, 2, 3, 4, 5, 6, 7, 10, 20, 30$. The PU LTE and WiFi number are set to 10, respectively. The total number of users in the network simulated both CR and primary are chosen, because it is the number of average users that use a WiFi and LTE network.
- The range of coverage of the AP and eNB are set to 200 m and 350 m, respectively. This was done to generate interference between the technologies.

All of the parameters used in the simulation are shown in Table 1. The same parameters were used for each type of decision method, in order to be compared.

5.2   Simulation Results

The (P_d) vs CR $users$ and the (P_{fa}) vs CR $users$ is presented as a cumulative distribution function (CDF) for all methods compared, as shown in Figs. 3 and 4. The proposed Coalition Decision method curve was obtained implementing and simulating the algorithm in NS-3, whereas the curves of Non-cooperative decision method and Centralized decision method were obtained implementing and simulating using MATLAB.

The P_d parameter of each simulation was obtained by dividing all the samples of each simulation where the detection was 1 (detected), for the number total of samples and the P_d parameter for each number of CR users was obtained by dividing the sum of all the P_d of each simulation for the number of simulations performed (21).

Figure 4 shows that the average obtained from P_{fa} for the solution proposed based on coalitions exceeds the performance of the centralized solution with which it was compared, but it is still lower than the solution based on a non-cooperative case. Therefore, the proposed algorithm compensates for this performance gap through the false average alarm reached. In summary, Figs. 3 and 4 show the performance trade off that exists between the gains achieved by

Table 1. System simulation parameters

Parameter	Value
LTE frequency	729 MHz
eNB cells	3
WiFi frequency	2400 MHz
LTE bandwidth	20 MHz
WiFi bandwidth	20 MHz
Tx power	0.037 mW
Rx power	0.06 mW
CR LTE UE	Variable
CR WiFi UE	Variable
Dual CR UE	Variable
Primary LTE UE	10
Primary WiFi UE	10
AP range of coverage	200 m
eNB range of coverage	350 m
Time of simulation	1200 s
Samples	16000
Traffic	TCP
Mobility model	Random Waypoint
Propagation model	Range Propagation Loss

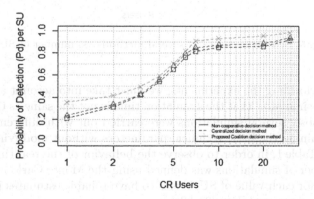

Fig. 3. Probability of detection of several methods vs. number of SU's.

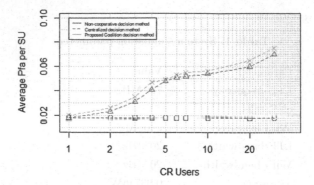

Fig. 4. Average false alarm probabilities of several methods vs. number of SU's.

collaborative detection through the game of coalitions in terms of the average missing probability and the cost in terms of average false alarm probability.

Figure 5 shows a detection accuracy diagram with respect to the SU number variation. If the amount of SU increases, the chances of having a Improvement in the channels to detect increases and thus also increases detection accuracy.

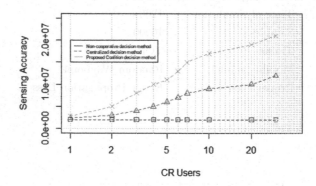

Fig. 5. Sensing accuracy of several methods vs. number of SU's.

Before performing the experiments, we must take into account an important factor for the simulator, that the simulation time is not the same as the real time. For this purpose, several simulations were carried out with different simulation times, maintaining the basic technical parameters without modifying which are indicated in Table 1, in order to observe the behavior of the real time.

The number of simulations was defined using the Monte Carlo method, with 21 iterations for each value of SU, this is to have reliable estimates in the distributions of the generated data [31,32].

We observe the linear and increasing behavior of Real Time vs Simulation time in Fig. 6.

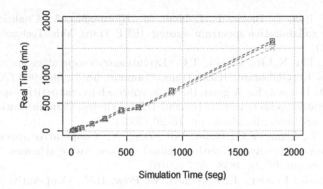

Fig. 6. Simulation time vs. real time

6 Conclusions

In this paper, we propose a collaborative spectrum detection method applied to cognitive mobile radio networks. We modeled the collaborative problem of decision and detection as a coalition game provided by mathematical tools of Game Theory, with a utility function and we obtained an algorithm for the formation of coalitions of SUs. The proposed coalition formation algorithm is based on the merge and split rules that allow the SUs that make up the coalitions in a cognitive mobile network to cooperate with each other to improve their P_d having as a limitation the cost in terms of P_{fa}. We characterize simulation scenarios with resulting network structures implementing the proposed algorithm in each of the nodes, analyze their performance and efficiency. In addition, the parameters of sensing accuracy and simulation time are observed. Simulation results showed that the proposed algorithm increase the P_d, P_{fa}, sensing accuracy and decrease the simulation time per SU compared to the non-cooperative case and the centralized case. The results showed that through the proposed efficient detection and decision algorithm, the SU can adapt and change the structure of the network autonomously and intelligently, if there are variations of parameters that can be environmental, power, distance, etc.

References

1. Ramani, V., Sharma, S.K.: Cognitive radios: a survey on spectrum sensing, security and spectrum handoff. Chin. Commun. **14**(11), 185–208 (2017)
2. Hu, F., Chen, B., Zhu, K.: Full spectrum sharing in cognitive radio networks toward 5G: a survey. IEEE Access **PP**(99), 1 (2018)
3. Luís, M., Oliveira, R., Dinis, R., Bernardo, L.: RF-spectrum opportunities for cognitive radio networks operating over GSM channels. IEEE Trans. Cogn. Commun. Netw. **3**(4), 731–739 (2017)
4. Wang, J., Feng, S., Wu, Q., Zheng, X., Xu, Y.: Hierarchical cognition cycle for cognitive radio networks. Chin. Commun. **12**(1), 108–121 (2015)

5. Saad, W., Han, Z., Basar, T., Debbah, M., Hjorungnes, A.: Coalition formation games for collaborative spectrum sensing. IEEE Trans. Veh. Technol. **60**(1), 276–297 (2011)
6. Wang, B., Liu, K.J.R., Clancy, T.C.: Evolutionary cooperative spectrum sensing game: how to collaborate? IEEE Trans. Commun. **58**(3), 890–900 (2010)
7. Niyato, D., Hossain, E.: A game-theoretic approach to competitive spectrum sharing in cognitive radio networks. In: 2007 IEEE Wireless Communications and Networking Conference, Kowloon, pp. 10–20 (2007)
8. Peh, E.C.Y., Liang, Y.C., Guan, Y.L., Zeng, Y.: Cooperative spectrum sensing in cognitive radio networks with weighted decision fusion schemes. IEEE Trans. Wirel. Commun. **9**(12), 3838–3847 (2010)
9. Chaudhari, S., Lunden, J., Koivunen, V., Poor, H.V.: Cooperative sensing with imperfect reporting channels: hard decisions or soft decisions? IEEE Trans. Sig. Process. **60**(1), 18–28 (2012)
10. ns-3 Model Library, Release ns-3.23. https://www.nsnam.org/docs/release/3.23/models/ns-3-model-library.pdf
11. Li, H., et al.: Utility-based cooperative spectrum sensing scheduling in cognitive radio networks. IEEE Trans. Veh. Technol. **66**(1), 645–655 (2017)
12. Abuzainab, N., Vinnakota, S.R., Touati, C.: Coalition formation game for cooperative cognitive radio using Gibbs sampling. In: 2015 IEEE Wireless Communications and Networking Conference (WCNC), New Orleans, LA, pp. 937–942 (2015)
13. Fenila Janet, M., Lavanya, S., Bhagyaveni, M.A.: Performance analysis of cooperative spectrum sensing in cognitive radio using game theory. In: 2016 International Conference on Wireless Communications, Signal Processing and Networking (WiSPNET), Chennai, pp. 2061–2065 (2016)
14. Hyder, C.S., Xiao, L.: Cooperative routing via overlapping coalition formation game in cognitive radio networks. In: 2016 25th International Conference on Computer Communication and Networks (ICCCN), Waikoloa, HI, pp. 1–6 (2016)
15. Palacios, P., Castro, A., Azurdia-Meza, C., Estevez, C.: Signal detection methods in cognitive mobile radio networks: a performance comparison. In: IEEE Latin-American Conference on Communications (LATINCOM), 2017 Workshop, Guatemala (2017)
16. Palacios, P., Castro, A., Azurdia-Meza, C., Estevez, C.: SVD detection analysis in cognitive mobile radio networks. In: 2017 Ninth International Conference on Ubiquitous and Future Networks (ICUFN), Milan, pp. 222–224 (2017)
17. Mathur, S., Sankaranarayanan, L., Mandayam, N.: Coalitions in cooperative wireless networks. IEEE J. Sel. Areas Commun. **26**, 1104–1115 (2008)
18. Han, Z., Liu, K.J.: Resource allocation for wireless networks: basics, techniques, and applications. Cambridge University Press, Cambridge (2008)
19. Shiryaev, A.N.: On optimum methods in quickest detection problems. Theory Probab. Appl. **8**(1), 22–46 (1963)
20. Saad, W., Han, Z., Debbah, M., Hjørungnes, A., Başar, T.: Coalitional games for distributed collaborative spectrum sensing in cognitive radio networks. In: Proceedings of IEEE INFOCOM, Rio de Janeiro, Brazil, April 2009
21. Foster, I., Kesselman, C.: The Grid: Blueprint for a New Computing Infrastructure. Morgan Kaufmann, San Francisco (1999)
22. Owen, G.: Game Theory, 3rd edn. Academic, London (1995)
23. Czajkowski, K., Fitzgerald, S., Foster, I., Kesselman, C.: Grid information services for distributed resource sharing. In: 10th IEEE International Symposium on High Performance Distributed Computing, pp. 181–184. IEEE Press, New York (2001)

24. Foster, I., Kesselman, C., Nick, J., Tuecke, S.: The physiology of the grid: an open grid services architecture for distributed systems integration. Technical report, Global Grid Forum (2002)
25. National Center for Biotechnology Information. http://www.ncbi.nlm.nih.gov
26. Ghasemi, A., Sousa, E.S.: Collaborative spectrum sensing for opportunistic access in fading environments. In: IEEE Symposium New Frontiers in Dynamic Spectrum Access Networks, Baltimore, USA, pp. 131–136, November 2005
27. Visotsky, E., Kuffner, S., Peterson, R.: On collaborative detection of TV transmissions in support of dynamic spectrum sensing. In: IEEE Symposium New Frontiers in Dynamic Spectrum Access Networks, Baltimore, USA, pp. 338–356, November 2005
28. Niyato, D., Hossein, E., Han, Z.: Dynamic Spectrum Access in Cognitive Radio Networks. Cambridge University Press, Cambridge (2009)
29. Myerson, R.: Graphs and cooperation in games. Math. Oper. Res. **2**, 225–229 (1977)
30. Saad, W., Han, Z., Debbah, M., Hjørungnes, A.: Network formation games for distributed uplink tree construction in IEEE 802.16j networks. In: Proceedings of IEEE Global Communication Conference, pp. 1–5, New Orleans, LA, December 2008
31. Alfonso, U.M., Carla, M.V.: Modelado y simulación de eventos discretos. Editorial UNED (2013)
32. Ramírez, I.C., Barrera, C.J., Correa, J.C.: Efecto del tamañoo de muestra y el número de réplicas bootstrap. Ingeniería y Competitividad **15**(1), 93–101 (2013)

Monitoring of Small Crops for the Measurement of Environmental Factors Through the Internet of Things (IoT)

Jorge Gomez[1]([✉])(iD), Alexander Fernandez[1], and Miguel Zúñiga Sánchez[2]

[1] Departamento de Ingenieria de Sistemas, Universidad de Cordoba,
Monteria, Colombia
jeliecergomez@correo.unicordoba.edu.co
[2] Departamento de Informatica, Universidad Tecnica de Babahoyo,
Babahoyo, Ecuador

Abstract. This paper shows the development of a small crop monitoring system through the measurement of environmental factors and the use of the Internet of Things (IoT). The purpose of this research article is the deployment of a system that allows the collection of data generated by environmental factors included in crop growth. Its objective is to monitor the processes in small-scale crops, as elements that ensure the food security of certain rural populations. This system allows the collection, interaction and management of the information provided by the monitored variables. The results show that the system can present complete information of controlled environmental factors.

Keywords: Small-scale crops · IoT · MQTT · Precision agriculture · Control of environmental variables · Food security

1 Introduction

There has been no other time in the history of humanity's development that has suffered as many changes as those that have happened in the last fifty years. Although technological development has brought great benefits, it is clear that these have not been distributed efficiently, increasing the inequality gap existing in already developed countries and those still in development.

Agriculture in its different forms is one of the methods used to guarantee a constant food flow. The impact it has had on humanity until today is clear, since it is the basis of past and current nourishment [1]. The generation of food security is given when people have constant physical and economic access to a sufficient amount of healthy, nutritious food, with which they can satisfy all their dietary needs and thus expect an active and healthy life [2].

The key aspects of food security are given by the availability of food referring to national or regional supply or production, the access to food understood as

M. Botto-Tobar et al. (Eds.): CITT 2018, CCIS 895, pp. 16–28, 2019.
https://doi.org/10.1007/978-3-030-05532-5_2

the ability to obtain food and the need to have resources for it and finally the use of food represented in the levels of nutrition obtained [2]. How much food security there is in a certain population can be known by making an analysis of said factors, and this can be a source of policies and programs that work to guarantee food security.

But today, achieving an efficient availability of food is undoubtedly linked to agricultural development and the management of production at different scales. However, this agricultural development that supplies the necessary food production is carried out through gigantic agroproductive operations with the capacity to supply these demands. Technological production directly impacts the use of vital resources such as water or the quality of the soil. This is mainly due to the need to use effective elements in pest control, fertilization and the extensive use of agrochemicals that affect the areas of influence of these crops [3].

Indeed, the need to face those environmental and economic challenges has made it necessary to look at other viable production alternatives to be created. This is how small crops begin to be an option at an environmental level: because they have used ancient crops techniques to interact with the environment, they cause little or no impact on it. This can ensure local food security where the communities are widely integrated for this purpose. At an economic level, production is specialized towards the native crops of each region and those effective for nutrition. This diminishes the need to use the classic crops that are previously supplied by large agricultural operations. This type of production is seen to a large extent in countries in development where they feed a large part of the population [4].

In this sense, the de-monopolization of the large agro-alimentary operations in the world is a valid approach for sustaining food security. Linking small farmers to this approach would ensure the integration of communities that could feed a huge number of people from their own self-supply, taking into account common socio-cultural aspects. This can achieve an effective use of the foods coming from each group of people.

In order to achieve the optimization and development of small crops, it is necessary to include technology in agriculture, since it can complement the knowledge acquired by farmers over generations. Making use of the knowledge they have earned, for example, balance can be achieved over combating pests using other insects and plants that allow nature to balance its environment and thus control other factors [4].

According to the above, this study intends to monitor environmental factors such as soil moisture, solar radiation, temperature and relative humidity, in order to maintain the ideal growth conditions of different types of crops. The proposal is the deployment of a monitoring and control system of these factors that allow obtaining data through devices that are used for the collection of information. These data are made available to the farmer through the use of technological platforms from the Internet of Things (IoT). The way the user interacts with the system is through a web application that provides permanent control and analysis of the information. The system allows generating the respective control alerts that can be received in a mobile app or in simpler cases by SMS-type messages. All this allows the small farmer to develop the necessary adjustments to the crop in real time, allowing to optimize its growth. By monitoring small crops, farmers not only improve the conditions of their crops, but also the possibility of implementing crop diversification by expanding the nutritional range with foreign crops. The following parts of this document analyze related studies in which the contributions related to the growth of crops are shown, such as precision agriculture that can be applied to this type of development with the incorporation of monitoring through the use of elements from the Internet of Things. Next, the initiatives for the development of this study are outlined. Then it is explained how the architecture of the system would be applied by studying the different processes that are used in the development of the proposed system. In the following part, the results that are related to the operation of the system and the different interaction with the user are discussed. Finally, the conclusions delivered by the development of the study are shown.

2   Related Work

The possibilities offered by systems based on the Internet of Things are directly related to its ability to allow its use in a number of sensors and devices. Through these sensors, it allows the development of a wide variety of applications with the possibility of taking the information obtained by these devices and making it available to users, according to their needs. This allows planning and controlling the development of the growth of different types of crops. With IoT applications, developing pollution control has been managed, as well as standardization and food control techniques and soil quality management among others with the purpose of increasing production and caring for public health [6].

The use of the IoT is currently linked to many fields of action. In cities, for example, it has increasingly become necessary to manage their basic infrastructure to improve the quality of life of its inhabitants. For example, there are studies that seek to implement environmental control platforms with the use of the IoT by obtaining, analyzing and controlling environmental variables in urban areas [7], in this case environmental data is collected through monitoring stations and then placed at the disposal of the authorities and the population.

In agriculture applications with the IoT, there are studies [8] that allow its use in small-scale crop optimization. The implementation of systems related to the monitoring of protected crops, in which the parameters that are involved with the growth and development of crops are analyzed, is based on the use of a network of sensors and actuators. These allow effective control by monitoring factors such as temperature, relative humidity, and volumetric water content in soil through a network of sensors and the use of IoT. The results of this study are reflected in the ease of application and control in crops. Low-cost production processes are compared to the poor configuration capabilities of the systems currently offered. In Europe, especially in the Mediterranean area, there is currently a broad growth of this type of crops and the possibility of applying systems like this.

There is another type of work that explores the development of a monitoring system of the IoT in precision agriculture for small-scale crops. The latter is understood as the art or science of using technology to improve crop production. This type of study resents the development of a prototype for a system that, based on a network of sensors and an IoT cloud, alerts the farmer when his crop must be irrigated. Once deployed, the wireless sensor network (WSN) cooperates with each of the other nodes of the same infrastructure autonomously to collect and transmit information to the base station [9].

The optimization of crops through the control of their environmental factors is presented with the development of a visual monitoring system for the estimation of water balance in vegetable crops using low cost camera systems. This allows the use of this sensor system to accurately estimate the water balance. This is achieved through the obtaining of images through a period of time. After its process, the percentage of greenness coverage (PCG) can be estimated. All this allows the system to calibrate the quantity of water that is needed for an optimal growth, allowing a substantial saving of this resource. The whole focus of this study is on the algorithmic process of the images, allowing knowing water consumption needs [10].

Regarding the control of environmental variables that can be used in the context of crop growth and optimization, focused on small areas, the implementation of a meteorological station in Acacias, Meta, where IoT and other tools are used, can be appreciated. This study seeks to provide techniques and tools in the design of autonomous devices, especially low cost and connected to the cloud, which serve in the development of intelligent systems aimed at the use of the Internet of Things [11].

3 Motivation

Colombia is currently in a situation where it is immersed in gigantic challenges to achieve development and get past difficult internal conflict, which have afflicted the country for decades. It is seeking to achieve social stability by trying to reach social equity. Based on this, programs that, in general, seek to consider countryside to make agricultural production one of the priorities have been developed. With this, the technological tools proposed in this study present viable alternatives to realize these purposes. The development of crops on a small scale makes it possible to deal more quickly with external factors that can strongly affect all aspects of food security, such as the decrease in production, crop growth and deficiency in nutritional quality. Among these factors, the slow but constant impact of global climate change can be highlighted.

Climate change begins to affect large-scale production, largely due to the decrease in vital resources such as water, soil quality, the unforeseen increase in solar radiation, and, as a consequence, bring imbalances in rainfall cycles and floods. The increase of arid areas where they did not exist before or with changes in the frequencies that appear in other areas can also be seen [5].

4 Proposal

This study shows the development of a system that allows the monitoring of small crops through the control of factors related to the growth and development of plants. For this purpose, a software architecture designed for the Internet of Things was designed, taking elements from precision agriculture, used in large-scale extensive crops and mass production, in order to be incorporated into small-scale agricultural production environments.

4.1 Theoretical Models Analyzed to Obtain the Samples

Soil moisture is one of the parameters that present a high need for control, since it is in the soil where all the growth of the plants that make up the crop takes place. Due to the different properties of the soil, it is necessary to know a general estimate of humidity, which represents a challenge, due to its lack of homogeneity. For the exploration of the different models destined for the estimation of data, multiple linear regression methods and some spatial correlation techniques have been incorporated by means of geostatistical methods. Some methods are described below.

Multiple Linear Regression Method. This statistical method adjusts a lineal function to a determined group of independent variables (given by Xj) approximating the dependent variable (Y) [12]. What is sought with this is the calculation of the values of the coefficients (β_i), as it can be appreciated in Eq. 1 below:

$$Y = \beta + \beta_0 x X_1 + \beta_2 x X_2 + \dots \beta_p x X_p + \varepsilon \tag{1}$$

In this case, the least squares method is used to estimate β_i. Error is defined as sum of square differences [13]. For the model, it is required of the input variables to be explanatory in relation to the output variable.

After choosing the input variables that are representative of the output variables, the multicollinearity is analyzed using the inflation factor of the variance in a normal least squares regression analysis, as shown in Eq. 2.

$$FIV = \frac{1}{1 - R_i^2} \tag{2}$$

Once the variance inflation factor was obtained, the magnitude of multicollinearity was analyzed, considering the size of FIV(β_i). Where FIV$(\beta_i) > 10$, it would have a high multicollinearity, where the values of the variables would not be reliable.

Inverse Distance Weighting Method (IDW). In this method, the sample points are weighted in the realization of the interpolation, developing this in such a way that the influence of one point in relation to the others decreases with the distance from the unknown point that is to be found.

This is achieved by weighting the points through the use of a weighting coefficient that will control the way in which the influence of the weighting is inversely proportional to the distance of the point to be predicted. Thus, the greater the weighting coefficient, the lower the effect that the points would have.

It is necessary to keep in mind that the quality of the interpolation result could decrease if it is found that the distribution of the data points of the samples is unequal, this can be seen in Eq. 3.

$$\hat{z} = \frac{\sum\limits_{i=1}^{n} Z(x_i).d_{ij}^{-\alpha}}{\sum\limits_{i=1}^{n} d_{ij}^{-\alpha}} \tag{3}$$

Estimation of Soil Moisture Using the Kriging Method. In the temporal space estimation models, the Kriging tool [14] is very useful for predicting data on a surface, as well as providing some measure of certainty or accuracy of predictions.

This is ideal for areas where it is difficult to collect samples due to the extension of the test field or the difficulty when extracting them. The possibility that this method presents is to determine the statistical relationships between midpoints by means of self-correlation, as they produce a higher prediction surface.

With the Kriging, it is possible to predict the distance or the direction between the different points of sample, which arrive to show a spatial correlation that comes to be used like explanation of the variation of the surface. This is achieved by adjusting a mathematical function to a certain number of sample points within a specific radius with which the output values of each sample area are determined.

The Kriging is given by the general formula that also has the interpolation process IDW, and is formed as a sum of data weighting (Eq. 4).

$$Z = \sum\limits_{i=1}^{N} \lambda_i Z(S_i) \tag{4}$$

The weighting will depend exclusively on the distance to the location of the prediction. It is important to note that the Kriging is based on the general spatial arrangement of the measured points.

This method allows generating the prediction of interpolation through the location of the rules of dependence and the realization of the prediction. For this, the creation of variograms and covariance functions is necessary, which allows to calculate the values of statistical dependence or spatial auto-correlation that later allow the adjustment of the model. Once this adjustment is made, it is necessary to make the prediction. The construction of the experimental semivariogram calculates the semivariancy of each point in relation to the others, which is given by Eq. 5:

$$v(h = d_{ip}) = \frac{1}{2n} \sum_{i=1}^{n} (f_i - f_p)^2 \tag{5}$$

The Kriging tool shows its application, which is the prediction of attribute values in the locations that were not taken in the initial sample. When making the different predictions, the Kriging weights are used, which are given from the semivariogram. Then, for the realization of a continuous surface, the predictions are made for each point or location in the study area that are based on the semivariogram and the spatial disposition of the values that have been measured closely.

The result of this tool can be seen in Fig. 1, which shows a sample prediction map through the interpolation of data using regionalized variables.

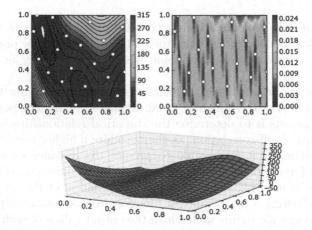

Fig. 1. Schematic of interpolated data surface.

In Table 1, it can be seen that the most efficient method is the Kriging, because a structural analysis is performed using the correlation functions such as the variogram. These calculate the weighted averages of the sample observations that come from the description of the correlation of points in space, which allows estimating values in places lacking information.

4.2   Conceptualization of the Proposed Architecture

The architecture is located within a client-server organization, in which a structuring in the form of layers, deployed throughout the proposed system, can be seen.

Data Capturing. This is done through the permanent reception of the information from the respective sensor array of each station located in the monitored

Table 1. Characteristics of data interpolation methods.

Proposal	Description	Statistical method	Average (zi)	FIV	Semi variogram	Reg. var.
Mlr	Analysis of the relationship between a dependent variable and other independent variables	Deterministic	Yes	Yes	No	No
Idw	Estimation of variable z from weighted averages	Deterministic	Yes	No	No	No
Kriging	Set of spatial prediction methods that is based on the minimization of the mean square error of prediction	Probabilistic	Yes	No	Yes	Yes

crop. The stations allow the connection through the use of IoT platforms in the cloud, using the MQTT protocol. In the same way, this also allows the management and calibration of the sensor system [15], so that later these data can be integrated to the following layers of systems.

Administration and Capture Processes. In this part, the main objective is the permanent collection of data made through the topics subscribed to each sensor in its respective arrangement. The protocol used in this layer comes from the family of M2M protocols [16], which is the MQTT protocol and allows the wireless and/or wired system to make the necessary connections. Information management is handled by an interface that collects the data sent by the device system.

Client Services Interface. The requests generated by the client, coming from the web interface, are sent to the next layer, in which the management of the system is processed. This layer also shows the responses of the different clients (web, mobile, webservice consumption, etc.), which are updated by HTTP protocol.

Administration and Management. Through the subscription of the PAHO-MQTT client to a broker of the Cloud-IoT platform, the link is made with the database to obtain the persistence of the data collected by the monitoring phase, which for this case may come from soil moisture, temperature, relative humidity and UV radiation.

The requirements of the clients are visualized in the interface thanks to the implementation of a Python script, which in turn implements OPS libraries. The submission topic is processed through a string that is the source of the data that becomes persistent in the system database, restarting the cycle of the new reading separated by a predetermined delay by the sensor array driver of the respective reading stations.

The underlying layer is responsible for the recovery and delivery of information. This will depend on the requirements made by users, as well as the arrangement of sensors. This process is handled by the system through the generation of queries. The organization of the system's architecture can be seen in Fig. 2.

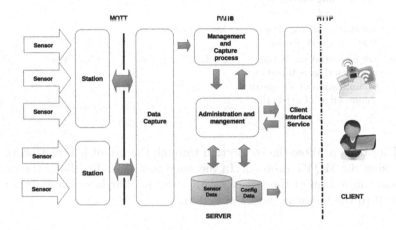

Fig. 2. System architecture.

Each station and its respective sensor array must verify the proper functioning through proper calibration tests. Then it proceeds with the reading of the data, originated in the process of monitoring the controlled factors and then they are sent using the Cloud-IoT platform, as can be seen in Fig. 3.

The sequence of the sending and transmission process, originating in the reading of the array of sensors, goes through the system until achieving persistence in the base of data (Fig. 4).

5   Results

Once the system is deployed, the data is obtained in real time and the update is developed automatically, allowing the user to verify the information in the web or mobile application. The view of the information in fact originates from the array of sensors, configured in scalar measurement format. The periodicity of reading for the collection according to the parameter to be measured is developed between one and thirty minutes.

This is due to the fact that the measurements vary according to the type of sensor, in this case for soil moisture a thirty-minute interval is determined, as well as the temperature, while the solar radiation is taken every minute. The process of generation of alerts is verified according to the design of thresholds for the adequate growth of crops, creating artificial conditions to force the development of alerts.

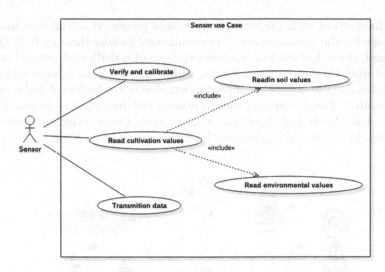

Fig. 3. Case of administration of sensor usage

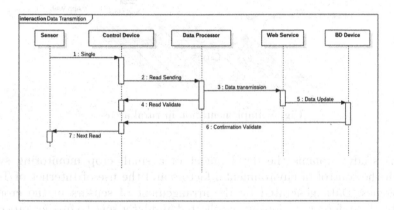

Fig. 4. Sending and transmission process sequence

5.1   Case Study in Small Crops in Rural Area

For crops grown in areas far from urban centers or rural areas and where the deployment of mobile telecommunications infrastructure is lower, it has some disadvantage compared to the crops studied in the periphery of cities. This is mainly due to the limited coverage and capacity of the same network, allowing some processes, especially real-time ones, not to be exploited. For this case, two solutions are presented, one which allows the crop processing stations to issue short text messages (SMS), which can be received in any type of mobile terminal. This is possible even without Internet connection and only using the basic platform of mobile communication services, so that alerts can be sent via SMS messages almost in real time. This solution allows traditional farmers to achieve integration with the technological tools presented in the monitoring of small crops for the measurement of environmental factors through IoT. On the other hand, the other solution proposes the use of a dedicated connection link to the Internet through satellite service, which would require a more structured organization and infrastructure of production, due to the technical and economic needs required. These solutions seek to present different options to small farmers, both traditional and those who tend to their crops using more advanced technology. In Fig. 5, the deployment for rural areas can be seen.

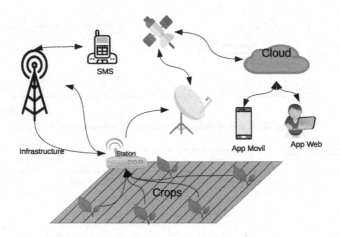

Fig. 5. Implementation in rural areas.

This study explains the development of a small crop monitoring system through the control of environmental factors and the use of Internet of Things technologies. Data generated by the arrangement of sensors in the crop oriented by the different stations were collected and later sent to further processing through subscription to a Cloud-IoT and the use of MQTT protocol. The collection infrastructure is based on free hardware, using the Arduino platform to manage the sensors and raspberry pi to control the shipping logic.

In this step of information gathering, the use of different statistical tools such as multiple linear regression analysis was analyzed for the process of soil moisture data. However, the use of this tool would be difficult because this method needs to incorporate other input variables different from the soil moisture. It can be seen that the multiple linear regression method is useful for indirect estimation of soil moisture.

The other method that was analyzed was the use of geostatistics tools such as the inverse distance weighting (IDW) and the application of simple Kriging to estimate the soil moisture of the cultivation area. This last tool is efficient predicting the data of the points not taken in the sample and, since it depends on the average relation between points, the estimation of the data is much more accurate and reliable. Therefore, it is an indication that the sample taken when processed will deliver a realistic estimate of the soil moisture in the study area.

This study seeks the development of tools that take advantage of IoT technologies, allowing applying this type of systems in any crop, especially those of small scale. The analysis of the collated information allows an effective control of the growth of crops, anticipating elements that could end up damaging the final production. With the generation of alerts, it is possible to prevent the effect caused by sudden changes that may put the growth of crops at risk. The use of MQTT protocol, designed for those sensors that consume little energy and little bandwidth, increase the possibility of implementing the system in rural and remote areas and at low costs.

The possibilities that this type of systems suggest are the implementation of another element of the IoT, carrying out the automated control of irrigation systems, pest control, and verification by images of the moment of growth and harvest. In addition, this type of monitoring would help the implementation of foreign crops adapted to other climates that must have very precise conditions for their growth. Hence, it would be difficult to achieve their success without the use of this type of studies.

Acknowledgments. This project was funded by the University of Córdoba, with the code Nro FI-01-16. We thank Professor Teobaldis Mercado and the Department of Agronomic Engineering.

References

1. Gomez, J., Castaño, S., Mercado, T., Garcia, J., Fernández, A.: Sistema de Internet de las cosas (IoT) para el monitoreo de cultivos protegidos. Ingenieria e Innovacion **5**(1), 27–36 (2017)
2. Salazar, L., Aramburu, J., Gonzalez-Flores, M., Winters, P.: Sowing for food security: a case study of smallholder famers in Bolivia. Food Policy **65**, 32–52 (2016)
3. Tolon, A., Lastra, X.: La agricultura intensiva del poniente Almeriense. Diagnostico e instrumentos de gestión ambiental. Revista Electrónica de Medio ambiente **8**, 18–40 (2010)
4. Altieri, M., Koohafkan, P.: Enduring Farms, 1st edn. Third World Network (TWN), Penang (2008)
5. Altieri, M., Nicholls, C.: Los impactos del cambio climatico sobre las comunidades campesinas y de agricultores tradicionales y sus respuestas adaptativas. Revista Agroecologia **3**, 7–28 (2008)
6. Popovic, T., Latinovic, N., Pesic, A., Zecevic, Z., Krstajic, B., Dukanović, S.: Architecting an IoT enabled platform for precision agriculture and ecological monitoring: a case study. Comput. Electron. Agric. **140**, 255–265 (2017)
7. Gómez, J., Marcillo, F., Triana, F., Gallo, V., Oviedo, B., Hernández, V.: IoT for environmental variables in urban areas. In: The 8th International Conference on Ambient Systems, Networks and Technologies (2017). Procedia Comput. Sci. **109**, 67–64
8. Cama-Pinto, A., Gil-Montoya, F., Gomez-Lopez, J., Garcia-Cruz, A., Manzano-Agugliaro, F.: Sistema inalambrico de monitorizacion para cultivos en invernadero. DYNA **81**(184), 164–170 (2014)

9. Sawant, S., Durbha, S.S., Jagarlapudi, A.: Interoperable agro-meteorological observation and analysis platform for precision agriculture: a case study in citrus crop water requirement estimation. Comput. Electron. Agric. **138**, 175–187 (2017)
10. González-Esquiva, J.M., Oates, M.J., García- Mateos, G., Moros-Valle, B., Molina-Martínez, J.M., Ruiz-Canales, A.: Development of a visual monitoring system for water balance estimation of horticultural crops using low cost cameras. Comput. Electron. Agric. **141**, 15–26 (2017)
11. Rodríguez, A., Figueredo, J.: Selection and implementation of a prototype weather station using IoT and tools Google. Actas de Ingeniería **2**, 219–225 (2016)
12. García, G., et al.: Determinacion de la humedad de suelo mediante regresion lineal multiple con datos TerraSAR-X. Revista de Teledetección **46**, 73–81 (2016)
13. Helsel, D., Hirsch, R.: Statistical Methods in Water Resources Techniques of Water Resources Investigations, Book 4, Chapter A3. U.S. Geological Survey, 295–297 (2002)
14. Giraldo, R.: Introducción a la Geoestadistica. Departamento de Estadistica, Universidad Nacional de Colombia, Bogota, Colombia (2002)
15. Wagle, S.: Semantic data extraction over MQTT for IoT centric wireless sensor networks. In: International Conference on Internet of Things and Applications (IOTA), vol. 26, pp. 227–232 (2016)
16. Luzuriaga, J.E., Perez, M., Boronat, P., Cano, J.C., Calafate, C., Manzoni, P.: Improving MQTT Data Delivery in Mobile Scenarios: Results from a Realistic Testbed. Mobile Information Systems (2016)

Management of SSL Certificates: Through Dynamic Link Libraries

Javier Vargas[1(✉)], Franklin Mayorga[1], David Guevara[1],
and H. David Martinez[2]

[1] Facultad de Ingeniería en Sistemas Electrónica e Industrial,
Universidad Técnica de Ambato, Ambato, Ecuador
{js.vargas, fmayorga, dguevara}@uta.edu.ec
[2] Universidad de Guayaquil, Guayaquil, Ecuador
hector.martinezvi@ug.edu.ec

Abstract. This article describes the process of creating a dynamic-link library for SSL certificate management. The use of these libraries is usually between client-server, for communication security. The programming of a dynamic link infrastructure entails a sequence of modules for the adaptation of the requirements of a client-server system. Each module is managed by external libraries, between them the OpenSSL libraries. The proposed infrastructure uses OpenSSL libraries in client-server communication environments, resulting in interoperability between programming languages for example, Java to C/C++ migration for the creation of a secure communication environment.

Keywords: Dynamic-link library · OpenSSL · Interoperability

1 Introduction

Information shared on the Internet or a communication network may be public, read-only or private, with authorized access only. The protection of this information is a key issue in computer security research. Information protection techniques or the communication channel through which it is transmitted involve the use of network security tools [1]. SSL and TLS validation certificates, public and private encryption keys, digital signatures are secure communication services [2], which allow the reliability of the transmission of information.

Referring to this type of computer or information security services involves a secure communication infrastructure, encryption and decryption algorithms, for example RSA an asymmetric encryption algorithm for SSL certificates [3].

On the other hand, we have OpenSSL a robust open source project with SSL/TLS security protocols [4], which sees the need to implement cryptographic mechanisms such as X.509, pkcs12, etc., for secure communication with SSL [5]. The configuration or programming of these security mechanisms are variants, putting the complexity of the information or data to be protected first.

Under the demand of the initial configuration of cryptographic mechanisms, programming can be both complex and simple: complex due to the interoperability between programming languages, compiled under C/C+++ [6], and the level of programming by

M. Botto-Tobar et al. (Eds.): CITT 2018, CCIS 895, pp. 29–40, 2019.
https://doi.org/10.1007/978-3-030-05532-5_3

including external libraries belonging to OpenSSL [7], simple by the migration between programming languages of C, C+++, assembler and Java so that they can interact with each other, to solve these types of problems is the use of JNI [8] gateways.

An SSL certificate in production or use is a reliable communication protocol [9]. The creation of these certificates involves a sequence of steps to create the RSA key and generate the certificate signature request CSR [10], where the use of the tools containing the OpenSSL libraries is not limited.

Creating a DLL or Dynamic Link Library makes it easier to manage certificates and program them. Each SSL certificate is encrypted within the library, including the private key and the encrypted certificate, a request must be sent to the server, so that the certificate generated by the client is signed with output in the valid '.p12' pkcs12 [11] format. For the creation of the signature, a trusted CA is created to validate and sign all managed SSL certificates within the secure communication infrastructure [12].

For further development, the dynamic link library is implemented in a system of certificate generation, warehouse generation and automatic code, referred to as: Tool for the Automatic Generation of Security Infrastructure in Communications using Java [13].

2 Related Works

OpenSSL is even more popular for SSH keys, each of these keys manages a certificate [14], which is generated with tools such as the OpenSSL CSR Tool [15]. Each certificate that contains an encryption key implemented in AES and RSA ensures the confidence of each of them. One of the main advantages of OpenSSL implemented protocols for different operating systems between Linux, Windows and others [16].

A security flaw in OpenSSL will probably cause more damage that an error in an unknown link library, these libraries will be created from the communication between the client and the server. One of the main causes of these vulnerabilities is the misunderstanding of the developers of the numerous options, parameters and return values of SSL libraries [17]. Creating a PKI Public Key Infrastructure that you can share between operating systems that use OpenSSL for security mechanisms are varied like Peer-to-peer PKIs [18].

For the Windows platform we have GnuWin which uses a dll that internally generates a connection that uses the Openssl libraries but only for Windows.

To use OpenSSL's Linux SSL Certificate Tools is commonly used to create the CSR and private key for many different platforms [19].

The development of an "JNI" gateway, for access from Java to functions OpenSSL cryptography not provided in the JCE library of the Java Virtual Machine, avoids resorting to an external provider. In this way, a Java project can be used to you can create a user certificate signed by the certification authority to use the OpenSSL certificate management infrastructure [20].

It is an automatic system that from Java allows to generate security warehouses necessary in security applications, either client/server SSL applications or generation applications and/or signature verification, secure database access applications, etc. Normally the generation of security stores is done manually with the, which is part of the Java Virtual Machine distribution [21].

Each of these tools are complementary to the library's suggestion. The use parameter between secure communication enables certified communication for applications in different programming and interoperability environments.

3 Compiler Architecture

The programming of the library is established in three modules: conversion, interpretation and compilation. For the first module of the conversion of source code to executable code in Java and C/C+++, the use of JNI is envisaged.

On the other hand, for the second module of the interpretation of OpenSSL libraries, it is stable in a client-server environment which manages the use of these libraries. And finally there is the module compilation of the dynamic link library in Visual C+++ [22], the compiler translates the source code and header programming language, thus generating a dynamic DLL link infrastructure.

3.1 Conversion Module

The Java source code contains the basic functions for generating a certificate, structured with the adaptation of the OpenSSL libraries: create_petition(...), convert_p12(...), and create_signature(...). Each function contains the user input variables of the SSL Certificate. The standard SSL certificate [23] contains the length of the key and the input parameters: name of the unit, location, etc. For this purpose, JNI migrates the native method that is created in Java to C, thus creating the base class file for the generation of the library (see Fig. 1).

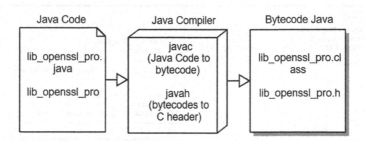

Fig. 1. JNI functions.

3.2 Programming

In the previous section the basic functions are mentioned, each function contains a programming segment based on the classification of the OpenSSL library; create_petition for the creation of the SSL certificate (see Fig. 2), then the RSA certificate encryption algorithm is generated. To continue with the dynamic link library segment of the code; convert_p12 generates the installable certificate with the respective private key.

```
//GENERATE FORMAT                                    //THE CERTIFICATE IS PRINTED p.12

//THE USER'S PRIVATE KEY IS OBTAINED                 out10=BIO_new(BIO_s_file());
   out11=BIO_new(BIO_s_file());                      BIO_write_filename(out10,certp12);
   BIO_read_filename(out11,privkey);
                                                     i2d_PKCS12_bio(out10, p12n);
   privatekey = PEM_read_bio_PrivateKey(out11, NULL, 0, "NULL");
   if (privatekey == NULL)                            BIO_free_all(out10);
   {
       printf("ERROR LOADING THE PRIVATE USER KEY       \n ");     printf("                              'cert_user.p12'"+
           fprintf(fd1," ERROR LOADING THE PRIVATE USER KEY    \n ");         " successfully    !!!! \n\n\n");
                                                          fprintf(fd1,"Certificate created    'cert_user.p12'"+
           printf("ENTER A KEY TO EXIT.              ");                " successfully     !!!\n\n\n");
       scanf("%s",&tecla);
       exit(0);                                          PKCS12_free(p12n);
   }                                                     fclose(fd1);

   BIO_free_all(out11);

       printf("LOADED THE PRIVATE USER KEY       \n ");
       fprintf(fd1," LOADED THE PRIVATE USER KEY       \n ");
```

Fig. 2. SSL Certificate format Creation.

In order to validate the certificates generated, it is necessary to have a certification signature. Each signature is encrypted based on the CA private key. The code segment processes the user request, generating a new SSL certificate (see Fig. 3) valid within the OpenSSL standards. The functions consumed are create_signature and create_signature_V2, the second one implemented a CA certification authority>openssl ca -config./CA/myCA.cfg -in req_recv.pem -verbose.

```
//Read the req.pem file for OPENSSL                  /* A new certificate is created              */
in_bio1 = BIO_new( BIO_s_file() );
BIO_read_filename( in_bio1, file );                  if (!(cert = X509_new()))
req = PEM_read_bio_X509_REQ ( in_bio1, NULL, NULL, NULL );    int_error(" Error creating X509 object      ");

if (req == NULL)                                     //set version number for the certificate (X509v3) and the serial number

{                                                    if (X509_set_version(cert, 2L) != 1)
    printf ("--->Error when opening REQ file     \n");     int_error(" Error setting certificate version      ");
    fprintf (fd1, "--> Error when opening REQ file    \n");   ASN1_INTEGER_set(X509_get_serialNumber(cert), serial++);

        printf(" ENTER A KEY TO EXIT:         ");    //The certificate summary is generated and signed with the CA's private key
        scanf("%s",&tecla);
        exit(0);                                     if (EVP_PKEY_type(CApkey->type) == EVP_PKEY_DSA)
                                                         digest = EVP_dss1();
}                                                    .....
else
printf(" read REQ petition.... !!!      req.pem\n\n\n");   if (!(X509_sign(cert, CApkey, digest)))
                                                         int_error(" Error signing certificate       ");
fprintf(fd1," read REQ petition.... !!!     req.pem\n\n\n" );
                                                     printf(" Signed petition for CA          \n\n\n");

                                                         BIO_free_all(in_bio1);
                                                         BIO_free_all(out);
```

Fig. 3. SSL Certificate format Validation.

3.3   Interpretation Module

This section uses the OpenSSL libraries for the generation of SSL certificates. Each library has multiple functions, methods, classes and more. The OpenSSL classes [24] used are: <openssl/bio.h> which handles SSL connections, <openssl/x509.h> validates the certificate, <openssl/pem.h> reads and writes the certificate based on the private key, <openssl/ssl.h> implements the protocol to use. It should be noted that these classes are those used within the research framework of the article, although there are implicitly more classes or libraries used.

In the previous section the basic functions are mentioned, each one contains a programming segment based on the classification of the OpenSSL library: create_request for the creation of the SSL certificate, convert_p12 generates the installable certificate with the respective private key, and to validate the generated certificates it is necessary to have a certification signature create_signature.

Each signature is encrypted based on the private key obtained by the CA. The code infrastructure processes the user's request, generating a new valid SSL certificate within the OpenSSL standards (see Fig. 4).

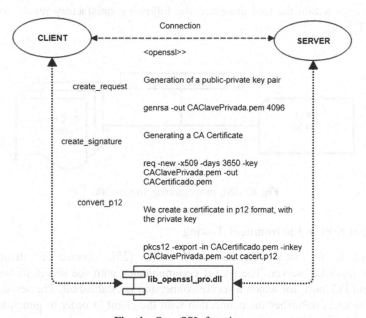

Fig. 4. OpenSSL functions.

3.4   Compilation Module

The library compilation receives all input files from the dynamic link infrastructure. Each file is grouped into blocks of executable code to later generate a dynamic link library of SSL certificate generation (see Fig. 5).

```
InitializeBuildStatus:
   Se creará "Release\lib_openssl_pro.unsuccessfulbuild" porque se especificó "AlwaysCreate".
ClCompile:
   stdafx.cpp
   dllmain.cpp
   funciones_openssl.cpp
   lib_openssl_pro.cpp
Link:
      Creando biblioteca C:\Documents and Settings\Administrador\Escritorio\lib_openssl_pro\Release\lib_openssl_pro.lib y obj
   Generando código
   Generación de código finalizada
   lib_openssl_pro.vcxproj -> C:\Documents and Settings\Administrador\Escritorio\lib_openssl_pro\Release\lib_openssl_pro.dll
FinalizeBuildStatus:
   Se eliminará el archivo "Release\lib_openssl_pro.unsuccessfulbuild".
   Aplicando tarea Touch a "Release\lib_openssl_pro.lastbuildstate".
```

Fig. 5. Compiler output.

4 Experimental Results

For the implementation of the DLL and execution tests of the same is stable within the Tool for the Automatic Generation of Security Infrastructure in Communications using Java, the tool manages the certificates and generates them automatically. The DLL execution tests within the tool presented the following satisfactory results to the end user (see Fig. 6).

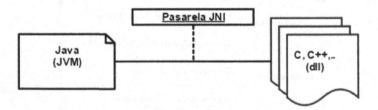

Fig. 6. JNI, programming framework.

4.1 Client-Server Environment Testing

The client is the one who sends the SSL [25], connection string via a socket_client/socket_server. The socket communicates with the server through an IP address and link port, for which a secure connection is established. The server through a socket_server, establishes the connection with the client in order to generate an SSL certificate (see Fig. 7).

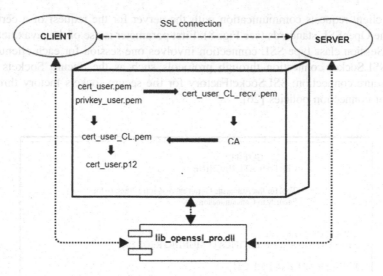

Fig. 7. Mechanism of the DLL lib_openssl_pro.

4.2   Client-Server Environment Results

The validation of the results within the client-server communication is the use of the tool as such, The following Table 1, where the DLL is implemented as one more library of the tool ().

Table 1. Versions of the certificate module

Merge dll.	Certificate management tool
v1.0 basic version	Sent string writeUTF/readUTF SSL connection with CA signed certificate stores
v1.1 openssl library	Openssl library is incorporated to create a req.pem request
v1.2 client size	The length of the req.pem file is calculated at the client and sent to the server
v1.3 storage array	The array bytes' space is reserved, we read the req.pem file in the client and send it to the server. The server reserves byte array space and receives the file, stores it in the byte array and prints it to the file req_recv.pem
v1.4 file request	The server signs the request and generates the cert_user.pem file
v1.5 file output	The server calculates the length of the cert_user.pem file and sends it to the client. The client reserves space in an array of bytes. The server then sends the cert_user.pem file to the client, receives it and prints it to the file
v1.6 pkcs12 finished	The client converts the cert_user.pem file together with the private key into a cert_user.p12 file

The client requests communication with the server for the request of a certificate within the OpenSSL standards (see Fig. 8). First parameter is use of the javax.net class, the SSLSession class type SSL connection involves one session for each client/server entity; SSLSocket connection through protocols such as the Secure Sockets Layer (SSL) secure connection; SSLSocketFactory for the secure sockets factory through a variety of connection policies [26].

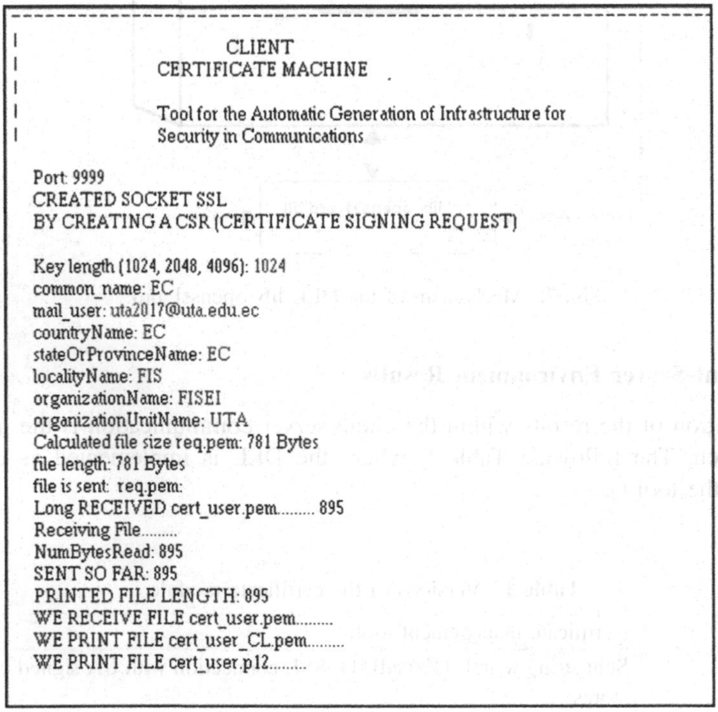

```
----------------------------------------------------------------
I                         CLIENT
I                   CERTIFICATE MACHINE  .
I
I           Tool for the Automatic Generation of Infrastructure for
I           Security in Communications

  Port: 9999
  CREATED SOCKET SSL
  BY CREATING A CSR (CERTIFICATE SIGNING REQUEST)

  Key length (1024, 2048, 4096): 1024
  common_name: EC
  mail_user: uta2017@uta.edu.ec
  countryName: EC
  stateOrProvinceName: EC
  localityName: FIS
  organizationName: FISEI
  organizationUnitName: UTA
  Calculated file size req.pem: 781 Bytes
  file length: 781 Bytes
  file is sent: req.pem:
  Long RECEIVED cert_user.pem......... 895
  Receiving File.........
  NumBytesRead: 895
  SENT SO FAR: 895
  PRINTED FILE LENGTH: 895
  WE RECEIVE FILE cert_user.pem.........
  WE PRINT FILE cert_user_CL.pem.........
  WE PRINT FILE cert_user.p12.........
```

Fig. 8. Client environment.

The server allows the connection with the client and asks the library if the client's request is valid, (see Fig. 9), in order to send the client, the request for an SSL certificate duly signed by the CA. Inside the library lib_openssl_pro the method create_signature_V2, is used to create a code block that allows to generate or load automatically the files organized with their details, using HashMap as initial capacity and the load factor for the files [27], then the client is sent the file already loaded in the server and signed, so that the client converts it into p12 file.

The results of the client/server context is the SSL certificate duly validated by the CA. Each certificate issued subsequently will be stored in a certification database on the server. To view the certificate, you can execute the following OpenSSL >openssl x509 command -in cert_user.pem -noout -text (see Fig. 10). In addition, each certificate generates a "p12" configuration file so that the user can install its certificate on its workstation.

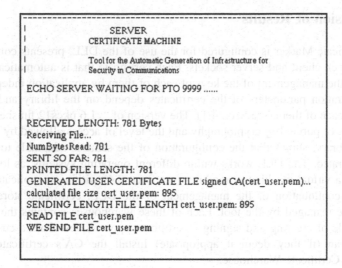

```
|                        SERVER
|                  CERTIFICATE MACHINE
|           Tool for the Automatic Generation of Infrastructure for
|           Security in Communications
|
ECHO SERVER WAITING FOR PTO 9999 ......

RECEIVED LENGTH: 781 Bytes
Receiving File...
NumBytesRead: 701
SENT SO FAR: 781
PRINTED FILE LENGTH: 781
GENERATED USER CERTIFICATE FILE signed CA(cert_user.pem)...
calculated file size cert_user.pem: 895
SENDING LENGTH FILE LENGTH cert_user.pem: 895
READ FILE cert_user.pem
WE SEND FILE cert_user.pem
```

Fig. 9. Server environment.

Fig. 10. Outputting an SSL certificate generated by the dynamic link library.

5   Discussion of Results

In the Certificate Marker is configured for the use of the DLL, presents compatibility results between client and server sockets. Each certificate that is automatically generated allows the management of the keys of each of them by application independently. The configuration parameters of the certificates depend on the library and the limit allowed for each of them (see Sect. 4.1). The version of "v1.6 pkcs12 finished", within the standards of public key cryptography and the level of access allowed by the socket inside the library, shows that the configuration of the same is adaptable to each certificate generated. The DLL works within different operating systems, as long as you have the java virtual machine or modules (see Sect. 3.4) within an application.

For the continuation of the management of the DLL, certificate stores will be created to be managed by the tool. Each of these warehouses contains the CA is an entity capable of creating and signing a certificate upon request from a customer, so customers can (if they deem it appropriate) install the CA's certificate in their Trusted CA Certificate Warehouse.

6   Conclusions and Future Work

The generation of a client/server tool facilitates the transmission of the file with the certificate duly signed by the entity in V1, without any problem when sending it at the request of the client, for the creation of certificates that allow identification on the Internet and reliably to web servers that establish secure communications through the SSL (Secure Socket Layer) protocol. They can be identified because they are accessed through addresses such as https://. Their issuance and use is subject to the SSL-Compliant Server Certificate Certification Policy.

Each SSL Certificate is automatically generated by the DLL and the internal manipulation of OpenSSL libraries that provide a set of accessible files for the user to install, configure and generate one or more certificates again.

As future work we are looking to implement a secure communication service using the DLL to work with various processes between clients and servers.

Acknowledgments. To the Ecuadorian Corporation for the Development of Research and Academia CEDIA, for research funding, development and innovation through CEPRA projects, in particular to the CEPRA-IX-2015 project; *Tool for the Automatic Generation of Security Infrastructure in Communications using Java.*

References

1. Kim, H., Wasicek, A., Mehne, B., Lee, E.A.: A secure network architecture for the internet of things based on local authorization entities. In: Proceedings - 2016 IEEE 4th International Conference on Future Internet of Things and Cloud, FiCloud 2016, pp. 114–122 (2016)
2. Ranjbar, A., Komu, M., Salmela, P., Aura, T.: An SDN-based approach to enhance the end-to-end security: SSL/TLS case study. In: Proceedings of the NOMS 2016 - 2016 IEEE/IFIP Network Operations and Management Symposium, pp. 281–288 (2016)

3. Loebenberger, D., Nüsken, M.: Notions for RSA integers. Int. J. Appl. Cryptol. **3**(2), 116–138 (2014)
4. Ghafoor, I., Jattalai, I., Durrani, S., Ch, M.T.: Analysis of OpenSSL heartbleed vulnerability for embedded systems. In: 17th IEEE International Multi Topic Conference: Collaborative and Sustainable Development of Technologies, IEEE INMIC 2014 - Proceedings, pp. 314–319 (2014)
5. Zhang, L., et al.: Analysis of SSL certificate reissues and revocations in the wake of Heartbleed. In: Proceedings of the ACM SIGCOMM Internet Measurement Conference, IMC, pp. 489–502 (2014)
6. Dietz, W., Li, P., Regehr, J., Adve, V.: Understanding integer overflow in C/C++. In: Proceedings - International Conference on Software Engineering, pp. 760–770 (2012)
7. Georgiev, M., Iyengar, S., Jana, S., Anubhai, R., Boneh, D., Shmatikov, V.: The most dangerous code in the world: validating SSL certificates in non-browser software. In: Proceedings of the ACM Conference on Computer and Communications Security, pp. 38–49 (2012)
8. Papadimitriou, S., Moussiades, L.: Combining Scala with C++ for efficient scientific computation in the context of ScalaLab. In: Lecture Notes in Engineering and Computer Science, vol. 2223, pp. 409–412 (2016)
9. Brubaker, C., Jana, S., Ray, B., Khurshid, S., Shmatikov, V.: Using frankencerts for automated adversarial testing of certificate validation in SSL/TLS implementations. In: Proceedings - IEEE Symposium on Security and Privacy, pp. 114–129 (2014)
10. Suga, Y.: SSL/TLS servers status survey about enabling forward secrecy. In: Proceedings - 2014 International Conference on Network-Based Information Systems, NBiS 2014, pp. 501–505 (2014)
11. Berbecaru, D., Desai, A., Lioy, A.: A unified and flexible solution for integrating CRL and OCSP into PKI applications. Softw. Pract. Exp. **39**(10), 891–921 (2009)
12. Roman Garcia, F.: Desarrollo de librerias de firma ciega para OpenSSL. Universitat Politecnica de Catalunya (2016)
13. Vargas, J., Guevara, D., Mayorga, F., Sánchez, F., Díaz, D.: Generación de librerías de código base para autenticación a través de certificados SSL generados automáticamente utilizando Java (2016)
14. Delaney, S.: Secure embedded communications. Electronic Products (Garden City, New York), **53**(4) (2011)
15. Chen, L., Tao, L., Li, X., Lin, C.: A tool for teaching web application security. In: Proceedings of the 14th Colloquium for Information Systems Security Education, pp. 17–24 (2010)
16. Aly, H., Elgayyar, M.: Attacking AES using bernstein's attack on modern processors (2013)
17. Atamli-Reineh, A., Paverd, A., Petracca, G., Martin, A.: A framework for application partitioning using trusted execution environments. Concurr. Comput. **29**(23), e4130 (2017)
18. Sohail, F., Ahmed, J., Habib, Z.: PKI based cryptographic module. Paper presented at the 17th IEEE International Multi Topic Conference: Collaborative and Sustainable Development of Technologies, IEEE INMIC 2014 - Proceedings, pp. 87–91 (2015)
19. Racine, J.: The Cygwin tools: a GNU toolkit for Windows (2000)
20. Zhang, H.R., Zeng, W.X., Jiang, T.H.: Realization of certificate authority using Java and OpenSSL. Appl. Res. Comput. **5**, 055 (2004)
21. Seidl, R., Goetze, N., Bauer-Hermann, M.: U.S. Patent No. 9,979,716. U.S. Patent and Trademark Office, Washington, DC (2018)
22. Yu, Y., He, W.: Design of acoustic emission monitoring system based on VC++. In: Proceedings of SPIE - The International Society for Optical Engineering, vol. 9794 (2015)

23. Jawi, S.M., Ali, F.H.M.: Rules and results for SSL/TLS nonintrusive proxy based on JSON data. In: 2016 6th International Conference on IT Convergence and Security, ICITCS 2016 (2016)
24. Tzvetkov, V.: Disaster coverable PKI model based on majority trust principle. In: International Conference on Information Technology: Coding Computing, ITCC, vol. 2, pp. 118–119 (2004)
25. Boopathi, M., Panwar, M., Goel, M.: SSL-Heartbleed bug. Int. J. Appl. Eng. Res. **10**(4), 9947–9956 (2015)
26. Pitt, E.: Scalable secure sockets. In: Pitt, E. (ed.) Fundamental Networking in Java, pp. 185–213. Springer, London (2006). https://doi.org/10.1007/1-84628-252-7
27. Pich, C., Nachmanson, L., Robertson, G.G.: Visual analysis of importance and grouping in software dependency graphs. In: Proceedings of the 4th ACM Symposium on Software Visualization, pp. 29–32. ACM, September 2008

IoT-Based System to Help Care for Dependent Elderly

Gleiston Guerrero-Ulloa[1,2], Carlos Rodríguez-Domínguez[2],
and Miguel J. Hornos[2(✉)]

[1] State Technical University of Quevedo, 120501 Quevedo, Ecuador
gguerrero@uteq.edu.ec
[2] Software Engineering Department, University of Granada,
18071 Granada, Spain
gleiston@correo.ugr.es,
{carlosrodriguez,mhornos}@ugr.es

Abstract. The aging of the population in most developed countries has increased the need of proposing and adopting systems to monitor the behaviour of elder people with cognitive impairment. Home monitoring is particularly important for caregivers and relatives, who are in charge of these persons in potentially risky environments (e.g., the kitchen, the bathroom, the stairs, go out alone to the street, etc.), while they perform their household activities. On the other hand, the paradigm of Internet of Things (IoT) allows the interconnection of everyday objects to implement sophisticate, yet simple-to-use, computer systems. In this paper, we analyse the existing IoT-based proposals to monitor elder people at home. Moreover, we propose a generic design of an IoT-based home monitoring system that allows caregivers, relatives and/or emergency services to be notified of potentially risky demeanours. Finally, some scenarios or situations are presented in order to better understand the proposal, and to validate its design to cover some common use cases.

Keywords: Assisted Living · Home monitoring · Elderly
Caregiver assistance · Access control to restricted areas

1 Introduction

Life expectancy has been steadily increasing all over the world for the past decades, and it is expected to continue so in the future. As a consequence, both the amount and the percentage of elder people have increased, especially in the most developed countries. This group of people usually suffer from multiple chronic diseases, which convert them into more fragile and dependent persons. Consequently, they demand further caring, also generating a health, social and familiar yet-to-be-solved challenge [1].

Many relatives of dependent old people take care of them, while they also take charge of the household keeping. Moreover, they usually must take responsibility of other activities and tasks. The concerns that these relatives commonly have regarding the well-being of the people who they take care of could be decreased through the implementation of computer systems to monitor them. In this regard, the most recent

© Springer Nature Switzerland AG 2019
M. Botto-Tobar et al. (Eds.): CITT 2018, CCIS 895, pp. 41–55, 2019.
https://doi.org/10.1007/978-3-030-05532-5_4

advances in Internet of Things (IoT) [2] could be of great interest to be able to implement a simple-to-use, yet technically complex, monitoring system.

Nowadays, IoT is an emerging research field with a potentially huge transformation effect in our societies. Home appliances, buildings, vehicles, daily objects, etc. are starting to be connected to the Internet, equipped with enough computing resources to be able to capture and analyse information to improve our lifestyle, work, education, etc. The projected impact of IoT over Internet and the worldwide economy is extensive. In fact, CISCO [3] predicted that over 50,000 million devices would be connected to the Internet in 2020.

Some IoT-based systems have been developed to help care for the elderly, with a view to reducing the costs required for the care of this group of vulnerable people. Some of them are systems patient caring within hospitals [4–7], while others perform remote patient monitoring [8–10]. In these systems, sensors collect data from people, as well as the objects they use and their physical environment. The collected data is processed by the system to obtain useful information that proactively and transparently can provide the users with helpful information to improve their lifestyle, thus converting usual environments into intelligent environments [11].

An intelligent environment implies the interconnection of different devices in a determinated physical space, so that computing devices automatically respond to human behaviour and needs. To achieve that goal, systems and applications must be developed to handle both context information [12] and user preferences [13], in order to adequately respond to the needs demanded by the assisted people. In fact, there are works related to intelligent systems and context-aware services [14–16] whose objective is to help elder people to live a more independent and safe life in their own homes [4].

In this paper, a system is proposed for the care of dependent elderly people who live with their caregiver, so it is necessary to identify each person according to their role, using non-intrusive devices. In this system, older people have access restrictions to certain areas of the home that are considered dangerous for them. The caregiver will receive notifications on his/her smartphone. In addition, the elderly will be able to receive notifications about activities that they should or can perform, such as taking their medications, watching his/her favourite TV program, etc.

We have followed the approach of using non-intrusive devices since we consider that dependent elderly people, especially if they have any cognitive problems, might find certain objects used to monitor them as intrusive (e.g., bracelets, smartphones, and body sensors [10, 17]). In practice, such a feeling would make them to take these devices away or to forget to carry the devices with them [18]. Equally intrusive can be considered video cameras, violating the privacy of the person under surveillance [19].

The rest of the paper is structured as follows. Section 2 presents some related work to the proposal presented herein. Section 3 describes the proposal, depicting its layered architecture and giving details about the functioning of each of its layers. Section 4 presents a scenario and a set of use cases to validate the proposal. Finally, Sect. 5 outlines the conclusions and some directions for future work.

2 Related Works

In recent years, many scientific contributions have been made in the field of IoT applied to the care and monitoring of older people. More specifically, most of these works are currently focused on monitoring the behaviour and health status of this group of people. A problem usually addressed in several recent contributions is fall detection. In this context, Odunmbaku et al. [20] propose a tele-health system, based on IO (Internet of Objects), which also allows monitoring elderly people suffering from Alzheimer's disease and the quality of their sleep. This system is capable of capturing the vital signs of the users and making them remotely accessible. De Luca et al. [9] propose an algorithm for fall detection based on the use of accelerometers and gyroscopes.

Monitoring the user behaviour, especially of people with cognitive impairment, is also a widely addressed problem in the literature. For instance, Cunha et al. [10] have developed a system to support the continuous and proactive care of the elderly. This system is based on the detection of ambient light from a mobile device, as an alternative to the use of body sensors, in order to create a ubiquitous and multiuser system to recognize, inform and alert about environmental changes and human activities at home. The system uses lights and sounds to alert about the actions of the monitored people. In addition, it recognizes some of their daily activities, identifying the individual and his/her movements in the house, by using RFID technology.

The improvement of the elderly independence, through the use of technology, is also a very prolific research area. In WITSCare [4], the researchers present an IoT-based system and implement a web application whose main objective is to help older people to live more safely at their own homes. WITSCare offers an analysis of contextual information (e.g., about daily activities). The system learns about users and allows creating rules to personalize services through a graphical interface. After the system learns enough about the user, it offers the contexts as services (universal contexts). However, the authors do not specify what happens when the person in question (from whom the system must learn about) lives with other people.

In the field of positioning and tracking of objects or people, both outdoors and indoors, several works have been published. Among them, Del Campo et al. [21] present an overview of middleware solutions designed for IoT in the domains of health and well-being. Likewise, they present as a case study an assistive technology that includes support for home monitoring of people with dementia. It is illustrated how a specific middleware designed for telemetry applications, the MQTT (Message Queuing Telemetry Transport), can be effectively applied in welfare scenarios, with different architectural options and communication technologies. Chu et al. [22] present the design of a robot with automatic tracking to help the elderly at home, being able to determine their location by using RSSI (Received Signal Strength Indication). In addition, using ultrasonic sensors and internal maps, the robot positions the people and creates a route to find them. If there is any obstacle in its path, it will automatically modify its route to avoid it. However, a limitation of this work is that it does not help prevent access to places that pose a potential danger to the person. On the other hand, Shang et al. [23] present the design of Foglight, which uses light sensors to position objects with an average precision of 1.7 mm. Mainetti et al. [24] propose an Ambient

Assisted Living (AAL) system that includes the continuous monitoring of the health status of the elderly through the data gathered from heterogeneous sources (for example, environmental sensors and medical devices). It is also able to offer real-time user positioning, either outdoors or inside the home. The collected data is analysed and, if necessary, notifications and alerts are generated.

IoT has also been widely applied to health monitoring of patients. Thus, Chen [5] proposes a system of acquisition of multi-physiological parameters for e-health. The system incorporates sensors installed in ZigBee terminal nodes, which are responsible of collecting the physiological parameters of the human body with low latency and transmitting them for their visualization in real time. Zanjal et al. [6] propose the use of IoT to remind patients of the intake of certain medications. On the other hand, Dziak et al. [7] address the problem of assisting elderly people living alone by covering certain healthcare needs, such as difficulty in mobility, symptoms of dementia or other health problems. To do this, they propose a both outdoors and indoors positioning system based on IoT that uses the accelerometer and the magnetometer, as well as pattern recognition, edge detection and an algorithm based on decision trees. In addition, the system identifies falls and daily activities, such as lying down, getting up, sitting down and walking, classifying them as normal, suspicious or dangerous. If necessary, it also notifies the medical attention staff about possible problems.

Another important research field is the one associated with smart homes. Dawadi et al. [25] perform a literature review to determine the most important applications to help the elderly within their home. These authors select 25 works, in which they identify as study topics, from most to least concern, the monitoring of: health, the kitchen, the living room, the bedroom, the security, the bathrooms (toilets), and the social connection, among others. They also identify the following objects as candidates for continuous monitoring: bed, lamp, mobile, medicine bottle, door, window, chair, stove, dishwasher, sink, kettle, fridge, TV, food cabinet, table and sofa. In their analysis, they conclude that the monitoring of these activities and objects is very useful for caregivers. On the other hand, they emphasize that the use of sensors is very frequent, and that the applications developed in the different works act only in very specific scenarios. Zhou et al. [26] present a model of context-aware information for smart homes, addressing the problem of home care services for the elderly (Elderly Homecare Services - EHS). To do this, they use the technique of constructing activity models and apply them for ADL (Activities of Daily Living) recognition. Although the proposal recognizes the activities performed by a person, they do not specify whether or not it addresses the recognition of the specific person who performs them. Davis et al. [27] carry out two studies on the use of lights to transmit information. In the first one, they explore the adequate characteristics of light (colour, frequency of changes and brightness) to promote context awareness, so they examine the preferences, perceptions and interpretations of environmental lighting configurations. In the second study, they determine if there were significant implications of the activity awareness through illumination, without affecting the mood or the social connection of the people. Although it was not tested with older adults, the presented results prompted us to propose the emission of light as part of the notifications.

Several of the works mentioned [10, 23, 26], linked to monitoring, positioning and smart homes, respectively, have similar objectives to the ones proposed in our work.

Likewise, the system presented in [24] emits alerts about events caused by older adults during their daily activities at home. However, in contrast to the proposal presented in this article, access to sites with high levels of danger is not restricted or monitored. More specifically, our proposal consists of an IoT-based system that allows the caregiver to monitor the elderly's activities, establishing areas and activities that are restricted or supervised. In addition, it allows us to provide reminders about routine daily activities that must be performed by the users supervised.

3 Proposed System

3.1 Motivation and Objectives

Many older people live in their homes accompanied and cared by their relatives/caregivers. However, in the literary review carried out, no studies have been found about helping these relatives/caregivers who live with them in their caring tasks. So far, the published works on this subject are clearly focused on proposing IoT-based systems that allow monitoring people and notifying their caregivers, family members and/or emergency health services about certain harmful events and alerts. For example, their vital signs are monitored, their location inside and outside the house, the falls they suffer are detected, etc. In addition to covering some of these aspects, in this work we propose a system that distinguishes whether the elderly is alone at home or with their caregiver(s), focusing especially on serving as an assistant and support tool for the latter. Consequently, the idea is to facilitate his/her caring tasks.

More specifically, the proposed system has 3 main objectives: (i) Blocking accesses (doors) to the rooms of the house that would pose a certain danger for the elderly, particularly for those who have cognitive problems. This contributes to an improved tranquillity on the side of the family member/caregiver, especially when the latter is away from home. (ii) Issuing notifications for those who are inside the house, making use of everyday objects (lights, speakers, etc.), and for those who are out of it, through the smartphone. The notifications may also be issued to alert/warn the elderly about certain activities that they are performing or have to perform. (iii) Informing family members who do not live or who are not at home with the elderly about the events that occur within it.

3.2 System Architecture

The architecture of the proposed system consists of 5 layers, which are depicted in Fig. 1. More information regarding layered-based architectures for cloud computing can be found in [28].

Sensors/Actuators Layer. It consists of a network of sensors/actuators, interconnected through Bluetooth and Wi-Fi, coupled to Arduino Uno boards and distributed throughout the home. The sensors will detect the signals corresponding to environmental events, which will be transmitted to the local computing layer. Actuators will receive from said layer the corresponding control commands to act on the physical environment.

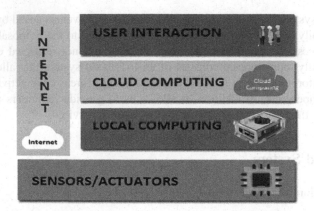

Fig. 1. Layered architecture of the proposed system.

In each of the entrances (doors) to the rooms that may pose a risk for the elderly, a sensors/actuators network node (SANN) will be installed. Each SANN will consist of a proximity sensor, RFID sensors [29, 30] and an Arduino board [31]. In addition, a notification node (NN) could be installed, which will integrate LED lights [27] and speakers, together with an Arduino Uno board, in those objects in which the elderly pays special attention (for example: a mirror, TV, etc.).

All the people (whether they are caregivers, relatives or elderly people) who live in the home will imperceptibly carry an RFID tag on their clothing that will store their identification data. The proximity sensor will detect when a person approaches a certain distance, being able to configure this distance (and set, for example, to 80 cm). When someone is at that distance or less from the door in question, the Arduino board will take the data captured by the RFID reader (corresponding to the RFID tag that the person carries) and will send the data to the central processing node, which is located at the local computing layer.

The speakers, as part of the NN, will allow reproducing different sounds or music [32], which will serve as warning or prohibition notifications, depending on the potential risk of the situation. Prohibition notifications will also prevent the elderly to perform certain tasks without the presence of their caregiver. In addition, the LED lights will serve as a visual complement to the auditory signal. Warnings will turn green LED lights on, while prohibition notifications will turn them red.

Local Computing Layer. It will be responsible for managing, validating and processing all the signals captured by the previous layer, as well as generating all the control signals. Its main functions consist of: identifying the person who approaches the entrances of the controlled rooms of the house, issuing notifications about the events that occurred and the orders sent by the caregivers from their mobile devices, as well as delivering the data for its storage in the cloud computing layer. It will consist of a Raspberry Pi [33] (central processing node) on which the database services will be executed, and the software for the control and administration of data.

When this layer receives data from the sensors/actuators layer, it will access the local data (stored in a database) and will make a query to identify a matching person.

In case the identified person is the elderly being supervised and an access to a restricted room is attempted, then it will issue control signals to prevent the door from opening and it will alert of the potentially harmful situation. For other unrestricted rooms, the layer will simply notify that the elderly has entered them.

This layer will manage the data of the people living in the house, introduced by means of a mobile application, and the configuration of the SANNs installed in the doors of the rooms whose access is to be controlled, so that it can deny and alert the access attempt, as well as temporarily disable one of the SANNs or the global system. In addition, it will keep the data updated in the cloud, which can be consulted by the caregivers/family members through a web application.

The layer will also communicate with the SANNs to obtain the data captured by the sensors and send the control commands to the actuators, after searching for matches with the data stored in the database to identify the person in question.

Cloud Computing Layer. This layer involves a (third-party) cloud server for hosting the database (which will contain the data sent by the local computing layer) and the web application, in addition to the web application server. Through the web application, family members/caregivers can be informed about the events that have occurred in the monitored home, as well as send notifications or commands (e.g., reminders, turning a certain light on/off, etc.) to the local computing layer.

The model MVC (Model-View-Controller) has been chosen (see Fig. 2) to develop the web application, which will facilitate its future maintenance. Since this application is hosted in the cloud, it can be accessed from any place and any device through an Internet connection. This application and the mobile application will share the same database.

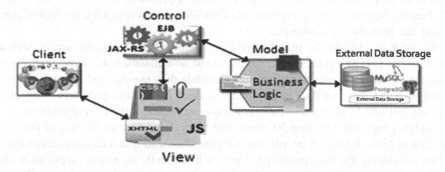

Fig. 2. Development model selected for the web application.

In addition, storage and processing in the cloud are designed with the possibility of implementing the system in different houses where older people live. Therefore, a single web application, hosted in a single domain, allows non-co-located users to use the same infrastructure, but only accessing their private information, thus reducing the costs that would entail the installation of multiple instances (one per address) of the web application.

User Interaction Layer. It consists of a mobile application and a web application. Its function will be to keep caregivers/relatives informed, when they are away from home. The applications will enable to send notifications and commands that will be processed by the local computing layer. More specifically, caregivers can use these applications to: configure the sensor network, enable/disable the system, issue/receive notifications and issue commands.

The notifications and commands may be issued by the system, the caregivers and/or the elderly (as long as they have the capacity to handle the mobile/web application). Likewise, the notifications and commands may be directed to be received by the caregivers, the elderly and/or the sensors/actuators layer to take any action.

The network nodes, when installed at the entrances of each room of the house, must be configured as completely restricted or potentially risky. To do this, the mobile/web application will interact with such nodes and store the corresponding data in the database, in both (local and cloud) computing layers. Moreover, the web application will allow the relatives to consult the events that occurred within the home(s) for which they have access permission to consult this information.

Internet Layer. Internet will be the communication network between the three upper layers, that is, it will serve to communicate and synchronize the local and cloud computing layers, and to communicate the user interaction layer with the computing ones.

3.3 Mobile Application Interfaces and Their Evaluation

In Fig. 3, four screenshots of the prototype user interface are depicted. Screenshot (A) shows the login screen, in which the application asks for the user's email and password, while Screenshot (B) presents the current menu options. The profile of the supervised people can be configured in the mobile application, as shown in Screenshot (C). Finally, Screenshot (D) presents a list of the locations in which the monitored older person has been during a timespan.

In order to validate the usability of the user interface, we make use of several contributions [34, 35], since we are willing to test an unfinished prototype application. Analysing users' reaction and their comments while they use the application is the key to improve the user interface and produce a final application prototype. The pilot usability test will be oriented to analyse the user experience. We have determined that the usability tests will last from 30 min to one hour, depending on the skill of the user. The first test will involve 5 people, but we plan to extend that analysis to more users before developing the final prototype. Users will test both the mobile application and the web application. The mobile application (.apk) is going to be sent by email to be directly installed on the users' smartphones. The mobile application will automatically collect usage statistics. The web application is going to be tested by each user in front of a computer connected to an intranet.

The evaluating users will be asked to fill out and sign the informed consent letter and fill in the form with their demographic data, including age, gender, experience in the use of mobile applications, and Internet experience. If the user has any comments regarding the applications, he/she should mention them and explain them to the member of the development team who is present during the test.

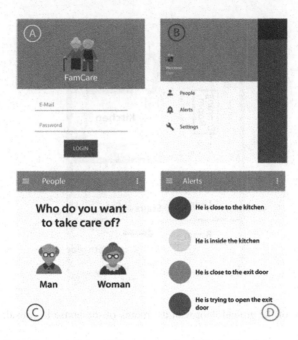

Fig. 3. Several screenshots of the proposed mobile application user interface.

4   Scenario and Cases to Validate the Proposal

In this section, we present a scenario and a series of cases that can occur within that scenario in order to validate the feasibility of the proposed system. Let us consider the scenario of a house with two (or more) floors. On the ground floor, depicted in Fig. 4, we find the living room and other spaces that will be considered for the implementation of our system. As shown in Fig. 4, there are 6 access points that can be assumed to be risky, 3 of which are completely forbidden: main entrance (A), and exit doors to the terrace (B and C), and 3 are precautionary: kitchen (D), stairs (E) and toilets (F). The system has been configured so that objects O1 and O2 reproduce a different sound when the elderly tries to access and/or enter each of these rooms in the house.

In all the cases considered, the system stores the data in the cloud (in addition to the local computing layer), so that they can be accessed through the web application from anywhere and from any device that has a browser installed and an Internet connection. The notifications are also sent to the mobile device [36] when the system reacts in some way.

Two situations have been considered: the first one, when the caregiver is in the house with the elderly person, and the second one, when the caregiver leaves the house and the old person is left alone. Below, we detail the cases that can occur in each of these two situations.

Fig. 4. Blueprint of the ground floor with the rooms of the house to consider for the tests.

4.1   Situation 1: Caregiver at Home

Let us suppose that the caregiver is on the top floor, and the elderly is sitting on the sofa in the living room (which is on the ground floor, as shown in Fig. 4), watching his/her favourite television program. Below, we will analyse a series of cases that can occur in this situation:

Case 1. The elderly stands up and goes to the bathroom, so the proximity sensor placed in F detects that he/she is approaching. The Arduino board at that point (F) calculates the distance with the information received from the proximity sensor. When it is less than the determined distance (for example, 80 cm), it takes the data read by the RFID sensor and sends this data to the central computer (Raspberry Pi). It searches in the database to identify the person and identifies the elderly. It then sends the appropriate control signals to the O1 and O2 objects so that the speakers reproduce the warning sound or music (configured according to the preferences of the inhabitants of the house) and the green LED lights turn on. When the caregiver listens to the music, he/she knows that the elderly has entered the bathroom. While the elderly remains in the bathroom, the music continues to play and the LED lights remain lit in green. When he/she leaves the bathroom, the speakers stop playing the music and the LED lights go off, so the caregiver knows that he/she has left the bathroom. In case the elderly stays for too long in it, the system could indicate that something might go wrong; thus, the caregiver would quickly go down to see what is happening.

Case 2. The elderly goes to the kitchen to take something from the fridge. The proximity sensor placed in D captures the nearness and the Arduino that is at that point calculates the distance similarly as done in the previous case. When the distance is within the considered range, it takes the data read by the RFID reader and identifies the elderly. Then the system sends the relevant commands to the objects O1 and O2 so that the speakers play the corresponding music (different from the bathroom) and the LED lights turn on, also in green, since it is a warning notification, as in Case 1. When the caregiver listens to that music, he/she knows that the elderly has entered the kitchen, and the moment the music stops playing and the LED lights go off he will know that the person has abandoned that place. If the elderly stays for too long in the kitchen, then the system will notify it, and the caregiver may go down to check if everything is going well. Hence, as this case is similar to Case 1, the system will act analogously in both cases, except in the reproduced music. Something similar will happen when the elderly approaches and goes up or down the stairs, except that the music played will be different from the one played in the mentioned cases. So, if the elderly falls down the stairs, the caregiver will quickly know it.

Case 3. The elderly approaches the door of the terrace, considered a restricted area to which he/she cannot access alone, given that he/she could then go out into the street and, as this person becomes easily disoriented, he/she would be lost. The proximity sensor placed in B detects that the elderly person brings near and the Arduino board of that SANN identifies him/her (as explained in the previous cases). Then, the system blocks the access door to the terrace, to ensure that the person cannot access that place, and sends the commands to the objects O1 and O2 to reproduce the corresponding sound or music of prohibition and turn on the red LED lights. When the caregiver listens to that sound or music, he/she knows that the elderly is trying to access the terrace. While the latter remains within the established distance range (about 80 cm, for example), the system will continue to play the music and the LED lights will light red. If the elderly stays there for a long time, then the caregiver could go down and persuade the elderly to return to the room or go out with him to the terrace. Something similar would happen if the elderly tries to open the other door that gives access to the terrace (C) or the one of the main entrance (A).

Case 4. The caregiver goes down the stairs, and goes to the bathroom, the kitchen, and the door of the terrace. As the system identifies the caregiver (making use of the signals detected by the SANNs placed in E, F, D and B respectively, when he/she is within the range of distance specified for each place), the corresponding doors are not blocked and commands are not issued to reproduce any sound or to switch on the LED lights.

4.2 Situation 2: Absent Caregiver

In this situation, the caregiver leaves the home, leaving the elderly alone at it, sitting on the couch in the living room, watching his favourite TV show. Now, we will analyse a series of cases that may occur in this situation:

Case 5. The elderly approaches the bathroom and the system detects it, like in Case 1. As a result, instead of sending the commands to objects O1 and O2 to play the corresponding music and turn on the green LED lights, the caregiver receives the notification on his/her smartphone by means of the mobile application, informing that the elderly has entered the bathroom. In addition, the mobile application turns on the flash of the caregiver's smartphone intermittently, which will remain that way until the elderly leaves the bathroom. Therefore, when the caregiver's smartphone flash goes out, the caregiver will know that the elderly has left that location. Something similar will happen when the elderly goes to the kitchen or the stairwell.

Case 6. The elderly approaches the door of the terrace. When the system detects him/her (as explained in Case 3), in addition to blocking the door to ensure that he/she cannot open it, it sends a notification to the caregiver's mobile application. If the caregiver considers it necessary, he/she could send notifications to the elderly person's smartphone (if he/she has one) or to another object in the environment (such as loudspeakers, for example) with a reassuring message. In addition, he/she could send a notification so that one of the other caregivers/family members approaches the home and checks for the status of the elderly person and reassures him/her, if necessary.

Case 7. The caregiver sees that returning home will take him/her longer than expected at the time of his/her departure, so he/she sends a notification directly to the person being cared for (if he/she is able to use his/her smartphone) and/or objects of the environment, to inform him/hem of the activities he/she must perform, such as: showering, taking a nap, taking some medicines, etc. As in the previous case, if the caregiver considers that the elderly needs direct attention, he/she could inform all the family members so that someone come to the home and give the elderly person the help he/she needs.

5 Conclusions and Future Work

We have presented a system especially intended to help caregivers or family members in their responsibility to ensure the well-being of the elderly people that they take care of, as well as to monitor, protect and assist the latter. In the literature review carried out, we have found systems that have been implemented/proposed with the aim of helping elderly people who live alone. However, from our point of view, such systems have not focused enough on the caregivers who share their lives with the elderly served. In addition, no systems have been found that control access to certain rooms, considered dangerous for people who have certain cognitive problems.

An outline of the architecture of the proposed system has also been presented, and each of the layers that integrate it (as well as its components) has been explained.

To validate the proposed system, we have presented a scenario and a series of possible cases within it, considering the two general situations that can occur in a dwelling with dependent elderly people in it: (1) these elderly people are left alone at home (because their caregivers have left); and (2) both the elderly people and their caregivers are at home.

Our proposal has to be tested with real users in their own homes. This will provide us a lot of information to improve the system, and especially its user interfaces regarding usability and adaptation aspects.

All of the monitoring data obtained will be stored, with the permission of the people involved, to be analysed and used later in a study on the behaviour of dependent older people with and without their caregiver present at home. The idea is to use the results that can be extracted from this analysis to implement systems that autonomously make increasingly intelligent decisions, in order to improve the well-being of the elderly people they are trying to serve. This task will occupy the authors' attention in the near future.

Additionally, the usability of the mobile and web applications will be tested with real users before developing a final prototype.

Security and privacy issues will be addressed in a future research paper, and the whole system implementation will be published as open source as soon as we finish producing a debugged source code and a detailed deployment documentation.

Finally, facial recognition techniques could be incorporated into the system to identify people and, depending on who they are, to allow them or not to access the different rooms of the dwelling. Decision making techniques could also be applied to automatically analyse the collected data in order to increase the accuracy of the alerts.

References

1. Kornfeld Mate, R., Fernández Lorca, M.B., Belloni Symon, C.L., Martín Larraín, P.P., Quinteros Reillan, M.C.: Personas Mayores y Demencia: Realidad y Desafíos. Pontificia Universidad Católica de Chile, Chile (2015). http://omayor.cl/wp-content/uploads/2016/05/PERSONAS-MAYORES-Y-DEMENCIA-FINAL-2.pdf
2. Perera, C., Zaslavsky, A., Christen, P., Georgakopoulos, D.: Context-aware computing for the Internet of Things: a survey. IEEE Commun. Surv. Tutorials **16**(1), 414–454 (2014)
3. Evans, D.: The Internet of Things - how the next evolution of the internet is changing everything. CISCO White Paper, pp. 1–11, April 2011. https://www.cisco.com/c/dam/en_us/about/ac79/docs/innov/IoT_IBSG_0411FINAL.pdf
4. Yao, L., Benatallah, B., Wang, X., Tran, N.K., Lu, Q.: Context as a service: realizing Internet of Things-aware processes for the independent living of the elderly. In: Sheng, Q.Z., Stroulia, E., Tata, S., Bhiri, S. (eds.) ICSOC 2016. LNCS, vol. 9936, pp. 763–779. Springer, Cham (2016). https://doi.org/10.1007/978-3-319-46295-0_54
5. Chen, W.: Design of a remote health monitoring system based on wireless sensor networks. In: International Conference on Applied Mechanics and Mechanical Automation (AMMA 2017), pp. 294–297 (2017). DEStech Transactions on Engineering and Technology Research
6. Zanjal, S.V., Talmale, G.R.: Medicine reminder and monitoring system for secure health using IOT. Proc. Comput. Sci. **78**, 471–476 (2016)
7. Dziak, D., Jachimczyk, B., Kulesza, W.: IoT-based information system for healthcare application: design methodology approach. Appl. Sci. **7**(6), 596–621 (2017)
8. Raad, M.W., Sheltami, T., Shakshuki, E.: Ubiquitous tele-health system for elderly patients with Alzheimer's. Proc. Comput. Sci. **52**, 685–689 (2015)
9. De Luca, G.E., Carnuccio, E.A., Garcia, G.G., Barillaro, S.: IoT fall detection system for the elderly using Intel Galileo development boards generation I. In: IEEE Congreso Argentino de Ciencias de la Informática y Desarrollos de Investigación (CACIDI 2016), pp. 1–6 (2016)
10. Cunha, M., Fuks, H.: AmbLEDs collaborative healthcare for AAL systems. In: IEEE 19th International Conference on Computer Supported Cooperative Work in Design (CSCWD 2015), pp. 626–631. IEEE (2015)
11. Augusto, J.C., Callaghan, V., Cook, D., Kameas, A., Satoh, I.: Intelligent environments: a manifesto. Hum. Centric Comput. Inf. Sci. **3**(1), 12 (2013)

12. Alegre, U., Augusto, J.C., Clark, T.: Engineering context-aware systems and applications: a survey. J. Syst. Softw. **117**, 55–83 (2016)
13. Oguego, C.L., Augusto, J.C., Muñoz, A., Springett, M.: A survey on managing users' preferences in ambient intelligence. Univ. Access Inf. Soc. **17**(1), 97–114 (2018)
14. Gil, D., Ferrández, A., Mora-Mora, H., Peral, J.: Internet of Things: a review of surveys based on context aware intelligent services. Sensors **16**(7), 1–23 (2016)
15. Hossain, M.A., Alamri, A., Almogren, A.S., Hossain, A., Parra, J.: A framework for a context-aware elderly entertainment support system. Sensors **14**(6), 10538–10561 (2014)
16. Abreu, C., Miranda, F., Mendes, P.M.: Smart context-aware QoS-based admission control for biomedical wireless sensor networks. J. Netw. Comput. Appl. **88**, 134–145 (2017)
17. Al-Shaqi, R., Mourshed, M., Rezgui, Y.: Progress in ambient assisted systems for independent living by the elderly. SpringerPlus **5**(1), 624 (2016)
18. Azimi, I., Rahmani, A.M., Liljeberg, P., Tenhunen, H.: Internet of Things for remote elderly monitoring: a study from user-centered perspective. J. Ambient Intell. Humaniz. Comput. **8** (2), 273–289 (2017)
19. Yared, R., Abdulrazak, B.: Toward context-aware smart oven to prevent cooking risks in kitchen of elderly people. In: Helfert, M., Holzinger, A., Ziefle, M., Fred, A., O'Donoghue, J., Röcker, C. (eds.) Information and Communication Technologies for Ageing Well and e-Health. CCIS, vol. 578, pp. 57–77. Springer, Cham (2015). https://doi.org/10.1007/978-3-319-27695-3_4
20. Odunmbaku, A., Rahmani, A.-M., Liljeberg, P., Tenhunen, H.: Elderly monitoring system with sleep and fall detector. In: Mandler, B., et al. (eds.) IoT360 2015. LNICST, vol. 169, pp. 473–480. Springer, Cham (2016). https://doi.org/10.1007/978-3-319-47063-4_51
21. Del Campo, A., Gambi, E., Montanini, L., Perla, D., Raffaeli, L., Spinsante, S.: MQTT in AAL systems for home monitoring of people with dementia. In: IEEE 27th Annual International Symposium on Personal, Indoor, and Mobile Radio Communications (PIMRC 2016), pp. 1–6. IEEE (2016)
22. Chu, H.C., Chien, M.F., Lin, T.H., Zhang, Z.J.: Design and implementation of an auto-following robot-car system for the elderly. In: International Conference on System Science and Engineering (ICSSE 2016), pp. 1–4. IEEE (2016)
23. Ma, S., Liu, Q., Phillip, C.-Y.: Foglight: visible light-enabled indoor localization system for low-power IoT devices. IEEE Internet Things J. **5**(1), 175–185 (2018)
24. Mainetti, L., Patrono, L., Secco, A., Sergi, I.: An IoT-aware AAL system for elderly people. In: International Multidisciplinary Conference on Computer and Energy Science (SpliTech 2016), pp. 1–6. IEEE (2016)
25. Dawadi, R., Asghar, Z., Pulli, P.: Internet of Things controlled home objects for the elderly. In: 10th International Joint Conference on Biomedical Engineering Systems and Technologies (BioSTEC 2017), vol. 5, pp. 244–251 (2017)
26. Zhou, F., Jiao, J.R., Chen, S., Zhang, D.: A context-aware information model for elderly homecare services in a smart home. In: ASME 2009 International Design Engineering Technical Conferences and Computers and Information in Engineering Conference, vol. 5. 35th Design Automation Conference, Parts A and B, pp. 1009–1018. The American Society of Mechanical Engineers (2009)
27. Davis, K., Owusu, E.B., Marcenaro, L., Feijs, L., Regazzoni, C., Hu, J.: Effects of ambient lighting displays on peripheral activity awareness. IEEE Access **5**, 9318–9335 (2017)
28. Singh, P., Jain, E.A.: Survey paper on cloud computing. Int. J. Innov. Eng. Technol. **3**(4), 84–89 (2014)
29. Amendola, S., Lodato, R., Manzari, S., Occhiuzzi, C., Marrocco, G.: RFID technology for IoT-based personal healthcare in smart spaces. IEEE Internet Things J. **1**(2), 144–152 (2014)

30. Chen, M., Gonzalez, S., Leung, V., Zhang, Q., Li, M.: A 2G-RFID-based e-healthcare system. IEEE Wirel. Commun. **17**(1), 37–43 (2010)
31. Piyare, R.: Internet of Things: ubiquitous home control and monitoring system using android based smart phone. Int. J. Internet Things **2**(1), 5–11 (2013)
32. Kanai, K., Nakada, T., Hanbat, Y., Kunifuji, S.: A support system for context awareness in a group home using sound cues. In: Second International Conference on Pervasive Computing Technologies for Healthcare (PervasiveHealth 2008), pp. 264–267. IEEE (2008)
33. Gill, A.Q., Phennel, N., Lane, D., Phung, V.L.: IoT-enabled emergency information supply chain architecture for elderly people: the Australian context. Inf. Syst. **58**, 75–86 (2016)
34. Cayola, L., Macías, J.A.: Systematic guidance on usability methods in user-centered software development. Inf. Softw. Technol. **97**, 163–175 (2018)
35. Quiñones, D., Rusu, C., Rusu, V.: A methodology to develop usability/user experience heuristics. Comput. Standards Interfaces **59**, 109–129 (2018)
36. Fiore, A., Caione, A., Zappatore, D., De Mitri, G., Mainetti, L.: Deploying mobile middleware for the monitoring of elderly people with the Internet of Things: a case study. In: Longo, A., et al. (eds.) IISSC/CN4IoT -2017. LNICST, vol. 189, pp. 29–36. Springer, Cham (2018). https://doi.org/10.1007/978-3-319-67636-4_4

VoIP System Dimensioning the Radio-Links and the VSAT of the MINTEL School Connectivity Project Through the TELCONET S.A. Network

Joffre León-Acurio[1]([✉]) [iD], Enrique Ismael Delgado Cuadro[1] [iD],
Luis Miguel Navarro Veliz[2] [iD], Miguel Botto-Tobar[1,3,4] [iD],
Luis Isaías Bastidas Zambrano[1] [iD], and Byron Oviedo[5] [iD]

[1] Universidad Técnica de Babahoyo, Babahoyo, Ecuador
{jvleon,edelgado,mbotto,lbastidas}@utb.edu.ec
[2] Telconet S.A., Guayaquil, Ecuador
luisnavarrove@hotmail.com
[3] Eindhoven University of Technology, Eindhoven, The Netherlands
m.a.botto.tobar@tue.nl
[4] Universidad de Guayaquil, Guayaquil, Ecuador
miguel.bottot@ug.edu.ec
[5] Universidad Técnica Estatal de Quevedo, Quevedo, Ecuador
boviedo@uteq.edu.ec

Abstract. Due to the constant changes that technology offers, it has allowed us to integrate various services to telecommunication networks, to improve solutions and offer advantages in connectivity and remote access to places where you do not have access to networks, problems with cellular coverage have allowed us to look for alternative ways of communication and to improve education in rural and urban areas deployed in the connectivity project between Telconet S.A. and Mintel. For which it is appropriate to design a network and to deploy a robust VoIP system through radio links guaranteeing high transmission rates, so you can expand and better the services that contribute to the development of telecommunications in Ecuador. The proposed system provides technical features that make the system more efficient and allow the incorporation of quality of service protocols that provide optimum service to the user with imperceptible latency, as well as the possibility of permanent VoIP service availability through a backup system that is part of the contingency plan allowing to have universal access to information technologies and thus to the society of knowledge.

Keywords: Network access · Imperceptible latency · Connectivity project
System backup

© Springer Nature Switzerland AG 2019
M. Botto-Tobar et al. (Eds.): CITT 2018, CCIS 895, pp. 56–71, 2019.
https://doi.org/10.1007/978-3-030-05532-5_5

1 Introduction

In recent years, the need to incorporate citizens from the most vulnerable sectors of the country into the information and knowledge society has become evident, which allows us to reduce digital illiteracy and provide more opportunities for people of limited resources, making them more competitive in the world of work.

By virtue of this, and to comply with the social responsibility that TELCONET S.A. has with the country, a contract has been signed between this company and the Ministry of Telecommunications and Information Society (MINTEL) that seeks to improve internet penetration in rural and marginal urban sectors of the province of Guayas, thus contributing With the increase in universal access to fundamental communication and information services, this contract aims to provide equipment to Computational Laboratories and National Level Connectivity Service.

These laboratories offer the possibility of accessing the internet from the schools that are included in the contract signed between MINTEL and TELCONET SA, however, because they are located in remote areas of the province of Guayas, should they arise. Interruptions in Internet service due to failures in the network, in most cases it is not possible to attend to the requirements of those affected immediately because there is no real-time communication between the schools and the staff. TELCONET SA technical assistance, mainly because in those communities there are no conventional or mobile telephony networks that allow them to report incidents in a timely manner. For this reason, solving a problem of this nature can take days and even weeks.

Under the current conditions it is not possible to guarantee availability of the 99.999% Internet access service in the educational units benefiting from the project led by MINTEL, due to the lack of an appropriate communication mechanism between schools and the service. Technician of TELCONET SA that allows to provide assistance in the event that failures arise in any device that conforms to the Computer Lab. The impact on the continuity of the internet service has an important impact on the normal development of the classes as well as on the fulfillment of the Digital Literacy Education Program of the beneficiaries of the project and therefore on the development of the communities involved [1].

For which we opted for the design of a VoIP infrastructure for the solution of the communication problem, using as voice transport a radio-link network [2] and a Vsat network [3], taking into account as the main point the design for VoIP infrastructure [4], and making the comparison in QoS.

2 VoIP and Its Elements in a System

2.1 VoIP

Voice over IP technology standardized through the H.323 specification issued by the ITU (International Telecommunication Union) it allows the voice signal to travel in data packets through IP networks in digital form.

VoIP/H.323's primary objective is to facilitate and ensure the interoperability between equipment of various manufacturers and establishes the aspects such as the suppression of rests, compression and addressing, and the establishment of elements that allow the interconnectivity with the traditional switched telephone network (PSTN). In the Fig. 1 shows the H.323 protocol tower [5].

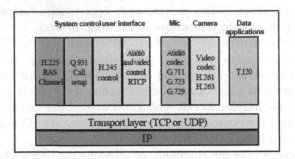

Fig. 1. H.323 protocol tower [5]

Figure 2 shows the H.323 architecture for terminal interoperability according to what is specified in the ITU2 standard [6].

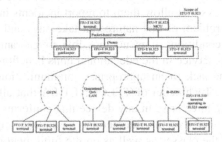

Fig. 2. Interoperability of terminals ITU-T H.323 [6]

2.2 Elements of a VoIP System

2.2.1 The Client

A Customer can be a Skype user or a user of a company that sells its IP telephony services through equipment such as ATAs (Analog Telephone Adapters) or IP phones or Softphones which is a software that allows calls to be made through a computer connected to the Internet [5].

2.2.2 Servers

Los servidores se encargan de manejar operaciones de base de datos, realizado en un tiempo real como en uno fuera de él. Entre estas operaciones se tienen la contabilidad, la recolección, el enrutamiento, la administración y control del servicio, el registro de los usuarios, etc.

2.2.3 The Gateways

The gateways are used to "terminate" the call, that is, the customer originates the call and the gateway ends the call, which is when a customer calls a landline or cell phone, there must be the part that makes that call possible. Through Internet, you can connect with a customer of a fixed or cellular telephone company [7] (Fig. 3).

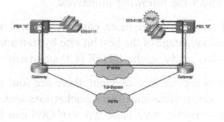

Fig. 3. Elements of a VoIP system [8]

2.3 Codecs

The voice must be encoded in order to be transmitted over the IP network. For this, codecs are used to guarantee the encoding and compression of audio or video for later decoding and decompression before being able to generate a usable sound or image. According to the codec used in the transmission, the required bit rate will be used. The amount of bitrate used is usually directly proportional to the quality of the transmitted data.

Among the most used VoIP codecs Are G.711, G723.1 and G.729 (specified by the ITU-T).

These codecs have the following coding bit rates.

- G.711: bit-rate de 56/64 Kbps
- G.722: bit-rate de 48,56 o 64 Kbps
- G.723: bit-rate de 5.3 o 6.4 Kbps
- G.728: bit-rate de 16 Kbps
- G.729: bit-rate de 8/13 Kbps

2.4 VoIP Latency

The latency is also called DELAY. This is not a specific problem of non-connection oriented networks and therefore of VoIP, rather it is a general problem of telecommunications networks. For example, the latency in satellite links is very high due to the distances that the information must travel.

Latency is technically defined in VoIP as the time it takes for a packet to arrive from the source to the destination.

Real-time communications (such as VoIP) and full-duplex are sensitive to this effect. Like jitter, it is a frequent problem in slow or congested links.

The latency or delay between the start and end points of the communication must be less than 150 ms. The human ear is able to detect latency of about 250 ms and

200 ms in the case of people who are quite sensitive. If that threshold is exceeded, the communication will fly annoying [9].

2.5 VoIP QoS

To improve the level of service, it has been aimed at reducing the bitrates used, for them we have worked under the following initiatives:

- The suppression of silences, gives more efficiency when making a voice transmission, since it takes advantage of the best bit rate by transmitting less information.
- Compression of headers applying the RTP/RTCP standards.

For the QoS quality of service measurement, there are four parameters such as bit rate, time delay (delay), delay variation (jitter), packet loss and echo.

For these types of drawbacks, three basic types of QoS can be implemented in the design.

- Best Effort: This method simply sends packets as they are received, without applying any real specific task. That is, it has no priority for any service, just try to send the packages in the best way.
- Integrated Service: This system has as its main function to pre-accord a path for the data that need priority, besides this architecture is not scalable, due to the amount of resource it needs to be reserving the transmission rate of each application.
- Differentiated Services: This system allows each network device to handle individual packets, and each router and switch can configure its own QoS policies to make its own decisions about the delivery of packages. Differentiated services use 6 bits in the Ip header.

3   Proposed Model for the Solution of the Problem

Within the solution the proposed solution to the problem of communication between schools and towards customer services of the company for damages that the data network may present, the following basic elements are analyzed:

- Determination of equipment requirements with technology such as Wireless Fidelity (Wi-Fi) and VoIP that will be supplied by TELCONET S.A. These equipment will be of high performance to ensure a high level of innovation in the last mile network.
- Determination of the technical characteristics of a local IP telephone exchange (the possibility of installing it in a computer of small dimensions type Microcomputer NUC will be evaluated). The innovative element is the use of a low power consumption computer with enough power to handle several phone calls simultaneously.
- Basic IP telephones for the installation of remote schools, a Gateway (Session) Protocol Initiation Protocol (SIP) for the interconnection of remote schools with destinations outside the project such as conventional telephone lines. In this way we ensure the possibility of crosses called to CNT in those schools where there is the possibility.

- Determine the technical characteristics of a router that will serve to make the dimensioning of the network dividing the Internet and Data services, also analyze the feasibility of installing a wireless controller Fidelity (Wi-Fi) being in charge of the centralized management of the access points, mesh architecture (Mesh) and user authentication. User traffic will not be tunneled from the access points to the controller, but will flow independently from them to their destination, minimizing the delay and supporting VoIP over WIFI.
- The installation of radio-relay equipment using Orthogonal Frequency Division Multiplexing (OFDM) brand Cambium Networks will be analyzed, carrying out point-to-point and point-to-multipoint links with a capacity of 50 Mbps Full Duplex and the different distances of said links with technical studies of the area of Fresnel and equipment configuration.

With this project direct communication between each of the schools will be allowe members of the MINTEL Connectivity Project. This is the main result. That is, obtain a better quality of communication between the schools and entities that intervene in the MINTEL Schools Connectivity Project, providing as added value the implementation of cutting edge telephony as are the VoIP networks that will help complement the excellent development carried out by the Connectivity Project.

In addition to providing the Ministry of Education with a practical solution for communication with the schools of the Project. This is a result important social: enable direct and quality communication elevated, between each of the member schools of the Project MINTEL connectivity and with other institutions. In addition, provide as an added value the implementation of VoIP that helps complement the excellent development of the Connectivity Project implemented by TELCONET S.A. and supported by MINTEL.

Submit to TELCONET S.A. a solution that could be offered to schools as part of their communication with destinations different from those mentioned in the Project. This is a result of business enterprise: install technologies designed, designed and fully implemented in Ecuador to present to TELCONET S.A. a solution that could be offered to schools as part of communicating them with destinations other than those mentioned in the project.

4 Solution Design

The design of the proposed solution requires the use of high technological equipment that guarantees the provision of a quality service, with imperceptible latencies to the end user, and quality standards that allow uninterrupted and efficient communication.

4.1 Research and Design

Prior to the selection of the equipment required for the implementation of the VoIP system, it is necessary to proceed with the elaboration of the respective design that fundamentally seeks to satisfy the minimum service demands determined by the contracting entity.

In order to meet the requirement, VoIP technology has been chosen to facilitate real-time communication between the administrators of the computer centers of the educational units and the TELCONET S.A. technical assistance center. In the present design, it concentrates exclusively on the technical characteristics of the communication network and on the quality of the transmission service.

To provide an IP telephony system, the installation of a telephone exchange based on VoIP protocols is essentially required. The entire telephone network would be centralized by a communications gateway that would provide the basic functionalities of a traditional telephone exchange together with other additional features.

The Gateway is based on the Session Initiation Protocol (SIP), which is a protocol of the session layer according to the OSI model (Open System Interconnection) [10] that facilitates signaling and allows creating, modifying and end sessions with one or more clients. Sessions include: telephone calls, multimedia data transfer and real-time conferences. Additionally, SIP allows the implementation of call routing policies in the system through the transport layer services of the OSI model. Figure 4 shows how the SIP protocol, located in the application layer of the TCP/IP model (Transmission Control Protocol/Internet Protocol), provides start and end services for voice and video calls at a higher level and for this purpose it is supported in TCP/IP transport layer protocols such as UDP (User Datagram Protocol), SCTP (Stream Control Transmission Protocol) and TCP [11].

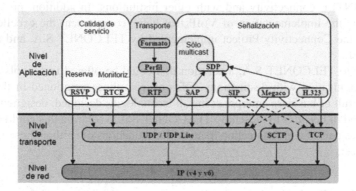

Fig. 4. Functionality of protocols involved in VoIP [12].

SIP makes use of network elements called proxy servers or SIP servers to help route requests to the user's current location, authenticate and authorize users.

From the foregoing it is evident that the first network element of the system design is the Gateway based on SIP protocol, implemented by a proxy server with built-in SIP functionalities.

Additionally, a router will be required that provides data routing capacity over the network, a switch that provides layer 2 services to clients, computers and IP telephones.

Figure 5 shows the design of the proposed IP telephone exchange, developed with the Packet Tracer ® software from Cisco Systems.

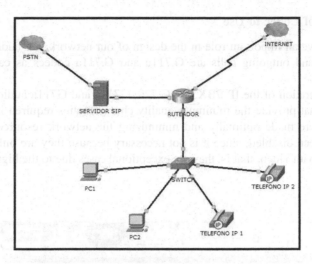

Fig. 5. Structure of an IP telephone exchange.

4.2 VoIP Phone System

In order to manage telephone resources based on IP telephony, TELCONET S.A has recommended the design of a virtual IPBX central developed by Denwa Technologies Corp. that allows managing more than 10 million users in its Data Center IP model [13].

In Fig. 6 you can see the operation interface of Denwa.

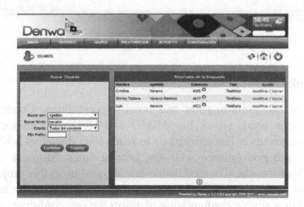

Fig. 6. Denwa operation interface [15].

Denwa is a highly versatile, totally graphic system that guarantees the efficient and continuous operation of the system using software tools, reducing the cost of implementation considerably without minimizing the quality of the service provided.

4.3   Choice of Codec to Use

The codecs have an important role in the design of our network, the audio codec used for incoming and outgoing calls are G.711u and G.711a codecs as can be seen in Fig. 7.

For the operation of the IP PBX, the G.729, G711u and G711a audio codecs have been chosen that provide the minimum quality characteristics required in such a way that the calls are made optimally and minimizing the network resources. The video codecs have been disabled, since it is not necessary because they are only enabled for IP telephones with video, that is, they are exceptional cases due to the high requirement in the network.

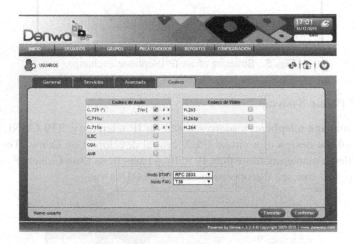

Fig. 7. Data from user codecs Denwa.

4.4   Radio Links

In order to carry out point-to-point and point-to-point links, Cambium Networks equipment has been used, which has MIMO and OFDM technology, the use of reflector type dish antennas has allowed us to reach long distances while maintaining high throughput and performance with low latency times. Moment of sending full duplex traffic. Dynamic adaptive modulation has allowed us in this project to maintain a high and robust modulation to the interference, guaranteeing the bit rate required by the MINTEL, with a simple configuration platform we can configure our links.

One of the most important advantages of Cambium Networks equipment is that it has 2 band options such as 5.4 GHz and 5.7 GHz, as having these bands has allowed us to have more alternative when choosing the best available frequency, prior to this election. Spectrum analysis has been carried out in the different repeaters of the project in order to prevent possible falls or intermittent links and ensure a better service [14] (Fig. 8).

Fig. 8. Cambium networks teams.

4.5 Fresnel Zone Studies

In order to design wireless links it is important to consider several factors that may affect our communication, among them the obstacles that may exist between the Master or Slave in the radio signals, and this is where you must perform calculations of the Fresnel zone, which it defines us an ideal value for a good wireless communication.

For the interconnection of the aforementioned schools, the establishment of radio links is required, which must provide minimum operating characteristics to guarantee the quality of the service.

Figure 9 shows the point-to-point and multipoint systems of the network in question.

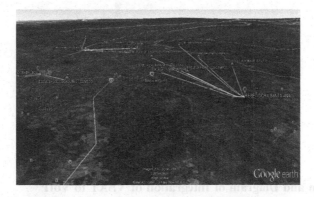

Fig. 9. Point-to-point and point-to-multipoint system.

In order to determine the feasibility of the radio links, the simulation is carried out where the technical characteristics of the equipment involved are taken into account, the topography of the environment and the propagation characteristics of the signal.

Figure 10 shows the topographic profile of the study carried out at the Lautaro Vera School belonging to the Salitre song to the Santa Ana repeater.

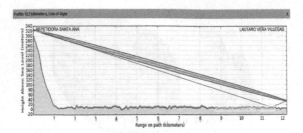

Fig. 10. Simulation of the link between Lautaro Vera Villegas School towards Node Santa Ana.

5 Platform and Diagram of Integration

5.1 Platform and Diagram of Integration of RF to VoIP

The integration platform between the terrestrial radiofrequency interface and the VoIP system is presented in the diagram of Fig. 11, as it can be seen, through wireless links of a system with point-multipoint topology, the telephone exchange is connected to TELCONET SA with the users, for this purpose it is made use of the towers and support structures previously described, as well as the necessary radiant elements to spread the information through the air interface, then the routing and network switching elements installed in each node they allow the reception and distribution of information towards each of the points.

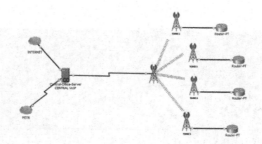

Fig. 11. RF to VoIP integration diagram.

5.2 Platform and Diagram of Integration of VSAT to VoIP

The integration platform between the satellite radiofrequency interface (Vsat) and the VoIP system is presented in the diagram of Fig. 12, as can be seen, through satellite link communication is established towards the points of each school, to its Once the information propagated by the space is received by a satellite that acts as a remote repeater, and then the signal is sent to the Hub, which is the earth station that allows to concentrate the information received and with the help of elements of commutation and routing, distributing it to the points of interest, based on this scheme the proposed system is technically operational and provides the minimum quality requirements to guarantee an optimal service with imperceptible latencies for the school.

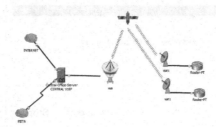

Fig. 12. Vsat to VoIP integration diagram.

6 Results of Radio-Link and VSAT

In order to observe the results obtained in the radio and Vsat links, a bandwidth test was performed occupying the WAN Killer tool, in which UDP traffic is sent with a rate of 10 Mbps, in this way we check if the link supports the traffic what is required (4 Mbps full duplex) for the Mintel project (Fig. 13).

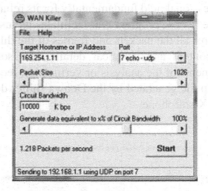

Fig. 13. Wan Killer menu.

We can see that the traffic of 10 Mbps is constant and does not have cuts or intermittences, this guarantees that when connecting our radio-link to the router and have real traffic consumption is not saturate or completely miss the communication causing intermittences, being able to support the bit rates that we need to establish a VoIP call (Fig. 14).

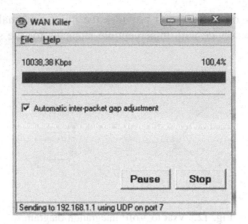

Fig. 14. Shipment of UDP packets.

7 Verification of Operation

In order to verify that the system is operating properly in the lower layers of the OSI model, it is necessary to use a network protocol analyzer software that is capable of reproducing the.cap extension files generated by the Denwa telephone exchange, for of this thesis makes use of Wireshark software, the same that is widely used as "sniffer" in the academic and professional field fundamentally for its reliability and versatility, as well as being a GPL-type license program that facilitates its installation and operation.

The Wireshark captures all the packets and frames of the different levels of the OSI model and shows its content and technical details, this software allows filtering according to the requirements of the analysis or verification required. Figure 15 shows the information of the cap file generated by the Denwa sniffer during the establishment of a call through the 3CX softphone.

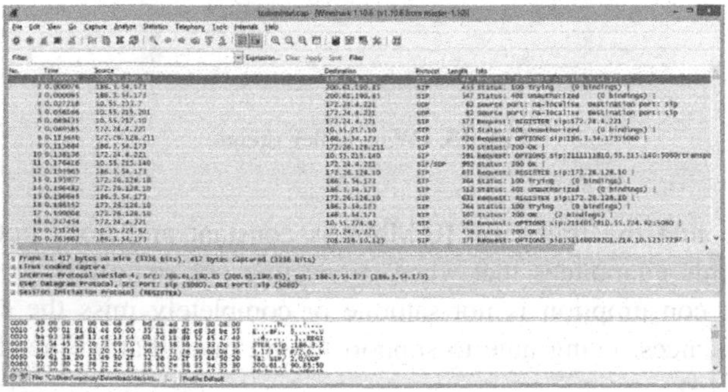

Fig. 15. Package capture in Wireshark.

As you can see, during the lapse of packet captures, all correspond to the SIP service of IP calls, when you open the VoIP call information window it is verified that the system has registered the calls made to the user that was taken as an example to the school "Pueblo Nuevo" and that has been processed by the PBX "tesismintel" as can be seen in Fig. 16.

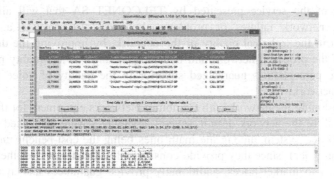

Fig. 16. VoIP call log in Wireshark.

The Wireshark allows visualizing the graphical packet analyzer, which facilitates observing the start, establishment and end of the VoIP call session, as can be seen in Fig. 17.

Fig. 17. Wireshark graphic analyzer.

As shown, the system works according to plan, verification of the operation of the system has been made using the Denwa telephone exchange, the 3CX softphone and the Wireshark network protocol analyzer that together have provided optimal results that guarantee the correct functioning of the PBX.

8 Conclusions

The system proposed in the present design, based on the results obtained from the network design simulations, once implemented, would provide a considerable improvement in communication between the schools that make use of it, and the customer service center of TELCONET SA, this improvement is not only due to an optimization of the service presented by TELCONET SA that will allow timely reporting of network failures or problems, but will also provide a substantial improvement in the technical quality of the network, by improving the design characteristics of the proposed network and by incorporating service quality protocols, a very accurate perception is guaranteed superior in the quality of voice transmitted through the network.

In dimensioning the network with Cambium Networks equipment for the point-to-multipoint link of the network design, several advantages were evidenced that potentiate the proposed system, among the main ones being the cost-benefit ratio of radio frequency equipment, since they provide considerable advantages over their competitors in relation to market prices, additionally provide guarantees and availability of permanent spare parts and finally, by making use of frequency bands allocated in the National Frequency Plan on a secondary basis, the cost for monthly payment of rates of use of the radio electric spectrum to the State.

The proposed telephone exchange Denwa Technology provides important features among which are its ease of use, the system is very user friendly, thus facilitating the recurrent use of these resources as well as the maintenance and configuration of the plant, the it is scalable, so it can be easily projected to a larger VoIP network by making small changes in its configuration and technological infrastructure.

Finally, a backup system has been designed that would take part in the Network Contingency Plan. This backup will guarantee the continuity of the service in emergent cases in which, due to force majeure, the main network is out of service.

References

1. Navarro-Veliz, L.: Sistemas VoIP: Diseño de proyectos de conectividad de escuelas atreves de la red de Telconet en la Provincia del Guayas. Pro-Sciences, vol. 1, no. 4, pp. 12–20, Noviembre 2017. ISSN: 2588-1000
2. Oñate-Monta, J., Zambrano-Herrera, D.: Diseño e Implementación de VoIP en redes inalámbricas wifi bajo el estándar de la IEEE 802.11g y superiores. Tesis de Grado, Ingeniería en Sistemas, Universidad Técnica de Cotopaxi, Latacunga (2010)
3. Rendon-Hernandez, R.: Análisis del método MFSP para contrarrestar los retardos en los sistemas satelitales en transmisiones de VoIP. Tesis de Grado, Ingeniería en Electrónica y Telecomunicaciones, Escuela Politécnica Nacional, Quito (2009)
4. Bulla, W., Fino, R.: Metodología de Diseño e implementación de soluciones de VoIP. Revista Visión Electrónica, Julio–Diciembre 2012, vol. 6, no. 2, pp. 93–102 (2012). ISSN: 1909-9746
5. Kaschel, H.C., Enrique San Juan, U.: Consideraciones Técnicas para Elaborar un Estándar Definitivo VoIP, Santiago de Chile (2012). http://sistemamid.com/

6. Unión Internacional de Telecomunicaciones (UIT), Recomendación ITU-T H.323 (2009). https://www.itu.int/
7. Cisco Systems Inc, Los gateways (2009). http://wwww.cisco.com/
8. Cisco Systems Inc, Elementos de un sistema de VoIP (2009). http://wwww.cisco.com/
9. LATENCIA DE VoIP, por 3CX. http://www.voipforo.com/QoS/QoS_Latencia.php
10. Internet Engineering Task Force (IETF) (1999)
11. Buenos Aires University, 2006 SIP: Session Initiation Protocol
12. Funcionalidad de protocolos involucrados en VoIP. http://www.voip.unam.mx/archivos/docs/Curso%20SIP_05012008.pdf, http://www.fiuba6662.com.ar/6648/presentaciones/2006/Informe%20SIP.pdf
13. Cambium Networks (2015). www.cambiumnetworks.com
14. Cambium Networks, características del reflector dish (2015). http://www.cambiumnetworks.com/
15. Denwa Technology Corp, Ipbx Denwa (2015). http://www.denwaip.com/

A Systematic Mapping Study of Specification Languages in Cloud Services Development

Jorge Bermeo Conto, Miguel Zúñiga-Prieto[✉],
and Lizandro Solano-Quinde

Departamento de Ciencias de la Computación,
Universidad de Cuenca, Av. 12 de Abril S/N, Cuenca, Ecuador
{jorge.bermeo,miguel.zunigap,
lizandro.solano}@ucuenca.edu.ec

Abstract. Specification languages offer abstractions and notations that facilitate the systematic and analytical reasoning about important aspects in a specific domain problematic. In a software engineering process domain, the usage of specification languages improve the quality and delivery time of the artefacts generated during the execution of the process activities. Cloud applications, or cloud services, are service-oriented applications whose consumption is constantly growing; however, their development require support for new roles and activities. In this work we are interested in knowing how specification languages are being used by researchers and practitioners to support the development of cloud services. This work presents a systematic mapping that provides guidance to determine the current state and to characterize the specification languages that support the service life cycle activities in a cloud services development domain.

Keywords: Cloud applications · Cloud services · Systematic mapping protocol
Specification languages · Service life cycle · Model driven development

1 Introduction

Cloud computing is a business model for delivering IT resources and applications (cloud resources) as services that can be accessed remotely on demand and over the Internet [1]. In this context, the set of data centers, hardware, software, and storage is known as cloud. The difference of this business model with the traditional resource delivery model is that: in a traditional model resources are delivered in the form of products sold or licensed to users, and then used locally in their technological infrastructure; whereas in cloud computing users purchase remote access to cloud resources.

Cloud applications are service-oriented applications that from a software engineering perspective are software provided as services [2]. These are distributed applications, usually composed of web services, which consume resources obtained from cloud providers during their execution. Unlike traditional software engineering, service-oriented applications require new roles and new development tasks. The service life cycle includes different stages, (i.e., design-time, run-time and change-time), as well as different stakeholders (service provider, application provider – service consumer – and service broker), where each stakeholder has different activities associated depending on the life cycle stage.

M. Botto-Tobar et al. (Eds.): CITT 2018, CCIS 895, pp. 72–88, 2019.
https://doi.org/10.1007/978-3-030-05532-5_6

The different activities of the service life cycle require developers to systematically reason about their related aspects. Specification languages are used in software engineering to improve the quality and delivery time of software systems by offering notations and abstractions that ease the reasoning about different aspects in a domain problem, helping to express system models. Among various distinctive approaches, which propose specification languages, we are interested in those that support and enable the analytical reasoning about service requirements at the service life cycle activities in the cloud applications development domain.

In this paper we conduct a systematic mapping in order to gather evidence and characterize specification languages that support the service life cycle activities in a cloud application domain, to identify the issues languages addressed by those languages, and to identify gaps in the existing research. This systematic mapping was based on a mapping protocol that we have already designed in [20], which was extended to improve its accuracy. To the best of our knowledge, this is the first systematic mapping with this objective.

2 Research Method

A systematic mapping study is a formalized and repeatable process that provides guidance for categorizing and summarizing existing information about a research question in an unbiased way. A systematic mapping study has three stages [3]: Planning, Conducting, and Reporting. We plan to perform a systematic mapping study by taking into account guidelines provided by [4–6].

2.1 Planning the Systematic Mapping

We formulated the mapping protocol based on the activities proposed by the systematic literature review guidelines and procedures described in [6], see Fig. 1.

Fig. 1. Systematic mapping protocol activities

2.1.1 Establishment of the Research Question

The research question was structured following the PICOC (Population, Intervention, Comparison, Outcome and Context) criteria [7]; however, our research focus was not comparison, consequently it was not included. We formulated the following research question: "How specification languages are being used by researchers and practitioners to support the life cycle activities of cloud services/applications development?". This allows us: (i) to categorize and summarize the current knowledge concerning the usage of specification languages, and (ii) to identify gaps in current research. Since our research question is too broad, it was decomposed into more detailed sub-questions. Table 1 shows these research sub-questions along with their motivation.

Table 1. Research sub-questions

Research sub-questions	Motivation
RQ1: How do specification languages support the life cycle activities of services?	To discover what activities of services' lifecycle are most frequently supported, which activity aspects are being specified, and which stakeholders are generally involved in the specification
RQ2: Which are the characteristics of the offered specification languages?	To discover characteristics of specification languages frequently offered, language syntax and semantics
RQ3: How do specification languages support the cloud paradigm?	To discover the delivery service model and the cloud environment used. Also, to find out the proposed infrastructure and whether it is supplier specific
RQ4: Which software development approaches do the specification languages support?	To discover which development approaches are being supported (e.g., agile, model-driven, incremental)

2.1.2   Definition of the Search Strategy

The search strategy included digital libraries and manual search approaches on conference proceedings and journals. The main digital libraries used to search for primary studies were: ACM Digital Library, IEEE Explore Digital Library, and Scopus. A search string defined by identifying the main concepts that represent the specification languages in the cloud services development domain was used to perform the automatic search on the selected digital libraries (see Fig. 2).

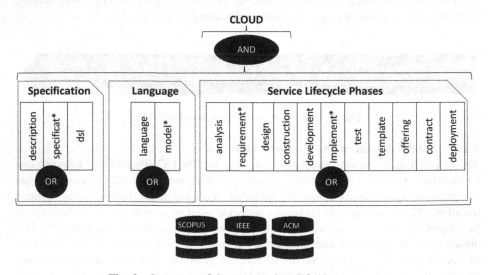

Fig. 2. Summary of the query string definition process

The search string included alternative terms for those main concepts (e.g., model or models for language); used the OR Boolean operator to join alternate terms and synonyms in each main concept, and the AND Boolean operator to join the main concepts. Table 2 shows the resulting query string. The search string was applied to the title and abstract of each article on all the sources, therefore, we modified it to fit the syntax and semantic of each digital library (see Table 2). In order to perform a consistent search, these search terms were also used in the manual search.

Table 2. Excerpt query string for each digital library

Library	Query string
IEEE	(("Abstract":cloud* AND ("Abstract":description OR "Abstract":specificat* OR "Abstract":dsl) AND ("Abstract":language OR "Abstract":model*) AND (Abstract:analysis OR "Abstract":requirement* OR "Abstract":design OR "Abstract":construction OR "Abstract":development OR "Abstract":implementation OR "Abstract":test OR "Abstract":template OR "Abstract":offering OR "Abstract":contract OR "Abstract":provisi* OR "Abstract":deployment)))
ACM	recordAbstract: (+(cloud*) + (description specificat* dsl) + (language model*) + (analysis requirement* design construction development implementation test template offering contract provisi* deployment))...
SCOPUS	TITLE-ABS ((cloud* AND (description OR specificat* OR dsl) AND (language OR model*) AND (analysis OR requirement* OR design OR construction OR development OR implementation OR test OR template OR offering OR contract OR provisi* OR deployment)))

2.1.3 Selection of Primary Studies

The selection of studies was performed through the multi-step process shown in Fig. 3. The period reviewed included studies published from 2006 to 2017 (inclusive), where the starting date was selected due to we wanted to know the influence of "Cloud Computing" on new approaches or proposals for specification languages, and in 2006 Amazon Inc. officially launched Amazon Web Services [8].

Fig. 3. Stages of selection of primary studies process

At the beginning, the search string was, manually or automatically, applied to all the sources (Stage 1), and the results were imported or copied to an Excel sheet, sorted by study title, then duplicates were eliminated (Stage 2).

Resulting studies retrieved as result of the automated or manual search were evaluated by the authors of this work in order to decide whether or not the studies are within the scope of this systematic mapping, and, hence, included. Evaluation was carried out by reading the title and abstract of each study. Only studies presenting specification languages that support the lifecycle activities associated with services in cloud environments were selected. Studies that met at least one of the following criteria were excluded: (i) Studies that do not focus on the cloud domain or do not propose specification languages. (ii) Studies that are systematic reviews, mapping reviews or introductory papers for special issues, workshops, tutorials, and mini-tracks. (iii) Studies that are less than four pages or presenting only recommendations, guidelines, or design principles. (iv) Duplicates of the same study in different sources (Stage 3). At Stage 4, if after reading a study's title and abstract it was uncertain whether it was a relevant work, a full-text skim was performed. Divergences in the selection were solved by consensus among the authors of this work. Studies were discarded based on the inclusion/exclusion criteria used on Stage 3.

Finally, in Stage 5, by using the resulting primary studies of stage 4, a reference harvesting and analysis was performed [9] in order to realize whether relevant studies were missed.

2.1.4   Quality Assessment

The quality assessment of the selected studies was carried out by applying a three-point Likert-scale questionnaire to evaluate the qualities shown in Table 3. Each question was applied and scored for each study, by the authors of this work, and the final score of each question was obtained by calculating the arithmetic mean of the authors' scores. Then, the overall total in a study was calculated adding the totals of every closed-question. The overall total of a study was used to identify representative studies, not to exclude them from this systematic mapping.

Table 3. Description of quality assessment

1. Problem definition of the study
2. Context in which the study was carried out
3. Describes the support used to deal with the identified problem
4. Type of validation conducted
5. Contributions of the study
6. Insights derived from the study
7. Limitations of the study
8. Relevance of the journal or conference proceedings where the study has been published

2.2 Data Extraction Strategy

The data extraction strategy consisted on providing a predefined set of possible answers for each research sub-question, allowing to ensure the application of the same extraction data criteria to all selected papers as well as facilitating their characterization. Next, the possible answers to each research sub-question are explained.

With regard to **RQ1**, a paper can be classified in one of the following answers (see Table 4):

Table 4. Extraction criteria for RQ1

EC1. Lifecycle phase for which the approach offers a solution [10]. The service life cycle model is composed by design-time and run-time processes. Design-time processes include: Requirements engineering, Business modeling, Service Design, Service Development, Services testing and Service implementation [11]. Run-time processes include: Service publishing, Service provision, Service monitoring, Service discovery, Service orchestration/composition, Service Negotiation, Service invocation, Application testing and Service monitoring [12]

EC2. Qualities of the service lifecycle activity specified. The qualities of the service lifecycle are functional and non-functional. Non-functional requirements have significant importance for cloud consumer; therefore, modeling those requirements play an important role as they allow a structured representation of such requirements. Pricing is one of the non-functional qualities that is specified in several studies [13]; additionally, we take into account whether a language supports the specification of the following aspects: functional, non-functional, service level agreement, architecture descriptions, service descriptions, implementation descriptions, deployment descriptions, execution environments, node characteristics, and constrains

EC3. Role to whom the language is expected to provide support. Service lifecycle phases are associated with a stakeholder or role [10, 14]. Architecture related stakeholders in service-oriented applications are: service provider, service consumer, and service broker [10]

With regard to **RQ2**, modeling languages syntax can be summarized as follows [15, 16]: abstract syntax, concrete syntax, and semantics. A paper can be classified in one of the qualities indicated in Table 5:

Table 5. Extraction criteria for RQ2

EC4. Abstract syntax of the modeling language. XML schema, UML library, UML profiles, Ecore and Grammar

EC5. Concrete Syntax of the modeling language. According to [15, 16]: Graphical, Graphical (UML-based), Graphical (Cloud MIGXpress), Textual (JSON-based), Textual (XML-based), Textual (YAML-based), Graphical + Textual (OVF based), Graphical (UML based), Textual (XML based) and Textual (XML based) + Graphical (VINO4Tosca)

EC6. Semantics of the modeling language. According to [15, 16]: English Prose, Mapping to TOSCA, Deployment Optimizer, Conformance Checker, Provisioning Engine, OpenStack, Deployment Optimizer, Deployment Engine, Open Nebula and Open Tosca

---

With regard to **RQ3**, a paper can be classified in one of the qualities indicates in Table 6:

Table 6. Extraction criteria for RQ3

EC7. Service delivery model. Cloud delivery models are pre-packaged combinations of cloud resources offered by cloud providers as services. The basic service delivery models are: (i) infrastructure as a service (IaaS): computing capabilities such as storage, processing and network are delivered as standardized services over internet, (ii) platform as a service (PaaS): development/run-time environments (prebuilt components and interfaces) offered to developers to build or run applications, (iii) software as a service (SaaS): software applications delivered as services, and finally, (iv) hybrid: enables match the IaaS, PaaS or SaaS
EC8. Cloud environment essential characteristics. In cloud computing, resources such as storage, processing, network and software platforms are available from data centers operated by cloud providers [17, 18]. Cloud environments offer the following essential characteristics [19]: (i) on-demand self-service: consumers can provision resources as needed automatically without requiring human interaction with service providers; (ii) broad network access: capabilities are available over the internet and accessed through standard mechanisms; (iii) resource pooling: resources offered by cloud providers are pooled in order to be used by multiple consumers using a multi-tenant model; depending on consumer demand, physical and virtual resources are dynamically assigned and reassigned; (iv) rapid elasticity: resources are provisioned and released, according with the actual demand, to rapidly scale outward and inward. Sometimes this task is carried out automatically
EC9. Deployment Model. There are four major cloud deployment models: (i) public cloud: the general public or a large industry group has access to the cloud infrastructure, (ii) private cloud: only one organization has access to the cloud infrastructure, (iii) hybrid cloud: a composition of two or more clouds that remain unique entities but are bound together by standardized or proprietary technology that enables data and application portability, and (iv) community cloud: a community that has common concerns shares the access to the cloud infrastructure
EC10. Cloud provider (supplier). A proposal may or may not be linked to specific supplier such as: Google, Amazon and Azure

With regard to **RQ4**, a paper can be classified in one of the qualities in Table 7:

Table 7. Extraction criteria for RQ4

EC11. Model driven development approach. A model-driven development approach (MDD, MDA or MDE), referred as MDA in this work, helps to solve the problem of heterogeneity of technologies and integration; therefore, it is of interest to determine if the primary studies propose solutions to support MDA
EC12. Incremental development approach. Service-oriented applications are usually developed in an incremental fashion by building reusable services that may interoperate with each other. In this context, it is of interest to determine if the primary studies propose solutions to support an incremental development approach

The template, showed in Table 8, is used to systematize the data extraction activities and to ease the management of the data extracted for each paper.

2.3 Selection of Synthesis Methods

Both, quantitative and qualitative synthesis methods were applied. During the quantitative synthesis the following activities were carried out: (i) the primary studies classified in each answer from the research sub-questions were counted; (ii) the primary studies classified in each bibliographic source per year were counted; and (iii) in order to report the frequencies of combining the results from different research sub-questions bubble plots were defined. Bubble plots, two x–y scatter plots with bubbles in category intersections, provide a map and provide a quick overview of a research field [5].

3 Conducting the Systematic Mapping

The application of the systematic mapping protocol generated the preliminary results shown in Fig. 4. As a result of the application of the search string to each source, 1359 papers were obtained, where 301 papers had been published in more than one source, therefore, those duplicates were removed, keeping only one of them, according to our search order (IEEEXplore, ACM and SCOPUS). Other papers were removed due to their title (736 papers), abstract (224 papers) or content (63 papers) were not related to the research question. The final selection included 15 research papers (see Appendix A), where 53% of the papers where published since 2015.

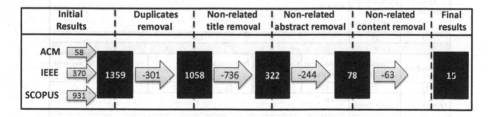

Fig. 4. Results of the conducting stage

4 Reporting Stage the Systematic Mapping

A summary of the overall results, presented in Table 9, shows the classification of the primary studies based on the answers to the extraction criteria that corresponds to our research sub-questions.

The mapping created by combining different research sub-questions and the analysis of the results are presented next.

With regard to *EC1: Lifecycle phase for which the approach offers a solution*, the results indicate that the main activities of the service lifecycle supported by the

Table 8. Excerpt data extraction strategy

RQ1: How specification languages support the life cycle activities of services?							
EC1: Lifecycle phase for which the approach offers a solution.							
Requirements engineering	Business modeling	Service Design	Service Development	Services testing	Service implementation	Service publishing	Service provision
☐	☐	☐	☐	☐	☐	☐	☐
Service monitoring	Service discovery	Service orchestration /composition	Service Negotiation	Service invocation	Application testing	Service monitoring	
☐	☐	☐	☐	☐	☐	☐	
EC2: Aspects of the service lifecycle activity specified.							
Functional	Non-functional	Service level agreement	Architecture descriptions	Service descriptions	Implementation descriptions	Deployment descriptions	Execution environments
☐	☐	☐	☐	☐	☐	☐	☐
Node characteristics	Constrains	Pricing	Others:_____				
☐	☐	☐					
EC3: Role to whom the language is expected to provide support.							
Service provider	Service consumer	Service broker					
☐	☐	☐					
RQ2: Which are the characteristics of the offered specification languages?							
EC4: Abstract Syntax.							
XML Shema	UML Library	UML Profiles	Ecore	Grammar	Others:_____		
☐	☐	☐	☐	☐	☐		
EC5: Concrete Syntax.							
Graphical	Graphical (UML-based)	Graphical (Cloud MIGXpress)	Textual (JSON-based)	Textual (XML-based)	Textual (YAML-based)	Graphical + Textual (OVFbased)	Graphical (UMLbased)
☐	☐	☐	☐	☐	☐	☐	☐
Textual (XMLbased)	Textual (XMLbased) + Graphical (VINO4Tosca)	Others:_____					
☐	☐	☐					
EC6: Semantics.							
English Prose	Mapping to TOSCA	Deployment Optimizer	Conformance Checker	Provisioning Engine	OpenStack	Deployment Optimizer	Deployment Engine
☐	☐	☐	☐	☐	☐	☐	☐
Open Nebula	Open Tosca	Others:_____					
☐	☐	☐					
RQ3: How specification languages support the cloud paradigm?					RQ4: Which software development approaches are supported by the specification languages?		
EC7: Service delivery model.					EC11: Software engineering paradigm is MDA.		
IaaS	PaaS	SaaS	Hybrid:_____		Yes	No	
O	O	O	O		O	O	
EC8: Cloud environment feature supported.					EC12: Incremental development approach.		
Dynamic provisioning	Pay-as-you-go principle	Elastically scale	Quality of service.		Yes	No	
☐	☐	☐	☐		O	O	
EC9: Deployment model.							
Private	Community	Public	Hybrid				
O	O	O	O				
EC10: Supplier.							
Google	Amazon	Azure	Supplier independent	Other:___			
O	O	O	O	O			

Table 9. Results of the conducting stage

Research question	Criteria	Possible answers	Results	
			# Studies	Percentage (%)
RQ1: How specification languages support the life cycle activities of services?	EC1: Lifecycle phase for which the approach offers a solution	Service deployment	5	28%
		Requirements engineering	4	22%
		Service composition	3	17%
		Business modeling	2	11%
		Service development	1	6%
		Service implementation	1	6%
		Service monitoring	1	6%
		Service evolution	1	6%
	EC2: Aspects of the service lifecycle activity specified	Service description	5	24%
		Deployment	4	19%
		Architecture	3	14%
		Functional requirements	2	10%
		Service level agreement	2	10%
		Pricing	2	10%
		Execution environments	1	5%
		Constrains	1	5%
		Others	1	5%
	EC3: Role to whom the language is expected to provide support	Service provider	10	63%
		Service consumer	5	31%
		Service broker	1	6%
RQ2: Which are the characteristics of the offered specification languages?	EC4: Abstract syntax	Others	5	33%
		XML schema	4	27%
		Grammar	4	27%
		UML library	1	7%
		UML profiles	1	7%

(continued)

Table 9. (*continued*)

Research question	Criteria	Possible answers	Results	
			# Studies	Percentage (%)
	EC5: Concrete syntax	Others	13	87%
		Graphical	1	7%
		Textual (XML-based)	1	7%
	EC6: Semantics	Others	13	87%
		English prose	1	7%
		Mapping to TOSCA	1	7%
RQ3: How specification languages support the cloud paradigm?	EC7: Service delivery model	IaaS	3	50%
		SaaS	2	33%
		PaaS	1	17%
	EC8: Cloud environment essential characteristics	Measured service	4	33%
		Rapid elasticity	3	25%
		On-demand self-service	2	17%
		Resource pooling	2	17%
		Broad network access	1	8%
	EC9: Deployment model	Private	2	33%
		Public	2	33%
		Hybrid	2	33%
	EC10: Supplier	Amazon	3	50%
		Azure	2	33%
		Other	1	17%
RQ4: Which software development approaches are supported?	EC11: Software engineering paradigm is MDA (MDD, MDE)	MDA	8	47%
		No MDA	0	0%
	EC12: Incremental development approach	Yes	1	6%
		No	0	0

analyzed proposals are *Service Deployment* and *Requirements Engineering*, with 28% and 22% of the papers reviewed, respectively.

Regarding to *EC2: Aspects of the service lifecycle activity specified*, the results indicate that the aspects of the life cycle covered by the reviewed papers are *Service Description, Deployment* and *Architecture*; with 24%, 19% and 14% of the papers reviewed, respectively.

With regard to *EC3: Role to whom the language is expected to provide support*, it was identified that *Service provider* and *Service consumer* are the stakeholder roles that receive most or the support offered by the reviewed proposals; which is, the 63% and 31% of the reviewed papers respectively. Where, service consumers (i.e., providers of cloud applications that buy cloud resources from cloud providers in order to deploy their applications) receive less support than the providers.

The results for *EC4: Abstract syntax of the modeling language,* revealed that the 17% of the reviewed papers propose the use of *XML Schemes*, whereas the other studies work with: *Web Ontology Language for Service (OWL-S)*, Cloud aCcounting Service (*aCCountS-DSL*), *PROTOKIT, Cloud-net, Goal SPEC language, Abstract Behavioral Specification language (ABS), Cloud Management Policy Language (CloudMPL)*, fusion between *UML2/SoaML, Neptune, CSS grammar, Protocol.bpel; Protocol.wsdl; deploy.xml* and *Own grammar.*

The results for *EC5: Concrete Syntax of the modeling language* indicate that only 8% of the reviewed papers propose a *Graphical* concrete syntax. In the same way, only 8% of the reviewed papers proposed a *Textual (XML-based)* concrete syntax. The remaining studies, around 83%, propose other types of concrete syntax, such as: *Textual (UML), Similar to class diagrams, Formalization, Textual (based on RELAX Language), Reserved keyword (Neptune developed with Ruby), Union of XML + JSON + YAML, Backus Naur form (BNF), Grammar notation, OPDL (Outsourcing Protocol Definition Language) GrammarRules, LDAP syntax.*

With regard to *EC6: Semantics of the modeling language*, it was identified that the 14% of the reviewed paper used *Mapping to TOSCA* and *English Prose*. The remaining papers use other semantics: *Formulas, ABS, Plain English sentences, Invocations of Neptune, mapped to BPEL constructs.*

The analysis of the results indicates that relating to *EC7: Service delivery model*, about 50% of the reviewed papers focuses on solutions for *IaaS*, whereas 33% of the studies focuses on *SaaS*, and the remaining studies (17%) on *PaaS*.

In relation to *EC8: Cloud environment essential characteristics*, among the main cloud characteristics supported *Measured service*, which accounts for 33% of the studies, whereas 25% of the studies reported *Rapid elasticity*.

The results for *EC9: Deployment Model* revealed that there are no preferences for the deployment models supported, all of them account for around 33% of the studies.

With regard to *EC10: Cloud provider,* the main cloud providers chosen in the reviewed papers are Amazon, Microsoft Azure and Eucalyptus.

With regard to *EC11: Model driven development approach*, around 47% of the studies apply the MDA approach, whereas 6% of the studies support and *Incremental development approach (EC12).*

Figure 5 shows the mapping results obtained from research extraction criteria EC4 and EC5 in comparison to extraction criteria EC1 and EC3. These results might indicate that:

- The majority of automated languages are service *Provider* oriented (*Provider* in EC3); where, there are almost no *Graphical Concrete Syntax* offerings (*Graphical* in EC5).
- *Service Deployment* life cycle phase (*Service Deployment* in EC1) is the most supported by specification languages. However, there is a need of service *Consumer* oriented proposals—service consumers could be developers of cloud applications that buy cloud resources from cloud providers in order to deploy their applications— (*Consumer* in EC3).

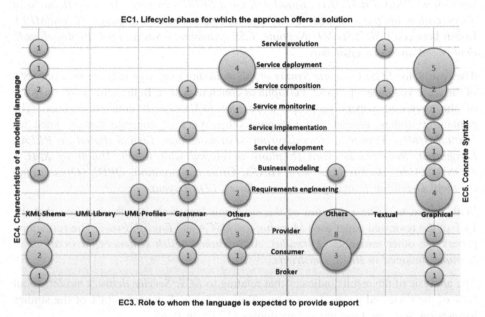

Fig. 5. Mapping results obtained from the combination of extraction criteria (EC4, EC5, EC1, EC3).

Figure 6 shows the mapping results obtained from research extraction criteria EC4 and EC5 in comparison to extraction criteria EC8 and EC11. These results might indicate that:

- The *Model Driven Development Approach* is being applied in specification languages that support cloud services life cycle (*MDA* in EC11). However, there are no *Graphical Concrete Syntax* offerings (*Graphical* in EC5); MDA is not likely used to support the creation of graphical editors.

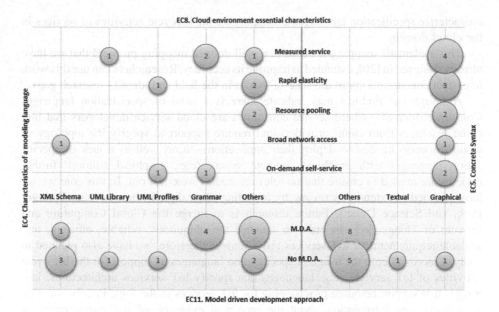

Fig. 6. Mapping results obtained from the combination of extraction criteria (EC4, EC5, EC8, EC11).

5   Threats to the Validity

The main limitations of this systematic mapping study are related to the study selection bias, data extraction inaccuracy, and study misclassification. Study selection bias can result when the selection of studies is incorrectly understood. We undertook this threat by defining our inclusion criteria to gather the largest possible amount of studies that fit into the specification languages in the cloud domain. Additionally, we chose the sources where studies about specification languages and cloud are normally published. However, we have excluded some libraries in the specification languages and cloud fields from this systematic review since we had no access to them. This could affect the validity of the results we presented. With regard to inaccuracy in extraction and study classification, the possibility of different reviewers extracting studies information in different ways, we attempted to reduce these threats by conducting the classification of the studies with three reviewers (the authors). In this context, as previously indicated divergences in studies selection were solved by consensus.

6   Conclusions

Specification languages are used in software engineering to improve the quality of software systems, easing developers to document their current activity decisions, as well as to improve their decision making in further life cycle activities. This paper presented a systematic study aimed to summarize the existing information that characterize specification languages as support for the lifecycle activities of services in the cloud domain.

This systematic mapping is based in a well-defined mapping protocol that we have already designed in [20], extended to improve its accuracy. Researchers can use this work to extract conclusions about the state-of-the-art in the field and identify research gaps.

Although our findings may indicate there is a need of specification languages Consumer oriented—where service consumers are cloud service developers that buy cloud resources from cloud providers and require support to specify the topology of cloud resources needed to deploy their applications—a, as well as a lack of specification languages with graphical concrete syntax (e.g., graphical editors); further reviews are needed to ensure that no relevant studies were left out. In this context, we have planned to extend this review by including other digital libraries (e.g., Springer Link, and Science Direct). Future research is to merge the Cloud Computing and Internet of Things (IoT) in order to satisfice the ubiquitous, reliable, efficient, and scalable requirements of IoT services provisioning; therefore, we have also planned to analyze more in-depth the usage of specification languages as support for the life cycle activities of IoT services (e.g. languages that specify IoT services architectures, languages that support resource provisioning for IoT services in the fog). Finally, we plan to collect more information about the empirical evidence of the effectiveness of usability evaluation methods for the Web.

Acknowledgements. This research is supported by the DIUC_XIV_2016_038 project.

Appendix A. Primary Studies Selected

[S001]   Alansari M, Almeida A, Bencomo N, Bordbar B (2015) CloudMPL: A Domain Specific Language for Describing Management Policies for an Autonomic Cloud Infrastructure.

[S002]   Alfonso C de, Caballer M, Alvarruiz F, Molto G, Hernández V (2011) Infrastructure Deployment Over the Cloud. In: 2011 IEEE Third International Conference on Cloud Computing Technology and Science. pp 517–521.

[S003]   Bezirgiannis N, Boer F de (2016) ABS: A High-Level Modeling Language for Cloud-Aware Programming. In: SOFSEM 2016: Theory and Practice of Computer Science. Springer, Berlin, Heidelberg, pp 433–444.

[S004]   Bunch C, Chohan N, Krintz C, Shams K (2011) Neptune: a domain specific language for deploying hpc software on cloud platforms. ACM Press, p 59

[S005]   Cavaleri A, Cossentino M, Lodato C, Lopes S, Sabatucci L Self-Configuring Mashup of Cloud Applications.

[S006]   Fan G, Yu H, Chen L (2016) Formally Modeling and Analyzing the Reliability of Cloud Applications. Int J Soft Eng Knowl Eng 26:273–305. https://doi.org/10.1142/s0218194016500121

[S007]   Johnsen EB, Schlatte R, Tarifa SLT (2013) Modeling Application-Level Management of Virtualized Resources in ABS. In: Formal Methods for Components and Objects. Springer, Berlin, Heidelberg, pp 89–108

[S008]   Kövesdán G, Asztalos M, Lengyel L Modeling Cloud Messaging with a Domain-Specific Modeling Language. 10

[S009]   Mangler J, Beran PP, Schikuta E (2010) On the Origin of Services Using RIDDL for Description, Evolution and Composition of RESTful Services. In: Proceedings of the 2010 10th IEEE/ACM International Conference on Cluster, Cloud and Grid Computing. IEEE Computer Society, Washington, DC, USA, pp 505–508

[S010]   Nassar M, Erradi A, Malluhi QM (2015) A Domain Specific Language for Secure Outsourcing of Computation to the Cloud. In: 2015 IEEE 19th International Enterprise Distributed Object Computing Conference. pp 134–141

[S011]   Pham LM, Tchana A, Donsez D, Palma N de, Zurczak V, Gibello PY (2015) Roboconf: A Hybrid Cloud Orchestrator to Deploy Complex Applications. In: 2015 IEEE 8th International Conference on Cloud Computing. pp 365–372

[S012]   Ponte N, Trinta F, Viana R, Andrade R, Garcia V, Assad R (2015) A Service-oriented Architecture for Billing Resources in IaaS Cloud Platforms. In: Proceedings of the 30th Annual ACM Symposium on Applied Computing. ACM, New York, NY, USA, pp 1719–1721

[S013]   Silva FAP da, Neto PA da MS, Garcia VC, Trinta FAM, Assad RE (2013) VeloZ: A Charging Policy Specification Language for Infrastructure Clouds. In: 2013 22nd International Conference on Computer Communication and Networks (ICCCN). pp 1–7

[S014]   Yi X, Huang B, Li C (2014) A Multi-properties Based Description Method of Cloud Manufacturing Services. In: 2014 International Conference on Service Sciences. pp 193–198

[S015]   Zuñiga-Prieto M, Insfran E, Abrahão S (2016) Architecture Description Language for Incremental Integration of Cloud Services Architectures. In: 2016 IEEE 10th International Symposium on the Maintenance and Evolution of Service-Oriented and Cloud-Based Environments (MESOCA). pp 16–23

References

1. Leavitt, N.: Is cloud computing really ready for prime time? Computer **42**, 15–20 (2009). https://doi.org/10.1109/MC.2009.20
2. Hamdaqa, M., Livogiannis, T., Tahvildari, L.: A reference model for developing cloud applications, pp. 98–103. SciTePress - Science and Technology Publications (2011)
3. Kitchenham, B., Charters, S.: Guidelines for performing systematic literature reviews in software engineering (2007)
4. Brereton, P., Kitchenham, B.A., Budgen, D., Turner, M., Khalil, M.: Lessons from applying the systematic literature review process within the software engineering domain. J. Syst. Softw. **80**, 571–583 (2007). https://doi.org/10.1016/j.jss.2006.07.009
5. Petersen, K., Feldt, R., Mujtaba, S., Mattsson, M.: Systematic mapping studies in software engineering, p. 10 (2008)

6. Kitchenham, B.: Procedures for performing systematic reviews. Keele, UK, Keele Univ. **33**, 1–26 (2004)
7. Petticrew, M., Roberts, H.: Systematic Reviews in the Social Sciences: A Practical Guide. Blackwell Publishing, Malden (2006)
8. Amazon Web Services, Inc.: What is cloud computing? - Amazon web services. https://aws. amazon.com/what-is-cloud-computing/. Accessed 29 May 2018
9. Littell, J.H., Corcoran, J.: Systematic reviews. In: The Handbook of Social Work Research Methods (2009)
10. Gu, Q., Lago, P.: A stakeholder-driven service life cycle model for SOA, pp. 1–7 (2007)
11. Wall, Q.: Understanding the service lifecycle within a SOA: design time (2006). http://www. oracle.com/technetwork/articles/entarch/soa-service-lifecycle-design3-099306.html. Accessed 29 May 2018
12. Wall, Q.: Understanding the service lifecycle within a SOA: run time (2006). http://www. oracle.com/technetwork/articles/grid/soa-service-lifecycle-run-099156.html. Accessed 29 May 2018
13. Bermayr, A., Grossniklaus, M., Wimmer, M.: D9.1 State of the art in modelling languages and model transformation techniques. ARTIST. Technische Universität Wien 51 (2013)
14. Matsumura, M.: The definitive guide to SOA governance and lifecycle management, p. 44 (2007)
15. Bjørner, D.: Software Engineering 1: Abstraction and Modelling. Springer, Heidelberg (2006). https://doi.org/10.1007/3-540-31288-9
16. Bézivin, J.: On the unification power of models. Softw. Syst. Model. **4**, 171–188 (2005). https://doi.org/10.1007/s10270-005-0079-0
17. Bergmayr, A., Wimmer, M., Kappel, G., Grossniklaus, M.: Cloud modeling languages by example, pp. 137–146. IEEE (2014)
18. Vaquero, L.M., Rodero-Merino, L., Buyya, R.: Dynamically scaling applications in the cloud, vol. 41, no. 1, pp. 45–52 (2011)
19. Mell, P., Grance, T.: The NIST definition of cloud computing (2011)
20. Conto, J.B., Zúñiga-Prieto, M., Solano-Quinde, L.: Description languages for the lifecycle activities of services in the cloud domain: a systematic mapping protocol. Journal MASKANA, Special Number: Proceedings of II Congreso I + D + Ingeniería - 2017 (2017, to be published)

Security and Privacy

Implementation and Detection of Novel Attacks to the PLC Memory of a Clean Water Supply System

Andres Robles-Durazno(✉), Naghmeh Moradpoor,
James McWhinnie, Gordon Russell, and Inaki Maneru-Marin

Edinburgh Napier University, Edinburgh, Scotland, UK
{a.roblesdurazno,n.moradpoor,j.mcwhinnie,
g.russell}@napier.ac.uk, 40291354@live.napier.ac.uk

Abstract. Critical infrastructures such as nuclear plants and water supply systems are mainly managed through electronic control systems. Such control systems comprise of a number of elements, such as programmable logic controllers (PLC), networking devices, sensors and actuators. With the development of online and networking solutions, such control systems can be managed online. Even though network connected control systems permit users to keep up to date with system operation, it also opens the door to attackers taking advantages of such availability. In this paper, a novel attack vector for modifying PLC memory is proposed, which affects the perceived values of sensors, such as a water flow meter, or the operation of actuators, such as a pump. In addition, this attack vector can also manipulate control variables located in the PLC working memory, reprogramming decision making rules. To show the impact of the attacks in a real scenario, a model of a clean water supply system is implemented on a Festo MPA rig. The results show that the attacks on the PLC memory can have a significant detrimental effect on control system operations. Further, a mechanism of detecting such attacks on the PLC memory is proposed based on monitoring energy consumption and electrical signals using current-measurement sensors. The results show the successful implementation of the novel PLC attacks as well as the feasibility of detecting such attacks.

Keywords: Industrial Control Systems (ICS) · Cyber attacks
PLC memory attack · Clean water supply system

1 Introduction

The evolution of Industrial Control Systems has improved the application of computer-based management systems in industrial settings. For instance, in water industries, the technology has improved the reliability and quality of water services, but as a result it has increased the likelihood of targeted cyber events that could lead to disruption in the water supply. Currently, Industrial Control Systems (ICS) are facing new threat vectors design to extract sensitive information or disrupt operations. One of the biggest recent attacks occurred in May 2017, using the WannaCry ransomware [1] that affected a considerable number of computers running Windows operating system across the

© Springer Nature Switzerland AG 2019
M. Botto-Tobar et al. (Eds.): CITT 2018, CCIS 895, pp. 91–103, 2019.
https://doi.org/10.1007/978-3-030-05532-5_7

globe. This attack affected not only desktop computers, but industrial and social infrastructure facilities as well. For instance, Renault, Nissan and Honda were forced to suspend operations because their facilities were infected. In another example, the ExPetr (Petya) attack [1], which was discovered in Jun 2017, affected power sector companies, transport industry and even the Chernobyl radiation monitoring station. Such attacks are becoming increasingly more sophisticated, and the risk of disrupting industry operations if growing.

Although cyber-attacks to critical infrastructures, such as water plants, have increased globally [2], growing awareness of the risk does not necessarily result in companies implementing better security protocols and safer systems. When cyber-attacks are identified publically, the focus is frequently on security breaches in industries such as banking and retail [3]. Although, according to a number of reports, cyber-attacks on vital infrastructure such as electrical grids and water distribution systems have increased considerably. For instance, on November 21st, 2001, hackers gained access to a clean water utility in Springfield, USA and destroyed a pump [4]. The attackers stole the access credentials by first breaking into a computer belonging to the utility's SCADA software vendor. The control system under attack kept turning on and off, resulting in the burnout of a water pump. According to the forensic report, the hackers may have had access to the water plant two months prior the attack. This attack resulted in about 56000 people without water.

This paper proposes a novel attack vector to the PLC memory and a mechanism of detecting this type of attack, by monitoring the energy consumption and other electrical signals. To validate this approach, a model of an un-interrupted clean water supply system was constructed a Festo MPA rig [5]. This paper is organized as follows. Section 2 describes the related work in the field. Section 3 gives a brief overview of the PLC operation. Sections 4 refers to the testbed used to conduct this research. Section 5 describes the attacks performed to the PLC memory. Section 6 proposes a new method of attack detection by analyzing energy traces. Section 7 indicates the results obtained. Section 8 presents the conclusions follows by references.

2   Related Work

In this section, existing work related to anomaly detection techniques for SCADA systems are discussed. Detecting attacks is challenging, as in particular attacks change over time and such attacks may be using previously unknown attack methods. For this reason the authors have focused on applying machine learning approaches to the task, with the goal of making such detection easier and more effective.

In [6], a behavior-based attack detection and classification scheme for a Secured Water Treatment (SWaT) system is proposed using machine learning algorithms. SWaT is an operational scaled down water treatment plant with six main processes, though they studied intrusions against only one of the processes. Here, Best-First Tree (BFTree) shows the best results in terms of precision and accuracy of detection and classification in comparison with their other eight selected machine learning algorithms. They used 18 attacks based on exploiting 10 different issues in three different subsystems to build the model to evaluate their selected nine machine learning algorithms. The three places that their attacks occurred were inflow into the process (4 attack types in total), outflow from the process (2 attack types in total), and the water level of the tank (4 attack types in total). Their attacks were based on the model proposed by [7] with the aim to mislead the PLC by providing false sensor or actuator information. For instance, for the attack on inflow, one of the attacks changed the operating value of the flow indicator sensor to above the normal operating range, which falsified input flow rate and gave a wrong impression to the PLC that the relevant sensor was faulty. In one of the outflow attacks, the value of the main pump's status was set to "closed". This made the PLC turn on the backup pump while the main pump was still running, which can damage pumps or burst pipes. Likewise, for an attack on the water level aspect of the tank, the value of the water level sensor was changed to below the normal minimum level, which in turn made the outflow and filtration process stop.

In [8], a Support Vector Machine (SVM) was employed, and a proposed an Intrusion Detection System (IDS) with a discriminant model to detect cyber-attacks on Industrial Control Systems (ICS) was presented. Their proposed model was based on a communication profile analysis which considers only packet intervals and packet length. Their testbed contained two water tanks prepared with control devices and controlled automatically. For their experiments, they created two datasets that included penetration test dataset and normal dataset each consisting of 10 sub datasets. While the former was constructed during the period of a four-stage penetration test, over which malicious and benign packets are labelled based on their source IP address, the latter was built throughout the normal operation of the system. For each dataset, packet interval and packet length was captured. For their penetration tests, they used the Metasploit Framework (Rapid7) and then Wireshark to capture packets. In their results they identified a significant difference between attack packets and normal packets in terms of packet intervals and packet lengths.

In [9], big data analysis and behaviour observation techniques were employed for cyber-attack detection within a simulated critical infrastructure: a pressurized water cooled nuclear reactor. The simulated system includes a water source, two water tanks, a condenser, a reactor, a generator, acid tank, and emergency coolant. In their simulation, each component has a corresponding observer to extract physical information about behavior and construct two datasets: one with a smaller and one with a larger number of features and events. They constructed features by taking the maximum, minimum, mean and median of water tank level, steam output, and energy creation for 32 mechanical components and 9 system components, which is sampled at 4 Hz (4 times every second) for a 24-h simulation. After specifying the constraints for the water tank, steam output, and energy creation, they observed the minimum and maximum levels regularly. If the levels recorded are lower or higher than the expected minimum or maximum values then the system behavior identified it as abnormal, otherwise it is identified as normal behavior. They then used five supervised data classifiers to detect attacks. Addressing their captured results, in the initial evaluation, the classifiers were able to produce a reasonably good accuracy, which in turn was significantly increased in their second evaluation by increased the number of the events as well as the number of the features captured per event.

In [10], unsupervised machine learning algorithms for anomaly detection in water treatment systems was examined using a dataset collected through the same SWaT testbed as [6], which was a scaled-down raw water purification plant. They applied and compared two unsupervised algorithms: Deep Neural Network (DNN) including a layer of Long Short-Term Memory (LSTM) architecture followed by feedforward layers of multiple inputs and outputs, and a one-class Support Vector Machine (SVM) in which DNN performs slightly better than one-class SVM in general. They used logs from the testbed that were available online [2] which contained benign and malicious events collected from network traffic, in addition to the data collected from all 51 sensors and actuators available in SWaT over eleven days of continuous operations. This included seven days of continuous normal operation in addition to four days of 36 attack scenarios representative of typical network-based attacks on Cyber-Physical Systems (CPSs). Generally, their attacks were based on hijacking and modifying network packets through the data communication link of the SWaT network, allowing for sensor data and actuator signals to be manipulated before reaching the PLCs, pumps, and valves.

In [11], an unsupervised Recurrent Neural Networks (RNN) for anomaly detection was proposed using a dataset collected through the SWaT. This considered only a single process (Process 1) out of six available processes of the testbed. Addressing their captured results, they were able to detect the majority of attacks with low false positive rate using their proposed RNN approach. The SWaT dataset is available online [2] and includes benign and malicious logs captured from the SWaT testbed [6]. The dataset collected over seven days of continuous normal operation and four days of malicious operation during which 36 attack scenarios were conducted. The attacks have been simulated by network packet hijacking and manipulation which results in sensor data and actuator signals to be manipulated before reaching the PLCs, pumps, and valves. For the data pre-processing stage, they treated all P1's sensors and actuators as a numeric attribute and normalized each feature by subtracting the mean and scaling to the unit variance given.

In [12], an unsupervised SCADA data-driven approach to detect integrity attacks on a simulated Water Distribution System (WDS) was proposed. This was based on k-nearest neighbour technique and includes two stages of: (1) automatic identification of consistent and inconsistent state of SCADA systems and (2) automatic extraction of proximity-based rules from the identified states to detect inconsistent states. They compared their proposed unsupervised learning approach with three other approaches, two of which are based on unsupervised learning and one is based on semi-supervised learning. Their proposed unsupervised approach shows better performance in terms of detection accuracy and efficiency. For their attack scenarios, they conducted man-in-the-middle attacks to manipulate process parameters such as: water flow, water pressure, water demand, water level, valve status, valve setting, pump status, and pump speed in the WDS server. To simulate a realistic scenario, the WDS server reads and controls these process parameters in response to message commands from a filed device. In total they used three datasets: (1) a publicly available dataset referred to as DUWWTP [13] which comes from the daily measuring of sensors in an urban waste water treatment plant and (2) their two simulated datasets. The DUWWTP includes 527 observations of 38 data nodes in which 14 of them are labelled as inconsistent. The simulated datasets include 10,500 observations from 23 data nodes for which 100 events are labelled as inconsistent.

Attacks documented in previous publications [6, 10, 11] employed attacks based on packet hijacking, manipulation and injection, as well as old techniques like man-in-the-middle attacks such as in [12], all of which could be detected by Network Intrusion Detection/Prevention Systems (IDS/IPS). In this paper the authors propose a different, novel attack targeting PLC memory. Additionally, a unique approach to detect attacks is proposed for PLC memory based on monitoring the energy consumption of the system.

3 PLC Operation

The operation of a PLC is straightforward. It makes decisions based on the program coded within it by a user. PLCs operate by running a scan cycle and repeat this many times per second [14]. Figure 1 represents the PLC scan cycle. When placed into run it checks on the hardware and software for faults, then it starts a three step process: input scan, program execution and output write or update [15] described as follows.

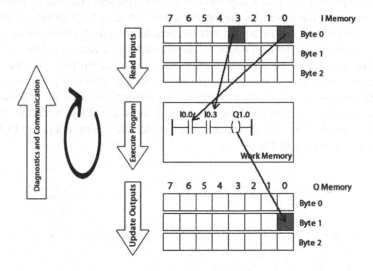

Fig. 1. PLC scan cycle

3.1 Input Scan

In this scan, the PLC takes a snapshot of the inputs and determines the state of the devices connected. Then it saves this information in a data table to use in the next step. This speeds up subsequent processing and maintains consistency in cases where an input changes in the period from start to the end of the program [15].

3.2   Execute Program

After getting the information from the inputs, the PLC executes a program, one instruction at a time, using only the memory copy of the inputs. In addition, during the program execution, the PLC may require information allocated in the working memory, such as a Process Variables (PV) or Set Point (SP).

3.3   Output Update

The outputs will be updated when the execution of the program ends, using the temporary values in memory. The PLC updates the status of the outputs by writing to the memory locations associated with each output [15].

4   Testbed

A model of an uninterrupted clean water supply system using the Festo MPA rig [5] was implemented to support the investigation. To simulate a clean water demand of a small town, a water demand model was constructed [20] which is represented in Fig. 2. The X-axis represents 24 h of a day and the Y-axis represents the value applied to the space of memory addressed to the proportional valve, which simulates the water demand in the town. It can be argued that the simulation only represents one week and in some cases the water demand might variate depending on various factors over longer periods. For instance, water demand during the summer might be higher than during the winter, or even during the holidays. However, for experimental purposes the water demand model ignores such variances. Figure 3 represents the network implementation where the attacker is connected to the control network along with the PLC and Supervisor Console. The sensors and actuators, which are connected to the PLC inputs and outputs, are shown in Fig. 4.

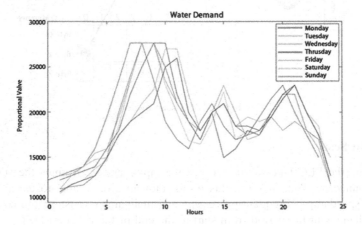

Fig. 2. Water demand models.

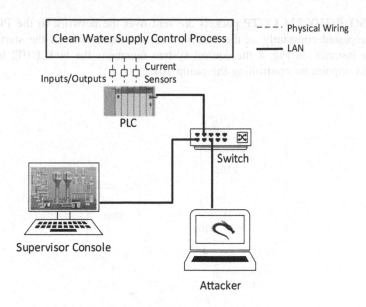

Fig. 3. Testbed implementation.

4.1 Normal Operation

An uninterrupted clean water supply system was modelled. In this model, the water reservoir is assumed to be a continuous naturally filtered water supply that is pumped up to the supply tank. Figure 4 represents the control process diagram implementation. In normal operation tank B101 simulates the clean water supply which is pumped up to the reservoir tank B102. The valve V102 simulates a non-return valve; therefore, the water does not return when the pump is not operating. The flow in the pipe is measured by a flowmeter FIC/B102. The ultrasonic sensor LIC/B101 placed at the top of tank B102 measures the water level. In this model, a cascade control aiming to maintain the required water level SetPoint (SP) is implemented. The ultrasonic sensor reading is the process variable PV for the cascade outer loop and the flowmeter reading is used as the process variable for the cascade inner loop. The proportional valve V106 simulates the water demand for a small town. Finally, the water returns to tank B101.

5 PLC Memory Corruption

The previous section showed a brief summary of the PLC operation. In this section three novel PLC memory corruption attacks are introduced.

5.1 Attack to the PLC Inputs

In this attack, the aim is to overwrite the bytes of memory assigned to the external sensors in the PLC. This attack affects the control process because the PLC uses wrong readings while executing the internal code that will define the PLC outputs.

Crafted ISO 8073/X.224 COTP packets are sent over the network to the PLC. This attack is repeated constantly as the PLC updates the input table at the start of each cycle. For instance, in Fig. 4 the control system maintains the tank B102 level at a determined setpoint by controlling the pump 101.

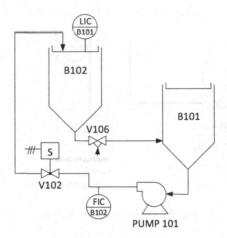

Fig. 4. Clean water supply system control diagram

The control process is configured to maintain the reservoir tank setpoint at 6 litres. In the first scenario, the attacker tampers with the memory used to hold data from the ultrasonic sensor, so that the tank appears to contain 1 litre of water. The reaction of the control system is to try and achieve the setpoint by speeding up the pump, which results in overflowing the B102 tank.

5.2   Attack to the PLC Outputs

In this attack, the aim is to overwrite the memory associated with the outputs in the PLC. The same attack logic is employed as in the previous attack. However, the main difference is in the devices targeted during this attack. The aim to overwrite the memory associated with the pump with the intention of increasing its speed to overflow tank B102 showed in Fig. 4. To achieve this, crafted packets are injected with values that require the pump work at 100% of its capacity. This is reminiscent of the Stuxnet [16] attack discussed earlier where the attack increased and decreased the values injected in the PLC Output memory. In this paper we plan to increase and reduce the speed of the pump at the time to emulate overflowing and emptying the tank B102.

5.3   Attacks to the PLC Working Memory

As discussed before, the PLC is composed of different memory elements, such as work memory, retentive memory, etc. The working memory contains the PLC code that is executed at runtime [14]. Process variables such as the setpoint are allocated in this part of the PLC memory. In this scenario, the memory associated with the setpoint variable is modified. Two different values can be controlled, namely the high and low setpoints for a system. In the attack the setpoint value is modified by steadily increasing and decreasing it. This is similar to the attack proposed in [17, 18]. However, they proposed a theoretical approach while in this work it is physically implemented.

6 Mechanisms of Attack Detection

The detection of attacks in control systems can be seen from different points of view because some of these systems are connected to corporate networks; as a result, they face targeted attacks like Stuxnet [16] and common attacks such as buffer overflow, SQL injection and more. In this paper, attack detection is implemented by monitoring the signal of the ultrasonic sensor and the flowmeter.

In the author's previous work, the feasibility of detecting cyber attacks was demonstrated in a control process by monitoring the energy consumption of the pump [19]. In the first attempt, this was by monitoring the energy consumption of the ultrasonic sensor and the flowmeter; however, these sensors consume a low amount of energy which makes monitoring the energy consumption difficult. For this reason, current sensors were used instead at the PLC Inputs for the ultrasonic sensor and the flowmeter. This means, for instance, it should detect any change to the setpoint variable by monitoring the input signal of the ultrasonic sensor. This signal is represented in volts (v).

7 Results

The results of the energy consumption records in the pump and voltage signals of the ultrasonic sensor and flowmeter are shown in Fig. 5. The shaded areas show each one of the attacks performed and they are explained as follows. Table 1 summarizes the attacks performed to the clean water supply system, in addition it also includes the shadow area represented in Fig. 5.

Attack on the PLC Working Memory. When the setpoint suffers a significant change, for instance from 6 litres to 9 litres, the pump starts speeding up to achieve the new setpoint, as a result, it consumes more energy than expected. In Fig. 5, the first shadow area from the left-hand side which marked with 1 shows this sudden change. The energy consumption of the pump might indicate that an attack is happening in the control system, although it does not indicate in which part of the control system it is happening. On the other hand, the ultrasonic sensor signal allows monitoring the water level in the reservoir tank, and when the setpoint increases, the ultrasonic sensor signal also increases. Thus, the energy monitored in the pump correlated with the ultrasonic sensor signal indicating the parts of the control system that have been affected. It can be argued that the PLC permits collecting and monitoring the energy of the ultrasonic sensor, as a result, it could allow detecting the increment in the setpoint using normal

Table 1. Summary of attacks to the PLC memory

Shadow Area	PLC Memory	Attack	Results
1	Working memory	- Setpoint	- Signal in the ultrasonic sensor increases/decreases - Energy consumption in the pump increases/decreases
2	PLC input	- Ultrasonic sensor reading	- Signal in the ultrasonic sensor increases/decreases - Energy consumption in the pump increases/decreases
3	PLC output	- Pump speed	- Signal from the ultrasonic sensor increases/decreases - Energy consumption in the pump increases/decreases
4	PLC input	- Flowmeter reading	- Energy consumption in the pump decreases
5	PLC input/output	- Pump speed - Ultrasonic sensor	- System unstable

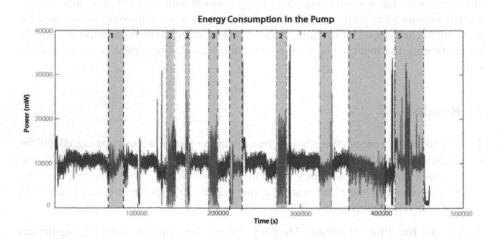

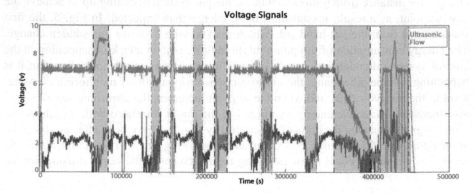

Fig. 5. Energy and voltage signals.

rules. However, in this scenario, detection does not rely on the information provided by the PLC because it might itself be compromised. For that reason, external and independent current sensors are preferred.

In the second scenario, when the setpoint goes from six litres to two litres the pump stops working, and the ultrasonic sensor signal decreases. In Fig. 5, the second shadow area from the left-hand side marked with 1 shows this change in the ultrasonic sensor and the pump. Until the setpoint is reached the energy consumption in the pump falls to zero along with the flow in the pipe. Afterwards, the pump starts working again to maintain the new setpoint. However, the energy used by the pump is lower than the normally used.

In the third scenario, the intention is to avoid the sudden change in the energy consumption of the pump and so the attack decreases the setpoint by one over time until the tank is empty. In Fig. 5, the third shadow area from the left-hand side marked with 1 shows this attack. It can be seen that the energy consumption of the pump does not suffer a considerable change. However, the signal in the ultrasonic sensor starts to decrease indicating that the tank starts to empty.

Attack to the PLC Inputs. In this case the memory associated with the ultrasonic sensor signal is overwritten by injecting a value that represents eight litres. As a result, the pump slows down and the reservoir tank is reduced to one litre of water. In Fig. 5, the first shadow area marked with 2 shows this attack. In the second attack, memory was overwritten with a value that represented one litre of water, and as a result, the pump started working at 100% of its capacity resulting in a rapid increase of water and an imminent overflow of the reservoir tank. This attack can be seen in the second shadow area marked with 2 in Fig. 5. It should be considered that the response of the control system to attacks depends on how it is designed and implemented. For this testbed a cascade control system was implemented. It worth mentioning that a different technique such as a Proportional Integral (PI) controller acting directly on the pump might produce different results to this attack.

In the next attack, the PLC memory addressed to the flowmeter was overwritten with a value that represents 4.1 litres per minute, which is the maximum value that the pump provides. This attack does not affect the operation of the control system, because this value is used for the inner loop of the cascade control, which is designed to handle high amounts of noise. Meaning that the control system is interpreting the attack as noise. In addition, the flow in this control system is low, which is another reason for the low impact of the attack. In Fig. 5, the shadow area marked with 4 shows this attack.

Attack to the PLC Outputs. In this scenario, the aim is to compromise the pump by overwriting the PLC output memory addressed to it. This increased and decreased the pump speed by injecting integer values into the PLC memory. In Fig. 5, the shadow area marked with 3 shows that the energy consumption in the pump starts to fluctuate. It can be concluded that this affected the control system, however, it does not cause a huge impact. Instead, this attack might lead to damage the pump over time and stop the process operation completely.

Multiple Attacks. In this scenario, an attack is executed on all the devices that are part of the control system at the same time, as a result, it affected the entire process operation. In Fig. 5, the grey area marked with 5 shows the behaviour of the control process. In this attack, the memory associated with the pump was overwritten with a small value aiming to slow down the pump. In addition, random values were injected in the memory associated with the ultrasonic sensor. At the end, the setpoint was modified to zero. During this attack, the control system operation is highly affected. It could be said that performing this type of attacks on real control systems might have the same effect compromising the water supply of a certain population.

8   Conclusions

In this paper, a novel attack vector is proposed for control systems which targets PLC memory corruption in three places: PLC input, PLC output, and PLC working memory. These attacks were demonstrated in a clean water supply system modelled in the Festo MPA Rig to show the impact of the attacks in a real scenario. The execution of these attacks showed that it is possible to disrupt the control system operation by overwriting the memory locations associated to PLC Inputs and Outputs. In addition, attacks were made which modified the setpoint variable located in the PLC working memory. It can be concluded that most published research proposes different types of theoretical attacks. However, practical implementations are needed to measure the impact of those attacks. It can be argued whether the theoretical attacks proposed are applicable in real implementations. Further, this paper extended our previous work by offering a mechanism of detection based on monitoring the energy consumption of the pump and the electrical signal from the ultrasonic sensor and the flowmeter. The results show the feasibility of detecting the attacks performed to the control system by monitoring the energy and voltage parameters. When reducing the setpoint by one until reaching the minimum setpoint, the energy consumption in the pump did not show a considerable change. However, the electrical signal in the ultrasonic sensor is reduced showing that the reservoir tank is emptying. In future work, the feasibility of attack detection in industrial control systems using control engineering techniques will be investigated.

References

1. Kaspersky: Threat Landscape for Industrial Automation Systems in H1 2017, 20 May 2018. https://ics-cert.kaspersky.com/reports/2017/09/28/threat-landscape-for-industrial-automation -systems-in-h1-2017/
2. Secure water treatment (SWaT) Dataset, 21 May 2018. https://itrust.sutd.edu.sg/research/ dataset/
3. Morris, T.H., Gao, W.: Industrial control system cyber attacks. In: Proceedings of the 1st International Symposium on ICS & SCADA Cyber Security Research 2013, Leicester (2013)
4. Bradley, T.: Water utility hacked: are critical systems at risk? PCWorld, 20 November 2011. https://www.pcworld.com/article/244359/water_utility_hacked_are_our_scada_systems_at_ risk_.html. Accessed 30 April 2018

5. FESTO: MPS® PA Compact Workstation with level, flow rate, pressure and temperature controlled systems. http://www.festo-didactic.com/int-en/learning-systems/process-automati on/compact-workstation/mps-pa-compact-workstation-with-level,flow-rate,pressure-and-tem perature-controlled-systems.htm?fbid=aW50LmVuLjU1Ny4xNy4xOC44ODIuNDM3Ng

6. Khurum Nazir, J., Goh, J.: Behaviour-based attack detection and classification in cyber physical systems using machine learning. In: Proceedings of the 2nd ACM International Workshop on Cyber-Physical System Security, Xi'an, China (2016)

7. Adepu, S., Mathur, A.: An investigation into the response of a water treatment system to cyber attacks. In: 2016 IEEE 17th International Symposium on High Assurance Systems Engineering (HASE) (2016)

8. Terai, A., Abe, S., Kojima, S., Takano, Y., Koshijima, I.: Cyber-attack detection for industrial control system monitoring with support vector machine based on communication profile. In: 2017 IEEE European Symposium on Security and Privacy Workshops (EuroS PW) (2017)

9. Hurst, W., Merabti, M., Fergus, P.: Big data analysis techniques for cyber-threat detection in critical infrastructures. In: 28th International Conference on Advanced Information Networking and Applications Workshops (2014)

10. Inoue, J., Yamagata, Y., Chen, Y., Poskitt, C., Sun, J.: Anomaly detection for a water treatment system using unsupervised machine learning. In: IEEE International Conference on Data Mining Workshops (2017)

11. Goh, J., Adepu, S., Tan, M., Lee, Z.: Anomaly detection in cyber physical systems using recurrent neural networks. In: 2017 IEEE 18th International Symposium on High Assurance Systems Engineering (HASE) (2017)

12. Almalawi, A., Yu, X., Tari, Z., Fahad, A., Khalila, I.: An unsupervised anomaly-based detection approach for integrity attacks on SCADA systems. Comput. Secur. **46**, 94 (2014)

13. Frank, A., Asuncion, A.: UCI machine learning repository, 12 May 2018. http://archive.ics. uci.edu/ml

14. Kamel, K., Kamel, E.: Programmable Logic Controllers: Industrial Control. McGraw-Hill Professional, New York (2013)

15. Bolton, W.: Input/output devices. In: Programmable Logic Controllers, Sixth Edn., Chap. 2, pp. 23–61. Newnes, Boston (2015)

16. Langner, R.: Stuxnet: dissecting a cyberwarfare weapon. IEEE Secur. Priv. **9**, 49–51 (2011)

17. Shames, I., Texeira, A., Sandberg, H., Johansson, K.: Revealing stealthy attacks in control systems. In: 2012 50th Annual Allerton Conference on Communication, Control, and Computing (Allerton) (2012)

18. Urbina, D., et al.: Limiting the impact of stealthy attacks on industrial control systems. In: Proceedings of the 2016 ACM SIGSAC Conference on Computer and Communications Security, Vienna (2016)

19. Robles-Durazno, A., Moradpoor, N., McWhinnie, J., Russell, G.: A supervised energy monitoring-based machine learning approach for anomaly detection in a clean water supply system. In: Cyber Security 2018 (2018). Accepted for publication

20. NORDPOOL: Market Data Nord Pool. NORDPOOL. https://www.nordpoolgroup.com/ Market-data1/Power-system-data/Consumption1/Consumption/ALL/Hourly1/?view=table. Accessed 30 April 2018

Vulnerabilities in Banking Transactions with Mobile Devices Android: A Systematic Literature Review

Pablo F. Ordoñez-Ordoñez[1,2]([✉]) [iD], Domingo D. Herrera-Loaiza[1] [iD], and Roberth Figueroa-Díaz[1] [iD]

[1] Facultad de Energía, Universidad Nacional de Loja,
Ave. Pío Jaramillo Alvarado, La Argelia, Loja, Ecuador
pfordonez@unl.edu.ec
[2] ETSI Sistemas Informáticos, Universidad Politécnica de Madrid,
Calle Alan Turing s/n, 28031 Madrid, Spain

Abstract. This qualitative systematic literature review (SLR) corresponds to the search for vulnerabilities in banking transactions by means of ANDROID Intelligent mobile devices and the incidents in the users. In these devices there is leaking information that is captured by hackers and with it the dissatisfaction of users to ignore how to treat these insecurities. For this, initially of between 123 studies, 18 were selected according to the search criteria corresponding to the research questions in vulnerability and incidence, it was mainly found the bank Phishing, the injections of malware in mobile applications and to a large extent victims of bank fraud.

Keywords: Mobile applications · Banking transactions
Software vulnerabilities · Mobile vulnerabilities
Android vulnerabilities

1 Introduction

The use of the applications on mobile devices Android is extremely high for its popularity, that is why it is increasingly increase the people who use this type of devices for entertainment and as a tool of work [13,14,28]. When conducting mobile banking transactions, users are not aware that they may be victims of any of the insecurities in banking services indicated in [10], so this paper is a systematic literature review of the vulnerability in banking transactions with Android mobile applications, in order to know the current situation of research carried out according to the research questions:

- **RQ1:** What frequent vulnerabilities exist in banking transactions for Android mobile devices?
- **RQ2:** How do these vulnerabilities affect users?

© Springer Nature Switzerland AG 2019
M. Botto-Tobar et al. (Eds.): CITT 2018, CCIS 895, pp. 104–115, 2019.
https://doi.org/10.1007/978-3-030-05532-5_8

In addition, according to [4] there is a top 10 of vulnerabilities in the mobile platform that is of great importance as related work.

The SLR was based on the protocol of [5,12], where RQ1 and RQ2 were raised. These questions were considered in order to systematize the findings of studies with vulnerable impact on mobile device users when performing tasks such as: online payments, news review, games and entertainment in general.

In Sect. 2, the SLR is executed, the result of which is described in Table 2. On the basis of these results, Sect. 3 presents the most notable details and the synthesis argued and discussed in the 18 primary studies and Sect. 4 concludes as research questions the consequences of the review, and specific lines of research for the future.

2   Review Protocol Development

2.1   Research Identification

The criterion for the choice of search sources was based on web accessibility and the inclusion of search engines that allow to carry out advanced queries, in this way the following were used: IEEE library [1], SCOPUS Library [8], Google Scholar [2] and OWASP [3].

For the choice of keywords it was considered: research questions and keywords of previously reviewed articles: Vulnerability, mobile applications, Bank transactions, mobile vulnerabilities, Android vulnerabilities, mobile Banking, security

Table 1. Bibliographic sources and search strings.

Search ID	String
B01 Scopus	((An android based) AND (based mobile device) AND (device application) AND (Games and multimedia))
B02 Scopus	((forensic investigation) AND ('onedrive' OR 'box' OR 'googledrive' OR 'dropbox') AND (applications) AND (android) AND (ios))
B04 Scopus	(title-abs-key (how current) AND title-abs-key (android) AND title-abs-key (malware seeks) AND title-abs-key (evade automated) AND title-abs-key (code analysis))
B05 Scopus	(ALL (automatic detection) AND ALL (correction) AND ALL (visualization) AND ALL (security vulnerabilities) AND ALL (mobile apps))
B06 OWASP	"owasp" + "mobile top 10" + "Vulnerabilities" + "vulnerabilidades" + "móviles"
B07 IEEE	"((("Publication Title": Security assessment) OR assessment of Mobile) AND Mobile Banking)"
B03 IEEE	(((("Document Title": Potential Vulnerability) AND Analysis) AND Mobile Banking) AND Applications)
B08 Google Scholar	"Systematic Literature Review:" + "Security Challenges of Mobile Banking" AND "Payments System"
B09 Google Scholar	"Examining" + "Security Risks" of "Mobile" + "Banking Applications" + "through Blog Mining"

assessment, Potential Vulnerability, Banking applications, security risks, mobile device.

Searches were performed using logical operators: (AND) and (OR) and the following inclusion criteria were considered for the search:

- Include as relevant the existing publications from 2012 onwards, as a result of the exponential indication of the Use of mobile devices.
- Search results in the area of science and computation, by the close relationship of technical analysis for further mitigation.
- Documents in Spanish and English language.
- Search the Abstract of the article for keywords.

The Table 1 correspond to the search chains (B01...B09) in the different bibliographic sources.

2.2   Selection of Primary Studies

Once the results were obtained with the searches, the following criteria were established for the selection and evaluation of primary studies:

- In the summary, you should be aware of the vulnerabilities and/or incidents that occur in the Mobile devices with ANDROID operating system.
- The title must be related to the investigation.
- The document must respond to RQ1 and/or RQ2.
- The conclusion must have relevant information for the investigation.

2.3   Data Extraction

The Table 2 presents the relevant information for each of the selected articles (S01...S18) according to the search by pointing out elements such as: type of vulnerability (RQ1) and incidence (RQ2) as research questions, study/article title, and findings as Relevant conclusions. These are the results:

Table 2. Data extraction from the primary studies.

Search ID - Source ID - Ref. Article title	
Vulnerability and/or incidence in users	Findings
B01 - S01 - [9] Games and multimedia implementation on heroic battle of surabaya: An android based mobile device application	
There is an impact on the change in lifestyle of mobile users for accessing information	The number of mobile users increases very rapidly. Interactive applications are developed that allow a better teaching especially in young people

(continued)

Table 2. (*continued*)

Search ID - Source ID - Ref. Article title	
Vulnerability and/or incidence in users	Findings
B02 - S02 - [7] Forensic investigation of OneDrive, Box, GoogleDrive and Dropbox applications on Android and iOS devices	
Forensic investigation of OneDrive, Box, GoogleDrive and Dropbox applications on Android and iOS devices Unsafe storage of information in the cloud The credentials, the information accessed in the cloud through mobile devices, could be recovered in the internal memory of the device The sessions and activities carried out in the cloud can be recovered in the backup	The information currently is stored in the cloud and is easily accessible by means of a mobile device, which could be recovered in the internal memory of the mobile device
B03 - S03 - [6] Potential Vulnerability Analysis of Mobile Banking Applications	
Potential vulnerabilities can be created from the permissions that the operating system grants to applications	Application developers generate vulnerabilities by default. Applications can generate vulnerabilities from permissions which could cause serious impacts on the system and applications The applications generate vulnerabilities, due to the lack of knowledge of the developer
B04 - S04 - [27] How Current Android Malware Seeks to Evade Automated Code Analysis	
Attack campaigns specifically to the ANDROID platform, exploit the tapjacking vulnerability. New Malware are detected as BadAccents	Malicious applications are spread through email and SMS messages. It detects new malware like the Android/BadAccents family. At present there are many campaigns of new threats to the ANDROID platform
B05 - S05 - [26] Automatic Detection, Correction, and Visualization of Security Vulnerabilities in Mobile Apps	
There is no confidentiality in sending data from mobile applications	The information that circulates from end to end is exposed to unauthorized observers To increase confidentiality, remote servers are implemented to protect the data, using techniques such as Value-Similarity

(*continued*)

Table 2. (*continued*)

Search ID - Source ID - Ref. Article title	
Vulnerability and/or incidence in users	Findings
B06 - S06 - [25] Weak Server Side Controls	
The weakness of controls on the server allows cybercriminals to scan open ports, applications, exploiting vulnerabilities through the injection of malicious code XSS Cross-Site Scripting Vulnerabilities, generated from the API, web service or web server applications are exploited through a mobile device	Attackers to find a vulnerability inject malicious code to perpetrate its purpose that is the theft of information from users Vulnerabilities are exploited through a mobile device, the same one that feeds malicious entries to the server, to violate them, this can produce unexpected sequences of events
B06 - S07 - [19] Insecure Data Storage	
Insecurity in Data Storage, when the user loses his mobile device, attacks can be made to access this medium using the EXPLOITS	Users losing their mobile device for any reason can be victims of attack through malware
B06 - S08 - [20] Insufficient Transport Layer Protection	
Insufficient Protection in the Transport Layer, as there is no encryption	Data encryption protocols must be used in the transport layer, with SSL/TLS
B06 - S09 - [24] Unintended Data Leakage	
Unintended Data Fugue, when developing mobile applications you can not control the security of the other systems that are going to interact or hardware with which you will interact so you can lose data	Developers must be trained so that each time they code new applications, they can take action on the possible leaks of information that may occur
B06 - S10 - [22] Poor Authorization and Authentication	
Poor Authentication and Authorization, due to the lack of security tokens, information can be lost, for example with the well-known "you want to save your password" [22]	You should not be confident at the moment that an application asks if you want to save or remember passwords, this can be displeasing to know that they are capturing the passwords
B06 - S11 - [16] Broken Cryptography	
Broken Cryptography, using proprietary data encryption algorithms may have holes through which attackers may violate a mobile application	Sometimes the methods of encryption of information (data) become an almost obsolete practice

(*continued*)

Table 2. (*continued*)

Search ID - Source ID - Ref. Article title	
Vulnerability and/or incidence in users	Findings
B06 - S12 - [17] Client Side Injection	
Lateral Injection Client, mainly occurs in ROOT users since having super user permissions can access files and leave doors open	Users who are not experts or do not know about the privileges that can be activated on their ANDROID devices are vulnerable in terms of information theft perpetrated by CYBER CRIMINALS
B06 - S13 - [23] Security Decisions Via Untrusted Inputs	
Security decisions that are not trusted via entries, mobile applications when interacting with other applications that are not trusted are vulnerable since there are some processes that may contain malware	Mobile applications should interact only with trusted applications that pass through a certified filter
B06 - S14 - [18] Improper Session Handling	
Inadequate Management of the session, it happens when we do not close the session for example when we leave open a session in some social network or electronic banking account among others	The naive users are those who are most subject to this vulnerability because they do not know the topic of login when being connected to the internet
B06 - S15 - [21] Lack of Binary Protections	
Lack of protection at the binary level, through reverse engineering can obtain confidential information from attackers, this happens when a programmer has not been the full author of the application	Developers must have absolute control of their application because otherwise they can be victims of attack by computer criminals
B07 - S16 - [15] Security assessment of Mobile- Banking	
SMARTPHONES are gaining use in front of the PCs, this does not cause much admiration due to the great benefits that the smart phones give	It is basically code injections on mobile devices that are not managed correctly by the user
Denial of Distributed Service (DDoS), services are not accessed by their legitimate users	It occurs due to easy access to stolen devices, taking into account the level of security that the device owns
Mobile malware, potentially affects the majority of users who do not have the necessary knowledge to mitigate this vulnerability	When developing an application the data is usually exchanged between client-server
Threats from third-party applications are dangerous when interacting with systems other than ANDROID without due security	Interaction with third-party applications, in which the code of other developers is not well known

(*continued*)

Table 2. (*continued*)

Search ID - Source ID - Ref. Article title	
Vulnerability and/or incidence in users	Findings
TCP-IP Spoofing, which is based on replacing an IP address with a false one	There are authentication patterns that are considered insecure, this is the case of the IP address change
Rear access doors, here malicious codes are captured that do not allow the proper functioning of the algorithm	Sometimes the methods of encryption of information (data) become an almost obsolete practice
Manipulation, users follow an inappropriate sequence in their SMARTPHONE re-directing it to another application	Access to unreliable applications by users, in which their data is vulnerable and very prone to theft
Exploits, is a vulnerability very well known by computer scientists but little for common users	Insecurity of communication between processes, easily the user can be redirected to another environment through false advertising, games etc.
Social engineering and Trojans are very common to violate access to mobile devices	Handling very weak information, a Trojan can easily be introduced to a device, as well as taking information through social engineering to naive users [15]
B08 - S17 - [11] Systematic Literature Review: Security Challenges of Mobile Banking and Payments System	
The improper use of the APIs, produces an insecurity in the operating system	Users and applications can have full control of mobile devices, as there is no control of priorities in the management of processes
B09 - S18 - [10] Examining Security Risks of Mobile Banking Applications through Blog Mining	
Banking Phishing, perhaps one of the most common perpetrated by cybercriminals	A fraud by cloning pages or applications, very well planned by hackers
WIFI networks without encryption, currently there are applications capable of easily breaching a WIFI network	Poor configuration in network equipment causes unsafe networks, even in the same homes being a gateway to cybercriminals
Vulnerabilities of mobile banking applications, with the development of fake ANDROID mobile applications hackers can impersonate original applications for false	Reverse engineering application in banking applications [10]

2.4 Data Synthesis

Table 3 shows the searches that generated 123 articles, of which 72 coincidences were recorded, where the number of articles reviewed was 51, of which 18 articles were selected according to the aforementioned search criteria.

Table 3. Summary of reviewed studies.

Sources	Found	Coincidences	Revised	Selected
SCOPUS	41	32	09	04
IEEE	47	28	19	02
OWASP	11	0	10	10
GOOGLE SCHOLAR	24	12	12	02
Totals	123	72	51	18

3 Discussion

What reflects [S01] is the unbridled increase of mobile users for its great features to perform online tasks (payments or purchases, transactions, news, games, etc.) and with this the change in the routine of users that has affected positive and negative way worldwide in terms of health education, history and many other factors that are already known by users. [S02] mentions the growing development of smartphones and with it the use that users give them to perform online tasks, specifically banking transactions, also points out some types of vulnerabilities to which users are exposed as the distributed denial of service attack (DDOS) called the third highest threat according to the FBI, in which the attacker plays the role of network for the scanning of open ports and thereby perpetrate the theft of information, also mention is made of other vulnerabilities such as malware (malicious software), Spoofing of TCP-IP in which the pirate gets access to the phone in an unauthorized way, backdoors installed by the same developers, modifications in applications, pieces of spy code (exploits) and the knowledge of social engineering with banking Trojans. Because of the lack of security in the servers, attackers can make contact with unencrypted data; it also mentions some protocols used by smartphones for information security, there are also some encryption algorithms that are used in the mobile data flow and a security method for banking systems in which authentication and the authorization. In [S03] it is clearly understood the vulnerability that exists when using different clouds to manage user information, it is referred to four (OneDrive, Box, GoogleDrive and Dropbox) that when used in different ANDROID and IOS devices, is It is easy to retrieve information using forensic techniques based on this article in the NIST 10 forensic guide and Martini's four-step forensic framework, demonstrating how you can retrieve information from mobile devices depending on your operating system version (ANDROID version 2.2. 2 and IOS version 4.3.5), this information is recorded in different files of the internal memory of the phone independently if it is restored to the device for later recovery, showing a complete history of task management performed by the user in that moment.

Regarding the permissions that the user gives to the ANDROID applications, [S04] finds: the normal, the dangerous, the signature and the system, of which the dangerous category is the one associated to the banking applications in which users could naively give permission without knowing the risk they run when their data are intercepted by attackers. In short, there are different types of licenses that users can give to ANDROID mobile applications, each allows with a degree of danger in terms of leakage that can be caused by misuse of them, causing severe damage when installed. Harmful applications in smart devices. Likewise, it is mentioned in [S05] the great ability that hackers have to introduce themselves to smartphones using sophisticated techniques (up to ANDROID version 4.4) for the theft of information, for this they use the so-called attack of tapjacking that is exploited by the Android/BadAccents, consists of the superposition of cloned windows that appear on the screen of the device, and that ask to enter personal data for an update required by the operating system in order to obtain super user permissions (ROOT), it is worth mentioning that they introduce this malware to the SMARTPHONES by means of text messages making fun of the security of servers with intersection of messages or voice calls.

In [S06] we detail the access that mobile applications have to the different types of data that the user has installed on their smartphone as very private information (bank accounts, passwords etc.). An application called ASTRAEA that is responsible for the mitigation of vulnerabilities in information leakage, which has its own security proxy, which makes the flow of data according to the application very secure by examining the information that passes from the end to the extreme.

At work [S17] the use of smart phones worldwide is highlighted, due to their banking services among others, which in turn classifies threats as broad, from telephone to telephone, and online, on the other hand that most malware is on google and the Android platform. Consequently, it explains that mobile users increase day by day so they can enter at any time the mobile banking to perform various tasks, this leads to the attackers to invent new methods (more sophisticated Trojans and malware in general as the forms to introduce them to the SMARTPHONES) in order to circumvent the security of said banking entities, likewise recommend the updates due to their equipment.

The authors of [S18] emphasize security in mobile applications and for this they refer to a study based on mining BLOG (method blog mining) that is about the search for blogs that contain information on security applications of banking mobile, encountering many coincidences such as threats and vulnerabilities (trojans, rootkits and viruses), phishing as insecure Wi-Fi networks; and with these a range of countermeasures such as data encryption, antivirus application updates, among others. They also talk about some malwares like: Zitmo, Banker, Perkel/Hesperbot, Wrob, Bankum, ZertSecurity, DroidDream and Keyloggers.

Regarding threats from third-party applications they secretly alter a banking application, so the author recommends the constant updating of applications from reliable sources, another huge vulnerability found is the famous phishing that deals with fraudulent applications (application clones)), unencrypted WIFI networks in popular places which allows the attacker to violate these networks due to its weak security and reverse engineering. For their part, they recommend integrating mobile security based on biometrics as well as intelligent technology based on monitoring in mobile banking applications.

4   Conclusion and Future Work

With the growing development of smart terminals (SMARTPHONES) and its extensive benefits to the user to improve the lifestyle, a number of vulnerabilities arise for both mobile platforms and operating systems in general, so that the desire for computer criminals steal confidential information from users, who for different reasons do not use their smartphone properly.

As mobile vulnerabilities are mitigated in different versions of the Android operating system, the attacker is at the forefront to take advantage of the minimum flaw that is in the current versions and thus act deliberately and especially violate banking applications.

The systematic review allowed to know the frequent vulnerabilities in the banking transactions by Android mobile devices, usually the user is not aware of what they happen, the ones that stand out are: Banking Phishing, Trojans and injections, unsafe storage in the cloud, campaigns to violate the ANDROID platform, insufficient protection when circulating data, insecurity in servers, lack of protection in the transport layer, involuntary data leakage, poor authentication and authorization, broken cryptography, ROOT users.

With respect to the incidence of use of banking transactions with smartphones in users, the increase in technology has partly facilitated their way of life due to the great benefits that smartphones have generated in their daily performance, the change in routine of users who use SMARTPHONES, has had a positive and largely negative impact, simply because they do not know deeply the good use of these smartphones and therefore are the victims of many bank frauds and information leakage.

Consequently, future work is needed to establish models of trust in mobile transactions and person-mobile research that minimizes the effects of the user when data security is concerned. Also, that from these results are generated recommendations for the mitigation of these incidents.

References

1. Google Scholar. https://scholar.google.com/
2. IEEE Xplore Digital Library. https://ieeexplore.ieee.org/Xplore/home.jsp
3. OWASP. https://www.owasp.org/index.php?search=&title=Special%3ASearch&go=Go

4. Sobre OWASP. https://www.owasp.org/index.php/Sobre_OWASP
5. Centro Cochrane Iberoamericano: Manual Cochrane de Revisiones Sistemáticas de Intervenciones, versión 5.1.0 (2011)
6. Cho, T., Kim, Y., Han, S., Seo, S.H.: Potential vulnerability analysis of mobile banking applications. In: 2013 International Conference on ICT Convergence (ICTC), pp. 1114–1115, October 2013. https://doi.org/10.1109/ICTC.2013.6675570
7. Daryabar, F., Dehghantanha, A., Eterovic-Soric, B., Choo, K.K.R.: Forensic investigation of OneDrive, Box, GoogleDrive and Dropbox applications on Android and iOS devices. Aust. J. Forensic Sci. 48(6), 615–642 (2016). https://doi.org/10.1080/00450618.2015.1110620
8. Elsevier B.V.: Scopus. https://www.scopus.com/home.uri
9. Handojo, A., Lim, R., Andjarwirawan, J., Sunaryo, S.: Games and multimedia implementation on heroic battle of surabaya: an android based mobile device application. In: Pasila, F., Tanoto, Y., Lim, R., Santoso, M., Pah, N.D. (eds.) Proceedings of Second International Conference on Electrical Systems, Technology and Information 2015 (ICESTI 2015). LNEE, vol. 365, pp. 619–629. Springer, Singapore (2016). https://doi.org/10.1007/978-981-287-988-2_69
10. He, W., Tian, X., Shen, J.: Examining security risks of mobile banking applications through blog mining. In: MAICS, pp. 103–108 (2015)
11. Islam, S.: Systematic literature review: security challenges of mobile banking and payments system. Int. J. u-and e-Serv. Sci. Technol. 7(6), 107–116 (2014)
12. Kitchenham, B.: Procedures for performing systematic reviews (2004)
13. Liang, C.: Subjective norms and customer adoption of mobile banking: Taiwan and vietnam. In: 2016 49th Hawaii International Conference on System Sciences (HICSS), pp. 1577–1585, January 2016. https://doi.org/10.1109/HICSS.2016.199
14. Njenga, K., Ndlovu, S.: On privacy calculus and underlying consumer concerns influencing mobile banking subscriptions. In: Information Security for South Africa (ISSA), pp. 1–9. IEEE (2012)
15. Nosrati, L., Bidgoli, A.M.: Security assessment of mobile- banking. In: 2015 International Conference and Workshop on Computing and Communication (IEMCON), pp. 1–5, October 2015. https://doi.org/10.1109/IEMCON.2015.7344489
16. OWASP: Broken Cryptography - Mobile Top 10 2014–M6. https://www.owasp.org/index.php/Mobile_Top_10_2014-M6
17. OWASP: Client Side Injection - Mobile Top 10 2014–M7. https://www.owasp.org/index.php/Mobile_Top_10_2014-M7
18. OWASP: Improper Session Handling - Mobile Top 10 2014–M9. https://www.owasp.org/index.php/Mobile_Top_10_2014-M9
19. OWASP: Insecure Data Storage - Mobile Top 10 2014–M2. https://www.owasp.org/index.php/Mobile_Top_10_2014-M2
20. OWASP: Insufficient Transport Layer Protection - Mobile Top 10 2014–M3. https://www.owasp.org/index.php/Mobile_Top_10_2014-M3
21. OWASP: Lack of Binary Protections - Mobile Top 10 2014–M10. https://www.owasp.org/index.php/Mobile_Top_10_2014-M10
22. OWASP: Poor Authorization and Authentication - Mobile Top 10 2014–M5. https://www.owasp.org/index.php/Mobile_Top_10_2014-M5
23. OWASP: Security Decisions Via Untrusted Inputs - Mobile Top 10 2014–M8. https://www.owasp.org/index.php/Mobile_Top_10_2014-M8
24. OWASP: Unintended Data Leakage - Mobile Top 10 2014–M4. https://www.owasp.org/index.php/Mobile_Top_10_2014-M4

25. OWASP: Weak Server Side Control - Mobile Top 10 2014–M1. https://www.owasp. org/index.php/Mobile_Top_10_2014-M1
26. Pistoia, M., Tripp, O., Ferrara, P., Centonze, P.: Automatic detection, correction, and visualization of security vulnerabilities in mobile apps. In: Proceedings of the 3rd International Workshop on Mobile Development Lifecycle, MobileDeLi 2015, New York, NY, USA, pp. 35–36 (2015). https://doi.org/10.1145/2846661.2846667
27. Rasthofer, S., Asrar, I., Huber, S., Bodden, E.: How current Android malware seeks to evade automated code analysis. In: Akram, R.N., Jajodia, S. (eds.) WISTP 2015. LNCS, vol. 9311, pp. 187–202. Springer, Cham (2015). https://doi.org/10. 1007/978-3-319-24018-3_12
28. Sugiono, E., Asnar, Y., Liem, I.: Android security assessment based on reported vulnerability. In: 2014 International Conference on Data and Software Engineering (ICODSE), pp. 1–6, November 2014. https://doi.org/10.1109/ICODSE.2014. 7062686

Computer and Software Engineering

Towards a Merged Interaction Design Pattern Focused on University Prospective Students: Results from a Pretest–Posttest Intervention Study

Shirley M. Martínez[1] and Omar S. Gómez[2]([✉]) [iD]

[1] Escuela Superior Politécnica de Chimborazo, Riobamba 060155, Ecuador
[2] Grupo de Investigación en Ingeniería de Software (GrIISoft),
Escuela Superior Politécnica de Chimborazo, Riobamba 060155, Ecuador
ogomez@espoch.edu.ec

Abstract. Usability in the software arena is a hot topic that has attracted the attention of researchers. Usability has been studied in different application contexts. In the context of Higher Education Institutions, some usability aspects have started to be incorporated into university websites. In this work, we present a merged interaction design pattern oriented to improve the usability experience of prospective students. The assessment of the pattern was done through a pretest-posttest intervention study, using a sample of 266 prospective students. Our results suggest that the use of an interaction design pattern has significantly improved the usability experience of the participants in this study.

Keywords: Usability · Navigability · Pretest-posttest study
Software engineering · University website · Higher education institution

1 Introduction

Nowadays, there is no doubt that the World Wide Web or WWW plays an important role in different sectors of society such as business, government, education, science, leisure, among others. Private and public organizations have benefited from this technology by offering information about their products or services through websites.

In the field of education, university websites offer the information of interest about degree programs they offer to prospective students. Although these websites should ideally reflect the needs of their users, the web design is often dictated by the technology used to develop and design them or by business objectives, not taking into account the needs of users [8]. As a result, searching for information of interest can be difficult for those who access these websites for the first time [3].

This situation has resulted in the owners of these websites, as well as the personnel involved in their design starting to study and incorporate aspects of usability in their university websites [17]. Although at present we have a body of knowledge that can help us to improve aspects of usability in these types of websites, we observe that there are still university websites that can be improved by taking usability aspects into account.

© Springer Nature Switzerland AG 2019
M. Botto-Tobar et al. (Eds.): CITT 2018, CCIS 895, pp. 119–132, 2019.
https://doi.org/10.1007/978-3-030-05532-5_9

An example of this is observed in the national arena (Ecuador). The search for information about bachelor's degree programs in different universities can be a complex task; this because each university offers a different structure on their website. In some cases, the required information is easy to find, but in other cases, it is difficult to access.

Due to prospective students are an important type of user, the owners and web designers must offer the necessary usability mechanisms that allow for this type of user to browse and find information of study programs in an agile and simple way.

In order to face this situation, in this work we present a merged interaction pattern focused on improving the navigability of university websites. This pattern is developed with the aim of facilitating the search for information of study programs for prospective students who wish to enroll in a given undergraduate university program. The proposed interaction pattern was implemented as part of a prototype for an Ecuadorian university website.

The proposed pattern was evaluated using a sample of 266 prospective students. As a research method, we conducted a pretest-posttest intervention study. Participants were assessed in two different time periods (sessions) using the website of an Ecuadorian university. One session without the interaction pattern developed (pretest or control) and the other session with the website prototype (posttest or the intervention) that includes the proposed interaction pattern (intervention).

The rest of the document is organized as follows: Sect. 2 presents the related work; meanwhile, Sect. 3 deals with concepts and basic terminology. In Sect. 4 the merged interaction pattern is presented. The research method used is described in Sect. 5. In Sect. 6, the results obtained are presented and finally, in Sect. 7, we present the discussion and conclusions.

2 Related Work

The study of usability in university websites has gradually begun to be of interest. For example, in [18], authors conducted a study in order to have more knowledge of how prospective students use university websites. A total of 55 students from four high schools participated in the study. Authors used a survey which addressed different aspects of a university website. Content, site architecture (organization), ease of navigation, speed of connection (download), focus on target audience, distinctiveness of site, and importance of graphics were among the aspects studied. Authors found that content, organization and ease of navigation were the most important aspects of a university website according to the participants.

In the work of [3], the author proposes a series of practices in order to help the developers and designers of university websites to improve the navigability and organization of their content.

In other work of [16], authors focused on evaluating nine different Jordanian universities. The evaluation was performed through a survey and the use of automated tools. Authors came up with a list of 23 website usability criteria.

In [8], authors carried out a study in order to identify factors affecting the usability of a sample of Lebanese universities websites. Authors found that management and leadership in the ICT department, user testing and ease of use were key factors that may affect the usability of university websites.

In the work of work [15], authors created a usability evaluation model, this model was used for evaluating ten university websites in Asia. The websites were evaluated in two phases. First authors conducted a survey using thirty participants (students) enrolled in three different universities. In this first stage, authors identified problems faced by the participants while interacting with the analyzed websites. The outcomes of the survey were used to create the usability evaluation model. This model consists of 17 measures divided into five feature categories such as website content, webpage design, navigation, page design layout and accessibility.

In the work of [6], authors examined the usability and user acceptance of various websites of African universities with the aim of identifying some criteria that best evaluate these aspects. Authors observed that interaction, appeal, application robustness and invisibility measures have a relevant impact on usability and user acceptance.

In the work of [19], authors evaluated the usability and accessibility of three university websites. Authors used two types of usability evaluation techniques: a questionnaire-based evaluation and a performance-based evaluation. Usability assessment was done by analyzing the observed task success rates, task completion times, post-task satisfaction ratings and the feedback of 68 participants.

Recently, in [7], authors studied the usability of 24 Ecuadorian university websites using data mining techniques. Authors found that 50% of the websites assessed meet certain usability standards. As we observe, the study of the usability in university websites has been performed either using participants or automated tools.

3 Basic Terminology

In this section, we present some basic terminology related to the topic addressed in this paper.

3.1 Usability

Different definitions of usability can be found in the literature; the usability definition is mainly based on the different attributes or factors by which it can be evaluated [9]. One of the first usability terms was coined in 1979 [4]. It was used to describe the effectiveness of human performance [4], In [20], it is defined as the ability of something to be used by humans in an easy and effective way. The ISO/IEC 25010 standard [11] defines usability as the degree to which a product or system can be used by specified users to achieve specified goals with effectiveness, efficiency and satisfaction in a specified context of use.

3.2 Navigability

The navigability is the ability of the user to be intuitively guided through a website. Usually, the navigability is integrated on the homepage of a website; it is closely related to meeting the needs of the different types of users that visit the site.

Consequently, it can be said that good navigability exists if a type of user finds the links that lead you to what you are looking for in the pages of the site (especially in the beginning) [12], thus having a good mechanism of navigation will positively influence the usability experience of the user.

3.3 Design Patterns

According to [2], a design pattern describes a problem that occurs continuously in our environment, and it describes the base solution to a particular problem. In general, patterns describe solutions to problems that occur repeatedly in our environment [1].

In the software engineering arena, design patterns follow a series of steps that describe the problem, the solution and its application, as well as its consequences [10].

We can find different types of patterns; on the one hand, we have the interaction design patterns that have the objective of solving usability problems. While the software design patterns are aimed to solve functional problems, both of these two pattern-based design models complement each other, and can be used together with successful results in the design of interactive applications [21].

Although both types of patterns are clearly intended to solve different problems, usability and functionality cannot be treated as independent aspects of an interactive application. The usability not only depends on the design of the interface but also on the design at the architecture level of the application; this means that a design decision at the functionality level will affect the usability, and vice versa.

4 Proposed Interaction Design Pattern

In this section, we present the merged pattern focused on prospective university students. Taking the pattern structure used in [10] as reference, we describe the proposed pattern.

Pattern name: Prospective Student

Intention: To improve the navigability and usability of universities websites.

Problem: Based on a focused problem, higher education institutions may have websites with different designs and content organization, which makes the search for information by prospective students a difficult and demanding activity.

Usability principles:
- Visibility of the system status.
- Recognize before remembering.
- Flexibility and efficiency of use.
- Aesthetic and minimalist design.

Context: The present pattern can be implemented in university websites with the aim of improving the browsing experience of prospective students who are looking for information regarding study programs.

Solution: With regards to the website's main menu, the use of a vertical dropdown menu is proposed [22], since it is necessary that the options of each section of the menu are directly visible.

We also suggest the use of breadcrumbs [22] as a solution to the problem of location that users may have when browsing the website; this also allows users to return to higher levels quickly because a hierarchical route is displayed at any given moment.

In this proposed pattern, the use of split navigation is also considered [22]. Having split navigation allows prospective students to change quickly between pages on different levels. It consists of having a home page (first level) and secondary thematic pages, the home page will contain the links of interest that the website has. By clicking on a link, the student will navigate to a second level or thematic pages.

The thematic web pages should contain an index to further levels (for example third and four webpage levels). All textual information is displayed on this thematic page. Users can switch between pages in the third and four levels by clicking on the index links. The links of the homepage of the split navigation will be grouped by means of a menu without header (headerless menu) [22]. This is a type of vertical menu that combines different menus using different visual clues instead of headers.

Finally, we propose that thematic pages be guided by doormat navigation [22], specifically speaking of the offered programs degrees section. It is important that prospective students be directed to the proper degree program. It will give them a quick overview of the programs offered without having to click on them.

Fig. 1. Example of the proposed pattern implemented in a university website prototype.

Consequences:
- It improves the navigability of prospective students, since links and contents are better organized.
- It reduces redundant links and the resulting website structure is minimalist and clean.

Benefits:
- It provides a user-friendly interface.
- The contents are presented in an orderly manner.
- The prospective student finds information of programs degrees more easily.

Example: An example of the proposed merged pattern is shown in Fig. 1. The pattern is implemented in a prototype of a university website.

Related patterns: vertical dropdown menu, breadcrumbs, split navigation, headerless menu, doormat navigation.

5 Method

In this section, we describe the steps involved in the creation and assessment of the proposed pattern. Figure 2 shows the steps we follow.

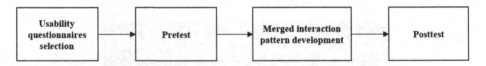

Fig. 2. Steps involved in the reported pretest-posttest intervention study.

5.1 Usability Questionnaires Selection

For the first step, we selected two widely known validated instruments specializing in the assessment of usability [13, 14]. The first instrument also known as "USE Questionnaire" (Usefulness, Satisfaction, and Ease of use.) proposed in [14], is a questionnaire composed of four sections that assess usefulness, ease of use, ease of learning and satisfaction. Each of these sections includes items to be answered using a seven point Likert scale (ranging from strongly disagree that represents a minimum value of 1 to strongly agree that represents a maximum value of 7).

The second instrument we chose is the one known as After-Scenario Questionnaire and is described in [13]. We chose this questionnaire in order to triangulate results. It evaluates aspects such as the ease of completing tasks, the time to complete a task and the adequacy of the support or help information (not considered for this study). The After-Scenario Questionnaire (ASQ) is a three-item questionnaire (also uses a seven point Likert scale, from strongly disagree to strongly agree) that addresses three aspects of user satisfaction with regards system usability: ease of task completion, time to complete a task, and adequacy of support information (on-line help, messages, and documentation; this item was not considered in our study because university websites do not usually make online help available).

Both questionnaires are intended to measure the perceptions of the users with regards to the usability of a determined software product, in our case, a university website. Once the usability questionnaires to be used were selected, we adapted them to Spanish.

5.2   Pretest

An Ecuadorian university website was selected as a control group for the pretest. We contacted to the management staff from a high school located in Riobamba, Ecuador and we explained the study to them. They were interested in our study and agreed to participate.

In this step, an initial sample of 274 prospective students (students in the last year of high school) participated in the pretest. These students belong to different specialization areas from this school. Table 1 shows the distribution of the participants.

Table 1. Summary of prospective students that participated in our study.

Specialization	Participants (n)
Informatics	25
Basic sciences	105
Accounting	64
Food preservation	38
Clothing industry	42
Total	*274*

The day of the pretest, we gave to participants directions of how to complete the usability questionnaires; we also gave the participants a couple of tasks they had to complete, such as looking for specific information in a defined university website.

Participants were asked to search specific information of three bachelor's program degrees. Participants only had ten minutes to complete this task. After the time assigned for this task was up, the participants were asked to respond to the questionnaires.

We also asked to participants to give comments and feedback of the tasks they performed. For example, we asked them to look out for and record any possible problems encountered while navigating through the university website.

For this study, we had access to a computer lab with 15 computers connected to the Internet. In conjunction with the teachers, we divided the participants into groups of 15.

5.3   Merged Interaction Pattern Development

Taking into account the comments and feedback of participants, we designed the merged interaction pattern described in Sect. 4. Once the pattern was designed we built a prototype of the university website used for the pretest. This prototype contains the designed merged pattern.

5.4   Posttest

Five weeks after applying the pretest and once the prototype containing the merged pattern was complete, we conducted the post-test. The same students that participated in the pretest also participated in the post-test. The same questionnaires with same directions were given to the participants. In this session, participants worked with the prototype developed, which included the merged interaction pattern.

It is worth noting that we had to remove eight measurements due to some participants not attended either the pretest or post-test sessions, thus resulting in a sample size of 266 participants. According to the study design used, it is necessary that the same participants in the two different sessions be exposed to the pretest and the intervention (posttest).

6   Results

In this section, we present the findings of the study with regards to each of the aspects assessed in the questionnaires used. Findings were examined by means of descriptive and inferential analysis.

6.1   Usefulness (First Questionnaire)

Usefulness is defined as the extent to which participants considered the information provided by the university website (actual [pretest] and the prototype [posttest]) to be useful. Table 2 shows a summary of the descriptive statistics observed in the pretest and the posttest (website prototype which implements the merged interaction pattern). For each participant, all of the items belonging to this aspect were averaged, so the mean and the median were calculated from the averages of the sample used. These two values (mean and median) are in the range of the Likert scale used (from strong disagree [the minimum value is 1] to strong agree [the maximum value is 7]).

Table 2. Descriptive statistics related to usefulness.

Session	n	mean	median	sd	min	max
Pretest	266	3.36	3.14	1.54	1	6.57
Posttest	266	5.95	6.43	1.12	1.86	7

As shown in Table 2, on average, participants yielded a higher score in the posttest that in the pretest, i.e. participants perceive the prototype to be more useful than the actual university website assessed. In order to visually assess the difference between the pretest and the posttest, we used a Bland-Altman plot [5] as shown in Fig. 3. A Bland-Altman plot or difference plot is used to analyze the agreement between two different essays or samples.

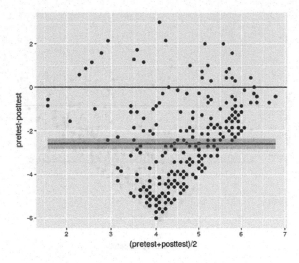

Fig. 3. Bland-Altman plot related to usefulness.

As shown in Fig. 3, the differences between the pretest and the posttest are mostly distributed below zero suggesting a difference of these two samples in favor of the posttest.

6.2 Ease of Use

This aspect refers to the ease with which participants were able to use or navigate through the university website. Table 3 shows the descriptive statistics with regards this aspect.

Table 3. Descriptive statistics for the ease of use aspect.

Session	n	mean	median	sd	min	max
Pretest	266	3.05	2.82	1.51	1	6.82
Posttest	266	5.98	6.36	1.11	1.27	7

On average, participants in the posttest session showed a better performance than the pretest (as shown in Table 3). Figure 4 shows the difference plot related to this aspect.

As we see, most of the differences shown in the Fig. 4 are distributed below zero, suggesting a difference in favor of the intervention (posttest session).

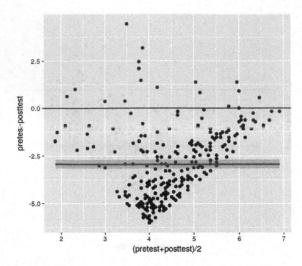

Fig. 4. Bland-Altman plot related to ease of use.

6.3 Ease of Learning

In this case, ease of learning is related to the amount of effort that participants expend learning to use the university website. Table 4 shows the descriptive statistics related to this aspect.

Table 4. Descriptive statistics related to ease of learning.

Session	n	mean	median	sd	min	max
Pretest	266	3.08	2.75	1.71	1	7
Posttest	266	6.08	6.5	1.19	1.75	7

Also for this aspect, participants showed a better score using the university website prototype than the actual university website. The difference plot (not shown due to the limitation of page space) also yielded a similar distribution to the observed in Figs. 3 and 4.

6.4 Satisfaction

It refers to the extent to which participants perceive the university website to meet their information requirements. Table 5 shows the descriptive statistics of the sample used.

Table 5. Descriptive statistics of the satisfaction aspect.

Session	n	mean	median	sd	min	max
Pretest	266	3	2.57	1.66	1	7
Posttest	266	6.05	6.43	1.17	1.57	7

As observed in Table 5, on average participants in the posttest session perceived a better degree of satisfaction than in the pretest session.

6.5   After-Scenario Questionnaire (Second Questionnaire)

In order to triangulate the results, we also used a second usability questionnaire. As mentioned in Sect. 5, this questionnaire is composed of three items. Table 6 shows the resulting descriptive statistics.

Table 6. Descriptive statistics related to the second questionnaire used.

Session	n	mean	median	sd	min	max
Pretest	266	3.18	3	1.81	1	7
Posttest	266	6.19	6.5	1.12	1.5	7

Results shown in Table 6 also suggest a better performance in the posttest session than in the pretest. The results yielded with this second questionnaire (After-Scenario Questionnaire [13]) are consistent with those of the first questionnaire (USE Questionnaire [14]). Figure 5 shows the resulting difference plot.

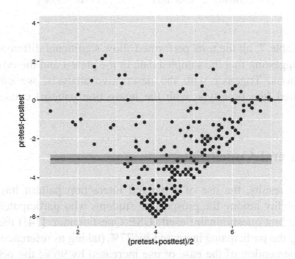

Fig. 5. Bland-Altman plot related to data of the After-Scenario Questionnaire [13].

As observed in Fig. 5, most of the differences are distributed below zero, suggesting a difference in favor of the posttest session.

6.6   Inferential Analysis

Once we have an exploratory analysis of the data sample, we proceed with an inferential analysis in order to examine possible significant differences of our pretest-posttest study.

Because the items of the two questionnaires used are measured with an ordinal scale (Likert scale), it is probable that the sampled data is not normally distributed. In this situation, a non-parametric inferential analysis is more useful. In our case, after conducting the Shapiro-Wilk normality test for each of the aspects of the both questionnaires, for each aspect, we rejected the null hypothesis (at an alpha level of 0.01) of this test in favor of a lack of normality of the data.

In order to compare the pretest and posttest for each aspect of the questionnaires, we used the Wilcoxon signed-rank test. Table 7 shows the results of this test.

Table 7. Inferential analysis using the Wilcoxon signed-rank test.

	Aspect	V	p-value
Questionnaire 1	Usefulness	33711	<0.001
	Ease of use	34326	<0.001
	Ease of learning	32968	<0.001
	Satisfaction	33319	<0.001
Questionnaire 2	Usability	31910	<0.001

As noted in Table 7, all the tests performed show significant differences at an alpha level of 0.001, suggesting that the sampled data in the pretest and the posttest belong to different populations. Together with the descriptive analysis, we observe that the intervention studied (the prototype with the interaction pattern) caused significantly different results.

7   Discussion and Conclusions

According to our results, the use of a merged interaction pattern has improved the perception of usability among the prospective students who participated in this study. In the case of the first questionnaire used (USE Questionnaire [14]) the perception of usefulness among the participants increased by 77% (taking as reference the average of the pretest); the perception of the ease of use increased by 96%; the perception of the ease of learning increased by 97%; the perception of satisfaction increased by 100%. Combining these four aspects, on average, the perception of the usability has increased by 93% in the university website prototype. A similar percentage is observed in the second questionnaire (After-Scenario Questionnaire [13]), participants perceived an increase of the usability by 95% with regards to the current university website (pretest). Both instruments yielded consistent results in favor of the merged interaction pattern proposed.

Although our results are promissory, it is necessary to conduct further research in order to make improvements or adaptations to the proposed pattern. Also, this work can serve as reference for conducting replications with other prospective students in other schools. The main contribution of the present work is the presentation and assessment of a merged interaction design pattern focused on university prospective students. As a concluding remark, the use of interaction design patterns in university websites help to increase the usability experience of prospective students.

References

1. Aedo, I., et al.: Ingeniería de la web y patrones de diseño. Pearson Educación, Madrid (2003)
2. Alexander, C., et al.: A Pattern Language: Towns, Buildings, Construction. Oxford University Press, p. 1216 (1977). ISBN 0-19-501919-9
3. Arosemena, K.: University web site navigation & content organization best practices: prospective students point of view. In: Fifth Euro-American Conference on Telematics and Information Systems, EATIS 2010, Panama (2010)
4. Bennett, J.L.: The Commercial Impact of Usability in Interactive Systems. In: Shackel, B. (ed.) Man-Computer Communication, Infotech State-of-The-Art, vol. 2, pp. 1–17. Infotech International, Maidenhead (1979)
5. Bland, J.M., Altman, D.: Statistical methods for assessing agreement between two methods of clinical measurement. The Lancet 327(8476), 307–310 (1986)
6. Booi, V.M., Ditsa, G.E.: Usability and user acceptance of university web portal interfaces: a case of south african universities. In: Stephanidis, C. (ed.) HCI 2013. CCIS, vol. 373, pp. 91–95. Springer, Heidelberg (2013). https://doi.org/10.1007/978-3-642-39473-7_19
7. Chamba, L., et al.: Analysis of usability of universities Web portals using the Prometheus tool - SIRIUS. Presented at the 19 April 2017
8. Daher, L.A., Elkabani, I.: Usability evaluation of some Lebanese universities web portals. In: 13th International Arab Conference on Information Technology, ACIT 2012 (2012)
9. Folmer, E., Bosch, J.: Architecting for usability: a survey. J. Syst. Softw. 70(1–2), 61–78 (2004)
10. Gamma, E., et al.: Design Patterns: Elements of Reusable Object-Oriented Software. Addison Wesley, New York (1997)
11. ISO/IEC 25010 - Systems and software engineering - Systems and software Quality Requirements and Ev. (SQuaRE) - System and software quality models (2010) by ISO/IEC
12. Kalbach, J., Gustafson, A.: Designing Web Navigation: Optimizing the User Experience. O'Reilly Media, Beijing, Sebastopol (2007)
13. Lewis, J.R.: IBM computer usability satisfaction questionnaires: psychometric evaluation and instructions for use. Int. J. Hum.-Comput. Interact. 7(1), 57–78 (1995)
14. Lund, A.M.: Measuring usability with the use questionnaire. Usability Interface 8(2), 3–6 (2001)
15. Manzoor, M., Hussain, W.: A web usability evaluation model for higher education providing universities of Asia. Tech. Dev. 31, 183–192 (2012)
16. Mustafa, S., Al-Zoua'bi, L.: Usability of the academic websites of Jordan's Universities an evaluation study. Presented at the 12 December 2009
17. Pierce, K.: Web site usability report for Harvard University. Capella University (2005)
18. Poock, M.C., Lefond, D.: How college-bound prospects perceive university web sites: findings, implications, and turning browsers into applicants. Coll. Univ. 77, 15–21 (2001)

19. Roy, S., et al.: A quantitative approach to evaluate usability of academic websites based on human perception. Egypt. Inform. J. **15**(3), 159–167 (2014)
20. Shackel, B.: Usability – context, framework, definition, design and evaluation. Interact. Comput. **21**(5–6), 339–346 (2009)
21. Tidwell, J.: Designing Interfaces: Patterns for Effective Interaction Design. O'Reilly Media, Beijing (2011)
22. Van Welie, M.: Interaction Design Pattern Library. http://www.welie.com/patterns/index. php

Gesture-Based Children Computer Interaction for Inclusive Education: A Systematic Literature Review

Pablo Torres-Carrión[1]([✉]) [iD], Carina González-González[2],
César Bernal-Bravo[3], and Alfonso Infante-Moro[4]

[1] Universidad Técnica Particular de Loja, San Cayetano Alto,
1101608 Loja, Ecuador
pvtorres@utpl.edu.ec
[2] Universidad de la Laguna, La Laguna, Santa Cruz de Tenerife, Spain
[3] Universidad Rey Juan Carlos, Madrid, Spain
[4] Universidad de Huelva, Huelva, Spain

Abstract. Gestural interfaces are closely related with cognition and physical activity, and can be powerful tools for cognitive training and motor skills. Their use has been proposed by researchers in various areas, including education, and within this field, inclusive education. In this study, a systematic literature review about children computer gestural interactions (touch, body, face and motion) and on its application to digital educational resources for learning disabilities has been conducted. Applying the Torres-Carrión method, a "conceptual mindfact" and research problem has been structured, as a basis to build the search script, to be applied in the selected scientific databases (Scopus, WoS and Google Scholar). Five research questions are proposed, which involves standards of gesture-based computer interaction for children, design guides, methods and instruments, non-invasive interaction environments and personalization of didactic resources for children with special needs, in particular children with Down' syndrome. As a final product, a list of relevant magazines and databases of the area has been obtained; 47 valid papers were analyzed to answer the research questions, and they are organized in a structured way, allowing the researcher to establish a valid context from which to focus future research.

Keywords: Gestural computer interaction · Children computer interaction
Inclusive education · Systematic review

1 Introduction

Tangible interfaces and tangible interaction approaches specializes on interfaces or systems that are physically embodied (be it in physical artifacts or in environments), and they include the tangibility and materiality of the interface, the whole body interaction, and the users interaction in real spaces and contexts. This involves a more natural interaction with information and a greater sense of control over it, while improving cognitive abilities and assimilation of information. The creation of such interfaces involves the development of sensors and their encapsulation in a variety of

© Springer Nature Switzerland AG 2019
M. Botto-Tobar et al. (Eds.): CITT 2018, CCIS 895, pp. 133–147, 2019.
https://doi.org/10.1007/978-3-030-05532-5_10

objects that can be of daily use. Tangible objects and gestural interfaces are closely related with cognition and physical activity, and can be powerful tools for cognitive training and motor skills [1–3]. So, one of the objectives of our work is to contribute to the knowledge about the research and applications of gestural interfaces in education, in particular, with children with learning disabilities, and more specifically, with children with Down' syndrome. For this reason, a systematic review of the scientific literature on these specific topics was conducted, in order to identifying research questions, as well as for justifying future research [4, 5].

In this systematic literature review we used an adaptation of the method proposed by Kitchenham [6] and Bacca [7] and adapted in a new methodology by Torres-Carrión [5], which divides the review process into three sub-parts: planning, conducting and reporting results. In our case we found 75 studies on Human-Computer Interaction, three of which specifically referenced gestural interactions in educational contexts. No studies were found for inclusive education. With this information in hand, we continued with the process by proposing five research questions involving standards for gesture-based learning, design guidelines, methods and instruments for educating persons with Down syndrome (DS), evaluating results in non-invasive interaction environments, and personalizing educational resources based on physical and cognitive needs.

As part of planning the search process, several general and specific inclusion and exclusion criteria were defined, along with some complementary inclusion and exclusion parameters. Variables were set up involving theoretical research, international standards and research methods adaptable to each item in order to steer the replies to the five research questions. Applying the search process to scientific articles yielded forty-three studies, which were properly sorted and coded with the aid of the Mendeley bibliographic management tool.

The report on the results provides tables and graphs that explain the answers to each of the research questions posed. A comparative analysis is then conducted of the results and the prior studies, as well as of the listing of studies selected and the potential research proposals. Finally, the findings of the study are presented, complemented with suggestions for possible applications of this methodological adaptation to subsequent systematic reviews of the scientific literature and the state of the art in new areas of research.

2 Method

We used the method for a systematic review of the literature by Torres-Carrión [5] adapted from Kitchenham [6] and Bacca [7], which divides the process into three main phases, as shown in the outline below:

- Planning
  - Identification of the need for review
    Current State of Natural Interaction
    Research Questions
    Mentefacto Conceptual

            Semantic Search Structure
            Related Systematic Reviews
            Selection of Journals
- Development of a review protocol
            Definition of inclusion and exclusion criteria
            Definition of analysis categories
            Preparing a data extraction form
- Conducting the review
  - Identification of research
  - Selection of primary studies
  - Study quality assessment
  - Data extraction and monitoring
  - Data synthesis & monitoring
- Reporting the review.

2.1 Planning

2.1.1 Current State of Natural Interaction

Studies on Human-Computer Interaction (HCI) are becoming increasingly relevant to technology designers and manufacturers, as well as to groups of people with some kind of disability and who require personalized equipment and sensors to enable them to interact with computers. This field of research is growing, primarily due to the expansion of mobile technology and the lower prices of sensors and devices used to carry out everyday activities, which often allows people to issue instructions to computers using common gestures or voice commands, a process known as Natural Interaction (NI).

2.1.2 Research Questions

CCI environments are becoming more prevalent thanks to the market availability of increasingly cheap and efficient sensors developed for the leisure, entertainment and health industries, and in particular for videogames and fitness. Their use has been proposed by researchers in various areas, including education, and within this field, in inclusive education [8]. Since we are interested in CCI based on natural interactions (gestures, touch, voice and motion) and on its application to digital educational resources that are customized to children's needs, we considered the following research questions:

- RQ1 – Of the standards that describe the gesture-based CCI, which are being applied in inclusive educational environments?
- RQ2 – How are design guides applied to inclusive educational gestural interfaces for children?
- RQ3 – What methods/instruments are considered in gestural inclusive interactions for children with Down syndrome in educational environments?
- RQ4 – How were the research results in non-invasive interaction environments evaluated?
- RQ5 – What processes were adapted to personalize interaction resources, considering each child's educational needs and disabilities?

2.1.3   Mentefacto Conceptual

In the Torres-Carrión methodology [5], the *mentefacto conceptual* allows the researcher to focus his attention on the real theoretical context of the investigation. Moving vertically can make the central concept more specific or general, as it moves down or up. In the right part the concepts that differ from the central one are detailed, in such a way that the researcher can discriminate with reference articles. On the left, the characteristics of the concept are located, as an input to locate the key words, part of the scientific thesaurus (Fig. 1).

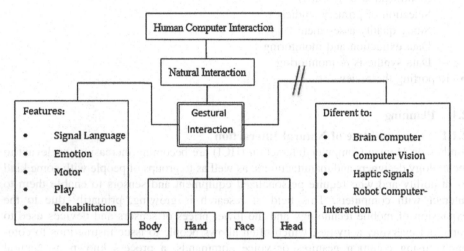

Fig. 1. Mentefacto conceptual about gestural interaction.

2.1.4   Semantic Search Structure

This data is the input of the consultations to the various databases that the researcher considers. The information is organized in five layers, being the first an abstraction of

Table 1. Semantic structure from thesaurus for searching specific papers

L1	Gestural Computer Interaction	`(gestur* OR hand* OR body OR leg OR mov* OR motor* OR motion OR fac* OR eye OR mobile OR touch*) AND (comput* OR automat*) AND (interact* OR interfac* OR recognit* OR track*)`
L2	+Child *	`AND (child* OR boy OR kid OR infant*)`
L3	+Education	`AND (educa* OR learn* or train*)`
L4	+Special Education	`AND (syndrome OR disabilit* OR inclusiv* OR special* OR disorder)`
L5	**Question**	Q1: **(Standard Interaction)** Q2: **(Design Guide)** Q3: **(Down syndrome)** Q4: **(Assessment AND Noninvasive environment)** Q5: **(Digital Learning Literacy)**

the *mentefacto conceptual*; the second a filtering to the specific population; the third and fourth refer to the subfield of application, which is education inclusive; and, the fifth layer is subdivided according to the five research questions. The semantic search structure is the input to perform a structure review, valid for two moments: (a) during the search for systematic reviews or related meta-searches; (b) in the specific search for documents related to each research question, which in this case are five (Table 1).

2.1.5   Related Systematic Reviews

Initially, it is important to identify previous studies on systematic reviews of the literature in our field of research so that our contribution can be original and useful to the scientific community. We conducted a systematic general search of the Web of Science (WoS), Scopus and Google Scholar databases, using a search syntax as similar as possible in all three platforms and adhering to the rules in place for each one. We were unable to find reviews of the literature that allow us to provide an answer to the research questions posed, thus requiring us to undertake this work in order to achieve our goal (Table 2).

Table 2. Recent studies on reviews of the literature involving natural Interaction in children for educational purposes

Study	Analysis	Papers reviewed
Sheu [9]	Analyzes research focused on "gesture-based computing in education" using an empirical approach that searched five academic databases, with a manual selection of papers (published between 2001 and 2013) that are then analyzed	59
Boucenna [10]	Although only one goal focuses on education (exclusive for autistic children), it provides a set of emerging resources and tools and strategies for enhancing their use	>100
Benton [11]	Considers the roles, responsibilities and activities in the design of technology projects adapted to inclusive educational needs, adapted by both students and teachers	46

2.1.6   Selection of Journals and Databases

The platform used for this initial filtering was "Primo de Ex Libris" (licensed to the library of the Universidad de La Laguna), specifically through its search engine, "Punto q". The platform automatically generates lists that are arranged into two groups, one for journals and another for databases.

Additionally, in the case of the DBs an initial filter was applied that left only the five databases with the most number of papers, as shown in Table 3. The final sum exceeds the resulting amount (508) because several papers are indexed in more than one DB. Identifying the databases used to index the scientific papers with the highest impact consolidates the secondary sources of research, facilitating future work.

Table 3. List of databases with the highest number of articles returned by the search

Database name – *listDB*	Number of papers
Scopus (Elsevier)	364
MEDLINE/PubMed (NLM)	234
Social Sciences Citation Index (Web of Science)	210
Science Citation Index Expanded (Web of Science)	190
ERIC (U.S. Dept. of Education)	134

Table 4. List of journals arranged by category based on JCR 2016

Ord	Journal name	N° of papers	JCR IF	Quartile	SJR	Google academic h5	*Ord*
JCR Science Edition							
1	Pediatrics	10	5,473	Q1	2,894	116	4593,27
2	Computers & Education	23	2,556	Q1	2,578	88	3334,22
3	PLoS ONE	9	3,224	Q1	1,300	161	1518,26
8	IEEE Transactions On Neural Systems And Rehabilitation Engineering	4	3,188	Q1	1,04 2	45	149,49
10	Physical Therapy	2	2,526	Q1	1,270	52	83,41
JCR Social Science Edition							
4	Journal Of Autism And Developmental Disorders	9	3,665	Q1	1,696	61	853,12
5	Child Development	3	4,061	Q1	3,065	64	597,45
6	Research in Developmental Disabilities	22	1,887	Q1	0,986	47	480,96
7	Journal of Learning Disabilities	7	1,901	Q1	1,596	34	180,52
9	Journal of Intellectual Disability Research	9	1,778	Q1	0,935	33	123,44
11	Computers In Human Behavior	1	2,694	Q1	1,582	75	79,91
12	Journal of Computer Assisted Learning	2	1,370	Q1	2,048	41	57,52

2.2 Development of a Review Protocol

2.2.1 Definition of Inclusion and Exclusion Criteria

For research purposes, it is necessary to define criteria for selecting journals related with our objectives and with the research questions posed.

General Criteria:

- Studies involving gestural interactions by children with technology devices and whose main purpose is inclusive education processes.
- Studies published in the last ten years, that is, between 2008 and 2017.

Specific Criteria:
The studies must comply with one or more of the following specifications:

- Studies on standards that include an analysis of gestures in child-computer interactions.
- Studies that present design guides for gesture-based, inclusive educational interfaces.
- Studies that share methods/instruments used in research on populations with Down syndrome and gestural interfaces.
- Studies that explain studies for validating research processes in non-invasive environments involving gestural interactions.
- Also considered is whether the studies present a methodology for designing a gestural interaction to make it more effective for individuals with learning disabilities.

Additional parameters were defined to exclude papers from consideration:

- Papers involving gestural interaction in environments not pertaining to HCI or for non-educational purposes.
- Journals that are not catalogued as scientific papers: editorials, book reviews, technical reports, data sets, etc.

2.2.2 Definition of Analysis Categories

In keeping with the methodology in Torres-Carrión [5] in this sub-stage we define a series of analysis categories, the criteria for which are based on the research questions posed at the start of the study. These categories will allow us to group studies depending on the criteria that enable a systematic response to the research questions (RQ).

- RQ1 – Of the standards that describe the gesture-based CCI, which are being applied in inclusive educational environments? In this section we consider variables from ISO 9241 (Ergonomics of human-system interaction) and all its parts.
  - ISO Title: based on ISO 9241 - Ergonomics of human-system interaction and IEC [12].
  - Categories of the standard: User performance/satisfaction, product, development process, life cycle processes [12].
  - Type of gestural interaction: ISO/DIS 9241-960 Framework and guidance for gesture interactions; ISO 9241-210 Human-centered design for interactive systems [13, 14].
  - Report new experimental standard of gestural analysis [12].
- RQ2 – How are design guides applied to inclusive educational gestural interfaces for children?
  - Phases and procedures: based on ISO 9241-210 Human-centered design for interactive systems [14].
  - Human factors: senses, memory and cognition.
  - Types of senses: light, sound, smell, movement, speech, touch and biological variables.

- Emotions or feelings in design: based on EMODIANA [15].
- RQ3 - What methods/instruments are considered in gestural inclusive interactions for children with Down syndrome in educational environments?
  - Educational target group: based on International Standard Classification of Education - UNESCO [16].
  - Research method.
  - Data collection method.
  - Range of mental age/natural age.
  - Technology for interaction: details on instruments and tools.
  - Type of interface: based on ISO 9241-210 Human-centered design for interactive systems [14].
  - Type of gestural interaction: ISO/DIS 9241-960 Framework and guidance for gesture interactions [13].
  - Report results from research.
- RQ4 - How were the research results in non-invasive interaction environments evaluated?
  - These variables apply only to research using non-invasive technologies.
  - Research method.
  - Assessment tools.
  - Report results from research.
  - Special need addressed: name and percent.
- RQ5 - What processes were adapted to personalize interaction resources, considering each child's needs and disabilities?
  - Detail of adaptation process.
  - Special need addressed: name and percent.
  - Detail of digital learning strategy (qualitative item) – if the scope of the research is pedagogical.

2.3   Conducting the Review

This process relies on the results from the previous phase: the inclusion and exclusion criteria and the list of journals (*listJournal_2*) given in Table 4. We followed the "Knowledge Discovery in Databases" (KDD) process [17] by conducting a continuous search in each of the journals and arranging the results based on the structure of the variables in the research questions. The five steps in this section follow the method by Torres Carrión [5], using Mendeley as software for the administration of the resulting scientific articles.

3   Reporting the Review

3.1   RQ1 – Of the Standards that Describe Gesture-Based CCI, Which Are Being Applied in Inclusive Educational Environments?

The standard that best references multi-touch interactions is ISO/IEC 14754, which defines the commands for the basic gestures for select, delete, insert space and line, move, copy, paste, scroll and undo actions, and also extends these actions to pen interfaces [37]. One of the new work standards in HCI is that associated with the muscle-computer interface (MCI), which despite having many elements of natural interaction, is mainly studied in the area of augmented reality (Table 5).

Table 5. Papers that apply the ISO 9241-960 and ISO 9241-210 standards

Of those that apply the ISO 9241 standard (Ergonomics of human-system interaction), those applicable to our study were selected: [12]		f
• ISO 9241-9: Environment	[18–26]	8
• ISO 9241-10: Interface	[20, 23, 24, 27–37]	14
• ISO 9241-11: Usability	[3, 24, 30, 32, 33, 35]	6
• ISO 9241-17: Interaction	[19, 23, 28, 30, 31, 35, 37–48]	18
Type of gestural interaction: [13, 14]		
• Body	[18, 23, 25, 27, 29, 30, 33, 34, 37, 39–41, 46, 49–51]	16
• Speech	[21, 36, 40, 52, 53]	5
• Touch	[20, 26, 35–38, 40, 45, 46, 48, 53–57]	15
• Hand	[22, 28, 54, 58, 59]	5
• Face	[47, 54, 58, 60]	4
• Eye	[3, 30]	2

3.2 RQ2 – How Are Design Guides Applied to Inclusive Educational Natural Interfaces for Children?

This question is closely related to the first. To answer it, we considered the standards presented, which were complemented with the design phases and processes, the human factors that are of interest in our field of research, and an additional consideration

Table 6. Papers that apply sub-categories of the design guide as per the ISO 9241-210 standard

Human factors:		f
• Senses	Every paper in the next sub-category (type of sense)	35
• Memory	[31, 43, 49, 61]	4
• Cognition	[18–22, 24, 26–28, 30–32, 34–36, 38, 39, 42, 43, 46, 49, 51, 53, 55, 56, 58, 59, 61, 62]	29
Type of sense:		
• Light	–	0
• Sound	[21, 36, 40, 52, 53]	5
• Smell	–	0
• Movement	[18, 22, 23, 25, 27–30, 33, 34, 37, 39–41, 46, 47, 49–51, 54, 58–60]	24
• Speech	[21, 36, 40, 52, 53]	5
• Touch	[20, 26, 35–38, 40, 46, 48, 53–57]	14
• Biological variables	–	0

involving an emerging topic, namely the user's emotional response during the interaction. Table 6 shows part of the classification, relating the human factors and type of
sense to the study needs and research questions.

3.3   RQ3 - What Methods/Instruments Are Considered in Gestural Inclusive Interactions for Children with Down Syndrome in Educational Environments?

Knowing the specifics of the literacy level, learning style and physiological conditions
of a person with Down syndrome (DS) is vital when planning their education,
preparing learning strategies and the resources for their interaction in the classroom
[63]. Of the papers studied, 16.28% involve specific studies carried out on this population, and one on *fragile X syndrome* [38], which also considers this sub-group. The
study by Tabatabaei [58] does not consider a formal academic activity, but rather uses
images of young children to establish differentiation patterns in images based on
specific facial features (Table 7).

Table 7.   Articles based on Target Group of Education (UNESCO sub-group) and age.

Target Group of Education: based on International Standard Classification of Education - UNESCO [16] (subcategory)		f
• Early childhood education	[59, 61]	2
• Primary education	[29, 44, 61, 64]	4
• Lower secondary or higher		0
Range of mental age/natural age		
• 0–3	[59]	1
• 4–6	[59]	1
• 7–9	[29]	1
• 10–12	[29]	1
• >12		0
• No specific	[44, 64]	2

3.4   RQ4 - How Were the Research Results in Non-invasive Interaction Environments Evaluated?

Of the list of papers studied, there were none of an experimental nature that considered
maintaining the everyday interaction and working setting. Parés [23] makes an effort by
studying the interactive design for children with autism and visual impairments, presenting as a result a protocol for a multi-sensory space that evaluates visual, aural and
vibrotactile stimuli. Although the author's design proposes non-invasive interaction
aspects, there is no method for letting the student maintain his/her interaction space;
instead, a removable space resembling a small room has to be installed to allow for
personalized interaction.

3.5   RQ5 – What Processes Were Adapted to Personalize Interaction Resources, Considering Each Child's Educational Needs and Disabilities?

Of the articles reviewed, 48.83% considered the personalization of resources in some way, at least theoretically and conceptually; of this group, it was mostly the studies on autism (28.57%) that emphasized the personalization of resources, followed by general SEN studies. We did not find any experimental studies in this group of papers that formally or informally describe the application of a platform for personalizing the educational resources of students in the classroom. Mahmoud [59] and Tabatabaei [58] share a model for an *Intelligent Tutoring System* applicable to Down syndrome (Mahmoud) and to speech disorders only.

4   Conclusions

- The methodological adapted to the method of Torres-Carrión [5], Kitchenham [6] and Bacca [7] can be used to confidently select scientific studies in a way that is organized and focused on the user's needs. The results of this systematic review confirm its validity in the field of scientific research, allowing researchers to locate databases, important scientific journals and leading and relevant researchers working in their area of study.
- The ISO 9241-960 (Ergonomics of Human-System Interaction) and ISO 9241-210 (Human-Centered Design for Interactive Systems) standards are the most widely applied in the area of child-computer gesture interaction, with ISO 9241-17: Interaction being prominent in the former and types of motor and touch interaction in the latter.
- The design guides for natural interfaces are partially applied in some studies, and underscore the cognition and sensory human factors. The most widely used sensors are for motion (motor) and touch. None of the studies considered an emotional assessment, either as a subjective or objective measure.
- The few studies on subjects with Down syndrome involved children 0 to 12 years of age, and do not consider subjects beyond primary education. The main technology used is virtual reality through Wii games, and artificial intelligence applications for early intervention in mathematics learning.
- No experimental studies were found that take place specifically in non-invasive interaction environments. Proposals for designing work protocols in multi-sensory spaces were proposed, but these require taking the student to this new interactive environment.
- Any experimental study describing the personalization of gesture-based interaction in inclusive educational environments for students with special needs has been found. Neither, about the use of gestural interaction platforms to personalize the educational resources for Down's syndrome students. Two models for Intelligent Tutoring Systems are proposed that rely on expert systems.

References

1. Torres-Carrion, P., González-González, C.S., Mora Carreño, A.: Methodology of emotional evaluation in education and rehabilitation activities for people with Down syndrome. In: XV International Conference on Human Computer Interaction, pp. 12–15 (2014)
2. Torres-Carrión, P.: Evaluación de Estrategias de Aprendizaje con HCI Kinect en alumnos con Síndrome de Down (2017). http://e-spacio.uned.es/fez/view/tesisuned:ED_Pg_CyEED-Pvtorres
3. Torres-Carrión, P., Gonzalez-Gonzalez, C.: Usability study of didactical resources to children with Down syndrome. In: Guerrero-Garcia, J., González-Calleros, J.M., Muñoz-Arteaga, J., Collazos, C.A. (eds.) Human-Computer Interaction Series, pp. 127–148. Springer, Heidelberg (2017). https://doi.org/10.1007/978-3-319-55666-6_7
4. Swartz, M.K.: The PRISMA statement: a guideline for systematic reviews and meta-analyses. J. Pediatr. Health Care. 25, 1–2 (2011)
5. Torres-Carrión, P., González-González, C., Aciar, S., Rodríguez-Morales, G.: Methodology for systematic literature review applied to engineering and education. In: EDUCON2018 – IEEE Global Engineering Education Conference. IEEE Xplore Digital Library, Santa Cruz de Tenerife - España (2018)
6. Kitchenham, B.: Procedures for Performing Systematic Reviews. Joint Technical report, Keele, UK (2004)
7. Bacca, J., Baldiris, S., Fabregat, R.: Augmented reality trends in education: a systematic review of research and applications. J. Educ. Technol. Soc. 14, 133–149 (2014)
8. Yarosh, S., Radu, I., Hunter, S., Rosenbaum, E.: Examining values: an analysis of nine years of IDC research. In: Proceedings of the 10th International Conference on Interaction Design and Children, pp. 136–144. ACM (2011)
9. Sheu, F.R., Chen, N.S.: Taking a signal: a review of gesture-based computing research in education. Comput. Educ. 78, 268–277 (2014)
10. Boucenna, S., et al.: Interactive technologies for autistic children: a review. Cognit. Comput. 6, 722–740 (2014)
11. Benton, L., Johnson, H.: Widening participation in technology design: a review of the involvement of children with special educational needs and disabilities. Int. J. Child-Comput. Interact. 3–4, 23–40 (2015)
12. Bevan, N.: International standards for HCI and usability. Int. J. Hum.-Comput. Stud. 55, 533–552 (2001)
13. ISO: ISO/DIS 9241-960. Ergonomics of human-system interaction - Part 960: Framework and guidance for gesture interactions, Geneva, Switzerland (2015)
14. ISO: ISO 9241-210:2010. Ergonomics of human-system interaction - Part 210: Human-centred design for interactive systems, Geneva, Switzerland (2015)
15. González-González, C.S., Cairós-González, M., Navarro-Adelantado, V.: EMODIANA: Un instrumento para la evaluación subjetiva de emociones en niños y niñas. Actas del XIV Congr. Int. Interacción Pers. (2013)
16. UNESCO: The International Standard Classification of Education 2011. UNESCO Institute for Statistics, Montreal, Quebec, Canada (2012)
17. Dhiman, A.K.: Knowledge discovery in databases and libraries. DESIDOC J. Libr. Inf. Technol. 31, 446–451 (2011)
18. Jarus, T., et al.: Effect of internal versus external focus of attention on implicit motor learning in children with developmental coordination disorder. Res. Dev. Disabil. 37, 119–126 (2015)

19. Cheng, Y., Huang, R.: Using virtual reality environment to improve joint attention associated with pervasive developmental disorder. Res. Dev. Disabil. **33**, 2141–2152 (2012)
20. Fernández-López, Á., Rodríguez-Fórtiz, M.J., Rodríguez-Almendros, M.L., Martínez-Segura, M.J.: Mobile learning technology based on iOS devices to support students with special education needs. Comput. Educ. **61**, 77–90 (2013)
21. Toki, E.I., Pange, J.: The design of an expert system for the e-assessment and treatment plan of preschoolers' speech and language disorders. Procedia - Soc. Behav. Sci. **9**, 815–819 (2010)
22. Cano, M.-D., Sanchez-Iborra, R.: On the use of a multimedia platform for music education with handicapped children: a case study. Comput. Educ. **87**, 254–276 (2015)
23. Parés, N., et al.: Starting research in interaction design with visuals for low-functioning children in the autistic spectrum: a protocol. Cyberpsychol. Behav. **9**, 218–223 (2006)
24. Mich, O., Pianta, E., Mana, N.: Interactive stories and exercises with dynamic feedback for improving reading comprehension skills in deaf children. Comput. Educ. **65**, 34–44 (2013)
25. Shih, C.-H., Shih, C.-T., Chu, C.-L.: Assisting people with multiple disabilities actively correct abnormal standing posture with a Nintendo Wii balance board through controlling environmental stimulation. Res. Dev. Disabil. **31**, 936–942 (2010)
26. Ahmed, S., Parsons, D.: Abductive science inquiry using mobile devices in the classroom. Comput. Educ. **63**, 62–72 (2013)
27. Crisco, J.J., Schwartz, J.B., Wilcox, B., Costa, L., Kerman, K.: Design and kinematic evaluation of a novel joint-specific play controller: application for wrist and forearm therapy. Phys. Ther. **95**, 1061–1066 (2015)
28. Cai, Y., Chia, N.K.H., Thalmann, D., Kee, N.K.N., Zheng, J., Thalmann, N.M.: Design and development of a Virtual Dolphinarium for children with autism. IEEE Trans. Neural Syst. Rehabil. Eng. **21**, 208–217 (2013)
29. Wuang, Y.-P., Chiang, C.-S., Su, C.-Y., Wang, C.-C.: Effectiveness of virtual reality using Wii gaming technology in children with Down syndrome. Res. Dev. Disabil. **32**, 312–321 (2011)
30. Lahiri, U., Bekele, E., Dohrmann, E., Warren, Z., Sarkar, N.: Design of a virtual reality based adaptive response technology for children with autism. IEEE Trans. Neural Syst. Rehabil. Eng. **21**, 55–64 (2013)
31. de la Guía, E., Lozano, M.D., Penichet, V.M.R.: Educational games based on distributed and tangible user interfaces to stimulate cognitive abilities in children with ADHD. Br. J. Educ. Technol. **46**, 664–678 (2015)
32. Seo, Y.-J., Woo, H.: The identification, implementation, and evaluation of critical user interface design features of computer-assisted instruction programs in mathematics for students with learning disabilities. Comput. Educ. **55**, 363–377 (2010)
33. Torrente, J., Freire, M., Moreno-Ger, P., Fernández-Manjón, B.: Evaluation of semi-automatically generated accessible interfaces for educational games. Comput. Educ. **83**, 103–117 (2015)
34. Stasolla, F., et al.: Computer and microswitch-based programs to improve academic activities by six children with cerebral palsy. Res. Dev. Disabil. **45–46**, 1–13 (2015)
35. Marco, J., Cerezo, E., Baldassarri, S.: Bringing tabletop technology to all: evaluating a tangible farm game with kindergarten and special needs children. Pers. Ubiquitous Comput. **17**, 1577–1591 (2012)
36. Shahin, M., et al.: Tabby talks: an automated tool for the assessment of childhood apraxia of speech. Speech Commun. **70**, 49–64 (2015)
37. Cantón, P., González, Á.L., Mariscal, G., Ruiz, C.: Applying new interaction paradigms to the education of children with special educational needs. In: Miesenberger, K., Karshmer, A., Penaz, P., Zagler, W. (eds.) ICCHP 2012. LNCS, vol. 7382, pp. 65–72. Springer, Heidelberg (2012). https://doi.org/10.1007/978-3-642-31522-0_10

38. Hall, S.S., Hammond, J.L., Hirt, M., Reiss, A.L.: A "learning platform" approach to outcome measurement in fragile X syndrome: a preliminary psychometric study. J. Intellect. Disabil. Res. **56**, 947–960, 14p. (2012)
39. Marti, P., Giusti, L.: A robot companion for inclusive games: a user-centred design perspective. In: 2010 IEEE International Conference on Robotics and Automation, pp. 4348–4353. IEEE (2010)
40. Keskinen, T., Heimonen, T., Turunen, M., Rajaniemi, J.-P., Kauppinen, S.: SymbolChat: a flexible picture-based communication platform for users with intellectual disabilities. Interact. Comput. **24**, 374–386 (2012)
41. Mombarg, R., Jelsma, D., Hartman, E.: Effect of Wii-intervention on balance of children with poor motor performance. Res. Dev. Disabil. **34**, 2996–3003 (2013)
42. Doyle, T., Arnedillo-Sánchez, I.: Using multimedia to reveal the hidden code of everyday behaviour to children with autistic spectrum disorders (ASDs). Comput. Educ. **56**, 357–369 (2011)
43. Dovis, S., Van der Oord, S., Wiers, R.W., Prins, P.J.M.: Improving executive functioning in children with ADHD: training multiple executive functions within the context of a computer game. A randomized double-blind placebo controlled trial. PLoS ONE **10**, e0121651 (2015)
44. Feng, J., Lazar, J., Kumin, L., Ozok, A.: Computer usage by children with Down syndrome: challenges and future research. ACM Trans. Access. Comput. **2**, 1–44 (2010)
45. Torres-Carrión, P., Sarmiento-Guerrero, C., Torres-Diaz, J.C., Barba-Guamán, L.: Educational math game for stimulation of children with dyscalculia (2018)
46. Jong, J.-T., Hong, J.-C., Yen, C.-Y.: Persistence temperament associated with children playing math games between touch panel and embodied interaction. J. Comput. Assist. Learn. **29**, 569–578 (2013)
47. Hamzah, M.S.J., Shamsuddin, S., Miskam, M.A., Yussof, H., Hashim, K.S.: Development of interaction scenarios based on pre-school curriculum in robotic intervention for children with autism. Procedia Comput. Sci. **42**, 214–221 (2014)
48. Fletcher-Watson, S., Pain, H., Hammond, S., Humphry, A., McConachie, H.: Designing for young children with autism spectrum disorder: a case study of an iPad app. Int. J. Child-Comput. Interact. **7**, 1–14 (2016)
49. Jelsma, D., Ferguson, G.D., Smits-Engelsman, B.C.M., Geuze, R.H.: Short-term motor learning of dynamic balance control in children with probable developmental coordination disorder. Res. Dev. Disabil. **38**, 213–222 (2015)
50. Sanna, A., Lamberti, F., Paravati, G., Rocha, F.D.: A kinect-based interface to animate virtual characters. J. Multimodal User Interfaces **7**, 269–279 (2013)
51. Levac, D., Rivard, L., Missiuna, C.: Defining the active ingredients of interactive computer play interventions for children with neuromotor impairments: a scoping review. Res. Dev. Disabil. **33**, 214–223 (2012)
52. Wagner, A., Rudraraju, R., Datla, S., Banerjee, A., Sudame, M., Gray, J.: Programming by voice. In: Proceedings of the 2012 ACM Annual Conference Extended Abstracts on Human Factors in Computing Systems Extended Abstracts - CHI EA 2012, p. 2087. ACM Press, New York (2012)
53. Tressoldi, P., Vio, C., Iozzino, R.: Efficacy of an intervention to improve fluency in children with developmental dyslexia in a regular orthography. J. Learn. Disabil. **40**, 203–209, 7p. (2007)
54. Rosenblum, S., Regev, N.: Timing abilities among children with developmental coordination disorders (DCD) in comparison to children with typical development. Res. Dev. Disabil. **34**, 218–227 (2013)
55. Campigotto, R., McEwen, R., Demmans Epp, C.: Especially social: exploring the use of an iOS application in special needs classrooms. Comput. Educ. **60**, 74–86 (2013)

56. Jones, A.C., Scanlon, E., Clough, G.: Mobile learning: two case studies of supporting inquiry learning in informal and semiformal settings. Comput. Educ. **61**, 21–32 (2013)
57. Hassan, A., Danish, Z.: Multi-touch user interfaces to treat social, communicative and collaborative impairments in children with autism: a review. Int. J. Comput. Appl. **117**, 35–39 (2015)
58. Tabatabaei, S.M., Chalechale, A.: Using DLBP texture descriptors and SVM for Down syndrome recognition. In: 2014 4th International Conference on Computer and Knowledge Engineering (ICCKE), pp. 554–558. IEEE (2014)
59. Mahmoud, A.F.A., Belal, M.A.F., Helmy, Y.M.K.: Towards an intelligent tutoring system to Down syndrome. Int. J. Comput. Sci. Inf. Technol. **6**, 129–137 (2014)
60. Gordon, I., Pierce, M.D., Bartlett, M.S., Tanaka, J.W.: Training facial expression production in children on the autism spectrum. J. Autism Dev. Disord. **44**, 2486–2498 (2014)
61. Visu-Petra, L., Benga, O., Tincas, I., Miclea, M.: Visual-spatial processing in children and adolescents with Down's syndrome: a computerized assessment of memory skills. J. Intellect. Disabil. Res. **51**, 942–952, 11p. (2007)
62. Imhof, B., Scheiter, K., Edelmann, J., Gerjets, P.: Learning about locomotion patterns: effective use of multiple pictures and motion-indicating arrows. Comput. Educ. **65**, 45–55 (2013)
63. Ratz, C.: Do students with Down syndrome have a specific learning profile for reading? Res. Dev. Disabil. **34**, 4504–4514 (2013)
64. Næss, K.-A.B., Melby-Lervåg, M., Hulme, C., Lyster, S.-A.H.: Reading skills in children with Down syndrome: a meta-analytic review. Res. Dev. Disabil. **33**, 737–747 (2012)

Portability Approaches for Business Web Applications to Mobile Devices: A Systematic Mapping

Viviana Cajas[1,3]([✉]), Matías Urbieta[1,2], Yves Rybarczyk[4],
Gustavo Rossi[1,?], and César Guevara[5]

[1] LIFIA, Facultad de Informática, Universidad Nacional de La Plata,
La Plata, Argentina
{matias.urbieta,gustavo.rossi}@lifia.info.unlp.edu.ar
[2] CONICET, Buenos Aires, Argentina
[3] Facultad de Ciencias Administrativas y Económicas,
Universidad Tecnológica Indoamérica, Quito, Ecuador
vivianacajas@uti.edu.ec
[4] Intelligent & Interactive Systems Lab (SI2 Lab),
Universidad de Las Américas, Quito, Ecuador
yves.rybarczyk@udla.edu.ec
[5] Centro de Investigación en Mecatrónica y Sistemas Interactivos (MIST),
Universidad Tecnológica Indoamérica, Quito, Ecuador
cesarguevara@uti.edu.ec

Abstract. Applications on mobile devices have had an exponential grow; however, there are business legacies 1.0 that have not migrated or have not been adapted due to the operating or economic cost involved in the required migration. The companies are not often aware of the benefits the mobile applications have to generate new business models. This paper aims to study the different approaches used in the portability of web applications 1.0 to mobile devices in the last decade, in order to identify the edges and perspectives of the area. A systematic mapping is carried out on the main databases in the area, such as SCOPUS, IEEE, and ACM. 44 articles are selected from 824 initials and are classified with respect to the approach, the type of research and contribution. This systematic review shows that while the technical achievements on the mobile development have been outstanding, there are still many issues to be solved for migrating Web applications.

Keywords: Portability approach · Web application · Systematic mapping
Mobile devices

1 Introduction

The companies have taken advantage of a series of benefits with the new business models that arise from Web applications 2.0 [1], positioning the end user as the protagonist, and the Web 3.0 [2] providing the semantics and the cloud. Some advantages of the e-commerce are: (i) to make a client segmentation and loyalty in situ

© Springer Nature Switzerland AG 2019
M. Botto-Tobar et al. (Eds.): CITT 2018, CCIS 895, pp. 148–164, 2019.
https://doi.org/10.1007/978-3-030-05532-5_11

[3], (ii) to brand image for its positioning in the mind of consumers [4], (iii) the payment using mobile devices at a lower cost through mobile business applications functioning as extensions of an organizational core, among others. Unfortunately, there is still a system barrier and a lack of standardization [5], so the need for a new unified design with functionality, synchronization, distributed processing has to be proposed [6]. In such a way the end users will not have problems with usability and business achievement of their strategy's goals.

Similarly, there are applications that could be framed within the term Web 1.0 [7]. These applications are characterized by serving static unidirectional content, in which the business website is designed obtaining immediacy in services for customers. The reader must note that there are applications remaining as legacies that have not migrated to modern technologies. Adapting a Web application to mobile can be time-consuming and have a high cost, in accordance with the complexity of building a light mobile app from a business site, avoiding inconsistencies or conflicts with business requirements [8]. With cross-platform, the software development becomes more complicated, because Android and iOS have different SDK, programming logic, and physical devices characteristics. This scenario constrains the designs and will perhaps double the cost [9]. Since legacy Web apps are not properly rendered by mobile devices requiring scrolling and zooming for accessing data and features, this makes the user's experience unsatisfactory. The correct layout on mobile is not the only drawback to solve, mobile applications are also used in a context that involves technical and functional challenges. There are others attributes to improve in the applications like the proactivity that allows the correct recovery of information against the cuts due to the limited connectivity or the distraction of the users. Moreover, the poor usability generates a digital gap enforced by certain aspects such as demographics, economy, education, geographical location and politics [10].

Because of the latter, this topic is increasingly important and it is necessary to investigate the most optimal solutions according to the approaches that emerged through this global problem. In order to provide an overall view of current trends on techniques and approaches we conduct a systematic mapping review which aims at answering the research question (RQ): Which approaches or strategies have been applied in the portability of legacy Web applications to mobile ones? This question motivates the study of the trends in the mobile area and identifying how the problem has been addressed in researches on this subject. The outcome of this research is expected to benefit both the industry and academy with an overview of tools, techniques and approaches which allows migrating systems to mobile solutions. Because the most users today are digital natives. Internet is their main tool, and they have mobile devices: smartphones, tablets and laptops, whereby companies that are not adapted with their business models to mobile devices run the risk of failing in the medium term, these models can arise through mobile applications. At the same way, software engineers without skills to provide optimal mobile solutions will be discarded in the workplace. This article is organized as follows: the related papers are defined in Sect. 2. The review planning is explained in Sect. 3, including the protocol, the research question, the search strategy, and the selection and extraction of criteria from the articles. The synthesis of relevant studies is then presented in Sect. 4. The discussion is presented in Sect. 5. Limitations are in Sect. 6. Finally, the conclusions and future work are contemplated in Sect. 7.

2 Related Work

By reviewing the literature, several studies were found related to the topics published which are summarized in Table 1. The findings described permit, to establish that most correspond to an informal literature, surveys or comparisons without defined research questions, without a search protocol that is evidenced or can be replicated for the extraction of information as a process of analysis of data.

Table 1. Main characteristics of related works

Author	Evaluation/Future work
Zimmerman et al. (2009)	Find the drawbacks of applications in the devices with small screens, which need to be deepened: legibility of the typography, the icons, the size, and orientation of the screen, navigation problems and audio that should be included in certain elements to increase understanding. Development a pilot project about a health application
Zhang et al. (2011)	Classify, synthesize, and compare the pros and cons of the main methods of adaptation. It raises 10 general guidelines to develop a method of adapting web pages for mobile devices
Alshahwan et al. (2011)	Experimental tests were performed between a SOAP architecture and another REST. Poses as future work, control the download process and find strategies to select an Auxiliary Mobile Host (AMH)
Deuschel et al. (2016)	Evaluate the applications covered with the main aspects of spatial perception: resizing and screen transition
Younas et al. (2016)	Survey examining the main model-based development approaches. Evaluation through phase compliance. (i) Requirements. (ii) Analysis. (iii) Design. (iv) Implementation. (v) Tests
Siebra et al. (2017)	The result of the review of 247 articles, was a classification scheme that merges the analyzed approaches. The authors conducted an experiment to assess the user experience of disabled people using the scheme

The systematic mapping presented in this document is different from previous studies because the goal is (i) to strictly compile the portability methodologies of business applications to mobile; (ii) to limit the period of time to the last 11 years (2006 period of introduction of the term Web 2.0 [7] to 2017). The procedure was carried out through a protocol performed in a systematic and rigorous manner, following the guidelines provided by Petersen [11], Kitchenham [12] and Brereton [13]. These guidelines aim to present a fair evaluation of a research subject using a reliable, rigorous and auditable methodology. The next section of this paper addresses the planning of the review, which includes the main objective, the research question, and the search string. Also explains the digital libraries used, the search period and the preview results. Finally details the inclusion and exclusion criteria.

3 Review Planning

The main objective of this systematic mapping [11] is to obtain an overview perspective of the portability of Web applications to mobile that allows determining the state of the topic and especially to focus on the current weaknesses to determinate future researches. According to Kitchenham et al. [12], a Systematic mapping study (also referred to as a scoping study) corresponds to a broad review of primary studies in a specific topic identifying what evidence is available on the topic. Based on the RQ "Which approaches or strategies have been applied in the portability of legacy Web applications to mobile ones?" the search terms are shown in Table 2, keywords and synonyms that compose the question were built based on Brereton et al. [13] steps that use the PICO criteria.

Table 2. Search terms

PICO	Keywords	Alternative words
Population	Portability	Adaptation, modernization, migration, transformation
Intervention	Legacy Application	Web application
Comparison	Mobile	Multi devices, small screens
Outcomes	Approach	Framework

The search string is: (Portability OR Adaptation OR Modernization OR Migration OR Transformation) AND (Legacy Application OR Web Application) AND (Mobile OR Multi devices OR Small Screens) AND (Approach OR Framework).

3.1 Search Execution

The search was centered in the period 2006-2017 because in 2006 emerged the concept of Web 2.0, introduced by Tim O'Reilly, and in 2007 the first iPhone was released setting the current mobile architecture. SCOPUS, IEEE Xplore, and ACM Digital Library were used to recover investigations endorsed by Institutes or Organizations that establish standards for the development of mobile apps, are the most representative in the area. Besides SCOPUS already includes the largest publishers in the world, such as IEEE, Elsevier, Emerald, Springer, and Wiley. However, technical reports, doctoral theses or unpublished results were not considered and also the Google Scholar search engine was not used because the results include gray literature. The search resulted in 824 articles: 355 in Scopus, 169 in IEEE and 300 in ACM.

3.2   Selection of the Investigations

First, the title and summary of the resulting studies gathered from index systems were carefully reviewed, and then irrelevant documents were rejected. If the researchers did not agree, the study was included or analyzed with the help of an independent mediator. The full papers were read to get a final list of the studies reviewed with respect to the defined inclusion/exclusion criteria:

(i) Inclusion criteria: Documents that meet the search string: journals, conferences and workshops, written in English and published from January 2006 to December 2017 (inclusive).

(ii) Exclusion criteria: Papers will be excluded from the study if they are: (i) papers out of topic, documents that do not focus on portability of web applications to mobiles or that were strictly related to hardware, networks or security; (ii) papers that are available only in the form of abstracts, slides, summary of a workshop presentation or surface studies; (iii) papers duplicates (same research in different databases or improved versions); (iv) other studies that mention portability of web applications to mobiles as a general introductory term, and (v) when there is no proposal related to portability among the specifics contributions listed in Sect. 3.4 as conceptual frameworks.

3.3   Scheme for the Data Extraction

In this section, we will introduce data extracted from founded studies and their classification. Later this information will be used for generating the visual summary accordingly to the classification [11]. The data extracted from each study are:

(i)   Basic metadata: title, author, and date of publication.
(ii) Type of research (based on Wieringa classification scheme [14]): opinion, personal experience, philosophical, proposal of a solution, validation of the proposal and evaluation.
(iii) Type of contribution (based on Kosar et al. [15] classification scheme [24]): process, model, prototype, tool, framework, mapping, and technique.
(iv) The scope of application: academy, industry, or mixed.

3.4   Synthesis of the Information

A quantitative synthesis method was used to present the results of this systematic mapping, and consists of counting, classifying the studies according to the dimensions and categories defined in the previous sections. The combinations of dimensions and categories are described using bubble charts and bars, statistics and frequency analyses. The next section answers the research question (RQ) evidencing the results obtained after analyzing the studies content.

4 Results

For being the study the first systematic mapping of legacies applications to mobiles corresponds to an important contribution to the subject. Table 3 presents the authors and title of the studies (all the quotes were entered and classified with the help of Mendeley [16]).

Table 3. Results of the research and filtering

No.	Author	Title
P1	Lehtonen et al.	Towards user-friendly mobile browsing [17]
P2	Di Santo et al.	Reversing GUIs to XIML descriptions for the adaptation to heterogeneous devices [18]
P3	Cheng et al.	An adaptive and unified mobile application development framework for java [19]
P4	He et al.	A flexible content adaptation system using a rule-based approach [20]
P5	Ennai et al.	MobileSOA: A Service Oriented Web 2.0 Framework for Context-Aware, Lightweight and Flexible Mobile Applications [21]
P6	Ahmadi et al.	Efficient web browsing on small screens [22]
P7	Kopf et al.	Adaptation of web pages and images for mobile applications [23]
P8	Eap et al.	Personalised mobile learning content delivery: a learner centric approach [24]
P9	Iñesta et al.	Framework and authoring tool for an extension of the UIML language [25]
P10	Xiao et al.	Mashup-Based Web Page Adaptation for Small Screen Mobile Device [26]
P11	Paternò, F.	MARIA: A universal, declarative, multiple abstraction-level language for service-oriented applications in ubiquitous environments [27]
P12	Ueyama et al.	Exploiting a generic approach for constructing mobile device applications [28]
P13	Paternò et al.	Desktop-to-mobile web adaptation through customizable two-dimensional semantic redesign [29]
P14	Armenise et al.	A tool for automatic adaptation of web pages to different screen size [30]
P15	Chmielewski et al.	Mobile interfaces for building control surveyors [31]
P16	Guirguis et al.	A smart framework for web content and resources adaptation in mobile devices [32]
P17	Li et al.	Web page layout adaptation based on WebKit for e-paper device [33]
P18	Koehl et al.	M.Site: Efficient content adaptation for mobile devices [34]
P19	Macbeth et al.	A Middleware Service for Image Adjustment and Filtering for Small Screens [35]

(continued)

Table 3. (*continued*)

No.	Author	Title
P20	Rajkumar et al.	Dynamic web page segmentation based on detecting reappearance and layout of tag patterns for small screen devices [36]
P21	Challiol et al.	Crowdsourcing mobile web applications [37]
P22	Shaari et al.	Achieving "One-Web" through customization and prioritization [38]
P23	Amendola et al.	Adapting CRM systems for mobile platforms: An MDA perspective [39]
P24	Chen et al.	Organization and correction of spatial data in mobile GIS [40]
P25	Albasir et al.	Smart mobile web browsing [41]
P26	Yun et al.	MobiTran: tool support for refactoring PC websites to smart phones [42]
P27	Sumit Pandey	Responsive design for transaction banking - a responsible approach [43]
P28	Coondu et al.	Mobile-enabled content adaptation system for e-learning websites using segmentation algorithm [44]
P29	Toile et al.	Adaptation of composite E-Learning contents for reusable in smartphone based learning system [45]
P30	Badam et al.	Polychrome: A cross-device framework for collaborative web visualization [46]
P31	Yang et al.	Panelrama: Enabling easy specification of cross-device web applications [47]
P32	Kovachev et al.	Direwolf: A framework for widget-based distributed user interfaces [48]
P33	Xiang et al.	Effective Page Segmentation Combining Pattern Analysis and Visual Separators for Browsing on Small Screens [49]
P34	Yin et al.	WebC: toward a portable framework for deploying legacy code in web browsers [50]
P35	Tseng et al.	Migratom.js: A JavaScript migration framework for distributed web computing and mobile devices [51]
P36	Sarkis et al.	MSoS: A Multi-Screen-Oriented Web Page Segmentation Approach [52]
P37	Wang et al.	Towards Web Application Mobilization via Efficient Web Control Extraction [53]
P38	Bouzit et al.	Evanescent Adaptation on Small Screens [54]
P39	Miján et al.	Supporting personalization in legacy web sites through client-side adaptation [55]
P40	Favre et al.	Modernizing software in science and engineering: From C/C + + applications to mobile platforms [56]
P41	G. Huang et al.	Programming Situational Mobile Web Applications with Cloud-Mobile Convergence: An Internetware-Oriented Approach [57]
P42	H. Li et al.	Extracting Main Content of Webpage to Enhance Adaptively Rendering for Small Screen Size Terminals [58]
P43	Bosetti et al.	An approach for building mobile web applications through web augmentation [59]
P44	Sarkis et al.	A multi-screen refactoring system for video-centric web applications [60]

The main results of this mapping show a total of 824 works was obtained out of which 681 were found out of topic, 25 as duplicate studies, 8 as conceptual frameworks, 7 as mappings or reviews considered in the related works section, 59 as papers that were purely directed to the development of mobile applications without considering migration. Therefore, 44 studies were considered relevant works for the mapping: 28 from Scopus, 7 from IEEE, and 9 from ACM, which corresponds to 5.4% of the search. This can be justified because SCOPUS is an indexing system, so its engine is more advanced and it includes a series of digital sources including IEEE and several ACM publications, for this reason, there were repeated studies when conducting the search also in IEEE. As for ACM and IEEE, the majority of studies resulting were the improvement of hardware and networks to mobile applications, for this reason, were excluded. Figure 1 presents the type of document: article, conference, and journal. These results show that International conferences are the most recognized events, in which researchers can propose their solutions for the remapping of mobile devices, at the other end, there are publications in journals that because of their high impact have a degree more demanding. Figure 2 shows the area of the studies: industry, academy and mixed. The predominate strategies come from the academy, being traditionally the cradle of entrepreneurship, then the industry, since the sector, both public and private, is the one that moves the economy of the countries. There are also joint works between these two Scopes of activity.

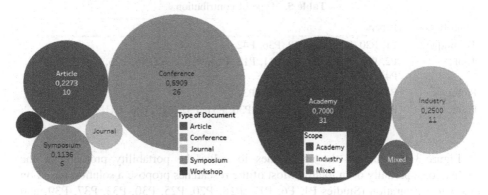

Fig. 1. Type of document   **Fig. 2.** Scope

Table 4 shows that: (i) 86,4% of the research efforts have been directed towards proposed solutions, (ii) 22,73% in process evaluation, (iii) 6,82% in adaptability process, (iv) 56,82% in verification and validation process, (v) 6,82% corresponds to studies based on experience, (vi) 4,55% with process evaluation, and (vii) 2,27% in verification and validation process. Also, there are validation studies in 6,82%, with adaptability process in 2,27% and modeling process in 4,55%. The main contribution of the studies is summarized in the following way: 45,45%, correspond to contributions that deliver tools, 22,7% correspond to frameworks, 15,92% are techniques, and 15,91% are prototypes.

Table 4. Scope Vs facet of research and contribution

	Experience	Proposed solution	Validation	Framework	Tool	Technique	Prototype
Process evaluation	4,55%	22,73%	0,00%	6,82%	11,36%	4,55%	4,55%
Adaptability process	0,00%	6,82%	2,27%	0,00%	4,55%	4,55%	0,00%
Modeling process	0,00%	0,00%	4,55%	2,27%	2,27%	0,00%	0,00%
V & V process	2,27%	56,82%	0,00%	13,64%	27,27%	6,82%	11,36%
Total	6,82%	86,37%	6,82%	22,73%	45,45%	15,92%	15,91%

Table 5 shows the grouping according to the contribution of each paper where the majority represents tools because allows testing the proposed methodology or solution. Then frameworks, which are a standardized set of concepts, practices, and criteria to approach a type of problem. After that are the techniques, which define procedures to perform software production tasks, and the prototypes are a limited representation of a product, it allows the parties to test it in real situations or to explore its use.

Table 5. Type of contribution

Contribution	Papers
Techniques	P1, P20, P23,P24, P29, P36, P42
Tool	P2, P3, P6, P7, P8, P9, P11, P13, P14, P16, P17, P19, P26, P34, P38, P39, P43, P44
Prototype	P4, P10, P12, P25, P27,P33, P37
Framework	P5, P15, P18, P21, P22, P28, P30, P31, P32, P35, P40, P41

Figure 3 summarizes the approaches to solve the portability problem of the applications, partially or in totally. Most of the researches propose a solution based on DOM restructuration (Studies P1, P6, P17, P18, P20, P25, P30, P33, P37, P39, and P43), then there are solutions based on Model Driven Development (P9, P13, P22, P23, P40). Then, the most used solutions implement Translators (P11, P12, P26, and P34), XML (P3, P4, P8, and P36), Specific Migrations (P2, P24, P29), and Multiscreen development (P7, P16, P31, P44). Only two studies present solutions about SOA (P5, P15). Finally, in the same number there are other solutions like Mashups (P10), Genetic Programming (P14), Artificial Intelligence (P19), Augmentation (P21), Prototypes (P26), Middleware (P28), Widgets (P32), Architecture (P35), Visualization Techniques (P38), cloud computing (P41) and Algorithms (P42).

Figure 4 presents a diagram XY in the category intersections that allow considering several categories at the same time and providing a quick overview of a field of study, scope of the research vs. type and contribution. The most common strategy like the proposed solution responds to how to create, delete, update, and move elements and content of the DOM tree of the pages to achieve personalization according to the

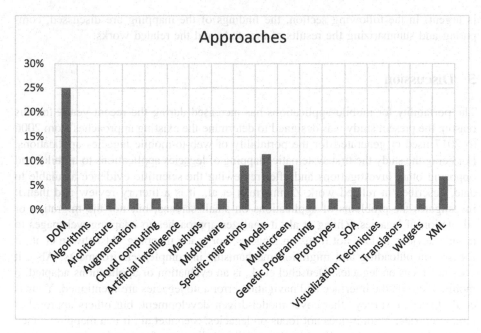

Fig. 3. Approaches

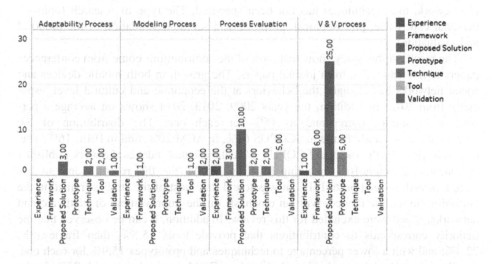

Fig. 4. Research scope vs. contribution

device. Model-driven engineering work (MDE in English) where contributions use metamodels to represent the problem to be solved and model transformations to obtain software applications. This is an efficient solution but it is semiautomatic because requires the programmer's assistance to complete the model whenever something new is urgent. In the following section, the findings of the mapping are discussed, comparing and summarizing the results of the study and the related works.

5 Discussion

The portability for mobile applications has increased during the recent years, for this reason, the present study was designed to determine the existing approaches from 2006 to 2017 used or generated for the portability of web-to-mobile legacies applications. For being the study the first systematic mapping of legacies applications to mobiles and opposing other investigations and after reviewing the scientific evidence available to date, described in related work Zimmerman et al., it is a literary review and then it investigates the problems of applications on small screens, but not the migration or adaptation of legacies. Zhang et al., it analyzes approaches to adapting web pages to mobile devices, it does not focus on legacies, nor is it a mapping. Alshahwan et al., it focuses on offloading and migration mechanisms in complex environments. Also, it does not focus on legacies. Deuschel et al., is an evaluation of applications adapted to mobile focus on the interface and navigation errors, no legacies are mentioned. Younas et al., these are surveys that cover model-driven development, but others approaches remain outside. Also, it does not focus on legacies. Siebra et al., it is a mapping aimed at detecting errors and requirements in mobile applications for people with some type of disability. In addition, in which no data have been found on the association between the validation field (academy, industry, mixed), the specific contribution of each study (framework, tool, technique) has not been specified. The type of research (opinion, personal experience, philosophical, proposal of a solution, validation of the proposal and evaluation).

The results of this study show that most of the contributions come from conferences papers 59,1% and 4,5% from journal papers. The growth in both mobile devices and social networks has changed the behaviors at the economic and cultural level, especially from 2012. In addition, the years 2009, 2013, 2014 shows on average a percentage of studies correspond to 15% for each one. The distribution of the investigations is mainly found in SCOPUS 64%, in ACM 20%, and in IEEE 16%. This can be justified by the fact that SCOPUS is a database that indexes the work published by various publishers [61] including IEEE and ACM. For this reason, some studies were repeated. In relation to IEEE, it was found that most of the studies framed in the portability to mobile devices with an emphasis on the improvement of hardware and networks, which were excluded for this review. In addition, it can be observed that the majority corresponds to contributions that provide tools 45,5%, then frameworks 22,7%; and with a lower percentage to techniques and prototypes 15,9% for each one.

The approaches are predominantly based on DOM manipulation with 25%. In the second position, the development of model-driven software (MDD) with 11,4% which produces only partially successful proposals, since they cannot guarantee a fully automatic process (a programmer is always required to code the modifications or details that have not been considered or situations that appear). Then, there are specific migrations, multiscreen development, and translators with the same percentage 9,1%. In fourth place come XML configurations. Solutions through SOA services comes next. Finally, in the same proportion, 2,3% are the algorithms, architecture, augmentation, cloud computing, artificial intelligence, mashups, middleware, genetic programming, prototypes, visualization techniques, and widgets. However, a design with the correct visualization on the screen of the mobile device does not solve all the problem that entails the adaptation to this type of applications. Some factors like the connectivity, speed of response, navigation, information, type of controls supported by the platform (Android vs. iOS) should be considered because an incompatibility on the controls affects the efficiency of the data entry.

The portability is varied; however, there is more emphasis in the adaptation of desktop web applications to mobile web applications, HTML, CSS, JavaScript or Jquery and to HTML5 with the corresponding variants in the types of file. On the other hand, there are improvements to existing technologies such as visualization technologies, genetic programming, among others. Additionally, it is observed that some innovations have been included in the adaptations. For example, the introduction of augmented reality, 3D, and the specific migrations, for example, C/C ++ to Haxe, Cobol to Java Web, Mario Kart 64 of Nintendo to Android, web applications to Python and Php. This study did not detect any evidence about the methodologies for the portabilization or migration of applications developed in licensed tools.

Finally, most of the research efforts have been directed towards solutions that contribute with tools, scope cover assessment processes, adaptability processes, and modeling processes. Additionally, half of the studies propose frameworks for the assessment and modeling processes. The minority of the studies contributes to techniques and prototypes that perform assessment processes and are in adaptability process. In addition, of the items included in the mapping, it can be mentioned that the research and validation methods used correspond to case studies, experiments with users, and also the development of prototypes or pilots. The case study facilitates the validation of the proposed solution when there are several applications in which the methodology was implemented, on the other hand, the evaluation with users generally corresponds to the validation of usability issues and determination of compliance with tasks, prototypes or simulations are suitable when you want to perform a partial test of the methodology or do not have the availability of the required hardware. The problem of threats of study validity and limitations is discussed in the next section.

6 Limitations

The main limitation lies in obtaining results that depend on the use of search tools integrated into the SCOPUS indexing system. Also the scanned digital libraries: ACM and IEEE. Searches were made using search strings defined by terms derived from the research question connected by Boolean operators in the range from 2006 to 2017. During the keyword search process, some sources may have been omitted, because the keywords used by some authors are synonymous with those used in this study. In order to reduce the validation risk of the analysis, the review of the articles was conducted independently by investigators and validated in a cross way. In this way, it was possible to control both false positives and negatives. Another limitation is that the negative results take longer to be published or cited in other publications to a lesser extent,

Kitchenham [19]. The next section provides a series of conclusions drawn from this study from this mapping and recommendations for future studies.

7   Conclusions and Future Work

In the last years, mobile applications have grown exponentially in all kinds of areas worldwide. These applications are part of the everyday life. This study represents the first systematic mapping that encompasses the portability methodology of legacy web applications to mobile devices during the last decade, selecting 44 papers according to their relevance to the topic. The main result shows that researches are required in order to: (i) have rich interfaces and not just get reformats with basic results; (ii) deepen the creation of tools that apply visualization strategies; (iii) get more use of hardware and intrinsic resources such as camera, geolocation, tactile and non-tactile commands, voice recognition, voice-to-text, mobility, haptic interfaces, holograms with adaptations that improve usability and access.

On the other hand, there is no evidence of any study on methodologies for the portability or migration of applications developed in licensed tools. The management of reports is not studied either, except in the case of visualization strategies of mobile cartography. Instructions must be created to standardize some topics related to the type of letter and other visualization aspects. It is also necessary to strengthen the security of mobile applications that manage core business with sensitive data. It was not observed the use of sensitive analysis tools or the adaptability of business workflows to mobile workflows or Markov models [62]. Finally, there are the need to create emergent protocols that can achieve connectivity without the Internet, that is, sustainable, ecological and progressive applications. In addition, there is a future planning to make a revision systematic of the literature to can describe plus deep each study with his efforts and gaps. To end, it is recommended to follow up the works that leave guidelines or conceptual frameworks to determine if already they were actually used or are pending implementation.

References

1. Díaz, F.J., Osorio, M.A., Amadeo, A.P.: Pasos necesarios para convertir una aplicación Web en una aplicación Web 2.0. In: XII Work. Investig. en Ciencias la Comput., no. 1900, pp. 541–546 (2010)
2. Shelly, G.B., Campbell, J.T.: Microsoft Expression Web 3: Comprehensive. Cengage Learning Inc., Boston (2010)
3. Shankar, V., Venkatesh, A., Hofacker, C., Naik, P.: Mobile marketing in the retailing environment: current insights and future research avenues. J. Interact. Mark. 24(2), 111–120 (2010)
4. González Romo, Z., Contreras Espinosa, R.: Apps como una posibilidad más de comunicación entre la marca y su público: un análisis basado en la valoración de los usuarios. Pensar la Publicidad Rev. Int. Investig. Public. 6(1), 81–100 (2012)
5. Sanaei, Z., Abolfazli, S., Gani, A., Buyya, R.: Heterogeneity in mobile cloud computing: taxonomy and open challenges. IEEE Commun. Surv. Tutorials 16(1), 369–392 (2014)

6. Bianco, P.: Desarrollo de Aplicaciones Basadas en XML Web Services para Dispositivos Móviles con Microsoft .NET Compact Framework, pp. 1–81 (2005)
7. O'Reilly, T.: What is web 2.0?: design patterns and business models for the next generation of software, no. 65, pp. 17–37 (2005)
8. Urbieta, M., Escalona, M., Luna, M., Rossi, G.: Detecting Conflicts and Inconsistencies in Web Application Requirements (2012)
9. Kitchenham, B., Pearl Brereton, O., Budgen, D., Turner, M., Bailey, J., Linkman, S.: Systematic literature reviews in software engineering - a systematic literature review. Inf. Softw. Technol. 51(1), 7–15 (2009)
10. Vázquez, C., et al: Comunicando Comunidades: Redes Informáticas y el Partido de La Matanza. Universidad Nacional de La Matanza (2008)
11. Petersen, K., Feldt, R., Mujtaba, S., Mattsson, M.: Systematic mapping studies in software engineering. In: EASE 2008 Proceedings of 12th International Conference on Evaluation and Assessment in Software Engineering, pp. 68–77 (2008)
12. Kitchenham, B., Charters, S.: Guidelines for performing Systematic Literature reviews in Software Engineering Version 2.3. Engineering 45(4ve), 1051 (2007)
13. Brereton, P., Kitchenham, B.A., Budgen, D., Turner, M., Khalil, M.: Lessons from applying the systematic literature review process within the software engineering domain. J. Syst. Softw. 80(4), 571–583 (2007)
14. Wieringa, R., Maiden, N., Mead, N., Rolland, C.: Requirements engineering paper classification and evaluation criteria: a proposal and a discussion. Requir. Eng. 11(1), 102–107 (2006)
15. Kosar, T., Bohra, S., Mernik, M.: Domain-specific languages: a systematic mapping study. Inf. Softw. Technol. 71, 77–91 (2016)
16. Mohammadi, E., Thelwall, M., Kousha, K.: Can Mendeley Bookmarks Reflect Readership ? A Survey of User Literature review Changes in scholarly reading habits in the digital era (2014)
17. Lehtonen, T., et al.: Towards user-friendly mobile browsing. In: Proceeding AAA-IDEA 2006 Proceedings of the 2nd International Workshop on Advanced Architectures and Algorithms for Internet Delivery and Applications Article No. 6 (2006)
18. Di Santo, G., Zimeo, E.: Reversing GUIs to XIML descriptions for the adaptation to heterogeneous devices. In: Proceeding SAC 2007 Proceedings of the 2007 ACM Symposium on Applied Computing, pp. 1456–1460 (2007)
19. Cheng, M.C., Yuan, S.M.: An adaptive and unified mobile application development framework for java. J. Inf. Sci. Eng. 23(5), 1391–1405 (2007)
20. He, J., Gao, T., Hao, W., Yen, I.-L., Bastani, F.: A flexible content adaptation system using a rule-based approach. IEEE Trans. Knowl. Data Eng. 19(1), 127–140 (2007)
21. Ennai, A., Bose, S.: MobileSOA: a service oriented web 2.0 framework for context-aware, lightweight and flexible mobile applications. In: Proceedings - IEEE International Enterprise Distributed Object Computing Workshop, EDOC (2008)
22. Ahmadi, H., Kong, J.: Efficient web browsing on small screens. In: Proceeding AVI 2008 Proceedings of the Working Conference on Advanced Visual Interfaces, pp. 23–30 (2008)
23. Kopf, S., Guthier, B., Lemelson, H., Effelsberg, W.: Adaptation of web pages and images for mobile applications. In: Proceedings, Multimedia on Mobile Devices 2009, vol. 7256, p. 72560C (2009)
24. Mey Eap, T., Gaševiü, D., Lin, F.: Personalised mobile learning content delivery: a learner centric approach. Int. J. Mob. Learn. Organ. 3(1), 84–101 (2009)
25. Iñesta, L., Aquino, N., Sánchez, J.: Framework and authoring tool for an extension of the UIML language. Adv. Eng. Softw. 40(12), 1287–1296 (2009)

26. Yunpeng, X., Yang, T., Qian, L.: Mashup-based web page adaptation for small screen mobile device. In: Proceedings - 5th International Conference on Wireless Communications, Networking and Mobile Computing, WiCOM 2009 (2009)

27. Paterno, F., Santoro, C., Spano, L.D.: MARIA: a universal, declarative, multiple abstraction-level language for service-oriented applications in ubiquitous environments. Comput. Interact. **16**, 19 (2009)

28. Ueyama, J., et al.: Exploiting a generic approach for constructing mobile device applications. In: Proceeding COMSWARE 2009 Proceedings of the Fourth International ICST Conference on COMmunication System softWAre and middlewaRE Article No. 12 (2009)

29. Goos, G., et al.: Desktop-to-mobile web adaptation through customizable two-dimensional semantic redesign. In: International Conference on Human-Centred Software Engineering HCSE 2010: Human-Centred Software Engineering, pp. 79–94 (2010)

30. Armenise, R., Birtolo, C., Troiano, L.: A tool for automatic adaptation of web pages to different screen size. In: ICEIS 2010 - Proceedings of the 12th International Conference on Enterprise Information Systems, vol. 5, pp. 91–98. HCI (2010)

31. Chmielewski, J., Walczak, K., Wiza, W.: Mobile interfaces for building control surveyors. In: Cellary, W., Estevez, E. (eds.) I3E 2010. IFIP AICT, vol. 341, pp. 29–39. Springer, Heidelberg (2010). https://doi.org/10.1007/978-3-642-16283-1_7

32. Guirguis, S.K., Hassan, M.A.: A Smart framework for web content and resources adaptation in mobile devices. In: 2010 The 12th International Conference on Advanced Communication Technology (ICACT) (2009)

33. Li, Q.-C., Zhang, Z.-Y., Ma, J., Zhang, J.: Web page layout adaptation based on webkit for e-paper device. In: 2011 14th IEEE International Conference on Computational Science and Engineering (2011)

34. Goos, G., et al.: M.Site: efficient content adaptation for mobile devices - Middleware 2012. In: Proceeding Middleware 2012 Proceedings of the 13th International Middleware Conference, pp. 41–60 (2012)

35. Macbeth, M, Wong, R.K.: A middleware service for image adjustment and filtering for small screens. In: Proceedings - 2012 IEEE 9th International Conference on Services Computing, SCC 2012 (2012)

36. Rajkumar, K., Kalaivani, V.: Dynamic web page segmentation based on detecting reappearance and layout of tag patterns for small screen devices. In: International Conference on Recent Trends in Information Technology, ICRTIT 2012 (2012)

37. Challiol, C., Firmenich, S., Bosetti, G.A., Gordillo, S.E., Rossi, G.: Crowdsourcing mobile web applications. In: International Conference on Web Engineering ICWE 2013: Current Trends in Web Engineering pp. 223–237 (2013)

38. Shaari, N., Charters, S., Churcher, C.: International Journal of Web Information Systems Achieving ' One-Web ' through customization and prioritization. J. Web Inf. Syst. **9**(3), 279–316 (2013)

39. Amendola, F., Favre, L.: Adapting CRM systems for mobile platforms: an MDA perspective. In: SNPD 2013 - 14th ACIS International Conference on Software Engineering, Artificial Intelligence, Networking and Parallel/Distributed Computing (2013)

40. Chen, F., Ma, X., Ni, S.: Organization and correction of spatial data in mobile GIS. J. Networks **8**(7), 1514 (2013)

41. Albasir, A., Naik, K., Abdunabi, T.: Smart mobile web browsing. In: 2013 International Joint Conference on Awareness Science and Technology & Ubi-Media Computing (iCAST 2013 & UMEDIA 2013) (2013)

42. Ma, Y., Fang, Y., Zhu, X., Liu, X., Huang, G.: MobiTran: tool support for refactoring PC websites to smart phones. In: Proceeding MiddlewareDPT 2013 Proceedings Demo & Poster Track of ACM/IFIP/USENIX International Middleware Conference Article No. 6 (2013)

43. Pandey, S.: Responsive design for transaction banking -a responsible approach. In: Proceeding APCHI 2013 Proceedings of the 11th Asia Pacific Conference on Computer Human Interaction, pp. 291–295 (2013)
44. Coondu, S., Chattopadhyay, S., Chattopadhyay, M., Chowdhury, S.R.: Mobile-enabled content adaptation system for e-learning websites using segmentation algorithm. In: SKIMA 2014 - 8th International Conference on Software, Knowledge, Information Management and Applications (2014)
45. Toile, H.: Adaptation of composite E-Learning contents for reusable in smartphone based learning system. In: 2014 International Conference on Advanced Computer Science and Information System (2014)
46. Badam, S.K., Elmqvist, N.: Polychrome: a cross-device framework for collaborative web visualization. In: ITS 2014 – Proceedings of 2014 ACM International Conference on Interactive Tabletops Surfaces, pp. 109–118 (2014)
47. Yang, J., Wigdor, D.: Panelrama: enabling easy specification of cross-device web applications. In: Proceedings of the 32nd Annual ACM Conference on Human Factors in Computing Systems - CHI 2014, pp. 2783–2792 (2014)
48. Kovachev, D., Renzel, D., Nicolaescu, P., Koren, I., Klamma, R.: DireWolf: a framework for widget-based distributed user interfaces. J. Web Eng. 13(3–4), 203–222 (2014)
49. Xiang, P., Yang, X., Shi, Y.: Effective page segmentation combining pattern analysis and visual separators for browsing on small screens. In: Proceedings - 2006 IEEE/WIC/ACM International Conference on Web Intelligence (WI 2006 Main Conference Proceedings), WI 2006 (2007)
50. Yin, J., Tan, G., Bai, X.L., Hu, S.M.: WebC: toward a portable framework for deploying legacy code in web browsers. Sci. China Inf. Sci. 58(7), 1–15 (2015)
51. Tseng, T.-L., Hung, S.-H., Tu, C.-H.: Migratom.js: a JavaScript migration framework for distributed web computing and mobile devices. In: Proceeding SAC 2015 Proceedings of the 30th Annual ACM Symposium on Applied Computing, pp. 798–801 (2015)
52. Sarkis, M., Concolato, C., Dufourd, J.-C.: MSoS: a multi-screen-oriented web page segmentation approach. In: Proceeding DocEng 2015 Proceedings of the 2015 ACM Symposium on Document Engineering, pp. 85–88 (2015)
53. Wang, S., et al.: Towards web application mobilization via efficient web control extraction. In: Proceeding Internetware 2015 Proceedings of the 7th Asia-Pacific Symposium on Internetware, pp. 21–29 (2015)
54. Bouzit, S., Chêne, D., Calvary, G.: Evanescent adaptation on small screens. In: Proceeding OzCHI '15 Proceedings of the Annual Meeting of the Australian Special Interest Group for Computer Human Interaction pp. 62–68 (2015)
55. Miján, J.L., Garrigós, I., Firmenich, S.: Supporting personalization in legacy web sites through client-side adaptation. In: Bozzon, A., Cudre-Maroux, P., Pautasso, C. (eds.) ICWE 2016. LNCS, vol. 9671, pp. 588–592. Springer, Cham (2016). https://doi.org/10.1007/978-3-319-38791-8_54
56. Favre, L., Pereria, C., Martinez, L., Pereira, C.: Modernizing software in science and engineering: from C/C++ applications to mobile platforms. In: Papadrakakis, M., Papadopoulos, V., Stefanou, G., Plevris, V. (eds.) ECCOMAS Congress 2016 VII European Congress on Computational Methods in Applied Sciences and Engineering Crete Island, Greece, pp. 5–10 (2016)
57. Huang, G., Liu, X., Lu, X., Ma, Y., Zhang, Y., Xiong, Y.: Programming Situational Mobile Web Applications with Cloud-Mobile Convergence: An Internetware-Oriented Approach (2015)

58. Li, H., Hu, M., Du, X., Zhu, X.: Extracting main content of webpage to enhance adaptively rendering for small screen size terminals. In: Proceedings - 2015 International Conference of Educational Innovation Through Technology, EITT 2015 (2016)
59. Bosetti, G.A., Firmenich, S., Gordillo, S.E., Rossi, G., Houben, G.-J., Bielikova, M.: An approach for building mobile web applications through web augmentation. J. Web Eng. 16 (2), 75–102 (2017)
60. Sarkis, M., Concolato, C., J.C. Dufourd, "A multi-screen refactoring system for video-centric web applications," Multimed. Tools Appl., pp. 1–28, 2017
61. Chen, L., Babar, M.A., Zhang, H.: Towards evidence-based understanding of electronic data sources. In: EASE 2010 Proceedings of 14th International Conference Evaluation & Assessment in Software Engineering, pp. 135–138 (2010)
62. Kleine Deters, J., Rybarczyk, Y.: Hidden Markov Model approach for the assessment of tele-rehabilitation exercises. Int. J. Artif. Intell. 16(1), 1–19 (2018)

Design of an Augmented Reality Serious Game for Children with Dyscalculia: A Case Study

Diego Fernando Avila-Pesantez[1,2(✉)] (iD),
Leticia Azucena Vaca-Cardenas[2] (iD), Rosa Delgadillo Avila[1] (iD),
Nelly Padilla Padilla[2] (iD), and Luis A. Rivera[3] (iD)

[1] National University of San Marcos, Lima, Peru
davila@espoch.edu.ec
[2] Polytechnic University of Chimborazo, Riobamba, Ecuador
[3] State University of North Fluminense, Rio de Janeiro, Brazil

Abstract. Numeracy skills are essential in the modern world. However, many children experience difficulties in learning mathematics. This disorder is known as Dyscalculia, and it has a negative impact on the children affected by it. The students might find difficult to work with numbers, mental calculations and mathematical functions and symbols. From this context, several studies agree using Serious Games as an assistive mechanism in therapies can improve the students' motivation, motor skills, and mathematical abilities. This article presents the design and a prototype of the Augmented Reality Serious Game named ATHYNOS for children with Dyscalculia. In the case study, forty children aged between 7–9 years with difficulties in learning mathematics from private and public primary schools, completed 4 weeks of computer game training for 15 min per day, twice a week. Results shown that children took significantly advantage from the training regarding basic numeracy, sequential order and mathematical reasoning, this game allows flexible adaptation to children's learning.

Keywords: Serious games design · ATHYNOS · Dyscalculia
Augmented Reality Serious Game

1 Introduction

Some of the most common learning disabilities that interfere with children's academic performance are Dyscalculia, Dyslexia, Dysgraphia, Attention Deficit Hyperactivity Disorder (ADHD), Language Processing Disorder, Dyspraxia and Executive Functioning [1, 2]. Regarding this specific work, Dyscalculia disorder was analyzed due to the negative affectations it has in learning or comprehending arithmetic of scholar age. Dyscalculia means a "disorder in the calculation." It is used to describe specific difficulties in learning mathematics [3]. Dyscalculia was first recognized in 2001 by the UK Department for Educational and Science and defined as: "A condition that affects the ability to acquire arithmetical skills. Dyscalculic learners may have difficulty understanding simple number concepts, lack an intuitive grasp of numbers, and have problems learning numbers facts and procedures..." [4]. Mainly, students diagnosed

M. Botto-Tobar et al. (Eds.): CITT 2018, CCIS 895, pp. 165–175, 2019.
https://doi.org/10.1007/978-3-030-05532-5_12

with Dyscalculia have difficulties with numeracy which can be an acquired condition as a result of brain damage or a developmental cognitive disorder [5].

Some indicators for this disability include a slow processing speed when engaged in math activities, trouble with sequencing order. Also, an inability to manage time in daily life, a tendency not to notice patterns, mathematical reasoning issues, difficulty in transferring knowledge, visual, spatial and perceptual difficulties, among others [6–8]. The most recent statistics suggest that about 5–7% of the school-aged population will face issues when solving Math problems [9]. In this sense, computer and emerging technologies may facilitate the process of mathematical exploration in dyscalculic learners. Several researchers have demonstrated the advantages of using game-based interventions, since children obtained improvement in basic facts such as adding, sub-tracting, multiplying, dividing; and grasping and remembering math concepts [10–13].

Consequently, Serious Games (SG) have been largely used in the development of therapies for different disabilities. SG focuses on computer games that are often designed with educational purposes [14]. Several benefits of SG have been reported, through improvements and efficacy on students, increasing their positive attitudes, motivation, self-perception, and their problem-solving approaches [15]. These SGs are the new trend in teaching and learning tools nowadays [16, 17] that are attractive to current students (digital native). Additionally, a challenging concern for SG is expanding innovations through technology-enhanced learning approaches such as Augmented Reality (AR).

AR is an emerging technology that adds extra virtual information on top of the perception of the real world, in real-time [18]. Importantly, this technology encourages its users to face new experiences; offering timely feedback, which is provided accordingly to each of the individual needs [19]. These emergent technologies together are evidencing more significant advantages in the teaching-training process. Therefore, the main motivation of this work is to design an Augmented Reality Serious Game (ARSG) to be used purposely to help children diagnosed with Dyscalculia based on educational and neuropsychological interventions. The execution of this work is mainly addressed to enhance the assimilation of arithmetic concepts using experimentation based on physical movements (using an interface), by means of working with virtual elements in real scholar settings. Consequently, the study aims to compare the results gathered after a training process with the experimental and control groups (the former using an ARSG prototype called ATHYNOS and the latter using traditional therapies). The Kinect sensor was used since it allows to have a natural user interface using 3D virtual environments.

The first section of this paper introduced in advance some aspects related to general information about Dyscalculia, Serious Games and Augmented Reality. The second section presents the ARSG development process. The third section delineates the research methodology. Finally, the paper describes the conclusion of the case study.

2   ATHYNOS Design Process

This research work was carried out in four phases (analysis, design, development, and evaluation) based on the software lifecycle [20] as shown in Fig. 1. The analysis phase includes the gather of the requirements and information about how the performance of children affected by Dyscalculia can be improved, to define the goals of the game, the analysis of pedagogical and therapeutic aspects, learning activities and gameplay factors [21, 22]. All of this using a child-centered approach that allowed us to identify the different elements to develop of the SG.

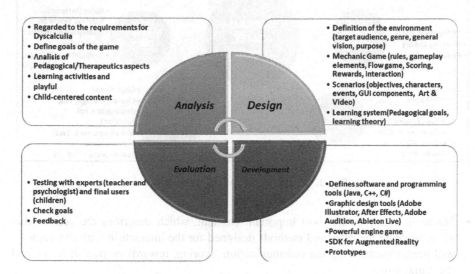

Fig. 1. Four phases of development ATHYNOS game.

Additionally, some aspects presented by [23, 24], were taken into account as significant when being used in therapeutic interventions, they help to boost the mathematical learning effectiveness in children with Dyscalculia. In this sense, the main factors considered for the present study were:

- The application of computer-based activities which allow participants to practice math facts, at the time they provide immediate feedback.
- Personal attempts are more effective.
- Repetition is necessary throughout interventions. It will help to enhance the learning process.
- The learning content must be segmented.

In the design phase, as it regards to the literature reviewed [25–30] SG are constituted by components that include Environment, Mechanic game, Scenarios, Game objects, learning system and Technical Spec that reflect the analysis specifications (see Fig. 2).

- *Environment* is a worldgame (physical or virtual) part of a ludic context; this promotes an emotional appeal which in the short term, ends up in attracting student's attention. The goal of the game must be clear to the player; thus, it is necessary to define the target audience, genre (racing simulation, puzzle, role-playing game, adventure, flight simulation among others) and level design.

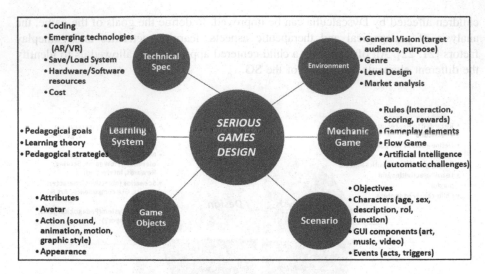

Fig. 2. Main components of game design.

- *Mechanic Game* is the most important element, which describes the actions that allow building the rules and methods designed for the interaction with the game. It will permit establishing the communication, scoring, rewards or punishments, and the game flow.
- *Scenario* is a description of a setting which requires the game player to overcome some challenges to achieve the defined goals [31]. It describes in detail the characters (age, sex, description, and function), which is essential in order to identify the sequential space of the game progress. Also, the GUI components (art, animations, music & video) ought to be established, and events like acts and triggers that invoke a transition.
- *Game objects* are virtual things included in the worldgame. They allow having a combination of skills such as decision making, moving, acting inside the game. They have a set of features (an appearance, duties, functions) and are able to create actions that describe the aesthetic representation of it [31].
- *Learning System* is the educational component. It is a fundamental pillar for the creation of SG as long as it concerns the construction of knowledge. Two essential elements are considered: *educational objectives*, and *pedagogical strategies*. Educational objectives are defined through the learning theories, related to the acquisition of intellectual or motor skills (reasoning operations, motor coordination, rapidity of reflexes and balance, oral expression, enhancing attention, concentration, memory capacity, time management to accomplish tasks, autonomy, critical thinking). This setting encourages the players to have an active role in their learning. On the other hand, the pedagogical strategies are diverse and can be deduced from the learning theories (constructivist, cognitivist, behavioral), the combination of them would build an appropriate instructional environment for the game.

- *Technical Spec* is the component where the planning is described from a technical perspective. Here, some questions will arise: Is there any new technology interested in developing the game? For instance, Augmented or Virtual Reality (AR/VR). What kind of specifications does the game engine need? What will the technologic cost be? Additionally, it describes the development platform, as well as any software tools and hardware required for the development of the game. It is necessary to specify if the game involves the use of the web, local area or wireless networks [26].

Additionally, this phase remarks how the educational objectives and the challenges of the game are related, which are developed implicitly [32].

In the development stage, the tools and software resources needed to develop the SG are detailed. The prototype was implemented in the Microsoft Windows platform. For the gaming engine, Unity 3D was chosen. It was combined with the C # high-level programming language. Plenty of tools were used for the graphic design (Adobe Illustrator, Adobe After Effects, Adobe Premiere Pro, Ableton Live, and Adobe Audition). The Software Development Kit (SDK) Vuforia was implemented for using the Augmented Reality application, this enables other devices to consolidate the game´s interfaces. All these tools were carefully handled, not to mention the best programming approach.

There are two roles (the end user and the expert) which complement the SG evaluation phase. They combine the different aspects developed in the previous steps. In this stage, goal validation, testing techniques, and feedback will be proved [33].

2.1 ATHYNOS Gameplay

A flowchart is one potential way to present the gameplay. This graphic organizer highlights all the different paths through the game's components a player would take and interact with (see Fig. 3).

ATHYNOS runs in windows platform using a Kinect sensor 2.0, which acts as a natural user interface for player and cards that integrate AR tags. At the beginning, the therapist explains to children the procedure to play ATHYNOS. After that, each player must log in to access the game by choosing an avatar and write his/her name. Then, the main menu is displayed. In ATHYNOS, the scenarios (Missing Character, Shape and Match) switch accordingly to the therapy game as shown in Fig. 4. Each one has three difficulty levels (beginner, intermediate, and advanced) which change depending on each player's skills and capabilities.

The player will have three card options displayed to choose from. Each of them is associated with a different scene through the AR tag. This tag loads the view of the game that can be operations of basic numeracy, geometric figures, sequential order and mathematical reasoning. The goal in *Match game,* for example, is corresponding the object on the left side with the right side of the machine located in the middle of the screen correctly. Inside the game, a database saves the number of achievements and failures occurred during the play mode and time records. In the end, the player and the therapist can see the results on the screen (see Fig. 5).

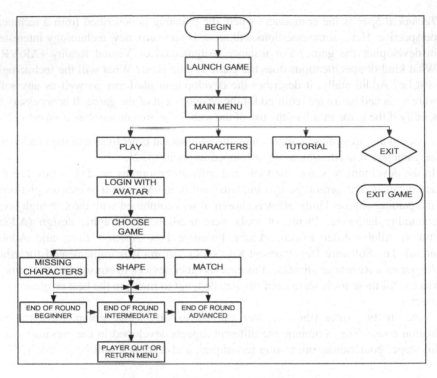

Fig. 3. ATHYNOS gameplay flowchart

Fig. 4. Screenshot of scenarios in ATHYNOS.

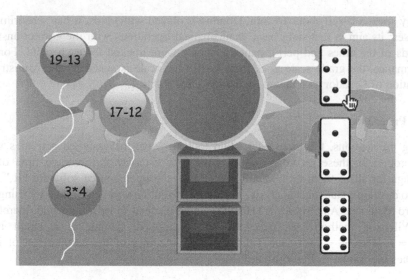

Fig. 5. Screenshot of mathematical reasoning scene.

3 Research Methodology

3.1 Participants

The group chosen for this study was made up by 18 boys and 22 girls, (M = 45%; F = 55%) of ages within 7–9 years; the average age was 7.95 years old (SD = 0.81). To prevent probable slant, the universe was separated randomly into two groups (20 children in each). These children are students from private and public primary schools from Riobamba City - Ecuador. The principals of the educational centers required a written permission from the children's parents before their participation in this research. For comparison purposes, two groups were set off; one was defined as Control Group (CG) which worked under a traditional therapy method using a domino game, and the other group was called Experimentation Group [31], which used ATHYNOS ARSG. Teachers and therapists were part of the research group. They conducted and applied intervention sessions, using Domino traditional method and ATHYNOS game. Children attended 2 weekly meetings during a month. Children participated randomly; each

Table 1. Education Ministry of Ecuador's Grades Scale

Quantitative	Qualitative meaning
10	Exceeds the learning
9	Master the learnings
7–8	Achieves the required learning
5–6	Is close to reaching the learning
≤ 4	Does not reach the necessary learning

Source: Art. 193. Scale for the application of the student assessment [34].

therapy session lasted about 15 min. Domino is played with cards. It has sensorimotor purposes; its aim is matching basic mathematical operations with the correct answer. Records of the times and performance accuracy were tracked for each child. For the performance, the grade scale goes from 1–10 (this scale is stated by the Ministry of Education of Ecuador as national regulation). See Table 1.

3.2   Procedure

During the sessions, the times each child took to solve the assigned activities were registered; with these records, it was possible to estimate the average time of all meetings for all of them individually. After that, the open source software "R." was used to develop a statistical analysis. The data distribution was determined by using the Shapiro-Wilk test. As a result, ATHYNOS game resulted to be not normal; therefore, the Wilcoxon method was necessary to be applied, having as a result a p-value = 6.748e−08 < 0.05 (See Table 2). The outcomes of the comparison of both therapies are shown in Fig. 6(a) and (b).

Table 2. Time statistic summary (Minutes)

Method	Min.	1st Qu.	Median	Mean	3rd Qu.	Max.
Traditional Domino	3.520	3.688	3.830	3.790	3.902	3.980
ATHYNOS	2.005	2.294	2.585	2.575	2.926	3.005

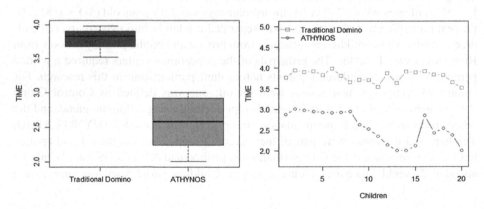

Fig. 6. (a) Boxplot of time distributions results in both method. (b) Exploratory analysis of Time.

Every right answer and failure was assigned with a grade to each child. This information was used to calculate the average score for every participant, this data in this study is called performance. Similarly, when using the Shapiro-Wilk test, ATHYNOS game was determined as not normal in its data distribution. Then, once more the Wilcoxon method was used, obtaining a p-value = 3.337e−05 < 0.5 (See Table 3). Comparative charts of performance results are presented in Fig. 7(a) and (b).

Table 3. Statistic summary of performance (Grades scale)

Method	Min.	1st Qu.	Median	Mean	3rd Qu.	Max.
Traditional Domino	6.225	6.495	7.000	6.984	7.406	7.850
ATHYNOS	7.225	7.475	8.113	8.064	8.495	9.000

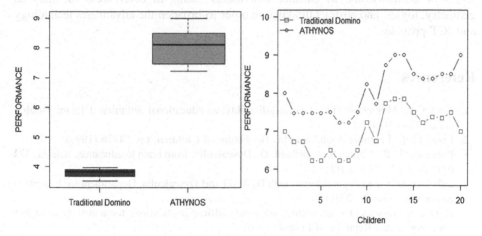

Fig. 7. (a) Boxplot of performance distributions. (b) Comparative analysis of performance between both groups.

3.3 Results

The results of the charts displayed above and the descriptive analysis of data confirmed that children take less time developing the assigned activities when working with the ATHYNOS method. The evidence shows that working with the Domino Traditional method increases the activities' execution time significantly. A clear improvement in the mathematical reasoning was evidenced in the experimental group through the analysis of their performance. The variability of the times resulted homogeneous for the experimental and the control group, which demonstrates that participants have similar skills when using either the Traditional Domino or ATHYNOS methods.

4 Conclusions

Serious Games have demonstrated to be a useful tool in the treatment and prevention of learning disabilities in children with Dyscalculia. In this case study, Serious Games and Augmented Reality were integrated by using the Kinect sensor as a natural interface user in different scenarios designed to motivate the emotional competencies of the participants of this research work. Evaluation of the learning through ATHYNOS games showed significant training effects in basic mathematical operation and sequential order. This game was well adapted to the needs of the participants. It promotes a spontaneous interaction of the children involved and encourages them to be permanently interested in mathematical problem-solving activities. A significant response and the time reduction during the therapeutic sessions helped to prove this theory. Children's interest and motivation also increased which was observed by the therapists during the experimentation. Moreover, the feedback from teachers and therapists was positive.

In the future, ATHYNOS must develop more scenarios to work with different levels of difficulty and so enhance individuals' skills in other areas of study as geometry, logics, and abstract thinking, in order to broaden the advantages technology and ICT provide.

References

1. Kass, C.E., Myklebust, H.R.: Learning disability: an educational definition. J. Learn. Disabil. **2**(7), 377–379 (1969)
2. Lyon, G.R.: Learning disabilities. In: The Future of Children, pp. 54–76 (1996)
3. Butterworth, B., Varma, S., Laurillard, D.: Dyscalculia: from brain to education. Science **332** (6033), 1049–1053 (2011)
4. DfES: Guidance to Support Pupils with Dyslexia and Dyscalculia. Department for Education and Skills, London (2001)
5. Doyle, A.: Dyscalculia and mathematical difficulties: implications for transition to higher education in the Republic of Ireland (2010)
6. Bird, R.: The Dyscalculia Toolkit: Supporting Learning Difficulties in Maths. Sage, London (2017)
7. Chodura, S., Kuhn, J.-T., Holling, H.: Interventions for children with mathematical difficulties: a meta-analysis. Zeitschrift für Psychologie **223**(2), 129 (2015)
8. Landerl, K.: Development of numerical processing in children with typical and dyscalculic arithmetic skills—a longitudinal study. Front. Psychol. **4**, 459 (2013)
9. Berch, D.B., Mazzocco, M.M.: Why is math so hard for some children? In: The Nature and Origins of Mathematical Learning Difficulties and Disabilities. Paul H Brookes Publishing (2007)
10. Cezarotto, M.A., Battaiola, A.L.: Contribuições do aprendizado multimídia para jogos com foco nas dificuldades da matemática (2017)
11. de Castro, M.V., Bissaco, M.A.S., Panccioni, B.M., Rodrigues, S.C.M., Domingues, A.M.: Effect of a virtual environment on the development of mathematical skills in children with dyscalculia. PLoS ONE **9**(7), e103354 (2014)
12. Göbel, S.: Serious games application examples. In: Dörner, R., Göbel, S., Effelsberg, W., Wiemeyer, J. (eds.) Serious games, pp. 319–405. Springer, Cham (2016). https://doi.org/10. 1007/978-3-319-40612-1_12
13. Katmada, A., Mavridis, A., Tsiatsos, T.: Implementing a game for supporting learning in mathematics. Electron. J. e-Learn. **12**(3), 230–242 (2014)
14. Liarokapis, F., De Freitas, S.: A case study of augmented reality serious games. In: Looking Toward the Future of Technology-Enhanced Education: Ubiquitous Learning and the Digital Native, pp. 178–191 (2010)
15. Ferrer, V., Perdomo, A., Rashed-Ali, H., Fies, C., Quarles, J.: How does usability impact motivation in augmented reality serious games for education? In: Book How Does Usability Impact Motivation in Augmented Reality Serious Games for Education?, pp. 1–8. IEEE (2013)

16. Qian, M., Clark, K.R.: Game-based learning and 21st century skills: a review of recent research. Comput. Hum. Behav. **63**, 50–58 (2016)
17. Torres-Carrión, P., Sarmiento-Guerrero, C., Torres-Diaz, J.C., Barba-Guamán, L.: Educational math game for stimulation of children with dyscalculia. In: Rocha, Á., Guarda, T. (eds.) ICITS 2018. AISC, vol. 721, pp. 614–623. Springer, Cham (2018). https://doi.org/10.1007/978-3-319-73450-7_58
18. Loijens, L.W., Brohm, D., Domurath, N.: What is augmented reality? In: Augmented Reality for Food Marketers and Consumers, p. 356. Wageningen Academic Publishers, Wageningen (2017)
19. Mikoski, G.S.: The New Digital Shoreline: How Web 2.0 and Millennials are Revolutionizing Higher Education. By Roger McHaney, Stylus Publishing, Sterling, VA (2011). xix⁺ 248 p. ISBN 978-1579224608. $29.95, Teaching Theology & Religion, 2013, 16 (S1)
20. Yusof, N., Rias, R.M.: Serious game based therapeutic: towards therapeutic game design model for adolescence. In: Book Serious Game Based Therapeutic: Towards Therapeutic Game Design Model for Adolescence, pp. 40–45. IEEE (2014)
21. Boyle, E., Connolly, T.M., Hainey, T.: The role of psychology in understanding the impact of computer games. Entertain. Comput. **2**(2), 69–74 (2011)
22. Cano, S., Arteaga, J.M., Collazos, C.A., Gonzalez, C.S., Zapata, S.: Toward a methodology for serious games design for children with auditory impairments. IEEE Latin Am. Trans. **14**(5), 2511–2521 (2016)
23. Kroesbergen, E.H., Van Luit, J.E.: Mathematics interventions for children with special educational needs: a meta-analysis. Remedial Spec. Educ. **24**(2), 97–114 (2003)
24. Lee Swanson, H., Sachse-Lee, C.: A meta-analysis of single-subject-design intervention research for students with LD. J. Learn. Disabil. **33**(2), 114–136 (2000)
25. Cezarotto, M.A., Battaiola, A.L.: Game design recommendations focusing on children with developmental dyscalculia. In: Zaphiris, P., Ioannou, A. (eds.) LCT 2016. LNCS, vol. 9753, pp. 463–473. Springer, Cham (2016). https://doi.org/10.1007/978-3-319-39483-1_42
26. Fullerton, T.: Game Design Workshop: A Playcentric Approach to Creating Innovative Games. CRC Press, Boca Raton (2008)
27. Motta, R.L., Junior, J.T.: Short game design document (SGDD): Documento de game design aplicado a jogos de pequeno porte e advergames Um estudo de caso do advergame Rockergirl Bikeway. Campinas Grande: Faculdade de Ciências Sociais Aplicadas FACISA (2013)
28. Rogers, S.: Level Up! The Guide to Great Video Game Design. Wiley, Hoboken (2014)
29. Schell, J.: The Art of Game Design: A Book of Lenses. AK Peters/CRC Press, Boca Raton (2014)
30. Schuytema, P.: Design de games: uma abordagem prática. Cengage Learning, Boston (2008)
31. Tang, S., Hanneghan, M.: Game content model: an ontology for documenting serious game design. In: Book Game Content Model: An Ontology for Documenting Serious Game Design, pp. 431–436. IEEE (2011)
32. Hamari, J., Shernoff, D.J., Rowe, E., Coller, B., Asbell-Clarke, J., Edwards, T.: Challenging games help students learn: an empirical study on engagement, flow and immersion in game-based learning. Comput. Hum. Behav. **54**, 170–179 (2016)
33. Mayer, I., et al.: The research and evaluation of serious games: toward a comprehensive methodology. Br. J. Educ. Technol. **45**(3), 502–527 (2014)
34. Ortega, W.: Instructivo para la aplicación de la evaluación estudiantil. In: Book Instructivo para la aplicación de la evaluación estudiantil. Ministerio de Educación del Ecuador, Quito (2013)

Software Estimation: Benchmarking Between COCOMO II and SCOPE

Cathy Guevara-Vega[1](✉) (iD), Andrea Basantes-Andrade[2] (iD),
Joseph Guerrero-Pasquel[1], and Antonio Quiña-Mera[1] (iD)

[1] Faculty of Engineering in Applied Sciences, Universidad Técnica del Norte,
Av. 17 de Julio y José Córdoba 5-21, EC100150 Ibarra, Ecuador
{cguevara,jdguerrerop,aquina}@utn.edu.ec
[2] Faculty of Education Science and Technology, Universidad Técnica del Norte,
Av. 17 de Julio y José Córdoba 5-21, EC100150 Ibarra, Ecuador
avbasantes@utn.edu.ec

Abstract. This article presents the result of a comparative study that best determines the most useful software assessment tool applicable to software development costs. This study was applied to Systems Engineering faculty students and teachers from Técnica del Norte University as well as to IT companies' end users. This research work carried out defined quantitative parameters, reflected on aspects regarding supplies, friendly user tools, methodologies, in addition to documentation and data language contained. These features were incorporated in a survey that allowed us to analyze the opinions and preferences of the respondents. The tools selected to carry out this process were SCOPE at a private environment and COCOMO II at a free environment. The results of this research showed that the best option for a software assessment tool applied to software development costs is COCOMO II with 83.33% over 75% of SCOPE.

Keywords: COCOMO II · SCOPE · Benchmarking · Software estimate

1 Introduction

The most concurrent problem in the development of software projects is to consider the estimation of software costs empirically because it causes loss of budget, unfair competition, and the price does not reflect quality and misuse of resources. It is evident that lack of knowledge about time, cost of development, lack of training, and complex systems generates a high failure rate in the software product delivery. According to CHAOS Report (2016), only 29% of software projects are successful.

This paper presents an overview of the most representative approaches to the estimation of requirements engineering that are a problem-solving support in early stages of software companies development; therefore, a comparative analysis between COCOMOII and SCOPE was carried out with the following defined criteria: expert recognition, search level, utilization, installation, function points, code lines, adaptation and reuse, tool type, and documentation, information and language of the tool.

© Springer Nature Switzerland AG 2019
M. Botto-Tobar et al. (Eds.): CITT 2018, CCIS 895, pp. 176–190, 2019.
https://doi.org/10.1007/978-3-030-05532-5_13

The starting point for software development is the management of requirements and estimation, which describes the needs of those involved in the project; the times, costs, resources necessary to control and plan the work in the next stages of development. However, the costs estimating process in software engineering is not an easy task, but if it is important for solve problems associated with the effort and time invested (Antúnez et al. 2016); (Nassif et al. 2016).

The resources approach understood as an estimated time, money, effort, staff and others, allows carrying out the activities for the construction of products associated to the project (Seville 2014). The success or failure of a project will depend on this initial step, since it shows all the necessary resources to carry out the software development requirements (Agredo 2016; Guerrero 2016); (Maleki et al. 2014). It is necessary to know that any estimate will never be exact because it involves many variables that are part of its calculation, and the estimator may fail to determine.

Authors such as Salam et al. (2016); Baumann et al. (2016); Dapozo et al. (2015) state that, a poor estimate of effort and duration of a software project, for software companies, can cause failure to meet deadlines, incomplete product delivery and loss of competitiveness; software development companies must continuously investigate alternatives that allow them to increase reliability of requirements estimation, to reduce risks and cost overruns in the development process (Londoño et al. 2008).

There are four factors that significantly influence the estimates: complexity, size, degree of structural uncertainty (requirements, functions and related information) and the availability of historical information (projects already carried out) (Seville 2014); however, authors such as Shekhar and Kumar (2016); Villareal (2017); Monterrey (2010) affirm that it is important to start from an initial estimate that reflects the historical data, the staff experience and reliability, the technical and technological analysis of the software tools.

Currently, there are several models that allow estimating costs in software development, for this research, COCOMO II and SCOPE were selected.

Constructive Cost Model (COCOMO II) is a target cost model that allows estimating cost, effort and duration of a software product development (Castillo et al. 2015), p. 2. It is utilized for planning and execution in which it manages projects or lines of software business, through a model that provides a framework for communicating business decisions among the interested parties of a software effort (CSSE. COCOMO® II 2017). It admits contract negotiations, analysis of process improvements, tool purchases, architectural changes, manufacturing offsets, component purchase; in addition, return on investment decisions with a real estimation base (Sharma 2011). The model consists of three models: composition of applications, early design and post architecture; each model offers increasing fidelity throughout the planning of the project and the design of the process (Santanach et al. 2012). On the other hand, SCOPE is a tool that helps to manage effectively software development and supports the International Function Point Group (IFPUG), and Function Point Analysis (FPA) methodology. With the FPA methodology, it is possible to estimate, compare, and manage projects and reliably invoice software development. Traceability and the ability to quantify changes are particularly important for contract negotiations in outsourced development (Morris 1994). In the SCOPE projects, metrics that meet the International Software Benchmarking Standards Group (ISBSG) are recorded: effort, defects, size, use, experience, technology cost drivers, environment, among others, in order to perform an Industry benchmarking and will inform its metrics in any of the selected recording levels (TotalMetrics.com).

The aim of this research was to determine the best tool for estimating software development costs between COCOMO II and SCOPE, so that professionals and students of careers related to Software Engineering be supported when choosing a tool of estimation, replacing the traditional empirical estimation. In addition, a prototype computer system was developed, which was estimated with the COCOMO II tool, in order to show the difference between the empirical estimate and the use of an estimation tool.

2   Methods and Materials

Research methodology was conducted in three main steps: research design, information gathering, and analysis and development phase. See Fig. 1.

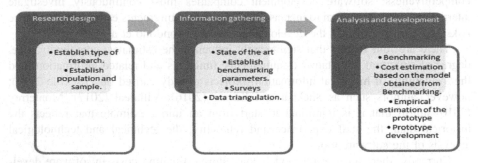

Fig. 1.   Research methodology.

2.1   Phase1 - Research Design

Investigation Type
The research involves a quantitative exploratory, documentary, and field-descriptive approach.

Population and Sample
The population or universe was formed by 12 faculty from the Computer Systems Engineering Major (CSEM), and 41 students prior to graduation from the same major at Universidad Técnica del Norte (UTN). This group of students played an important role to develop the study because of their professional training and experience gained in field-related internships. This has given them enough competence to develop different types of software projects (10 projects approximately) and empowered them to have critical thinking skills regarding complex issues, as cost estimation, for example. In addition to this, 7 professional software developers with an average experience of 5 years in the software business were considered: 2 project managers and 5 master software developers from different companies in the city of Ibarra - Ecuador.

In these terms, the universe population was ultimately conformed by 60 people, to whom a survey was applied as the means of a primary method technique in order to obtain empirical evidence. See Table 1.

Table 1. Study population.

Population	Number
Students CISIC	41
Faculty CISIC	12
Software developers	7
Total	60

2.2 Phase 2 – Information Gathering

State of the Art
The construction of the state of the art was carried out since September 2017, through virtual access to the different indexed databases (Scopus, SCimago, Ebsco and Pro-Quest) at the library in Universidad Técnica del Norte and through Google Scholar. 37 important references were identified as highly related to the topic. We sought to understand why it is better to use a cost-estimation software tool, rather than simply making empirical approximations. For this purpose, we selected two models, one as a free-type character COCOMO II and the other one as a privative-type character SCOPE, evaluated with competitive benchmarking, which allows to perform analysis based on public information about the selected tools (Llorente 2016).

Benchmarking Parameters
After establishing the state of the art, the benchmarking parameters were determined, which served to evaluate the models COCOMO II and SCOPE. See Table 2.

Table 2. Benchmarking parameters.

Parameters	Description
Offer	Tool recognition at professional level as well as among the future professional through international projection focused on web environments and search results
User friendliness	When understanding tool complexity, it is important to contemplate each installation process until the end apart from recommendations made by users that have previously used these tools
Methodologies	At this point, methodologies used by other cost assessment tools take into account the span number allowed
Type of tool	The online/offline accessibility that a tool is capable of providing was evaluated in addition to professionals' preference for the payment of tools/the acceptance of free tools
Information documentation	The process of having a clear understanding of the information and documentation submitted by the tools have was verified
Tool language	Language is considered an important factor for the understanding of user friendliness

Surveys
The survey consisted of 18 questions and it was validated by 3 experts in the area of software engineering from Universidad Técnica del Norte. They assessed relevance, relationship with the objectives, writing coherence and clarity of each of the questions. The final revised document had 13 questions, which were applied as a pilot test to 10 randomly chosen students, and thus verify its reliability and validity.

Data Triangulation
Data triangulation in the survey and the state of the art were carried out with the purpose to eliminate redundant information and, therefore, obtain a representative perspective regarding software development estimation costs. Data processing and analysis was conducted by using Microsoft Excel 2016 and SPSS statistical package for social research, and by crossing the variables, it was possible to establish the results of the investigation.

2.3   Phase 3 - Analysis and Development

Benchmarking
By using the Likert scale, also known as the added scale since the score of each unit of analysis is the result of the sum of the ranges granted to each item (García-Sánchez et al. 2011), it was possible to evaluate individual attitudes or predispositions in specific social contexts.

In the comparative analysis of the COCOMO II and SCOPE models, the benchmarking parameters established in Table 2 and the results obtained in the survey were considered to identify which among these models is the best option. Table 3 shows the first alternative of assessment which serves to identify whether the benchmarking parameters set out in Table 5 are met. Likewise, Table 4 represents the second assessment alternative that allows to transform the qualitative assessment into quantitative, as well as to establish the benchmarking results.

Table 3. First assessment alternative.

Alternative	Value
Yes	1
No	0

Table 4. Second assessment alternative.

Alternative	Value
Very good	5
Good	4
Normal	3
Bad	2
Quite bad	1

Table 5. Parameters assessment

Characteristics	COCOMO II	Likert estimate	SCOPE	Likert estimate
Function points	Yes	1	Yes	1
Code lines	Yes	1	No	0
Adaptation and reuse	Yes	1	No	0
Desk tool	Yes	1	Yes	1
Online tool	Yes	1	No	0
Free of charge	Yes	1	No	0
Official page	Yes	1	Yes	1
Video tutorials	Yes	1	Yes	1
Manual	Yes	1	Yes	1
Acknowledgement by experts	Good	4	Good	4
Degree of search	Good	4	Normal	3
Installation	Normal	3	Normal	3
Utilization degree	Normal	3	Normal	3
Documentation degree	Good	4	Good	4
Language tool	Normal	3	Quite good	5
	Total	30	Total	27

Prototype Requirements

As an initial step, 12 user stories were collected, from which 9 functional requirements were extracted. See Table 6.

Table 6. Prototype requirements.

Functional requirements
User management
Students management
Faculty management
Thesis process
Thesis student report
Comprehensive examination student report
Thesis correcting/editing students/tutor report
Opposing faculty report
Dissertation marks

Cost Estimation and Prototype Development

Once the benchmarking was done, the COCOMO II technique was applied to measure effort, time, cost and personnel involved in the development of a computer system prototype, this with the purpose of automating the CSEM – UTN "Granting-Degrees Work Monitoring" system. Functional requirements in terms of COCOMO II are presented as internal logical files, external interface files, external inputs, external outputs and external queries, with their respective Data Element Type (DET), Record Element Type (RET) and File Type Referenced (FTR). These were valued according to their complexity based on the table of ranges defined by the COCOMO II methodology. See Table 7.

Table 7. Function points and weight determination.

Internal software files	DET	RET	Complexity degree
Users	5	1	Low
Students	6	1	Low
Faculty	6	1	Low
Thesis work	3	1	Low
Thesis	11	2	Low
Comprehensive examination	7	1	Low
Correcting and editing	6	1	Low
Marks	6	1	Low
Dissertation	3	1	Low
External input	**DET**	**FTR**	**Complexity degree**
User input	7	1	Low
User update	7	1	Low
User removal	3	1	Low
Student input	7	1	Low
Student update	7	1	Low
Student removal	3	1	Low
Faculty input	7	1	Low
Faculty update	7	1	Low
Faculty removal	3	1	Low
Thesis work input	5	1	Low
Thesis work update	5	1	Low
Thesis work removal	3	1	Low
Thesis input	13	1	Low
Thesis update	13	1	Low
Thesis correcting and editing	3	1	Low
Comprehension test input	9	1	Low
Comprehension test update	9	1	Low
Removal comprehension test	3	1	Low
Correcting and editing input	8	1	Low
Correcting and editing update	8	1	Low
Correcting and editing removal	3	1	Low
Marks input	8	1	Low

(*continued*)

Table 7. (*continued*)

Internal software files	DET	RET	Complexity degree
Marks update	8	1	Low
Marks removal	3	1	Low
Dissertation input	5	1	Low
Dissertation update	5	1	Low
Dissertation removal	3	1	Low
External output	**DET**	**FTR**	**Complexity degree**
User queries	4	1	Low
Student queries	6	1	Low
Faculty queries	6	1	Low
Dissertation queries	4	1	Low
External queries	**DET**	**FTR**	**Complexity degree**
Locating thesis	7	1	Low
Locating comprehensive exams	7	1	Low
Locating thesis marks	7	1	Low
Locating thesis dissertation	6	1	Low
Locating thesis correcting and editing	8	1	Low
Locating dissertation thesis marks	8	1	Low
Locating comprehensive exams marks	7	1	Low

The next step was to calculate the unadjusted function points (AFP) based on the weight of the complexity factor. See Table 8.

Table 8. Unadjusted function points calculation.

Function points	Complexity						
	Low	Weight	Mid-level	Weight	High	Weight	Total
External input	27	X 3		X 4		X 6	81
External output	4	X 4		X 5		X 7	16
External queries	7	X 3		X 4		X 6	21
Internal software files	9	X 7		X 10		X 15	63
External interface files		X 5		X 7		X 10	0
Total (PFSA)							181

Finally, scale factors and cost drivers were established (See Tables 9 and 10), with which prototype estimation indicators were calculated. See Eqs. 1, 2, 3 and 4.

Table 9. Defined scale factors.

Defined scale factors	Detail	Rate	Value
PREC (Precedence)	Previous experience level in contrast to product to be developed	High	2.48
FLEX (Flexibility)	Demand level in compliance with pre-established requirements, time frame and interface specification	Extra high	0
RESL (Architecture and risk assessment)	Aspects related to critical risk item expertise to be tackled in the project	Low	5.65
TEAM (Team cohesion)	Difficulties of synchronization between project participants	High	2.19
PMAT (Process maturity)	Fulfillment of each area, evaluating compliance degree by the respective baselines	Nominal	4.68
Total			15

Table 10. Defined cost drivers.

Defined drivers cost	Detail	Rate	Value
RCPX	Product's reliability and complexity	High	0.83
RUSE	Required reusability	Nominal	1
PDIF	Plataform complexity	Low	0.95
PERS	Pessonnel's aptitudes	Low	0.87
PREX	Perssonnel's expertise	Low	1.12
FCIL	Facilities.	Nominal	1
SCED	Required development schedule	Low	1.1
Total effort multiplier			0.845

Equation 1. Indicator - Nominal effort calculation.

$$PM_{NOMINAL} = A * (Size)^B$$

$$A = Constant = 2.94$$

$$Size = Constant\,based\,on\,Language * PFSA$$

$$PFSA = 181$$

$$Size = 53(Java) * 181(PFSA) = 9593\,SLOC = 9.593\,KSLOC$$

$$B = Software\,Savings\,and\,Spending\,Scale\,B = 0.91 + 0.01x \sum_{j=1}^{5} SF_j$$

$$B = 0.91 + 0.01(15)$$

$$B = 1.06$$

$$PM_{NOMINAL} = 2.94x(9.593)^{1.06}$$

$$PM_{NOMINAL} = 2.94x10.99$$

$$PM_{NOMINAL} = 32.31\, Months - Per\ Person$$

Equation 2. Indicator - Adjusted Effort Estimate.

$$Abstract.PM_{AJUSTADO} = PM_{NOMINAL}x\Pi(ME_i)$$

$$PM_{AJUSTADO} = 32.31x0.845$$

$$PM_{AJUSTADO} = 27.30\, Months - Per\ person$$

Equation 3. Indicator - Development Time Estimate.

$$TDEV = \left[3.67xPM^{(0.28\,+\,0.2(B-0.91))}\right]$$

$$TDEV = \left[3.67x27.30^{(0.28\,+\,0.2(1.06-0.91))}\right]$$

$$TDEV = \left[3.67x27.30^{(0.28\,+\,0.2(1.06-0.91))}\right]$$

$$TDEV = \left[3.67x27.30^{0.31}\right]$$

$$TDEV = [3.67x2.79]$$

$$TDEV = 10.24\, Months$$

Equation 4. Indicator - Cost Estimate.

$$Cost = effort * salary$$

$$Cost = 27.30 * 375$$

$$Cost = 10237.5\, USD$$

2.4 Prototype Empirical Estimation

Empirical estimation was performed by allocating necessary periods of time to complete the tasks immersed in the functional requirements presented in Table 6. The costs were established based on their experience by the work team, consisting of a development leader and two programmers (See Table 12). Being this an empirical method, it was not possible to determine with certainty what eventualities may the developed product have.

3   Results

3.1   Survey Results

The Most Relevant Outcomes from the Survey are Presented Below

Six out of ten people say that it is necessary to use a tool of any kind to estimate costs. This is because there seems to be a projection of resources adjusted to the reality in software development processes. In terms of awareness and use of a cost estimation tool, the results are divided. 50% do not know about any, while 25% use SCOPE, 23.3% use COCOMO II and 1.7% use another type. However, 1% of people who have experience in its use, express that it is difficult to do it. More than 90% of the people surveyed believe that a tool for estimating costs would help them to optimally develop a software project, however, 69.5% say they would not pay for a license of use. Four out of ten people know about institutions that use cost estimation tools, obtaining thus better results than just using an empirical estimation. Regarding the documentation obtained through the tools under study, the results coincide with 60% of easy availability.

3.2   Benchmarking Results

Similarly, as with the results obtained in the survey, it is emphasized that the use of a tool for cost estimation is highly important. In order to determine which of the tools presented greater benefits and acceptance, aspects such as marketing or recognition for each tool were considered. The study showed that the two proposed models are good and widely known; However, the best option seemed to be COCOMO II with 83.33% over 75% for SCOPE.

There are quite a few methodologies that allow to estimate costs. From these, "Function Points" is the one with most relevance and use, and it is covered by both tools. However, the others offered by COCOMO II should also be considered to make an estimate, thus obtaining estimations by lines of code and by reusing projects that have already been carried out, providing greater ease in the use of COCOMO II tool.

The availability of a tool in its different forms, online and as a desktop application, is important because it reflects the portability it allows to have in different operating systems. An important consideration is the type of tool being used. These days, there is a greater preference for free tools with free access, being COCOMO II the one which takes the lead in this regard.

The documents, information and videos obtained from the tools, greatly facilitate its understanding and proper use. The two tools have official websites, tutorial videos and user manuals that help to learn about them. When asking the survey respondents about the relevance of the information provided, they highlight the fact that it is convenient and good for the user, nevertheless, it should be considered that the majority of this documentation is written in English. COCOMO II and SCOPE satisfy this aspect at the same level. The fact that a tool may allow to choose the language for its operation, represents a relevant feature. Not all tools allow to select another language different from the one than comes set as a default feature. SCOPE presents wide flexibility and a list of languages that make it easier to use, unlike COCOMO II, which is only managed with one language.

3.3 Prototype Estimation Results with COCOMO II and an Empirical Method

The estimation made with COCOMO II regarding the prototype shows the following results: effort required in 27.3 month-person, 10.2 months, a cost of 10,237.22 dollars and approximately a personnel of 3 people per prototype (See Fig. 2). These results were calculated based on scale factors and cost drivers specified in the materials and methods section.

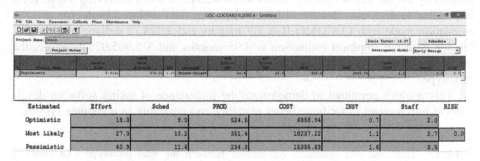

Fig. 2. Application of COCOMO II.

With respect to the empirical method, the prototype presents the following results for time and cost indicators. See Table 11.

Table 11. Time results indicator/empirical method.

Functional requirements	Estimated time (Weeks)	Equivalent to (months)
User management	1.5	0.375
Students management	1.5	0.375
Faculty management	1.5	0.375
Thesis process	5	1.25
Thesis student report	2.5	0.625
Comprehensive examination student report	2	0.5
Thesis correcting/editing students/tutor report	2	0.5
Opposing faculty report	2	0.5
Dissertation marks	3	0.75
Total	21	5.25 Months

Table 12. Indicator results/cost empirical method

Work team	N° of people	Estimated cost (Per Month)
Project leader	1	450 USD
Programmer	2	375 USD
Total	3	825 USD

Prototype overall cost estimation was obtained by multiplying estimated cost (per month) by the number of months, which was $ 4,331.25. When observing Table 13, it is possible to determine that the difference between the developed prototype and the estimation made with COCOMO II is 1.7 months and 3,224.72 dollars; and the difference with the empirical estimation is 4.95 months and $ 5,905.97; therefore, the estimation with COCOMO II showed more real values for the development of this prototype.

This analysis permitted to demonstrate the importance of taking software development into account to facilitate better planning and reliability in computer systems.

Table 13. Time and cost indicators comparison between the final prototype COCOMO II development assessment stage and the empirical estimate.

Item	Estimated time (Months)	Total cost
Developed prototype	8.50	7,012.50 USD
COCOMO II assessment	10.20	10,237.22 USD
Empirical estimate	5.25	4,331.25 USD

4   Discussion

With the global review of the results it is established as a generality, that the knowledge of cost estimating tools in the academic and business environment is limited, despite its various advantages to optimize resources in the software development process, users are not willing to pay licenses to use those tools. It is inferred that when making a comparison between tool characteristics the cost factor is very important when deciding which ones to acquire and use.

The exceptions that were presented were that public institutions, by law they must use free software in their projects, being a definitive factor to choose one of the exposed tools. Another exception showed that 5% of the survey respondents knew absolutely nothing about the subject, its benefits and limitations.

In accordance with the results of Salam et al. (2016), Gómez et al. (2015) and Sharma (2013), and the findings of this research refer to the use of the COCOMO II tool to perform the estimation of software development costs in order to increase the accuracy in the estimation.

The results show the use of a traditional process of software development, unlike the results of Góngora et al. (2013) that use models of product line development; nevertheless, the two studies carried out conclude that the use of COCOMO II is the best alternative for estimating costs. It should be noted that the competitive bench-marking conducted between COCOMO II and SCOPE is an unpublished work, which serves to demonstrate the trend of use in the research environment.

It is suggested to develop more exhaustive studies in the estimation models and that are applied in the software industry, since the percentage of institutions that do not use this type of solutions are the majority. Finally, the application of estimation models improves costs, resources, and time in the development of software projects.

5 Conclusion

Through the selection of criteria resulting from the survey aimed at people, profes-sionals in software development and the career of Computer Systems Engineering, valued with the Likert scale, the most feasible tool for estimating software development costs was COCOMO II. This was chosen as the best alternative for the estimation of an application developed in the CISIC - UTN career.

In the development of the prototype applying COCOMO II it was shown that the time and cost indicators of the prototype were estimated in a more real way, unlike the empirical estimate, which determined the importance and improvement when esti-mating the software development in the planning phase.

For the estimation to be faithful to the development of the software, it must be done in conjunction with the development methodology, considering that if at some point during the development stage, the initial requirements change or are modified, it will be necessary to make a new estimate with the new added requirements.

If the estimation of the cost, effort and development time of a software project is inaccurate, in many cases it leads to its failure; therefore, the COCOMO II model will allow software developers to make better decisions in the planning of software development projects.

Software development companies must continually investigate alternatives that allow them to increase the reliability of the requirements, to reduce risks and cost overruns in the development process (Londoño et al. 2008).

References

Antúnez, T., Valdovinos, R., Marcial, J., Ramos, M., Herrera, E.: Estimation of development costs, case study: reactor quality management system TRIGA mark III. Cuban J. Comput. Sci. 10(1), 215–228 (2016)

Nassif, A.B., Capretz, L.F., Ho, D.: Enhancing use case points estimation method using soft computing techniques. arXiv:1612.01078 (2016)

Sevilla, P.: Planning and Estimation of Software Projects (2014). http://sevillajarquin.udem.edu.ni/wp-content/uploads/2014/01/Planificacion-y-Estimacion-de-Proyectos-de-Software.pdf

Agredo, C.: Estimation of software (2016). https://www.ceiba.com.co/es/estimacion-de-software

Guerrero, L.P.C.: Management in software projects. Technol. Res. Acad. 4(2), 12–19 (2016)

Maleki, I., Ebrahimi, L., Jodati, S., Ramesh, I.: Analysis of software cost estimation using fuzzy logic. Int. J. Found. Comput. Sci. Technol. (IJFCST) 4(3), 27–41 (2014)

Salam, A., Khan, A., Baseer, S.: A comparative study for software cost estimation using COCOMO-II and Walston-Felix models. In: The 1st International Conference on Innovations in Computer Science & Software Engineering, (ICONICS 2016), 15–16 December 2016 (2016)

Baumann, F., Milutinovic, A., Roller, D.: Software engineering inspired cost estimation for process modelling. In: Conference: ICBPM 2016, At London, UK. World Academy of Science, Engineering and Technology Int. J. Econ. Manag. Eng. **10**(2), 576–586 (2016). https://waset.org/publications/10003773/

Dapozo, G., Ferraro, M., Medina, Y., Pedrozo-Petrazzini, G., Lencina, B., Irrazábal, E.: Estimation of software: methods oriented to the agile management of projects, web development and early estimation. Work presented at the XVII Workshop of Researchers in Computer Science, Salta (2015)

Londoño, L., Anaya, R., Tabares, M.: Requirement-oriented requirements analysis according to the software industry. EIA J. **9**, 43–52 (2008)

Shekhar, S., Kumar, U.: Review of various software cost estimation techniques. Int. J. Comput. Appl. (0975 – 8887) **141**(11), 31–34 (2016)

Villareal, C.: 7 common mistakes in software development projects – Northware (2017). http://www.northware.mx/7-errores-comunes-en-proyectos-de-desarrollo-de-software/

Monterrey, T.: Estimation of software (2010). ftp://sata.ruv.itesm.mx/portalesTE/Portales/Proyectos/2841_BienvenidaAdmonProy/materiales/modulo3/HP209_21feb.pdf

Castillo, C., Rodríguez, F., Gutiérrez, J., Sánchez, M.: Estimation model of the effort, time and cost of developing a management software. Off. Sci. Res. J. **6**(2) (2015)

Sharma, T.N.: Analysis of software cost estimation using COCOMO II. Int. J. Sci. Eng. Res. **2**(6), 1–5 (2011)

Santanach, A., Vargas, J.E., Ramírez, L., Prieto, D.R., Ramos, M.: Proposal of a method of estimating time and effort for the release. RCC J. **13**(1), 12–13 (2012)

Morris, P.: SCOPE Introduction (1994). http://www.totalmetrics.com/scope-project-sizing-software

Llorente, J.: Benchmarking Introduction (2016). http://gestion-calidad.com/wp-content/uploads/2016/09/Benchmarking.pdf

García-Sánchez, J., Aguilera-Terrats, J., Castillo-Rosas, A.: Technical guide for the construction of attitude scales. Odiseo Electron. J. Pedagogy **8**(16) (2011). http://www.odiseo.com.mx/2011/8-16/garcia-aguilera-castillo-guia-construccion-escalas-actitud.html

Gómez, A., López, M., Migani, S., Otazú, A.: A Software Project Estimation Model (2015). https://es.scribd.com/document/290028359/Material-2-COCOMO

Sharma, H.K.: E-COCOMO: the extended cost constructive model for cleanroom software engineering. Database Syst. J. **4**(4), 3–11 (2013)

Góngora, M., Picota, P., Clunie, C.: Cost estimate methods comparison in software product lines (SPL). RUTIC J. **1**(2), 18–19 (2013)

CSSE. COCOMO® II (2017). http://sunset.usc.edu/csse/research/cocomoii/cocomo_main.html

Tosan Bingamawa, M., Kamalrudin, M.: A Review of Software Cost Estimation: Tools, Methods, and Techniques, pp. 2–4 (2016). https://doi.org/10.13140/rg.2.2.18980.48008

Proactive Approach to Revenue Assurance in Integrated Project Management

Gilberto F. Castro[1,2] ⓘ, Anié Bermudez-Peña[3](✉) ⓘ,
Francisco G. Palacios[1] ⓘ, Fausto R. Orozco[1] ⓘ,
Diana J. Espinoza[4] ⓘ, and Inelda A. Martillo[1,2]

[1] Facultad de Ciencias Matemáticas y Físicas, Universidad de Guayaquil,
Guayaquil, Ecuador
{gilberto.castroa, francisco.palacioso, fausto.orozcol,
inelda.martilloa}@ug.edu.ec
[2] Facultad de Ingeniería, Universidad Católica Santiago de Guayaquil,
Guayaquil, Ecuador
{gilberto.castro, inelda.martilloa}@cu.ucsg.edu.ec
[3] Facultad 2, Universidad de las Ciencias Informáticas, Havana, Cuba
abp@uci.cu
[4] Facultad de Jurisprudencia, Ciencias Sociales y Políticas,
Universidad de Guayaquil, Guayaquil, Ecuador
diana.espinozavi@ug.edu.ec

Abstract. In project management organizations, it is advisable to conduct a proactive and positive management to improve the implementation of processes. Moving forward in a project without a proactive approach to risk management is likely to lead to a greater number of problems and income leaks, because of unmanaged threats. Revenue assurance allows to reduce costs and maximize the income in organizations, for them it applies statistical techniques, risk management, scope, and time. The objective of this work is to present a proactive approach for revenue assurance that is applied in Integrated Project Management. Risk management is developed with a proactive approach, based on the application of PMBOK and computing with words techniques for planning and qualitative risk assessment. For validation, the proposal is applied in a real environment, using data from concluded projects, criteria of multiple experts and soft computing techniques. A final analysis is carried out that shows the great advantages of the proposal with respect to the results obtained with the traditional PMBOK technique. The proposed method is integrating into a platform for project management that support decision-making in organizations and have many functionalities for revenue assurance.

Keywords: Revenue assurance · Integrated Project Management · Risk management

© Springer Nature Switzerland AG 2019
M. Botto-Tobar et al. (Eds.): CITT 2018, CCIS 895, pp. 191–204, 2019.
https://doi.org/10.1007/978-3-030-05532-5_14

1 Introduction

Integrated Project Management requires a harmonious development between technologies, resources and integral management systems in order to obtain competitive projects of high quality. It is not possible to direct projects using state-of-the-art technologies with modern equipment using obsolete steering systems [1].

Integrated Project Management, supported by professional computer systems, allows to carry out an execution schedule and show the progress of the project through management indicators. It allows one to manage the problems and their causes so that one can make decisions based on a previously established strategy of priorities. When carrying out a characterization of Integrated Project Management, the following aspects are identified:

- Presence of numerical and linguistic data.
- Vagueness in the concepts for decision making.
- Uncertainty and inaccuracy in the data and appreciation of people.
- Changing conditions in the execution environment of the projects.

Mismanagement of projects and inadequacies in the handling of data in the Integrated Project Management cause innumerable economic losses with high social impact.

To be successful, an organization must commit to addressing management proactively and consistently throughout the project. A conscious selection should be made at all organization levels to actively identify and procure effective management during the life of a project [2]. Project management must be supported by the use of information systems that help decision-making.

Project risks have their origin in uncertainty that is present in all projects. Known risks are those that have been identified and analyzed, which makes it possible to plan answers for them. Known risks that cannot be managed proactively must be assigned a contingency reserve. Unknown risks cannot be managed proactively; therefore, a management reserve can be assigned to them. Negative project risk that has materialized is considered a problem [3].

Project risk can exist from moment the project starts. Moving forward in a project without a proactive approach to risk management is likely to lead to a greater number of problems, as a result of unmanaged threats. According to the research carried out, the current solutions in the area of revenue assurance are based mostly on reactive approaches and do not adequately use active or proactive strategies.

In project management organizations, projects are conceived to achieve compliance with the strategic objectives of the entities that generate them and can be grouped in the form of programs to achieve a common goal. In addition, the organization by programs allows a more efficient use of the resources assigned to the projects, considering the priorities that are established for them [4].

In these types of organizations, despite efforts to improve efficiency and management efficiency, there are still many difficulties and situations that generate revenue losses [5, 6]. In project management there are several situations that have a significant impact on the success of projects and in revenue assurance [7–13]. Among the most common problems are:

- Errors in the definition of the project scope, which generally cause bad estimates in costs, affecting revenue and profits.
- Errors in the planning, control, and monitoring of projects, with respect to the partial coverage of requirements defined in the scope or because the plan is not understood by members of the organization.
- Little attention to the risks of the project, which frequently causes a slight override in project costs.
- Use of the wrong technology, in the case of information technology projects, is reflected in bad architectural decisions that generate delays, re-work and affect the profits of organizations.

As a strategy to help solve some of these problems, in this work, a proactive approach for revenue assurance is presented. As part of the novelty of the work, the proposed approach combines proactive techniques of risk management and identification of situations that generate income leaks in Integrated Project Management.

The rest of this paper is structured as follows. Section 2 provides the bases related to revenue assurance and project management standards. Section 3 presents the proactive approach for revenue assurance in Integrated Project Management. Evaluation and results are described in Sect. 4. Finally, conclusions and feature work are presented.

2 Related Works

2.1 Bases of Revenue Assurance

Revenue assurance is an interdisciplinary field that combines statistical techniques, risk management, scope, time, data analysis, among other techniques. Revenue assurance as an area of knowledge arose in the late 1970s in the telecommunications sector, as a discipline oriented to the protection and recovery of financial resources of organizations [14–16]. In this context, definitions have emerged to describe the subject matter of this discipline. Among them, Acosta says that "it consists in seeking, identifying and eliminating the technical and structural causes that give rise to the leakage of revenue directed to two dimensions: the maximization of revenue and the minimization of costs" [16].

With the development of this discipline called revenue assurance along with new spaces for specialists training and the creation of standards, emerge TM Forum [14, 15] and the Global Association of Revenue Assurance Professionals GRAPA [17, 18]. TM Forum promotes a model for evaluating the maturity of organizations in the implementation of revenue assurance processes. This maturity model has five levels: initial, repeatable, defined, managed, and optimized.

GRAPA states that among the main reasons that cause loss of revenue in telecommunications are the integration of organization processes and the adoption of standards [19]. This situation is similar in Integrated Project Management, but with the difference that costs, budgets, and planning gain relevance in these other environments. According to GRAPA, among the most used techniques in revenue assurance are: risk analysis, exchange analysis, process analysis, systems analysis, and statistical analysis.

Likewise, both GRAPA and TMForum agree on the existence of lines open to research, among which are proactivity in revenue assurance and prevention over classical techniques for recovery of income.

In general, techniques proposed for revenue assurance worldwide are still insufficient both for telecommunications companies where they arise and for Integrated Project Management. Often the implemented solutions constitute black boxes supported by proprietary tools. Full impact of the information management with these external tools is not known for sure. It has been identified that many of those problems affect the efficiency and the effectiveness of revenue assurance processes.

2.2 Project Management Standards

Integrated Project Management is instituted by institutions and standards dedicated to the formalization of methods of organization and work. These institutions include the Project Management Institute (PMI) with its PMBOK standard [3], the Software Engineering Institute (SEI) with the Capability Maturity Model Integration (CMMI) [20], the International Project Management Association (IPMA) [21] and the ISO with its standards 10006 and 21500 [22].

There is convergence in techniques and good practices for risk management focused mainly on ISO 21500 and PMBOK standards. Some of the principal techniques proposed by PMBOK and ISO 21500 for risk management, which have the greatest influence on revenue assurance, are:

- Analysis of variation, trends and reserve analysis.
- Categorization of risks and prioritization.
- Evaluation of probability and impact of risks.
- Evaluation of the quality of risk data.
- Expert judgment, SWOT analysis, checklist.
- Measurement of technical performance.
- Revaluation and risk audits.
- Strategies for negative risks or threats.
- Strategies for positive risks or opportunities.
- Strategies of response to contingencies.
- Technical diagramming: cause and effect, process flow, influence diagrams.
- Techniques of information gathering.

In this work we apply SWOT analysis proposed by PMBOK. This technique examines the project from each of the strengths, weaknesses, opportunities, and threats (SWOT) perspectives [3]. For risk identification, it is used to increase the breadth of identified risks by including internally generated risks. The technique starts with the identification of strengths and weaknesses of the organization, focusing on either the project, organization, or the business area in general. SWOT analysis then identifies any opportunities for the project that may arise from strengths, and any threats resulting from weaknesses. The analysis also examines the degree to which organizational strengths may offset threats and determines if weaknesses might hinder opportunities.

We also apply the document analysis for risk management. Risks may be identified from a structured review of project documents, including, but not limited to, plans, assumptions, constraints, previous project files, contracts, agreements, and technical documentation [3]. Uncertainty or ambiguity in project documents, as well as inconsistencies within a document or between different documents, may be indicators of risk on the project.

CMMI relates the generic and specific practices applicable to risk management [20]. However, it does not propose concrete algorithms to achieve it. It focuses on manual work and exhaustive documentation of processes, rather than on the determination of faults and errors from the data analysis.

As a strategy to solve these problems in Integrated Project Management, the authors developed research associated with the application of data mining and soft computing techniques. In [23] an active learning method is applied with the intervention of experts for outlier detection that affect revenue assurance. However, the proactive strategy remains as pending work and in this work it is given a solution.

3 Proactive Approach for Revenue Assurance

The method proposed for revenue assurance consists of three fundamental parts: organization diagnosis, managing risk with a proactive approach, and evaluating results for decision-making. Figure 1 shows the process outline to follow to apply the proactive approach for revenue assurance.

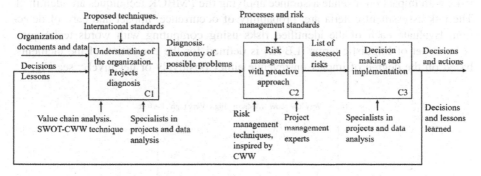

Fig. 1. Process to apply the proactive approach for revenue assurance

Following the activities in Fig. 1, the diagnosis and understanding of the processes of the organization are first made. For this, the group of experts with sufficient knowledge of the process of generating the organization values is selected.

The group of experts builds the sequence of primary and support activities, which form the value chain of the organization. Primary activities are those related to production, logistics, marketing, and after-sales services. Support activities are those that support the development of primary activities, such as administration, technological development and purchases of goods and services. For each activity, the margin is calculated, which is the difference between the total value and the total costs incurred to perform the value generating activity.

Based on the analysis of value chain, a SWOT matrix is constructed, identifying elements that influence each primary activity both in reduction of costs and in improvement of revenues and that affect the margin of each activity.

In this identification and evaluation of elements that influence the revenue of the organization, six groups are identified:

1. New services or products, generators of new revenue.
2. Sources of errors that affect the use of opportunities or that generate revenue losses.
3. Errors or possible anomalous situations that enhance threats affecting revenue.
4. Activities to mitigate or avoid threats.
5. External risks and external sources that can cause loss of revenue.
6. Activities based on strengths that help avoid or mitigate loss of revenue from threats.

These six groups allow experts to evaluate each element that influences revenue, grouped by their nature. Elements of groups 2, 3 and 5 concentrate the internal or external factors, the possible sources of errors and other anomalous situations that affect the revenue. Elements of groups 4 and 6 are recommended actions and will be used following a proactive approach in stage 2 of the proposed method. The elements of group 1 are aimed at exploiting the opportunities and will be considered following a proactive approach in stage 2 of this method.

In the second stage of the proposed method, a new technique based on computing with words [24] is introduced in the qualitative risk analysis processes. To do this, the risks with impact on revenue assurance applying the PMBOK techniques are identified. The risk assessment criteria are: probability of occurrence, impact and ease of detection. Evaluate each of the identified risks using computing with words techniques. A basic set of linguistic terms (LBTL) is defined for the evaluation of the elements, based on the degree of impact on revenue either positively or negatively, see Fig. 2.

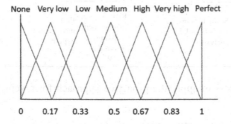

Fig. 2. Linguistic variable "Impact", used in the risks evaluation

Following the 2-tuples model of computing with words, expert evaluations are added, consolidating the same for each element to be evaluated. Upon completion, the identified risks and their impact on revenue assurance processes are taken into account.

To mitigate, avoid or enhance each element based on its impact on revenue, the experts propose a set of actions to be executed. Generally, actions of different groups can be executed in parallel.

In the last stage of the method, the results are evaluated, the impact for organization of the detected risks is estimated and a detailed analysis is carried out. When you reach this step you have two groups of situations aimed at recovering revenue:

- Set of risks that are avoided or mitigated, allowing to reduce the flight of revenue.
- Set of measures taken proactively to mitigate or eliminate risks, but which have a cost of implementation that should also be considered in revenue assurance.

There are various impact estimation techniques for a set of activities aimed at risk management and the proactive treatment of revenue assurance. To estimate the economic impact of these situations, the following techniques are proposed:

Estimation Technique. It is based on estimating three values: (1) most probable amount (M) to be recovered based on a realistic assessment of the expert, (2) amount to be recovered based on an optimistic approach (O) based on the best possible scenario, and (3) the pessimistic recovery amount (P) based on the analysis of the worst scenario for the recovery. Then we proceed to calculate the estimated value using Eq. (1).

$$ce = \frac{O + 4M + P}{6} \tag{1}$$

Ascending Estimation Technique. In this case, an estimate is made of what was recovered for each of the detected risks and this result is consolidated by adding the amounts in monetary units associated with each activity. In case it is difficult to estimate the impact of an activity, it is decomposed into lower level components for a more detailed analysis and then the estimates are consolidated respecting the built hierarchy.

Technique Based on Network Analysis. This technique is based on the construction of a network in such a way that each node represents a possible state of the organization in different situations of risks. The edges represent the possible decisions and each edge is labeled by a vector with the following characteristics [25, 26].

- The first component represents the probability of making the decision or of the occurrence of a risk.
- The second component represents one of the following elements: cost of making the decision, positive economic impact in the event of an opportunity, negative economic impact in the event of a threat.

With this structure, a set of classical techniques associated with working with networks can be applied to estimate the economic impact of different revenue assurance scenarios, among which are: Bayesian networks [27], maximum flow algorithm, Dijkstra algorithm, and Floyd algorithm [28] to determine the path with minimum cost of the organization.

For this decision-making, the use of information systems combined with expert judgment is proposed. The following recommendations must be followed:

- Involve members in the search for solutions.
- Apply information systems that allow the management by cuts and the use of objective indicators that cover the areas of knowledge.
- Prioritize in the decision-making activities of the value chain with the greatest impact on revenue and profits.

Decision-making techniques can help prioritize risk response strategies. Multi-criteria decision analysis uses a decision matrix to provide a systematic approach for establishing key decision criteria, evaluating and ranking alternatives, and selecting a preferred option [3].

The cycle between the third step and the first one, allows to continue adapting the revenue assurance method to the organization according to the maturity reached during continuous improvement. In addition, it serves to take into account the decisions made and the lessons learned in future analysis of revenue assurance of the organization.

4 Results and Discussion

For validation, methodological triangulation of methods and experts are applied in the comparison of the proposed proactive approach for risk management against the PMBOK technique. An experiment is carried out to validate the risk management proposal proactively associated with revenue losses. The traditional technique proposed in PMBOK is compared with the technique based on the 2-tuple model of computing with words.

For experimentation, a database of concluded projects was used from the repository belonging to the Project Management Research Laboratory [29]. This database has fourteen real software development projects, which are already closed and it is known how their risks behaved.

For validation, a group of six project management experts who did not participate in the selected projects was taken, whose data is reflected in Table 1.

Table 1. Characterization of experts for risks evaluation

Total experts	6
Number of Doctors	4
Number of Masters	2
Average years dedicated	18,8
Standard deviation	9,8
Minimum number of years dedicated	14
Maximum number of years dedicated	37

Eighteen of the most common risks in this scenario were taken into account, covering all areas of knowledge of project management [30, 31].

The experts were given enough information that characterizes each project to carry out the risk assessment. The experts evaluated, by consensus, each risk in each project using the method proposed by PMBOK which we will call Risks-PMBOK. The experts independently, evaluated each risk in every project using the 2-tuples model of computing with words (Risks-CWW).

The mean square error (MSE) committed in the project p (Ep) was calculated according to the two variants of evaluation methods, see Eq. (2).

$$E_p = \frac{1}{18} \sum_{i=1}^{18} (D_i - Y_i)^2 \tag{2}$$

Where D_i is what really happened in the risks, that is the desired output. Being Y_i the output given by the different evaluation methods for each risk. Finally, the mean squared errors calculated according to each method were compared for each of the projects. In the analysis of the results, it was identified that the Risk-PMBOK method obtained a total of 146 in the square errors, while in the Risk-CWW method it was 71.55. As shown graphically in Fig. 3, the best results are obtained with the Risk-CWW assessment method.

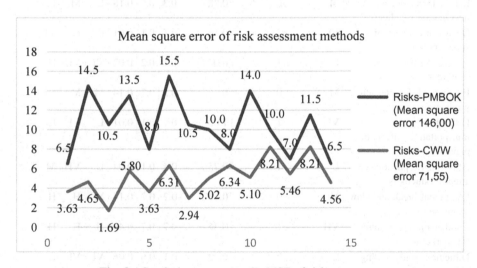

Fig. 3. Graph that represents the MSE of risk assessment

The following Table 2 shows an example of risk analysis for the evaluation of project 1 taking into account the methods Risk-PMBOK and Risk-CWW. In this table, after the list of risks, the second column exposes the value with which the risk in this project was evaluated in terms of impact. For each of these risk assessments linguistic terms are used: None (N), Very low (VL), Low (L), Medium (M), High (H), Very high (VH), and Perfect (P), that this last case was used by those experts who considered that the impact of the risk was the maximum.

Then, two comparisons of the mean square error appear. First, calculating the quadratic distance of the Risk-PMBOK method with respect to the evaluation that had the risk in the project when it occurred (expected output), whose value was 6.5 for the

Table 2. Example of risk analysis for the evaluation of a project. Where P is the probability, I the impact and D the ease of detection of the risk.

Risks	Linguistic value	Comparison of methods (MSE)		Risk-PMBOK method Experts			Risk-CWW method Expert 1			...
		6.5	3.63							
		Distance SQR PMBOK	Distance SQR CWW	P	I	Exp	P	I	D	...
Loss of human resources, conditions	M	1	1.60	0.5	0.6	0.3	H	H	H	...
Low level of HR training	L	0	0.64	0.2	0.6	0.12	L	M	M	...
Few incentives to the team, low production	H	0	0.22	0.8	0.6	0.48	H	H	VH	...
Bad team conformation	L	1	0.00	0.3	0.6	0.18	L	M	L	...
Disinterested client who does not participate in meetings	L	1	0.07	0.2	0.8	0.16	M	L	L	...
Late delivery of information by client	M	0	0.28	0.3	0.6	0.18	L	M	L	...
Delays in delivery of suppliers	VL	1	0.16	0.1	0.1	0.01	L	L	VL	...
Increase in the prices of resources	L	1	0.04	0.1	0.2	0.02	VL	VL	H	...
Energetic difficulties affect production	M	0	0.16	0.2	0.7	0.14	M	M	VL	...
Difficulties with transportation, affects the plan	VL	1	1.00	0.1	0.1	0.01	L	VL	L	...
Atmospheric phenomena affect productivity	L	1	0.75	0.4	0.1	0.04	L	VH	M	...
Equipment break and slow maintenance	M	0	0.16	0.2	0.7	0.14	M	H	H	...
Cumbersome procedures for marketing	VH	1	0.36	0.7	0.7	0.49	H	H	H	...
Difficulties with bidding requirements	L	0	0.02	0.1	0.6	0.06	VL	VL	L	...
Difficulties with the definition of architecture	VL	1	0.36	0.1	0.6	0.06	VL	VL	L	...
Lack of leadership in project leaders	L	4	0.04	0.1	0.1	0.01	L	VL	L	...
High external pressure, causes planning and execution errors	M	0	0.11	0.5	0.5	0.25	M	M	M	...
Low levels of reuse	VL	0	1.28	0.1	0.3	0.03	L	L	M	...

case of project 1. Then the same is compared, but with the proposed method (Risks-CWW), where the value of the error was 3.63, this being a better result.

As can be seen among the advantages of the proposed method is the ease for interpretability of results when expressing both expert evaluation and final results in words.

Proposed method also allows simultaneous assessment of multiple experts, and as you can see the results of the two methods are different. None of the risks evaluated with the traditional PMBOK method had high exposure despite the high probability or impact of some. In addition, the final order after the evaluation that is important for the response to the risks was also different, the proposed method being superior. The computing with word method was also more intuitive and allowed a better interpretation of results by using linguistic terms instead of numerical values.

The proposal was implemented on the GESPRO platform due to its versatility and the large number of functionalities for revenue assurance [29], among which are:

- Module for data analysis and revenue assurance, which integrates libraries in R for detection of anomalous data.
- Module for risk management, applicable for proactive analysis.
- Scorecard with indicators and early warnings, aimed at detecting shortcomings in the planning and execution of projects.
- Reach and quality management regarding the coverage of the requirements in the schedule and quality control.
- Management and prediction of project costs based on the behavior of data.
- It allows one to manage portfolios of projects with their respective execution schedules and to control the progress of them.

Figure 4 shows a view of the risk management module as part of the revenue assurance subsystem in the GESPRO tool.

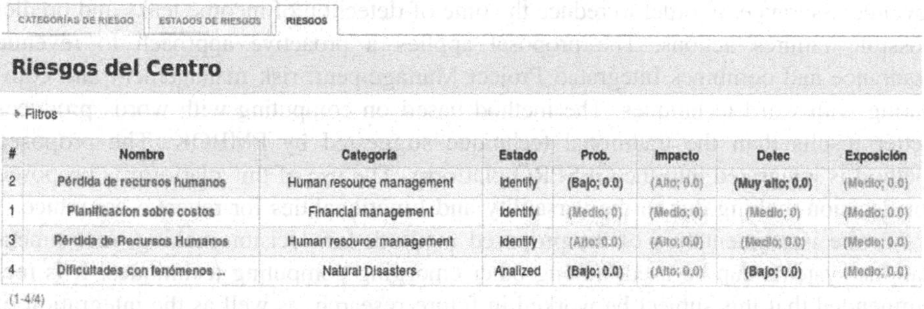

#	Nombre	Categoría	Estado	Prob.	Impacto	Detec	Exposición
2	Pérdida de recursos humanos	Human resource management	Identify	(Bajo; 0.0)	(Alto; 0.0)	(Muy alto; 0.0)	(Medio; 0.0)
1	Planificacion sobre costos	Financial management	Identify	(Medio; 0)	(Medio; 0)	(Medio; 0)	(Medio; 0.0)
3	Pérdida de Recursos Humanos	Human resource management	Identify	(Alto; 0.0)	(Alto; 0.0)	(Medio; 0.0)	(Medio; 0.0)
4	Dificultades con fenómenos ...	Natural Disasters	Analized	(Bajo; 0.0)	(Alto; 0.0)	(Bajo; 0.0)	(Medio; 0.0)

Fig. 4. View of risk management module in GESPRO platform

Figure 5 shows a view of the risk assessment. Note that the tool allows multiple criteria in risk assessment by multiple experts.

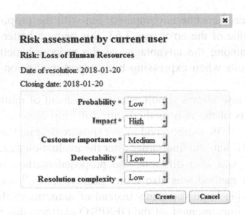

Fig. 5. View of risk assessment in GESPRO

With the application of the proposal in the GESPRO tool, a total of fourteen information technology development centers have benefited, in which more than two hundred projects are managed and where more than five hundred users converge. In addition, the model was implemented in the Ecuadorian company QuitusServices, dedicated to the provision of information technology and communication services [32]. In this company, with the application of the proposed model, an amount of 500 USD was recovered in one month. This amount is obtained from the analysis of the behavior of income, costs and leakage of income of the company during the six months of application of the model.

5   Conclusions

The need to combine reactive with proactive strategies was identified as a trend in revenue assurance, in order to reduce the time of detection of income leaks and predict possible failures actions. The proposal applies a proactive approach to revenue assurance and combines Integrated Project Management, risk management and computing with word techniques. The method based on computing with words produces better results than the traditional technique suggested by PMBOK. The proposed method is integrated into the GESPRO platform. The use of this platform is proposed for decision-making due to the versatility and functionalities for revenue assurance.

In the instrumentation of the proposed method, for decision-making, recommendations systems can be used, among other emerging computing techniques. It is recommended that this subject be worked in future research, as well as the integration of proactive, reactive and active management in revenue assurance for Integrated Project Management.

References

1. Delgado, R.: La Dirección Integrada de Proyecto como Centro del Sistema de Control de Gestión en el Ministerio del Poder Popular para la Comunicación y la Información, CENDA, Caracas, Venezuela (2011)
2. PMI: IBM: Keys to Building a Successful Enterprise Project Management Office. Project Management Institute, New York (2015)
3. PMI: A Guide to the Project Management Body of Knowledge. PMBOK® Guide, 6th edn. Project Management Institute, Pennsylvania, EE.UU (2017)
4. Paquin, J.P., Gauthier, C., Morin, P.P.: The downside risk of project portfolios: the impact of capital investment projects and the value of project efficiency and project risk management programmes. Int. J. Project Manag. **34**(8), 1460–1470 (2016). https://doi.org/10.1016/j.ijproman.2016.07.009
5. The Standish Group International: The CHAOS Manifesto. The Standish Group International, Incorporated (2014). https://www.projectsmart.co.uk/white-papers/chaos-report.pdf
6. The Standish Group International: Standish Group 2015 Chaos Report. The Standish Group International, Inc., New York (2015). https://www.infoq.com/articles/standish-chaos-2015
7. Burke, R.: Project Management: Planning and Control Techniques, 5th edn. Wiley, Hoboken (2013)
8. Schwalbe, K.: Information technology project management. Cengage Learning, 7th edn. Cengage Learning, Boston (2015)
9. Phillips, J.: PMP, Project Management Professional (Certification Study Guides), Sybex, 7th edn. McGraw-Hill Osborne Media (2013)
10. Leach, L.P.: Critical Chain Project Management, 1st edn. The North River Press, Artech House, Great Barrington (2014)
11. Verzuh, E.: The Fast Forward MBA in Project Management, 5th edn. Wiley, New York (2015)
12. Fischer, H., Dreisiebner, S., et al.: Revenue vs. costs of MOOC platforms. Discussion of business models for xMOOC providers based on empirical findings and experiences during implementation of the project iMOOX. In: 7th International Conference of Education, Research and Innovation (ICERI2014), IATED, pp. 2991–3000 (2014)
13. Wojnar, K.: Comparison between ISO 21500 and PMBOK® Guide 5th Edition. Theoretical background and practical usage of ISO 21500 in IT projects (2013)
14. TM Forum: Revenue Assurance a survey pre-result blog: Lack of cross-functional mandate holds back change, say Revenue Assurance professionals (2014). https://inform.tmforum.org/features-and-analysis/2014/12/revenueassurance-survey-2014-maturity-rise/
15. TM Forum: Revenue Assurance practitioner blog: do we need a new approach to revenue assurance in the digital world? & Seeing is believing: Setting revenue assurance KPIs (2014). https://inform.tmforum.org/
16. Acosta, K.: Aseguramiento de ingresos: una actividad fundamental en las empresas de telecomunicaciones. Revista Ingeniería Industrial **29**(2), 1–6 (2008)
17. Mattison, R.: The Telco Revenue Assurance Handbook. XiT Press, Oakwood Hills (2005). http://www.grapatel.com/A-GRAPA/07-Library/RABook.asp#top
18. Mattison, R.: The Revenue Assurance Standards? Release 2009. GRAPA. XiT Press, Oakwood Hills (2009). http://www.grapatel.com/members/viewfile.asp?file=stdbook
19. GRAPA: The Global Revenue Assurance Professional Association (GRAPA) Professionalizing the Information, Communications and Technology Industry (2016). http://www.grapatel.com/

20. Software Engineering Institute: CMMI para Desarrollo, Versión 1.3. Mejora de los procesos para el desarrollo de mejores productos y servicios. Technical report, Software Engineering Institute, EE.UU (2010). http://www.sei.cmu.edu/library/assets/whitepapers/Spanish%20Technical%20Report%20CMMI%20V%201%203.pdf
21. IPMA: International Project Management Association (2015). http://www.ipma.world/
22. ISO: ISO 21500:2012 Guidance on Project Management. International Organization for Standardization (2012)
23. Castro, G.F., et al.: PRODanalysis, un Sistema para el Aseguramiento de Ingresos Basado en Minería de Outliers. INNOVA Res. J. 1(7), 18–36 (2016)
24. Herrera, F., Martinez, L.: A 2-tuple fuzzy linguistic representation model for computing with words. IEEE Trans. Fuzzy Syst. 8(6), 746–752 (2000)
25. Merigó, J.: New extensions to the OWA operators and its application in decision making. Department of Business Administration, University of Barcelona, Ph.D. (2008)
26. Merigó, J.M., Yager, R.R.: Norm aggregations and OWA operators. In: Bustince, H., Fernandez, J., Mesiar, R., Calvo, T. (eds.) Aggregation Functions in Theory and in Practise. AISC, vol. 228, pp. 141–151. Springer, Heidelberg (2013). https://doi.org/10.1007/978-3-642-39165-1_17
27. Nielsen, T.D., Jensen, F.V.: Bayesian Networks and Decision Graphs, 2nd edn, p. 448. Springer, New York (2009)
28. Vattai, Z.A.: FLOYD-warshall in scheduling open networks. Procedia Eng. 106–114 (2016). https://doi.org/10.1016/j.proeng.2016.11.598
29. Castro, G.F., et al.: Platform for project evaluation based on soft-computing techniques. In: Valencia-García, R., Lagos-Ortiz, K., Alcaraz-Mármol, G., del Cioppo, J., Vera-Lucio, N. (eds.) CITI 2016. CCIS, vol. 658, pp. 226–240. Springer, Cham (2016). https://doi.org/10.1007/978-3-319-48024-4_18
30. Paselli, L.: The Project Management Advisor: 18 Mayor Project Screw-Ups, and How to Cut Them Off at the Pass, p. 167. Financial Times Prentice Hall (2004)
31. STS Sauter Training and Simulation: Comparing PMBOK Guide 4th, PMBOK Guide 5th and ISO 21500, STS Sauter Training and Simulation (2016). http://www.pmi-netherlands-chapter.org/images/stories/PMI-data/chapternews/pmbokiso.pdf
32. QuitusServices, Portal corporativo compañía de servicios informáticos. Guayaquil-Ecuador (2018). https://businessredmine.herokuapp.com/portal/quitusservices

User-Centered-Design of a UI for Mobile Banking Applications

Diana Minda Gilces[(✉)] [iD] and Rubén Fuentes Díaz [iD]

Universidad de Guayaquil, Guayaquil, Ecuador
{diana.mindag, ruben.fuentesdi}@ug.edu.ec

Abstract. A rapid increase in the number of smartphone users and wireless internet subscribers has brought about a digital revolution. Today, mobile devices serve not only as a medium of voice communication, but are also used to streamline daily activities. For instance, mobile banking allows clients to conduct financial transactions remotely using a mobile device such as a smartphone or tablet. As the influence of mobile technology continues to grow, financial institutions need to develop applications that guarantee customer usability. Ergo, there is a need to explore the role user interface design plays in enhancing the usability of a mobile application. This document describes the design and evaluation processes of the user interface of a mobile banking application that provides three functions: payments, balance inquiries and transfers. An experiment is carried out to test two different user interface prototypes. The prototypes differ in the implementation of Nielsen heuristics' for user interface design. Prototype A is designed empirically, whereas prototype B is based on the application of Nielsen's rules. Usability tests results demonstrate that credit union customers appraise the user interface designed according to the heuristics as more usable than the empirical one.

Keywords: User centered design · User interface · Mobile banking application
Usability · Heuristics

1 Introduction

Latin America is undergoing a process of expansion in the use of Information and Communication Technologies (ICT), characterized by a growth in the number of Internet users and, above all, the explosion of cellular mobile telephony [1]. The banking industry has become aware of this trend towards mobility betting strongly on the development of mobile banking (m-banking), a service that allows customers to perform financial transactions remotely by using a smartphone or tablet [2, 3]. It differs from online banking in that it uses an app, provided by the financial institution for the customer to login into a bank's mobile website to carry out banking transactions, payments and text message (SMS) banking [3]. In 2016 [4] estimated 1.2 billion m-banking users in the region and reported that 90% of the banks have at least 3 mobile technologies in their relationship with customers, from which mobile apps reached almost 96% of use.

© Springer Nature Switzerland AG 2019
M. Botto-Tobar et al. (Eds.): CITT 2018, CCIS 895, pp. 205–219, 2019.
https://doi.org/10.1007/978-3-030-05532-5_15

Ecuadorian renowned banks have adopted m-banking, however, this is not the case of credit unions.[1] According to [5] the number of credit unions in Ecuador grew 12.8% in relation to 2015; this indicates that credit union membership is on the rise. At the moment, credit union members need to wait in lines for long periods of time at the institution to perform basic transactions such as reviewing the account balance in their savings account [6, 7]. This is impractical and leads to time loss, in turn, there may be customers who prefer to open an account at an institution that provides mobile banking apps and access their accounts through their smartphones from anywhere in the world. The advent of smartphones provides an opportunity for credit unions to innovate their processes and provide a better service to their customers [1–3, 8].

Mobile app interfaces use touchscreens as the main source of input. Their design usually follows heuristics or "rules of thumb" [9, 10] originally intended for desktop software. However, traditional user interface design may not be totally compatible with the mobility context, it presents different constraints to developers. For instance, the controls and keyboards on smartphones can be particularly difficult to read and understand because mobile screens are smaller [11]. Additionally, mobile apps are often used in non-work settings, meaning that there is a high chance that the user may face distractions or problems like limited connectivity or a draining battery. Therefore, it is important for mobile app developers to ensure that their applications provide customer usability.

1.1 Usability

The term usability refers to the degree of ease with which consumers use a software application to achieve a specific goal [12]. ISO 9241-11 officially defines it as "the extent to which a product can be used by specified users to achieve specified goals with effectiveness, efficiency and satisfaction in a specified context of use". Usability studies [12, 13] have been carried out in different contexts and several models have been proposed to quantify and evaluate usability in Human-Computer Interaction. Recently the mobile context has gained increased research attention, findings in [3, 9, 14] suggest that mobile user interface design is a critical factor in achieving customer usability.

1.2 Related Work

The foundations of Human-Computer Interaction research and practice were established over 20 years ago, yet they remain an active area of study. Gould and Lewis [9] stressed three principles of design in 1980 which included "an early and continuous focus on users and their tasks". Since the involvement of end-users throughout the design process of software products, several studies [10, 13–17] have explored the influence of user interface design in software usability. The majority of them coincide

---

[1] A credit union is a financial non-profit organization which main role is to provide a safe space for savings and loans at reasonable rates; commonly established by people with a common background. Their main appeal to members is that any profit earned by the institution is either invested back into the credit union or paid out to members as a dividend.

in the application of Nielsen Heuristics to build and test usability of software products. Nielsen Heuristics include ten rules: (1) Visibility of system status, (2) Match between system and the real world, (3) User control and freedom, (4) Consistency and standards, (5) Error prevention, (6) Recognition rather than recall, (7) Flexibility and efficiency of use, (8) Aesthetic and minimalist design, (9) Help users recognize, diagnose, and recover from errors, and (10) Help and documentation [15].

This study aims to determine if Nielsen Heuristics exert an influence on the level of usability of a mobile banking application. To do so, this paper focuses on two main objectives: (i) to design two (2) different user interfaces prototypes for the same mobile banking app; one which lacks design rules and another which follows Nielsen Heuristics to support a user centered design approach. (ii) to test the usability of each user prototype by analyzing Key Performance Indicators and surveying credit union customers regarding the ease of use of each of the user interface.

2 User-Centered-Designed-Interface

The mobile banking application design followed the User Centered Design (UCD) methodology. The main concept of UCD is that only by understanding the domain of work in which users are engaged, usability can be enhanced and human-computer interaction facilitated [14]. UCD is standardized in ISO 13407 and describes four essential UCD activities to follow: (1) "Understand and specify the context of use"; (2) "Specify the user and organizational requirements"; (3) "Produce design solutions"; and (4) "Evaluate designs against requirements". This section describes each of the activities in the methodology for the deployment of the mobile banking application user interfaces. Activities 1 and 2 are grouped together as one, named Context of Use and activities 3 and 4 are described individually.

2.1 Context of Use

The target audience in this study are customers of the credit unions in Guayaquil, Ecuador. To obtain the number of representative users needed for the sample, a fieldwork was carried out in which each of the establishments considered in this study were visited to determine the total number of members for each one of them and add them up to figure out the total population. It should be noted that the group of credit unions listed in this study are the ones which were willing to provide all the required information; some credit unions were discarded because they do not provide the m-banking service and thus could not be included in the mobile banking application. Table 1 shows the names and number of members for the credit unions considered in this research.

The total number of members is used to calculate the sample. As stated in [6] the formula to calculate the sample in finite populations is:

$$n = \frac{Nk^2 p \cdot q}{e^2(N-1) + k^2 \cdot p \cdot q} \tag{1}$$

Table 1. Credit Unions included in the m-banking app.

	Credit Unions	Number of members
1	Armada Nacional	11,000
2	Universidad de Guayaquil	7000
3	Águilas de Cristo	820
4	Los Andes Latinos Ltda.	1,500
5	C.T.E.	1,735
6	La Dolorosa	9000
7	Esperanza y Desarrollo	530
	Total Credit Union Members	**31,585**

$$n = \frac{31.585 \times 1,96^2 \times 0,5 \times 0,5}{0,05^2 \times (31.585 - 1) + 1,96^2 \times 0,5 \times 0,5} = 379,55 \rightarrow 380$$

The number of representative users that will participate in the prototyping and testing of the mobile banking application are 380 customers.[2] This is the same population for which [6] evaluated the predisposition of credit union users in Guayaquil to use a mobile banking app for their transactions. As suggested by [3, 4, 7, 8] among the various banking transactions, the most commonly included in m-banking are balance inquiries, transfers and payments. Therefore the mobile banking app should allow the user to access their account and perform at least the three banking features mentioned above. To identify, clarify, and organize the mobile banking application's user requirements, uses cases of the UML methodology are applied. A use case is made up of a set of possible sequences of interactions between a software system and its users in a specific environment to achieve a particular goal [18]. The use cases for the login and payments features of the m-banking app are described below in Tables 2 and 3 respectively.

According to [1–3, 5] among the available mobile operating systems, the two dominant platforms of the market share globally are Android (70%) and iOS (21%). In Ecuador Samsung Galaxy models are the most popular around users in the sample [6]. Their average screens size is between 5.0 and 5.5 in., so the Android prototypes are created within that screen dimensions. For the iPhone series, the most demanded models in 2017 were the iPhone 6 and iPhone 7 with a screen size of 4.7 in. and are also prototyped.

2.2   Nielsen Heuristics

This research focuses on the application of Nielsen's Usability Heuristics for User Interface Design within the UCD Methodology. Partly, because it involves less number

---

[2] Where: n = sample size, N = population, k^2 = 1.96 (constant that must not be less than 95%), $e = 0.05$ maximum allowable error[2], $p = 0.50$ (probability that the outcome will occur) and $q = 0.50$ complementary probability.

Table 2. Login use case

Use Case	UC – 1 Login
Descriptions	Entry of the parameters (username and password) required to access the mobile app
Actions	Once the user has logged in, the user can check his balance, make payments and transfer money among the various credit unions
Assumptions	The user must hold an account in a credit union to log in and access the app functionalities
Steps	1. User must enter their username in the first text box 2. Then, enter the corresponding password in the second text box 3. Press the "ingresar" button of the application
Variations	No variations are considered for the process

Table 3. Payments Use Case

Use Case	UC – 4 Payments
Descriptions	The customer pays for a commodity using their smartphones
Actions	User selects a payment method and pays for a service or commodity
Assumptions	The user has logged in into the app
Steps	1. User selects a payment method: credit card or savings account balance 2. They select the service or commodity they need to pay for 3. The payment goes through and credit/balance is updated 4. A notification message shows up indicating the payment was successful
Variations	The user does not have enough credit and a popup warning message appears indicating the transaction cannot be completed

of guidelines and for the fact that it was the most popular UCD approach in the 90s. Because of the nature of the mobile banking app and findings in [6, 7] regarding consumer preferences rules 1, 2, 3, 5 and 8 are selected to build and test the prototypes in this study. The selected heuristics are detailed in Table 4.

2.3 Produce Design Solutions

The term prototype refers to a modifiable working example through which a new model or a new version of an existing product can be derived [9]. Originating from User-Centered Design, prototyping has also become a popular method for user-based validating design concepts in service design and development [19]. The principal use of prototyping is to help the representative customers and developers agree on the software requirements. To create and test the two sets of prototypes for each operating system, the online usability tool Quant-UX was employed. This software provides the means to design, test and analyze interactive prototypes; its main advantage is that it allows real time execution of the prototypes as if the users were testing a real app [20]. For each operating system a set of two interfaces are prototyped. Prototype A lacks design rules whereas Prototype B is created by following the five selected guidelines in

Table 4. Nielsen Heuristics applied to the UCD

Principle	Description
Visibility of system status (S) (S)	The system should always keep users informed about what is going on, through appropriate feedback within reasonable time
Coincidence between the system and the real world (R.) (R.)	The system should speak the users' language, with words, phrases and concepts familiar to the user, rather than system-oriented terms. Follow real-world conventions, making information appear in a natural and logical order
User control and freedom (C) (C)	Users often choose system functions by mistake and will need an "emergency exit" clearly marked to leave the unwanted state without having to go through an extended dialogue. Support undo and redo
Error prevention (E) (E)	Error messages is a careful design that prevents a problem from occurring in the first place. Eliminate error-prone conditions or check them and present users with a confirmation option before committing to action
Aesthetic and minimalist design (D) (D)	Dialogues should not contain information that is irrelevant or rarely needed. Each additional unit of information in a dialogue competes with the relevant units of information and diminishes their relative visibility

Nielsen Heuristics. Each of the interfaces consists of a total of seven screens. For the purposes of this document, two screens are analyzed; the Login screen and the Payments Screen, for which each Use Case is documented in the previous section. A legend including the abbreviation of each heuristic is used to specify where in the screen Nielsen guidelines are applied.

Android Prototypes: Figure 1 portrays the Login and Payments views for Prototype A. These screens were created empirically. The Login screen shows the logo at the top of the screen and the title "IDENTIFICACION DEL USUARIO" below it. There exists two buttons, login (ingresar) and register (registrarse). The payments screen for Prototype A displays the logo, screen title "PAGOS" and 5 buttons. The first button allows the customer to select a credit card to pay for commodities, the other button pays for each of commodity using the savings account. An arrow shaped button is located at the top of the screen to go back to the previous view.

Figure 2 shows the Login and Payments views for Prototype B. These were created following Nielsen's heuristics. Both screens display the m-banking app name and logo at the top of the screen. This is standardized through all of the screens in the app. The titles "IDENTIFICACION DEL USUARIO" and "PAGOS" remain in the same position. In the Login screen, popup windows with warning texts appear next to the username and password textboxes to prevent the customer from entering wrong information. The first button in the Payments screen is replaced by two circled shaped checkboxes to select whether the customer would like to pay for commodities using a

Fig. 1. Android Prototype A views

credit card or their credit union savings account. The rest of the buttons are replaced by a vertical scroll viewer that allows the user to select which commodity they will be paying. The arrow shaped button at the top of the screen is now located at the bottom of the screen, with the sign "ATRAS" The application of Nielsen Heuristics is labeled through the semaphore like indicators. The login page in Prototype A is enhanced in the design of Prototype B by the application of the Error Prevention Heuristics, labeled E in Fig. 2. The remaining Heuristics are applied in the Payments Screen.

Fig. 2. Android Prototype B views

iOS Prototypes. The same user interface prototypes were built for the iOS Operating System. Figure 4 shows iOS Prototype A, the user interface which lacks design rules. The Login and Payments provide the same features as in the Android prototype in Fig. 1, with the slight variation in the Payments view where the button to select the payment method is omitted. For the iOS platform when selecting the commodity to pay, a popup window appears to use the payment data stored on the phone or the credit union savings account. Additionally icons indicating the type of commodity to pay are shown along with the name of each basic service. The arrow shaped button is located at the top of the screen to go back to the previous view.

Fig. 3. iOS Prototype A views

Figure 4 shows the Login and Payments views for iOS Prototype B. It resembles the view for the Android Platform in Fig. 2. The Login view applies the Error Prevention Heuristics and the Payments view applies all the remaining four heuristics. The visibility of System Status is applied through a Text Label "Cómo desea pagar" that indicates the customer that a payment is about to be performed. The view in Fig. 3 is modified to Match the Real World (heuristic labeled R) by asking the customer how they will like to make the payment (this is suited so that it matches the views in ATMs). The scroll view is also included in Prototype B in order to select the commodities to pay for. This feature corresponds to the Minimalistic Design Heuristic (D) and also matches real world touchscreens found at credit union establishments. To enhance user control and freedom the back button is located at the top with "ATRAS" (back) sign to indicate that the payment can be cancelled (Control heuristic labeled C).

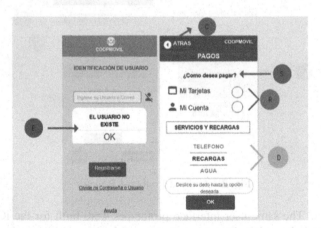

Fig. 4. iOS Prototype B views

3   Prototype Testing

After designing a total of 7 screens for each of the prototypes, it was important to test their usability. The Quant-UX provides the means to simulate the operation of the prototypes. The links to each of the prototypes simulators were included in a Google

Form[3] and sent to the WhatsApp number or email of each of the credit union customers that were selected to participate in the user centered design.

The usability evaluation of each prototype is double-factored. To determine which prototype offers the best user experience, an analysis of the First-click-heat map of the views is executed. The interpretation of these results is later backed-up by a survey to the credit union members.

3.1 Quant-UX First Click Heatmaps

Quant-UX provides a testing feature named Heat Maps. A Click Heat Map is a well-established method to analyze user interaction, they are fairly easy to read and help user interface designers corroborate ideas about primary and secondary tasks and detect the spots where unexpected behavior and other usability issues might occur. Click heat maps visualize where the users have clicked. The more the users click on a certain area, the hotter (more reddish) the area gets. Thus, the elements in the area are likely important for the user [20].

In this user-centered design the tasks for each interface is identified and prioritized in use cases for each operation. The primary widgets[4] are those that should be visualized and clicked first, according to the order of steps listed in the use case. When evaluating the user interface design, primary widgets should be easy to find and clicked frequently.

The Key Performance Indicators in this analysis are: Widget Clicks, First Clicks and Time-Before-Clicks. Widget-Clicks indicate how many times a certain widget was clicked. The gauge shows the absolute number of clicks, the position of the ring shows the relation to all other widgets in the prototype. First Widget Clicks indicate how many times a certain widget was clicked directly after a screen was loaded; they first show which widgets catch the most attention of the users. The gauge shows the absolute number, and the position visualizes the relation to the screen loads. The Time Before Click displays how many seconds the users took in average until they interacted the first time with the given widget. In general elements in the top are expected to have shorter times the elements at the bottom of a screen [16, 20]. A comparison of Prototype A vs. Prototype B for the Login and Payments Views of each of the operating systems is detailed below.

Android Comparisons of Prototype A vs. Prototype B

Login View: In this view, as stated in the Use Case in Table 2 the user should start the action by entering the username and password if they have already registered their information in the app. The TextBox2 widget that is meant for the user to enter their username is the widget with the least Time-Before-Click.

The image in Fig. 5 shows that Prototype A has a shorter Time Before Click (5 s) than the same element in Prototype B (7 s). However it also depicts that the TextBox2

---

[3] A full-featured forms tool that comes free with a Google account. It allows the user to add standard question types, drag-and-drop questions and customize the form with simple photo or color themes, and gather responses in Forms or save them to a Google Sheets spreadsheet.

[4] A component of an interface that enables a user to perform a function or access a service.

widget in Prototype A has a Widget Click KPI of 81 and a First Clicks KPI of 51. Prototype B indicates a Widget Click KPI of 38 and a First Clicks KPI of 30. The ratio of First Click/Widget Clicks is smaller in Prototype A (0.62) than in Prototype B (0.78) meaning that out of the total clicks, in Prototype B the probability of TextBox2 of being clicked first is greater.

Based on this quantification Prototype B is considered to provide a higher degree of usability when compared to Prototype A.

Payment View: In Fig. 6 the heat map in the left side (Prototype A) displays a greater number of "hot" areas compared to Prototype B. This indicates that credit union customers scrolled around more in Prototype A than in Prototype B.

The widget with the smallest Time Before Click in Prototype A is "Button", which displays the "Mis Tarjetas" option. This matches the Payments Use Case in Table 3 which states that the user should first select the payment method. The Time Before Click KPI is 5 s. In Prototype B, the RadioBox widget set for the "Mis Tarjetas" option has a Time Before Click of 4 s, meaning it took less time for the credit union customers to identify where to start the Payment Use Case. This interpretation is backed up by the fact that by calculating the First Click/Widget Click ratio for each of the prototypes, Prototype A (0.13) shows a smaller ratio than Prototype B (0.72). This suggest that there's a higher chance in Prototype B for the user to click the widget that corresponds to the first step in the Payments Use Case. According to this heat map analysis, Prototype B would most likely provide the highest degree of usability.

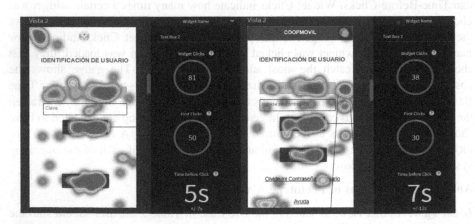

Fig. 5. Android Prototype A vs Prototype B Login View

iOS Comparisons of Prototype A vs. Prototype B

Login View: There is an interesting observation regarding this view. The first element clicked in both Prototypes is not the TextBox2 widget as in the Android platform. As seen in Fig. 7, the item with the least Time Before Click in Prototype A was the Button2 which corresponds to the Register button, which is clicked 4 s after the view is loaded.

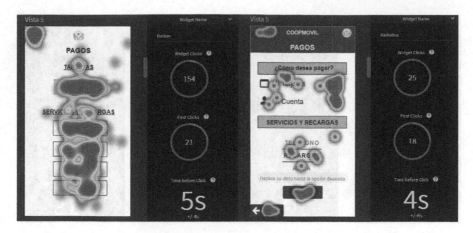

Fig. 6. Android Prototype A vs Prototype B Payments view

Prototype B displays much more hotspots than Prototype A. The Info Button located at the top of the view has the shortest Time Before Click (1 s). The First Click/Widget Clicks ratio for the Info Button Prototype B (0.80) is very high compared to the ratio of element TextBox2 (0.16) in Prototype A. This most likely means that the credit union users that were being surveyed probably simulated the prototypes in such a realistic way that they intended to actually register their accounts and look for information on how to interact with the mobile banking application, as sated in the Use Case in Table 2.

Based on this analysis it is possible to argue that even though none of the prototypes match the operations listed in the Login Use Case in Table 2, there is a need to clear out customers doubts by adding an info button or help label. Prototype B includes a help label at the bottom of the screen, meaning that this would be the most usable prototype. This interpretation is supported by the fact that the info button has the lowest Time Before Click KPI. It is suggested that the help label is deleted and the content that it displays should be moved to the top at the info button.

Payments View: Figure 8 shows that regarding the payments view, the first click hot spots resemble those of Android; although the Time Before Click KPI is smaller for both prototypes in the iOS platform.

The hottest hotspot in prototype A is Icon3, which is the widget that allows the customer to recharge credit in their phones or cable TV service. It has a Time Before Click KPI of 2 s. By dividing the First Click KPI over the Widget Clicks KPI for that element, the ratio is 0.73. Prototype B displays the RadioBox widget meant to select the payment method "Mis Tarjetas" as the one with the hottest spot and thus the one with the smallest Time Before Click (5 s). The First Click/Widget Clicks ratio for this element is 0.48.

Comparing these data with the Payments Use Case in Table 3 it can be stated that Prototype B would have a higher degree of usability as perceived by the customer.

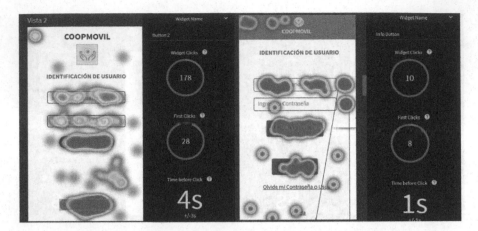

Fig. 7. iOS Prototype A vs Prototype B Login view

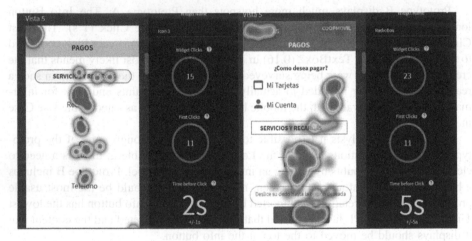

Fig. 8. iOS Prototype A vs Prototype B Payments view

After comparing the Login and Payments Views Heat Maps of Prototypes A and B for both of the operating systems and determining Prototype B would most likely present the highest degree of usability.

3.2   Survey Results

A survey is used to validate the results in the First Click Heat Map analysis. This consisted of four questions regarding the level of comfort credit union customers perceived when simulating the prototypes. There were only two possible answers for each question: Prototype A or Prototype B. The questions address each of the 5 Nielsen Guidelines selected for this study and are listed below

Q1: Which of the two prototypes provides a better visibility of the system status?
Q2: Which of the two prototype presents more understandable phrases or dialog boxes for the use of the mobile application?
Q3: Which of the two prototypes provided more control to browse the app and enter data?
Q4: Which of the two prototypes provides better error prevention?
Q5: In general terms, which of the two prototypes was the most intuitive and user-friendly?

Android Survey Results:
As shown in Fig. 9, for the Android Operating System, Prototype B is considered the most usable in the evaluation of each of the Nielsen Heuristics by credit union customers. All of the answers to the questions score above 60% acceptance. The question

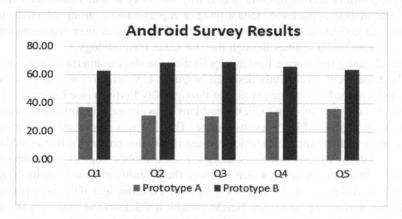

Fig. 9. Android survey results

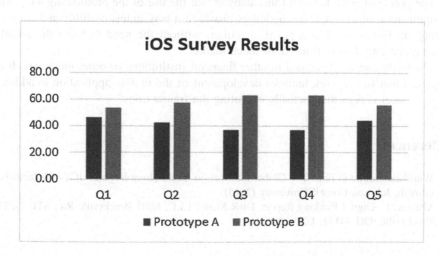

Fig. 10. iOS survey results

with the highest percentage is Q3 with 69.2% meaning that the Control heuristic is the most appreciated by credit union customers in the Android platform.

In iOSystem, Prototype B is also considered the most usable in the evaluation of each of the Nielsen Heuristics by credit union customers. As described in Fig. 10, all of the answers to the questions score above 50% acceptance. The questions with the highest percentage are Q3 and Q4 with 63% meaning that Control and Error Prevention are the most valued by the customers for this operating system.

4   Conclusions

The main objective of this research was to apply the User Centered Design approach in order to build and test two interface prototypes, one which lacks design rules and another which follows five out of the ten Nielsen Heuristics.

To successfully accomplish this goal, it was necessary to understand the context of use of the mobile application. Establishing a representative group of credit union customers to collect needs from, proved invaluable to asses user requirements and define software functionalities through the Use Case methodology.

After defining the mobile banking application needs, the interface prototypes for each Use Case were successfully designed in Quant-UX; which was also used later to test the level of usability of each prototype through Key Performance Indicators in First Click HeatMaps. Though First Click HeatMaps provide meaningful information, the interpretation of this KPI is very subjective. Thus, it was important to support this interpretation with the survey, in which Nielsen Heuristics prove effective in enhancing customer usability of user interfaces designed for a mobile context, regardless of its operating system. Prototype B, which followed the usability guidelines in its design, is perceived as easier to use by costumers in both Android and iOS. This perception matches our analysis of First Click HeatMaps which validates the study and the use of the User Centered methodology.

The principal contribution of this study is that the use of the prototyping tools and the application of the UCD Methodology provided a way to test usability and confirm findings in [10, 13–17] in a practical setting, without the need to build the mobile banking app and deploy it in the financial market.

The study can be replicated in other financial institutions or other industries. It is suggested that future work includes development of the mobile application to address further concerns regarding actually executing the transactions.

References

1. World Economic Forum: The Global Information Technology Report - ICTs for Inclusive Growth, Johnson Cornell University (2015)
2. Marous, J.: Digital Banking Report, DBR Media LLC, 8803 Brecksville Rd., STE 7-223, Brecksville, OH 44141, USA (2017)

3. Sharma, N., Kaur, R.: M-Services in India: a study on mobile banking and applications. In: 10th International Conference on New trends in Business and Management: An International Perspective, vol. 6, no. 2 (2016)
4. Fenu, G., Luigi, P.P.: An analysis of features and tendencies in mobile banking apps. Procedia Comput. Sci. **56**, 26–33 (2015)
5. Centro de Estudios Monetarios Latinoamericanos: Panorama del dinero en América Latina y el Caribe, Mexico (2017). E-ISBN 978-607-7734-86-4
6. Fernanda, L., Peralta, S., Guzhnay, T., Dayanna, Z.: PROPUESTA PARA LA CREACIÓN DE UNA APLICACIÓN MÓVIL PARA LOS CLIENTES DE LAS COOPERATIVAS DE AHORRO Y CRÉDITO DE LA CIUDAD DE GUAYAQUIL. Univerisdad de Guayaquil, Guayaquil (2017)
7. Cooharojananone, N., Atchariyachanvanich, K.: Case studies of user interface design on internet banking websites and mobile payment applications in Thailand. In: Uesugi, S. (ed.) IT Enabled Services. Springer, Vienna (2013). https://doi.org/10.1007/978-3-7091-1425-4_10
8. Paredes, O.C.: Striking the Balance in Microfinance, Quito, Ecuador, World Council of Credit Unions (WOCCU), pp. 242–260 (2008)
9. Weichbroth, P., Sikorski, M.: User interface prototyping. techniques, methods and tools, Uniwersytetu Ekonomicznego w Katowicach (2015). ISSN 2083-8611
10. Guimbreti, F.: Foundations for designing and evaluating user interfaces based on the crossing paradigm. ACM Trans. Comput. Hum. Interact. **17**(2), 9 (2010)
11. Budiu, R., Nielsen, J.: iPad app and website usability (2010). http://www.nngroup.com/reports/mobile/ipad/ipad-usability_1st-edition.pdf. Accessed 10 Apr 2018
12. Trivedi, M.C., Khanum, M.A.: Role of context in usability evaluations: a review. Adv. Comput. Int. J. (ACIJ) **3**(2), 69–78 (2012)
13. Geisen, E., Bergstrom, J.R.: Usability testing for survey research, 9 October 2017. https://www.uxmatters.com/mt/archives/2017/10/usability-testing-for-survey-research.php. Accessed 10 Apr 2018
14. Leitão, R., Ribeiro, J., de Barros, A.C.: Design and evaluation of a mobile user interface for older adults: navigation, interaction and visual design recommendations. Procedia Comput. Sci. **27**, 369–378 (2014)
15. Fico, G., Fioravanti, A., Arredondo Waldmeyer, M.T., Leuteritz, J.P., Guillén, A., Fernandez, D.: A user centered design approach for patient interfaces to a diabetes IT platform. In: Annual International Conference of the IEEE Engineering in Medicine and Biology, pp. 1169–1172 (2011)
16. Schnall, R., et al.: A user-centered model for designing consumer mobile health (mHealth) applications (apps). J. Biomed. Inform. **60**, 243–251 (2016)
17. Darejeh, A., Singh, D.: A review on user interface design principles to increase software usability for users with less computer literacy. J. Comput. Sci. **9**(11), 1443–1450 (2013)
18. Constantine, B.: Universitat Pompeu Fabra, Barcelona (2014). http://www.dtic.upf.edu/~jblat/material/diss_interf/notes/nidia/ucd.pdf. Accessed 1 May 2018
19. Constantinescu, G., Kuffel, K., King, B., Hodgetts, W., Rieger, J.: Usability testing of an mHealth device for swallowing therapy in head and neck cancer survivors. Health Inform. J. (2018)
20. Quant-UX (2016). https://www.quant-ux.com/#features.html. Accessed 10 Apr 2018

How to Govern VSE Teams: Experiences Through a Model and Case Study

René Arévalo[1] and Carlos Montenegro[2(✉)]

[1] Universidad Politécnica Salesiana, Quito, Ecuador
aarevalo@ups.edu.ec
[2] Escuela Politécnica Nacional, Quito, Ecuador
carlos.montenegro@epn.edu.ec

Abstract. The software development organizations need an understanding of the governance process and their practical approach to reach their strategic goals, a subject where there is a research opportunity. This study proposes a model type artifact to govern Very Small Entities (VSE) Teams for Software Development. The model design is based on COBIT 5 and IT governance best practices, with structural and dynamic governance components. The validation is done through the model application, in a case study, in a Public Sector Organization, using a SCRUM software process. The model application allows the appropriate responses to the software development needs and facilitate the solution of the problems in the project development. Besides, a survey shows that in a developing country, the model applicability can be generalizable. Thus, the study tests a tool for the practitioners and academics and contributes to the growth of the current knowledge concerning the Software Development Governance.

Keywords: Software Development Governance · VSE · COBIT
DSR · SCRUM

1 Introduction

Information Technology Governance (ITG) has been defined as the strategic alignment of IT with the Business such that maximum business value is achieved through the development and maintenance of adequate Information Technology (IT) control and accountability, performance and risk management [1]. ITG can be implemented by combining various *relations, structures,* and *processes* [2, 3]. One of the products of IT processes is the software applications, whose productivity is an indicator that supports the ITG activities [4].

Dubinsky *et al.* [5], consider governance has emerged in the last few years as critical to the success of software development, a result of an increased focus on teamwork. Governance of software teams includes practices of defining and executing decision rights and mechanisms to empower the development process to be governed.

The software product development implies two elements: (i) The Software Process Management (SPM); that is, the software product development, based on the requirements agreed between the stakeholders, and using a specific development process [6];

M. Botto-Tobar et al. (Eds.): CITT 2018, CCIS 895, pp. 220–232, 2019.
https://doi.org/10.1007/978-3-030-05532-5_16

and, (ii) Software Development Governance (SDG), which ensures that the results of a software organizations business processes meet the strategic requirements of the organization; it includes chains of responsibility, authority, and communication (structural component), and measurement and control mechanisms (dynamic element) [7].

The study of Sommer et al. [8] considers that SPM is changing through the emergence and perform of agile principles into existing SPM frameworks. This process varies in SPM governance assets, even though this aspect is not yet described in the current literature. Alike, Talby et al. [9] about SPM conclude that the governance iterations can be unified within agile development iterations, which can be useful in identifying issues and resolving them in an efficient and timely manner.

On the other hand, SDG is a process that is not yet mature; many companies do not manage it properly. According to Chulani et al. [7], the software development organizations that wish to reach their strategic goals successfully need an understanding of governance and their approach to it. A significant impediment to this understanding is that many software development managers, developers and the broader development organizations as a whole seem confused about precisely what SDG is, and what constitutes good governance.

In the described context, this work contributes to a proposal to improve the application of the SDG in VSE type work teams. Here, it is adopted the VSE teams definition, until 25 people [10, 11], and it poses a model based on the best IT governance practices, and uses an agile software development process, as an SPM component to probe the artifact.

2   Background

COBIT 5 provides a framework that assists enterprises in achieving their objectives for the governance and management of business IT; the tool helps enterprises to create value from IT by maintaining a balance between realizing benefits and optimizing risk levels and resource use. Alike, according to ISACA [6], COBIT is generic and useful for companies of all sizes, whether commercial, not-for-profit or in the public sector.

In the opinion of Maglyas et al. [12], the company size affects the goals and activities of SPM. Therefore, companies of different sizes require different approaches to the adoption of SPM activities. That is the role of software development management, but small firms are likely to govern via non-formal structures, processes, and relational mechanisms; and, large organizations will typically adopt more explicit, formal governance arrangements.

Van Wyk [13] suggest that the adherence to governance principles within agile software development projects is a concern for IT project managers and organizations at large. Er et al. [14] analyze the organizations that aim to adopt the right governance structure for their projects based on their characteristics and the tools to be aligned with this arrangement, embracing the principles from the field of Transaction Cost Economics.

Bannerman [15] poses an SDG meta-management approach regarding structures, processes, and relational mechanisms, as governance cells (Fig. 1).

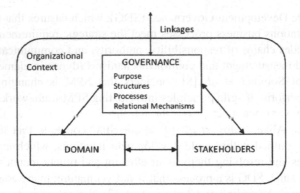

Fig. 1. Governance conceptual cell [15]

A governance cell applies to the activities of a particular domain (such as the whole corporation, IT, data management, architecture, projects or software development) and is associated with a set of stakeholders (such as governance proponents, governance actors, domain members and influential third parties). Each cell usually interlinks with one or more another related governance cell, vertically and/or horizontally to form an integrated governance infrastructure for the organization; this enables a pattern or framework of governance to be established that suits the needs of the organization.

3   Methodology

Design Science Research (DSR) approach is used in this work. DSR has been developed over the last years [16, 17]. The paradigm has been used in several domains: IT Management [18], Information Systems [19], and Business Processes Management [20], among others. According to Hevner *et al.* [17], DSR constitutes a pragmatic research paradigm that encourages the creation of innovative artifacts to solve real-world problems. Thus, DSR combines a focus on IT artifacts with a high priority for its relevance in the application domain.

DSR uses two phases: Design and Evaluation. A criterion for model design as a search process is a top-down design, where, as relevant, successively specific models and best practices for the new artifact, are included. In the Evaluation Phase, as a DSR option [16], the observational method of Case Study is used. A survey is utilized to identify the current state of the SDG on the model application context.

Also, DSR provides a stage of feedback for the designed artifact since the Evaluation Phase [16, 19]. The structures and the relational mechanisms of the Governance Cells were revisited and redefined according to the experiences in the Case Study. The last version of the model is documented.

The qualitative technique of Participant Observation contributes to the experiences of the observer-as-participant [21, 22]. In this study, one researcher on partial time acted as a participant in the generation and explanation of the model, and in planning implementation activities; and, additionally, one researcher on full-time, served as the

Project leader in the Case Study and carried out the development efforts, jointly with the enterprise personnel.

Figure 2 shows the methodological structure and the phase sequence, where is included the Literature Review as the background to the current study.

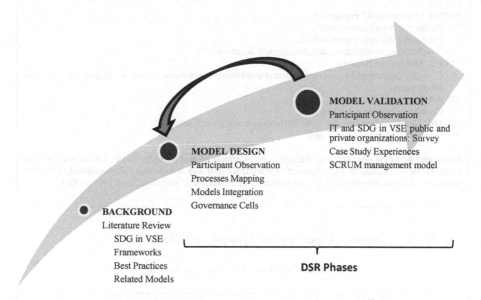

MODEL VALIDATION
Participant Observation
IT and SDG in VSE public and
private organizations: Survey
Case Study Experiences
SCRUM management model

MODEL DESIGN
Participant Observation
Processes Mapping
Models Integration
Governance Cells

BACKGROUND
Literature Review
SDG in VSE
Frameworks
Best Practices
Related Models

DSR Phases

Fig. 2. Structure and sequence of DSR based methodology

4 Designing the Model for SDG

The design of the SDG proposed in this study is based on the following components:

1. The reviews of Van Grembergen *et al.* [2], Bannerman [15], and De Haes *et al.* [23], from which the concept of governance mechanisms is extracted.
2. COBIT 5 [6], contributes to a set of governance best practices, as well as a set of proven and validated processes [24].

These contributions are organized in the model, as follows:

(a) A structural governance cell, with its corresponding hierarchical structures and chains of responsibility, authority, and communication to empower people within the organization where the software product is developed [7, 25–27].
(b) A governance dynamic cell, with its corresponding structures, measurement, and control mechanisms, to verify that software developers, project managers and others within the organization where the software product is developed, correctly perform their functions and responsibilities [8, 25–27].

Following, the summary of the Governance Structural cell is showed (Table 1).

Table 1. Governance structural component

Governance Cell: Structural Component
Purpose. Establish the governance structural component required for the software development process
Structures. Create the governance structure for the software development process
Processes   **APO01**. Manage the IT Framework   01. Define the organization chart.   02. Establish roles and responsibilities.   04. Communicate of objectives and management direction.   **APO02**. Manage the Strategy   01. Consider the current business environment and business processes, as well as company strategy and future goals.   **APO08**. Manage Relationships   03. Coordinate and communicate.   **MEA01**. Monitor, Evaluate and Asses Performance and Compliance.   01. Establish a monitoring approach
Relational Mechanisms. Promote the active participation of stakeholders and collaboration between them. Promote strategic dialogue and active participation of key stakeholders. Rewards and incentives for the association. Business / IT shared objectives understanding. Multifunctional jobs rotation.

In the same manner, is specified the dynamic cell (Table 2).

Table 2. Governance dynamic component

Governance Cell: Dynamic Component
Purpose. Establish the dynamic component of governing required for software development, i.e., the measurement and control mechanisms to verify that software developers, project managers, and others stakeholders appropriately perform their roles and responsibilities
Structures. Create the dynamic structure of governance for the software development process
Processes   **APO02** Manage Strategy   **APO11** Manage Quality   **APO12** Manage Risk   **BAI01** Manage Programs and Projects   **BAI02** Manage Requirements Definition   **BAI04** Manage Availability and Capacity   **BAI08** Manage Knowledge   **MEA01** Supervise, Evaluate and Evaluate Performance and Compliance.   01. Establish a monitoring approach.   02. Set performance and compliance goals.   03. Collect and process performance and compliance data.   0.4 Collect and process timely and accurate data aligned with the business approaches raised.
Relational Mechanisms.   Stakeholders participation based on Active Principle.   Key stakeholder collaboration.   Association rewards and incentives.   Strategic dialogue and shared learning.   Active conflict resolution ("no avoidance").   Training in business and IT.

5   Case Study in a Public-Sector Organization (PSO)

5.1   The Software Development Governance in a Developing Country

The context of the Case Study application is identified through a survey about SDG into Ecuador, a developing country.

With the help of the Undersecretary of Electronic Government [29] and the Ecuadorian Software Association AESOFT [30], at the investigation date (April 2017), are identified 150 companies, which formally develop software in Pichincha, Central Government Headquarters of Ecuador. A sample of 108 surveys is defined using 95% of confidence level and 5% of error. It is obtained 74 answered questionnaires (68.5%), according to the detail of Table 3. The final reached error value of the survey is 8.1%.

Table 3. Summary of surveys per team size

Team size	Private	Public	Total of enterprises
1–4	17	3	20
5–25	18	15	33
+25	12	9	21
Total	47	27	74

The survey consists of twenty questions. The questions 1 to 4 $[Q_1-Q_4]$ are related to the type of company. Questions $[Q_5-Q_{14}]$ are about data associated with the application of ITG in the organization, based on ITG definition [1]. Questions $[Q_{15}-Q_{20}]$ are about the use of SDG practices in the software development process, based on best practices [6]. Each question Q_i is answered between range 0 (No, Not at all) and 5 (Total, Completely). The Cronbach's alpha coefficient [31] of the results is 0.931, corroborating the internal consistency of the instrument.

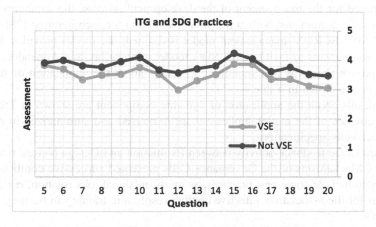

Fig. 3. ITG and SDG practices in VSE and Not-VSE teams

With the use of t-Test is concluded that the behavior about the practices of ITG and SDG on VSE and Not-VSE teams are similar with 95% of confidence, and a positive covariance that evidences the direct proportionality of the data. The Not-VSE shows best individual assessment for each question (Fig. 3).

Alike, the public and private sector companies have similar behavior, also with a covariance value greater than zero (Fig. 4).

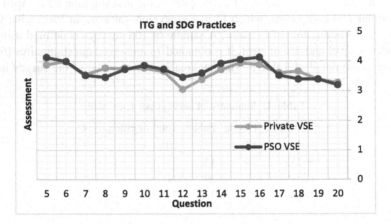

Fig. 4. ITG and SDG practices in VSE teams

5.2   The Case Study Details

The designed model was applied to software development for a PSO, the Eugenio Espejo Hospital (EEH) of the Health Ministry of Ecuador, to improve the Operating Rooms information manage, a critical institutional issue. There were ten stakeholders: seven from the EEH and three from the organization in charge of development.

Complementarily, from SCRUM it is extracts the hierarchical structure and the roles required for the management of the development process, the structures or containers of the requirements, both at the project level and for each iteration [28]. Thus, a modified SPM-SCRUM management model is defined; the model provides the management components to facilitate the SDG model application. See Appendix A.

The project time was four months. The details about the application of structural component are shown in Table 4.

The details about the application of dynamic component are shown in Table 5.

All activities of the model application are immersed and summarized in previous governance cells specifications.

Regard to the feedback activity between Evaluation and Design phases, mainly the Relational Mechanisms of the Governance Cells presented successive conflicts. It was necessary to include some best practices, as multifunctional jobs rotation, rewards and incentives for the association, effective conflict resolution, training in business and IT, and others.

Table 4. Governance structural component application

Governance Structural Component Application
Governance Structure
Project Manager: Director of the Teaching and Research Area - EEH. **Development Manager**: 1 Business Expert - EEH **SCRUM Master**: 1 Researcher, project leader **SCRUM Team Member**: 2 Researcher Assistants **Product Owner - Business Expert**: 1 EEH Officer, who knows the management of Operating Rooms **Reception Committee**: 1 member per area: Teaching and Research, ICT, Clinical and/or Surgical Specialties **Direct and indirect stakeholders:** Teaching and Research, Clinical and/or Surgical Specialties, Hospital of the Day, Statistics, ICT.
Processes
Align, Planning and Organize (APO)
AP01 Manage the IT Framework The Project Manager is responsible for: *01 Define the organizational structure.* - Appoints the officials who will collaborate in the project, according to their skills or knowledge related to the management of operating rooms. *02 Establish roles and responsibilities.* The areas of Teaching and Research, Clinical and/or Surgical Specialties, Daily Hospital and Statistics, provide the information required for the management of operating rooms. - The responsibilities for the functionalities to be implemented come from an agreement between the interested parties. When there is a conflict, the development manager will make the final decision. - The development manager, with the advice of the ICT official, will agree with the leader of the project, the scope, the requirements to be implemented, the development platform and the metrics of progress measurement and quality management. - Any new requirement or adjustment must be processed through the development manager. - The developer must train the test managers to use the agreed metrics and run the tests, using standardized processes. *04 Communicate the management of the objectives and the direction.* The development manager is responsible for: - Communicate knowledge and understanding of objectives, scope and agreed on development requirements for management, areas, and users **APO02 Manage the Strategy** *01 Consider the current business environment and business processes, as well as company strategy and future goals* - The Unit of Teaching and Research Management has as a mission, to incite the activities of formation of the professionals of the health and investigation and to manage the agreements of collaboration with academic institutions AP08 Manage Relationships The Development Manager is responsible for: *04 Coordinate and communicate.* - Work with stakeholders and coordinate the final delivery of the software application.
Monitor, Evaluate, and Assess (MEA)
MEA01 Monitor, Evaluate and Asses Performance and Compliance. *01 Establish a monitoring approach* The Development Manager and the designated ICT official, are responsible for: - Establish a collaborative process among stakeholders to develop and maintain a monitoring and control scope approach. - The interested parties will issue individual and joint reports of their appreciation about the fulfillment of the agreed requirements.
Used Relational Mechanisms
- The principle of active participation of stakeholders - Collaboration between the main stakeholders - Strategic dialogue and active participation of key stakeholders - Rewards and incentives of the association

Table 5. Governance dynamic component application

Governance Dynamic Component Application
Structures
- IEEE 830 standard format for the specification of functional and non-functional requirements that the application must satisfy.   - The stack structure of the product: Single key of stack log, Priority register of requirement, Description, Estimating effort, No. Sprint in which it is performed, Additional comments, Validation criteria, Person assigned as responsible, Use case or user story
Processes
Align, Planning and Organize (APO)
APO01 Manage the IT Management Framework   The development manager, project leader, and TICS official are responsible for: - Adopt standard IEEE830 format for the specification of functional and non-functional requirements.   - Adopt SCRUM for the management of the application development project.   - Adopt UWE, for the development of the application using the best practices of Web Engineering, to elaborate the use case diagrams, a diagram of the entity physical relation of the database, diagram classes, sequence, navigation, presentation, of processes.   - Establish verification and acceptance criteria for User manuals, installation manual, and technical manual.   **APO11 Manage Quality**   The owner of the product and the three officials designated as members of the reception committee are responsible for: - Verify and communicate compliance with the requirements agreed upon between the parties, for each iteration.   - Report the functionality, usability, and navigability of each component delivered at the end of each iteration.   - Apply the recommendations reported in the acceptance tests of each element at the end of the iteration.   **APO12 Manage Risk**   -The owner of the product, SCRUM master, and designated TICS official are responsible for: - Verify that the components and the final product meet the norms and requirements of IT, about the securities and development platform.   - Verify that the software complies with the laws and regulations of the institution.
Build, Acquire & Implement (BAI)
BAI02 Manage the Requirements Definition   The product owner, master SCRUM and the project manager are responsible for: - Raise the document of the specification of requirements between the interested parties, using the standard IEEE830.   - Negotiate the scope of the report of the specification of requirements between the involved parties, the product owner, master SCRUM and the project administrator.   - Determine the number of iterations to build the product. Four was the estimated number.   - Determine the time of the duration of the iteration. The estimated time was one month (30 days)   - Determine the time required to deliver the necessary technical documentation and conduct the acceptance and compliance tests of the final product.   **BAI08 Manage Knowledge**   The product owner, lead researcher, and research assistant are responsible for: - To raise the necessary technical documentation to guarantee the maintainability of the software, user manual, technical manual, and installation manual.
Monitor, Evaluate, and Assess (MEA)
MEA01 Supervise, Evaluate and Evaluate Performance and Compliance.   The developer and the product owner are responsible for: - Establish a mechanism to collaborate with stakeholders to establish tools to verify compliance with requirements, performance, and conformity of the software product.
Used Relational Mechanisms
- The principle of active participation of stakeholders   - Collaboration among key stakeholders   - Dynamic conflict resolution. There was a change of director in IT, which brought instability to the project because the new official initially did not know the authority of the official assigned as the owner of the product, which is corrected by the project manager.

At the project end, two surveys were run to evaluate the model among the participants:

a. The first one was oriented to verify if the application of the model contributed positively to the project management, from the perspective of the project manager, obtaining a valuation of 4.3/5. The principal identified lacks are generated due to the Public-Sector Organizations undesirable characteristics: low stability of the officials, and lack of continuity of policies and even procedures.
b. The second one was oriented to check if the model contributed in a positive way to the process of the software product development, from the perspective of the stakeholders; the valuation was 4.65/5. The central lack was the initial difficult to understand the coexistence of technical and governance tasks.

6 Discussion and Conclusions

The designed model aided to the problem and solution understanding. As DSR establishes, the selected case study allowed investigating a phenomenon within a real corporative context; it is cataloged as a representative for inferring some generalizable knowledge to related cases. The model application demonstrates his feasibility and utility; however, it is necessary to test it in other controlled case studies, as a future work option.

Significant themes to highlight in the results of the model application are the following:

a. The existence of a mechanism to collaborate with stakeholders to verify compliance with requirements, performance, and conformity of the product received jointly.
b. The definition of the stack structure of the product, that possibilities clear mechanisms of monitoring and evaluation of the software product.
c. Assignment of Operational and government officials for raising the necessary technical documentation to guarantee the maintainability and operability of the software product.
d. A governance structure which allows driving the potential conflicts, as it happened in the case study.

The developed model can be seen as a combination of reference models to processes improvement. Here was not necessary to use a complicated combination process, due to the use of agile SCRUM process as SPM, which complete the scenario to probe the SDG model. However, the background can be employed with other team characteristics, out of the agile environment, focusing on the ITG and IT Management integration.

Another issue related to the model is the COBIT use. Several studies are establishing the adoption difficulties [2, 32, 33]. The case study is evidence that it is possible to use specific COBIT components to improve the processes, in little groups. For a practical approach, it is important to extract the necessary information of COBIT and transforms it into a specific case template, as is made in this work.

Also, the work contributes to an exploratory study related to the ITG and SDG practices in Ecuador. The study results can constitute an initial reference for other regional countries, due to the cultural and economic similitudes. The main findings are the following: (i) The ITG and SDG practices are identical in VSE and Not-VSE teams; Not-VSE shows best individual assessment for each involved theme in ITG and SDG issues; and, (ii) The ITG and SDG practices are similar in PSO and private organizations.

Despite DSR use that promotes the generalization objective, the main identified limitation of the work is the possible results generalization regarding the company size, due to the influence of this parameter on VSE team behavior, as has been studied by Maglyas et al. [14] In the case study, the company size has a fixed value. Considering the study results about ITG and SDG practices, it is supposed that the others parameters, VSE team size and company type (public/private), do not influence the model application outcomes with another SPM. Therefore, an interesting issue is the possibility to apply the model in Not-VSE teams and/or private organizations and achieve similar results as in this work.

It is notorious the lack in SDG research, despite the importance of the theme and that VSE groups are widely spread around the world. In the context, this study contributes to providing a practical tool for the practitioners and academics and on the growth of the current knowledge concerning SDG for VSE type teams. Nevertheless, as an opportunity, further research is needed in the field of VSE-SDG and its relationship with SPM options.

Appendix A: SCRUM Management Model (SPM_SCRUM)

The model has three-phase execution, based on the best practices (See Fig. 5). The first phase refers to the initial conceptualization of the software development process in which the goal is to understand the problem that is being proposed, to suggest the solution jointly with the business owner, based on a clear understanding of the requirements of the problem and agreed metrics for product evaluation. The second phase corresponds to the iterative process that allows the construction of the software through increments or partial deliveries of functional software. The third stage refers to the control and monitoring of the software development project.

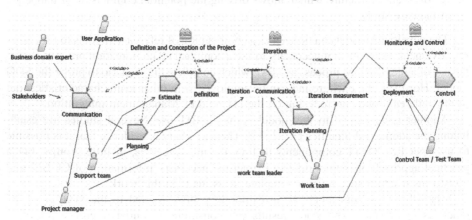

Fig. 5. SCRUM management model

References

1. Webb, P., Pollard, C., Ridley, G.: Attempting to define IT governance wisdom or folly?. In: 39th International Conference on System Sciences, Hawaii (2006)
2. Van Grembergen, W., De Haes, S.: Enterprise Governance of Information Technology. Springer, New York (2015). https://doi.org/10.1007/978-0-387-84882-2
3. Almeida, R., Pereira, R., Mira da Silva, M.: IT governance mechanisms: a literature review. In: Proceedings of the 4th International Conference IESS, Porto, Portugal, 7–8 February 2013
4. Castro, M., Hernandes, C.: A metric of software size as a tool for IT governance. In: Proceedings of 27th Brazilian Symposium on Software Engineering, SBES 2013 (2013)
5. Dubinsky, Y., Ravid, S., Rafaeli, A., Bar-Nahor, R.: Governance mechanisms in global development environments. In: Sixth IEEE International Conference on Global Software Engineering (2011)
6. ISACA: COBIT 5.0. A business framework for governance and management of IT (2012)
7. Chulani, S., Williams, C., Yaeli, A.: Software development governance and its concerns. In: Proceedings of the 1st International Workshop on Software Development Governance (2008)
8. Sommer, A., Dukovska-Popovska, I., Steger-Jensen, K.: Agile product development governance – on governing the emerging scrum/stage-gate hybrids. In: Grabot, B., et al. (Eds.): APMS 2014, Part I, IFIP AICT (2014)
9. Talby, D., Dubinsky, Y.: Governance of an agile software project. In: SDG 2009, Vancouver, Canada (2009)
10. O'Connor, R.V., Laporte, C.Y.: Software project management in very small entities with ISO/IEC 29110. In: Winkler, D., O'Connor, Rory V., Messnarz, R. (eds.) EuroSPI 2012. CCIS, vol. 301, pp. 330–341. Springer, Heidelberg (2012). https://doi.org/10.1007/978-3-642-31199-4_29
11. Sánchez-Gordón, M.-L., Colomo-Palacios, R., de Amescua Seco, A., O'Connor, R.V.: The route to software process improvement in small- and medium-sized enterprises. Managing Software Process Evolution, pp. 109–136. Springer, Cham (2016). https://doi.org/10.1007/978-3-319-31545-4_7
12. Maglyas, A., Nikula, U., Smolander, K.: Comparison of software product management practices in SMEs and large enterprises. In: Cusumano, M.A., Iyer, B., Venkatraman, N. (eds.) ICSOB 2012. LNBIP, vol. 114, pp. 15–26. Springer, Heidelberg (2012). https://doi.org/10.1007/978-3-642-30746-1_2
13. Van Wyk, L., Marnewick, C.: Applying governance principles to improve agile project success. In: International Association for Management of Technology IAMOT 2016 (2016)
14. Er, N., Erbaş, C., Ervaş, B.: Software development governance: a case study for tools integration. In: Modern Software Engineering Concepts and Practices: Advanced Approaches, Information Science Reference, pp. 315–332 (2011)
15. Bannerman, P.: Software development governance: a meta-management perspective. In SDG 2009, Vancouver, Canada (2009)
16. Hevner, A., Ram, S., March, S., Park, J.: Design science in information systems research. MIS Q. 28(1), 75–105 (2004)
17. Hevner, A., Chatterjee, S.: Design Research in Information Systems. Springer Publishing, New York (2010). https://doi.org/10.1007/978-1-4419-5653-8
18. Helfert, M., Donnellan, B. (eds.): EDSS 2011. CCIS, vol. 286. Springer, Heidelberg (2012). https://doi.org/10.1007/978-3-642-33681-2

19. Peffers, K., Rothenberger, M., Kuechler, B. (eds.): DESRIST 2012. LNCS, vol. 7286. Springer, Heidelberg (2012). https://doi.org/10.1007/978-3-642-29863-9
20. Tremblay, M.C., VanderMeer, D., Rothenberger, M., Gupta, A., Yoon, V. (eds.): DESRIST 2014. LNCS, vol. 8463. Springer, Cham (2014). https://doi.org/10.1007/978-3-319-06701-8
21. Given, L. (ed.): SAGE: The SAGE Encyclopedia of Qualitative Research Methods. SAGE Publications, Los Angeles (2008)
22. Mason, J.: Qualitative Researching. SAGE Publications, London (2002)
23. De Haes, S., Van Grembergen, W.: Information Technology Governance. Models, Practices, and Cases. IGI Publishing, Hershey (2008)
24. ISACA: COBIT 5: Enabling Processes (2012)
25. Noll, J., Beecham, S., Richardson, I., Canna, C.: A global teaming model for global software development governance: a case study. In: IEEE 11th International Conference on Global Software Engineering (2016)
26. Kofman, A., Yaeli, A., Klinger, T., Tarr, P.: Roles, rights, and responsibilities: better governance through decision rights automation. In: SDG 2009 (2009)
27. ISO IEC: ISO/IEC TR 29110-1 Systems and software engineering—Lifecycle profiles for Very Small Entities (VSEs) (2016)
28. SCRUMstudy™: A Guide to the Scrum Body of Knowledge (SBOK™ Guide), VMEdu, Inc. (2016)
29. SNAP-Ecuador: Subsecretaría de Gobierno Electrónico. http://www.administracionpublica.gob.ec/subsecretaria-de-gobierno-electronico/#. Accessed 2017
30. AESOFT-Ecuador: AESOFT. http://aesoft.com.ec/. Accessed 2017
31. Heal, R., Twycross, A.: Validity and reliability in quantitative research, Evid.-Based Nurs., 66–67 (2015)
32. Mangalaraj, G., Singh, A.: IT governance frameworks and COBIT - a literature review. In: Twentieth Americas Conference on Information Systems, Savannah (2014)
33. Bartens, Y., De Haes, S., Lamoen, Y., Schulte, F., Voss, S.: On the way to a minimum baseline in IT governance: using expert views for selective implementation of COBIT 5. In: 48th Hawaii International Conference on System Science (2015)

Maturity Level of Software Development Processes in SMEs Guayaquil

Vanessa Jurado Vite[✉], Shirley Coque Villegas,
and Guillermo Pizarro Vásquez

Universidad Politécnica Salesiana (UPS), Campus Centenario,
Robles 107 y Chambers, Guayaquil, Ecuador
{vjurado,scoque,gpizarro}@ups.edu.ec

Abstract. The software process improvement has gained a lot of space in recent years; the Software Engineering community has developed models that improve the software process. Knowing the reality of software development companies is fundamental for the application of some process improvement model. In the case of SMEs, due to lack of resources, this improvement may be unattainable. In this document, we present an analysis of the processes and activities that are considered by the CMMI process improvement models, Competisoft and ISO/IEC 29110. The aspects that must be fulfilled are established within the different activities that correspond to two processes: planning/management of the project and development/implementation of software; the instrument was designed and 10 SME software developers were evaluated. The results obtained indicate that the companies surveyed do not comply with all the aspects required to complete the initial level of a process improvement model.

Keywords: Maturity level · Software development processes
Software process improvement

1 Introduction

In order to establish an improvement of processes in a company, it is necessary to identify the situation of the activities that correspond to the processes of the business model. For SMEs that develop software products it is essential to consider a set of strategies that allow them to properly manage their processes [1], an inefficient process can derive in various problems like a low quality product, low productivity of the development team or products that do not correspond to what is requested by the clients. Being SMEs an engine of the global economy, which development contributes to the generation of foreign exchange and employment at a global level [2], it is important to carry out an analysis of the current situation of the activities to establish which processes are not responding to internationally accepted norms or standards and that can generate the problems described above. The improvement of software processes has been considered in several models into development of software products, each process contains a set of activities, which are associated with aspects that must be met and that must be properly documented, in such a way to consider it as successfully

© Springer Nature Switzerland AG 2019
M. Botto-Tobar et al. (Eds.): CITT 2018, CCIS 895, pp. 233–244, 2019.
https://doi.org/10.1007/978-3-030-05532-5_17

executed by the company. This article presents an analysis of the process improvement models, with the objective of determining the most relevant processes into development process, which can be found in Sect. 2. The activities of the selected processes are analyzed and the aspects of the activities are presented in Sect. 3, once the aspects that are going to be consulted to the SMEs are defined, the results obtained in Sect. 4 are presented. Section 5 is devoted to the discussion of the results obtained, whose purpose is to establish which points can be improved for software development SMEs. Finally, conclusions with Sect. 6.

2 Analysis of Process Improvement Models

To carry out the research work, three models of process improvement were considered, CMMI, Competisoft and ISO/IEC 29110. Those models provide a set of activities and processes that support companies to achieve the improvement of the quality of their software product. It is important for small software developers to have the necessary

Table 1. Process areas/Activities of the software improvement models

CMMI	COMPETISOFT	ISO/IEC 29110
Configuration Management (CM)	Process management	Project Planning (PM)
Measurement and Analysis (MA)	Resource management	Project Execution (PM)
Project Monitoring and Control (PMC)	Human resources management	Project Evaluation and Control (PM)
Project Planning (PP)	Management of Goods, Services and Infrastructure	Project Closing (PM)
Process and Product Quality Assurance (PPQA)	Knowledge Management	Software Implementation Start (SI)
Requirements Management (REQM)	Project management	Software Requirements Analysis (SI)
Supplier Agreement Management (SAM)	Software Development	Architecture and Detailed Software Design (SI)
Integrated Project Management (IPM)	Software Maintenance	Software Construction (SI)
Organizational Process Focus (OPD)		Software Integration and Testing (SI)
Focus on Processes of the Organization (OPF)		Product Delivery (SI)
Organizational Training (OT)		
Product Integration (PI)		
Requirements Development (RD)		
Risk Management (RSKM)		
Technical Solution (TS)		
Validation (VAL)		
Verification (VER)		

tools that allow them to enhance their capacity to produce high quality software [3]. The following is a description of the process improvement models considered:

CMMI is a maturity model that works on two levels: maturity and ability. It has 22 process areas, which are divided into categories: support, project management, process management and engineering [4].

The Competisoft project was developed for small software development organizations and uses a model with 10 process areas, cataloged in: top management, management and operation [5].

The ISO/IEC 29110 standard was developed considering the profiles of small companies. It offers a framework that consists of 5 parts: general vision, reference framework and taxonomy, evaluation guide, specification of the profiles and the management and engineering guide. It develops 10 activities, grouped in the processes: project management (PM) and software implementation (SI) [6].

The previous three models converge in various areas, processes and activities. In order to determine the activities that software development SMEs should prioritize, we proceeded with the analysis of the process areas described in Table 1.

The models proposed for the study handle areas of processes that have similarities. To determine these coincidences, the process areas that CMMI handled were analyzed against the process areas of Competisoft, then the process areas of Competisoft against the activities of ISO/IEC 29110 and finally, the CMMI process areas against the activities of ISO/IEC 29110. Subsequently, a selection of ISO/IEC 29110 activities was carried out as well as the CMMI and Competisoft process areas where there were more similarities in the management of processes and activities. Table 2 shows the results obtained from the information and selection crossings. The (X) in the table indicates the

Table 2. Summary of related processes between CMMI, Competisoft and ISO/IEC 29110

CMMI	Competisoft Project Management	Software Development	Competisoft ISO
Project Monitoring and Control (PMC)	X	X	Project Execution (PM)
Project Planning (PP)	X		Project Planning (PM)
Requirements Management (REQM)	X	X	Software Requirements Analysis (SI)
Integrated Project Management (IPM)	X		Product Delivery (SI)
Product Integration (PI)		X	Software Integration and Testing (SI)
Requirements Development (RD)		X	Software Construction (SI)
Validation (VAL)	X	X	Software Integration and Testing (SI)
Verification (VER)	X	X	Project Evaluation and Control (PM)

process area of Competisoft that relates to CMMI process areas and those of ISO/IEC 29110. In other words, the aspects that CMMI controls within the process area Monitoring and Control of the Project (PMC) Competisoft controls in the process areas of Project Management and Software Development, and ISO/IEC within the project Execution activity.

Table 3. Aspects to be considered in the Project Planning/Project Management

Act.	Aspects
Planning	The project document must have: • Definition of Scope and objectives • Description of general requirements • Definition of the development process • Definition of Roles and responsibilities • Definition of activities, dependencies and deliverables • Assignment of time to activities according to historical and goals to be met and generation of calendar • Risk analysis and contingency plan • Definition of Project configuration management (repository, version control system, permissions, etc.)
Execution	• The work methodology of the project should be made known to the project team • There must be a predefined communication and implementation plan • Project information should be distributed to the Task Force as a whole or each member should at least receive the information they need • The project team must know the tasks to be performed and the estimated time for completion • The project team must keep track of the progress of their tasks • It must continue identifying, categorizing and establishing treatment to the new and existing risks of the project • There must be a decision process regarding the acceptance of change request • Revision meetings must be generated with the work team • All costs generated must be recorded
Evaluation & Control	• Conduct an evaluation of the project plan that determines compliance with the scope of this • Conduct frequent meetings with the project team to resolve problems and difficulties encountered • Keep a record of the problems and the solutions proposed • Update the project plan to reflect the real progress of the project • Monitor the risks during the development of the project and update the Risk Management Plan with the new possible risks
Closing	• The project team must know the project closing date • The delivery protocol must be fulfilled • Generate a report of general suggestions • There must be a policy of process measurements • Generate a report of measurements according to the defined policies • Identify lessons learned • Incorporate lessons learned into the knowledge base

3 Processes and Minimum Activities to Reach Maturity Level

The project management and software development have been considered in the three models Competisoft, CCMI and the ISO/IEC 29110 standard for their control and improvement. Based on the activities defined in ISO/IEC 29110 that control different properly applied aspects that can lead to SMEs to have a first level of maturity in their development processes. These aspects were developed by carrying out an analysis of the work carried out in [7, 8] and adapted to the reality of the SMEs that work in the Ecuadorian context.

Given that the three models determine that the most relevant processes are project management and software development, the set of descriptors of each activity, which we will call as aspects, were established for each process as shown in Tables 3 and 4.

Table 4. Aspects to be considered in the Process Development/Project Implementation

Act.	Aspects
Start	• The team must know the initial tasks of the project • The team must know what is needed to start the implementation of Software • Assign tasks at least for the first week of project execution
Requirements analysis	• Conduct frequent meetings with stakeholders to capture requirements • Focus all the requirements of the stakeholders within a single requirement specification document • Possess a specialized environment to show the product to the stakeholders • There must be a person in charge of verifying the correct documentation of the requirements and of prioritizing the attention of the requirements
Architecture and software design	• Own a set of technologies (technological stack) defined by each type of project Software • Know if the system will communicate with other existing systems or if it will provide services to existing systems in the organization • Have an outline of the system's deployment infrastructure • Have a format to document the Architecture and Detailed Design of the Software • Check the validity of the Software Architecture Document • Record the traceability of the Software Components designed towards the requirements • Addressing Change Requests that impact on Software Architecture • Define and design the Software Components, their interfaces and the relationships between them • Document the relationships of the Software Components Example: UML diagrams, diagrams, flow diagrams, etc.

(continued)

Table 4. (*continued*)

Act.	Aspects
Software construction	• Have coding standards • Have standards for the development of database components • Have a set of reusable Software Components for each projects • Follow policies for the Software Components versioning • Perform unit tests • Count on metrics for code coverage • The development team must know and verify compliance with the metrics • Rules to define the development of the Software Components as finished Example: compilable code, 90% covered and added to the versioning repository.
Integration and testing	• Perform tests with the integrated software in different environments • There must be a procedure to declare an error or failure in the system • Define acceptance criteria for the execution of tests • Perform Software tests in an automated and manual way • There must be a procedure in case an integrated Software deployment fails
Product delivery/Closing	• The Operation and Maintenance Manuals must be documented and verified • The User Manual must be documented and verified • The system must be ready for deployment in the production environment • Verify that the delivery requirements indicated in the Acceptance Act are met • There must be steps to follow to deploy the system in the production environment • Attempt to meet the changes requested by stakeholders after the deployment of the system in production

4 Results

To measure the level of maturity of the software development processes in Guayaquil's SMEs, and taking as reference the mentioned aspects, an instrument of 62 questions was developed to measure compliance of the mentioned aspects by the software developers.

The instrument was applied in 10 software development companies of the city of Guayaquil, of which 56% indicated having up to 8 years of experience in the market, the remaining 46% indicated having 9, 17 and 38 years of experience. They were consulted about the number of projects they handle per year, the results were divided into three groups. The first group indicates handling up to 5 projects per year, the second one manages up to 20, and the third more than 20. The 56% of the samples

Table 5. Compliance of aspects by software development SMEs

Processes	Activities	# Aspects	# of aspects with full compliance	# of aspects with medium compliance	# of aspects with low compliance
Planning Process/Project Management	Planning	8	4	3	1
	Realization/Execution	9	3	5	1
	Evaluation & Control	5	1	1	3
	Closing	7	2	0	5
	Total	**29**	**10**	**9**	**10**
Development Process/Project Implementation (Software Development)	Start	3	3	-	-
	Requirements analysis	4	-	3	1
	Architecture & software design	7	1	6	-
	Software construction	8	2	4	2
	Integration and testing	5	1	2	2
	Product delivery/Closing	6	4	2	-
	Total	33	11	17	5
	Totals		21	26	15

indicated that they work with less than 10 workers, 33% with less than 50, and only 11% say they have more than 100 workers on their payroll.

When analyzing the answers provided by the VSEs, it was found that none of them comply with all the aspects in order to have a first level of maturity of software development processes. 22% meets over 90% of aspects, so that would be the closest companies have maturity level of development processes, another 22% meets less than 70% of the aspects and the remaining 56% are percentages of compliance between 70% and 89%.

The process improvement models establish aspects that indicate the levels of maturity of the software process, so that a company achieves a level of maturity in either CMMI, Competisoft or ISO/IEC 29110 the compliance of the set of aspects must be total for each process. In this study we have considered not only the total compliance, it was determined to create two ranges of validity to establish aspects of medium compliance, corresponding to the aspects that are met between 89% to 40%, and the second rank that was called low compliance going from 39% to 0%.

Table 5 shows the number of aspects that are fulfilled within the companies surveyed, for example in the Planning activity of the Project Planning/Management process, 8 aspects are considered, of which 4 are fully met, while 3 of they are met mildly and only 1 aspect has a lower compliance. In the process of Planning/Project Management of the 29 aspects, raised 10 aspects (34.48%) are fully met by all the members of the sample, while the process of Development/Implementation of the

Table 6. Compliance of aspects by software developers Project Planning/Management Process

Aspects with full compliance	Aspects with medium compliance	Aspects with low compliance
Activity: Planning		
– Definition of Scope and Objectives – Description of General Requirements – Definition of Roles and Responsibilities – Definition of Activities, dependencies and deliverables	– Definition of the development process – Assignment of time to activities according to historical and goals to be met, and generation of calendar – Definition of Project configuration management (repository, version control system, permissions, etc.)	– Risk analysis and contingency plan
Activity: Realization/Execution		
– Distribution of project information to the Work Team as a whole or each member receives the information they need – Knowledge of the tasks to be performed and the estimated time for completion by the project team – Generation of review meetings with the work team	– Knowledge of the project work methodology by the project team – Record of progress of tasks, by the project team – Existence of a communication plan and predefined implementation – Existence of a decision process regarding the acceptance of change request – Record of all costs generated	– Identification, categorization and establishment of treatment to the new and existing risks of the project
Activity: Evaluation & Control		
– Frequent generation of meetings with the project team to solve the problems and difficulties encountered	– Update of the project plan to reflect the real progress of the project	– Evaluation of the project plan that checks compliance with the scope – Record of the problems encountered and the solutions proposed – Monitoring of risks during the project development and updating of the Risk Management Plan with the new possible risks
Activity: Closing		
– The project team must know the project closing date – Compliance with the delivery protocol		– Generation of a general suggestions report – Identification of lessons learned – Incorporation of lessons learned to the knowledge base – Existence of process measurement policy – Generation measurements report according to the defined policies

software has a total compliance of 11 aspects (33.33%). Table 6 shows the aspects grouped by their compliance (Table 7).

Table 7. Compliance of aspects by software developers Development Process/Project Implementation (Software Development)

Aspects with full compliance	Aspects with medium compliance	Aspects with low compliance
Activity: Start		
– The team must know the initial tasks of the project – The team must know what is needed to start the implementation of Software – Assignment of tasks, at least for the first week of project execution		
Activity: Requirements Analysis		
	– Frequent meetings with stakeholders to capture requirements – Concentration of all stakeholder requirements within a single requirements specification document – Specialized environment to show the product to the stakeholders	– Existence of a person in charge of verifying the correct documentation of the requirements and of prioritizing the attention of the requirements
Activity: Architecture & Software Design		
– Existence of a format to document the Architecture and Detailed Design of the Software	– Knowledge of whether the system will communicate with other existing systems or whether it will provide services to existing systems in the organization – Attention of Change Requests that impact Software Architecture – Verification of the validity of the software architecture document – Existence of a set of technologies (technological stack) defined by each type of project Software – Existence of outline of the system deployment infrastructure – Traceability record of the Software Components designed towards the requirements	

(continued)

Table 7. (*continued*)

Aspects with full compliance	Aspects with medium compliance	Aspects with low compliance
Activity: Software Construction		
– Existence of a set of reusable software components for projects – Performing unit tests	– Existence of standards for the development of database components – Policies for the versioning of the Software Components – Existence of coding standards – Existence of rules to define the development of the Software Components once they are finished	– Existence of metrics for code coverage – Knowledge/compliance of the development team on metrics for code coverage
Activity: Integration and Testing		
– Conducting the tests with the integrated software in different test environments	– Definition of acceptance criteria for the execution of tests – Existence of a procedure to declare an error or failure in the system	– Testing of Software in an automated and manual way – Existence of a procedure in case of failure of deployment of integrated Software
Activity: Product Delivery/Closing		
– Preparation of the system for its deployment in the production environment – Verification of compliance with the delivery requirements indicated in the Acceptance Act – Existence of steps to follow to deploy the system in the production environment – Attention to the changes requested by the stakeholders after the deployment of the system in production	– Documented and verified Operation and Maintenance manuals – User Manual documented and verified	

5 Discussion

The software process improvement models establish the minimum parameters that the companies dedicated to software development must comply with. When analyzing the results obtained, we can affirm that none of the companies surveyed possess the levels of maturity in their processes, because none of them fulfilled all the aspects raised in this study. It is also observed that, although the Planning/Management process has a higher percentage of aspects that are fulfilled with respect to the Development/Implementation process, there exists a non-significant difference percentage. When comparing the results of the Aspects of medium and low compliance, we can appreciate that the Planning/Management process presents the greatest problems of non-compliance.

Activities that represent strengths in the study were found, since the disadvantages found are minor, these activities belong to the Development/Implementation process:

start, architecture & software design, and product delivery/closure. The weaknesses found within this process are requirements analysis, and integration & testing.

No strengths were found in the project Planning/Management process. The most visible weaknesses on SMEs are found in the evaluation & control activities and the closing activities, since those have the highest non-compliance percentage.

The aspects with low compliance identified in this study are related to risk management, knowledge management, process measurement and the existence of metrics for code coverage. These aspects are not being considered as a priority within the companies surveyed, which could cause serious problems in the quality of the product and in the progress of the organizations.

Within the risk management of the project, the aspects with low compliance: risk analysis and contingency plan; identification, categorization and establishment of treatment to the new and existing risks of the project; the monitoring of risks during the development of the project and update of the risk management plan with the new possible risks. In [9] it is mentioned that there is a common agreement that risk always implies two dimensions, one of them is the effect on the objectives, which means if the risk becomes a reality it will have consequences for the project. For this reason, the aspects presented are important, since they can mean the difference between the success or failure of the project.

The aspects with low compliance, related to knowledge management are: generation of general suggestions report; identification of lessons learned; Incorporation of lessons learned to the knowledge base. As mentioned in [10] citing Rodríguez (2002) to generate a true competitive advantage in the organization, effective knowledge management is necessary.

For the measurement of processes, the aspects with low compliance: existence of policy of process measurements, generation of report of measurements in accordance with the defined policies. In [11] it is stated that companies recognize processes and their optimization as success factors, and process measurement provides the tools for such optimization.

The aspects with low compliance related to code coverage: existence of metrics for code coverage; knowledge/compliance of the development team on metrics for code coverage. The code coverage allows measuring the quality of the tests [12], therefore it is necessary to have metrics that allow this measurement, and perform more exhaustive tests, so that there are fewer error situations without testing.

6 Conclusions

The software process improvement models CMMI, Competisoft and ISO/IEC 29110 converge in the improvement of two fundamental processes: Project Planning/Management and Project Development/Implementation.

The software development SMEs that were part of the study do not have the minimum requirements to ensure maturity of their software development processes, but it is demonstrated that, with a little work in certain aspects, they may be able to improve and obtain the desired level.

With respect to the process of Development/Implementation of the project, it was presented as the process with the most strengths and that could achieve the initial level of maturity, if the aspects with medium and low compliance are improved.

The project Planning/Management process is the one with the highest levels of non-compliance; the aspects related to risk management, knowledge management, process measurement and code coverage, although they are factors that can affect the success or failure of the project, are not being considered by the SMEs, and it is in these areas where improvement efforts should be concentrated.

References

1. Pino, F.J., García, F., Piattini, M.: Priorización de procesos como apoyo a la mejora de procesos en pequeñas organizaciones software. In: XXXIII Conf. Latinoam. Informática CLEI 2007 (2007)
2. Cabello, S.Y.T.: Importancia de la micro, pequeñas y medianas empresas en el desarrollo del país. Lex (2014)
3. Coque-Villegas, S., Jurado-Vite, V., Avendaño-Sudario, A., Pizarro, G.: Análisis de experiencias de mejora de procesos de desarrollo de software en SMEs. Cienc. Unemi **10** (25), 13–24 (2018). Analysis of experiences of improvement of software development processes in SMEs
4. Najjar, S.K., Al-Sarayreh, K.T.: Capability maturity model of software requirements process and integration (SRPCMMI). In: Proceedings of the International Conference on Intelligent Information Processing, Security and Advanced Communication, pp. 68:1–68:5 (2015)
5. Oktaba, H., Piattini, M., Pino, F.J., Orozco, M.J.: Competisoft: mejora de procesos software para pequeas y medianas empresas y proyectos. Alfaomega (2009)
6. Laporte, C.Y., Séguin, N., Villas Boas, G., Buasung, S.: Small tech firms: seizing the benefits of software and systems engineering standards. ISO Focus **4**(2), 32–36 (2013)
7. Ramos, C., Mendoza, L.: Implementación del estándar ISO/IEC 29110-4-1 para pequeñas organizaciones de desarrollo de software. Universidad Peruana De Ciencias Aplicadas (2014)
8. ProSoftCol, Guía Metodológica de Mejora de Procesos de Construcción de Software Adaptada Para Mismes_DS Colombianas (2010). http://pegasus.javeriana.edu.co/ ~CIS1030IS04/documentos.html
9. Zulueta, Y., Despaigne, E., Hernández, A.: La gestión de riesgos en la producción de software y la formación de profesionales de la informática: experiencias de una universidad cubana. REICIS. Rev. española innovación, Calid. e Ing. del Softw. **5**(3) (2009)
10. Marulanda Echeverry, C.E., López Trujillo, M.: La gestión del conocimiento en las SMES de Colombia. Rev. virtual Univ. católicadel norte **1**(38), 158–170 (2013)
11. Melcher, J.: Process Measurement in Business Process Management: Theoretical Framework and Analysis of Several Aspects. KIT Scientific Publishing, Karlsruhe (2014)
12. Fontela, M.C.: Cobertura entre pruebas a distintos niveles para refactorizaciones más seguras. Facultad de Informática (2013)

Integration and Evaluation of Social Networks in Virtual Learning Environments: A Case Study

Alexandra Juma[1], José Rodríguez[1], Jorge Caraguay[2],
Miguel Naranjo[3], Antonio Quiña-Mera[2],
and Iván García-Santillán[2(✉)]

[1] Postgraduate Institute, Universidad Técnica del Norte, Ibarra, Ecuador
{apjumaa, jlrodriguez}@utn.edu.ec
[2] Department of Software Engineering, Faculty of Applied Sciences,
Universidad Técnica del Norte, Ibarra, Ecuador
{jacaraguay, aquina, idgarcia}@utn.edu.ec
[3] Faculty of Education, Science and Technology, Universidad Técnica del Norte,
Ibarra, Ecuador
menaranjo@utn.edu.ec

Abstract. Higher education institutions objective is to establish a quality learning process in which faculty members and students may use the most suitable digital communication channel. In this context, this study's intention is to integrate and evaluate the social networks Twitter and Facebook in the Virtual Learning Environment (VLE). The study was conducted in a Technological Institute (ITSI) to determine the level of impact virtual communication has on faculty and students. In order to accomplish this goal, a Moodle platform was implemented with the following services: (i) user authentication (ii) cloud storage and file sharing and (iii) Twitter extension for message replication processes from VLE-ITSI to social networks. The proposal evaluation was performed using (i) usability and satisfaction metrics set up by the ISO/IEC 9126 standard and (ii) through a statistical analysis. The results from the standard application and the Wilcoxon statistical testing proved that social networks integration with the VLE-ITSI significantly contribute to faculty-student digital interaction during educational processes.

Keywords: Virtual Learning Environment · Social networks · Usability
Satisfaction · ISO/IEC 9126 · Moodle

1 Introduction

The use of learning management systems is a current tendency. Its main purpose is to contribute to the virtual communication between the faculty personnel and students who are the main actors in education and learning processes [1]. Education and learning processes are different processes but they develop jointly. Education is provided by a person (faculty member) while learning is done by a student. The educational process takes place when a communication bond is formed between both education and learning

© Springer Nature Switzerland AG 2019
M. Botto-Tobar et al. (Eds.): CITT 2018, CCIS 895, pp. 245–258, 2019.
https://doi.org/10.1007/978-3-030-05532-5_18

[2]. For this process to be carried out, higher education institutions have at their disposal a variety of IT tools and information sources so that students, as natural digital native, use social networks to set up virtual communication [3].

A group of people able to share ideas and to get involved in discussions of common interest constitutes a social network. The increasing use of social networks enables to take advantage of such tools for educational purposes. Nowadays, students potentially use social media far more than face-to-face communication [4]. The integration of social networks into learning practices has become a key element to complement and improve the traditional classroom education [5].

The use of Virtual Learning Environments (VLE) has become widespread and established in the academic world. It has become a dynamic and versatile working tool supporting contents management, academic processes as well as collaborative learning [6]. VLE may improve the quality of education enabling educators to review and evaluate students using available communication networks [7].

However, there are some drawbacks such as access and frequent use of VLE by students. This is often since the channel of virtual communication between users is not appropriate, and therefore it does not provide satisfaction to the people involved [8]. The quality of virtual communication in a teaching-learning system is important and plays a role in the use and efficiency of the platform [9]. Considering new trends in content distribution and the latest social skills, it would be a good idea to expand VLE's functionality by incorporating them within other platforms and apps like Facebook and Twitter, among others [10]. Nevertheless, usability issues might impede the use of every VLE feature and limit some learning objectives [11].

Web 2.0 technologies, which include social networks, have incorporated specific features that enhance students' constant collaboration in the learning process [3]. The educational potential of social networks relies on speed and diversity of connection between students. In this context, academic contents including contributions and online comments may be provided synchronously or asynchronously [12]. Interaction practices stimulate thinking [13] and since students are familiarized with social networks environment, it is more effective for students to perform their learning activities in an environment in which they feel more comfortable [14].

From this overview, the purpose of this study is to integrate and evaluate the social networks Twitter and Facebook particularly at VLE-ITSI to determine the impact virtual communication has between faculty personnel and students. The evaluation is carried out in the following two ways: (i) by measuring user satisfaction and usability of the VLE-ITSI by using ISO/IEC 9126 standard and (ii) by statistical analysis using Wilcoxon hypothesis testing and box-plot to compare the satisfaction of related user groups. This is the main contribution to the research.

Some existing studies serve as theoretical-scientific support for the research proposal because they address social networks within the academic field of higher education. These studies are listed below:

Díaz et al. [10] pointed to the benefits of integrating VLE to social networks. On the one hand, they involved various sectors of the academy to extend the outreach of academic activities. On the other hand, they extended VLE functionality to reach students through their social habits. Contreras and Navarro [15] showed the importance of users' satisfaction in the learning processes when using educational platforms.

Therefore, it may be concluded that there was an improvement in faculty-student interaction and communication thanks to the use of various synchronous or asynchronous communication tools. Alfonso-Cuba [16] stated that the quality of virtual education is based on Web environments that meet the current usability standards. Web environments study the way educational resources are accessed by students regardless of their ICT proficiency and the type of technology available to them. Mendes et al. [3] analyzed the impact of using Moodle and Facebook as learning media on a set of 159 students. Then, it was announced that Moodle linked to a Facebook plug-in were used to support learning activities outside the classroom. Moodle was used especially for formal communication with faculty members whereas Facebook was used for informal communication with peers.

Next, the research methodology used in this study is presented.

2 Materials and Methods

2.1 Participants

The study was conducted at "Instituto Tecnológico Superior Ibarra" [17] in Ecuador, during the September 2017 – March 2018 academic period. Participants were faculty members, students as well as administrative personnel who are the users of the VLE. The target group was composed of 12 Faculty members, 136 IT students, 73 Graphic Design students and 10 administrative staff, i.e. a total population of 231 users. 144 users were selected as a representative sample following the simple random sampling technique [18] using the most common values in the calculation formula (95% confidence level and 5% margin of error).

2.2 VLE-ITSI Platform Design

2.2.1 VLE Integration and Social Networks

VLE-ITSI integration, under Moodle Platform's version 3.4 [19] and social networks Twitter y Facebook cover three fundamental technological aspects: (i) VLE-ITSI user authentication through OAuth2; (ii) cloud storage and file sharing using Google Drive; and (iii) messages replication from VLE-ITSI to social networks using a Twitter extension.

2.2.2 User Authentication Through OAuth2

The Moodle native component OAuth Service [20] was configured in order to add authentication methods in the VLE-ITSI. This component enables to use the OAuth2 authorization protocol [21], by consuming the exchange protocol and data manipulation API REST (Representational State Transfer), to allow the authentication of Google user accounts [22] and Facebook [23]. This process involves the preliminary set up of those accounts in its own portals so that an Client ID and Secret password are obtained to grant access to REST API from VLE-ITSI [24] allowing the interaction between both technologies.

2.2.3 Cloud Storage and File Sharing

The Moodle Repository extension [25] was configured to enable the use of Google Drive Services for file sharing regardless of their size directly from the Cloud saving storage space on the VLE-ITSI server. Google Drive was chosen due to its connectivity with HTTP domains such as ITSI (http://www.itsivirtual.com/). Other services like Microsoft's OneDrive only allow interconnection via the SSL secure protocol (Secure Socket Layer).

2.2.4 Message Replication from VLE-ITSI to Social Networks

First, two user accounts were created for the exclusive use of the VLE-ITSI, one on Twitter (@ItsiVirtual) and another on Facebook (@ItsiEVA). Secondly, a module for Moodle was programmed and installed. It uses the Twitter library OAuth2 [26] as shown in Fig. 1. This allowed to create and replicate tweets automatically from VLE-ITSI to Twitter.

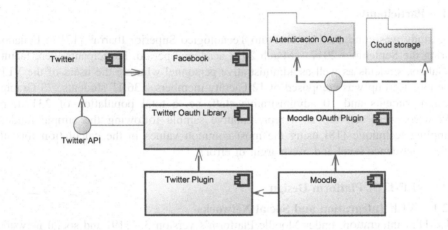

Fig. 1. Component diagram of the connection between Moodle, Twitter and Facebook

The Facebook application was registered on Twitter (Settings and Privacy option) to have access authorization to Twitter, in order to synchronize the exchange of tweets between both apps, generating a new communication channel (Twitter and Facebook) between faculty members and students.

2.3 VLE-ITSI Platform Evaluation

To evaluate the quality and satisfaction of VLE-ITSI with social networks, two procedures were carried out: (i) adopting usability and satisfaction metrics through ISO/IEC 9126-2 Standards -External Metrics- [27] and 9126-4 -Quality in use- [28], respectively; and (ii) through a statistical analysis based on Wilcoxon test and box-plot. The evaluation procedures are explained below.

2.3.1   Usability and Satisfaction Metrics Based on ISO/IEC 9126
Table 1 lists characteristics, subcharacteristics and metrics used in ISO/IEC 9126 Standard, which were consensually selected with the project's stakeholders (VLE administrator and ITSI's School Principal). These measures are relevant to determine the impact of the integration of VLE-ITSI with social networks on students, teachers and administrative personnel. Each column of Table 1 is detailed below:

(a) **Characteristic:** Quality attribute measuring the VLE-ITSI.
(b) **Sub-characteristics:** Breakdown items of the characteristic. In this study, four sub-characteristics were used to determine usability (understandability, learnability, operability and attractiveness) and one for quality in use (satisfaction).
(c) **Metric name:** Specific measures which evaluate the VLE-ITSI. They are related to digital communication between teachers and students rather than to the functionality of the platform.
(d) **Sub-characteristic's weight:** The following percentages were chosen by the project's stakeholders: 70% usability and 30% quality in use, considering the aim of this study, number of subcharacteristics and number of metrics. Then, the assigned weight is divided by the number of subcharacteristics, e.g. to determine the usability this formula was applied $0.7/4 = 0.175$ and for quality in use $0.3/1 = 0.3$.
(e) **Metric's weight:** Such value was obtained by dividing subcomponent's weight by the number of metrics assigned to each one of them, e.g. the formula $0.175/7 = 0.025$ for understandability and $0.3/3 = 0.1$ for satisfaction.
(f) **Method of Application:** For data gathering purposes: (i) survey (ii) observation (iii) satisfaction questionnaire [29].
(g) **Summation:** Calculated using the following Eq. (1):

$$T = \sum_{i=1}^{5} f_{i*i} \tag{1}$$

Where i represents the Likert scale level (5 levels) and f_i the relative frequency (%) calculated from absolute frequency measures (using some application method) and also considering the size of the sample (144 users). The Likert scale consists of referring the questions to the respondents, who must choose between five answer alternatives which reflect their degree of agreement or disagreement (the maximum acceptance value is 5 and the minimum is 1).

(h) **Score:** Determined by Eq. (2):

$$P = \frac{T * Metric's\,weight}{5} \tag{2}$$

where constant 5 represents the number of levels in the Likert scale and the other two variables being as previously detailed.

Table 1. Characteristics, subcharacteristics, usability metrics and quality in use according to ISO/IEC 9126.

1.	2.	3.	4.	5.	6.	7.	8.
Usability	Understandability	Completeness of description	0.175	0.025	Survey	4.8	0.024
		Demonstration accessibility		0.025	Observation	4.7	0.024
		Demonstration accessibility in use		0.025	Observation	4.6	0.023
		Demonstration effectiveness		0.025	Observation	4.7	0.024
		Evident functions		0.025	Observation	4.6	0.023
		Function understandability		0.025	Survey	4.9	0.025
		Understandable input/output		0.025	Observation	4.9	0.025
	Learnability	Ease of function learning	0.175	0.035	Survey	4.6	0.032
		Ease of learning to perform a task in use		0.035	Observation	4.7	0.033
		Effectiveness of the user documentation and/or help system		0.035	Survey	4.7	0.033
		Effectiveness of user documentation and/or help systems in use		0.035	Observation	4.9	0.034
		Help accessibility		0.035	Observation	4.6	0.032
	Operability	Operational consistency in use	0.175	0.019	Survey	4.6	0.017
		Error correction		0.019	Observation	4.6	0.017
		Default value availability in use		0.019	Observation	4.7	0.018
		Message understandability in use		0.019	Survey	4.6	0.017
		Operational error recoverability in use		0.019	Observation	4.9	0.019
		Time between human error operations in use		0.019	Observation	4.6	0.017
		Customizability		0.019	Observation	4.7	0.018
		Operation procedure reduction		0.019	Observation	4.9	0.019
		Physical accessibility		0.019	Observation	4.7	0.018
	Attractiveness	Attractive interaction	0.175	0.088	Survey	4.6	0.081
		Interface appearance customizability		0.088	Observation	4.9	0.086
Quality in use	Satisfaction	Satisfaction scale	0.300	0.100	Satisfaction questionnaire	4.9	0.098
		Satisfaction questionnaire		0.100	Satisfaction questionnaire	4.9	0.098
		Discretionary usage		0.100	Satisfaction questionnaire	4.9	0.098
		Total	**1.000**	**1.000**			**0.953**

2.3.2 Satisfaction Metrics Based on Statistical Analysis

An ad hoc questionnaire of 5 questions adapted from SUMI -*Software Usability Measurement Inventory*- [30] was submitted to the target group in order to statistically evaluate the satisfaction of VLE-ITSI users before and after the integration with social networks. This test allows to assess the user's perception and also determine the impact on digital communication between teachers, students and administrative personnel. Table 2 shows the questionnaire questions and the variables being measured.

Table 2. Ad hoc satisfaction questionnaire adapted from SUMI [30]

Questions	Variables
1. How would you rate VLE-ITSI user friendliness?	Satisfaction
2. To what degree can you understand the information provided by VLE-ITSI?	Understandability
3. Considering its security features, would you recommend VLE-ITSI to your colleagues?	Reliability
4. Do you enjoy the sessions on the VLE-ITSI?	Attractiveness
5. Has VLE-ITSI helped you overcome virtual communication drawbacks?	Communication

Using the outcomes of the questionnaire, a statistical analysis was performed applying Wilcoxon hypothesis test [31] to compare satisfaction levels between user-related groups as shown in Sect. 3. This non-parametric test was used due to the nature of the variables under study.

The adapted questionnaire used the 5-level Likert scale. The individual scores were summed and this total was compared to the expected value to check whether it was favorable or not [32].

Next, the results obtained in this study are presented.

3 Results and Discussion

Once the VLE-ITSI has been integrated to social networks like Twitter and Facebook, the evaluation outcomes are analyzed based on two points of view: (i) ISO/IEC 9126 Standard; and (ii) statistical analysis.

3.1 Usability Analysis and Quality in Use in Accordance with ISO/IEC 9126

Table 1 (column 8) shows the result obtained after applying the measuring instruments (methods of application) to the 144 user sample to determine the acceptance of the implemented platform. The sum of the weighted scores from the VLE-ITSI evaluation is $x = 0.953$ which means that it is in the range $0.8 < x \leq 1$ according to the scale established in Table 3, whose values are between [0 and 1], (1 being the best score).

Table 3. Acceptance range in accordance with ISO/IEC 9126 [28].

Scale	Range
Strongly agree	$0.8 < x \leq 1$
Agree	$0.6 < x \leq 0.8$
Uncertain	$0.4 < x \leq 0.6$
Disagree	$0.2 < x \leq 0.4$
Strongly disagree	$0 < x \leq 0.2$

The VLE-ITSI integration with Facebook and Twitter has been ranked as "Strongly agree" fulfilling usability characteristics and quality in use according to ISO/IEC 9126 standard evaluation model.

Figure 2 shows the comparison between the expected values –maximum- (Column 5 in Table 1) and values obtained (Column 8 in Table 1) in the VLE-ITSI evaluation. It must be mentioned that the difference between both expected and obtained values is not significant so the virtual communication channel between users is not only appropriate but also highly satisfactory.

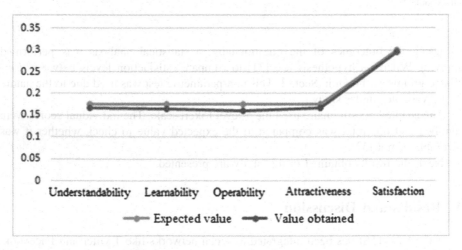

Fig. 2. Comparison between expected values (maximum) and values obtained in usability and quality in use in accordance with ISO/IEC 9126 standard.

3.2   Analysis of Satisfaction According to Statistical Analysis

In order to determine whether there were statistical differences between the original VLE-ITSI and the Facebook-Twitter platform integration, satisfaction metrics were assessed through an adapted SUMI questionnaire [30] of five questions (Table 2). As mentioned above such statistical differences are meant to verify the influence of virtual communication in faculty-students-administrative personnel exchange. In this test, the Likert Scale (5 levels) was used and the questionnaire was applied to the same sample of 144 user before and after integrating social networks to VLE-ITSI.

In this statistical analysis, the type of variables as well as the sample used were considered. In this case, the measured variables are of ordinal type (Likert Scale) and the sample is related (i.e. the same group of individuals). Therefore, the statistical test applied included the Wilcoxon theory [31]. This theory consists in a non-parametric test applied to two related samples and it attempts to discuss whether the results produced by both samples differ or not. Specifically, the null hypothesis (H_0) will show that the starting distributions of the populations from which the samples were obtained are the same, whereas the alternative hypothesis (H_1) shows difference between both distributions [33]. Here, both hypothesis were established as follow:

H_0: There are no significant differences in the level of virtual communication between faculty members and students before and after the implementation of social networks at VLE-ITSI.

H_1: There are significant differences in the level of virtual communication between faculty members and students.

The statistical analysis were performed using the IBM SPSS Statistics software version 24 [34]. The decision rule in the hypothesis test was the following:

If $p\_value > 0.05$ then H_0 is accepted, otherwise H_1 is accepted. The p_value represents a *Sig. Asymptotic* value shown in Table 4.

3.2.1 Wilcoxon Test

As shown in Table 4, the values of asymptotic significance (*p-value*) for every test are less than 0.05. This means that, according to the decision rule, hypothesis H1 is validated. Therefore, it is concluded that there are significant differences in the level of virtual communication using VLE-ITSI before and after integration with Facebook and Twitter.

Table 4. Wilcoxon statistical evidence

	Satisfaction after – before	Understandability after – before	Reliability after – before	Attractiveness after – before	Communication after – before
Z	–6.952	–8.074	–7.827	–7.782	–7.548
Sig. asymptotic value (bilateral)	0.000	0.000	0.000	0.000	0.000

Furthermore, the Wilcoxon signed-rank test was used to compare both related measures and to determine whether the statistical difference between them was due to randomness or not [33]. Table 5 shows the results obtained from the test applied to the satisfaction questionnaire.

It is observed that for each indicator (variable), positive ranks (average rank) prevail over the negative ones and the even ones, indicating that using VLE-ITSI integration had a favorable impact on faculty-students virtual communication, thanks to the Facebook-Twitter implementation.

Table 5. Wilcoxon signed-rank test

		N	Average rank	Sum of ranks
Satisfaction after – before	Negative rank	0	0.00	0.00
	Positive rank	105	53.00	5565.00
	Even	39		
	Total	**144**		
Understandability after – before	Negative rank	0	0.00	0.00
	Positive rank	138	69.50	9591.00
	Even	6		
	Total	**144**		
Reliability after – before	Negative rank	0	0.00	0.00
	Positive rank	135	68.00	9180.00
	Even	9		
	Total	**144**		
Attractiveness after – before	Negative rank	0	0.00	0.00
	Positive rank	114	57.50	6555.00
	Even	30		
	Total	**144**		
Communication After – before	Negative rank	0	0.00	0.00
	Positive rank	124	62.50	7750.00
	Even	20		
	Total	**144**		

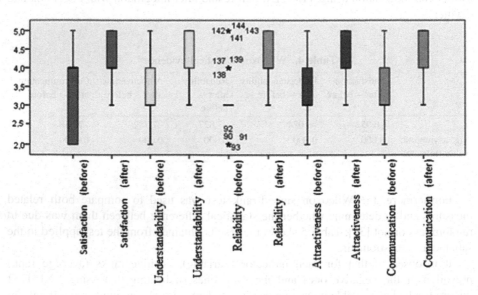

Fig. 3. Box plot of the five variables measured before and after social networking integration to VLE-ITSI.

3.2.2   Box-Plot

It is used for qualitative variables (ordinal in this case) representing the median (thick line inside the box) as well as other parameters related to its dispersion [29]. Figure 3 shows a box-plot showing the five variables measured before and after the integration of social networks to VLE -ITSI.

The five variables (satisfaction, understandability, reliability, attractiveness, communication) increased by at least one level in the Likert Scale, demonstrating a compelling impact to users' general satisfaction in regards to the use of VLE-ITSI.

3.3   Discussion

The findings of this study are consistent with those from [3] in the sense that students in both analyses showed higher levels satisfaction by having VLE (Moodle) linked to the social network Facebook. Likewise, results are in line with [35] which highlights that the integration of social networks to Moodle makes VLE access more effective and as a consequence far more appealing. However, despite advantages of IT tools convergence in the educational field, there are other disadvantages found in [5] where it is claimed that using Facebook in an academic environment may be the cause of distraction and consequently it may divert the learning process as students access social content.

Finally, it is recommended, as future work, to carry out this study considering the ISO/IEC 25000 standard known as SQuaRE Software Product Quality Requirements and Evaluation [36] instead of ISO/IEC-9126. In addition, a comparison of specific activities involving social and VLE objects could be addressed later, such as: cloud storage, file sharing, messages replication, among other tasks.

4   Conclusions

This research work performs the integration of the virtual learning environment (Moodle) to social networks Facebook and Twitter to enhance virtual communication between faculty, student and administrative personnel of the "Instituto Tecnológico Superior Ibarra" (Ecuador). The proposal assessment is performed through usability and quality in use metrics defined in the software quality model ISO/IEC 9126 (Table 1) but also through a non-parametric statistical analysis using the Wilcoxon test (Table 4) including a Box Plot (Fig. 3). The results show that final users are satisfied with the integration of the VLE-ITSI with the social networks Facebook and Twitter (Table 5). The five variables measured (satisfaction, understandability, reliability, attractiveness, communication) increased a level on the Likert scale (Fig. 3), improving the virtual communication between faculty personnel and students. As future work, it is recommended to conduct this study considering the ISO/IEC 25000 standard.

References

1. Vialart, N.M., Medina, I.: Programa educativo para el empleo de los entornos virtuales de enseñanza aprendizaje dirigido a los docentes de enfermería (Educational program for the use of virtual teaching-learning environments aimed at nursing teachers). Rev. Cubana Tecnol. Salud 9(1), 79–89 (2018). https://www.revtecnologia.sld.cu/index.php/tec/article/view/1025
2. Borroto, E.R., Vicedo, A., Cires, E.: La comunicación en el proceso enseñanza-aprendizaje (curso 27) (Communication in the teaching-learning process (course 27)). Editorial Universitaria, La Habana, Cuba (2014). (Rodríguez, G.J.B. (ed.))
3. Mendes, L., Guerra, H., Mendes, A., Rego, I.: Facebook vs moodle: surveying university students on the use of learning management systems to support learning activities outside the classroom. In: 10th Iberian Conference on Information Systems and Technologies (CISTI), Aveiro, pp. 1–4 (2015). https://doi.org/10.1109/cisti.2015.7170464
4. Mueller, J., Della, M.R., Del Giudice, M.: Social media platforms and technology education: Facebook on the way to graduate school. Int. J. Technol. Manage. 66(4), 358–370 (2014). https://doi.org/10.1504/IJTM.2014.065005
5. Petrovic, N., Jeremic, V., Cirovic, M., Radojicic, Z., Milenkovic, N.: Facebook versus Moodle in practice. Am. J. Distance Educ. 28(2), 117–125 (2014). https://doi.org/10.1080/08923647.2014.896581
6. Cantabella, M., López-Ayuso, B., Muñoz, A., Caballero, A.: Una herramienta para el seguimiento del profesorado universitario en Entornos Virtuales de Aprendizaje/A tool for monitoring lecturers' interactions with Learning Management Systems. Rev. Esp. Doc. Cient. 39(4), 1–15 (2016). https://doi.org/10.3989/redc.2016.4.1354
7. Razali, S.N., Shahbodin, F., Ahmad, M.H., Nor, H.A.M.: Integrating learning management system with Facebook function: the effect on perception towards online project based collaborative learning. Int. J. Adv. Sci. Eng. Inf. Technol. 7(3), 799–807 (2017). https://doi.org/10.18517/ijaseit.7.3.1310
8. Solórzano, F.N., García, A.: Una concepción teórico-metodológica para el aprendizaje en red en la Universidad Politécnica Salesiana del Ecuador (A theoretical-methodological conception for online learning at the Universidad Politécnica Salesiana del Ecuador). Congr. Univ. 5(4), 175–190 (2016). https://www.congresouniversidad.cu/revista/index.php/rcu/article/download/766/728/
9. Oliveira, L., Figueira, Á.: Social network analytics in formal and informal learning environments with EduBridge social. In: Costagliola, G., Uhomoibhi, J., Zvacek, S., McLaren, B.M. (eds.) CSEDU 2016. CCIS, vol. 739, pp. 296–316. Springer, Cham (2017). https://doi.org/10.1007/978-3-319-63184-4_16
10. Díaz, F.J., Schiavoni, A., Osorio, M.A., Amadeo, A.P., Charnelli, M.E.: Integración de plataformas virtuales de aprendizaje, redes sociales y sistemas académicos basados en Software Libre. Una experiencia en la Facultad de Informática de la UNLP (Integration of virtual learning platforms, social networks and academic systems based on Free Software). In: 10th Simposio sobre la Sociedad de la Información (SSI), 41JAIIO, pp. 58–70 (2012). Accessed http://41jaiio.sadio.org.ar/sites/default/files/5_SSI_2012.pdf
11. Babu, R., Singh, R.: Enhancing learning management systems utility for blind students: a task-oriented, user-centered, multi-method evaluation technique. J. Inf. Technol. Educ. 12, 1–32 (2013)
12. Chávez, J.: Las redes sociales en la educación superior (Social networks in higher education). Rev. Educ. Desarro. Soc. 8(1), 102–117 (2014)

13. Dahdal, A.M., Kisswani, N.M.I.: The integration of social media in the delivery of unit materials: a comparative examination of the experience of Macquarie University and Qatar University. In: 5th International Conference on e-Learning (ECONF), Manama, pp. 301–311 (2015). https://doi.org/10.1109/econf.2015.71
14. Rachael, K.F.I., Yun, H.: Facebook – a place for learning activities? In: 2013 Proceedings of the World Congress on Engineering & Computer Science (WCECS), vol. I, pp. 1–5 (2013)
15. Contreras, J., Navarro, M.: Sistema de administración de contenidos de aprendizaje (Learning content management system). UNID Editorial Digital, Distrito Federal, Estado de México (2015)
16. Alfonso-Cuba, I.M.: Universidad 2012. Curso corto 17: Usabilidad en la Educación: Garantía de la calidad de la Educación Virtual (University 2012. Short course 17: Usability in Education: Quality assurance of Virtual Education Year: 2012). Editorial Universitaria, La Habana, Cuba (2012)
17. ITSI: Portal del Instituto Tecnológico Superior Ibarra (2018). http://www.itsi.edu.ec Accessed 08 Feb 2018
18. Lind, D., Marchal, W., Wathen, S.: Statistical Techniques in Business and Economics, 16th edn. McGraw-Hill Education, New York (2014)
19. Moodle: Moodle 3.4 (2018). https://moodle.org/. Accessed 08 Feb 2018
20. Moodle: OAuth 2 services (2018). https://docs.moodle.org/34/en/OAuth_2_services. Accessed 08 Feb 2018
21. Moodle: OAuth 2 authentication (2018).https://docs.moodle.org/34/en/OAuth_2_authentication. Accessed 08 Feb 2018
22. Moodle: OAuth 2 Google service (2018). https://docs.moodle.org/34/en/OAuth_2_Google_service. Accessed 08 Feb 2018
23. Moodle: OAuth 2 Facebook service (2018). https://docs.moodle.org/34/en/OAuth_2_Facebook_service. Accessed 08 Feb 2018
24. VLE-ITSI: Virtual Learning Environment of the ITSI (2018). http://www.itsivirtual.com/. Accessed 08 Feb 2018
25. Moodle: Google Drive repository (2018). https://docs.moodle.org/34/en/Google_Drive_repository. Accessed 08 Feb 2018
26. Moodle: OAuth 2 Twitter service (2018). https://docs.moodle.org/34/en/OAuth_2_Twitter_service. Accessed 08 Feb 2018
27. ISO: Software Engineering. Software Product Quality. Part 2: External Metrics (2003). https://www.iso.org/standard/22750.html
28. ISO: Software Engineering. Software Product Quality. Part 4: Quality Metrics in Use (2003). https://www.iso.org/standard/39752.html
29. Alonso-Dos-Santos, M.A.: Investigación de mercados: manual universitario. (Market research: university handbook). Ediciones Díaz de Santos, Madrid, Spain (2017)
30. Alva, M.E.: Metodología de Medición y Evaluación de la Usabilidad en Sitios Web Educativos Educational Website Usability/Measuring and Evaluating Methods (Disertación doctoral). Universidad de Oviedo, España (2005). http://di002.edv.uniovi.es/~cueva/investigacion/tesis/Elena.pdf
31. Sáez, J.M.: Investigación educativa: fundamentos teóricos, procesos y elementos prácticos: enfoque práctico con ejemplos, esencial para TFG, TFM y tesis (Educational research: theoretical foundations, processes and practical elements: practical approach with examples, essential for TFG, TFM and thesis). UNED - Universidad Nacional de Educación a Distancia, Madrid, Spain (2017)
32. López, J.M., López, L.M.: Manual de investigación de mercados turísticos (Tourism market research manual). Larousse - Ediciones Pirámide, Madrid (2016)

33. Bouso, J.: El paquete estadístico R (Colección Cuadernos Metodológicos, 48) (The statistical package R (Collection Cuadernos Methodological, 48). CIS - Centro de Investigaciones Sociológicas, Madrid, Spain (2013)
34. IBM SPSS: IBM SPSS Statistics (2018). https://www.ibm.com/analytics/ec/es/technology/spss/
35. Berssanette, J.H., de Francisco, A.C., Frasson, A.C., Ferreira, F., Ranthum, R.: Facebook social network integration with learning platform Moodle. Espacios 38(10), 7 (2017)
36. ISO: ISO/IEC 25000 - Software Product Quality Requirements and Evaluation - SquaRE (2016). http://iso25000.com/index.php/en/iso-25000-standards

Towards the Implementation of a Software Platform Based on BPMN and TDABC for Strategic Management

Erik Sigcha⦿, Villie Morocho⦿,
and Lorena Siguenza-Guzman[✉]⦿

Department of Computer Sciences, Faculty of Engineering,
University of Cuenca, Cuenca, Ecuador
erik.sigchaq@ucuenca.ec, {villie.morocho,
lorena.siguenza}@ucuenca.edu.ec

Abstract. The strategic management of resources and processes has become a key element to enable industries to achieve their goals of minimising costs and maximising profits. Business Process Management (BPM) and Time-Driven Activity-Based Costing (TDABC) are two important tools that allow business managers to identify both activities performed and resources used within a company. Therefore, taking advantage of the integration of these tools may result in a deeper analysis of the state of a company.

This paper presents the development of a platform for integrating Business Process Management Notation (BPMN), to represent and store process flows, and TDABC, to obtain an estimation of their associated costs. To achieve this aim, the study reviews some methodologies used for modelling costing-oriented processes and for estimating process costs. The resulting software is a tool to support the first three phases of the BPM lifecycle, i.e., process identification, discovery and analysis, and the TDABC calculations.

Keywords: BPMN · TDABC · Strategic management · Management Costs

1 Introduction

In recent years, production companies have focused on performing strategic management of resources and processes. In fact, these two practices have a direct impact on the achievement of corporate objectives of any company. Indeed, strategic process management allows companies to align their internal activities with their objectives; and resource management helps to identify the efficiency with which these inputs are used within these activities. Among the disciplines applied to process management, Business Process Management (BPM) is the one most widely used in business and academic fields [1]. BPM comprises a set of principles, methods and tools that combines knowledge of information technologies, administrative sciences and industrial engineering with the aim of improving the processes of an enterprise [1]. The main idea of BPM is to develop a process-oriented organisation, eliminating activities that do not add value and improving the process flow within the limits of the company [2]. BPM is implemented in

© Springer Nature Switzerland AG 2019
M. Botto-Tobar et al. (Eds.): CITT 2018, CCIS 895, pp. 259–273, 2019.
https://doi.org/10.1007/978-3-030-05532-5_19

organisations through a series of steps and activities, called BPM life cycle. The BPM life cycle, presented in Fig. 1, can be summarised in six phases: identification, discovery, analysis, redesign, implementation, and control and monitoring [3].

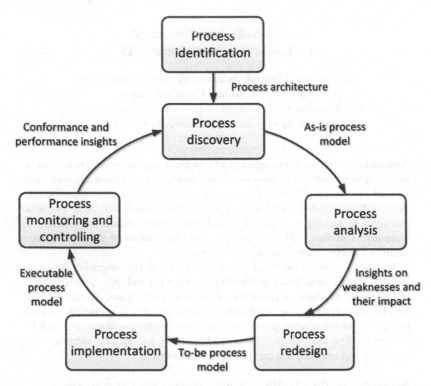

Fig. 1. BPM lifecycle (Source: Dumas et al. Fundamentals of BPM, Springer-Verlag 2013)

In practice, the application of the BPM life cycle is made with the support of modelling tools and process engines. BPM engines are capable of executing process models built using tools based on the BPMN (Business Process Management Notation) [4]. The objective of BPMN is to provide a notation that is easily understood by all members of a company, such as analysts, technical developers and decision makers [5]. When executing a process model, a BPM engine generates information that serves as an input to monitor and control the processes, which allows evaluating their performance and, therefore, optimising their operation.

In Latin America, many companies want to improve the management of their human, material and technological resources using the detailed information that provides BPM systems. For these companies, the identification, discovery and analysis phases of the BPM cycle acquire greater importance, since a diagnosis of their current state will be necessary, to identify processes and practices which need to be enhanced. In line with the process management paradigm, a complete and integrated diagnosis should also offer detailed information about costs related to each identified process.

To this end, an accounting management system offers several tools to make correct cost estimations. Time-Driven Activity-Based Costing (TDABC), through the use of time equations, adequately captures the diversity of processes and also provides accurate information on costs; a fundamental aspect for companies to detect possible internal inefficiencies, as well as development opportunities [6]. The TDABC system utilises two parameters: the cost per unit of resource time used, and the estimated time needed to perform an activity [7].

A tool providing support for process management and their corresponding costs in the early stages of the BPM life cycle would be highly convenient. A previous study that presented an analysis and design of a software tool applying TDABC for the management of processes and costs is reported in [8]. This software tool aims to support the management and analysis of information obtained from assembly companies before process redesign and optimisation. In that work, the tool constructed was intended to assist the early stages of the BPM life cycle, i.e., identification, discovery and process analysis; especially for companies that do not apply BPM yet and want to obtain an initial diagnosis before automating their processes. For that purpose, two goals were proposed: (1) documenting the analysis and design of software for the management of costs and processes applying TDABC, and (2) verifying if the development of the software allowed overcoming TDABC limitations. To achieve the first goal, the aspects to be considered during the software's life cycle were reviewed, emphasising the analysis and software design phases. Because of this analysis, a SCRUM-based development methodology was obtained with a set of resulting products proposed for each development phase. SCRUM is an approach for managing software development projects that introduces the ideas of flexibility, adaptability and productivity. To achieve the second goal, critical analysis was performed to determine whether the implementation of dedicated software to calculate processes costs reduces the limitations and/or improves the advantages of the TDABC costing systems.

The current paper presents a continuation of the study developed in [8], i.e., implementation and validation of a software tool for processes and costs management in assembly companies, applicable in the BPM phases of identification, discovery and analysis of processes. The resulting platform uses BPMN for process flows representation and TDABC for analysis of their costs. Additionally, the proposed work verifies if the described platform meets the objectives of improving benefits and reducing limitations of the TDABC system. The paper is organised as follows: Sect. 2 describes the tools and methodologies applied to software implementation. Section 3 summarises the results obtained when implementing and validating the platform with data collected from several case studies. The results are discussed in Sect. 4. Finally, the last section presents conclusions and briefly outlines the future directions for this work.

2 Materials and Methods

The materials and methods used to implement the platform include the following elements: methodology and tools for development, type of process modelling, a methodology for process cost estimation and methodology for software validation. Each element is described in more detail below.

2.1   Materials and Methods for Software Development

The work referenced in [8] resulted in the following elements needed to initiate the construction phase: (1) a software architecture, (2) a SCRUM-based software development methodology, (3) requirements and use case documents, (4) a conceptual data model, and (5) a plan to perform the implementation and validation. Based on the software architecture and the conceptual data model, a software tool evaluation was presented [9]. Here, the evaluation considers the characteristics of the data to be processed, the features to be implemented in the platform, and some comparison of programming tools, see [10–13]. The resulting programming environment is shown in Table 1.

Table 1. Programming environment used the process and cost management software.

Characteristics	Software tools
Programming language	Java (JDK 1.8)
Framework	Java server faces
IDE	NetBeans IDE 8.2
Web server	GlassFish Server 4.1.1
DBMS	PostgreSQL 9.3
Style and design tools	Bootsfaces 1.2 (Bootstrap based) Primefaces 5.2
Testing tools	JUnit
BPMN library	BPMNJS 0.22.1

To implement the functionalities of the platform, a planning task based on use cases compliance was considered. For this purpose, each use case was broken down into several resulting products or programming deliverables. More details on the use cases and software requirements are reported in [9]. A catalogue of macro functionalities implemented in the platform is as follows:

1. **Process Management.** Set of functions and interfaces that allow creating, updating, reading and deleting process information. For process information input, a diagram editor based on the BPMN 2.0 standard was considered.
2. **Business Data Management.** Set of forms and functions that allow entering, modifying, viewing and deleting information from entities belonging to the company. To accelerate the implementation of these functionalities, the Java Server Faces (JSF) framework was used. JSF allows automatically generating interfaces and programming functions to perform the "Create, Read, Update and Delete" (as an acronym CRUD) operations on database records.
3. **Process and Costs Analysis.** Software functions and interfaces that allow users to obtain results of cost estimates and process duration times using the TDABC costing system.
4. **Reporting.** Functionalities and interfaces to extract the results of the processing performed by the process and cost management platform as information reports.

5. **Software Configuration.** Features to manage general parameters of the software configuration. These include access control to the platform, user management, language, currency or default parameters for calculations and data entry.

These macro functionalities allow the process and cost management platform to fulfil its two main objectives: (1) to provide support for the management of process information of assembly companies, and (2) to provide a simple tool for cost analysis of these processes. To achieve these aims, the BPMN notation was selected as a means to represent processes and to analyse their costs using TDABC. For this reason, it was necessary to analyse the symbols provided by BPMN to identify the information that best contributes to cost estimation.

2.2 TDABC-Oriented BPMN Modelling

BPMN allows to represent a wide variety of process configurations for a diversity of audiences, providing three modelling styles: (1) Orchestration, (2) Choreography and (3) Collaborations [14]. Orchestration modelling is used to model internal processes of an organisation, since it allows to represent processes whose execution can be automated in a process engine, and processes which have been modelled only for documentation purposes and cannot be executed automatically [14]. Since the process diagrams generated in the BPM identification and process discovery phases are not executable process models, the BPMN Orchestration modelling was chosen to estimate process costs; where the only requirement was to specify processes flows from start to finish.

To specify a process model, BPMN offers a large number of symbols or elements that fulfil the objectives of being simple and easy to understand; and, at the same time, it can handle the high level of complexity that may arise when modelling business processes of an organisation [14]. BPMN elements may be grouped into those that have specifications for control of process flows and those that do not. Among the symbols used to specify process flows are Events, Activities, Gates, Sequence Flows and Message Flows. The elements not having semantics to control process flows are Lanes, Artifacts, Pools and Associations. The symbols related to the control of process flows were mainly used for process modelling oriented to costs estimation using the TDABC system; since they provide information on the activities that are performed and their order of execution. Figure 2 depicts the BPMN elements considered for modelling, oriented to the costing of processes by TDABC, with the information details provided by each element to estimate costs.

Notice from Fig. 2 that only a set of basic elements were selected from all the symbols provided by BPMN. These basic elements require complementary information provided by the Business Data Management module. Both Pools and Lanes were only implemented for representation purposes. Elements such as Types of Tasks, Attached Events and Artifacts were not considered, since they do not provide information to the costing and are more oriented to specify aspects of automation during execution in process engines. The selection of this set of basic elements was validated by the fact that the processes identified in the companies, used as case studies, can be modelled entirely using these symbols.

2.3   TDABC Implementation Methodology

The development of the Process and Cost Analysis functions is based on the steps defined in [15], which are illustrated in Fig. 3. These steps allowed estimating the process cost represented in BPMN using the TDABC costing system. Next, there is a detailed explanation of each step followed to estimate processes costs.

BPMN ELEMENTS	DATA FOR TDABC COSTING
EVENTS	
◯ START	- First activity performed.
◎ INTERMEDIATE	- Waiting time (minutes).
⬤ END	- End of the process - Last activity performed
ACTIVITIES	
Task — TASK	- Cost of the activity (Cost of using the resources in the activity) - Duration of the activity (minutes)
Subprocess — SUBPROCESS	- Cost of the subprocess (Cost of activities performed within the subprocess) - Duration of the subprocess (minutes)
GATEWAYS	
✕ EXCLUSIVE	- Represents a decision point in the process that evaluates the state of the process and breaks the flow into one of the possible flows. This generates more than one possible sequence of activities and cost for the process.
◇ INCLUSIVE	- Represents a decision point where the state of the process is evaluated and breaks the process flow into one or more flows.
✛ PARALEL	- Represents two or more concurrent task performed during the process.
SEQUENCE	
⟶ NORMAL FLOW	- Order in which the activities are executed

Fig. 2. BPMN elements for TDABC costing in the process and cost management platform.

1. **Identification of resource groups.** The first step requires resources data belonging to the company be available in a database. The minimum data required for a resource is Name, Type of Resource (e.g. human, material, technological or general), Availability (hours per month) and Resource Cost (salary or cost per period). The grouping is performed with records of the company resources, implying that resources must be assigned to the processes in which they are used. This can be accomplished by Activity (human, material and technological resources) or by

Process (General Resources). When creating records of processes or activities, the software tool requests to do the allocation of the resources, which allows saving the information of the resource groups by processes.

2. **Estimation of the total cost of each resource group.** Once the information generated in Step 1 is available, the software tool allows seeing which resources are used in each process and their costs for a certain period. The costs of all resources must be estimated within the same period, which may be monthly or yearly. To estimate the total cost of the resources per process, a sum of the costs of each resource is obtained.

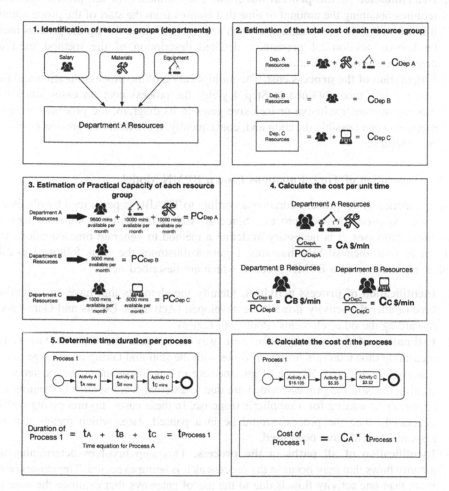

Fig. 3. Steps to estimate the process costs using TDABC.

3. **Estimation of practical capacity for each resource group.** In this step, all values of the theoretical resource capacity are adjusted to a single period (monthly). To do this, an estimate is made for values available in periods different from the monthly

ones. Once the theoretical capacity monthly value has been calculated for all resources identified in Step 1, the practical capacity of each resource is obtained by multiplying its theoretical capacity by its estimated practical capacity (i.e., 80% human resources and 85% material and equipment resources [7]). The result of this step is the practical capacity of each resource in minutes per month.

4. **Calculation of cost per unit of time.** The time unit used in TDABC is the minute; therefore, to calculate the cost per minute, the monthly cost value of each resource group is divided by the practical capacity in minutes gotten in the previous step. In this way, the cost per minute of each resource in the process is obtained.

5. **Determination of the process duration.** The estimation of the process duration requires obtaining the amount of time that elapses from the start of the process until it finishes. For this, the duration of each activity performed during the process must be known. Section 2.4 presents a detailed description of the method used to determine the process duration.

6. **Calculation of the process cost.** The multiplication of the process duration and the cost per unit time obtained in Step 4 yields the process cost. In cases when the process contains exclusive or inclusive gates in its diagram, the process can have more than one possible duration and, consequently, more than one process cost will be generated.

2.4 Generation of Time Equations from a BPMN Model

The estimation of the process duration according to TDABC is performed by obtaining the time equation for each process. Since BPMN is used in the software tool to represent processes, it is necessary to define a method to generate time equations for processes from their BPMN diagrams. Figure 4 illustrates the steps followed to calculate the duration of a BPMN process, which are described next.

1. **Identification of process activities.** Identify the elements that have an execution time or alter the activity flows to be developed (Activities, Events and Gateways), discarding the other elements (Pools and Lanes).

2. **Estimation of the activity time.** One way to estimate the time activity is by measuring time intervals from interviews with the staff and taking an average of the observed values [16]. In case of intermediate events, these mean the existence of waiting times in the process, which are due to external factors, such as waiting for approvals or waiting for a supplier's response. In these cases, no processing cost is generated, since the process would be in a paused state, which means that no resources would have been used.

3. **Identification of all paths in the process.** This step involves determining all activity flows that may occur in the process as it is being executed. The existence of more than one activity flow is due to the use of gateways that evaluate the state of the process at a certain point and, depending on some condition, separate the flow of activities in several routes. If gateways are not used in the process diagram, there will be only one possible flow of activities. However, if gateways are used then one of the following situations will be possible:

1. The exclusive gateway separates the process flow in two or more paths, which are mutually exclusive.
2. The parallel gateway represents that certain activities are executed simultaneously in a process flow, and it does not depend on conditions.
3. The inclusive gateway is a mix between inclusive and parallel gateways, depending on a condition. It separates the flow into two or more routes, which may be executed in parallel.

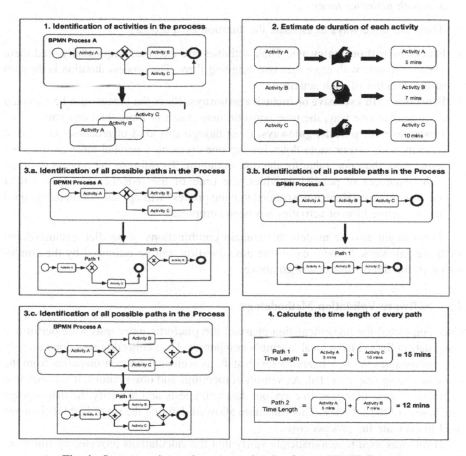

Fig. 4. Steps to estimate the process duration from a BPMN diagram.

In summary, depending on some condition, a process model that uses the exclusive or inclusive gateways will have several paths for being executed. This will cause that several possible flows of activities will be available with their respective duration.

4. **Calculation of time length for each identified path.** Estimating the process duration entails assessing the duration of each identified path, which is calculated

with Eq. (1). This will depend on the existence of gateways in the BPMN diagram of the process.

$$D = t_p = \sum a_i \tag{1}$$

D = process duration
t_p = path direction
a_i = path activities times

There are three ways to estimate the duration of a process:

1. **Processes without gateways.** Their activities are executed sequentially, and there are no elements with more than one outgoing flow. The process duration is the sum of the duration of each activity.
2. **Processes with exclusive or inclusive gateways.** Since the process can be executed in more than one way, the time equation may result in more than one value.
3. **Processes with parallel gateways.** Even though this kind of processes contains a gateway with two or more flows leaving one element, a parallel gateway does not cause more than one value for the time equation. To estimate the process duration with sequences of parallel activities, the time of the sequence having a longer duration is taken. Here, it is assumed that the process will operate continuously until the last active flow of activities has been completed.

There might also be models that contain combinations of parallel, exclusive and inclusive gateways. In these cases, the time duration will be estimated by the combination of the three ways described above.

2.5   Software Validation Methodology

Once completed the implementation phase of the platform, entry tests were performed using data collected from local assembly companies. Data collection was done directly in the companies through interviews with staff, as well as from measurements from the processes being operated [16]. As a result of meetings and observations, it was possible to obtain process files used to carry out data entry tests and to verify the data storage capabilities of the software. This validation allowed defining the set of BPMN elements used to estimate the process costs.

JUnit[1] was used to automatically verify that the calculations provided by functions of times and costs in processes, activities and resources produce the expected results. A final aspect regarding the software validation phase was evaluating compliance with requirements identified in the analysis and design phase. This evaluation verified the fulfilment of all functionalities outlined in the software design stage [8].

---

[1] JUnit, https://junit.org/junit5/.

3   Results

The main result obtained from this work is the construction of a software platform for processes and costs management. This platform allows saving and analysing information of processes in production companies. The BPMN notation is used for process representation and TDABC for estimating process costs. In addition, this software system facilitates data analysis of processes identified in the first two phases of the BPM life cycle, providing an overview of the current state of the company's costs and allowing the redesign of processes to optimise the resource utilisation of the company.

Figure 5 presents the software architecture used to develop the process and cost management platform, which is based on the Model-View-Controller architecture style. The **Model block** provides a set of classes that allow access to database records through programming data objects. The **View block** contains all the HTML pages, BPMN model templates, JavaScript libraries and other resources necessary for the operation of the application interfaces. The **Controller block** has been divided into three sub-blocks: Processing, Entity Management and Application Management. The Processing sub-block contains all functions required for formatting data, performing basic mathematical calculations, as well as functions to execute the TDABC costing, and processing the BPMN model data. The Entity Management sub-block is responsible for creating, updating, retrieving or deleting records from the database by using classes contained in the Model block. Finally, the Application Management sub-block contains all features required to assure proper functioning of the software, such as user authentication, handling of user sessions, security filters and software configuration.

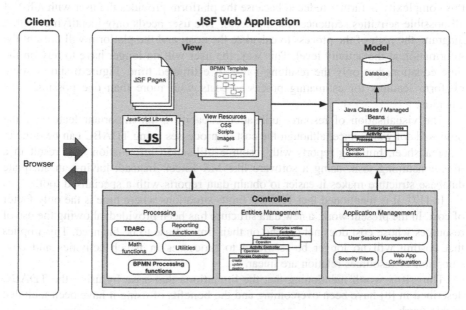

Fig. 5. The software architecture of the platform for calculating process costs.

To perform a cost estimation based on TDABC and BPMN, it was necessary to conduct an analysis of elements of the BPMN 2.0 standard used to estimate costs by processes. This analysis verifies: (1) which BPMN elements are available in the BPMN-JS library, (2) what information is provided by each element, (3) what data affects the times and costs calculations, (4) what elements are oriented to the automation of processes and (5) which elements are most used in the process identification phase. Because of this analysis, a BPMN modelling style was proposed, oriented to estimate costs using the TDABC approach.

Another result worth mentioning is an algorithm for calculating costs of processes from their BPMN process diagram. This functionality is based on a series of steps to estimate the costs of a process using TDABC [15]. To execute the costing function, in addition to the process flow, information of the company, such as personnel, resources, departments and roles is required, which is provided by the Business Data Management module of the platform. To develop this costing function, the steps defined in [15] were considered.

4 Discussion

The simplicity provided by TDABC to estimate costs and BPMN to represent the process flow is exploited in the proposed platform. It is well recognised that both BPMN and TDABC are elements that facilitate identifying processes to support improvement in performance and to reduce their costs.

The reduction of complexity in the estimation of costs using time equations allows a TDABC user to calculate processes costs based upon its characteristics. In this work, this complexity is further reduced because the platform provides the user with a list of all possible activities sequences for a process. The user needs only identifying, with a diagram, the path of the process to calculate the cost; and the platform will present the information at the activity level. This way, the user will no longer have to rely on the time equation, but only the resulting value of estimated time. Figure 6 shows some platform features for estimating processes costs with more than one possible time equation.

The visualisation of resource utilisation capacity is an important feature of the proposed software, since, although the cost of processes using TDABC can be done in a spreadsheet, building reports with resource utilisation information may result in a time-consuming task, using a software like MS Excel. Instead, having an adequate database structure makes it easier to obtain data reports with a specialised tool.

In [17], it is mentioned that TDABC limits situations where time is the only factor of cost. In the present work, a new data structure has been provided, allowing the use of resources whose cost does not depend on their time of use to be financed. This implies that costing will no longer be restricted to processes in which activities and consumption of resources relation are linear.

Thus, it is worth mentioning that the limitations that arise by using the TDABC described in [8] have been overcoming and the benefits of using it have been included in this work.

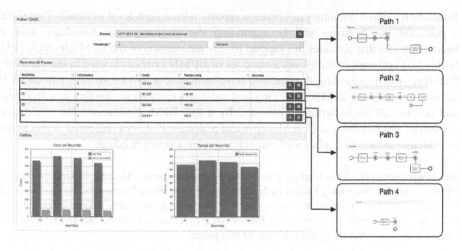

Fig. 6. Platform's interface for calculation of time equations.

5 Conclusions

This paper shows how the integration of the BPMN modelling technique with the TDABC costing system was accomplished to estimate processes costs in assembly companies. The use of BPMN to store and represent processes flows and activities in the company, as well as, the use of TDABC to perform cost analysis and process durations, allow obtaining accurate information about the process costs. This way, managers may identify expensive processes executed within the company and, which activities cause high costs. Besides facilitating the representation of processes, the application of BPMN 2.0 allows ensuring compatibility with process engines based on this standard.

The software platform for process and cost management presented in this work implements some improvements concerning the prototype version suggested in [18]. Among these improvements are the following: (1) use of BPMN notation for process representation, (2) cost calculation oriented to production companies, (3) storage of information of production companies. In addition, it is possible to extract various data reports, such as, process cards, process diagrams for documentation and process queries by operators, material or technological resources, which serve as inputs for the construction of internal manuals in the company or compliance with regulatory laws.

A possible limitation of the platform is regarding the process engine. The process and cost management platform allows an invariant analysis over time, adequate as an initial diagnosis, but with deficiencies at the moment of requiring an updated analysis. This limitation can be reduced by manually updating all the resources data, times and frequencies of each process, or obtaining data from an ERP software, using database connections. Even so, it would not be possible to reach a level of detail comparable to that of the information generated by a process engine, since this type of software is aimed at supporting the BPM life-cycle. Process engines, such as Bizagi[2] or

---

[2] Bizagi, https://www.bizagi.com/.

BonitaSoft[3], allow obtaining information reports with a high level of detail. Therefore, a potential improvement will be expanding the platform's functionalities until it becomes a tool that provides full support for the automation of the BPM life-cycle [15]. In this first software version, only a basic set of BPMN symbols is used in the platform; therefore, when expanding the platform functionalities, it will be necessary to check if the costing-oriented BPMN modelling and the costs estimation function can represent and process all the information provided by a full BPM application. The evaluation version of the Process and Cost Management Software Platform presented in this paper is available at http://imagine-platform.cidi.ingenieria.ucuenca.edu.ec.

Acknowledgements. This work is part of the research project "Modelo de Gestión para la Optimización de Procesos y Costos en la Industria de Ensamblaje" supported by the Research Department of the University of Cuenca (DIUC). The authors gratefully acknowledge the contributions and feedback provided by the IMAGINE Project team. In particular, special thanks to Eliezer Colina for reviewing the last draft of this paper.

References

1. van der Aalst, W.M.P., Rosa, M.L., Santoro, F.M.: Business process management. Bus. Inf. Syst. Eng. **58**, 1–6 (2016). https://doi.org/10.1007/s12599-015-0409-x
2. Kujansivu, P., Lönnqvist, A.: Business process management as a tool for intellectual capital management. Knowl. Process Manag. **15**, 159–169 (2008). https://doi.org/10.1002/kpm.307
3. Dumas, M., La Rosa, M., Mendling, J., Reijers, H.A.: Fundamentals of Business Process Management. Springer, Heidelberg (2013). https://doi.org/10.1007/978-3-642-33143-5
4. Geiger, M., Harrer, S., Lenhard, J., Casar, M., Vorndran, A., Wirtz, G.: BPMN conformance in open source engines. In: 2015 IEEE Symposium on Service-Oriented System Engineering, pp. 21–30 (2015)
5. Aagesen, G., Krogstie, J.: BPMN 2.0 for modeling business processes. In: vom Brocke, J., Rosemann, M. (eds.) Handbook on Business Process Management 1. IHIS, pp. 219–250. Springer, Heidelberg (2015). https://doi.org/10.1007/978-3-642-45100-3_10
6. Everaert, P., Bruggeman, W., De Creus, G.: Sanac Inc.: from ABC to time-driven ABC (TDABC) – an instructional case. J. Account. Educ. **26**, 118–154 (2008). https://doi.org/10.1016/j.jaccedu.2008.03.001
7. Kaplan, R.S., Anderson, S.R.: Time-Driven Activity-Based Costing: A Simpler and More Powerful Path to Higher Profits. Harvard Business School Press, Boston (2007)
8. Merchán, E., Sigcha, E., Morocho, V., Cabrera, P., Siguenza-Guzmán, L.: Análisis y diseño de un software de gestión de procesos y costos en empresas de ensamblaje. Maskana **9**(1), 79–88 (2018). https://doi.org/10.18537/mskn.09.01.08
9. Merchán E.: Análisis y diseño de software en la aplicación de TDABC para el sector productivo mediante el uso de metodologías ágiles. Master Thesis, University of Cuenca (2018)
10. Aruoba, S.B., Fernández-Villaverde, J.: A comparison of programming languages in macroeconomics. J. Econ. Dyn. Control **58**, 265–273 (2015). https://doi.org/10.1016/j.jedc.2015.05.009

---

[3] BonitaSoft, https://es.bonitasoft.com/.

11. Dávila, M.R.: Investigación en Progreso: Estudio Comparativo de la Incidencia de los Lenguajes de Programación en la Productividad Informática. Rev. Latinoam. Ing. Softw. **4**, 255–258 (2017). https://doi.org/10.18294/relais.2016.255-258
12. Pantoja, L., Pardo, C.: Evaluando la Facilidad de Aprendizaje de Frameworks mvc en el Desarrollo de Aplicaciones Web. Publicaciones E Investig. **10**, 129–142 (2016). https://doi.org/10.22490/25394088.1592
13. Aránega Hernández, A.: Almacenes de datos: Análisis de ventas de una compañía (2015)
14. von Rosing, M., White, S., Cummins, F., de Man, H.: Business process model and notation —BPMN. In: Von Rosing, M., Scheer, A.W., Von Schcc, II. (eds.) The Complete Business Process Handbook, pp. 433–457. Elsevier, Waltham (2015)
15. Everaert, P., Bruggeman, W., Sarens, G., Anderson, S.R., Levant, Y.: Cost modeling in logistics using time-driven ABC: experiences from a wholesaler. Int. J. Phys. Distrib. Logist. Manag. **38**, 172–191 (2008). https://doi.org/10.1108/09600030810866977
16. Andrade Serrano, E., Elizalde Lima, B.: Levantamiento de procesos de ensamblaje de televisores para la empresa Suramericana de motores Motsur Cia. Ltda (2018). http://dspace.ucuenca.edu.ec/handle/123456789/29718
17. Namazi, M.: Time-driven activity-based costing: theory, applications and limitations. Iran. J. Manag. Stud. Qom. **9**, 457–482 (2016)
18. Siguenza-Guzman, L., Cabrera, P., Cattrysse, D.: TD-ABC-D: time-driven activity-based costing software for libraries. In: 80th IFLA General Conference and Assembly, Lyon, France (2014)

Calyx and Stem Discrimination for Apple Quality Control Using Hyperspectral Imaging

Israel Pineda[1]([2])(ID), Nur Alam MD[2](ID), and Oubong Gwun[2]

[1] Ecuador Metropolitan University, Quito 170523, Ecuador
ipineda@umet.edu.ec
[2] Chonbuk National University, Jeonju 54896, South Korea
uzzalnp@gmail.com, obgwun@jbnu.ac.kr

Abstract. The production of high-quality food products needs an efficient method to detect defects in food, this is particularly true in the
production of apples. Hyperspectral image processing is a popular technique to carry out this detection. However, the stem and calyx of the
apple provoke frequent detection errors. We analyze the spectrum of our
apple data set, propose an algorithm that uses the average of the principal components of two regions of the spectrum to identify the defects, and
couple this detection routine with a two-band ratio that discriminates the
calyx and stem. Our study considers the spectral range between 403 nm
and 998 nm. Our results include the detection of scab, bruise, crack,
and cut with and without stem and calyx. We describe all the necessary parameters provided by our spectral analysis. Our algorithm has
an overall accuracy of 95%. We conclude that our algorithm effectively
detects defects in the presence of stem and calyx.

Keywords: Hyperspectral imaging · Two-band ratio
Defect detection

1 Introduction

The apple industry has traditionally invested in manual and time-consuming
processing of fruits to provide high-quality apples to its consumers. Nowadays,
however, the interest in automated processing techniques keeps increasing yielding a vast amount of work in this field. These new developments help to reduce
production costs and to increase competitiveness thanks to its capabilities, efficiency, and accuracy.

Hyperspectral imaging systems use a wider range of the electromagnetic spectrum to analyze and understand the data. These systems were originally developed for use in areas such as astronomy but have found application in agriculture
and more specifically in food quality control.

The vast majority of studies aimed for food quality control concentrate on
finding the optimal band for the defect detection of hyperspectral imaging. The

© Springer Nature Switzerland AG 2019
M. Botto-Tobar et al. (Eds.): CITT 2018, CCIS 895, pp. 274–287, 2019.
https://doi.org/10.1007/978-3-030-05532-5_20

optimal band is the band that, after the proper spectral analysis, seems to provide the best characteristics to execute image processing techniques. This is advantageous because if we know the fittest band we can execute fast algorithms. On the other hand, there have been fewer studies about the use of the full spectrum of the images. One possibility in this direction is the use of dimension reduction, for example, principal component analysis.

Previous work includes different approaches. Citrus fruit surface detection based on a multispectral image analysis and the PCA was introduced with a defect detection rate of 91.5% [6]. This method is susceptible to image orientation. Another work includes the detection of common defects on oranges [5], a hyperspectral image system was built for acquiring the reflectance images of orange samples in the spectral region between 400 nm and 1000 nm. The hyperspectral images of samples were evaluated using PCA.

Li et al. [5] reported the use of PCA and two-band ratio for orange defect detection with a detection rate of 92.6%. Wang et al. [11] reported a stepwise discriminant analysis to identify jujube insect infestations with 97% detection rate. Lee et al. [2] used a simple two-band ratio equation to detect apple defects with 93% detection rate. Zhang et al. [13] studied peach defects with multivariate analysis and two-band math with 93.3% detection rate.

In this paper, we propose a method to detect defects in the skin of apples. Our method uses the average of two principal components of different regions of the spectrum, visual and near-infrared, to detect defects. This kind of intensity-based methods usually have problems discriminating the stem and calyx of the fruit. These techniques wrongly regard the stem and calyx as defects. Our method includes the discrimination of stem and calyx using a two-band ratio to avoid detection errors. The selection of the regions for defect detection and the bands for the two-band ratio come from the analysis of the spectrum of our data, mainly using the principal component analysis. The proposed method can detect the defects of apple with high accuracy (95%) independently of the orientation of the apple in the image.

2 Resources

2.1 Hyperspectral Imaging System

In this section, we describe the Hyperspectral Imaging System (HIS) that acquires the data. Figure 1 shows the corresponding diagram of our laboratory setup and its con-figuration [3]. The hyperspectral camera is the iXon DU-860 Electron Multiplying Charge Coupled Device (EMCCD) with 1.4/35 C-mount lens (Schneider Optics, Hauppauge, USA). This is a line-by-line scan camera and can capture a total of 125 spectral bands in the range 403 998 nm. Illumination is provided by a pair of 150-watt quartz tungsten halogen (QTH) lamps in the direction of the field of view, the system is inside a dark room (enclosure).

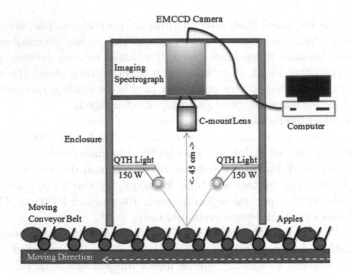

Fig. 1. The scheme shows the setup used to obtain the data set. The hyperspectral line scanner captures the apples as they pass through a dark room, the apples are carried through by a rotating conveyor belt. Then, the images are transferred to the computer for processing.

2.2 Apple Data Set

In the previous subsection, we described the configuration of the environment where we obtained the hyperspectral images containing the apples. Now, we describe the images itself.

Our data set has 369 apple samples. These samples have been separated and labeled into two classes: apples with defects (295) and apples without defects (74). The defects of the apples include scab, bruise, crack, and cut. For both, images with or without defect, we also include images with the stem and calyx. For analysis purposes we have subdivided our data set in images with scab (70), bruise (40), crack (65), cut (60), defect with stem (45), defect with calyx (15), normal (59), normal with stem (10), and normal with calyx (5). Figure 2 shows examples of our dataset.

3   Methods

3.1   Overview

We propose an algorithm able to detect several diseases in the skin of apples using hyperspectral image processing. In addition, our algorithm can identify the stem and calyx of the apples to avoid detection errors that are frequently caused by these parts of the fruit This section describes the multiple steps we propose. The algorithm starts with a hyperspectral image provided by the camera and then executes a sequence of steps until deciding if the input image contains an apple with or without a defect. Figure 3 shows the overview of the process.

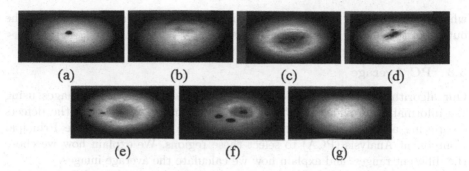

(a)   (b)   (c)   (d)

(e)   (f)   (g)

Fig. 2. Data set with different apple skin types: scab (a), bruise (b), crack (c), cut (d), stem (e), calyx (f), and normal (g). Images are from the 729.3 nm wavelength.

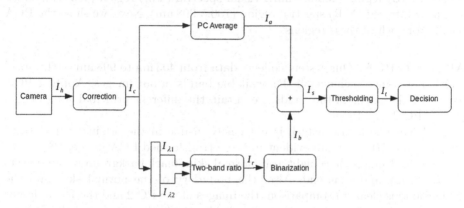

Fig. 3. Steps of the proposed apple defect detection algorithm

3.2 Correction

Hyperspectral cameras capture information and noise. The noise occurs mainly due to the non-uniform intensity of the different light sources and the dark current [9]. The dark current is a small electric current in the sensor of the camera when no light is entering [8]. Thus, the first step is to correct the hyperspectral input image I_h to account for these irregularities.

The correction uses a couple of references images, one for absolute brightest (white) and one for absolute darkness (black). The white reference image I_w is taken from a Teflon whiteboard with 99% reflectance. The black reference image I_d is taken with the lens of the camera closed, this ensures 0% reflectance. The white and black reference images reduce the influence of the intensity variability and the dark current of the camera. The following equation describes the correction procedure.

$$I_c = (I_h - I_d)/(I_w - I_d) \times 100 \tag{1}$$

where I_d is the black reference image and I_w is the white reference image. The output of this step is the corrected image I_c.

3.3   PC Average

Our algorithm identifies the defects of the apples in the input images using the information provided by the hyperspectral image. We identify the defects computing an average of different regions of the spectrum. We use Principal Component Analysis (PCA) to select these regions. We explain how we chose the different ranges, and explain how we calculate the average images.

The PCA of the hyperspectral images can be performed for different wavelength regions. In this study we work with three different regions: all bands spectral (AB) region (403 998 nm), visual spectral (VIS) region (403 695.7 nm), and near-infrared (NIR) spectral region (700.5 998 nm). Next, we show the PCA results for each of these regions.

All Bands PCA. Our system collects data from 403 nm to 998 nm of the spectrum. This range includes all the available bands in our images. Appling PCA to the whole range, all the bands, we obtain the different principal components (PC-1, PC-2, ..., PC-n).

A defect like bruise, which is not easily visible in the original single band image in Fig. 2(b), is more evident in these transformed PCA images: Fig. 4(b).

The PC-1 images have light gray normal skin, black background, and defects except bruise and stem-end. Also, the boundary of the normal skin and the background is clear. In comparison, the images of the PC-2 and the PC-3 do not have a clear boundary among the normal skin, the background, and the defects. The PC-2 images have light gray normal skin and background and in some cases, the PC-3 images have black normal skin and background, in other cases, it has light gray normal skin and background. The PC-1 images have no texture on the normal skin and around the defects, but the images of PC-2 and PC-3 have some texture like dots or smudge on the normal skin and around the defects.

Thus, it is easier to identify the defects of the apple in the PC-1 images than it is to identify them in the PC-2 or PC-3 images.

VIS Region PCA. Figure 5 shows the first three principal components in the visual spectral range (403 695.7 nm). Generally, the VIS-region spectral images are darker than the NIR-region spectral images. Especially the PC-2 images of the VIS-region are particularly darker than the PC-2 images of the NIR-region. In the PC-2 and PC-3 images, the images have texture on the normal skin and around the defects. In the VIR-Region, the PC-1 images have the best contrast and no texture as well as that of AB and NIR-regions.

NIR Region PCA. Figure 6 shows the first three principal components images. Generally, the NIR-region spectral images are a little brighter than the VIS-region spectral image. Especially the PC-2 images of NIR-region are much

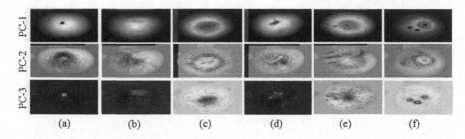

Fig. 4. First three principal components using all the bands in the range 403 998 nm. Each row presents the first, second, and third principal component respectively. Each column presents a different disease: scab (a), bruise (b), crack (c), and cut (d). Also, the stem (e), and the calyx (f) are presented.

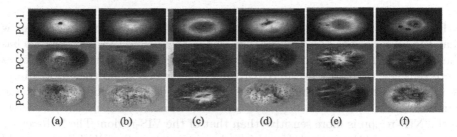

Fig. 5. First three principal components using the visual spectral range (403 695.7 nm). Each row presents the first, second, and third principal component respectively. Each column presents a different disease: scab (a), bruise (b), crack (c), and cut(d). Also, the stem (e), and the calyx (f) are presented.

brighter than the PC-2 images of the VIR region. In the NIR-region, the PC-1, images have the best contrast among the other type of PC too.

Selection of Regions. Hyperspectral images carry a lot more information than regular images. Thus, it is important to use the proper tool for dimension reduction and to identify the different ranges that provide the most useful information. For example, from our experiments, we identified that the defects of the apple are clearer in the PC1 image of the VIS region while the NIR region provides higher contrast.

The PC images have different reflectance features. For example, the apple defects in the PC-1 images of the VIS-region are shown more clearly than those in the PC-2 images of the VIS-region (Fig. 5). And the PC-1 images of NIR-region are a higher contrast than the PC-3 images of the VIS-region.

Until now, we decided that the PC-1 images provide greater variance so those are the ones that we will use in our algorithm. However, we still must decide which ranges of the spectrum we are going to use. The PCA of the hyperspectral image was carried out for three regions: AB, VIS, and NIR. In selecting the PC images to implement the proposed method, there are seven options: AB, VIS,

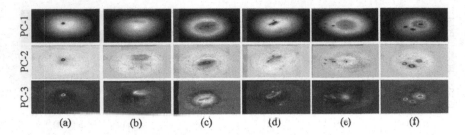

Fig. 6. First three principal components using the NIR-region range (700.5 998 nm). Each row presents the first, second, and third principal component respectively. Each column presents a different disease: scab (a), bruise (b), crack (c), and cut (d). Also, the stem (e), and the calyx (f) are presented.

NIR, AB/VIS, AB/NIR, VIS/NIR, and AB/VIS/NIR. Our experiments show that VIS/NIR has the best performance among them. The VIS/NIR average has the best performance because the reflectance of the defects in the VIS-region is more sensitive than that in the NIR-region like the crack and the cut of Fig. 8. Namely, the size and the color of those defects in the VIS-region are larger and darker than that in the NIR-region. In contrast, the reflectance of the normal skin in the NIR-region is more sensitive than that of the VIS-region. The NIR-region has no texture in the normal skin region. Averaging these two PC-1 images could increase the possibility to take advantage of the clear defects of the VIS-region and the clear normal skin of NIR-region simultaneously. This means that the best way to use the method is using the PC average between the VIS and NIR regions.

Figure 7 shows the average of the PC-1 from the VIS and NIR regions. We explain the detail of the average computation in the next subsection.

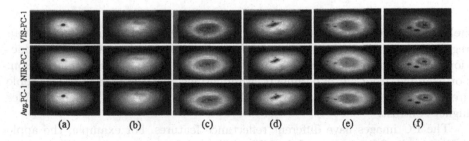

Fig. 7. Representative PC-1 images of the two groups of the spectral (VIS, NIR) regions and the average PC-1 for scab (a), bruise (b), crack (c), cut (d), stem (e), and calyx (f).

Average Computation. To take advantage of those features, we propose a method to average the PC images. In this method, the average $PC(I_a)$ is obtained by selecting PCs from VIS and NIR regions and averaging them through the following equation:

$$I_a = (I_{vis} + I_{nir})/2, \tag{2}$$

where the I_{vis} is the first principal component of the visual spectral region and I_{nir} is the first principal component of the near-infrared region.

3.4 Two-Band Ratio

Stem and calyx of apples can be challenging to process. Their intensity difference with respect to the rest of the apple makes it easy to confuse them with defects. It is possible to see in the dataset that the stem and calyx look like defects to the naked eye. The discrimination of the stem and calyx of the fruit uses the two-band ration technique. The first step is to identify which are the best bands for this task. Then, we can use the two-band ratio to avoid detection errors.

Bands Selection for Ratio. The spectral data analysis of the apple skin types was carried out. First, the region of interest (ROI) of the apple skin types was found, and the reflectance data of the ROI were averaged. Figure 8 shows the averaged reflectance data. In Fig. 8, we found the two bands; one is the band in which the local minimums of the stem and calyx-end are similar to each other, and the other is the band in which local maximum of the stem-end exists.

From the spectral analysis of Fig. 8, there are two possible band ratio combinations: (873.3/676.5) or (916.4/676.5). The former is set for stem and the later for calyx. So, an experiment was performed to know which set of the two sets has better image contrast. Figure 9 shows the results. The first row 676.6 shows similar minimum reflectance value for both the stem and calyx in the same band. The second row shows the maximum reflectance for the stem. The third row shows the maxim reflectance for the calyx. The fourth row 916.4/676.5 and the fifth row 873.3/676.5 are the two-band ratios on the bandwidth (916.4 nm, 676.5 nm) and (873.3 nm, 676.5 nm) respectively. In the experiment, two-band ratio images of 873.3/676.5 nm, and 916.4/676.5 nm were very similar to each other as shown in the fourth and fifth row of Fig. 9. Because it is not possible to decide which set of the images is better manually, another test is required.

From this analysis, we can also identify the optimal band (729.3 nm), later we use this band for comparison purposes.

The first operand of the two-band ratio was decided to be the reflectance of the wavelength 676.5 nm. It would be beneficial to make the reflectance of the two-band ratio large if a local maximum reflectance were used as the second operand of the two-band ratio. So, wavelength 873.3 and wavelength 916.4 were selected as the candidates of the second operator, which are the local maximum reflectance of the stem-end, and the calyx-end respectively.

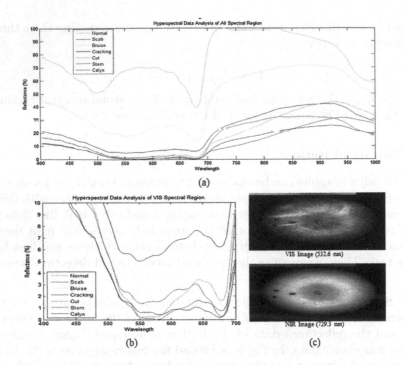

(a)

(b)   (c)

Fig. 8. The average representative ROIs reflectance spectra obtained from apple samples with different types of apple skin. (a) AB-region (403 nm to 998 nm), (b) VIS-region (403 nm to 695.7 nm), and (c) Comparison with the defect images of the same apple from VIS (532.6 nm) and NIR (729.3 nm) regions.

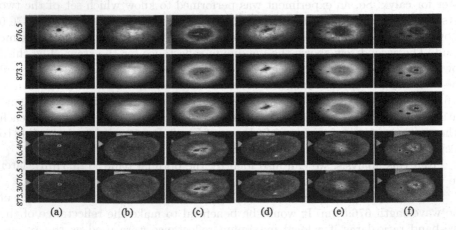

(a)   (b)   (c)   (d)   (e)   (f)

Fig. 9. Representative reflectance images (676.5-, 873.3-, and 916.4 nm), and two-band ratio images (873.3-/676.5 nm, 916.4-/676.5 nm) for (a) Scab, (b) Bruise, (c) Crack, (d) Cut, (e) Stem-End, and (f) Calyx-End.

Two-Band Ratio Calculation. We propose two-band reflectance ratio, which was used for defects detection on the peach and the citrus [4,10]. A two-band ratio can enhance or reduce the contrast between features by dividing a measure of reflectance for the pixels in one image band by the measure of reflectance for the pixels in the other image band [5]. Usually, it can be used to reduce whatever is common in two images and exaggerate from what they are different. Two-band ratio was found using the local minimum and maximum values for an image through the following equation:

$$I_r = I_{\lambda 2}/I_{\lambda 1},$$ (3)

where $I_{\lambda 1}$ is the maximum and $I_{\lambda 2}$ is the minimum reflectance as selected in the previous subsections.

3.5 Binarization

Next, we transform the ratio image (I_r) to a binary image (I_b) through global thresholding $(T1 = 3.5)$. The threshold is selected by analysis of the profile shown in Fig. 10. Then, a morphological operation is applied to reduce any undesired noise and to fill the holes. The selected morphological operations are opening and dilation with a disk-2-kernel structuring element.

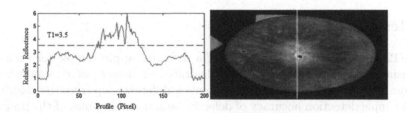

Fig. 10. Two-band ratio image (873.3/676.5). Spectral-profile plot (left) and corresponding red vertical line (right). Stem-end region of the apple can be identified in the right plot by thresholding.

3.6 Addition

In this stage, the average PC image (I_a) and the filtered binary I_b are added pixel-wise. This gives the new image (I_s). This creates a compensated image (I_s).

3.7 Thresholding

The compensated image (I_s) is used to generate a new binary image (I_t) with a gray threshold $(T2 = 0.28$ from Fig. 12) and a brightness inversion and it is denoted as the binary (I_t). The new binary (I_t) consists of black pixels representing normal skin and white pixels representing defects. Opening and dilation morphology operations with a disk-2-kernel structuring element is added before doing the binary conversion above.

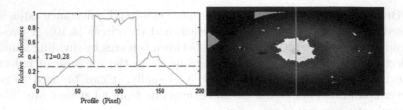

Fig. 11. Compensated I_s image from Fig. 3. Spectral-profile plot (left), corresponding red vertical line (right). The pixels of stem-end region have almost same and large value but those of other region except stem-end have different value. (Color figure online)

3.8 Decision

In succession, the area of the white pixels in the apple object boundary is calculated to serve as the decision criteria. Define the threshold and return true or false depending on the existence of a defect. If the area of that white pixels is greater than or equal to an area threshold, the apple of the image is considered as a defective one, otherwise as a normal one. The area threshold can be adjusted by the condition such as the texture difference of an apple skin. If the texture on an apple is heavy, the performance of the proposed system can be reduced.

4 Results

Figure 12 shows the detection results of a defective apple sample for each skin type using the proposed method. The illustrated six defects were randomly chosen from the test dataset. Each row presents a different step from the algorithm.

The apple detection accuracy of defective and normal apples of the proposed method was examined using 369 independent images. The other methods used for comparison are similar to what we have presented but we change the regions used in the identification of the defects. In other words, we compare average PCA (our method), all bands PCA, NIR region PCA, VIS region PCA, and optimal band PCA. There was no change in other parts of the algorithm. In the materials section, we described our data set. We used this dataset here to show the result of our experiments.

The average apple defect detection rate of the proposed method is 0.95. And that of the comparison group: AB PC-1, NIR PC-1, VIS PC-1, and optimal band are 0.86, 0.87, 0.84, and 0.89 respectively. It is interesting that the average apples detection rate of the optimal band, 0.89, that has only a single band without PCA processing, is higher than that of the PCA processed with a single PC-1 image (AB PC-1:0.86, NIR PC-1:0.87, and VIS-PC-1: 0.84). But the average apple detection rate could increase by averaging the VIS-region, PC-1 image, and NIR-region PC-1 image (AvgPC-1 2R: 0.95).

The detection rate of each skin type is very different from each other. In the proposed method, the detection rate of normal and normal with a stem is 1.0, but that of a bruise is 0.78, and normal with calyx is 0.8. The detection rate of

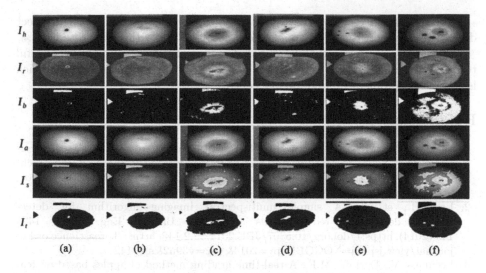

Fig. 12. Detection results of defective apple samples: scab (a), bruise (b), crack (c), cut (d), stem (e), and calyx (f).

the other skin types, except bruise and the defects with normal with calyx, is over 0.96, which is comparatively high.

5   Conclusions

We proposed and evaluated a hyperspectral image processing algorithm to detect apple defects. We included a two-band ratio routine that helps to discriminate between the stem and calyx of the fruit which is a challenging problem for intensity-based detection. After an analysis of the spectral information, we adopted an average of the VIS region and NIR regions to detect the defects of the apples. The hyperspectral analysis was carried out dividing the hyperspectral range into three regions: VIS, NIR, and AB. The reflectance of each region was analyzed and PCA for each region was carried out.

In the reflectance analysis, the apple images of VIS-region had a dark gray color with texture. Therefore, if only the images of the VIS-region were used, the texture could be classified as a defect. And the defects like the bruises of NIR-region had a bright gray color. It becomes difficult to identify the normal skin with the defects if only the images of NIR-region were used. These features of the hyperspectral data were almost the same as those of the PC-1s obtained from the PCA processing. Both regions must be fully used and the setting of the threshold should be set with close attention.

Also, we found a similar local minimum reflectance bandwidth of stem and calyx in the hyperspectral data. From this value, the similar reflectance ratio of stem and calyx could be obtained so that it could identify most of all the stems and calyxes. We used bands 878.3 and 676.5 for the ratio after evaluation of the spectral data.

The evaluation results showed that the proposed method has better defect detection rate than the basic apple defect detection algorithm, the rate is 95%.

We have provided a new technique that aids in this process and that is useful to avoid detection errors produced by the presence of the stem and calyx, which is a common problem in food quality control.

References

1. ElMasry, G., Wang, N., Vigneault, C.: Detecting chilling injury in red delicious apple using hyperspectral imaging and neural networks. Postharvest Biol. Technol. **52**(1), 1–8 (2009). https://doi.org/10.1016/J.POSTHARVBIO.2008.11.008, https://www.sciencedirect.com/science/article/pii/S0925521408003220
2. Lee, H., et al.: A simple multispectral imaging algorithm for detection of defects on red delicious apples. J. Biosyst. Eng. **39**(2), 142–149 (2014). https://doi.org/10.5307/JBE.2014.39.2.142, http://koreascience.or.kr/journal/view.jsp?kj=NOGGB5&py=2014&vnc=v39n2&sp=142
3. Leemans, V., Destain, M.F.: A real-time grading method of apples based on features extracted from defects. J. Food Eng. **61**(1), 83–89 (2004). https://doi.org/10.1016/S0260-8774(03)00189-4, https://www.sciencedirect.com/science/article/pii/S0260877403001894
4. Li, J., et al.: Multispectral detection of skin defects of bi-colored peaches based on vis-NIR hyperspectral imaging. Postharvest Biol. Technol. **112**, 121–133 (2016). https://doi.org/10.1016/j.postharvbio.2015.10.007
5. Li, J., Rao, X., Ying, Y.: Detection of common defects on oranges using hyperspectral reflectance imaging. Comput. Electron. Agric. **78**(1), 38–48 (2011). https://doi.org/10.1016/J.COMPAG.2011.05.010, https://www.sciencedirect.com/science/article/pii/S0168169911001256
6. López-García, F., Andreu-García, G., Blasco, J., Aleixos, N., Valiente, J.M.: Automatic detection of skin defects in citrus fruits using a multivariate image analysis approach. Comput. Electron. Agric. **71**(2), 189–197 (2010). https://doi.org/10.1016/J.COMPAG.2010.02.001, https://www.sciencedirect.com/science/article/pii/S016816991000013X
7. Mehl, P.M., Chen, Y.R., Kim, M.S., Chan, D.E.: Development of hyperspectral imaging technique for the detection of apple surface defects and contaminations. J. Food Eng. **61**(1), 67–81 (2004). https://doi.org/10.1016/S0260-8774(03)00188-2, https://www.sciencedirect.com/science/article/pii/S0260877403001882
8. Merken, P., Vandersmissen, R.: Dark current and influence of target emissivity. Technical report (2016)
9. Polder, G., van der Heijden, G.W., Keizer, L.P., Young, I.T.: Calibration and characterisation of imaging spectrographs. J. Near Infrared Spectrosc. **11**(3), 193–210 (2003). https://doi.org/10.1255/jnirs.366, http://journals.sagepub.com/doi/10.1255/jnirs.366
10. Qin, J., Burks, T.F., Zhao, X., Niphadkar, N., Ritenour, M.A.: Development of a two-band spectral imaging system for real-time citrus canker detection. J. Food Eng. **108**(1), 87–93 (2012). https://doi.org/10.1016/j.jfoodeng.2011.07.022
11. Wang, J., Nakano, K., Ohashi, S., Kubota, Y., Takizawa, K., Sasaki, Y.: Detection of external insect infestations in jujube fruit using hyperspectral reflectance imaging. Biosyst. Eng. **108**(4), 345–351 (2011). https://doi.org/10.1016/J.BIOSYSTEMSENG.2011.01.006, https://www.sciencedirect.com/science/article/pii/S1537511011000183

12. Wen, Z., Tao, Y.: Building a rule-based machine-vision system for defect inspection on apple sorting and packing lines. Expert Syst. Appl. **16**(3), 307–313 (1999). https://doi.org/10.1016/S0957-4174(98)00079-7, https://www.sciencedirect.com/science/article/pii/S0957417498000797

13. Zhang, B., et al.: Hyperspectral imaging combined with multivariate analysis and band math for detection of common defects on peaches (prunus persica). Comput. Electron. Agric. **114**, 14–24 (2015). https://doi.org/10.1016/J.COMPAG.2015.03.015, https://www.sciencedirect.com/science/article/pii/S0168169915001003

Perso2U: Exploration of User Emotional States to Drive Interface Adaptation

Julián Andrés Galindo[1,2(✉)], Raúl Mazo[3,4],
and Edison Loza-Aguirre[1]

[1] Departamento de Informática y Ciencias de la Computación,
Escuela Politécnica Nacional, Ladron de Guevera E11-253,
Quito 170517, Ecuador
{julian.galindo,edison.loza}@epn.edu.ec
[2] University Grenoble Alpes, CNRS, LIG, 38000 Grenoble, France
[3] Université Paris 1 Panthéon – Sorbonne, CRI, 90, rue de Tolbiac,
75013 Paris, France
raul.mazo@univ-parisl.fr
[4] Universidad Eafit, Grupo GIDITIC, Medellín, Colombia

Abstract. Taking into account dynamic user properties such as emotions for interfaces adaptation at runtime is a challenging task. To deal with this issue, we propose to personalize user interfaces at runtime based on user's emotions. This approach depends on emotion recognition tools to allow an Inferring Engine to deduce user emotions during the interaction. However, this inference releases many emotions without aggregating them. It makes more difficult the interpretation of user experience. Thus, we explore the feasibility of inferring similar emotional states (negative, positive and neutral) by grouping individual emotions. To achieve our goal, this paper reports on the results of an experiment to compare detected emotional states from different face recognition tools in web interaction. It evidences that it is feasible to infer similar emotion states (positive, negative, and neutral) from different emotion recognition tools, and the level of this similarity is still premature to have a robust categorization.

Keywords: User interface adaptation · Inferring engine · Emotion recognition
Face detection · Runtime

1 Introduction

Currently, Human-Computer Interfaces are expected to dynamically adapt to changes which may occur in their context of use (user, platform and environment) while preserving usability [1]. Such adaptation should deal with dynamic user properties such as the emotions felt by users during the interaction. In fact, emotions are recognized as important to the interpretation of experience [2, 3], and recently, they have been considered as affective responses of design elements [4]. Thus, the use emotions for user interfaces (UI) adaptation is a subject of great interest to practitioners and researchers [5].

As previous approaches in UI adaptation suggest (e.g. [5–7]), the key point for applying UI modifications relies on the emotions interpretation. In [9], we proposed an

© Springer Nature Switzerland AG 2019
M. Botto-Tobar et al. (Eds.): CITT 2018, CCIS 895, pp. 288–301, 2019.
https://doi.org/10.1007/978-3-030-05532-5_21

architecture, Perso2U, for UI adaptation by understanding user experience attached to emotions. The inferring engine of this architecture can deduce detected emotions from face recognition tools during UI interaction. However, the success of UI adaptation depends on finding relevant user responses, such as the emotions. Thus, a crucial part of the architecture is emotion detection and its interpretation to get results for adaptation rules.

Nowadays, there are many emotion commercial recognition tools such as Microsoft API, FaceReader, and Affdex. These tools usually provide recognition for seven basic emotions with some uncertainty. In spite of this, previous contributions [12] have demonstrated that it is feasible to have similar emotions values with different tools such as similar levels of happiness or anger. A fact which is considered as the first step for a generic architecture releasing many emotions to analyze, different intensity values and a complex user experience understanding.

Further, a question emerges independently from the tool used for detecting emotions: Is it feasible to interpret user experience in web interaction by using emotional states such as positive, negative or neutral? This question motivates us to compare two face emotion recognition tools and to hypothesize that, from these tools, it is possible to group emotions and provide similar states during interaction independently of the recognition tool. Hence, to identify this similarity, we conduct an experiment with 45 users across 4 websites. This paper describes the results of this experiment in terms of two aspects: (1) the potential identification of similar emotion states and (2) the level of this similarity to have a robust categorization of emotion states to be considered in Perso2u.

This paper is organized as follows. The following section presents related work about UI adaptation to emotions. The third section details Perso2u, an architecture to personalize the UI based on emotions. Then, we present an experiment that compares the emotion recognition tools to show the possibility of grouping emotions in states to be used for adaptation, followed by its results and limitations. The last section summarizes our contributions and presents future work.

2   Related Work

Modeling user emotions is a topic that has been largely studied (e.g. [8–12]). In such works, emotions are generally used to interpret user's tasks such as communication, learning, and tutoring. However, they are a few the contributions (e.g. [5, 6, 13, 14]) that rely on emotion recognition to drive adaptation to the UI. In this section, we are particularly interested in the genericity for inferring similar emotional states. We will explore the manner of inferring emotional responses to understand whether the inference is performed by grouping emotions in states.

Nasoz [5] proposed an adaptive intelligent system relying on the recognition of affective states from physiological signals (sensors) based on a multimodal affective user interface architecture [19]. This approach provides six key points: user emotion representation, emotion analysis, and recognition, user's emotion modeling, adaptation to emotions and emotional expressions and synthesis. The emotion inference depends only on emotion recognition tools (e.g., facial analysis) while the UI adaptation relies on a neural network algorithm.

In spite of this, this approach exhibits some limitations. First, it combines *individual* inferred emotions with user static information (e.g. personality, age or gender) to infers the changes on the UI. These *not-aggregated* emotions include anger, panic, sleepiness, and frustration. Thus, even when the emotions are detected by sensors such as a Galvanic Skin Response and other technologies such as voice or face recognition can also be used, it uses individual emotions values to deduce the user experience (satisfaction) instead of some emotion aggregation method.

The Affect and Belief Adaptive Interface System (ABAIS) [6, 15] allows adaptation that may affect displays, icons, notifications and custom user personalization. It is implemented by an architecture based on four modules: user state assessment, impact prediction, strategy selection, and GUI Adaptation. The first one is in charge of the emotion inference, which combines user information and a rule-based approach to infer the affective user state (user satisfaction). Although this module may be used with different recognition tools, detected emotions are limited to anxiety which limits the use of emotion categorization by using states.

In their work, Meudt et al. [13] propose an approach based on the analysis of historic interactions to identify the cause of an emotion and then driving UI adaptation. In this work, the interaction involves humans and robots, as a very specific kind of human-computer interaction domain. Many emotion classification methods are considered such as the wheel of emotions [16], the Geneva emotion wheel [17, 18], valence arousal dominance [19] and the Self-Assessment Manikin (SAM) [20]. Although, these methods could potentially classify emotions into states whether it is automatic or manual, their architecture does not implement them. Therefore, the lack of evidence in application defines a gap to understand and evaluate the potential impact of using this approach in real-time systems interaction.

Finally, UI adaptation is also addressed by using patterns in [14, 21]. In these works, the authors proposed an architecture to trigger the adaptation of UI according to emotions detected automatically in a model-based development with facial analysis and eye tracking. They used FaceReader to detect emotions, which potentially makes the architecture independent from the emotion recognition tool. The UI changes include colors or structure executed by an experimental prototype at runtime. Emotions are explicitly defined as states; however, this conception uses individual emotions rather than positive, negative or neutral states. To illustrate, a user's emotion could be recognized and assigned to the variables <EmotionalState> and <BiometricState> with the values "angry" and "95" respectively. It means that all emotional states are really expressed by one of the universal emotions (e.g., angry or happy) without considering an aggregation of emotions.

To summarize, four architectures have been proposed for dealing with UI adaptation to emotions. Even when they infer user emotions independently from the tool, they neither take into account aggregated emotions nor support all possible UI adaptations, particularly UI structure. Also, they deal with a few measured emotions. To avoid these drawbacks, we propose an architecture called Perso2U in the next section.

3 Perso2U Architecture

The Perso2U architecture (Fig. 1) is composed of three linked components [22]: the Inferring Engine ❶, the Adaptation Engine ❻, and the Interactive System ❾. The Inferring engine is in charge of dynamically deducing the values of the context of use (users with their emotions, platform, environment). The emotions are detected thanks to external tools such as MicrosoftApi or FaceReader. Then, the emotion Wrapper ❸ filters and aggregates the gathered emotions values to find whether the current user emotion is positive, negative or neutral. Currently, the architecture takes only these three values into account to show the interest of the approach. This can be extended, if necessary, with no impact on the architecture. Lastly, inferred emotions are sent to the Adaptation Engine with other contextual information.

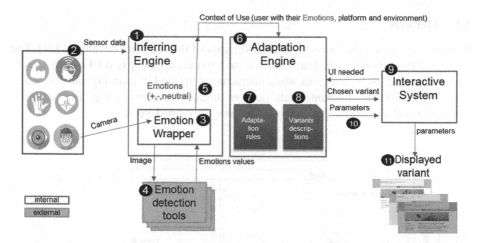

Fig. 1. UI adaptation architecture based on emotions.

The main function of the Adaptation Engine is the selection of the right adaptation to be applied to the UI. Based on the contextual information ❺ [23], the Adaptation Engine selects a UI variant (i.e., a predefined UI structure) among all available variants for the needed UI. Then, the Adaptation Engine computes the UI parameters (e.g., background-color, font, widgets selection) for even better adapting the chosen variant to the context of use. After this, it displays the variant and gives the computed parameters (variant and parameters) to the interactive system module, which is in charge of applying the parameters and displaying the variant, hence presenting the appropriate adapted UI.

4 Experimental Study

The experimental study aims at showing that it is feasible to (i) aggregate detected emotions by using Perso2U and (ii) provide similar results (positive, negative and neutral) independently from the tool. Thus, from any detection tool, the inferring engine can use this benefit to be able to send appropriate emotions states (positive, negative and neutral) to the adaptation engine. We will use two detection tools Microsoft emotion API and FaceReader. Therefore, the experiment hypotheses are:

H1: *there exist similarity on the emotion states retrieved by both tools with the detected emotions at using Perso2U.*
H2: *the level of the similarity is good enough to have a robust categorization of emotions into states.*

4.1 Methods

In the context of a travel website, four UI versions of the site were developed [24]. The content of the websites is similar; however, the versions differ by two UI quality factors which influence users' emotions while interacting with the UI: usability and aesthetics. Thus, by combining different levels (low vs. high) across two UI quality attributes (aesthetics and usability), Fig. 2 shows the four developed versions.

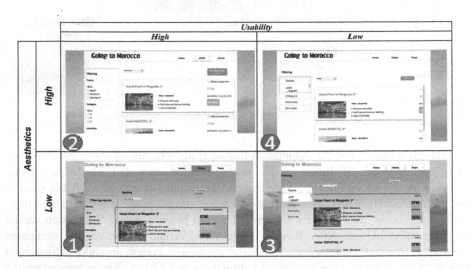

Fig. 2. Four variants of a web site user interface.

4.2 Participants

Forty-five persons participated in the study, with the following distribution for each website version: 13 (website1 - low aesthetics/high usability), 10 (website2 - high aesthetics/high usability), 12 (website3 - low aesthetics/low usability), and 10 (website4 - high aesthetics/low usability). The experiment sample included 53% (24) male aged from 19 to 67 years old and 47% (21) female from 23 to 63-year-old participants (mean male age 34, $\sigma = 11.66$ and mean female age 27 with $\sigma = 12.25$).

4.3 Procedure and Tasks

Each subject was assigned to only one version of the travel website. During the interaction with the website, user emotions were detected automatically. To ensure that participants are involved enough in the UI interaction, they answered an online questionnaire corresponding to three tasks to achieve: (1) look for a 5-star hotel offering a visit to the desert, (2) look for a specific hotel with a breakfast plan and lastly (3) look for a hotel circuit in a specific location. For instance, users responded to the following questions in the first task:

How many 5-star hotels offer a visit in the desert?
What is the name of the hotel that you found?
What city is this hotel located in?
What is the minimum price per person for this stay?

4.4 Interaction Data and Images Correction

The following interaction triple data set is captured during the experiment: User, UI, and the survey, resulting in 8 × 67 × 41 attributes respectively for 45 users. For the *User,* User features as the unique user identification from 1 to 45, Age and gender. The User emotions, happiness, contempt, fear, anger, sadness, disgust, neutral and surprise (Ekman emotions plus contempt, surprise and neutral) with values from 0 to 1. The *UI* includes *the* UI id: the website id from 1 to 4, UI variant: The web page where the user is interacting (e.g.100 = w1/home.html for website1 and 200 = w2/home.html for website2). A UI interaction set was defined. It includes the specific UI element and time (hour, minute, second and millisecond) in which the user is interacting by giving a click on it (e.g. check box, image, link, tab, etc.).

However, before being able to compare emotions detected by tools, some image corrections are needed. As a matter of fact, to get usable values from tools, participants were asked to have a not predefined position (e.g. rigid head). But some images were not good enough for an interpretation with FaceReader (Tool2). Thus, a face image correction was made for FaceReader for every image. The correction was made by adding a white rectangle at the bottom of the image without affecting the user's face. As a benefit, it was possible to improve the image detection, quality to detect emotion values as illustrated in Fig. 3.

With these corrections, we finally obtain 1730 images with an average of 38 images by the user. Moreover, each image corresponds to a timestamp, a UI variant (website version + current page) used and the users' characteristics. We name an observation the tuple of data with a timestamp, seven emotions (disgust, anger, fear, sadness, contempt, neutral and happiness), UI variant, users' age and users' gender. An observation corresponds to an image, so we retrieved 1730 observations with 11 values inside each tuple for a total of 19 030 values.

Before correction (300x260).   *After correction*(300x320).

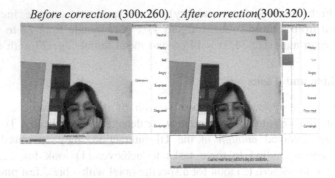

Fig. 3. FaceReader image correction.

4.5   Measures and Analysis

During interacting with the travel website, pictures of the participants are taken every 10 s. Next, these pictures have been sent to the 2 emotions detection tools. Once both the interaction data and images correction process were performed, some steps were performed to analyze the data. First, regarding the nature (positive, negative and neutral) or valence of each emotion defined in a circumplex model [25], the following aggregation was proposed for each detected emotion for both detection tools:

negative = maximum value <fear, sadness, anger, disgust, contempt>
positive = happiness
neutral = neutral

To remark, the maximum value (intensity) of all negative emotions is considered as the negative emotional state of a user. It follows the definition of *overall felt intensity* by [26] which ensures that the final intensity value is the maximum value in a time t. Thus, from all negative emotions detected in a *t* instance, the negative state corresponds to the *overall felt intensity* among them.

However, happiness and neutral does not require this treatment as they are the only ones in each category. To illustrate, for website1, if <fear1 = 0.2, sadness = 0.6, anger = 0.2, disgust = 0.1 && contempt = 0.3 > then Negative1 is equal to 0.6 which represents the maximum negative emotion state in tool 1 for one user in a particular time at interacting with the UI.

Second, to facilitate the analysis, a contingency table was designed as illustrated in Table 1. It compares the emotional states inferred for both detecting tools. Based on these values (from a to i) as a [3 × 3] matrix, the following measures were computed: *p-value of the Pearson chi-Squared test, Overall similarity,* and *the Cohen's Kappa.* Finally, the following set of measures is computed for tool1 (FaceReader) and tool2 (Microsoft Api):

P-value of the Pearson Chi-Squared Test: It computes the Pearson's product-moment correlation [27]. It expresses whether there is an association of the detected emotion states (positive, negative and neutral) between both detecting tools.

Table 1. Contingency table design.

		inf2 (tool2)		
		+	-	**neutral**
inf1 (tool1)	+	a	b	c
	-	d	e	f
	neutral	g	h	i
Overall similarity = (a+e+i) / (a+b+c+d+e+f+g+h+i)				

Overall Similarity: it computes the similarity or agreement rate of the detected emotion states between tool1 and tool2 [28]. It underlines preliminary how well both of tools agreed with the categorization of emotions into states.

The Cohen's Kappa: It computes how strong is the level of similarity or agreement of the detected emotion states between both detecting tools [29]. It helps to understand how robust is the similarity among tools by removing the effects caused by randomness.

5   Results

User emotions were detected as well as the emotion states illustrated in Fig. 4. It shows the detections performed by tool2 while users were interacting with one of the four UI versions. To clarify, the three detections at the top evidence the different levels of emotion's intensity with 55, 23 and 55% for fear, disgust and happiness. Each emotion represents the maximum detected value in each category (negative and positive). For instance, the first user evoked the highest negative level (fear) of 55%, which is supported by his particular facial expressions (eyebrows raised and pulled together, raised upper eyelids and lips stretched) while she was interacting with website3 (low level of aesthetics and usability).

Then, values for the contingency table were computed. Table 2 shows the compiled results of the inferring process to gather the emotional states similarities among the tools. A total of 280 similarities were retrieved where 243 agreements are distributed in 233, 9 and 1, which correspond respectively to neutral, negative and positive states. The remaining 37 values are spread into the differences in the emotional states. For instance, there were 11 dissimilarities across negative and neutral for tool1 and tool2 respectively.

Thus, concerning H1, the results confirm that there exist similarity or agreement between tool1 and tool2 at detecting emotion states (positive, negative and neutral) with a p-value = 8.23e−06. (χ^2(4, N = 280) = 28.89, p <0.01, ϕ = 0.22). Moreover, the feasibility of similar emotional states among tools is supporting by the *Overall similarity* metric with a rate of 83.24%. Therefore, there is an agreement of the identified emotional states between tool1 and tool2 with a similarity rate of almost 83%.

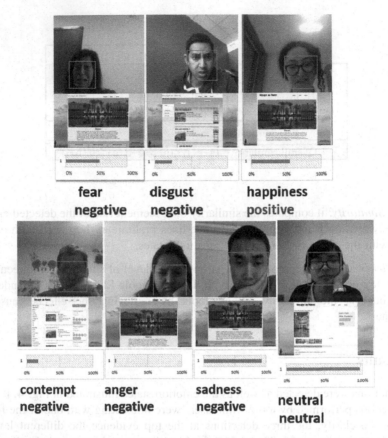

Fig. 4. Emotion detections and emotional states inferred by using tool2.

Table 2. Contingency table values between tool1 and tool2.

		inf2 (tool2)			
		+	-	neutral	total
inf1 (tool1)	+	1	0	3	4
	-	2	9	11	22
	neutral	6	25	223	254
	total	9	34	237	280

In what respects to H2, the results evidence a Cohen's Kappa of 0.24 (95% CI: [0.10, 0.38]), indicating a fair agreement in the detected emotion state among the emotion recognition tools. Overall, although there is evidence of similar criteria for detecting emotion states in the inferring engine at using two different tools, the magnitude of the agreement needs a deeper treatment to increase its reliability.

6 Threats to Validity

The experiment allows us to validate our two hypotheses: (H1) there exist similarity or agreement between tool1 and tool2 at detecting emotion states (positive, negative and neutral) with (1) a p-value lower than 0.01, and (2) 83% of similarity among tools. Concerning H2, the level of the similarity is good enough to have a robust categorization of emotions into states; particularly, this hypothesis is partially validated due to the fear magnitude of agreement found.

Some concerns should be evoked regarding the experiment nature. First, all emotion recognition tools detect user's macro expressions given by their faces without considering other biometric signals such as galvanic skin response, heart rate, video trace analysis, and eye tracking. Measures which may provide more insights to complement or validate our results.

Second, our UI adaptation architecture based on emotions advocates all elements of the context of use (user, environment, platform), which are not fully considered. For instance, environment changes such as noisy and light variations, day timeline or the user device (e.g. tablet) to access to the UIs.

The concerns in H2 can be addressed in two directions. First, our results suggest that some emotional states may be more relevant than others. For instance, some users may have a more significant emotional state regarding other factors such as age [30], gender [31, 32] or day timeline [33]. It is being more positive at facing some issues in the UI with aged rather than young users. Second, the consideration of more emotions (e.g., calm, relaxed or exited) into the positive category may growth the retrieved agreements between both detecting tools. Elements which should be considered for a deeper exploration to have a robust categorization.

7 Implications for the Perso2U Inferring Engine

The experiment described in Sect. 4 shows mainly that it is feasible to aggregate detected emotions with similar results (positive, negative and neutral) independently from the tool. The calculation relies on the user's emotions detected at runtime by any of both emotion detection tools. However, to articulate this capacity into Perso2U, it is necessary to define inferring rules implemented in functions inside the Inferring Engine. Then it can send a new context of use with the user's emotion states to the Adaptation Engine for adapting UI appropriately.

Figure 5 shows the implementation of such rules where three new functions were introduced: *setContextUseUserEmotionState_positive, setContextUseUserEmotion State_negative* and *setContextUseUserEmotionState_neutral.*

> *setContextUseUserEmotionState_positive:* computes the positive emotion state of the user and update the user component in the context of use.
> *setContextUseUserEmotionState_negative:* computes the negative emotion state of the user and update the user component in the context of use.
> *setContextUseUserEmotionState_neutral:* computes the neutral emotion state of the user and update the user component in the context of use.

```
//Inferring rules to detect user emotion states
//emotion state: positive
function setContextUseUserEmotionState_positive(happinessValue)
{
    contextUse.user.positiveValue=happinessValue;
    console.log("inferring Engine: positive emotion state=",
    contextUse.user.positiveValue);
}
//emotion state: negative
function setContextUseUserEmotionState_neutral(contemptValue,
fearValue,angerValue,disgustValue,sadnessValue)
{
    contextUse.user.negativeValue=max(contemptValue,
    fearValue,angerValue,disgustValue,sadnessValue);
    console.log("inferring Engine: negative emotion state=",
    contextUse.user.negativeValue);
}
//emotion state: neutral
function setContextUseUserEmotionState_neutral(neutralValue)
{
    contextUse.user.neutralValue=neutralValue;
    console.log("inferring Engine: neutral emotion state=",
    contextUse.user.neutralValue);
}
```

Fig. 5. Inferring engine rules to detect emotion states into Perso2U.

This implementation follows the highlights provided in Subsect. 4.5 and the architecture shown in Fig. 2. In our implementation, once emotions are detected by the emotion Wrapper (emotion recognition tools) ❸ in a time instance, the Inferring Engine ❶ is able to call the new three functions to dynamically and essentially update the context of use (e.g., contextUse.user.positiveValue = happinessValue;). Consequently, a new context of use is sent to the Adaptation Engine ❻. In general, the introduction of this inferring rules allows the inferring engine to update the context of use by adding the user emotion states in a dynamic and simple manner to advocate an appropriate adaptation. Further experiments will be needed to formally evaluate the automatic detection of emotions as an aggregation of emotions coming from different tools against the declared user experience (manual declaration).

8 Conclusion and Perspectives

This paper presents an architecture called Perso2U conceived to adapt the UI regarding emotions and an experiment to shows the similarity of detected emotional states by grouping individual emotions. It validates that (1) it is feasible to infer similar emotion states (positive, negative, and neutral) from different emotion recognition tools, and (2) the level of this similarity is still premature to have a robust categorization. These results are the key-element in a UI adaptation system to detect emotions, infer emotion states, adapt the UI and finally release an improved version.

Other experiment considerations could be used to strengthen the current results. Mainly, the use of more emotions in the positive category or the identification of relevant emotions per user could be used to increase the level of similarity. This would provide to the inferring engine a more reliable categorization as well as a more precise adaptation.

It would also be interesting to reinforce the current prototype by introducing relevant work in psychology related to other user characteristics such as age, gender, and personality. Furthermore, the consideration of contextual information about the environment and platform would consolidate our approach. Moreover, our experimental results can be overlapped with other existing technologies to uncover emotions during interaction such as galvanic skin response, heart rate, voice and eye recognition. Coupling this biometric knowledge into the adaptation engine would expand the interpretation of emotional states in real-time.

Moreover, the inferring engine (Perso2U) is able to update the context of use with emotion states thanks to the positive validation of the feasibility of using an aggregation method. However, as we pointed out, further experiments would be needed to evaluate the coherence between the detected emotion states and the declared user experience in real-time.

Although the study provides a spotlight of open questions to make the states' categorization more robust, it underlines the feasibility to inferring similar emotional states by grouping individual emotions in such manner that the inferring engine is preliminary able to interpret user experience regarding emotion's states to conduct UI Adaptation at real-time.

References

1. Calvary, G., Coutaz, J., Thevenin, D., Limbourg, Q., Bouillon, L., Vanderdonckt, J.: A unifying reference framework for multi-target user interfaces. Interact. Comput. **15**(3), 289–308 (2003)
2. Reeves, B., Nass, C.: How people treat computers, television, and new media like real people and places. CSLI Publications and Cambridge University Press Cambridge, UK (1996)
3. Carberry, S., de Rosis, F.: Introduction to special Issue on 'affective modeling and adaptation'. User Model. User-Adapt. Interact. **18**(1–2), 1–9 (2008)
4. Cyr, D.: Emotion and website design. In: Soegaard, M., Dam, R.F. (eds.) The Encyclopedia of Human-Computer Interaction. The Interaction-Design Foundation, Aarhus (2013)
5. Nasoz, F.: Adaptive Intelligent User Interfaces With Emotion Recognition. University of Central Florida Orlando, Florida (2004)
6. Hudlicka, E., McNeese, M.D.: Assessment of user affective and belief states for interface adaptation: application to an air force pilot task. User Model. User-Adapt. Interact. **12**(1), 1–47 (2002)
7. Martins, C., Faria, L., De Carvalho, C.V., Carrapatoso, E.: User modeling in adaptive hypermedia educational systems. Educ. Technol. Soc. **11**(1), 194–207 (2008)
8. de Rosis, F., Novielli, N., Carofiglio, V., Cavalluzzi, A., Carolis, B.D.: User modeling and adaptation in health promotion dialogs with an animated character. J. Biomed. Inform. **39**(5), 514–531 (2006)

9. Rowe, J., Mott, B., McQuiggan, S., Robison, J., Lee, S., Lester, J.: Crystal island: a narrative-centered learning environment for eighth grade microbiology. In: Workshop on Intelligent Educational Games at the 14th International Conference on Artificial Intelligence in Education, pp. 11–20, Brighton, UK (2009)
10. Forbes-Riley, K., Litman, D.: Designing and evaluating a wizarded uncertainty-adaptive spoken dialogue tutoring system. Comput. Speech Lang. 25(1), 105–126 (2011)
11. Porayska-Pomsta, K., Mavrikis, M., Pain, H.: Diagnosing and acting on student affect: the tutor's perspective. User Model. User-Adapt. Interact. 18(1–2), 125–173 (2008)
12. Graesser, A.C., et al.: The relationship between affective states and dialog patterns during interactions with AutoTutor. J. Interact. Learn. Res. 19(2), 293 (2008)
13. Meudt, S., et al.: Going further in affective computing: how emotion recognition can improve adaptive user interaction. In: Esposito, A., Jain, L.C. (eds.) Toward Robotic Socially Believable Behaving Systems, vol. 105, pp. 73–103. Springer International Publishing, Cham (2016)
14. Märtin, C., Rashid, S., Herdin, C.: Designing responsive interactive applications by emotion-tracking and pattern-based dynamic user interface adaptation. In: Kurosu, M. (ed.) HCI 2016, Part III. LNCS, vol. 9733, pp. 28–36. Springer, Cham (2016). https://doi.org/10.1007/978-3-319-39513-5_3
15. Hudlicka, E.: Increasing sia architecture realism by modeling and adapting to affect and personality. In: Dautenhahn, K., Bond, A., Cañamero, L., Edmonds, B. (eds.) Socially Intelligent Agents. Multiagent Systems, Artificial Societies, and Simulated Organizations, pp. 53–60. Springer, Boston (2002). https://doi.org/10.1007/0-306-47373-9_6
16. Plutchik, R., Kellerman, H.: Theories of Emotion, vol. 1 of Emotion: Theory, Research, and Experience. Academic Press, New York (1980)
17. Scherer, K.R.: What are emotions? and how can they be measured? Soc. Sci. Inf. 44(4), 695–729 (2005)
18. Fischer, G.: User modeling in human–computer interaction. User Model. User-Adapt. Interact. 11(1–2), 65–86 (2001)
19. Russell, J.A., Mehrabian, A.: Evidence for a three-factor theory of emotions. J. Res. Pers. 11(3), 273–294 (1977)
20. Bradley, M.M., Lang, P.J.: Measuring emotion: the self-assessment manikin and the semantic differential. J. Behav. Ther. Exp. Psychiatry 25(1), 49–59 (1994)
21. Märtin, C., Herdin, C., Engel, J.: Model-based user-interface adaptation by exploiting situations, emotions and software patterns. In: International Conference on Computer-Human Interaction Research and Applications (2017)
22. Galindo, J., Dupuy-Chessa, S., Céret, E.: Toward a UI adaptation approach driven by user emotions. In: Presented at the ACHI07, Nice, France (2017)
23. Céret, E., Dupuy-Chessa, S., Calvary, G., Bittar, M.: System and method for magnetic adaptation of a user interface. TPI2015053 déposé via France INPI le 7 juillet 2015, 2ème dépôt le 7 juillet (2016)
24. Dupuy-Chessa, S., Laurillau, Y., Céret, E.: Considering aesthetics and usability temporalities in a model based development process. In: Actes de la 28ième conférence francophone sur l'Interaction Homme-Machine, pp. 25–35 (2016)
25. Posner, J., Russell, J.A., Peterson, B.S.: The circumplex model of affect: an integrative approach to affective neuroscience, cognitive development, and psychopathology. Dev. Psychopathol. 17(3), 715–734 (2005)
26. Steunebrink, B.R., et al.: The Logical structure of emotions (2010)

27. Pearson, K.X.: On the criterion that a given system of deviations from the probable in the case of a correlated system of variables is such that it can be reasonably supposed to have arisen from random sampling. Lond. Edinb. Dublin Philos. Mag. J. Sci. **50**(302), 157–175 (1900)
28. Karl Pearson, F.R.S.: Mathematical Contributions to the Theory of Evolution. Dulau Co, London (1904)
29. Cohen, J.: A coefficient of agreement for nominal scales. Educ. Psychol. Meas. **20**(1), 37–46 (1960)
30. Hume, D.: Emotions and moods. In: Robbins, S.P., Judge, T.A. (eds.) Organizational Behavior, pp. 258–297. Pearson Prentice Hall, Upper Saddle River (2012)
31. Larsen, R.J., Diener, E.: Affect intensity as an individual difference characteristic: a review. J. Res. Pers. **21**(1), 1–39 (1987)
32. Diener, E., Sandvik, E., Larsen, R.J.: Age and sex effects for emotional intensity. Dev. Psychol. **21**(3), 542 (1985)
33. Watson, D.: Mood and Temperament. Guilford Press, New York (2000)

Mobile Based Approach for Accident Reporting

Luis Wanumen[1]([✉]), Judy Moreno[2]([✉]), and Hector Florez[1]([✉]) [ID]

[1] Universidad Distrital Francisco Jose de Caldas, Bogotá, Colombia
{lwanumen,haflorezf}@udistrital.edu.co
[2] Compensar Unipanamericana – Fundación Universitaria, Bogotá, Colombia
jmmorenoo@unipanamericana.edu.co

Abstract. When facing car accidents a lot of people are not prepared to respond or provide first aids to injured passengers. This paper presents the architecture and operation of a mobile tool equipped with a panic button to notify the situation to relatives of injured people in traffic accidents. The application has the necessary information to allow any passerby to be the first person to assist in this situation. The application provides critical information to enable a passerby to display relevant patient clinical information such as blood type, allergies, etc. With the panic button, a passerby can know victim information such as allergic reactions. The construction of the application follows the guidelines of the design science methodology, which consists in considering the research as base for creating the final product. In addition, the results of acceptance technology were measured with the Technology Acceptance Model that allows evaluating the perceived usefulness and ease of use. Finally, possible improvements for the mobile application are presented.

Keywords: Mobile assistant · Mobile panic application
Mobile reporting

1 Introduction

Since the introduction of smart phones, mobile technologies have contributed from many perspectives to the development of both software and hardware. In the last years, a mobile device offers a lot of smart functionalities that can be accessed with higher speed but lower price than before. Thus, smart devices are very attractive to people and almost everyone in the world already own at least one [9].

Regarding emergency situations, the most important feature for every panic application is concrete communications [5]. Then, nowadays tablets and smart phones can help people to connect with their health care providers, sharing personal and private information in an emergency events and helping to keep open the communication channels with proper people [6,7].

In most of the circumstances the smart phone of the affected people is the first tool to contact their relatives [8]. Several systems have been developed to reduce

© Springer Nature Switzerland AG 2019
M. Botto-Tobar et al. (Eds.): CITT 2018, CCIS 895, pp. 302–311, 2019.
https://doi.org/10.1007/978-3-030-05532-5_22

the response time and thus to reduce fatalities [2]. Thus, smart phones have played an important role in the implementation of systems to detect and report car accidents [1]. In some cases, the smart phone information is collected and analyzed through Dynamic Time Warping (DTW) in order to (a) determine the accident level, (b) reduce false positives (c) notify accident location and (d) notify medical information of injured people. Nevertheless, car accident reporting based on information provided by the smart phone peripherals such as accelerometer could be false or unreliable.

If an accident is detected in real time, many advantages are presented in the attention of that incident. In this context, the use of mobile applications could reduce detection times of emergency. Some countries have developed services to automatically detect car accidents based on the information provided by smart phones sensors.

Taking into account that nowadays smart phones are everywhere and have network connectivity, they are able to keep connected in order to immediately inform accidents to relevant people [1]. Thus, the development of a mobile application that allows reporting an accident gains great importance. On the one hand, it does not require installing expensive electronic equipment in the car. On the other hand, it improves communication between emergency aid personnel and hospital doctors.

In this work, we present *MAICAR (Mobile Application for Injured in a Car Accident Reporting)*. This application helps to rapidly and efficiently report traffic accidents. To face this problem *MAICAR* is provided with: (1) a contact manager, (2) an agenda to record personal health information, (3) a mobile assistant for emergency calls that delivers dependable information to the right people, and (4) a close friends locator.

MAICAR has the role administrator, who is the person that installs the application in his/her smart phone and can potentially have an accident. In addition, the role guest refers to the passerby, who approaches the person injured in the accident. The action of detecting close friends is automatically invoked by *MAICAR*. The guest is only able to view the results of this operation. In order to ensure that the design and development of *MAICAR* will have a positive impact, the research methodology called *Design Science* was used.

The paper is structured as follows. Section 2 presents the methodology, which is based on design science. Section 3 illustrates the approach for accident reporting. Section 4 presents the results of the work. Finally, Sect. 5 concludes the paper.

2   Methodology

The Design science research included two paradigms in Information System research: behavioral science and design science. On the one hand, the behavioral science attempts to develop and verify theories that explain or predict human or organizational behavior. On the other hand, design science attempts to extend the frontiers of human and organizational capabilities by creating new and innovative artifacts.

In the case of mobile application development for accident reporting, the following the aspects were taken into account:

- Aspects concerned to the environment
  - Strategies to request assistance in case of car accident
    * Proactive strategies to request assistance
    * Silent strategies to request assistance
  - People to request assistance in case of car accident
    * Relatives
    * Friends
  - Company to request assistance in case of car accident
    * Insurance company
    * Transit Police
    * Fire department
    * Hospital
  - Infrastructure to request assistance in case of car accident
    * Mobile Device
    * Sensor for automatic call
  - Applications to request assistance in case of car accident
    * Mobile Application
- Aspects concerned to the knowledge Base
  - Techniques to request assistance in case of car accident
    * Request assistance directly
    * Communicate a relative about the emergency
    * Communicate a friend about the emergency
    * Remote assistance
  - Methods to request assistance in case of car accident
    * Use of text messages
    * Use of panic button
    * Phone call
  - Theories to request assistance in case of car accident
    * Ambulatory emergency care protocols
    * Emergency care protocols by firefighters
    * Emergency care protocols by doctors

Figure 1 shows The Information System Research Framework based on Design science Research [11]. The framework has 4 subsystems as part of the Information System Research layer. Such subsystems were related to mobile applications development and specifically to *MAICAR* application development:

- Contact Management. It is based on the Android APIs for the storage of contacts in the smart phone. It allows storing the contact information that can be used in case of emergency. Contacts can be: guest, passerby, friend, owner, and relative.

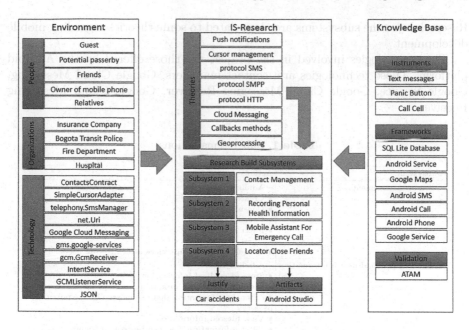

Fig. 1. Information system research framework based on design science research.

- Recording Personal Health Information. It allows adding additional information for the contacts stored by the contact management system. Such information is medical information that can be consulted by different actors depending the roles configuration made by the user. This subsystem not only allows storing information but also allows configure the type of information that each actor of the system can access.
- Mobile Assistant for Emergency Call. It deploys the initial view of the system, when an accident occurs. It presents the elements to be used by any user in order to send emergency information to predetermined contacts. This subsystem is supported by several technological services such as push notification, cursor agenda management, Short Message Service (SMS) protocol, among others. It is important to mention that the SMS service depends on the service contracted with the communications provider. Then, the system must optimize this resource in order to avoid additional charges. In addition, the information to be send using SMS must be selected strategically in order to inform assertively the accident situation.
- Locator Close Friend. It searches the location of closest friend ordered by distance in order to contact them. It is important to mention that the closest contacted friends must enable the option to share location. The system provides the services to agree location sharing between users.

Previous subsystems are related to (a) the environment layer, which contains people, organizations, and technology; and (b) the knowledge base layer, which includes instruments, frameworks, and validation. Furthermore, in the IS-

Research layer the subsystems are also related to some theories regarding mobile development.

The technologies involved in the project are those offered by the Android platform. Those technologies are: contact managers, Google Cloud Messaging, Google Service, Google Cloud Messaging Receiver, Google Cloud Messaging Receiver.

Table 1. Subsystems actions

Subsystem	Actions
Contact management	– Administrator • Create Users • Consult all users • Consult close users • Filter users – Guest • Consult users who are close after filtering users
Recording personal health information	– Administrator • Store of medical information • View all medical information • Filter the information that can be seen by the potential passerby • View filtered information • Filter information that can be sent to friends • Filter information that can be viewed by the user *guest* • Check clinical information to be delivered to contacts – Guest • View predefined information to the user *guest*
Mobile assistant for emergency call	– Administrator • Call all friends • Call close friends – Guest • Call close friends
Locator close friends	– Administrator • Display location close friends • Display location of a specific friend • Filter friends who are considered on visualization – Guest • Visualize close friends – System • Detect close friends • Detect location of a specific friend

Table 1 shows the actions that are allowed by the administrator and the user of each subsystem. In addition, the table shows the executed actions by the system that were not invoked directly by a user.

3   Approach

In this work, we designed and built *MAICAR*, which is a mobile based system developed in Java programming language using the Android software development kit (SDK) and the environment called Android Studio based on IntelliJ IDEA. When the application starts, the button called *Car accident report* is available permanently regardless the user.

(a) Screenshot   (b) Reporting an accident (c) Contacting recipients

Fig. 2. *MAICAR*

The user *Guest* does not need to be registered to report the accident. Figure 2a presents a screenshot of *MAICAR*.

When an accident occurs, usually the affected passenger does not have time to use the application. Thus, the application allows another user to send the report without registering. Figure 2b presents a screenshot of *MAICAR* when another user has pressed the button *Car Accident Reporting*.

When the report of the accident has been completed, the application displays the list of contacts, who have received the report. Figure 2c presents this operation.

The four subsystems of the approach are described below:

1. **Contact Management.** The contact management subsystem allows the administrator to create users and consult those who are nearby. The administrator can filter the contact and classify them as visible or invisible to the guest. The screenshot shown in Fig. 3a allows the administrator to disable those contacts who will not be visible to the administrator. Although these users are not shown, if they are closer than other users they will be notified through a text message.
2. **Recording Personal Health Information.** The recording system shown in Fig. 3b allows the administrator to store medical information; however, the user *Guest* just can view previously authorized information by the administrator. In the reporting subsystem the administrator can decide which clinical information can be delivered to specific contacts.
3. **Mobile Assistant for Emergency Calls.** Using the subsystem, which is presented in Fig. 3c, the user *Guest* can call close contacts and send them previously authorized information.

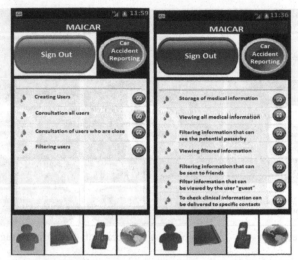

(a) Contact Management (b) Recording   Personal
                        Health Information

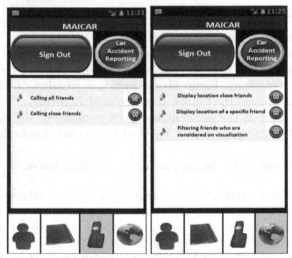

(c) Mobile Assistance for (d) Locator Close Friends
Emergency Calls

Fig. 3. *MAICAR* subsystems

4. **Locator Close Friends.** This subsystem calculates the proximity of a user
   regarding the current location of the administrator cell phone. Figure 3d
   presents the screenshot of this subsystem.

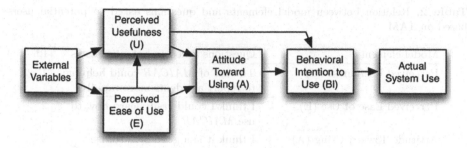

Fig. 4. Technology acceptance model [3]

4 Results

The prototype developed can be used whether there is a technological acceptance associated with the mobile application. Research is needed to find out how users are willing to accept and use a specific technology. Int his way, the model called *TAM (Technology Acceptance Model)* suggests that when users discover a new technology, there are several factors that influence their decisions regarding how and when they will download, install, and use such technology [3,10]. For this reason, the TAM model has been selected as the validation method for the prototype.

The TAM model includes two fundamental aspects [4]:

- Perceived usefulness (U). This aspect is defined as *the degree to which a person believes that using a particular system would enhance his or her job performance*
- Perceived ease-of-use (E). This aspect is defined as *the degree to which a person believes that using a particular system would be free from new or extra effort*

The TAM model also includes: External Variables, which refers to elements that cannot be controlled by the user, Attitude Toward Using (A), which refers to the level of satisfaction of the user, Behavioral Intention to Use (BI), which refers to the behavior presented by user when an application is used, and Actual System Use that determines how the application is used by users.

Figure 4 shows the Technology Acceptance Model. This model formed the basis of Table 2 in which the questions asked to potential users of *MAICAR* and its relationship with model elements are presented.

Thus, we performed a survey in which we requested users to give their opinion regarding the questions presented above. The survey was submitted by 197 people: 113 men and 84 women. The results are shown in Table 3.

Based on the results, we can observe that security is one aspect that women want. It is possible that women seek mechanisms that make them feel safe. In addition, it is possible, that *MAICAR* provides security to women. Somehow the

Table 2. Relation between model elements and questions asked to potential users based on TAM

Model elements	Questions asked to potential users	Id
Perceived Usefulness (U)	The use of *MAICAR* could help me to report accidents more rapidly	1
Perceived Ease of Use (E)	I think I could easily learn how to use *MAICAR*	2
Attitude Toward Using (A)	I think it is a good idea to use *MAICAR* to report the accidents	3
Behavioral Intention to Use (BI)	I have the intention to use *MAICAR* when it becomes available on Google Play	4

Table 3. Survey results

Id	Men who approved factor	Women who approved factor	Passing rate for men	Passing rate for women
1	70	69	61.95%	82.14%
2	87	72	76.99%	85.71%
3	91	76	80.53%	90.48%
4	79	74	69.91%	88.09%

results show that women appreciate more such applications than men. Consequently, *MAICAR* can be offered to women in order to gain users while the app becomes well known.

5   Conclusions

Traffic accidents often occur with little or no warning. Thus, a novel approach to report accident is a real contribution to the society. However, this kind of systems demand a lot of technology elements that need to be used with a proper methodology in order to ensure the success in the development of the system.

MAICAR is a novel approach to offer injured people of car accidents an oportunity to be assisted by different actors. Nevertheless, there are some situations that are out of the scope of *MAICAR*. For example, sometimes it is not possible to use the victim's smart phone and the passerby must be an honest person. Then, as future work, it is good to take into account, how the application should react when the passerby has not good intentions with the victim of the accident.

The Science should create projects that delve into researching about what information must provide a mobile application to the first responder specifically for this kind of projects.

References

1. Aloul, F., Zualkernan, I., Abu-Salma, R., Al-Ali, H., Al-Merri, M.: iBump: smartphone application to detect car accidents. In: 2014 International Conference on Industrial Automation, Information and Communications Technology (IAICT), pp. 52–56. IEEE (2014)
2. Boukerche, A., Zhang, M., Pazzi, R.W.: An adaptive virtual simulation and real-time emergency response system. In: 2009 IEEE International Conference on Virtual Environments, Human-Computer Interfaces and Measurements Systems, VECIMS 2009, pp. 360–364. IEEE (2009)
3. Davis, F.D.: User acceptance of information technology: system characteristics, user perceptions and behavioral impacts. Int. J. Man-Mach. Stud. **38**(3), 475–487 (1993)
4. Davis, F.D., Bagozzi, R.P., Warshaw, P.R.: User acceptance of computer technology: a comparison of two theoretical models. Manag. Sci. **35**(8), 982–1003 (1989)
5. Djajadi, A., Putra, R.J.: Inter-cars safety communication system based on android smartphone. In: 2014 IEEE Conference on Open Systems (ICOS), pp. 12–17. IEEE (2014)
6. Faiz, A.B., Imteaj, A., Chowdhury, M.: Smart vehicle accident detection and alarming system using a smartphone. In: Computer and Information Engineering (ICCIE), pp. 66–69. IEEE (2015)
7. Fernandes, B., Gomes, V., Ferreira, J., Oliveira, A.: Mobile application for automatic accident detection and multimodal alert. In: 2015 IEEE 81st Vehicular Technology Conference (VTC Spring), pp. 1–5. IEEE (2015)
8. Takizawa, O., Hosokawa, M., Takanashi, K., Hada, Y., Shibayama, A., Jeong, B.P.: Pinpointing the place of origin of a cellular phone emergency call using active RFID tags. In: 2008 22nd International Conference on Advanced Information Networking and Applications-Workshops, AINAW 2008, pp. 1123–1128. IEEE (2008)
9. Tangtisanon, P.: Android-based surveillance car. In: TENCON 2014-2014 IEEE Region 10 Conference, pp. 1–4. IEEE (2014)
10. Venkatesh, V., Davis, F.D.: A theoretical extension of the technology acceptance model: four longitudinal field studies. Manag. Sci. **46**(2), 186–204 (2000)
11. Von Alan, R.H., March, S.T., Park, J., Ram, S.: Design science in information systems research. MIS Q. **28**(1), 75–105 (2004)

Systematic Mapping Study of Architectural Trends in Latin America

Diana Alomoto[1](✉), Andrés Carrera[1](✉), and Gustavo Navas[1,2](✉)

[1] Universidad Politécnica Salesiana, Quito, Ecuador
{dalomoto,acarreraj}@est.ups.edu.ec,
gnavas@ups.edu.ec
[2] IDEIAGEOCA Research Group, Quito, Ecuador

Abstract. Software architecture has become an important aspect on systems development; however, despite the fact that there are several architectures that are already popular in the computer world, they do not seem to fully meet the demands of the developer due to the fact that system requirements are becoming increasingly stringent. This paper aims to carry out a systematic mapping study that allows publicizing the different architectures used in research accomplished in Latin America. For the study, numerous articles searches were executed in different bibliographic databases from acknowledged scientific journals, where several articles were obtained and through filters a total of 10 articles were obtained with which this project was worked on. Applying the systematic mapping process, a series of analyses were carried out on the selected scientific articles that allowed a detailed study of the investigations, which led to a varied collection of data that determined the focus of the studies when applying architecture to their systems. The final results of this work show that the scientific articles analyzed are focused on proposing new architectures based on existing ones.

Keywords: Software architecture · Systematic mapping study
Latin America

1 Introduction

In recent years software architecture implementation has become an essential point for the construction of systems because it provides a solid foundation on which software can be built. Software architecture "plays a key role as a bridge between needs and execution. By providing an abstract description of a system, architecture exposes certain properties while hiding others" [1].

This work implements a Systematic Mapping, a method that does not aim to answer a specific question, but rather collects, describes and catalogues the available evidence related to a topic of interest [2]. There are several methods for research such as:

- Systematic Mapping Review: Provides an overview of a research area, and identifies the quantity, type of research and results available [3].

M. Botto-Tobar et al. (Eds.): CITT 2018, CCIS 895, pp. 312–326, 2019.
https://doi.org/10.1007/978-3-030-05532-5_23

- Systematic Literature Review: A form of secondary study that uses a well-defined methodology to identify, analyze and interpret all available evidence related to a specific research question in a way that is unbiased and repeatable [4].
- Systematic Mapping Study: This is based on a broad review of primary studies in a specific topic that aims to identify what evidence is available on the topic [4].

2 Related Works

There are several studies that implement Systematic Mapping Study in different areas; however, SMS studies specifically in software architecture are limited. Below are some articles that study previously mentioned topics, but the context is different from that presented in this paper. It is worth stressing that none of these articles focuses on the study of architectural trends in a specific geographical space.

Li applies SMS to collect data from scientific articles related to software architecture and to identify in which types of architecture activities knowledge-based approaches are employed [5].

Liang implements SMS to SMS to evaluate articles that implement agile methodologies and software architecture in their studies. This article provides an extensive overview of several aspects such as practices, methods, benefits and costs of combining architecture and agile methodologies [6].

Tofan provides a systematic overview to determine the approach to architectural decisions, this document aims to analyze past work and future plans through studies published between 2002 and 2012 in different virtual libraries [7].

The articles mentioned above were used as a guide to analyze the application of SMS in each of the works, although the implementation of SMS in software architecture is different. Whilst the implementation of software architecture is mentioned in general, no specific type of architecture is named.

In this paper, the main objective of SMS's implementation is to present what types of software architectures are used by authors in articles implemented in Latin America. We could not find papers in which the location is a parameter of study; therefore it is not possible to make a comparison of specific results.

3 Research Methodology

This work is based on the systematic mapping process proposed by Paternoster [8] in 2014 as an adaptation of the diagram published by Petersen [9] in 2007.

According to the article published by Kai Petersen [9], Systematic Mapping Study has been recommended for studies related to software engineering. This methodology provides a process to obtain research reports and results through mapping of scientific papers [9]. Systematic Mapping Process presented by Paternoster [8] includes two more stages (rigor and relevance, synthesis) that were considered essential for the development of this research (Fig. 1).

Process steps

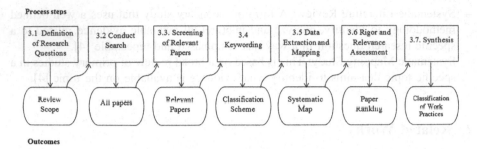

Outcomes

Fig. 1. Systematic Mapping Process [8]

3.1 Definition of Research Questions

Systematic Mapping Study (SMS) application aims to analyze the type of architectural methods used in software projects in Latin America. The following questions were asked in order to achieve this objective (Table 1).

Table 1. Definition of search questions

	Research questions	Motivation
RQ1.	What types of software architectures are used in Latin America?	Identify the software architectures that have been proposed, applied or studied
RQ2.	What is the main objective for the implementation of software architecture?	Analyze the main reason why the authors decided to apply software architecture to their systems
RQ3.	What is the most used architectural trend?	Determine which is the architectural trend used in the articles

3.2 Conduct Search

Keywords used for article search were based on different virtual libraries results; the search string established in this study was ("software architecture" AND "Latin America") because it presented more precise results related to the research topic. In addition, the search string was modified according to the established structure of each virtual library.

The search strings ("computing architecture" AND "Latin America") ("agile architecture") AND "Latin America" were tested but the results were too large and vague.

In addition, when searching with these strings in IEEE Xplore virtual library, most of the articles found contained topics related only to "Latin America" but without any relation to the main search string "computing architecture" or "agile architecture". For this reason, these strings were not considered although the results were higher than those of the other virtual libraries, they were inaccurate and inconsistent (Table 2).

This search string selection is due to the fact that there are not many academic articles that expose the topic of software architecture, unlike topics such as agile architecture and computing architecture that have been analyzed and presented by several authors. In this study, the use of article search tools was not necessary because the number of documents was minimal and the selection of documents could be done manually.

Table 2. Keywords for searching in virtual libraries

Virtual library	Search string	Results
ACM Digital Library	("software architecture") AND "Latin America"	0
	("computing architecture") AND "Latin America"	2
	("agile architecture") AND "Latin America"	0
Scopus	("software architecture") AND "Latin America"	3
	("computing architecture" AND "Latin America")	1
	("agile architecture" AND "Latin America")	0
IEEE Xplore	("software architecture") AND "Latin America"	34
	("computing architecture") AND "Latin America"	5827
	("agile architecture") AND "Latin America"	43717
Web of Science	("software architecture") AND "Latin America"	4
	("computing architecture") AND "Latin America"	0
	("agile architecture") AND "Latin America"	0

3.3 Screening of Relevant Papers

From 41 articles found (Table 2), 10 articles contained topics related to software architecture in Latin America. Several aspects of inclusion and exclusion (Table 3) were used into account in order to choose the appropriate articles. Once the articles were selected, we made a classification by language: Spanish, English and Portuguese (Table 4). It should be noted that language was not a point of exclusion in this paper as well as publication's year, however; it is worth mentioning that papers found were published between 2006 and 2017.

Table 3. Criteria for inclusion and exclusion of articles

Inclusion	Exclusion
- Scientific articles that contain topics related to software architecture and are applied in Latin America - Peer review - Publication's year is not considered	- Repeated articles - Articles not related to the software architecture - Articles those are related to software architecture but not applicable in Latin America - Dark literature

Table 4. Classification by language

Article title	Language
P1: Declarative and flexible modeling of software product line architectures [10]	Spanish
P2: Evaluation of software development through an MDA tool: a case study [11]	Spanish
P3: Incidence of software quality attributes in the design, construction and deployment of Cloud architectural environments [12]	Spanish
P4: Two-level software architecture for context-aware mobile distributed systems [13]	Spanish
P5: Towards a reference software architecture for improving the accessibility and usability of open course ware [14]	English
P6: Transpiler-based architecture for multi-platform web applications [15]	English
P7: Usage of social and semantic web technologies to design a searching architecture for software requirement artefacts [16]	English
P8: An architectural model for situation awareness in ubiquitous computing [17]	Portuguese
P9: Architectural requirements as basis to quality of software engineering environments [18]	Portuguese
P10: Using expert systems for investigating the impact of architectural anomalies on software reuse [19]	Portuguese

3.4   Keywording

This step is based on the classification scheme process (Fig. 2) used in Petersen's [9] research, this process starts with abstracts reading and a filter to select keywords to be able to structure the classification scheme.

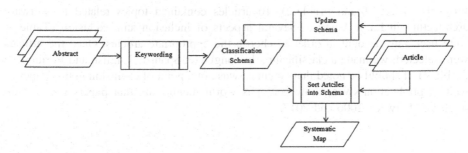

Fig. 2. Classification scheme steps [9]

The steps are detailed below:

– **Abstract**
  From 10 articles selected a reading of each abstract was made, if it was related to the research it was included in the selected articles list. In some cases abstract was not comprehensible so was read the content of the article and if it was related to the topic of interest then it was included in the list, otherwise it was eliminated from the options. In this filter 10 articles were related to the research topic, for this reason none were discarded.

– Keywording

The aim of this stage is to find words in common between all the articles. Ten scientific articles were classified by language and divided into three groups according to the language of each article. (Table 4).

With ATLAS TI tool was made a 'word cloud' of each group of articles previously classified by languages getting a number of words for each group (Table 5).

Table 5. Number of words per language

Language	Number of words
Spanish	3519
English	2641
Portuguese	2513

In this step three filters were made and will be explained below:

- *First filter*

  From 8673 words found among all the articles, was performed an elimination filter by articles, pronouns and words without relevance to the research topic. In Spanish language group, 4 documents were evaluated, so words with fewer than 4 repetitions in the 'word cloud' list were removed from this filter because the word was less likely to have at least one repetition in each article.

  Groups of documents with Portuguese and English language, words with less than 3 repetitions were eliminated due to the fact that 3 documents were evaluated in each of the groups. At the end of this filter was obtained 3 lists corresponding to the groups established above.

- *Second filter*

  A base list of common words related to software architecture was made with the Spanish language word group, as this group contains more documents; this list was compared with the other documents of the corresponding language groups.

  In total, 51 words were left that were considered the most optimal. It should be noted that these words were not consistent in all the articles.

- *Third filter*

  This filter consisted on discarding words that were not coincidental in all the articles. The result is a list of 10 words that are repeated at least once in each article, including the number of repetitions of each word in each of the articles classified by language.

When performing these filters the final list of words represents the keywords among all the documents evaluated. Table 6 shows the words that had been sorted according to the order of appearance in all the articles, with the word 'software' being the top of the list and the most frequently repeated in all documents.

Table 6. Word Filtering

WORDS	Spanish					Portuguese				English				TOTAL
	P 1	P 2	P 3	P 4	T.C	P 1	P 2	P 3	T.C	P 1	P 2	P 3	T.C	
Software	50	30	87	14	181	2	116	49	167	37	32	62	131	479
Architecture	3	15	15	33	66	13	55	7	75	22	25	22	69	210
Development	4	59	11	6	80	1	34	1	36	2	13	23	38	154
Systems	1	21	5	14	41	1	40	32	73	2	9	5	16	130
System	17	36	16	16	85	2	7	10	19	2	1	12	15	119
Engineering	15	1	7	3	26	4	27	8	39	5	2	37	44	109
Components	14	15	8	5	42	2	5	39	46	2	5	6	13	101
User	1	12	4	12	29	13	6	11	30	3	1	30	34	93
Design	3	9	18	2	32	6	16	8	30	7	13	4	24	86
Results	2	8	2	1	13	5	4	5	14	2	11	16	29	56

– **Classification schema**

Because of the matching words in all the articles were only 10. Classification scheme consisted in some cases on joining words to create sentences and in others only words that were considered important were chosen and searched in all the articles to find matches.

Table 7. Classification scheme

SPANISH	P1	Abstraction level	Internal variability	Reduction of development time	Software Product Line	Visual declarative Language FVS
	P2	MDA	Interoperability	Reduction of development time	Portability	Usability
	P3	ISO,IEC 12207	Product Quality	Software Life Cycle	Cloud Computing	Reusability / Reference Architecture
	P4	Layered Architecture	Abstraction level	Mobile Devices	Distributed Mobile Systems	Architecture CC (Composite Capability)
ENGLISH	P5	Reference Architecture	Usability	Accessibility	Software Product Line	Reusability / Interoperability
	P6	Reduction of development time	Layered Architecture	MVC Architecture	Cloud Instances	Web environments
	P7	Semantic Web	End user	Layered Architecture	Web environments	Re-use of products
PORTUGUESE	P8	Usability	Ubiquitous Computing	Interoperability	Mobile Devices	Architecture for 'situation awareness'
	P9	ISO,IEC 12207	Client/server architecture	Reference Architecture	Product quality	MVC Architecture
	P10	Reuse of Architectural components	End user	Software Life Cycle	Architectural evolutionary systems	Detection of architectural anomalies

Table 7 shows the phrases with matches that were found, as well as key phrases for each of the items that do not necessarily have repetitions.

In some cases the written word was not found explicitly but the content referred to one of the phrases, so they were included in the table.

3.5 Data Extraction and Mapping

Table 7 was considered as the basis for various classifications and data extraction. Three types of classifications were made, which will be detailed as follows:

- **Classification by type**

  O *Platforms:* OCW, Web Environments.
  O *Architectures:* MDA, Reference Architecture, Layered Architecture, CC Architecture, MVC Architecture, Client/Server Architecture and Architecture for 'Situation Awareness'.
  O *Characteristics:* Product quality, Architectural anomalies, Reuse of products, Reuse of architectural components, Abstraction level and internal variability.
  O *Tools:* Mobile device.
  O *Attributes:* Development time reduction, Reusability, Interoperability, Usability, Portability and Accessibility.
  O *Systems:* Software product line, Architectural evolutionary systems, Mobile distributed systems and Ubiquitous computing.
  O *Standard:* ISO/IEC/IEEE 12207.
  O *Processes:* Software lifecycle, Semantic Web.
  O *Languages:* Visual declarative language FVS.
  O *Technology:* Cloud Computing, Cloud Instances.

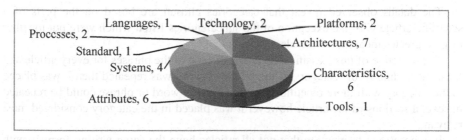

Fig. 3. Classification by type

The types chosen group certain general characteristics that in some way encompass their uses and operations, as can be seen in the illustration (Fig. 3) each of the types has specified the number of elements it contains.

The *platforms* group together web environments and Open Course Ware that are mentioned in certain articles.

There are *architectures* that are used and some articles may even use several architectures at once, but for the case of the classification scheme the most important ones have been taken from each article and listed.

Characteristics and attributes refer to the expectations that the research aims to achieve, final products or improvements that are managed and tried to obtain, in addition to correcting the inconveniences that appear, different elements that contribute to the objectives of the articles were grouped in tools and systems.

One *standard* that may have been found relevant to research is ISO/IEC/IEEE 12207 which refers to the life cycle processes of the ISO organization's software.

In the *language* grouping we could find the declarative visual language FVS on which one of the scientific articles studied is based.

The *technology* that could be observed with more relevance is Cloud Computing which is mentioned in some articles.

Finally, a general grouping of the stages, periods and organized works are the *processes* where software and semantic web life cycles are found.

- **Classification by content**

We made a classification of the terms found by sections of the scientific articles. It was divided into 8 sections explained below:

- Abstract/Objectives
- Introduction/Development: Two subcategories are derived from this section.
  - Applies
  - Research/Testing/Assessments
- Conclusions/Results
  - Based on
  - Proposes
- Related works/Future works

The details observed reveal that categories chosen are based on the parts of a scientific article with the exception of the subcategories listed which were put together to give greater meaning to the classification.

The objective of this classification is search each of the phrases for every article and locate according to the category, if the phrase or word was repeated then it was placed in the category with more repetitions, meaning that a word or phrase could be repeated in several sections of the article however it was placed in the category considered most relevant.

It is necessary to mention that not all articles have the same writing formats with exception of (Abstract, Introduction, and Conclusions) which are parts of an article. For this reason we have unified sections of the articles that we consider to be similar. As can be seen from the graph (Fig. 4), the category with the highest number of words or phrases is "Abstract/Objectives" followed by "Based on".

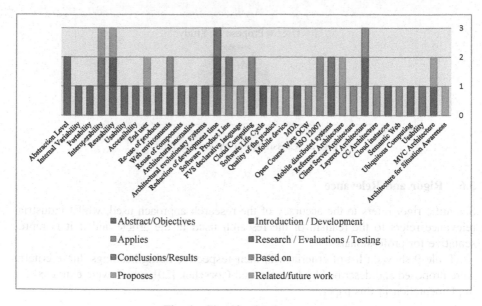

Fig. 4. Classification by content

- **Classification by architectures**

In this classification the main architectures used in each scientific article were searched, although several articles used different architectures. This classification is only based on the most relevant architectures of each article (Table 8). It was divided into 3 groups (Use, Study and Propose).

Table 8. Classification by architectures

P1	Software architecture product line	Use
P2	MDA (Model Driven Architecture)	Study
P3	Reference architecture	Study
P4	Two-Tier architecture in layers	Propose
P5	Reference architecture	Use
P6	Transpiler-based architecture	Propose
P7	Search architecture	Propose
P8	Architecture for 'situation awareness'	Propose
P9	Reference architecture	Propose
P10	ARCHIDES tool architecture	Use

As illustrated in the graph (Fig. 5), 50% of the articles seek to propose their own architecture to provide solutions to various problems, followed by 30% that use architectures that are already known in software development and finally 20% study architectures to evaluate either to develop quality models or to test the selected architecture.

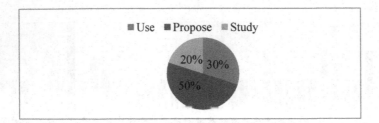

Fig. 5. Classification by architectures

3.6 Rigor and Relevance

Scientific rigor refers to the accuracy of the research approach used, whilst industrial relevance refers to the realism of the research used in the article and if it is representative for professionals.

Table 9 shows a list of criteria with their respective rating headings, these criteria were proposed and described by Ivarsson and Gorschek [20], which were extracted for implementation in this paper.

Table 9. Evaluation criteria for rigor and relevance [20]

Rigor	Relevance
• Context described	• Subjects
• Study design described	• Contexts
• Validity discussed	• Scale
	• Research method
Qualification	*Qualification*
- Strong description (1)	- Contribute to relevance (1)
- Medium description (0.5)	- Do not contribute to relevance (0)
- Weak description (0)	

After the criteria of rigor and relevance were established, Tables 10 and 11 shows an individual evaluation of each of the scientific articles studied, according to the weighting described previously.

Table 10. Rigor assessment

RIGOR										
Criteria	P1	P2	P3	P4	P5	P6	P7	P8	P9	P10
Context described	1	1	1	0.5	0.5	1	1	0.5	0.5	1
Study design described	0	0	1	0.5	0	0.5	1	0.5	1	0
Validity discussed	0	0	0	0	0	0.5	0	0	0	0

Table 11. Relevance assessment

RELEVANCE										
Criteria	P1	P2	P3	P4	P5	P6	P7	P8	P9	P10
Subjects	1	1	1	1	1	1	1	1	1	1
Context	1	1	1	1	0	1	1	1	1	1
Scale	1	1	1	0	0	0	1	1	0	0
Research method	1	1	1	1	1	1	1	1	1	1

Illustration (Fig. 6) compares the final results acquired by the evaluation, making a total sum of partial results for each article. Rigor results are lower compared to those of relevance. According to these results it can be determined that the articles studied have a greater focus on the realism of the research method; however, there is a lack of precision in the applied research approach.

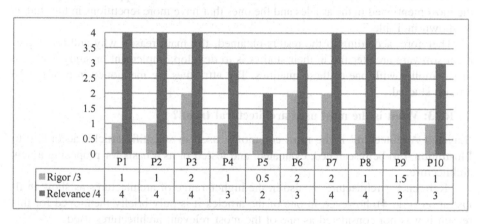

Fig. 6. Comparison of results between rigor and relevance

3.7 Synthesis

According to the data collected and the results analyzed, we answer to the first research questions that motivated this work.

– RQ1: What types of software architectures are used in Latin America?

According to Table 7 presented as our classification scheme; the architectures that were most used in the scientific articles are: MVC Architecture, Reference Architecture, Layered Architecture, MDA Architecture, and Client/Server Architecture.

Architectures previously mentioned were used in the articles either to use, study, or as a basis for proposing another type of architecture.

It is worth mentioning that the architectures presented were not the only ones mentioned in the articles as shown in Table 8, however, architectures mentioned previously have acquired more relevance in their respective studies, besides, are already known in software development.

– RQ2: What is the main objective for the implementation of software architecture?

Illustration (Fig. 3) shows a classification by type in which there are two groups that present the greatest number of elements, these groups are.

- *Attributes:* in this group there are elements that stand out as quality attributes, among which are evident: reduction of development time, reusability, interoperability, usability, portability, accessibility.
- *Characteristics:* this group refers to elements that were mentioned in the articles such as: product quality, architectural anomalies, product reuse, reuse of architectural components, level of abstraction, internal variability.

A study of the two previously presented groups determined that the scientific articles focus on the quality attributes because the elements that appear in this group are the most mentioned in the articles and the ones that have more repetitions in the studies as shown in Table 7.

Therefore, according to the results obtained, the main reason why authors implement software architecture in their studies is to develop, implement or study a system that complies with one of these qualities. The attributes are mentioned in 6 of the 10 articles studied.

– RQ3: What is the most used architectural trend?

'Layered Architecture' is the most commonly used in scientific articles according to Illustration 4 to be researched, evaluated, and tested or as a basis for proposing a new architecture.

'Reference Architecture' is also in the higher range of architectures as show in illustration (Fig. 4), however, in one of the articles it is only briefly mentioned for this reason it was not considered as one of the most relevant architectures used.

Therefore, it is evident that the architectural trend most used in the scientific articles developed is the 'Layered architecture', being considered as the preferred architecture for researches in Latin America.

4 Conclusions

Software architecture has become a focal point for carrying out work concerning the development or study of computer systems that has had a growing impact in recent years in Latin America. As it was demonstrated in this paper there are a great variety of software architectures that have been applied, studied or proposed for different projects, however, according to the data collection 50% of the articles propose software architectures while 30% use and 20% study architectures already known in the technological field.

'Layered Architecture' was determined as a trend from the results obtained, in the articles that study or use this architecture, abstraction level and reduction in development time stand out as common characteristics.

Systematic study carried out served as a starting point for a more specific understanding of the software architectures used in Latin America, the different preferences, the most used and the most stable ones for users, so that we can statistically agree on the trends that could be related to future work.

The results of the study carried out in this work reflect the scarcity of articles referring to software architecture that have been published in Latin America, as can be seen only 10 articles were found which are divided into three different languages this shows that the number of articles that were studied is reduced compared to other studies that implement SMS.

References

1. Garlan, D.: Software architecture: a travelogue. In: Proceedings of the on Future of Software Engineering - FOSE 2014 (2014). https://doi.org/10.1145/2593882.2593886
2. James, K., Randall, N., Haddaway, N.: A methodology for systematic mapping in environmental sciences. Environ. Evidence, 5(1) (2016). https://doi.org/10.1186/s13750-016-0059-6
3. Marques Samary, M.: Charla Systematic Review. https://users.dcc.uchile.cl/
4. Kitchenham, B.: Guidelines for performing Systematic Literature Reviews in Software Engineering. (2007)
5. Li, Z., Liang, P., Avgeriou, P.: Application of knowledge-based approaches in software architecture: a systematic mapping study. Inf. Software Technol. (2013). https://doi.org/10.1016/j.infsof.2012.11.005
6. Tofan, D., Galster, M., Avgeriou, P., Schuitema, W.: Past and future of software architectural decisions – a systematic mapping study. Inf. Software Technol. 56 (2014). https://doi.org/10.1016/j.infsof.2014.03.009
7. Yang, C., Liang, P., Avgeriou, P.: A systematic mapping study on the combination of software architecture and agile development. J. Syst. Software 111 (2016). https://doi.org/10.1016/j.jss.2015.09.028
8. Paternoster, N., Giardino, C., Unterkalmsteiner, M., Gorschek, T. and Abrahamsson, P.: Software development in startup companies: a systematic mapping study. Inf. Software Technol. 56(10) (2014). https://doi.org/10.1016/j.infsof.2014.04.014
9. Petersen, K., Feldt, R., Mujtaba, S., Mattsson, M.: Systematic Mapping Studies in Software Engineering (2007)
10. Asteasuain, F., Perez Vultaggio, L.: Declarative and flexible modeling of software product line architectures. IEEE Latin Am. Trans. 14 (2016). https://doi.org/10.1109/tla.2016.7437236
11. Duarte, J., Tonanez, M., Cernuzzi, L., Lopez, O.: Evaluation of software development through an MDA tool: a case study. IEEE Latin Am. Trans. 6 (2008). https://doi.org/10.1109/tla.2008.4653855
12. Cabrera, S., Abad, E., Danilo Jaramillo, H., Poma, G., Verdum, J.: Incidence of software quality attributes in the design, construction and deployment of Cloud architectural environments. In: 2015 10th Iberian Conference on Information Systems and Technologies (CISTI) (2015). https://doi.org/10.1109/cisti.2015.7170460

13. Medina Acosta, M., Lopez Dominguez, E., Gomez Castro, G., Pomares Hernandez, S., Medina Nieto, M.: Two-level software architecture for context-aware mobile distributed systems. IEEE Latin Am. Trans. **13**(4) (2015). https://doi.org/10.1109/tla.2015.7106376

14. Morales, G., Benedí, J.: Towards a reference software architecture for improving the accessibility and usability of open course ware. In: Proceedings of the 11th European Conference on Software Architecture Companion Proceedings - ECSA 2017 (2017). https://doi.org/10.1145/3129790.3129796

15. Andres, B., Perez, M.: Transpiler-based architecture for multi-platform web applications. In: 2017 IEEE Second Ecuador Technical Chapters Meeting (ETCM) (2017). https://doi.org/10.1109/etcm.2017.8247456

16. Chicaiza, J., López, J., Piedra, N., Martínez, O., Tovar, E.: Usage of social and semantic web technologies to design a searching architecture for software requirement artefacts. IET Software **4**(6) (2010). https://doi.org/10.1049/iet-sen.2010.0046

17. Lopes, J., Souza, R., Gadotti, G., Pernas, A., Yamin, A., Geyer, C.: An architectural model for situation awareness in ubiquitous computing. IEEE Latin Am. Trans. **12**(6) (2014). https://doi.org/10.1109/tla.2014.6894008

18. Nakagawa, E., Maldonado, J.: Architectural requirements as basis to quality of software engineering environments. IEEE Latin Am. Trans. **6**(3) (2008). https://doi.org/10.1109/tla.2008.4653856

19. Jullian Oliveira do Nascimento, R., Andre Guerra Fonseca, C., Dantas de Medeiros Neto, F.: Using Expert Systems for Investigating The Impact of Architectural Anomalies on Software Reuse. IEEE Latin Am. Trans. **15**(2) (2017). https://doi.org/10.1109/tla.2017.7854635

20. Ivarsson, M., Gorschek, T.: A method for evaluating rigor and industrial relevance of technology evaluations. Empirical Software Eng. **16**(3) (2010). https://doi.org/10.1007/s10664-010-9146-4

Augmented Reality as a Methodology to Development of Learning in Programming

Mónica Daniela Gómez Rios[1(✉)] and Maximiliano Paredes Velasco[2]

[1] Universidad Politécnica Salesiana, Cuenca, Ecuador
mgomezr@ups.edu.ec
[2] Universidad Rey Juan Carlos, Móstoles, Spain
maximiliano.paredes@urjc.es

Abstract. Learning programming is a complicated task and there is a high rate of students' failure or desertion. It requires the student to think abstractly and acquire a high level of affinity and discipline. It requires the student to think abstractly and acuire a high level of affinity as well as discipline. The basis is to find studies based on the development of tools for learning programming, which attract a high level of students' attention. The purpose is to carry out an analysis of the main characteristics, advantages and disadvantages of augmented reality as a learning methodology for programming, as well as the tools necessary for its development. After the review, we have found different types of applications which purpose range from business applications, maintenance support and equipment assembly to the development of kinesthetic skills. Regarding the support in learning, this is applied in different areas of study, with very few results in programming. It is intended to make a proposal of an augmented reality model for learning programming. Its high potential in education serves as support for pedagogical activities and the development of cognitive skills. However, there are still problems, such as the dependence of a device with a camera and special capabilities that support its proper functioning. Another impediment is that; the use of technology can be a cause of distraction when teaching a class. Nevertheless, all this with the advance of technology and research related to the subject of study, can certainly be overcome.

Keywords: Augmented reality · Computer science · Programming
Learning

1 Introduction

Augmented Reality (AR) is a technology that increases reality with computer-generated images of two or three dimensions (CGI), objects and/or information, and allows users to interact with them [1]. RA is used today to facilitate certain tasks in different areas of study such as, learning, entertainment, maintenance, assembly, among others. The methodology developed in this research has consisted in carrying out in first place a search of works in relevant magazines and congresses, in order to subsequently carry out an analysis of the characteristics of the tools, advantages/disadvantages they present. After this analysis, a study of the work analyzed in the scope of application in the design of an AR model for learning programming was carried out. The general scheme

© Springer Nature Switzerland AG 2019
M. Botto-Tobar et al. (Eds.): CITT 2018, CCIS 895, pp. 327–340, 2019.
https://doi.org/10.1007/978-3-030-05532-5_24

of augmented reality is through the use of a technological device, which allows us to visualize different sources of information of a physical object within the real world with virtual components. While in virtual reality all its environment is virtual, forming together the mixed reality. We are in the era of technology where the highest percentage of students uses an electronic device such as; a smartphone, a tablet or a computer. Augmented reality is characterized for being a feature-based system: visualization, interactivity, communication, graphic representation three-dimensional and object recognition [2]. In addition, it plays a very important role in the development of different activities and tools that are integrate as a support for learning at different levels of study and areas of development [3]. Its implementation is not simple since there are many difficulties that are presented at the pedagogical level, it is important to verify the enthusiasm of the students, the acceptance and adaptation in the use of space tools, which today is still used in many educational entities. Due to its dynamic content, it will always be more attractive for the student in any type of study, this leads to the fact that student is interested in the use of interactive tools that help in their learning process [4], the opinion of parents is an indicator of importance in the use of this type of tools specially for students of a basic level [5]. When applying the use of technology, we may take into account not only technological aspects, but the application of pedagogical methods. This would reduce the impact on the student's distraction and increase the commitment for a good use. Another important aspect to take into account is the degree of satisfaction of the students against the use of certain technology, in terms of the advantages and shortcomings that this may present, which would serve as a basis for building an effective learning tool in a future. The objective of this work is to present the characteristics and importance of the use of augmented reality and its different applications. As a learning tool, it is proposed to develop an application based on technology of Augmented Reality in the area of programming, which is relevant because there are no previous works that try to define an AR model for programming learning. In the future, this system will be evaluated by students of the same subject, who work with the tool in front of those who learn in the traditional way, and evaluate said results. Next, the details of the components and applications that include the use of augmented reality.

2 Components and Applications of Augmented Reality

Augmented Reality has several domains of use, identifying two large types of components or structures thereof. In this section we will see the components first and then a general review of the RA application.

2.1 RA Components

The general scheme of augmented reality is based on three components: the devices with camera, the software and the trigger or activator. With camera devices we have any kind of device ranging from a PC, mobile to a wearable. For software features, it is understood as any program that allow to make the necessary transformations to provide information additional that is required of the object captured by the camera. On the other hand, we have the triggers or activators, which are those formats of recognition to be treated as specifiers to the recognition of an object and they are used to link the printed content with the digital one. The Augmented Reality can be distinguished by two types, the one that employs markers or images and Augmented Reality based on position, and serve to locate and overlay a layer of information about points of interest, called POI (point of interest) of our environment, using GPS (Global Positioning Systems), accelerometers and compasses. For other part, we have augmented reality applications that employ markers or images which work with codes, which are nothing more than a way of representing information visually to allow its automatic reading, fast and without errors. Being the main difference between the different formats that exist, the way of representing the information and the amount of data they can store. As the most used until today we have the QR codes (Quick Response), whose meaning is rapid response code, which is an evolution to the barcode, the QR is a two-dimensional bar code or 2D matrix, which was developed by Denso Wave Corporation in 1994 [6], which, being two-dimensional, they read the code in both directions and can contain up to 7,089 numbers, being able to include images within their code, are composed by three squares in the corners that allow the reader to detect the position of the QR code and a series of scattered squares that encode the alignment and synchronization. There are other types of markers which, like the QR are arrays of two-dimensional points, but can create as specific identifiers of an object. For the present work what is intended with these markers is that, if the user focuses on them using a device, the result is information of a 3D object superimposed from different angles, that present details or add-ons including multimedia applications.

2.2 Hardware and Software Features

Augmented reality works with hardware devices and components of software, which are developed together to form an application. In regards of the hardware, the central device used for reality increased its a camera, which can be included in any mobile device, being the most used cell phones, tablets, binoculars. As for software components, there are a lot of tools and applications, the most used are detailed below. At the level of operating system, we have Android and iOS, as another component we have the ARToolkit libraries, used to track video in real time of position and orientation of the camera regarding the activators. They use markers or labels for recognition, also uses the library Vuforia as platform or SDK development kit [1] as well as Metaio [7]. As another package of components we have JSARToolKit for applications of augmented reality with the Web along with HTML5, which serves to include multimedia functions and access to hardware, in this case the camera's user through the getUse-Media API. Regarding the use of multimedia, among the most used we have Unity3D, it's a game engine that can integrate with Vuforia [8] and 3D Studio Max for a complete 3D modeling, animation and rendering [9], and among the most important languages of java programming, javascript, C#. Several applications use augmented reality technology. Some of them in learning, so in the next section you will see the related work.

3 Related Work

La realidad aumentada ha sido utilizada para diferentes aplicaciones, con variados tipos de interacción. A continuación, veremos algunos ejemplos de su utilidad y su aplicación en el aprendizaje.

3.1 Applications with RA

There are applications with augmented reality that support the realization or analysis of different types of processes, we can mention some work done, for example, in the support in aircraft maintenance using mixed reality [10]. On the other hand, we have in the development of virtual prototypes in workplaces to simulate equipment management configurations that may result dangerous [11]. Tools which serve as guidance for technicians during courses of maintenance and training of industrial equipment [12]. Another area in identity verification, is by reconstructing the face of one person [13]. In addition to this as a tourist level, allowing the user recognize different data and aspects of a city [14], make trips and allow tourists explore new interesting sites according to the places they visit and be able to visualize interesting details in the environment [15]. On the other hand, it has used augmented reality in the reconstruction of objects, such as the reconstruction of objects of a church that was based on a historical and artistic analysis of historical monuments to reconstruct them at reproduce a visual impression close to the original [16]. Another type of interesting applications are the creation of a calendar in Tokyo, which has different technological applications from the use of reality increased, sensory interaction to the use of smell and different sounds by touching a calendar photo per month to review the features respective events that happen within the city, to be able to touch some of the photographs and feel the texture of the paths or tabs, as well as also smell the freshly cut grass, feel the touch and smell the glass in the photography and much more [17].

3.2 Use of RA in Education

Augmented reality is being used in different areas of study, as a support to the learning process in a dynamic and interactive way, where the student can develop their skills visually and build your own knowledge There are several areas in which student uses as support tools implemented with reality increased, and in most cases have yielded positive results for their academic performance, making students feel more motivated, improve their level of knowledge and increase their skills to remember or memorize in shorter periods of time [18]. The areas in which there is greater precedence are in computer science, medicine, architecture, history, among others. For learning programming, the result is scarce, but in Sect. 7 in the design of the proposal some examples of the results obtained are presented.

There are some examples of applications in which the use of augmented reality has benefited learning in different study areas. We can mention in the science area of the computing with an example of hardware component analysis for computer architecture [19]. Another example is in the use of ICTs [20], as well as the use of labels for different areas of computer science and technologies [21]. In the area of Architecture

Applications have been made to improve the urban planning process [22] In addition to the use of augmented reality, there are tools that are applied to virtual reality in improving the design process in terms of the structural properties and the assembly of system components architectural [23]. The Augmented Reality technology in combination with the use of telephones Mobile offers many possibilities to evaluate, in situ, projects of architecture, urban design, construction processes and studies of the historical heritage. In the area of Earth and space sciences, they found applications for the geographical learning of a terrain by expanding objects in a book with RA [24]. In the agriculture for review of topics related to horticulture, gardening and landscaping [25] Several applications have implemented augmented reality with the application of concept maps, such as in the area of science at the primary level [26], as well as in the review of the day and night and the lunar phases. In the area of Technological Sciences in electricity is used in the ratio of the elements in an electrical circuit [27], another of the fields is where a test was carried out before and after the use of the RA and of traditional learning with very positive results, having a positive evaluation of the students in the classroom [28]. Another are in, History with applications that serve to a tourist and learning level, where the visitor acquires extensive and detailed knowledge of objects belonging to the built heritage of a city [29]. In the reconstruction of historic buildings [30]. In the area of mathematics for subarea of linear algebra, where the student can observe exercises of vectors through a game [31]. Augmented reality is used in different levels of study, and this is the reason why is used in primary level, applying in the study of numbers through a book of games for preschoolers using an old literature, The Thirsty Crow [32]. Based on kinesthetic learning there are also applications like learning mathematical concept graphics and its derivations to obtain speed and acceleration depending on any position given by the user's movement [33], being evaluated in the classroom these works satisfactorily. Another of the scenarios is the development of teaching resources for students of Mathematics I of the

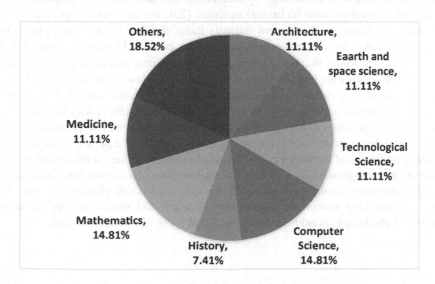

Fig. 1. Subjects in which augmented reality is used for education.

Technological Institute of Monterrey [34]. In Medicine and subarea of anatomy for learning the human skeletal structure [35] and in radio therapy [36]. Much of the tools have been evaluated within the classroom, using augmented reality with the support of a teacher or guide, under different modes of interaction, such as: books [37], games [31], robot's assembly [38], among others. Below, presents in general form according to indicated theory, the different types of subjects in which augmented reality is used for education (see Fig. 1).

From what has been exposed through the use of augmented reality for learning, the evaluation results present a series of advantages and disadvantages, which we present in the following section.

4 Benefits and Disadvantages

The augmented reality for the learning process or education, can be seen in the works mentioned in the previous point, which have great potential because of their dynamic content, reinforcing the student learning to improve their skills when viewing objects stimulating their learning, not only individually but in a way collaborative Several results show that the use of devices with augmented reality improve the learning experiences of the students, resulting in important characteristics such as improving level of interest and enjoyment the use of tools [19], in addition, allows merging the real world with the virtual world for different areas of study, more and more educational institutions are using tools of interaction as support for learning, currently the future Teachers and students need to replace traditional methods of reading with an interactive 3D application as a positive influence on the educational process [39]. On the other hand, when talking about drawbacks, these can be presented at the software or hardware level, one of them being orientation of the camera to focus on objects [40], another is the ability of investment in technology by institutions and adaptability in teachers, versus the use of technology with traditional methods [29], we must take into account that students learn whenever the content interests them, that is why it depends to a large extent on the material and the presentation of the content. In general, some authors comment on their results that the use of a virtual environment usually causes a high level of distraction in students because the use of a device in class, often causes students to perform another type of task or have display problems because not all devices work Likewise for specifications in terms of hardware or software, this is why there are areas that require the presence of a guide that covers their concerns and work in conjunction with the tool, between one of the impacts is that the gender of a person has a dominant influence on the use of technology, in the case of the males, it has an advantage in terms of use of technological tools, which is not due to biological factors but social factors [22]. The augmented reality with respect to the learning process, plays a very important role. The following section details the use of augmented reality as support for the learning methodology, in addition to the different types of interaction used.

5   AR as a Learning Methodology

The level of learning of a student depends on a large extended of methods and functions that a tutor develops in the classroom to correctly guide a student or the type of tool that contributes to their learning autonomously, one of the techniques used today is gamification, for being one of the most interactive methods where the student learns through games giving very good results in the learning. The augmented reality on the other hand, focuses on the dynamic interaction to perform different types of practical activities facilitate the learning process and the acquisition of knowledge of the students in the classroom. With the use of Augmented Reality, the Learning is done visually by interacting with images or multimedia contents that help to remember and memorize in the short term the proposed theme, others, are the use of conceptual maps of the contents of the subject, which help to synthesize and relate components [29]. On the other hand, the student develops a constructivist type of learning to whom interprets, elaborates, and experiences his learning. Constructivism is the basis of the use of the RA in reference to learning methods, and develops in different types, such as endogenous constructivism that emphasizes the importance of the apprentice's exploration during learning, the exogenous constructivism with a strong emphasis on students who build actively represent their own representation of knowledge with materials such as, instruction sheets and guidelines, and dialectical constructivism where the student interacts with other students and with the support of a teacher in materials such as; debate sessions, use of social networks, among others [19]. Direct experiences with the use of augmented reality allow the student to visualize closely elements that are not available in a physics with 3D format, which facilitates access to knowledge of different ways, improving traditional methods, but we still cannot leave totally isolated the traditional methodology, but on the contrary complement it with technology, through the use of textbooks, maps conceptual concepts, prototypes, specific locations and more. The RA components facilitate student access complementary concepts to expand information related to the subject or content of a subject, between activities or projects, which allows each student to continue to deepen in what is indicated or is find interested Typically tutors will find different benefits of the use of augmented reality according to the objectives of its exhibition, as well as in the development of activities or projects, being this type of technology adaptable to the requirements and needs of users. (see Fig. 2).

The previous figure, summarizes the fundamental characteristics that benefit the learning process through the use of augmented reality.

There are different physical and behavioral phenomena that influence the interaction of a user versus the use of technology, as well as different dynamic forms of the user in their interaction with reality increased, starting with the main types of interaction, first in the educational area, which mostly through books or conceptual maps where the images are the fundamental axis with which, the student visualizes the characteristics of the object through the identification of the same by means of QR codes or personalized codes that are captured by a camera and incorporate multimedia applications to include sound, videos, images and to be able to review in detail a set of characteristics and contents that help support learning by medium of interactions, for

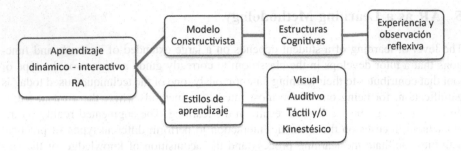

Fig. 2. General characteristics of learning with RA.

example, the Gagak application, which develops the concept of virtual book with augmented reality, this type of interaction is based on its majority to Billinghurst's Magic Book [32]. Another type of interaction is outside of the educational environment, such as in museums to observe geological objects, paintings, historical monuments. In the cities, the view of different buildings that makes up a cultural heritage and it turns as a tourist learning guide, in universities, to identify the campus or locations of different areas. In the marketing area, the user can interact with the product and review its details. The different forms of interaction are extended until you interact with kinesthetic components, used for physical activities in place to listen or visualize, for example the Kinect tool, a Motion detection device, equipped with camera, sensor infrared depth detection, microphone and a dedicated processor [33], and the type of interaction to verify step by step the assembly process of equipment or maintenance [41]. Our interest is focused on the learning process of programming through the use of augmented reality technology. The following section presents the importance of programming and therefore the development of applications that serve as support.

6 AR in Learning Programming

The importance of learning to program opens a world of possibilities. There are several tools that help you learn how to program. These characteristics and development are detailed of a programming learning tool by using RA.

6.1 Importance of Programming

In education refers the subject of Fundamentals of Programming as one of the most questioned in different areas of engineering, due to the results obtained in the students. One of the topics outlined by students in general is the difficulty in establish a logic in the development of algorithms from the management of control structures, loops, functions, the use of parameters and the scope of the variables [42], to the handling of events in the programming object oriented. Many of the causes of this problem is the lack of motivation, the use of different learning styles, knowledge previous in programming, and on the contrary to this, students who have experience in programming, which can cause a high degree of competitiveness compare to other students, leading this to the fact that, the other students may lose interest and as a consequence the teacher has to take the content of the subject. Most technologies are developed based on a programming language, for this reason it has become a challenge that at a very young age there are different means and techniques to improve and support the learning of programming.

6.2   Applications in the Area of Programming

The current learning in the field of programming, especially in the object-oriented, has led to execute different learning methods, but determining the effectiveness requires an analysis that evaluate the results regarding its use, there are support tools that can go hand by hand with the guidance of a teacher or instructor, we talk about a new paradigm of programming called "Real Word Programming (RWP)", where the user develops their own applications, specifying actions and conditions in the real world without using a computer desktop [43], and this is where most applications are headed. Among the most used tools today we have Scratch Community Blocks (see Fig. 3), which allows children to access, analyze and visualize code execution by dragging understandable commands to their level of knowledge and see the corresponding animation [44], other derivatives such as Minecraft [45] and Snap [46], another example is the educational robot Thymio for administration of events, where students through a tablet are reviewing in real time the executed event of the robot, which helps the student to have programming logic in terms of handling events [47]. Currently, there are different types of tools to support the learning of programming, as well as continue researching to improve them by conducting tests and studies, such is the case of the Beling.co website, which aims to facilitate learning basic programming for Indonesian teenagers from a fun way [48].

Fig. 3. Examples of tools to learn to program. Scratch.

Different types of tools that serve as support for learning programming, with different types of characteristics, forms of interaction and pedagogical methods are being developed. In the next section, a proposal is made to develop an application that uses augmented reality as a support technology for learning programming.

7 AR Design Proposal for Learning the Programming

As a result of the review, we find a large percentage of applications focused on education and applications in general that use augmented reality technology. Regarding its relation with the area of the programming applying the augmented reality, the result was scarce. Presented as projects that aim to achieve their objectives in terms of computer literacy through a series of applications for learning programming using augmented reality [49]. On the other hand, applications have been developed for students who begin to learn to program, oriented to students of the elementary school, through a game the student develops reasoning abilities by breaking down the problem into parts and forming a sequence [50]. Similar to this, there are applications in the area of robotics, which includes programming-oriented processes to give basic instructions to a robot. Based on these studies and the importance of the development of skills within the field of learning programming [51].

The authors are working on a prototype that exploits the benefits of AR in education for learning programming. Although, even prototype is in a very initial version, we want to present in this section the general idea of it. Therefore, it is proposed to develop a tool that cooperates interactively with the student in the process of learning using augmented reality technology, for this, The student must have a device at his disposal "a mobile", which with a web camera recognizes the labels that are immersed in the programming algorithm and help to visualize the detail of the algorithm components by using of multimedia, in later use the recognition of text that in this case would be the algorithm code to decipher as an interpreter of commands, and incorporate the interaction in terms of questions you can request the student through the same platform, this would be through utilities provided by artificial intelligence

Fig. 4. Outline of the proposal.

systems, taking as input data questions recorded by students and how output data simulation of the code used. (see Fig. 4).

General scheme of system development of augmented reality for learning programming.

8 Discussion and Conclusions

The review developed in this research shows us that the different types of applications developed through the use of augmented reality technology, have contributed to benefit in different areas of study, its adaptation as a complement to traditional learning has led users to feel more attracted to interact with the applications. It should be noted that one of the damages presented in different works indicates that its use is threatened by the direct dependence of a digital camera device on more than the characteristics in terms of capacity for its better functioning. On the other hand, the use of mobile devices during the development of a class, can be a distraction for the student, this leads to the need to take into account this type of factors that can be attributed in the development of the application which is detailed as a proposal. However, advances in technology and the continued use of mobile devices are growing and teachers are the ones who complement the tasks in the classroom through the support of technology. The authors believe that the important thing would be that its use does not interfere in the level of concentration of the students but on the contrary serves as a complement in the learning. It should be noted as an advantage that the augmented reality implemented in a system for any type of area, attracts the level of user attention and this technology is booming with new trends, which motivates us to develop a tool that includes the use of augmented reality for learning programming, since the results obtained in the revision of this area are few and even more with the inclusion of augmented reality in their applications. Taking into account the advantages and disadvantages described above, with respect to the use of augmented reality in the teaching process. The authors believe that the application of AR can help considerably for the development of the tool and this serves so that the student acquires basic knowledge of programming, starting from the concept of variable, constant and step of parameters in subprogramming.

References

1. Jamali, S.S., Shiratuddin, M.F., Wong, K.W., Oskam, C.L.: Utilising mobile-augmented reality for learning human anatomy. Procedia - Soc. Behav. Sci. **197**, 659–668 (2015)
2. Zheng, S.: Research on mobile learning based on augmented reality. Open Journal of Social Sciences **3**, 179 (2015)
3. Diegmann, P., Schmidt-Kraepelin, M., Van den Eynden, S., Basten, D.: Benefits of augmented reality in educational environments-a systematic literature review. In: Wirtschaftsinformatik (2015)
4. Diaz, C., Hincapié, M., Moreno, G.: How the type of content in educative augmented reality application affects the learning experience? Procedia Comput. Sci. **75**, 205–212 (2015)
5. Cascales, A., Pérez-López, D., Contero, M.: Study on parent's acceptance of the augmented reality use for preschool education. Procedia Comput. Sci. **25**, 420–427 (2013)

6. Kan, T., Teng, C., Chou, W.: Applying QR code in augmented reality applications (2009)
7. Majid, N.A.A., Husain, N.K.: Mobile learning application based on augmented reality for science subject: Isains. ARPN J. Eng. Appl. Sci. **9**, 1455–1460 (2014)
8. Chen, C.H., Ho, C., Lin, J.: The development of an augmented reality game-based learning environment. Procedia - Soc. Behav. Sci. **174**, 216–220 (2015)
9. Luis, C.E.M., Mellado, R.C., Díaz, B.A.: PBL methodologies with embedded augmented reality in higher maritime education: augmented project definitions for chemistry practices. Procedia Comput. Sci. **25**, 402–405 (2013)
10. Rios, H., González, E., Rodriguez, C., Siller, H.R., Contero, M.: A mobile solution to enhance training and execution of troubleshooting techniques of the engine air bleed system on Boeing 737. Procedia Comput. Sci. **25**, 161–170 (2013)
11. Grajewski, D., Górski, F., Zawadzki, P., Hamrol, A.: Application of virtual reality techniques in design of ergonomic manufacturing workplaces. Procedia Comput. Sci. **25**, 289–301 (2013)
12. Garza, L.E., et al.: Augmented reality application for the maintenance of a flapper valve of a Fuller-Kynion type M pump. Procedia Comput. Sci. **25**, 154–160 (2013)
13. Mayáns-Martorell, J.: Augmented user interface. Procedia Comput. Sci. **25**, 113–122 (2013)
14. Grüntjens, D., Groß, S., Arndt, D., Müller, S.: Fast authoring for mobile gamebased city tours. Procedia Comput. Sci. **25**, 41–51 (2013)
15. Zarzuela, M.M., Pernas, F.J.D., Calzón, S.M., Ortega, D.G., Rodríguez, M.A.: Educational tourism through a virtual reality platform. Procedia Comput. Sci. **25**, 382–388 (2013)
16. Laska, T., Golubkov, S., Tsimbal, I., Petrova, Y.: Multimedia information resource. The Church of the savior on ilyina street in Novgorod the great. Procedia Comput. Sci. **25**, 315–321 (2013)
17. Olalde, K., Guesalaga, I.: The new dimension in a calendar: the use of different senses and augmented reality apps. Procedia Comput. Sci. **25**, 322–329 (2013)
18. Majid, N.A.A., Mohammed, H., Sulaiman, R.: Students' perception of mobile augmented reality applications in learning computer organization. Procedia - Soc. Behav. Sci. **176**, 111–116 (2015)
19. Redondo, E., Fonseca, D., Sánchez, A., Navarro, I.: New strategies using handheld augmented reality and mobile learning-teaching methodologies, in architecture and building engineering degrees. Procedia Comput. Sci. **25**, 52–61 (2013)
20. Pacheco, B.A.: The development of augmented reality systems in informatics higher education. Procedia Comput. Sci. **25**, 179–188 (2013)
21. Kose, U., Koc, D., Yucesoy, S.A.: An augmented reality based mobile software to support learning experiences in computer science courses. Procedia Comput. Sci. **25**, 370–374 (2013)
22. bin Hanafi, H.F., Said, C.S., Ariffin, A.H., Zainuddin, N.A., Samsuddin, K.: Using a collaborative mobile augmented reality learning application (CoMARLA) to improve improve student learning (2016)
23. Abdelhameed, W.A.: Virtual reality use in architectural design studios: a case of studying structure and construction. Procedia Comput. Sci. **25**, 220–230 (2013)
24. Ramírez, P., et al.: Explora México: a mobile application to learn Mexico's geography. Procedia Comput. Sci. **25**, 194–200 (2013)
25. de Herrera, J.L., et al.: Tutorial 2.0 on technical drawing 3D and visualization. Procedia Comput. Sci. **25**, 108–112 (2013)
26. Chen, C.: An augmented-reality-based concept map to support mobile learning for science. Asia-Pac. Educ. Res. **25**, 567–578 (2016)
27. Matcha, W., Rambli, D.R.A.: Exploratory study on collaborative interaction through the use of augmented reality in science learning. Procedia Comput. Sci. **25**, 144–153 (2013)

28. González, M.A., Santos, B.S.N., Vargas, A.R., Martín-Gutiérrez, J., Orihuela, A.R.: Virtual worlds. Opportunities and challenges in the 21st century. Procedia Comput. Sci. **25**, 330–337 (2013)
29. Novotný, M., Lacko, J., Samuelčík, M.: Applications of multi-touch augmented reality system in education and presentation of virtual heritage. Procedia Comput. Sci. **25**, 231–235 (2013)
30. Soto-Martín, O.: 3D reconstruction & traditional illustrations, a non-invasive resource for the practice and teaching of conservation and restoration of cultural heritage. Procedia Comput. Sci. **25**, 247–250 (2013)
31. Nishizawa, H., Shimada, K., Ohno, W., Yoshioka, T.: Increasing reality and educational merits of a virtual game. Procedia Comput. Sci. **25**, 32–40 (2013)
32. Tomi, A.B., Rambli, D.R.A.: An interactive mobile augmented reality magical playbook: learning number with the thirsty crow. Procedia Comput. Sci. **25**, 123–130 (2013)
33. Ayala, N.A.R., Mendívil, E.G., Salinas, P., Rios, H.: Kinesthetic learning applied to mathematics using kinect. Procedia Comput. Sci. **25**, 131–135 (2013)
34. Salinas, P., González-Mendívil, E., Quintero, E., Ríos, H., Ramírez, H., Morales, S.: The development of a didactic prototype for the learning of mathematics through augmented reality. Procedia Comput. Sci. **25**, 62–70 (2013)
35. Hamrol, A., Górski, F., Grajewski, D., Zawadzki, P.: Virtual 3D atlas of a human body–development of an educational medical software application. Procedia Comput. Sci. **25**, 302–314 (2013)
36. Flinton, D.: Competency based assessment using a virtual environment for radiotherapy. Procedia Comput. Sci. **25**, 399–401 (2013)
37. Rambli, D.R.A., Matcha, W., Sulaiman, S.: Fun learning with AR alphabet book for preschool children. Procedia Comput. Sci. **25**, 211–219 (2013)
38. Alrashidi, M., Alzahrani, A., Gardner, M., Callaghan, V.: A pedagogical virtual machine for assembling mobile robot using augmented reality (2016)
39. Martín-Gutiérrez, J., García-Domínguez, M., Roca-González, C., Sanjuán-HernanPérez, A., Mato-Carrodeguas, C.: Comparative analysis between train-ing tools in spatial skills for engineering graphics students based in virtual reality, augmented reality and pdf3d technologies. Procedia Comput. Sci. **25**, 360–363 (2013)
40. Alsaggaf, W., Hamilton, M., Harland, J.: Mobile devices in computer programming lectures: Are CS lecturers prepared for mobile learning? (2012)
41. Luis, C.E.M., Marrero, A.M.G.: Real object mapping technologies applied to marine engineering learning process within a CBL methodology. Procedia Comput. Sci. **25**, 406–410 (2013)
42. Bosse, Y., Gerosa, M.A.: Why is programming so difficult to learn? Patterns of difficulties related to programming learning mid-stage. ACM SIGSOFT Softw. Eng. Notes **41**, 1–6 (2017)
43. Masui, T.: Real-world programming (2000)
44. Dasgupta, S., Hill, B.M.: Scratch community blocks: supporting children as data scientists (2017)
45. Minecraft - Sitio oficial
46. Snap - Sitio Oficial
47. Balderas, A., Ruiz-Rube, I., Mota, J.M., Dodero, J.M., Palomo-Duarte, M.: A development environment to customize assessment through student's interaction with multimodal applications (2016)
48. Fadhilah, S., Santoso, H.B., Goodridge, W.: Interaction design evaluation and improvement of beling. co: an online basic programming learning website (2016)

49. Ortega, M., et al.: iProg: development of immersive systems for the learning of programming (2017)
50. Goyal, S., Vijay, R.S., Monga, C., Kalita, P.: Code bits: an inexpensive tangible computational thinking toolkit for K-12 curriculum (2016)
51. Magnenat, S., Ben-Ari, M., Klinger, S., Sumner, R.W.: Enhancing robot programming with visual feedback and augmented reality (2015)

Analyzing Mid-Air Hand Gestures to Confirm Selections on Displays

Orlando Erazo[✉], Ariosto Vicuña, Roberto Pico, and Byron Oviedo

Universidad Técnica Estatal de Quevedo, Quevedo, Ecuador
{oerazo,avicuna,rpico,boviedo}@uteq.edu.ec

Abstract. The use of applications based on mid-air gestures has been increasing during last years, but there are still challenges to be addressed. One of them is the type of hand gestures that should be employed in specific scenarios and/or tasks. A particular case is the selection of an item on a display or surface, with the following confirmation of that selection. Thought several gestures have been proposed to confirm a selection, user interface designers should know the differences between them to make an appropriate decision. Therefore, we analyzed a set of confirmation hand gestures using performance metrics and subjective measures to make comparisons between the chosen gestures. According to our results, all the studied gestures can be perceived to be intuitive, but hover was the best gesture for confirming a selection. The reported findings should help designers to make distinctions between confirmation gestures and made decisions according to the desired scenarios.

Keywords: Mid-air hand gestures · Confirmation gestures
Touchless interaction · Natural user interfaces · Human-computer interaction

1 Introduction

The use of mid-air gestures as a style of interaction with computers has increased in recent years. The development of new low-cost hands and body tracking devices (such us Leap Motion and Intel RealSense) have contributed to develop applications in a variety of scenarios that go beyond entertainment. Healthcare [1], education [2], tourism [3] and public spaces [4] are just some examples where this interaction style provide advantages such us hygiene and security. Despite these advantages, there are still some challenges that should be addressed before deploying applications of this type.

One of the challenges that researchers and/or user interface (UI) designers should manage is the type of gestures to use in specific scenarios and/or tasks. An example of these tasks is the set of gestures used to select items on a screen. In this case, a system could display a set of selectable items. Then, a user can explore the items using gestures performed at a distance of the display or interactive surface. Once the user has made a decision, s/he needs to perform another gesture to confirm the selection, which is named *confirmation gesture* [4].

Although this type of tasks may not be too difficult to learn and perform, current findings are not enough to allow UI designers making distinctions between the proper

© Springer Nature Switzerland AG 2019
M. Botto-Tobar et al. (Eds.): CITT 2018, CCIS 895, pp. 341–352, 2019.
https://doi.org/10.1007/978-3-030-05532-5_25

confirmation gestures according to their needs. Some research efforts have been made to tackle this problem. On the one hand, Erazo and Pino [5] and Walter et al. [4] defined a set of gestures that could be used to select items on a display. In fact, Walter et al. [4] proposed a set of gestures to confirm the selection of an item as part of a design space for public displays, but their study did not cover all the described components. On the other hand, Schwaller and Lalanne [6] studied several strategies for pointing and selecting in the air focusing mainly on performance and effort. Despite the usefulness of the analysis of the selected strategies, more work is needed as the authors concluded.

Considering this landscape, we performed an analysis of several confirmation mid-air hand gestures. The candidate gestures come from previous works such as [4, 5]. We concentrate only on the most commonly used gestures, which have not been compared between them yet. Specifically, this research was conducted trying to answer the questions: Which are the differences between confirmation gestures? Is a particular confirmation gesture better than the others? Consequently, we analyzed the selected gestures considering performance and subjective measures to make comparisons between them.

As a result, this paper contributes with more insights about touchless hand gestures. In other words, the differences between several confirmation gestures are analyzed and discussed focusing on options that may help increase user performance. Thus, the findings reported here should help UI designers to distinguish between confirmation gestures before making a decision for the desired scenario.

2 Related Work

Departing from the fact that people use gestures to communicate between them, UI designers are now employing gestures to enable the communication between users and computers. Users can stand up or sit down at a distance from a display to perform the corresponding gestures using their hands or other body parts to interact with a software application. Then, the application recognizes the set of gestures previously defined/selected by implementing the needed algorithms.

Nowadays, UI designers can use various methods to select gestures and define the gesture set or *gesture vocabulary* [7] for an application. Some existing methods require user participation to collect and analyze data (e.g., [8–10]), whereas other methods are based on models to select gestures without asking user participation (e.g., [5, 11]). In the former case, designers generally ask users their opinions about the gesture(s) that best match a command, and then, compute a score of agreement [8, 9]. Using these methods designers can define a gesture vocabulary, but they cannot analyze other aspects of gestures. The second option refers to the use of evaluation models that allow estimating user performance and provide a framework to describe and reflect on problems without involving users. In this case, designers have to apply some formulas to compute the values of a specific metric, and next, select the gestures with the best scores. Examples of these models are those ones to forecast user performance time [5] and gesture difficulty [11]. Despite the usefulness of these methods to choose gestures and analyze interface designs, they are not focused on gestures for specific tasks.

A different approach followed by some researchers is the analysis of gestures for specific tasks or scenarios. Table 1 contains some examples of these gestures with their descriptions. In this sense, Nancel et al. [12] proposed and studied several mid-air input techniques for navigation on wall-sized displays. They considered the possibility of employing bimanual and unimanual input, and device-based and free-hand techniques. Although this work provides recommendations about techniques to navigate efficiently in very large multiscale environment, it focused only on mid-air pan-and-zoom. Hespanhol et al. [13] also studied mid-air gestures for interacting with large displays. They investigated four gestures (dwelling, grabbing, pushing and lassoing) that could be used to select items, but they focused on the intuitiveness and effectiveness of them. Likewise, Yoo et al. [14] evaluated mid-air gestures to support selection and navigation in large displays using (1) point-and-dwell and (2) push and grab-and-pull. It is interested to note that they found the "participants considered point-and-dwell to be more accurate but slower compared to push and grab-and-pull". Finally, Koutsabasis and Domouzis [10] focused on browsing and selecting images using mid-air gestures. Though the authors analyzed quantitatively only the techniques for browsing, they conducted a gesture elicitation study as a first step. The majority of participants proposed push gestures for making selections in that study.

Table 1. Examples of mid-air hand gestures.

Gesture	Description
Dwell (hover)	Hold a hand (on a target) a fixed time
Push (tap)	Move a hand toward the front a certain distance
Grip (grab) & release	Close and open a hand
Swipe	Move a hand from right to left or vice versa
Wave	Wave a hand toward the front

Based on these works, we could conclude that dwell is the best gesture for confirming selected items because it is more intuitive and accurate, although designers should take into account "it needs to be tuned in terms of dwelling time to be made more effective" [13]. However, there is also evidence that some users could prefer using pushing instead of dwelling. Therefore, we consider these studies are not enough to reach a "final conclusion".

There are a couple of works following other methods that could also contribute to our analysis of confirmation gestures. The first one proposes a design space for mid-air selection techniques on public displays [4]. Dwell, swipe, push, pointing, grip and wave are the gestures proposed as part of this design space to confirm a selection. Moreover, point and swipe were proposed as selection/browsing gestures. The authors concluded that users successfully used point + dwell for selecting items when no hint was provided, but they also stated that their proposal was not fully explored. Then, Erazo and Pino [5] performed a systematic bibliographic review with the aim of finding the most used mid-air gestures. The results showed that tap, swipe, dwell and grip were the preferred gestures. The authors also estimated the times for these gestures, but they did not make individual comparisons because the main goal of the study was to formulate a predictive model.

These related works allowed us deciding the gestures to be analyzed in our study. Given that we are not interested on finger-based gestures and that swipe gestures could be preferred mainly for browsing items, we selected three gestures: hover, tap and grip&release.

3   Materials and Method

This section describes the performed study with the aim of comparing the chosen gestures for confirming selections. The study was carried out in a controlled environment. It consisted in performing the selected gestures to interact with the developed application. We collected quantitative data and users' opinions as part of the study. The corresponding details are explained below.

3.1   Apparatus

A custom software application was utilized to carry out the study taking into account particularly related work as [5]. This application consisted in allowing users to answer some multi-choice questions by selecting one out of five possible answers (Fig. 1, left). Each participant had fifteen seconds to read each question and make a decision. Then, the question disappeared, the participant pointed to the desired option, and, s/he finally performed a mid-air gesture (i.e., tap, hover and grip&release) to confirm the answer (Fig. 1, right).

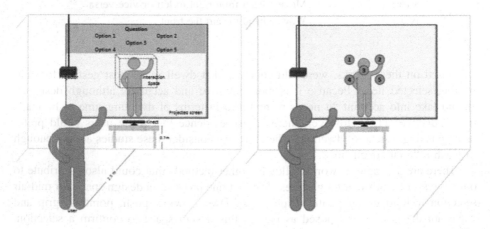

Fig. 1. Setup used in the study.

The experimental software was developed using Microsoft Visual C# and Kinect for Windows SDK. It logged time marks and attempts while participants performed the gestures. Its interface used an augmented reality parading blending user interface controls and the real environment. This idea have been successfully used in previous works (such us [1, 5]), which also provided additionally design guidelines such as feedback given to users.

The hardware setup consisted of a notebook, a Microsoft Kinect sensor and a projected screen (Fig. 1). The Kinect sensor was connected to the notebook to allow tracking users' hand position and recognizing gestures. It was placed at a height of 0.7 m. and below the screen. The notebook was connected to the projected screen with a 1360 × 768 pixels resolution. Participants stood 2.5 m away from the Kinect to interact with the software and perform the tasks.

3.2 Participants

Thirty healthy participants (mean age 19 years, SD = 2; 27 right-handed; 21 male) were recruited from our campus to carry out the study. They were attending the first or the second year of System Engineering. All participants self-declared to have no previous experience on mid-air gestures. These features and other demographic characteristics were collected in a final questionnaire. Moreover, the subjects were not paid for participation, and written informed consent was obtained from all of them before starting the study.

3.3 Data Collection

The metrics of interest were collected in various ways. First, time and attempts were captured automatically using the application. Gesture execution times were computed as the period of time since a user put a hand over the button and the gesture was recognized by the application. If the application could not recognize a gesture, that gesture was counted as a failed attempt (and the participant had to repeat it). Second, participants filled out a survey about their experience using the application. The questionnaire was adapted from [15] (see Table 2 below); it has also been applied in related works such as [2]. In general, the questions cover issues of physical operation, fatigue, comfort, speed and accuracy, and overall usability. Participants were instructed to answer the questions using a 7-point Likert scale. Third, we requested participants to rank the chosen gestures according to their preferences for the gestures to confirm a selection. Finally, participants were requested to freely comment about the use of the gestures and experienced problems.

3.4 Procedure and Design

In general, participants received written instructions to perform three tasks guided by the software. Instructions for the first task were provided after a general explanation and signing the informed consent. The participants had enough time to read these instructions, which referred to the way to execute the gestures for answering (i.e., if they had to use tap, hover or grip&release and how to execute every one). Next, participants placed in the designated area when they were ready to start, and the first question was showed on the screen. The questions were prepared bearing in mind participants' background. Moreover, several practice questions were used to allow the participants to learn to use the software and the gestures before starting the experimental questions/tasks. After finishing the first task, the participants were allowed resting for a couple of minutes, and then, they received the instructions for the following task.

A within-subjects design was used where the participants performed three tasks. The task order was counterbalanced using balanced Latin squares. Fifteen questions were answered randomly using only one gesture in each task. The whole experiment lasted less than one hour per participant in all cases.

4   Results

4.1   Time and Attempts

Figure 2 shows the mean times required to perform each gesture. Hover was the fastest gesture (1000 ms) as the feedback time was set on 500 ms, while tap and grip&release gestures had almost the same time (1155 ms and 1146 ms respectively). The measured differences were statistically significant for gestures as revealed in an analysis of variances ($F_{2,29} = 6.12$, $p < 0.005$). Moreover, pairwise comparisons showed a significant effect between tap and hover, and between hover and grip&release. The other comparison did not meet the five percent threshold for significance.

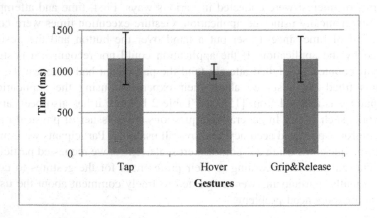

Fig. 2. Gesture execution times. Error bars indicate 1 SD.

Similar to the gesture execution times, the analysis of variances showed that the difference in the mean number of attempts (Fig. 3) was statistically significant ($F_{2,29} = 10.76$, $p < 0.001$). Performing pairwise comparisons we found that tap-hover and hover-grip&release were significantly different, whereas the condition tap-grip&release was not significant.

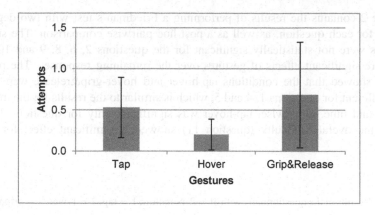

Fig. 3. Mean number of attempts per gesture execution. Error bars indicate 1 SD.

4.2   Questionnaire

The results obtained from the subjective data collected with the questionnaire are presented in Fig. 4 and Table 2. Figure 4 shows the results corresponding to the participants' perceptions after doing the experimental tasks. In general, hover was the best one in almost all cases. The exception is question 8, but the mean values of hover are very close to the values of the other two gestures. Tap and grip&release have different positions being the second one slightly better than tap.

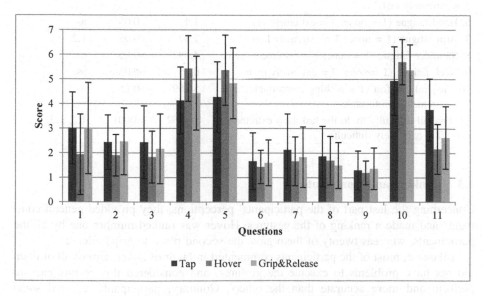

Fig. 4. Questionnaire results. Error bars indicate 1 SD.

Table 2 contains the results of performing a Friedman's test with two degrees of freedom for each question, as well as a post hoc pairwise comparison. The subjects' responses were not statistically significant for the questions 2, 6, 8, 9 and 10, while there were significant effects of gestures over the remaining responses. The post hoc analyses showed that the conditions tap-hover and hover-grip&release were significantly different for questions 1, 4 and 5, which is similar to the results for the measured attempts and time. Otherwise, tap-hover was significant only for questions 3 and 7. Finally, the overall difficulty (question 11) showed a significant effect for all the gestures.

Table 2. Results of the questionnaire with df = 2. Notation: 1 = tap, 2 = hover, 3 = grip&release, ns = not significant.

Question	χ^2	p	Post hoc comparisons
1. Facility to learn the task (1 = extremely easy; 7 = extremely difficult)	14,552	<0.005	1:2, 2:3
2. Mental effort to do the task (1 = extremely low; 7 = extremely high)	5,136	>0.05	ns
3. Physical effort to do the task (1 = extremely low; 7 = extremely high)	6,382	<0.05	1:2
4. Accurate during the task (1 = extremely low; 7 = extremely high)	21,515	<0.0001	1:2, 2:3
5. Speed to do the task (1 = extremely slow; 7 = extremely fast)	12,452	<0.005	1:2, 2:3
6. Hand fatigue (1 = none; 7 = extremely high)	1,4	>0.05	ns
7. Arm fatigue (1 = none; 7 = extremely high)	7,37	<0.05	1:2
8. Shoulder fatigue (1 = none; 7 = extremely high)	4,082	>0.05	ns
9. Neck fatigue (1 = none; 7 = extremely high)	0,25	>0.05	ns
10. General comfort (1 = nothing comfortable; 7 = extremely comfortable)	5,769	>0.05	ns
11. Overall difficulty to do the task (1 = extremely easy; 7 = extremely difficult)	21,152	<.0001	1:2, 1:3, 2:3

4.3 Ranking and Comments

Concerning the last part of the participants' perceptions, they provided general comments and made a ranking of the gestures. Hover was ranked number one by all the participants, whereas twenty of them gave the second place to grip&release.

Likewise, most of the participants commented in favor of hover; almost all of them did not have problems to execute the gestures, and considered this gesture easy to perform and more accurate than the others. Contrary, participants reported some problems to accomplish tap and grip&release gestures due to its nature (move the hand toward the front, and close and open the hand). For this reason, some participants suggested improving the provided feedback and accuracy. Despite the possible problems experienced with tap and grip&release, the participants said these two gestures are still acceptable.

5 Discussion

At the beginning of this paper we posed two questions concerning the differences between confirmation gestures. Therefore, in this section we discuss these differences based on the three considered aspects: gesture execution time, number of attempts, and participants' perceptions.

According to the measured time, the fastest gesture is hover, but it has the best time due to the feedback time used in our study. The used feedback time is based on previous works [5, 16], but other researchers and commercial system have utilized greater values [4, 17, 18]. Increasing the feedback time will result in an increment of the total time to perform a hover, and hence, it will be slower. Although the subjects' perceived speed gave results consistent with the measured time, the fact of using a higher feedback time can be disadvantageous in scenarios such as text entry in the air as it could impact the speed [19]. On the other hand, the mean times to perform tap and grip&release gestures are almost the same, but the second one could be analyzed as two different strokes (see for example [5]). In other words, the subjects had to perform a grip followed by a release gesture to make a selection in this study, but that selection could also be made by performing a grip or by performing a release. Lower values can be obtained doing this division [5] which may conduct to increase performance. Consequently, concerning time, hover would be the best one but employing the feedback time used here, although using grip or release independently may outperform hover.

Regarding accuracy, hover is definitely the best gesture. This fact is supported by the low number of attempts before performing the gesture correctly, which is also consistent with the participants' opinions (question 4). This result is expected because, to perform a hover, it is only necessary to keep the hand on the button and wait until the feedback is completed. In fact, we observed during the experiment most errors when performing hover gestures were counted due to target reentries. Additionally, other researches that compared hover with other gestures have reported lower error rates using this gesture [17]. Finally, it is expected that users would have better accuracy using hover in comparison to other gestures when no further instructions or hints are provided [4].

On the other hand, we included five questions concerning the perceived fatigue and comfort. Participants said they experienced some fatigue in hand, arm, shoulder, and neck, but this fatigue was very low (less than or equal to 2.1 for all gestures and body parts). Furthermore, only the reported arm fatigue was significant (question 7) with a difference between tap and hover, which could be attributed to the move of the hand toward the front. Although these results might conduct to think perceived fatigue is not a good a metric to compare confirmation gestures, it should be studied in more detail. Actually, other metrics can be used to analyze fatigue in a different way (for example [17, 20]).

Finally, the quality of this gesture set to make selections is ratified by the results obtained from the remaining questions. The participants said the gestures were in general easy to learn, required low mental and physical effort, and with a low overall difficulty. Moreover, the perceived comfort reported by the participants was high (greater than 5 for all gestures). This evidence supports the idea that the analyzed gestures can be good enough to confirm the selection of items. However, it is necessary to take into account the difference observed from our data between the facility to learn the gestures and the overall difficulty to perform them, for example, hover is easier than the other gestures.

6 Conclusions and Future Work

In this paper we analyze several mid-air hand gestures that are used to confirm the final selection of items on displays. Tap, hover and grip&realease were compared using collected quantitative data and users' opinions. According to our results, the three gestures can be perceived to be intuitive (which is consistent with related works), but hover was the best gesture for confirming a selection. This finding is also in agreement with previous works that suggest that hover is the most intuitive gesture [13], perceived to be more accurate and preferred as confirmation gesture [14], especially when no hints or instructions are given [4]. Nevertheless, hover gestures should be used with care because they need to be tuned in terms of hovering time [13] and some users may prefer using other gestures [10].

UI designers could still use tap and grip&release as confirmation gestures instead of hover based on the scores they reached in this study. Tap is similar to grip&release according to our results (though the second one was slightly better than the first one). Moreover, some users may prefer using tap for confirming selections [14], whereas other users may perceive it to be more difficult. All in all, hover may be easier but slower than the other gestures for confirming selections.

Future work should include experimentation using other scenarios and other gestures. Firstly, we employed an augmented reality parading in this study, but the application can also use a graphical user interface to allow the user making selections. Secondly, the feedback provided to users and the sensor accuracy could be improved. For example, future experimental software could include not only visual and auditory feedback; haptic feedback could also be provided to feel the sensation of pushing the hand (e.g., [21, 22]). Lastly, other gestures may be explored/proposed for making selections in mid-air, e.g., conducting a gesture elicitation study as a first step (similar to [10]).

Acknowledgments. This work was supported by FOCICYT 2017–2018 (Universidad Técnica Estatal de Quevedo, Ecuador).

References

1. Erazo, O., Pino, J.A., Pino, R., Fernández, C.: Magic mirror for neurorehabilitation of people with upper limb dysfunction using kinect. In: Proceedings of HICSS 2014, pp. 2607–2615. IEEE Press (2014)
2. Erazo, O., Baloian, N., Pino, J.A., Ochoa, S.F.: Designing hand gesture interfaces for easing students participation from their spot. In: Proceedings of the 21st International Conference on Computer Supported Cooperative Work in Design, pp. 133–138. IEEE (2017)
3. Minda Gilces, D., Matamoros Torres, K.: A kinect-based gesture recognition approach for the design of an interactive tourism guide application. In: Botto-Tobar, M., Esparza-Cruz, N., León-Acurio, J., Crespo-Torres, N., Beltrán-Mora, M. (eds.) CITT 2017. CCIS, vol. 798, pp. 115–129. Springer, Cham (2018). https://doi.org/10.1007/978-3-319-72727-1_9
4. Walter, R., Bailly, G., Valkanova, N., Müller, J.: Cuenesics: using mid-air gestures to select items on interactive public displays. In: Proceedings of MobileHCI 2014, pp. 299–308. ACM Press (2014)
5. Erazo, O., Pino, J.A.: Predicting task execution time on natural user interfaces based on touchless hand gestures. In: Proceedings of IUI 2015, pp. 97–109. ACM Press (2015)
6. Schwaller, M., Lalanne, D.: Pointing in the air: measuring the effect of hand selection strategies on performance and effort. In: Holzinger, A., Ziefle, M., Hitz, M., Debevc, M. (eds.) SouthCHI 2013. LNCS, vol. 7946, pp. 732–747. Springer, Heidelberg (2013). https://doi.org/10.1007/978-3-642-39062-3_53
7. Nielsen, M., Störring, M., Moeslund, Thomas B., Granum, E.: A procedure for developing intuitive and ergonomic gesture interfaces for HCI. In: Camurri, A., Volpe, G. (eds.) GW 2003. LNCS (LNAI), vol. 2915, pp. 409–420. Springer, Heidelberg (2004). https://doi.org/10.1007/978-3-540-24598-8_38
8. Vatavu, R.D.: User-defined gestures for free-hand TV control. In: Proceedings of EuroiTV 2012, pp. 45–48. ACM Press (2012)
9. Piumsomboon, T., Clark, A., Billinghurst, M., Cockburn, A.: User-defined gestures for augmented reality. In: Kotzé, P., Marsden, G., Lindgaard, G., Wesson, J., Winckler, M. (eds.) INTERACT 2013, part II. LNCS, vol. 8118, pp. 282–299. Springer, Heidelberg (2013). https://doi.org/10.1007/978-3-642-40480-1_18
10. Koutsabasis, P., Domouzis, C.K.: Mid-air browsing and selection in image collections. In: Proceedings of AVI 2016, pp. 21–27. ACM Press (2016)
11. Erazo, O., Pino, J.: Estimating the difficulty of touchless hand gestures. IEEE Latin Am. Trans. 12(1), 17–22 (2014)
12. Nancel, M., Wagner, J., Pietriga, E., Chapuis, O., Mackay, W.: Mid-air pan-and-zoom on wall-sized displays. In: Proceedings of CHI 2011, pp. 177–186. ACM Press (2011)
13. Hespanhol, L., Tomitsch, M., Grace, K., Collins, A., Kay, J.: Investigating intuitiveness and effectiveness of gestures for free spatial interaction with large displays. In: Proceedings of PerDis 2012. ACM Press (2012)
14. Yoo, S., Parker, C., Kay, J., Tomitsch, M.: To dwell or not to dwell: an evaluation of mid-air gestures for large information displays. In: Proceedings of OzCHI 2015, pp. 187–191. ACM Press (2015)
15. Douglas, S.A., Kirkpatrick, A.E., MacKenzie, I.S.: Testing pointing device performance and user assessment with the ISO 9241, part 9 standard. In: Proceeding of SIGCHI Conference on Human Factors in Computing Systems (1999)

16. Müller-Tomfelde, C.: Dwell-based pointing in applications of human computer interaction. In: Baranauskas, C., Palanque, P., Abascal, J., Barbosa, S.D.J. (eds.) INTERACT 2007. LNCS, vol. 4662, pp. 560–573. Springer, Heidelberg (2007). https://doi.org/10.1007/978-3-540-74796-3_56

17. Hincapié-Ramos, J.D., Guo, X., Moghadasian, P., Irani, P.: Consumed endurance: a metric to quantify arm fatigue of mid-air interactions. In: Proceedings of CHI 2014, pp. 1063–1072. ACM Press (2014)

18. Markussen, A., Jakobsen, M.R., Hornbæk, K.: Selection-based mid-air text entry on large displays. In: Kotzé, P., Marsden, G., Lindgaard, G., Wesson, J., Winckler, M. (eds.) INTERACT 2013. LNCS, vol. 8117, pp. 401–418. Springer, Heidelberg (2013). https://doi.org/10.1007/978-3-642-40483-2_28

19. Jones, E., Alexander, J., Andreou, A., Irani, P., Subramanian, S.: GesText: accelerometer-based gestural text-entry systems. In: Proceedings of the SIGCHI Conference on Human Factors in Computing Systems, pp. 2173–2182. ACM (2010)

20. Borg, G.: Borg's Perceived Exertion and Pain Scales. Human Kinetics, Champaign (1998)

21. Kamal, A., Li, Y., Lank, E.: Teaching motion gestures via recognizer feedback. In: Proceedings of IUI 2014, pp. 73–82. ACM Press (2014)

22. Pfeiffer, M., Schneegass, S., Alt, F., Rohs, M.: Let me grab this: a comparison of EMS and vibration for haptic feedback in free-hand interaction. In: Proceedings of the 5th Augmented Human International Conference. ACM (2014)

Educational Software Development in Ecuadorian Universities: A Systematic Mapping Study

Jessica Guerra-Gaibor[1](✉) ⓘ, Angel Cuenca-Ortega[2] ⓘ,
and Mariela Tapia-León[2] ⓘ

[1] Guayaquil, Ecuador
jguerrag7@gmail.com
[2] Universidad de Guayaquil, Guayaquil, Ecuador
{angel.cuencao,mariela.tapial}@ug.edu.ec

Abstract. *Context*: Ecuadorian universities to guarantee a quality higher education, contribute to the country's growth and train student researchers, allow to develop undergraduate theses as final career work to obtain their professional degree. *Objective*: In this paper, we present a systematic mapping study of the educational software development in the undergraduate theses done in Ecuadorian universities. *Method*: A systematic mapping study was conducted with a set of six research questions to analyze the undergraduate theses considered as the primary studies, dated from 2000 to 2017. *Results*: From a total of 522 undergraduate theses retrieved by an initial search string, 42 undergraduate theses were selected. This research classifies, quantifies, and qualifies the educational software development that has contributed to the education of Ecuador. We observe that 54,76% of the software developed is applied in elementary education, most of them are the tutorial type, and the pedagogical objective that has been mostly covered is to improve teaching-learning. *Conclusions*: Although universities are interested in developing educational software, there is a declining interest in the last two years analyzed. Also, it is necessary to develop educational software that covers other little attended pedagogical areas.

Keywords: Educational software · Undergraduate theses
Educational applications · Systematic mapping

1 Introduction

The academic regime regulations of the institutions of higher education of Ecuador, based on the Organic Law of Higher Education LOES [1] establishes the academic and disciplinary requirements necessary for the approval of a university career. In this context, one of the academic requirements that students must meet to obtain an undergraduate degree is to carry out a final degree project at the end of their career. This project is the result of research, academic or artistic, in which students demonstrate the knowledge acquired throughout their academic training. There are several options for the final project, where undergraduate theses could be one of them. This project consists of solving a daily life problem or through the revision of criticisms

© Springer Nature Switzerland AG 2019
M. Botto-Tobar et al. (Eds.): CITT 2018, CCIS 895, pp. 353–368, 2019.
https://doi.org/10.1007/978-3-030-05532-5_26

using scientific methods within their area of study. Once the students finish the work, they must present it before a committee, who will be responsible for approving their theses according to parameters that are framed within the law of each university.

Due to the importance in the teaching-learning process, either as a teaching tool or as a form of knowledge construction, this research presents a classification and a qualitative and quantitative analysis of the educational software development in the undergraduate theses done in Ecuadorian universities. This information is important; however, there is currently no work that shows the results that we present in this research.

In 2014, Ecuador created the network of open access repositories RRAAE[1], whose functions are to collect, manage, organize, and make available all the research works published by Ecuadorian universities. They could be undergraduate theses, masters theses, doctoral theses or scientific papers. Our selected search source is RRAAE.

Our Contribution. In this paper, we present an analysis of the educational software development in the undergraduate theses in computer science dated from 2000 and 2017, and determine the following: (i) the undergraduate theses that have developed educational software in the defined range, (ii) the educational levels in which the software has been applied, (iii) the areas of knowledge covered with the software, (iv) the software category to which the educational software belongs, (v) the technology has been used for the software development, and (vi) the pedagogical objectives of the educational software.

Plan of the Paper. The rest of the paper is organized as follows. Section 2 defines the basic concepts about the educational software. Section 3 describes the relevant works that are related to our research. Section 4 details the process of the systematic mapping. Section 5 shows the results of the study. Section 6 discusses the findings made in the previous section and their relation to the general objectives of this work. Also, it describes the possible limitations and threats to validity found in this mapping. Finally, we present the conclusions and future works in Sect. 7.

2 Theoretical Framework

Educational software is aimed at facilitating the teaching-learning process. Teachers and students use it as a tool to build knowledge. It is essential in the learning environments because it allows increasing the mastery of skills assisted by a computer. However, not all educational software achieves this purpose. An educational software must have the following: it must have *objectives*, it must have a *form of presenting information*, there must be a *structure of content*, it must allow *interaction* with the user and subsequent *evaluation* [2]. Based on the skills required to improve, the software can be classified as follows [3]:

- **Exercisers.** Presents the student with problems to solve them on a topic and provides immediate feedback.

---

[1] *Red de Repositorios de Acceso Abierto, RRAAE* (http://rraae.org.ec/).

- **Tutorials.** Guides for the student on a topic and activities associated with it. A student will apply what they have learned in the guide.
- **Simulators.** Represent processes or phenomena visually and attractively. It proves with events that are dangerous for people or difficult to experiment in reality.
- **Educational games.** Use games as a tool for learning. They have entertainment values that involve competency.
- **Problem-solving.** Programs that teach through explanations and give the steps to follow to solve problems.

3 Related Works

This section reports a series of studies, which have previously analyzed ungraduated theses. To the best of our knowledge, this paper is the first to investigate the research questions proposed in Table 1.

A bibliometric analysis of the ungraduated theses in two Venezuelan universities in the area of education dated from 1990 to 1999 is presented in [4]. This study focuses on determining the indicators that describe trends in the use of information sources for the students of these universities, i.e., [4] does not have the same focus of our research.

Another notable work is presented in [5]. This work offers an analysis of the quality of the abstracts of the undergraduate thesis carried out in the Ecuadorian universities, i.e., its scope is different from our research.

Finally, in [6], an analysis of the Latin American undergraduate and postgraduate theses was presented, whose objective is to generate knowledge through virtual learning environments dated from 2001 to 2010. The main difference with our work is that we have investigated the educational software developed in the undergraduate theses, and they analyzed the virtual learning environments.

4 Research Method

A systematic mapping is a study that categorizes and summarizes all relevant research on a topic of interest and makes a visual representation. Our systematic mapping aims to classify, quantify and qualify the educational software development in the undergraduate theses done in Ecuadorian universities. This section reports the research questions and details of the steps that we perform in this systematic mapping study according to the guidelines provided by [7].

4.1 Research Questions

Raising appropriate research questions is considered as of high importance for a systematic mapping. This work will answer the research questions (RQs) given in Table 1 to achieve its aim. Each question allows determining different aspects of the software, such as pedagogical objectives, application levels, and methodology applied to software development. The search range defined is 2000 to 2017 because in RRAAE there is no previous information to that date. Until the year 2014, the data of the undergraduate theses was a responsibility of the universities [8]. Currently, this information has not yet been fully uploaded to the repository of RRAAE. Furthermore, the analyzed works are written in Spanish because within the analyzed range there were

Table 1. Research question

Research question	Motivation
RQ1: How many educational software was developed between 2000 and 2017?	Quantify the undergraduate theses that have developed educational software during the defined range
RQ2: What the educational levels at which the educational software was applied?	Determine which are the educational levels where the educational software developed was applied
RQ3: What are the areas of knowledge that educational software was applied?	To discover what are the areas of knowledge where the educational software developed was applied
RQ4: How was the educational software developed?	Grasp how the platforms, tools, programming languages and methodologies that are used for the development of software
RQ5: What is the type of educational software developed?	Identify the type of educational software developed
RQ6: What are the pedagogical objectives of the educational software developed?	Pinpoint which the pedagogical objectives where the educational software developed was applied

only theses in that language. Table 1 shows the research questions addressed in this study and their motivations.

4.2 Search Strategy

The search strategy was based on the identification the main words of terms used in research questions and to combine with logical operators "AND" and "OR", to decrease the effect of the differences in terms.

Regarding the search method, we used both manual and automatic search. First, the automatic search has been done by using the search string[2] that is given in Table 2, which represents the basic terms related to developed software in the theses (see Table 3). After, we manually browsing the retrieved documents of theses.

4.3 Selection of Studies

As explained above, we used both manual and automatic search. We start the search by using the search string in Table 2 within RRAAE between the years 2000 and 2017.

---

[2] The search strings defined are in Spanish, such as the undergraduate theses analyzed.

Table 2. Search string defined for the systematic mapping study

Search string
Title-Abs-key = ("software educativo" OR "sistemas" OR "software" OR "aplicación") and Year between(2000 and 2017)

The initial set of undergraduate theses can be used to determine the total of software developed. After performing the automatic search, duplicate works are excluded, and we delimited the selection of the primary study regarding inclusion/exclusion criteria.

The following are the inclusion criteria applied:

- Undergraduate theses aimed at the development of educational software.
- The date of publication in the RRAAE within the period 2000 to 2017.

The following are the exclusion criteria applied:

- Theses that do not contain the search terms shown in Table 2.
- The same undergraduate thesis in different search sources.
- Educational software without evidence of being finished.

4.4 Classification of Studies

To conduct a systematic mapping is necessary a classification process that guarantees to include only relevant works on the development of educational software [7]. The following are the tree tasks defined for the process: (1) Apply the search strategy. (2) Read the titles, abstracts, and keywords to apply the inclusion criteria. (3) Apply the exclusion criteria by reading the works entirely to demonstrate that the software is finished, either through the visualization of certificates or screenshots.

After having queried on RRAAE using the search strings presented in Table 2 and removed the duplicates, the most relevant works were selected using a set of inclusion/exclusion criteria, 42 theses were considered as the primary study[3] (see Table 3).

Table 3. Search results and primary study

Source	Date of search	Research results	Primary study
RRAAE	2017/12/20	522	42

4.5 Strategy for Data Extraction and Synthesis

The strategy for data extraction and synthesis is based on a series of possible answers for each research question. Table 4 shows the defined strategy in this research, where the first column defines an identifier of the question, and the second column defines the classification criteria used for the delimitation of the questions.

---

[3] Table 14 shows the detail of the undergraduate theses considered as the primary study.

Table 4. Data extraction and synthesis strategy used

Id	Criteria
RQ1	C1. Year of Publication
	C2. Universities
RQ2	C1. Levels of Education
RQ3	C1. Areas of Knowledge
RQ4	C1. Development Platform
	C2. Development Tool
	C3. Programming Language
	C4. Development Methodology
RQ5	C1. Types of Educational Software
RQ6	C1. Pedagogical Objectives

5   Results

We performed this systematic mapping study according to the procedure described in Sect. 4. We first present the study search and selection results in Sect. 5.1 and from Sect. 5.2 to 5.11 answers to the RQs defined in Table 1.

5.1   Study Search and Selection Results

By applying the search strategy, we identified a set of 522 ungraduated theses. After, we applied the inclusion criteria from reading the titles, abstracts, and keywords. This step process produced a list of 96 primary study candidates. This list was refined through full theses reading and the application of exclusion criteria. As a result of the selection process, depicted in Fig. 1, 42 theses were identified as the primary study.

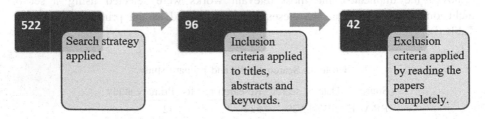

Fig. 1. Classification process of primary studies

As defined in Sect. 5, each question has different criteria applied. For example, given the RQ1 of Table 4, we can note that it has two criteria, C1 and C2. Therefore, the answers RQ1.C1 and RQ1.C2 answer RQ1. In the same way, for the rest of the questions. The following sections present the result for each search question.

5.2   RQ1.C1. Year of Publication

The total of educational software developed (and undergraduate theses analyzed) in the defined range is 42. Figure 2 presents the number of educational software developed per year. We notice that two theses were developed in 2010. In the next years, software development is ascending, and the most productive year to create educational software was 2015. However, there is a declining interest in 2016 and 2017.

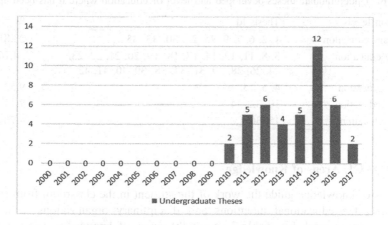

Fig. 2.   Number of educational software developed per year

5.3   RQ1.C2. Universities

Table 5 lists all the universities and the total of analyzed theses produced. We observe that the *Universidad Estatal Península de Santa Elena (UPSE)* has 30,95% of the software developed. i.e., UPSE developed more software than other universities.

Table 5.   Universities and undergraduate theses developed

Id	University	Thesis Id	%
EPN	Escuela Politécnica Nacional	1, 2	4,76
ESPOCH	Escuela Superior Politécnica de Chimborazo	3, 4	4,76
PUCE	Pontificia Universidad Católica del Ecuador	5, 6	4,76
UCE	Universidad Central del Ecuador	7, 8, 9, 10, 11, 12	14,29
UCUENCA	Universidad de Cuenca	13, 14	4,76
ESPE	Universidad de las Fuerzas Armadas	15	2,38
UNEMI	Universidad Estatal de Milagro	16, 17, 18	7,14
UPSE	Universidad Estatal Península de Santa Elena	19, 20, 21, 22, 23, 24, 25, 26, 27, 28, 29, 30, 31	30,95
UNACH	Universidad Nacional de Chimborazo	32, 33	4,76
UPS	Universidad Politécnica Salesiana	34, 35	4,76
UNIANDES	Universidad Regional Autónoma de Los Andes	36	2,38
UTA	Universidad Técnica de Ambato	37, 38	4,76
UTB	Universidad Técnica de Babahoyo	39	2,38
UTN	Universidad Técnica del Norte	40, 41, 42	7,14

5.4 RQ2.C1. Education Levels

Table 6 presents the education levels where the software is being applied. We observe that the *primary education* level is the most applied (23 theses), and the lowest education level is *higher education* (2 theses).

Table 6. Undergraduate theses developed and level of education where it has been applied

Education levels	Thesis Id	%
Secondary education	1, 2, 6, 7, 9, 25, 27, 30, 33, 35	23,81
Primary education	3, 8, 11, 12, 14, 17, 18, 19, 20, 21, 22, 23, 24, 26, 28, 29, 31, 37, 38, 39, 40, 41, 42	54,76
Special education	4, 5, 13, 16	9,52
Nursery education	10, 32, 34	7,14
Higher education	15, 36	4,76

5.5 RQ3.C1. Areas of Knowledge

The areas of knowledge guide the work of the student in the classroom from subjects that reflect the educational intentions and disciplinary organizations to facilitate teaching-learning work [9]. Table 7 shows the areas of knowledge covered by the educational software developed. We notice that *foreign language* and *interdisciplinary module* areas only have one work done. Similarly, the *social sciences* and *language and literature* have 2 and three works, respectively.

Table 7. Areas of knowledge of educational software

Areas of knowledge	Thesis Id	%
Electives	2, 7, 12, 24, 30, 33, 35, 40, 41	21,43
Natural sciences	10, 17, 18, 20, 25, 29, 31, 42	19,05
Social sciences	22, 23	4,76
Foreign language	37	2,38
Language and literature	5, 14, 21	7,14
Mathematics	6, 8, 9, 11, 15, 19, 26, 34, 39	21,43
Interdisciplinary module	27	2,38
Others	1, 3, 4, 13, 16, 28, 32, 36, 38	21,43

5.6 RQ4. C1. Development Platforms

Table 8 presents the platforms on which educational software has been developed. We note that 28 of the 42 educational software use *desktop* platform, and *mobile* technology has only three educational software developed.

Table 8. Platforms for which educational software has been developed

Platform	Thesis Id	%
Desktop	2, 3, 6, 7, 8, 9, 11, 13, 14, 15, 16, 17, 18, 19, 20, 21, 22, 23, 24, 25, 26,27, 28, 29, 32, 35, 37, 40	66,67
Mobile	4, 36, 38	7,14
Web	1, 5, 10, 12, 30, 31, 33, 34, 39, 41, 42	26,19

5.7   RQ4.C2. Software Development Tools

Table 9 presents the software development tool used. The most used is *Microsoft Visual Studio* with 12 software developed. On the other hand, the less used tools are *Eclipse IDE, Ninja IDE* and *ToolBook* with one software for each one. Also, the theses 17, 27, 39 and 42 do not mention the development tools used.

Table 9. Development tools used

Tool	Thesis Id	%
Adobe Flash	3, 10, 14, 35, 40	11,90
Android Studio	4, 36	4,76
Eclipse IDE	32	2,38
Neobook	7, 8, 12, 19, 21, 22, 23, 24, 25, 26, 29	26,19
Netbeans IDE	5, 15, 16	7,14
Ninja IDE	1	2,38
ToolBook	41	2,38
Visual FoxPro	20, 30	4,76
Microsoft Visual Studio	2, 6, 9, 11, 13, 18, 28, 31, 33, 34, 37, 38	28,57
Unspecified	17, 27, 39, 42	9,52

5.8   RQ4.C3. Programming Languages

Table 10 presents the list of all programming languages used by the software development. We observe that *Java* is the most widely used programming language with six software developed. The second programming languages most used are *C#* and *Visual Basic* with five software developed for each one. Also, there are 14 works, whose development language cannot be defined, since it is generated by the tool that has been used for software development (tool details are in Table 9).

Table 10. Programming language used for the educational software development

Language	Thesis Id	%
ActionScript	3, 10, 14, 35, 40	11,90
ASP.NET	37	2,38
C#	6, 28, 38, 31, 33	11,90
Java	4, 5, 15, 16, 32, 36	14,29
PHP	34, 39	4,76
Python	1	2,38
Visual Basic	2, 9, 11, 13, 18	11,90
Generated by tool	7, 8, 12, 19, 20, 21, 22, 23, 24, 25, 26, 29, 30, 41	33,33
Unspecified	17, 27, 42	7,14

5.9   RQ4.C4. Development Methodologies

Table 11 shows the methodology applied to the software development. In 25 under-graduate theses, the methodology is not specified. *DESED* is the widely applied methodology with four software developed. The second methodology most applied is *Cascade* model and *RUP* with two software developed for each one. Each other have one work developed.

Table 11. Software development methodologies used

Methodology	Thesis Id	%
Desarrollo de software educativo, DESED [10]	10, 35, 40, 41	9,52
Diseño de Interfaces de Usuario Multimediales para Aprendizaje, DIUMPA [11]	3	2,38
Cascade Model [12]	6, 28	4,76
Prototype Model [12]	32	2,38
Object Oriented Hypermedia Design Method, OOHDM [13]	38	2,38
Método de Producción de Software en Ambientes Web, OOWS [14]	5	2,38
Rapid Application Development, RAD [15]	36	2,38
Rational Unified Process, RUP [12]	1, 15	4,76
SCRUM [12]	31	2,38
User-Centered Design, UCD [16]	34	2,38
Ingeniería Web Orientada a Objetos basada en UML, UWE [17]	33	2,38
Extreme Programming, XP [12]	4	2,38
Unspecified	2, 7, 8, 9, 11, 12, 13, 14, 16, 17, 18, 19, 20, 21, 22, 23, 24, 25, 26, 27, 29, 30, 37, 39, 42.	59,52

5.10   RQ5.C1. Types of Educational Software

Table 12 shows the total of works done, where the type that has the most software developed is Tutorial with 26 theses created, followed by *problem solving* with 6 theses. On the other hand, the type that has fewer software developed is *simulators*.

Table 12. Types of educational software developed

Type	Thesis Id	%
Exercisers	7, 9, 13, 20, 29, 39	14,29
Tutorials	1, 2, 3, 5, 12, 14, 17, 18, 19, 21, 22, 23, 24, 25, 27, 30, 32, 33, 34, 35, 36, 37, 38, 40, 41, 42	61,90
Simulators	28	2,38
Educational games	10, 16, 31	7,14
Problem solving	4, 6, 8, 11, 15, 26	14,29

5.11   RQ6.C1. Pedagogical Objectives

Table 13 lists the pedagogical objectives and the corresponding undergraduate theses. We notice, the *interactive environment* and *teaching-learning* have the largest amount of educational software developed with 31 and 39 theses, respectively. On the other hand, the objectives of improving *cognitive skills*, *motor skills* and *logical reasoning* have 3 theses for the first two, and 4 for the latter.

Table 13. Pedagogical objectives covered by educational software

Pedagogical objective	Thesis Id	%
Interactive environment	1, 2, 3, 5, 6, 7, 8, 9, 10, 11, 12, 14, 15, 18, 19, 20, 21, 22, 23, 26, 28, 29, 30, 34, 35, 37, 38, 39, 40, 41, 42	73,81
Intellectual skills	3, 7, 14, 16, 19, 20, 29, 36, 42	21,43
Teaching-learning	1, 2, 3, 4, 5, 6, 7, 8, 9, 10, 11, 12, 14, 15, 16, 17, 18, 19, 20, 21, 22, 23, 24, 25, 26, 27, 28, 29, 30, 31, 33, 34, 36, 37, 38, 39, 40, 41, 42	92,86
Cognitive skills	14, 16, 19, 22, 26, 42	14,29
Motor skills	7, 20, 28	7,14
Critical thinking	22, 26, 28	7,14
Creative reasoning	2, 3, 7, 12, 28, 36, 39	16,67
Logic reasoning	7, 8, 26, 28	9,52

6 Discussion

This section discusses our main findings and insights about the software developed in the undergraduate theses at Ecuadorian universities.

6.1 Main Remarks

This work aims to determine the current state of the educational software developed in the undergraduate thesis at Ecuadorian universities. Therefore, after analyzing the results, we have the following remarks:

- There is no research related to the educational software developed in the undergraduate theses, demonstrating that it is a relatively new area.
- The result of the mapping evidence how the software of the undergraduate theses has been developed, which shows that few methodologies application exists to the software development. Therefore, this aspect should be improved.

6.2 Study Limitations

The main limitation of our systematic mapping is based on defining a correct search string. During the mapping, we could observe that the same search string tags many works not related to the research topic. For example, when searching for "educational software" is obtained a extended amount of works not related to educational software.

6.3 Threats to Validity

As in most empirical studies, a systematic mapping is threatened by way of the research was conducted. Our work presents the following threat: the search source was limited to RRAAE, which is the digital node of all the repositories of the universities of Ecuador. However, there were theses that we did not have full access through RRAAE because the university owns restricted their access only on-site, i.e., within the university campus. In this case, the review was carried out with the abstract.

7 Conclusion and Future Work

In this paper, we analyzed the educational software development in the undergraduate theses produced in Ecuadorian universities dated from 2000 and 2017. The 42 theses considered as primary study allowed the development of this systematic mapping study. The main contribution of this research is to classify, quantify, and qualify the undergraduate theses that have developed educational software in Ecuadorian universities. Our research allows people or companies interested in educational software to know in detail how many, which ones, and the type of educational software developed in Ecuador, and with this information to perform future research. The growth of the educational software development in the undergraduate thesis was from the year 2010. The most significant amount of educational software was developed in the year 2015, where the pedagogical objective of the numerous amount of developed software is teaching-learning. However, there is a declining interest in the last two years analyzed. We do not know the reasons, but it could be future work.

An interesting fact is that only 14 of the 32 Ecuadorian universities that integrate the RRAAE have developed educational software. We cannot determinate the reasons because it is beyond the scope of this work, but it remains as a research topic future.

Regarding the educational software development process, it was possible to identify the platforms, tools, programming languages and methodologies used for its development. However, we note that many jobs do not describe the applied methodology. Determining what the reasons are beyond the scope of this investigation. Determinate the reasons can be a future work.

Finally, another future work is to ascertain whether the analyzed software is being used for the proposed goal. If the software is not being used, to determinate the reasons.

Appendix A. Undergraduate Theses Analyzed

In this appendix, we list all undergraduate theses analyzed in our systematic mapping study. Table 14 shows the thesis identifier and description[4], grouped by the university.

Table 14. Undergraduate theses analyzed

Id	Description
Escuela Politécnica Nacional	
1	J. P. Chimborazo y M. J. Viñamagua, «*Desarrollo de un software educativo con interfaz multimedia, interactiva para mejorar el proceso enseñanza-aprendizaje...*», 2014
2	S. M. Quirumbay, «*Software educativo de informática aplicada a la educación para mejorar las habilidades tecnológicas en los estudiantes de primer...*», 2014
Escuela Superior Politécnica de Chimborazo	
3	S. I. Armas y D. E. Olmedo, «*Estudio de la ingeniería en diseño para la implementación de entornos virtuales de aprendizaje orientado a niños...*», 2011
4	A. D. Guamán, «*Sistema informático basado en pantallas táctiles para la enseñanza de los niños con síndrome de down del Instituto de Educación Especial Ibarra*», 2011
Pontificia Universidad Católica del Ecuador	
5	J. Urdiales, «*Sistema de soporte a la enseñanza y comprensión del lenguaje español escrito y simbólico para niños con discapacidad auditiva*», 2012
6	D. R. Urrutia, «*Elaboración y aplicación de un software educativo para la enseñanza aprendizaje de sistemas de ecuaciones lineales en la U. E. "Santiago de Quito"*», 2012
Universidad Central del Ecuador	
7	X. F. Pazmiño, «*Software educativo en el aprendizaje de computación en niños de séptimo año de educación general básica, del Colegio Liceo del Valle*», 2013

(continued)

---

[4] The title of the theses have been limited to save space.

Table 14. (*continued*)

Id	Description
8	L. E. Alvarez, «*Uso de los recursos didácticos tecnológicos para la optimización del aprendizaje de matemática de las niñas de séptimo año de educación básica ...*», 2013
9	W. A. Quilumba, «*Software educativo en el proceso de enseñanza aprendizaje de los Instrumentos de medida de precisión en los estudiantes del tercer año de ..."*», 2016
10	D. M. Iza y A. M. Villa, «*Diseño y desarrollo de un software educativo infantil para niños y niñas de preescolar de la U. E. Sagrados Corazones de Rumipamba...*», 2016
11	N. D. J. Vallejo, «*Software educativo para la enseñanza de vectores en los estudiantes de décimo año de la Unidad Educativa Darío Figueroa*», 2013
12	S. D. L. Á. Remache, «*Influencia de los recursos tecnológicos utilizados por el docente en el rendimiento académico de los estudiantes de 9no año en la computación...*», 2013
Universidad de Cuenca	
13	G. A. Suárez y A. S. Guerrero, «*Sistema de apoyo para la detección de niños con dislexia de 4 a 6 años de edad*», 2010
14	J. K. Rodríguez, «*Diseño e implementación de un software educativo interactivo en el aprendizaje de los poemas para los estudiantes del primer grado de ...*», 2012
Universidad de las Fuerzas Armadas	
15	F. G. Morales, «*Implementación de un simulador educativo para el aprendizaje de la asignatura de métodos numéricos utilizando software libre para la Esc. Ing. ...*», 2015
Universidad Estatal de Milagro	
16	J. T. Robalino y S. P. Solis, «*Estudio de las herramientas metodológicas que se utilizan en el proceso de enseñanza - aprendizaje en el área de inclusión escolar...*», 2015
17	N. M. Roldan y L. L. Murillo, «*Incidencia de un software educativo en el aprendizaje del bloque curricular no. 3 de ciencias naturales*», 2015
18	S. E. Rosso y T. Barreiro, «*Incidencia de un software interactivo en el aprendizaje de ciencias naturales en los estudiantes de octavo año de educación general ...*», 2015
Universidad Estatal Península de Santa Elena	
19	G. M. Rodríguez, «*Creación e implementación de un software educativo de matemática para mejorar el proceso enseñanza – aprendizaje de los estudiantes del 6to ...*», 2015
20	M. D. P. Villao, «*Herramientas tecnológicas para mejorar el proceso de aprendizaje de la asignatura de ciencias naturales del noveno año de educación básica...*», 2012
21	A. P. Rodríguez, «*Elaboración de un software educativo de leyendas y cuentos para fortalecer la enseñanza de la asignatura de lengua y literatura de ...*», 2015
22	G. M. Ramírez, «*Creación e implementación de un software educativo de estudios sociales para el desarrollo de las habilidades cognitivas de los estudiantes ..."*», 2015
23	L. J. Villao, «*Creación e implementación de un cd interactivo multimedia de tradiciones peninsulares para el fortalecimiento de la identidad cultural en los estudiantes ...*»2016
24	F. A. Pita, «*Creación e implementación de un software educativo para mejorar el conocimiento tecnológico en el área de computación en los estudiantes de 8vo ...*»2015
25	V. L. Rivera, «*Creación e implementación de un software educativo de estrategias ecopedagógicas para la aplicación en la asignatura de entorno natural ...*», 2015
26	M. E. Tumbaco, «*Creación e implementación de un software educativo de matemática para fortalecer el proceso enseñanza – aprendizaje en docentes y estudiantes ...*», 2015

(*continued*)

Table 14. (*continued*)

Id	Description
27	M. A. Lainez, «*Creación e implementación de un software educativo para optimizar el aprendizaje significativo en la asignatura de emprendimiento y gestión ...*», 2014
28	J. J. Reyes, «*Aplicación del dispositivo kinect, en el sistema multimedia para elaprendizaje del primer año básico, en la Esc. Cp. "Leonardo Abad Astudillo"*», 2017
29	P. I. Yagual, «*Software educativo en el área de entorno natural y social para los estudiantes del tercer grado, Esc. "Virgiliu Drouet Fuentes"*», 2017
30	F. S. Tigrero, «*Elaboración e implementación de un software educativo para mejorar el proceso de aprendizaje de la asignatura redes de área local en el segundo ...*», 2014
31	J. A. Caiza, «*Desarrollo de una aplicación web utilizando el motor gráfico unity 3d para la asignatura entorno natural y social, caso práctico Unidad Educativa*», 2014
Universidad Nacional de Chimborazo	
32	J. E. Guamán y O. F. Vega, «*Diseño de un software educativo para tv digital*», 2016
33	M. E. Vinces y W. D. Campaña, «*Desarrollo de un sistema vía web para procesos de aprendizaje constructivista, orientado a la educación secundaria a distancia...*», 2015
Universidad Politécnica Salesiana	
34	J. F. Basantes y P. A. Calero, «*Creación de ambientes virtuales interactivos 3d para el aprendizaje de matemática bajo tecnología web enfocado enseñanza preescolar*», 2011
35	J. C. Cucuri y L. F. Jaya, «*Desarrollo de un software educativo interactivo como refuerzo didáctico para el interaprendizaje de la asignatura de informática ...*», 2012
Universidad Regional Autónoma de los Andes "Uniandes"	
36	D. F. Quisi, «*Diseño e implementación de una aplicación para dispositivos android en el marco del proyecto pequeña y pequeños científicos de la U. P. Salesiana*», 2016
Universidad Técnica de Ambato	
37	P. M. Toapanta, «*Influencia del material interactivo en la enseñanza aprendizaje del idioma ingles de los estudiantes de quinto, sexto y séptimo año de educación ...*», 2012
38	C. E. Arcos, «*Implementación de un software ducativo utilizando técnicas de inteligencia artificial, realidad virtual y realidad aumentada para el 4to año ...*», 2010
Universidad Técnica de Babahoyo	
39	N. R. Ilbay, «*Innovacion de un software educativo interactivo como refuerzo didáctico para el interaprendizaje de la asignatura de matemáticas aplicada ...*», 2016
Universidad Técnica del Norte	
40	R. R. Guaján, «*Sistema educativo multimedia para 2do año de educación ...*», 2011
41	R. N. Moreta, «*Sistema educativo multimedia para 1er año de educación ...*», 2011
42	J. M. Alba y N. M. Chicaiza, «*Propuesta de uso de software educativo como material didàctico para la enseñanza - aprendizaje de las ciencias naturales con los...*», 2015

References

1. Presidencia de la República del Ecuador: Ley Orgánica de Educación Superior (LOES), de Ámbito, objetivo, fines y principios del sistema d educación superior (2010)
2. Reyes Caballero, F., Fernández Morales, F.H., Duarte, J.E.: Herramienta para la selección de software educativo aplicable al área de tecnología, Entramado, vol. 11, p. 1 (2015)

3. Cennamo, K., Ross, J., Ertmer, P.: Types of educational software, p. 6 (2010)
4. Jiménez, E.: Análisis bibliométrico de tesis de pregrado de estudiantes venezolanos en el área educación: 1990–1999, Revista Iberoamericana de Educación (2004)
5. Tapia León, M., Rivera Villalta, M.C., Lujan Mora, S., Barros Bastidas, C.I.: Análisis de la calidad de los resúmenes de tesis de grado de las universidades del Ecuador respecto a normas internacionales. Revista Ciencia de la Documentación (2017)
6. Esquivel Gámez, I., Edel Navarro, R.: El estado del conocimiento sobre la educación mediada por ambientes virtuales de aprendizaje: Una aproximación a través de la producción de tesis de grado y posgrado, Revista mexicana de investigación educativa (2013)
7. Kitchenham, B., Charters, S.: Guidelines for performing systematic literature reviews in software engineering. In: Proceeding of the 28th International Conference on Software Engineering (2007)
8. Red Nacional de Investigación y Educación del Ecuador: Una herramienta que crea e intercambia información para el beneficio de las universidades ecuatorianas, CEDIA (2016)
9. Ministerio de Educación: Currículo, Educacion.gob.ec (2017). https://educacion.gob.ec/curriculo-areas/. En línea. Último acceso: 20 Dec 2017
10. Peláez Camarena, G., López Azamar, B.: Metodología para el Desarrollo de Software Educativos (DESED), p. 42 (2006)
11. Marmolejo Cueva, M.C.: Nueva metodología de interfaces de usuario para el desarrollo multimedial destinado al aprendizaje, Escuela Superior Politécnica de Chimborazo (2008)
12. Pressman, R.S.: Metodología de desarrollo, de Ingeniería del software. Un enfoque práctico, Séptima ed. The McGraw-Hill (2010)
13. Rossi, G., Schwabe, D., Lyardet, F.: Web application models are more than conceptual models. In: Chen, P.P., Embley, D.W., Kouloumdjian, J., Liddle, S.W., Roddick, J.F. (eds.) ER 1999. LNCS, vol. 1727, pp. 239–252. Springer, Heidelberg (1999). https://doi.org/10.1007/3-540-48054-4_20
14. Pastor, O., Fons, J., Pelechano, V., Abrahão, S.: Conceptual modelling of web applications: the OOWS approach. In: Mendes, E., Mosley, N. (eds.) Web Engineering, pp. 277–302. Springer, Heidelberg (2005). https://doi.org/10.1007/3-540-28218-1_9
15. Martin, J.: de Rapid Application Development. Macmillan Publishing, Indianapolis (1991)
16. Norman, D.A., Draper, S.W.: User centered system design. New perspectives on human-computer interaction (1986)
17. Koch, N., Kraus, A.: The authoring process of the UML-based web engineering. In: First International Workshop on Web-Oriented Software Technology (2001)

Computational Intelligence

A Real-Time Method to Remotely Detect a Target Based on Color Average and Deviation

Henry Cruz[1](✉), Juan Meneses[2], and Gustavo Andrade-Miranda[3]

[1] Universidad de las Fuerzas Armadas-ESPE, Sangolquí, Ecuador
hocruz@espe.edu.ec
[2] Research Center on Software Technologies and Multimedia Systems
for Sustainability (CITSEM), Technical University of Madrid, Ctra. Valencia,
Km. 7, 28031 Madrid, Spain
[3] Facultad de Ingeniería Industrial. Av. Las Aguas, Universidad de Guayaquil,
Guayaquil, Ecuador

Abstract. This paper presents a new semiautomatic method to remotely segment a target in real-time. The aim is to obtain a fast distinction and detection based on RGB color space analysis. Firstly, a pixel of the desired target manually is selected and evaluated based on weighing different surrounding areas of interest (A_i). Later, statistical measures, identification of deviation parameters and the subsequent assignation of identifiers (ID's) that are obtained from the color information of each region A_i. The performance of the algorithm is evaluated based on segmentation quality and computation time. These tests have been performed using databases as well in real-time and accessed in remote way (distance from the control-site 8.828.12 km) to prove the robustness of the algorithm. The results revealed that the proposed method performs efficiently in tasks as; objects detection in forested areas with high density (jungle images), segmentation in images with few color contrasts, segmentation in cases of partial occlusions, images with low light conditions and crowded scenes. Lastly, the results show a considerable decrease of the processing time and a more accurate detection of a specific target in relation with other methods proposed in literature.

Keywords: Segmentation · Average color · Identifiers · Specific target
Time processing

1 Introduction

Several methods for detecting a specific or multiple target have been proposed in the literature [1]. Most of them are focused on appearance modelling, segmentation-based techniques, localization strategies and classification-based techniques. As a clarification, the segmentation is the process of dividing an image into regions by classifying the pixels according to common attributes. Ideally, all regions found have physical interpretations and correspond to the objects in a scene. The segmentation algorithms are used to detect, identify, recognize and track a single or multiple objects in a scene.

© Springer Nature Switzerland AG 2019
M. Botto-Tobar et al. (Eds.): CITT 2018, CCIS 895, pp. 371–383, 2019.
https://doi.org/10.1007/978-3-030-05532-5_27

Therefore, its applications are countless in different areas such as, e.g. remote sensing, recognition, traffic regulation, smart cities, social networks, augmented reality, smart cars, smartphones, computer vision, robotics, automation, medicine, games, biometric recognition, video analysis, annotation and tagging, content based on image retrieval, photo manipulation, video analysis, annotation and tagging, content based image retrieval, photo manipulation, image based rendering, intelligent video surveillance, scene understanding, among others [2–5]. On the other hand, the classification-based techniques seek to fulfil the key task of categorizing an image with robustness in terms of accurate detection [6, 7]. The classification-based techniques segment each of the objects that compose the image based on a set of features that better describe each of them. Some of the common features used are: texture, shape, brightness, contour energy, and curvilinear continuity, among others. According to Richards and Jia [8], the methods for supervised classification are mostly used for quantitative analysis (especially in remote sensing) based on different pixel-characteristics classifications.

One of the most challenging tasks in the detection of specific targets is the ability to efficiently extract their features. The literature shows the need to control variables depending on object or environment variations such as texture, colour, shape, dimensions, lighting variations, viewpoint, scale, occlusion and clutter [9, 10]. Another complex problem is the cluttering given the fact that the objects that surround the targets are very similar, causing false positives detections. It is a difficult task that still must be improved [11]. In order to reduce cluttering caused by colour variations and to improve the specific target detection with a minimum segmentation processing time, the Average and Deviation Segmentation Method (ADSM) has been proposed.

The ADSM starts with a manual pixel values acquisition of a specific target. This selection serves two purposes: the first is to get information about the average colour of the object of interest and to establish the desired region of interest (ROI). The second is to generate identifiers (ID's) in each ROI to localize the specific target. The RGB values have been widely used in the literature to obtain an accurate detection of a specific objective [12]. Other methods found in the literature include; light intensity variation [13], texture information [14], super-pixels resolution [15], Haar-like features [16] and saliency [17].

ADSM evaluates different areas of interest, which is a common practice in remote sensing where the spatial variability and texture of the image are considered [18]. Normally, rather than considering only the spectral characteristics of a given pixel, a group of pixels is used as literature suggests [19]. Lastly, the final segmentation is performed considering different areas of interest and different morphological operations. These kinds of detection method try to simulate the behaviour of a photo interpreter, permitting the recognition of homogeneous areas based on their spectral and spatial properties.

The paper is organized as follows. Section 2 details the ADSM methodology for detects a specific target. Section 3 shows the results obtained based on the Caltech 101 dataset [11] and Ecuadorian rainforest images obtained from an Unmanned Aerial Vehicle system (UAV's) of the Ecuadorian Air Force Research and Development Center (CIDFAE). Section 4 presents the discussion, and Sect. 5 the conclusions and future works.

2 Materials and Methods

This section provides a detailed explanation of the methodology carried out to detect a specific target. The object detection is based on properly ordered steps, which are described below (see Fig. 1 as an illustration):

1. Image acquisition
2. Selection of target coordinate (p_i) and evaluation areas (A_i)
3. Average and Deviation Segmentation Method (ADSM)
   a. Color average
   b. Deviation estimation
4. Post processing (acquisition of ROI's and ID's characterization)
5. Labeling (ID's contrasting)
6. Detected object.

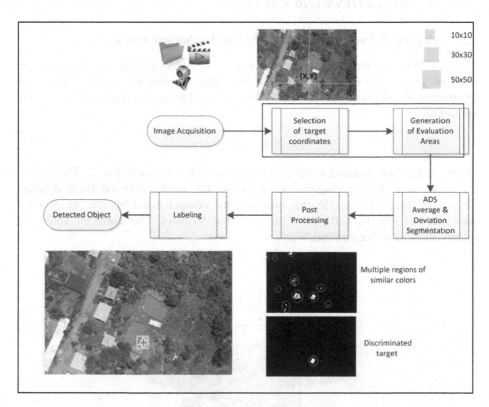

Fig. 1. Graphical representation of the steps followed to detect a target using ASDM.

2.1 Image Acquisition and Database

A total of 500 images are taken from the Caltech 101 [11] and CIDFAE database. The CIDFAE database has 1250 images of the Ecuadorian rainforest obtained from an Unmanned Aerial Vehicle system (UAV's) of the Ecuadorian Air Force Research and Development Centre (CIDFAE). The images resolutions are: RGB24 (320 × 240 pel), RGB24 (640 × 480 pel) and I240 (1280 × 1024 pel). This database is classified as confidential.

In order to evaluate the performance of the ADSM algorithm in the real-time over long distances and with bandwidth limitations, a remote experiment was done. The remote test has been performed between the CITSEM (Madrid-Spain 40°23'22.6"N 3° 37'35.9"W) as control site and CIDFAE (Ambato-Ecuador 1°12'41.5"S 78° 34'28.1"W) as terminal site. The approximate distance between both labs is around 8.828.12 km. The procedure was done using a P2P communication protocol, the resolutions of the images obtained remotely are: UYVY (352 × 210 pel), UYVY (352 × 480 pel) and UYVY (720 × 480 pel).

2.2 Selection of Target Coordinate (P_i) and Evaluation Areas

The ADSM is a semiautomatic method, where, is necessary to choose manually the pixel of interest (pi) inside the specific target that we want to segment. The color information of the pixels that surround pi is taken and three areas (A_i) of different size are defined as:

$$p_i \in A_1 \in A_2 \in A_3 \tag{1}$$

Where each area is included in the next larger one as it is shown in Fig. 2. The sizes of the areas were defined empirically based on the results obtained from different observation trials. The results that minimize the computational burden are obtained with areas of size 10×10, 30×30 and 50×50 pixel. Therefore, the following relationships have been established:

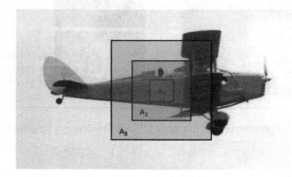

Fig. 2. Three areas of interest are defined around the pixel of interest p_i (center pixel of all areas).

$$p_i(r, g, b) \in A_1, A_2, A_3,$$

$$\text{Where; } A_i = \left(A_i^r, A_i^g, A_i^b\right) \tag{2}$$

$$\text{Such that: } p_i^r \in A_i^r, p_i^g \in A_i^g, p_i^b \in A_i^b.$$

The RGB components of the pixel p_i (r, g and b) are taken in each area, and they are weighted differently according to the size of the area.

2.3   Average and Deviation Segmentation Method (ADSM)

The segmentation by color average and deviation is divided in two steps. The first one computes the average value of the colors inside and around the target; and the second one computes the deviation of the average to find out the ROI. The complete procedure to detect and segment the targets is illustrated in Fig. 3.

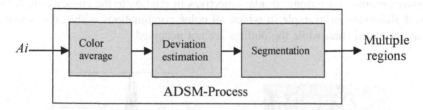

Fig. 3. Illustration of the ADSM algorithm.

2.3.1   Color Average

The segmentation process starts by computing the statistical average of the RGB values inside each of the three areas of interest A_i. To ensure the detection and discrimination of a specific target, the pixels belonging to A_i are weighted taking into account the distance with the target coordinate p_i. The lower the distance, the higher the weight w_i:

$$w_1 > w_2 \geq w_3 \tag{3}$$

w_1, w_2, and w_3 correspond to the weights of the A_1, A_2, and A_3, respectively, in this case the weights was calculated based on several empirical tests. Considering the relation (3), the total weight value, Q_k, over all areas A_i is computed through the following expression:

$$Q_k = \sum_{i=1}^{3} \sum_{j=1}^{n_j} p_j^k * w_i, \tag{4}$$

Where n_j is the number of pixels in each A_i, p_j^k is the pixel value of the RGB component k and w_i are the weights given to each area. From (4), the weighted average value, Q_{mk}, is computed as the division among Q_k and the weighted sum of the whole evaluated pixels:

$$Q_{mk} = \frac{Q_k}{\sum_{i=1}^{3} Ai * w_i},$$

(5)

Being, Q_{m1} the average value of the red component, Q_{m2} the average value of the green component and Q_{m3} the average value of the blue component. Lastly, those values are used as a reference to search similar targets around the images.

2.3.2 Deviation Parameters

It is not straightforward to find objects using only Q_{mk} information as the targets are not necessarily uniform. Therefore, an extended search area is computed; specifically a deviation parameter to widen the valid range around the average color that is used.

To effectively evaluate the pixels that correspond to a specific target, deviation limit is defined. The deviation limit allows obtaining valid colors based on Q_{mk} value. This procedure permits to determine similar objectives in relation to the chosen pixel value. Figure 4 illustrates an example in which all color combinations within the deviation limit are accepted meanwhile the outliers are not accepted.

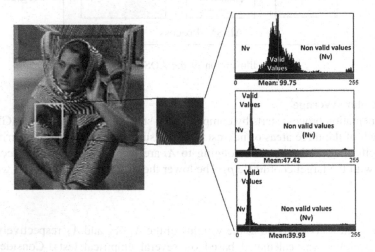

Fig. 4. Estimation of valid color ranges

To determine the deviation limits, three assumptions are made:

1. The maximum values of each color component are denoted as R_m, G_m, B_m and the most representative averages are named as R_{mx}, G_{mx}, B_{mx}, respectively.
2. The identification and detection of the target of interest depends on an area of maximum interest (Ai_m), the maximum value of each RGB component is extracted from the area of maximum interest and denoted as R_{max}, G_{max} and B_{max}.

3. The deviation restricts the detection error, therefore a tolerance interval (*TI*) is
   defined as $TI = \{a, b\}$:

$$a \leq D_{RGB} \leq b, \tag{6}$$

where D_{RGB} is the deviation for each RGB component. Considering the presented
assumptions, the relation of difference values for $R_{max}, G_{max}, B_{max}$ and R_{mx}, G_{mx}, B_{mx} are
computed as:

$$D_R = R_{max} - R_{mx}, \tag{7}$$

$$D_G = G_{max} - G_{mx}, \tag{8}$$

$$\text{and} \quad D_B = B_{max} - B_{mx}. \tag{9}$$

D_R, D_G and D_B are the initial deviations for each RGB component. The obtained
deviations are analyzed to obtain single reference value as $D_{Rmx} \bigvee D_{Gmx} \bigvee D_{Bmx}$, which
lies inside *TI* such as:

$$\forall \{D_R, D_G, D_B\} \exists ! D_{Rmx} \bigvee D_{Gmx} \bigvee D_{Bmx} | a \geq D_{aRGB} \geq b \tag{10}$$

From (10) it can be inferred that:

$$D_{RGBf} < a; D_{RGBf} = a \wedge D_{RGBf} > b; D_{RGBf} = b. \tag{11}$$

D_{RGBf} is the final deviation that has to be applied to each RGB component to obtain
valid values for carry out the segmentation. Lastly, each of the image pixels is analyzed
considering the valid RGB range. Hence, every pixel with a color value inside this
range is marked as a possible target pixel. The method works due that the pixel
majority is classified in a threshold (deviation) where pixels are grouping with similar
color range.

2.3.3 Post Processing (Acquisition of ROI's and ID's Characterization)

Within the post processing, different morphological operations are applied to keep the
shape features of the target. Specifically, to distinguish the target region from the
unwanted parts.

Firstly, dilation is used on the binary image obtained via segmentation. Later, the
dilated image is subtracted from the former image to obtain the edges. In this way, a
closed contour is obtained for each segmented object. Lastly, the detected contours are
filled, and an erosion process is performed.

2.3.4 Labeling (ID's Contrasting)

Once all the objectives are obtained through segmentation, it is necessary to discriminate the specific target. For this reason, a special characterization through identifiers
(ID's) and labeling has been developed.

Firstly, the coordinates of all detected regions are obtained and an identifier (ID) is assigned to each region generating a matrix of ID's. To discriminate the target region, the coordinates of the detected regions are compared with the coordinates of the initially selected pixel, and the ID of the coincident region is selected while the rest are discarded:

$$\forall\{ID_1, ID_2, ID_3, \ldots\ldots, ID_n\} \exists! O_i | ID_i\{x, y\} \simeq IO_i\{x, y\} \tag{12}$$

where O_i is the object of interest, ID_n are the ID's of n regions, ID_i is the identifier of the region of interest and IO_i the identifier of the target region. From (12), the algorithm compares the matrix of ID's with the value of the IO_i, if it is a match with the value of the chosen pixel; it is chosen as the final identifier. Finally, a bounding box is used to better visualize the results, and the data of the location and center of mass is depicted. The complete process is illustrated in Fig. 5.

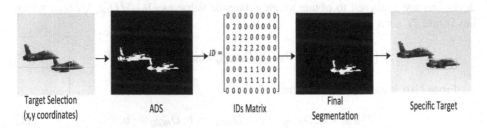

Target Selection   ADS   IDs Matrix   Final   Specific Target
(x,y coordinates)   Segmentation

Fig. 5. Description of the characterization process through ID's.

2.4   ADSM Implementation

A graphical interface developed in Matlab R2012a and R2013b is implemented. Through the interface the detection and discrimination of a specific target can be visualized. This graphic interface additionally includes a classifier of successes and failures. Through this tool, it was possible to perform image assessments in the control site and terminal site. In the control site, a computer with an Intel (R) DualCore with 2.13 GHz processor, 2 GB RAM and 64 bit OS was used. For remote testing in CIDFAE, a computer with an Intel (R) Core (TM) i7 3.4 GHz processor, 7.49 GHz, RAM, 64 bit OS and electro-optical camera has been employed.

3   Experimental Results

Experimental tests have been performed within the research center CITSEM (Spain) and the CIDFAE (Ecuador). The experiments focused on proving two types of evidence: segmentation quality, and processing time.

3.1 Segmentation Quality

The present method focuses on better response times and more accurate detections; segmentation is designed to achieve both purposes. To verify the quality of the segmentations achieved with ADSM, the framework proposed by Martin [20], Creiver [21] and Wang et al. [22] have been used. The tests are based on the comparison between expert segmentation and automatic segmentation. In particular Global Consistency Error (GCE), Local Consistency Error (LCE) as well as Object Level Consistency Error (OCE) developed by Polak [23], are used. GCE and LCE are defined as:

$$GCE = \frac{1}{n}\min\left\{\sum_i E(S_h, S_a, p_i), \quad \sum_i E(S_a, S_h, p_i)\right\} \tag{13}$$

$$LCE = \frac{1}{n}\sum_i \min\{E(S_h S_a, p_i), E(S_a, S_h, p_i)\} \quad \forall GCE \leq LCE, \tag{14}$$

E represents the local refinement error, S_h is the expert image segmentation, S_a is the ADSM segmentation, p_i interest pixels relationship and n the number of pixels. The OCE is defined as follows:

$$OCE(S_h, S_a) = \min(E_{h,a}, E_{a,h}) \tag{15}$$

OCE defines an accuracy error, given the measured errors $E_{h,a}$ and $E_{a,h}$ based on penalization for over-segmentation and under-segmentation. Different trials are carried on between ADSM segmentation and expert segmentation using the database detailed in Sect. 2.1. As a matter of illustration, a sample of ten cases is presented and the results are depicted in Table 1.

Table 1. Results of the segmentation quality for LCE, GCE and OCE

Img.	1	2	3	4	5	6	7	8	9	10	Avg.
LCE	0.04	0.01	0.01	0.01	0.06	0.01	0.04	0.01	0.02	0.03	0.03
GCE	0.04	0.01	0.01	0.01	0.06	0.01	0.04	0.01	0.02	0.03	0.03
OCE	0.08	0.02	0.06	0.04	0.07	0.05	0.06	0.02	0.03	0.05	0.05

The results show an average value of 0.03 with LCE and GCE and 0.05 with OCE. Figure 6 illustrates some examples of the final segmentations obtained using ADSM.

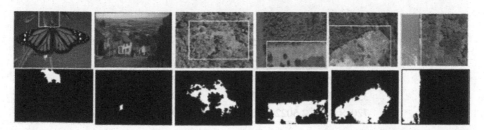

Fig. 6. Illustration of six images with its respective ADSM segmentation.

Additionally, the segmentation performance of ADSM is compared with the Region Growing based technique [24] and Chan-Vese algorithm [25] using the GCE as a metric. These methods were considered because show high performance for segmentation of the ROI's [12] [24, 25]. The results are shown in Table 2.

Table 2. GCE results of three different segmentation methods

Method	Average GCE
Region growing	0.0522
Chan-Vese	0.0167
ADSM	**0.030**

ADSM performs well (0.03 GCE average) in comparison with the other techniques. However, the aim of ADSM is to ensure fast target detection rather than a perfect segmentation.

3.2 Computational Cost

The computational cost of ADSM, Region Growing and Chan-Vese is computed for the whole database. The average values of the execution time (te), as well as the execution time plus processing time (tp) of each method, are compared. Te and tp are computed by the following relations (16) and (17):

$$te_T = \frac{1}{n}\sum_{i=1}^{n} te_i \tag{16}$$

$$tp_T = \frac{1}{n}\sum_{i=1}^{n} te_i + tp_i. \tag{17}$$

Where, te_i is the average execution time and represents the total time spent in the segmentation, n is the number of tests performed, and tp_T is the average execution time plus processing time. tp_T includes the time for labeling (made through ID's) and target discrimination until the target object is identified. Table 3 shows the tp values obtained with the electro-optical camera through remote access (in special external environmental conditions).

Table 3. Time processing average of 500 images (s) using electro-optical camera

Image size	ADSM	Chan-Vese	Region growing
352 × 210	1.2083	2.3276	2.0647
352 × 480	1.5215	3.2769	2.9549
720 × 480	2.5022	5.8171	4.9409

Comparing the times in Table 3, it can be observed that the computational time of ADSM is the lowest. In Table 4, the percentages of processing time reduction, ADSM in comparison to region growing and Chan-Vese also are shown.

Table 4. Percentages of processing time reduction, ADSM in comparison with region growing and Chan-Vese

	ADSM with Electro-Optical camera		
Method	352×210	352×480	720×480
Chan-Vese	48.09%	53.57%	56.99%
Region growing	41.48%	46.84%	49.36%
Average	44.79%	50.01%	53.18%

4 Discussions

An essential part of this work is the efficiency and effectiveness of detections in areas of dense vegetation, especially images of the Ecuadorian jungle, precisely other methods describe the difficult to get precision in these environments [26, 27]. The algorithm developed through ADSM, detect and discriminate a specific target despite the difficulty to differentiate objectives with similar color.

In relation to the segmentation quality test, ADSM performs well in general but it is overcome by the Chan-Vese method. ADSM is perfect for applications as surveillance, reconnaissance as well as remote sensing applications, where the response time and precise detection is primary that a perfect segmentation.

The results obtained remotely via electro-optical camera (Tables 3 and 4) show an overall reduction in tp when ADSM is used. This reduction is proportional to the resolution of the image and the speed of data transmission for remote access. ADSM presents a significant improvement in the tp parameter when is compared against region growing and Chan-Vese method. The worst tp are the ones obtained with Chan-Vese followed by region growing method, 5.81 seg, 4.94 seg, respectively.

5 Conclusions and Future Works

ADSM has been developed to obtain specific target detection and discrimination within multiple objects of similar colors. This method is based on the proposal to combine a calculation of an average color value together with deviation parameters that generate a novel method for real-time detection. ADSM has also contributed to solve some problems related with false positives in the detection of specific targets, especially in scenarios with color saturation such as jungle or forest. The proposal allows an efficient detection and discrimination of specific targets with low computational costs. ADSM do not use other attributes such as texture or morphology however show high performance.

The remote access tests have enabled to execute the graphical interface based on the developed method and the implemented algorithm, checking the robustness of the application in real environmental conditions. A natural extension of this work is to develop a specific target tracking within multiple objects through ADSM, this must ensure an accurate tracking into real environmental conditions and ensure low processing rates.

Acknowledgments. Henry Cruz Carrillo gives thanks the Technological Scientific Research Center of the Ecuadorian Army (CICTE) for the collaboration obtained.

This work was sponsored by Spanish National Plan for Scientific and Technical Research and Innovation, project number TEC2013-48453-C2-2-R.

Henry Cruz Carrillo gives thanks Ecuadorian Air Force Research and Development Center (CIDFAE) for the collaboration obtained.

References

1. Xin, Z., Yee-Hong, Y., Zhiguang, H., Hui, W., Chao, G.: Object class detection: a survey. J. ACM Comput. Surv. (CSUR) **46**(1), 101–151 (2013)
2. Tsai, M.K.: Automatically determining accidental falls in field surveying: a case study of integrating accelerometer determination and image recognition. Safety Sci. J. **66**, 19–26 (2014)
3. Galceran, E., Carreras, M.: A survey on coverage path planning for robotics. J. Robot. Auton. Syst. **61**(12), 1258–1276 (2013)
4. Cabrera, R., Tuytelaars, T.: Boosting masked dominant orientation templates for efficient object detection. Computer Vis. Image Und. J. **120**, 103–116 (2014)
5. Andrade-Miranda, G., Godino-Llorente, J.I.: Glottal gap tracking by a continuous background modeling using inpainting. Med. Biol. Eng. Comput. **55**, 2123–2141 (2017)
6. Dong, J., Xia, W., Chen, Q., et al.: Subcategory-aware object classification. In: IEEE Conference on Computer Vision and Pattern Recognition (CVPR), pp. 827–834 (2013)
7. Chia, A., et al.: Structural descriptors for category level object detection. IEEE Trans. Multimedia **11**(8), 1407–1421 (2009)
8. Richards, J., Xiuping, J.: Remote sensing Digital Image Analysis: An Introduction, 4th Edition, Chap. 8, pp. 193–338. Springer, Heidelberg (2005). https://doi.org/10.1007/3-540-29711-1
9. Everingham, M., Van Gool, L., Williams, C., Winn, J., Zisserman, A.: The PASCAL visual object classes (VOC) challenge. Int. J. Comput. Vis. **88**(2), 303–338 (2010)
10. Maggio, E., Cavallaro, A.: Video Tracking Theory and Practice, 3rd edn, pp. 3–120. Wiley, Hoboken (2011)
11. Lei, F., Fergus, R., Perona, P.: Learning generative visual models from few training examples: an incremental Bayesian approach tested on 101 object categories. Computer Vis. Image Underst. **106**(1), 59–70 (2007)
12. Pérez, P., Hue, C., Vermaak, J., Gangnet, M.: Color based in probabilistic tracking. In: Proceedings of 7th European Conference Computer Vision, pp. 661–675 (2002)
13. Ross, D., Lim, J., Lin, R., Yang, M.: Incremental learning for robust visual tracking. Int. J. Comput. Vis. **77**, 125–141 (2008)
14. Avidan, S.: Ensemble tracking. IEEE Trans. Pattern Anal. Mach. Intell. **29**(2), 261–271 (2007)
15. Wang, S., Lu, H., Yang, F., Yang, M.: Superpixel tracking. In: Proceedings of IEEE International Conference Computer Vision, 1323–1330 (2011)

16. Grabner, H., Bischof, H.: On-line boosting and vision. In: Proceedings of IEEE Conference on Computer Vision and Pattern Recognition, pp. 260–267 (2006). https://doi.org/10.1109/cvpr.2006.215

17. Lui, Z., Zou, W., Le Meur, O.: Saliency tree: a novel saliency detection framework. IEEE Trans. Image Process. **23**(5), 1932–1952 (2014)

18. Seo, Y., Lee, K.: Category classification of multispectral image data using spatial information in the small image region. IEEE Geosci. Remote Sens. Symp. **4**, 1978–1980 (1993)

19. Jianghong, S., Zhongming, Z., Qingye, Z., Yanfeg, W.: An algorithm for eliminating the isolated regions based on connected area in image classification. IEEE Geosci. Remote Sens. Symp. **5**, 3058–3061 (2004)

20. Martin, D., Fowlkes, C., Tal, D., et al.: A database of human segmented natural images and its applications to evaluating segmentation algorithms and measuring ecological statistics. In: Proceedings of International Conference Computer Vision, Vancouver, pp. 416–425 (2001)

21. Crevier, D.: Image segmentation algorithm development using ground truth image data sets. Comput. Vis. Image Understand. **112**(2), 143–159 (2008). https://doi.org/10.1016/j.cviu.2008.02.002

22. Wang, M., Li, R.: Segmentation of high spatial resolution remote sensing imagery based on hard-boundary constraint and two-stage merging. IEEE Trans. Geosci. Remote Sens. **52**(9), 5712–5725 (2014)

23. Polak, M., Zhang, H., Pi, M.: An evaluation metric for image segmentation of multiple objects. J. Image Vis. Comput. **27**(8), 1223–1227 (2009)

24. Herwitz, S.R., et al.: Imaging from an unmanned aerial vehicle: Agri- cultural surveillance and decision support. Comput. Electron. Agricult. **44**(1), 49–61 (2004)

25. Chan, T.F., Vese, L.A.: Active contours without edges. IEEE Trans. Image Process. **10**(2), 266–277 (2001)

26. Cruz, H., Eckert, M., Meneses, J., Martínez, J.F.: Precise real-time detection of nonforested areas with UAVs. IEEE Trans. Geosci. Remote Sens. **55**(2), 632–644 (2017)

27. Cruz, H., Eckert, M., Meneses, J., Martínez, J.F.: Efficient forest fire detection index for application in unmanned aerial systems (UASs). Sensors **16**(6), 893, 1–15 (2016). https://doi.org/10.3390/s16060893

A Hybrid Approach of Recommendation via Extended Matrix Based on Collaborative Filtering with Demographics Information

Priscila Valdiviezo-Díaz[1,2]([✉]) and Jesus Bobadilla[2]([✉])

[1] Computer Science and Electronic Department,
Universidad Técnica Particular de Loja, Loja, Ecuador
pmvaldiviezo@utpl.edu.ec
[2] Universidad Politécnica de Madrid, Madrid, Spain
jesus.bobadilla@upm.es

Abstract. In view of the growth in the use of methods based on matrix factorization, this research proposes an hybrid approach of recommendation based on collaborative filtering techniques, which exploits demographic information of the user and item within the factorization process, considering an extended rating matrix in order to generate more accurate prediction. In this paper we present an approach of collaborative filtering that is at least as accurate as the biased matrix factorization models or better than them in terms of precision and recall metrics. Several experiments involving different settings of the proposed approach show predictions of improved quality when extended matrix is used. The model is evaluated on three open datasets that contain demographic information and apply metrics to measure the performance of the proposed approach. Additionally, the results are compared with the traditional bias-based factorization model. The results showed a more expressive precision and recall than the model without demographic data.

Keywords: Collaborative filtering · Demographic information
Extended matrix · Matrix factorization · Recommender system
Sparse data

1 Introduction

Some techniques for filtering information in recommender systems may be used the most well known are those that are based on Content Based Filtering (CBF) and Collaborative Filtering (CF) [1]. Content-based Filtering Systems can be designed to recommend items similar to those that a pre-determined user likes in the past. These items could be documents, books, news, songs, movies, and websites, among others. Collaborative filter system (CF) bases its predictions and recommendations on the qualifications or behaviors of other users in the system [2]. In these recommender systems, users' behaviors are influenced by the hidden interests of users [3], information that is very important to know in order to provide better recommendations. On the other hand, there is hybrid filtering, in which the recommender system generates recommendations that combine characteristics of different filtering techniques. The

© Springer Nature Switzerland AG 2019
M. Botto-Tobar et al. (Eds.): CITT 2018, CCIS 895, pp. 384–398, 2019.
https://doi.org/10.1007/978-3-030-05532-5_28

most common combinations are collaborative filtering with content-based filtering or collaborative filtering with demographic filtering [4, 5].

Recommendation systems are traditionally applicable in different domains considering two types of entities, users and items. In these systems, according to [6] the context where a recommendation is provided is overlooked. Context information can be obtained explicitly or implicitly, that is, directly from the user, the environment, by observing the user's interactions with items or by feedback of the user's preference on various previously recommended topics.

In the literature is possible find some works related to the Recommender Systems applied to a variety of areas such as e-commerce, education, health, etc., where it is necessary to use certain techniques and methods for the recommendation process, among them are Matrix Factorization methods [7] that are currently receiving more attention mainly in the decomposition of latent variables. According to [8], the reason for MF favoured over other CF-based approaches is not only in its outstanding performance and simplicity but also in its ability to incorporate with additional information, for example: In [9], propose a recommender system for user by combining collaborative filtering with transaction data such as the estimated rating, the demographic information of the user, and the similarity of the item. A study on the role of the Matrix Factorization in collaborative filtering is presented by [10] where matrix factorization models is presented as an SVD to address the challenges of collaborative filtering algorithms, which can serve as a roadmap for research in this area.

In [11] indicate Matrix Factorization formalism has not been explored with the typical modeling of content and peer learning preferences, which has not been discussed in the context of these. Also, the use of contextual data to transform users and items into a single space of latent factors and the use of rating information together with these latent factors to generate recommendations is a largely unexplored area [12].

Models analyzed in the literature present good results and work best in sparse datasets; however, the number of parameters they use for both users and items are often large, which increases the complexity of the models. Most of the studies that use demographic information make use of the biased model [13–16], in our case we also propose the use of the biased factorization model but with a smaller number of parameters within a hybrid model that integrates user and item demographic information within the factorization process considering an extended rating matrix.

Therefore, motivated by the collaborative filtering models used for the recommendation, we propose merging demographic information with user ratings as a single hybrid model of latent factors, less complex than those mentioned in the study of art.

Our approach differs from the analyzed models because in addition to knowledge of the user and item information, the concept of integrated extended matrix (rating matrix R linked to the demographic values matrix) is incorporated and no separate factorization of the demographic information is done, as related works do. Therefore, factor vectors are learned from the observed ratings and the demographic information of the user or item, this is done by applying the optimization method called gradient descent [17].

The rest of the paper is organized as follows:

Section 2: Literature review on collaborative filtering models that incorporate either demographic information of the user or the item or both. Section 3 describes the extended matrix hybrid approach, Sect. 4: Experiments and Sect. 5: Conclusions and future work.

2 Literature Review

The following is a series of recent studies using Matrix factorization (MF) in the field of Collaborative Filtering (CF) recommender systems. A well-known work is the one proposed by [13], which proposes an extension of the bias-based MF model, called SVD ++, which integrates implicit and explicit user feedback into a new factorization model of neighbors where the training is similar to the model of latent factors. Based on this work in [14] make an adjustment to the SVD method, when they calculate the product of vectors P and Q. It is a latent factors approach that integrates user metadata and items and implicit feedback within of a unified model based on bias, considering demographic information.

Works such as the one presented by [18], use two matrices: the one of ratings and the demographic information matrix of the item, they work with Bayesian Networks to obtain probability distributions for the estimation of ratings. The topology of the model is layered, the first layer is CF, and the second is CB. The results obtained are predicting the rating using the content-based component, considering only collaborative filtering information, using the traditional algorithm based on the Pearson correlation, and a hybrid approach considering both.

Similarly, [19] present several extensions to the basic MF algorithm, taking into account user attributes when generating predictions of ratings. They consider both demographic attributes, explicitly provided by users, and the implicit attributes that are derived from the texts generated by users. In both cases, they use dimensionality reduction techniques to obtain compact representations of the users, which consist of a small number of latent factors. In [15], a model based on neighbors and the latent factor model based on bias is presented, which integrates implicit feedback, added as a set of weights, and considering the set of all the items for which the user provides an implicit preference, they also incorporate an aggregate compensation variable for the reference estimates. In [20] propose a new version of the recommendation model gSVD ++, proposed in Manzato [16], which is an extension of the SVD ++ algorithm [13], and consists of incorporating structured attributes of items within the factorization process in order to improve the accuracy of the system. These authors in their new version use hierarchies of topics extracted automatically as metadata. The algorithm is combined with the Bayesian Personalized Ranking (BPR) technique, in order to provide a better personalized ranking of the items to users who use only implicit comments. In [21], a latent factor model is proposed that calculates the accuracy and efficiency by reducing the number of latent features of users or items that make it less complex than the regularized SVD proposed by Simon Funk. In the proposed approach, the number of latent factors of the items varies according to the dataset, but the number of latent factors of the user is constant and equal to one. In this way, this model decreases the number of latent factors to train compared to regularized SVD.

The use of combined user profiles is proposed in [8], learned from the items seen by the user as a new latent variable in the models of latent factors (Implicit-SVD and Explicit-SVD). They use factorization models based on the user's feedback and based only on the user's ratings. They add an additional parameter to control the influence of the user features factor and the items, analyze the impact of this parameter for the model they propose.

On the other hand, the MF based framework [22], provides a better use the intrinsic structure of user-item rating matrix and content-based information. MF in context-aware CF recommender system has been used [23], specifically using a dataset with geographic information and another dataset with musical information. Using the MF based CF as the best opinion for group recommender system has been presented by [24]. Other current work is presented by [25], applics the users' implicit interaction records with items to efficiently process massive data by employing association rules mining. Similar work is presented by [26], they calculate the norm of a vector of factors of the attributes obtained from the demographic information of the users as part of an MC algorithm (matrix completion) combined with the neighbor model to incorporate auxiliary user data. Other studies of great interest are related to Latent Dirichlet Allocation (LDA) for collaborative filtering are the presented by [27], who utilize a hybrid approach in making recommendations, that is, by employing LDA to discover the latent semantic structure (hidden) in the documents that users have read, which includes the distribution of words on latent topics and the distributions of latent topics on documents. Similarly, the authors in [28] propose a new approach to improve standard CF based recommenders by utilizing LDA to learn about the latent properties of the items expressed in terms of the proportion of topics, which is derived from their textual description. The user's topic preferences are inferred by the same latent space based on her historical rating. This method has had considerable success in recommender systems, for example [29], by proposing a probabilistic method for recommendations that is content unaware inspired by LDA, and which uses the behavior of users in order to provide recommendations.

In [30], the authors propose a new schema for making three-layer recommendations, namely user-interest-item. This system is based on collaborative filtering. The main objective is to aid the understanding of the interactions between the users, items, and interests of users. These authors consider the increase of user interest by means of personalized ratings. Other study show thc use Bayesian approach into the MF model is the presented by [31], they propose two novel latent factor model, which incorporate both socially influenced feature value discrepancies, and socially-influenced conditional feature value discrepancies. Wang and Blei [32] presents a hybrid model (Collaborative Topic Model - CTR) for recommending scientific articles to users based on both content and other users' ratings. They combine these approaches in a probabilistic model based on topic modeling.

Unlike these approaches, our proposal incorporates the extended matrix concept into factorization process.

3 Description of the Extended Matrix Hybrid Approach

In our proposal, the approach based on collaborative and content-based filtering is combined in a latent factor model using a matrix that integrates both the user's feedback (example: ratings) and the demographic information to make more adjusted recommendations by considering the approximation of user preferences through hidden variables. These preferences are estimated taking into account both user or item features and the rating of other users.

In this approach, the attributes of items and users are mainly of interest. To illustrate an example of the setting of extended matrix we considering the information of dataset of MovieLens, in this case, the item features is the genre of the movie, and the users who rated these items. From the perspective of a user, we have the characteristics of gender, age and occupation, plus the items that were rated by those users. The objective is to combine the original rating matrix with all the information on demographic features extracted in a single model. Figure 1 illustrates the extended matrix.

	User Features																
	movie					genre		age					occupation				
	I1	I2	..	..	Iy	F	M	A1	A2	..	..	An	O1	O2	...	..	Oz
U1	5	0	0	3	0	1	0	1	0	0	0	0	1	0	0	0	0
U2	0	3	0	5	0	0	1	0	1	0	0	0	0	1	0	0	0
...	0	2	4	0	0	1	0	0	0	0	1	0	0	0	1	0	0
...	1	0	0	0	5	1	0	0	0	1	0	0	0	0	0	1	0
Ux	0	2	0	0	3	0	1	0	0	0	0	1	0	0	0	0	1
IF1	1	1	0	0	0	0	0	0	0	0	0	0	0	0	0	0	0
IF2	0	1	1	0	0	0	0	0	0	0	0	0	0	0	0	0	0
..	0	0	0	1	1	0	0	0	0	0	0	0	0	0	0	0	0
..	1	0	0	0	0	0	0	0	0	0	0	0	0	0	0	0	0
IFa	1	0	1	0	0	0	0	0	0	0	0	0	0	0	0	0	0

(Item Features labels the lower rows)

Fig. 1. Extended matrix with demographic information

We need to complete the lower right part of our extended matrix with zero values to keep the matrix designed rectangular form.

Considering the input data, the user information is represented in a binary matrix Lu of dimension $N * MU$, where N represents the number of users and MU the number of users features (Table 1). When the user is described by that characteristic $Lu_{i,j} = 1$, otherwise it is 0. Similarly, it happens with the information of the item, it is represented by a binary matrix Li of dimension $M * MI$. The ratings are also represented by an R matrix of size $N * M$, where users are represented in the rows and items in the columns.

After building the extended matrix, collaborative filtering is applied to estimate the missing ratings. Considering this notation, the latent factor vectors p and q, are initialized randomly from a uniform distribution.

It is expected that this type of extended matrix with content-based features will improve the performance of rating prediction.

Table 1. List of notations

Notations	Definition
R	Ratings Matrix
$r_{u,i}$, $\hat{r}_{u,i}$	Real rating and prediction rating
N	Number of users
M	Number of items
MU	Number of columns (attributes) with demographic values
MI	Number of item features
K	Number of latent factors
Lu	User features matrix
Li	Item features matrix
P	Latent factor matrix associated with users
Q	Latent factor matrix associated with the items
b_u	Vector of users biases
b_i	Vector of items biases
β	Regularization parameter for user factor and item factor
λ	Regularization parameter for the biased factor
α	Learning rate
μ, μ_{ext}	Overall average rating and Extended Overall average rating

3.1 Biased Matrix Factorization

According to [26] the matrix factorization methods consist of factorize a data matrix. MF models map users and items into a space of latent factors of dimensionality K, where a high correspondence between the factors of the users and the items leads to a recommendation [1]. The basic model of matrix factorization, is to find for each user a vector $p_u \in \Re^K$ that measures the interest that the user has in the items, and a vector $q_i \in \Re^K$ for each item, which measures the degree to which the item possess those factors [6]. Then, the user-item interactions are modeled as a scalar product among their corresponding vectors, such as:

$$r_{u,i} = q_i^T p_u \qquad (1)$$

The resulting product denotes the estimated rating of a user towards an item.

A variant of this method are biased matrix factorization, since much of the variation observed in the ratings is due to the effects associated with users or items, known as bias. Formally, an initial reference estimate of each user-item pair is estimated using the bias involved in the rating, denoted by $b_{ui} = \mu + b_u + b_i$, where μ is the global average of ratings, b_u and b_i represent the user bias and item bias respectively, which can be estimated with the gradient descending method. Thus the biases equation presented in [6] is given by.

$$r_{u,i} = b_{ui} + q_i^T p_u \qquad (2)$$

3.2   Formulation About Proposed Approach

This proposal is based in collaborative filtering model based on biases.

Unlike the base models, the model proposed in this research integrates both user and item information in a single factoring model considering the integrated extended matrix concept (ratings + demographic values). It is also possible to use the model only with demographic information of the user or only with demographic information of the item, obtaining two different approaches, one based on demographic information of the user and another based on demographic information of the item as [12], unlike these authors we integrate these two models in a single hybrid model that can use all the available demographic information.

The proposed approach of factorization is based on bias but with a smaller number of parameters within the extended matrix hybrid model. Thus, the model is learned from the observed ratings and the available demographic information of the user or item. In this way, in our approach the input matrix to the model would be formed by the union of the Rating matrix (R) with the matrix Lu to obtain the extended training matrix. Based on this matrix the overall average rating is denoted by μ_{ext}.

Latent factor vectors of Eq. (2), which compute the prediction, are complemented with latent factors of the available demographic information. These are initialized from a uniform distribution considering the following:

Definition 1: Let Q a latent factor matrix associate to items, where q_i is the row vector corresponding to row i of Q. when we working only with user demographic data, item features matrix Q is extended with latent factors of user profiles.

$$Q \in \Re^{(M + MU)^* K}$$

Where the vector q_i takes values in the $(M + MU) \times K$ matrix (Q) associated to items.

Definition 2: Let P be a latent factor matrix associate to users, where p_u is the row vector corresponding to the row u of P. when we considering item features, P is extended with latent factors of item profiles.

$$P \in \Re^{(N + MI)^* K}$$

Where the vector p_u takes values in the $(N + MI) \times K$ matrix (P) associated to users.

Integrating user and item demographic information, both matrices P and Q are extended.

Likewise, the bias vectors also are extended and must be computed considering the corresponding dimension just as it was done with latent vectors, hence: $b_u \in \Re^{(N + MI)}$, $b_i \in \Re^{(M + MU)}$.

Then, the model is trained by minimizing the sum of the squared error between the predicted rating and the current rating. So, p and q vectors and those of the biases are updated after each iteration using the equations of baseline model algorithm based on bias [19], but considering as input of model the extension of: rating matrix, latent matrix, and bias. Vectors p and q would be learned from the ratings and demographic values. To learn the factor vector, we minimized the regularized squared error on the set of known rating, utilizing the stochastic gradient descendent.

4 Experimentation

In this section, we show three different ways to apply this approach according to the selected dataset. The experiments were performed with three datasets, which are described below:

4.1 Datasets

- MovieLens (100k): is a collection of user ratings about movies. The range of ratings values is 1–5. This dataset contains a total of 100,000 ratings, out of a total of 1682 movies that have been rated by 943 users. All selected users have rated at least 20 movies. The selected dataset contains demographic information of users and items (age, gender, occupation and zip) of users.
- Book-Crossing (BX): contains the book rating information. The ratings are explicit, expressed on a scale of 1–10 (higher values denote a higher appreciation) or implicit, expressed by 0. Demographics data are provided ('location', 'age') if available. In addition, there is information based on content such as: ('book-title', 'book-author', 'year-of-publication', 'publisher'). This dataset consists of 278,858 users who have rated 271,379 items. Because of the memory limitation in our machine, we chose the users who rated more than 7 items and the items that have more than 5 ratings by the users. In this way a subset of 120367 ratings, of 2030 users and 1821 items was obtained.
- FilmTrust: collecting 1,508 users, 2,071 movies and 35,497 ratings (scaled from 0.5 to 4.0 with step 0.5). It also contains 1,853 trust ratings that are issued by 609 users. The trust ratings in FilmTrust are binary.

For the training and testing the split technique was considered, where each dataset is randomly split into train and test set (70% training, 30% test set). In both dataset, the same users and items are considered. That is, that in training dataset all the users and items are included, but not all the ratings. The remaining ratings are used to test the model. After 150 iterations we have reached some acceptable level of convergence.

4.2 Data Processing

The proposed approach exploits explicit information such as ratings, demographic information of the user and items. In the case of MovieLens: age, gender and occupation, and information on items such as the genre of the movies. To integrate the demographic information of the user as part of the general user-item matrix, a pre-processing of the attributes that refer to this information is done. For example, age was pre-processed in order to group users within the same age group. Seven age groups or ranges are defined: less than 18, 18–24, 25–34, 35–44, 45–49, 50–55, and greater than 56. The gender field receives similar treatment, if the user is a man or a woman would be assigned 1 in the corresponding column. As for the occupation each one is placed as a column in the matrix *Lu*. The processing of the demographic information of the item is similar, the genres of the movies are placed as columns and 1 indicates that the movie is of that genre and 0 that it is not, the movie can be of more than one genre.

In the case of BX, information such as age and location is used for the users, and for the books, the year of publication. The users were grouped by age ranges, 8 ranges were obtained. In reference to location 20 countries were configured. The books were also grouped by the year of publication, 9 ranges were established. Because the feature of dataset vary in scale $\{1,..., 10\}$, feature transformations such as normalization is apply. In our case, we proceed to normalized rating, in a scale of $\{1,..., 5\}$, this is obtained according to the following expression:

$$r_{u,i}^* = trunc(\frac{R + min(R)}{2}) \tag{3}$$

The function trunc returns a numeric vector containing the integers formed by truncating a decimal number. This normalization is done before applying the technique used.

For the experimentation with the dataset FilmTrust was considered only user demographic information as the trust ratings given by users. For this was necessary normalizes *Lu* for obtained better results. The values of *Lu* were normalized as follows:

$$Lu_{i,j}^* = 3maxLu + Lu_{i,j} \tag{4}$$

Then, *Lu* Matrix is linked with R for form the extended matrix.

With the other dataset when normalizing *Lu* or *Li*, the result was similar than without normalizing the demographic values, for this reason the results shown are with 1/0 values for the demographic data.

4.3   Evaluation Metrics

The model was evaluated considering the demographic data as part of the factorization of the matrix, in terms of Precision and Recall in the recommendation process.

The Mean Absolute Error (MAE) is used, which measures how close the system's prediction is with the user's real ratings for each item considering the absolute deviation between the predicted rating and the user's actual rating. For which the following equation is used.

$$MAE = \frac{\sum_{i=1}^{N} |p_i - r_i|}{N} \tag{5}$$

Where N is the number of real values of the test set, r is the real rating, and p the predicted rating.

To measure the quality of the recommendations, the Precision and Recall metrics described in [33] are used. Precision represents the probability of a recommended item being relevant and Recall represents the probability of a relevant item being recommended. These techniques involve the creation of the so called confusion matrix. An item is Relevant if its rating is greater or equal to 4, No Relevant if the value of the rating is less than 4. The item is Recommendable if it is within the TopN-recommendations defined in the experiment and if it has been rated.

To demonstrate the effectiveness of the proposed approach, the results are compared with the recommendation approach BiasedMF: Extend the MF baseline approach by adding user and item bias.

4.4   Results Analysis

Parameters Influence

The regularization parameters in the proposed approach are of great importance because such parameters have considerable effects on the performance of predictions. We explore the impact of regularization parameters for the proposed approach. Figure 1(a) shows the impact (MAE) of parameter β for BX, FilmTrust, and MovieLens, Fig. 1(b) shows the predicted quality (MAE) based on K parameter for each dataset. We can see that the proposed model achieve optimal MAE values for small values of β in the three datasets, when this parameter is ranged in [0, 1]. Experimental results show that $\alpha = 0.01$ and $\lambda = 10$ are proper values for BX dataset, when integrated demographic information both users and items. While $\alpha = 0.01$ and $\lambda = 3$ are more suitable for FilmTrust dataset with user demographic information. Finally $\alpha = 0.01$ and $\lambda = 0.0001$ is better for MovieLens integrating demographic information both users and items.

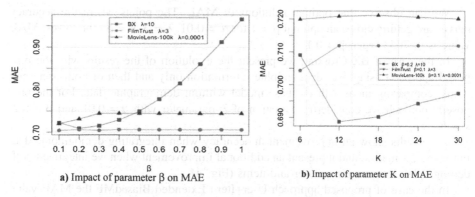

a) Impact of parameter β on MAE   b) Impact of parameter K on MAE

Fig. 2. Impact of parameter β and K on MAE for BX, FilmTrust, MovieLens using k = 6, $\alpha = 0.01$

The main conclusion from graph into Fig. 2 when the proposal approach is used, predictions quality is significantly affected when selecting small *k* value.

4.5   Comparison with Other Model

To better understand the effects of hyperparameters on the performance of the recommender dataset, the MAE variation results obtained using Biased MF and Extended Biased MF for FilmTrust, are showed in the Fig. 3.

The main conclusions are: (a) User-Extended Biased MF provides better accuracy results than the baseline do, when we integrated information demographic in the rating matrix. (b) The predictions quality is affected when we change values of regularizations parameters.

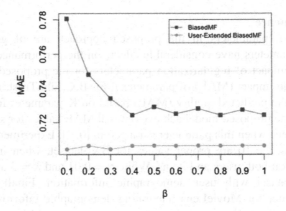

Fig. 3. MAE result using FilmTrust, $k = 6$, $\lambda = 3$.

We can observe that optimal solutions of MAE. The points where the accuracy curves are getting closer an optimal $\beta = 1$ for $\alpha = 0.01$, $\lambda = 3$, $k = 6$. The lowest MAE value is 0, 7043 when $\beta = 0.1$

In the case of BX-Crossing we present the evolution of the results with the proposed approach using user demographic information only and then of both users and items, comparing them with the base model without demographic data. For the proposed approach we considering variation of λ parameter with $\alpha = 0.01$ and $\beta = 0.2$, $k = 6$.

The results show an improvement in accuracy when integrating demographic data in the ratings matrix, and it present an additional improvement when we integrated both demographic information of user and items (Fig. 4).

In the case of proposed approach User+Item Extended BiasedMF the MAE value decreases up 0.7089 with increasing the regularizations parameter $\lambda = 10$. Similarly, on MovieLens 100k dataset using Extended Biased MF we obtained an improvement in accuracy in comparison with Biased MF without demographic data, for example: The MAE for BiasedMF is 0,72268, and for Extended BiasedFM is 0.7198.

Precision and Recall of this algorithm is shown in next figure for MovieLens dataset. All methods were compared at top 5 and top 40 recommendations (Fig. 5).

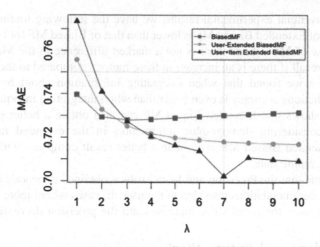

Fig. 4. Comparison between BiasedMF and proposed approach, user-based demographic information (User-Extended BiasedMF), and both (User + Item Extended BiasedMF). BX dataset.

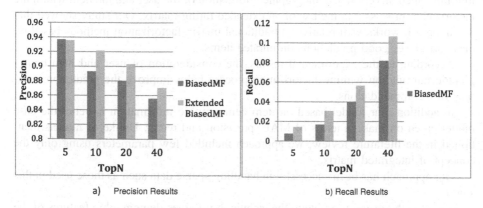

Fig. 5. Comparison of Precision and Recall metrics for our proposed approach and Biased MF, MovieLens dataset.

4.6 Discussions

As described above, the most important aspect of the proposed method are results obtained of measures the quality of the predictions and recommendations. The best results of these metrics for each dataset are shown in the summary table.

Table 2. Best Precision and Recall of BiasedFM, Extended BiasedFM

Dataset/Algorithm	Precision		Recall	
	BiasedMF	Extended BiasedMF	BiasedMF	Extended BiasedFM
BX	0.7634	0.9012	0.0377	0.0395
Filmtrust	0.7123	0.7391	0.0079	0.0051
MovieLens 100k	0.8557	0.8704	0.0819	0.1067

From the eventual experimental results, we have the following findings.

The MAE of Extended Biased MF is lower than that of Biased MF for FilmTrust and BX. In the case of MovieLens there is not a marked difference in the MAE, but with precision and recall if there is an increase in these metrics compared to the base model.

From Fig. 3 we found that when integrating information about both users and items, the predictions accuracy is even better than when integrating information only of user. Table 2 shows that Extended Biased MF can also obtain a better precision and recall when considering demographic information in the extended rating matrix. Therefore, Extended Biased MF can obtain a better result compared with Biased MF without demographic data.

We conclude that the Precision and Recall values obtained depended on the length of the list of recommendations provided to the user. In cases where more movies were returned to the user, the recall value increased and the precision decreased.

5 Conclusions and Future Work

In this paper, we present an approach of recommendation based on collaborative filtering which incorporate demographic information of the user and the item within the factorization process, via the use of an extended rating matrix. Our study showed that this approach works well relative to traditional matrix factorization methods based on bias and makes good predictions on unrated items.

According to the experimental results, the consideration of user and item demographic information whiting factorization process helps improve the prediction accuracy of recommendations.

In addition, our model based on item demographic information is better the base model based on bias, in terms of MAE, precision and recall. Unlike of models mentioned in the literature review, we approach included few parameters using only the concept of integrated matrix.

Our approach has been successful in handling sparse data such as those used in this study.

To solve the sparsity problem, the technique involves demographic features of the user and the item. In some cases, the features of the user are grouped according to the type of characteristics, reducing the dimensionality of the space of the demographic information of the user or the item and therefore of the extended matrix.

As future work, the proposed approach can be extended to learn the parameters of the model in order to improve the recommendations. It can also be extended to the use of other dataset that include demographic information and compare with other baseline models such as those mentioned in the related works.

References

1. Lops, P., De Gemmis, M., Semeraro, G.: Recommender Systems Handbook. Springer, Boston (2011). https://doi.org/10.1007/978-0-387-85820-3
2. Ekstrand, M.D., Riedl, J., Konstan, J.: Collaborative filtering recommender systems. Found. Trends® Hum.-Comput. Interact. **4**, 81–173 (2010)

3. Liu, Q., Chen, E., Member, S., Xiong, H., Ding, C.H.Q., Chen, J.: Enhancing collaborative filtering by user interest expansion via personalized ranking. IEEE Trans. Syst. Man Cybern. Part B Cybern. **42**(1), 218–233 (2012)
4. Adomavicius, G., Tuzhilin, A.: Toward the next generation of recommender systems: a survey of the state-of-the-art and possible extensions. IEEE Trans. Knowl. Data Eng. **17**(6), 734–749 (2005)
5. Bobadilla, J., Ortega, F., Hernando, A., Gutiérrez, A.: Recommender systems survey. Knowl.-Based Syst. **46**, 109–132 (2013)
6. Adomavicius, G., Tuzhilin, A.: Context Aware recommender systems. In: Ricci, F., Rokach, L., Shapira, B., Kantor, Paul B. (eds.) Recommender Systems Handbook, pp. 217–253. Springer, Boston, MA (2011). https://doi.org/10.1007/978-0-387-85820-3_7
7. Koren, Y., Bell, R., Volinsky, C.: Matrix factorization techniques for recommender systems. IEEE Comput. Soc. **42**(8), 42–49 (2009)
8. Zhang, H., Nikolov, Nikola S., Ganchev, I.: Exploiting user feedbacks in matrix factorization for recommender systems. In: Ouhammou, Y., Ivanovic, M., Abelló, A., Bellatreche, L. (eds.) MEDI 2017. LNCS, vol. 10563, pp. 235–247. Springer, Cham (2017). https://doi.org/10.1007/978-3-319-66854-3_18
9. Tiwari, S.K., Potter, H.: An approach for recommender system by combining collaborative filtering with user demographics and items genres. Int. J. Comput. Appl. **128**(13), 16–24 (2015)
10. Kumar Bokde, D., Girase, S., Mukhopadhyay, D.: Matrix factorization model in collaborative filtering algorithms. In: 4th International Conference on Advances in Computing, Communication and Control, ICAC3 2015 (2015)
11. Hong, L., Davison, B.D.: Co-Factorization machines: modeling user interests and predicting individual decisions in twitter. In: Proceedings of the Sixth ACM International Conference on Web Search and Data Mining, pp. 557–566. ACM (2013)
12. Wilson, J., Chaudhury, S., Lall, B.: Improving collaborative filtering based recommenders using topic modelling. In: IEEE/WIC/ACM International Joint Conferences on Web Intelligence and Intelligent Agent Technologies, pp. 340–346, August 2014
13. Koren, Y.: Factor in the neighbors. ACM Trans. Knowl. Discov. Data **4**(1), 1–24 (2010)
14. Santos, E.B., Garcia, M., Goularte, R.: Evaluating the impact of demographic. IADIS Int. J. WWW/Internet **12**(2), pp. 149–167 (2014)
15. Di Fu, T., He, Z.: A combined collaborative filtering model for recommender system, **1**(2), pp. 1–5 (2013)
16. Manzatog, M.G.: SVD++: supporting implicit feedback on recommender systems with metadata awareness. In: 28th Symposium on Applied Computing – SAC 2013, Coimbra, PT. ACM (2013)
17. Schenkel, J.F.: Collaborative Filtering for Implicit Feedback system by including context. University of Oslo, Oslo (2017)
18. De Campos, L.M., Fernández-Luna, J.M., Huete, J.F., Rueda-Morales, M.A.: Combining content-based and collaborative recommendations: a hybrid approach based on Bayesian networks. Int. J. Approx. Reason. **51**(7), 785–799 (2010)
19. Seroussi, Y., Bohnert, F., Zukerman, I.: Personalised rating prediction for new users using latent factor models. In: Proceedings of the 22nd ACM Conference on Hypertext Hypermedia - HT 2011, January 2011, p. 47 (2011)
20. Manzato, M.G., Domingues, M.A., Marcacini, R.M., Rezende, S.O.: Improving personalized ranking in recommender systems with topic hierarchies and implicit feedback. In: Proceedings of the international Conference on Pattern Recognition, pp. 3696–3701 (2014)
21. Kumar, B.: A novel latent factor model for recommender system. JISTEM-J. Inf. Syst. Technol. Manag. **13**(3), 497–514 (2016)

22. Li, Y., Wang, D., He, H., Jiao, L., Xue, Y.: Mining intrinsic information by matrix factorization-based approaches for collaborative filtering in recommender systems. Neurocomputing 249(Suppl. C), 48–63 (2017)
23. Baltrunas, L., Ludwig, B., Ricci, F.: Matrix factorization techniques for context aware recommendation. In: Proceedings of the Fifth ACM Conference on Recommender Systems, RecSys 2011, New York, NY, USA, pp. 301–304. ACM (2011)
24. Ortega, F., Hernando, A., Bobadilla, J., Kang, J.H.: Recommending items to group of users using matrix factorization based collaborative filtering. Inf. Sci. 345(Suppl. C), 313–324 (2016)
25. Najafabadi, M.K., Mahrin, M.N., Chuprat, S., Sarkan, H.M.: Improving the accuracy of collaborative filtering recommendations using clustering and association rules mining on implicit data. Comput. Hum. Behav. 67(Suppl. C), 113–128 (2017)
26. Gogna, A., Majumdar, A.: Latent Factor Models for Collaborative Filtering (2017)
27. Chang, T.-M., Hsiao, W.-F.: LDA-based personalized document. In: PACIS (2013)
28. Wilson, J., Chaudhury, S., Lall, B.: Improving collaborative filtering based recommenders using topic modelling. In: IEEE/WIC/ACM International Joint Conferences on Web Intelligence (WI) and Intelligent Agent Technologies (IAT), pp. 340–346 (2014)
29. Xie, W., Dong, Q., Gao, H.: A probabilistic recommendation method inspired by latent Dirichlet allocation model. Math. Probl. Eng. 2014, 1–10 (2014)
30. Liu, Q., Chen, E., Member, S., Xiong, H., Ding, C.: Enhancing collaborative filtering by user interest expansion via personalized ranking. IEEE Trans. Syst., Man, Cybern., Part B: Cybern. 42, 218–233 (2012)
31. Zafari, F., Moser, I.: Modelling socially-influenced conditional preferences over feature values in recommender systems based on factorised collaborative filtering. Expert Syst. Appl. 87, 98–117 (2017)
32. Wang, C., Blei, D.M.: Collaborative topic modeling for recommending scientific articles. In: Proceedings of the 17th ACM SIGKDD International Conference on Knowledge Discovery and Data Mining, KDD 2011, pp. 448–456 (2011)
33. Herlocker, J.L., Konstan, J.A., Terveen, L.G., Riedl, J.T.: Evaluating collaborative filtering recommender systems. ACM Trans. Inf. Syst. 22(1), 5–53 (2004)

Simple Bayesian Classifier Applied to Learning

Byron Oviedo[1]([⊠]) [iD], Cristian Zambrano-Vega[1] [iD], Joffre León-Acurio[2] [iD], and Alina Martinez[1] [iD]

[1] Faculty of Engineering Sciences, Quevedo State Technical University,
Quevedo, Ecuador
{boviedo,czambrano,amartinez}@uteq.edu.ec
[2] Babahoyo Technical University, Babahoyo, Ecuador
http://www.uteq.edu.ec, https://www.utb.edu.ec/

Abstract. In this article, we propose the use of a new simple Bayesian classifier (SBND) that quickly learns a Markov boundary of the class variable and a network structure relating class variables and the said boundary. This model is compared with other Bayesian classifiers, then experimental tests are carried out for which 31 well-known ICU databases and two bases of artificial variables have been used. With these databases we compare the results obtained by such algorithms studied in the state of the art such as Naive Bayes, TAN, BAN, RPDag, CRPDag, SBND and combinations with different metrics such as K2, BIC, Akaike, BDEu. The experimental work was done in Elvira software.

Keywords: Bayesian networks educational analysis ·
Bayesian classifier · Educational analysis

1 Introduction

Learning can be defined as 'any process, through which a system improves its efficiency' [6]. The ability to learn is considered a central feature of intelligent systems [9], and this is why a lot of effort and dedication have been put on the research and development of this topic. The development of knowledge based systems has motivated research in the area of learning with the aim of automatizing the knowledge acquisition process, what is considered one of the main problems in the building of these systems. For some time, algorithms for learning without Bayesian networks restrictions, especially those based on the metric + search paradigm have been considered inadequate for competitive construction of classifiers based on Bayesian networks [1]. This perception is being changed due to the development of generic networks learning methods, which are very competitive [1]. Bayesian networks (without structural restrictions of any kind) can also be used for classifying. In this case, classifiers are referred to as non-restricted Bayesian net-works. These will be used in this paper too. Any Bayesian network can be used in supervised classification, for which it is enough to use

© Springer Nature Switzerland AG 2019
M. Botto-Tobar et al. (Eds.): CITT 2018, CCIS 895, pp. 399–409, 2019.
https://doi.org/10.1007/978-3-030-05532-5_29

the Markov blanket of the case variable. It is necessary to consider that a non-restricted Bayesian classifier has a higher expressive power than a structurally restricted model [8].

In this paper we present a new classifier, which we have called Simple Bayesian classifier, consisting in a generic Bayesian network, but learned from a voracious techniques.

2 Simple Bayesian Classifier

SBND is a new simple Bayesian classifier designed to simplify this activity. To start using this classifier, we will need a PARENTS function, which, given a variable X_i and a set of candidates, can calculate the best parents set in X_i among that set of candidates. The parents set is returned in Π_i and at the same time gives back a numerical value constituting the Score of this variable, given that set of parents meas-ured by a Bayesian Score.

This PARENTS function is the one making a heuristic search for the best set of parents among a set of candidates and this occurs by adding and removing parents as long as the score improves. The idea is to start introducing C as a root node in the Bayesian network $\mathscr{B}$ and keep a set of nodes $\mathbf{X'}$ of the attributes already introduced in the net (initially empty) [13].

Different Score metrics $Score(X_i, \mathbf{A}|\mathscr{D})$ measuring the suitability of $\mathbf{A}$ as X_i parents set can be used (these metrics can be BDEu, BIC, K2 o Akaike).

Since we assume to have a procedure PARENTS(X_i, CANDIDATOS, Π_i), which calculates the best set of parents Π_i from X_i using the selected metric, and returns the value of this optimum metric, when implementing this function we will have a voracious algorithm, which starts with an empty Π_i and keeps adding and removing form Π_i the variable producing the highest metric increase, until there is not any possible improvement. In these conditions the values for each $X_i \in \mathbf{X} \setminus \mathbf{X'}$ variable is calculated:

$$Infor(X_i, C) = \text{PADRES}(X_i, \mathbf{X'} \cup \{C\}, \Pi_i) - \text{PADRES}(X_i, \mathbf{X'}, \Pi_i')$$

Infor $Infor(X_i, C)$ calculates the differences among the best X_i metrics with parents set chosen between $\mathbf{X'}$ including C and without including C in the candidates. Intuitively, it is a measure of X_i and C conditional dependency, given the already included variables. This value is always theoretically higher or equal to zero, but it could be negative since the best parents set is calculated approximately [13].

Once this value has been calculated for each $X_i \in \mathbf{X} \setminus \mathbf{X'}$ variable, $X_{max} = \arg\max_{X_i \in \mathbf{X} \setminus \mathbf{X'}} Infor(X_i, C)$ is selected. This would be the variable providing most information about the C class according to the already introduced variables. If $Infor(X_{max}, C) > 0$, then this variable provides additional information about C and is inserted in the network and in $\mathbf{X'}$. Its parents set is calculated with PARENTS($X_{max}, \mathbf{X'} \cup \{C\}, \Pi_i$). In theory, $C \in \Pi_i$, always, since otherwise $Infor(X_{max}, C) = 0$, although due to the voracious nature of the procedure, $C \notin \Pi_i$, what is a remote possibility.

In other words the variable giving most information is added to the network provided that the information is positive, and is considered, as well as its parents set, the best parents set provided by this function. Since the information is positive, the class variable should be supposed to be included in the parents set. The algorithm ends if the function $Infor(X_{max}, C) \leq 0$ [13].

The main characteristics of this classifier are:

- Learns an arbitrary Bayesian network with a subset of initial variables directly influencing this variable. In this sense, it can be considered an algorithm, which calculates a Markov boundary, because it intends to obtain a set of such variables that, once obtained, the rest of the variables are independent.
- The class variable is always a root node and there are links from this node to the rest of the attributes (except for very few occasions due to the approximate nature of the parents calculation). It is, in this sense, similar to other Bayesian classifiers, where there is always a link from the class to each of the attributes.
- The arrangement of the attributes in based on selecting in a voracious way those providing most information on the class, given the selected attributes. In this way the most relevant attributes are introduced first. Obtaining the network with the best metrics is not based on the space of the attributes order, but in obtaining the maximum information for the class. It can even be some network quality lose in this sense, but the algorithm gains speed [13].

3   Experimentation

In this section experimental tests are carried out through using 31 well - known to ICU databases [11] and two bases including artificial variables. The databases can be seen in Table 1. With these two databases. The results obtained by the algorithms mentioned in the state of art, namely Naive Bayes [15], TAN [7], BAN [3], SBND [12], RPDAG and C-RPDAG [1,9] are compared to other combinations with different metrics, namely K2 [4], BIC [14], Akaike [2], BDEu. These methods build up classifiers constituting generic Bayesian networks equivalent in independence and equivalent in classification. The experimental work was made at Elvira [5].

Table 1 provides a brief description of each database characteristics, including the number of instances, attributes, and the states for the class variable. These data sets have been preprocessed as follows: continuous variables have been discretized using the procedure proposed by [10], and the instances having non definite or missing values were removed. For this pre-processing stage, the results obtained by [1] have been used.

4   Results

The results obtained by each classifier and its combinations with the studied metrics can be observed in Tables 2, 3, 4 and 5 (due to their size, they have been divided in 4).

Table 1. Description of the databases

Database	Instances	Attributes	Classes
adult-d-nm	45222	14	2
australian-d	690	14	2
breast-no-missing	682	10	2
car	1728	6	4
chess	3196	36	2
cleve-no-missing-d	296	13	2
corral-d	128	6	2
crx-no-missing-d	653	15	2
diabetes-d-nm	768	8	2
DNA-nominal	3186	60	3
flare-d	1066	10	2
german-d	1000	20	2
glass2-d	163	9	2
glass-d	214	9	7
heart-d	270	13	2
hepatitis-no-missing-d	80	19	2
iris-d	150	4	3
letter	20000	16	26
lymphography	148	18	4
mofn-3-7-10-d	1324	10	2
nursery	12960	8	5
mushroom	8124	22	2
pima-d	768	8	2
satimage-d	6435	36	6
segment-d	2310	19	7
shuttle-small-d	5800	9	7
soybean-large-no-missing-d	562	35	19
splice.dbc	3190	60	3
vehicle-d-nm	846	18	4
vote	435	16	2
waveform-21-d	5000	21	3

Below some non-parametric tests are made of the differences among the different methods in determining the best classifying algorithm, It is important to indicate that the means value for each of the algorithms has been included, as well. The best means is obtained by CRPDAG-BDEu with an 88.354 value,

Table 2. Results with ICU database

Database	SBND BDE	SBND BIC	SBND Ak	SBND K2	TAN	NBayes
adult-d-nm	85.255	85.213	85.405	85.963	85.295	83.090
australian-d	86.667	85.797	86.232	86.667	85.362	85.652
breast-no-missing	97.370	97.662	96.053	97.515	96.196	97.662
car	94.097	85.067	93.635	94.097	94.214	85.299
chess	97.496	96.214	97.653	97.121	91.989	87.765
cleve-no-missing-d	82.115	82.126	80.759	82.103	79.724	82.414
corral-d	99.231	100.0	99.167	99.231	99.231	85.962
crx-no-missing-d	85.916	86.375	86.671	87.140	86.974	86.678
diabetes-d-nm	78.780	79.040	78.908	79.429	77.997	77.341
DNA-nominal	96.171	96.203	93.943	95.983	94.822	95.418
flare-d	82.268	82.268	82.738	82.268	83.018	80.395
german-d	74.0	73.6	71.8	72.3	73.6	75.5
glass2-d	85.882	81.066	84.007	85.882	85.257	83.493
glass-d	73.355	64.545	71.494	69.134	73.852	73.853
heart-d	81.111	81.111	82.593	82.963	82.963	83.333
hepatitis-no-missing-d	90.0	90.0	90.0	86.25	86.25	85.0
iris-d	94.0	95.333	95.333	94.667	94.0	94.667
letter	81.565	74.015	85.655	85.36	86.320	73.6
letter-d	84.320	74.365	84.81	84.615	85.775	73.935
lymphography	77.571	81.620	80.381	80.381	79.048	81.762
mofn-3-7-10-d	92.522	90.790	100.0	93.501	91.237	85.425
nursery	91.890	91.705	97.469	94.537	92.261	90.332
mushroom	100.0	98.523	99.274	100.0	99.963	95.495
pima-d	79.166	79.560	78.259	79.429	79.038	77.994
satimage-d	85.144	82.316	86.807	85.812	88.252	82.440
segment-d	94.459	93.550	95.022	94.372	95.151	92.208
shuttle-small-d	99.741	99.552	99.534	99.759	99.069	99.052
soybean-large-no-missing-d	91.278	84.496	90.918	93.409	94.298	91.269
splice.dbc	96.238	96.270	91.944	96.364	94.796	95.454
vehicle-d-nm	65.849	65.013	70.451	64.892	69.986	61.829
vote	94.715	94.952	95.640	95.174	94.498	90.338
vote-no-missing	95.396	95.375	94.704	95.169	94.244	90.095
waveform-21-d	82.84	82.34	81.9	83.5	83.1	81.84
media	87.770	86.244	88.156	88.030	87.810	85.048

followed by SBND Akaike with 88.156. The basic non parametric test used is Friedman, since it has more than 2 associated samples.

The null hypothesis (H_0) being contrasted is that the answers associated to each of the treatments have the same probability distribution or distributions

Table 3. Results with ICU database

Database	BAN Learning BDEu	BAN Learning BIC	BAN Learning K2
adult-d-nm	85.534	85.472	84.906
australian-d	84.638	86.812	84.203
breast-no-missing	97.662	97.662	97.664
car	93.517	85.414	94.213
chess	96.151	95.745	96.995
cleve-no-missing-d	81.069	79.713	78.701
corral-d	100.0	100.0	98.462
crx-no-missing-d	86.063	86.986	84.681
diabetes-d-nm	78.387	78.389	78.127
DNA-nominal	95.292	95.418	93.158
flare-d	82.830	82.831	83.298
german-d	75.3	75.3	74.1
glass2-d	85.882	85.221	85.846
glass-d	72.013	76.190	74.762
heart-d	82.963	82.222	82.963
hepatitis-no-missing-d	88.75	87.5	88.75
iris-d	94.0	94.0	94.0
letter	84.715	74.880	87.965
letter-d	85.56	77.34	86.945
lymphography	85.0	82.333	74.857
mofn-3-7-10-d	87.617	90.865	93.804
nursery	91.860	91.883	94.892
mushroom	100.0	100.0	100.0
pima-d	78.775	78.780	79.040
satimage-d	88.361	85.175	87.506
segment-d	95.281	92.900	95.195
shuttle-small-d	99.052	99.776	99.741
soybean-large-no-missing-d	93.424	93.418	89.860
splice	95.329	95.705	94.107
vehicle-d-nm	70.689	70.102	69.384
vote	94.493	93.811	92.659
vote-no-missing	93.092	93.552	92.875
waveform-21-d	82.94	82.62	83.5
media	88.090	87.211	87.791

with the same means against the alternative hypothesis stating that at least the distribution of one of the means differs from the others.

The values that will be used in these tests can be seen in Table 6, where the average order of the algorithms are presented. The best performance is shown by SBND K2 algorithm.

Table 4. Results with ICU database

Database	RPDag-BDEu	RPDag-BIC	RPDag-K2
adult-d-nm	85.748	85.576	85.339
australian-d	85.797	85.362	85.797
breast-no-missing	97.662	97.662	97.662
car	93.228	85.878	94.040
chess	97.152	94.931	96.871
cleve-no-missing-d	82.115	81.770	80.425
corral-d	100.0	100.0	100.0
crx-no-missing-d	86.371	86.068	84.387
diabetes-d-nm	79.429	79.040	79.170
DNA-nominal	95.857	96.360	95.450
flare-d	82.268	82.268	82.268
german-d	74.4	74.2	73.8
glass2-d	84.632	84.044	82.169
glass-d	67.294	65.823	73.788
heart-d	80.370	81.481	82.963
hepatitis-no-missing-d	87.5	90.0	86.25
iris-d	96.0	95.333	94.667
letter	83.185	74.835	86.65
letter-d	86.085	74.87	86.325
lymphography	76.905	75.524	74.952
mofn-3-7-10-d	100.0	93.808	96.829
mushroom	100.0	100.0	100.0
nursery	93.465	91.312	94.792
pima-d	79.299	79.299	79.301
satimage-d	84.911	79.285	84.911
segment-d	94.199	94.589	95.325
shuttle-small-d	99.690	94.862	99.534
soybean-large-no-missing-d	89.148	86.096	93.064
splice	95.956	96.238	96.363
vehicle-d-nm	64.902	61.584	64.066
vote	94.720	94.947	95.185
vote-no-missing	94.709	95.153	93.092
waveform-21-d	79.98	81.06	83.320
media	87.666	86.038	87.841

Friedman test's results are shown in Table 7, where a value lower than 0.05 is seen, thus rejecting the null hypothesis and it is determined that the differences measure the statistically significant distributions of the different methods.

When the differences detected are significant, Holm's test is applied for comparing the control algorithm (the best classified) to the rest. Holm's is a multiple

Table 5. Results with ICU database

Database	CRPDag-BDEu	CRPDag-BIC	CRPDag-K2
adult-d-nm	85.257	85.463	85.372
australian-d	86.667	86.232	84.348
breast-no-missing	97.662	97.662	97.664
car	93.228	85.878	94.040
chess	96.621	95.713	96.277
cleve-no-missing-d	81.747	81.057	78.724
corral-d	100.0	100.0	100.0
crx-no-missing-d	86.981	87.135	83.308
diabetes-d-nm	78.387	77.996	78.127
DNA-nominal	96.422	96.202	83.519
flare-d	83.020	82.830	82.738
german-d	73.4	74.1	74.0
glass2-d	86.471	85.221	85.882
glass-d	74.329	70.519	73.377
heart-d	82.593	82.222	82.963
hepatitis-no-missing-d	90.0	83.75	86.25
iris-d	94.0	94.0	94.0
letter	83.845	75.135	87.01
letter-d	86.55	77.34	87.195
lymphography	76.905	80.333	76.333
mofn-3-7-10-d	100.0	93.808	96.829
mushroom	100.0	100.0	100.0
nursery	93.465	91.312	94.792
pima-d	78.775	78.910	78.910
satimage-d	87.553	85.175	86.667
segment-d	95.325	92.900	94.978
shuttle-small-d	99.741	99.707	99.707
soybean-large-no-missing-d	89.859	90.025	93.590
splice	96.332	96.332	90.157
vehicle-d-nm	70.929	72.228	71.517
vote	93.811	93.346	93.351
vote-no-missing	92.854	92.860	93.330
waveform-21-d	82.94	82.74	83.46
media	88.354	86.913	87.528

Table 6. Average score of the algorithms

Algorithm	Ranking
SBND BDE	7.676470588235294
SBND BIC	9.264705882352944
SBND Akaike	7.73529411764706
SBND K2	5.955882352941175
TAN	8.249999999999998
NaiveBayes	11.382352941176473
BAN Learning BDEu	7.058823529411763
BAN Learning BIC	7.955882352941175
BAN Learning K2	7.823529411764705
RPDag Learning BDEu	7.661764705882354
RPDag Learning BIC	9.20588235294118
RPDag Learning K2	7.191176470588233
CRPDag Learning BDEu	6.2647058823529385
CRPDag Learning BIC	8.823529411764708
CRPDag Learning K2	7.749999999999998

Table 7. Friedman test's results

Test	P Value	Hypothesis
Friedman	1,542E−4	Rejected

comparison test, by means of which we confront SBND with K2, the best classifying value, with the rest of the algorithms.

Table 8 shows Holm test's results for 0.05 significance level and Table 9 for 0.10 significance level.

In the first place it was considered $\alpha = 0.05$. P values in Holm test is $P \leq 0.0045$. This value is compared to the rest of the algorithms based on the right column of Table 8. It can be observed that this algorithm is significantly better than Naive Bayes, SBND BIC, RPDag Learning BIC and there are no significant differences with the rest of the algorithms.

In the second place, $\alpha = 0.10$ significance level is considered, P value in Holms test is $P \leq 0.01$. With this value multiple comparisons with the values in the right column of Table 9 are made. It can be determined that our control algorithm SBND with K2 classifies better than Naive Bayes, SBND BIC, RPDag Learning BIC, CRPDag Learning BIC algorithms and there are no significant differences with the rest of the algorithms.

Table 8. Holm Table for $\alpha = 0.05$

i	Algorithm	$z = (R_0 - R_i)/SE$	p	Holm
14	NaiveBayes	5.0029586834427615	5.645704442401309E-7	0.0035714285714285718
13	SBND BIC	3.0505845630748563	0.0022839635380862903	0.0038461538461538464
12	RPDag Learning BIC	2.9963519486201924	0.0027323088004595057	0.004166666666666667
11	CRPDag Learning BIC	2.643839954664876	0.00819714047525547	0.004545454545454546
10	TAN	2.1150719637318978	0.03442381432538883	0.005
9	BAN Learning BIC	1.8439088914585775	0.06519641907813004	0.0055555555555555556
8	BAN Learning K2	1.7218855089355838	0.08509026052283775	0.00625
7	CRPDag Learning K2	1.6540947408672533	0.09810826450210172	0.0071428571428571435
6	SBND Akaike	1.6405365872535898	0.10089364763218327	0.008333333333333333
5	SBND BDE	1.586303972798925	0.1126703715408176	0.01
4	RPDag Learning BDEu	1.57274581918526	0.11577768575893127	0.0125
3	RPDag Learning K2	1.1388849035479442	0.2547511629904382	0.016666666666666666
2	BAN Learning BDEu	1.0168615210249505	0.3092193106086886	0.025
1	CRPDag Learning BDEu	0.28472122588698523	0.7758577275237244	0.05

Table 9. Holm tabla para $\alpha = 0.10$

i	Algorithm	$z = (R_0 - R_i)/SE$	p	Holm
14	NaiveBayes	5.0029586834427615	5.645704442401309E-7	0.0071428571428571435
13	SBND BIC	3.0505845630748563	0.0022839635380862903	0.007692307692307693
12	RPDag Learning BIC	2.9963519486201924	0.0027323088004595057	0.008333333333333333
11	CRPDag Learning BIC	2.643839954664876	0.00819714047525547	0.009090909090909092
10	TAN	2.1150719637318978	0.03442381432538883	0.01
9	BAN Learning BIC	1.8439088914585775	0.06519641907813004	0.011111111111111112
8	BAN Learning K2	1.7218855089355838	0.08509026052283775	0.0125
7	CRPDag Learning K2	1.6540947408672533	0.09810826450210172	0.014285714285714287
6	SBND Akaike	1.6405365872535898	0.10089364763218327	0.016666666666666666
5	SBND BDE	1.586303972798925	0.1126703715408176	0.02
4	RPDag Learning BDEu	1.57274581918526	0.11577768575893127	0.025
3	RPDag Learning K2	1.1388849035479442	0.2547511629904382	0.03333333333333333
2	BAN Learning BDEu	1.0168615210249505	0.3092193106086886	0.05
1	CRPDag Learning BDEu	0.28472122588698523	0.7758577275237244	0.1

5   Conclusions

In this article we have introduced a Bayesian classifier known as SBND which is based in quickly obtaining an easy to learn and very competitive Markov's boundary. This classifiers is fast to learn and very competitive as compared to other classifiers of the state of art. Various experiments were made using 31 well known in the ICU databases and two bases of artificial variables.

SBND classifier's performance in some examples is dependent on the metric being used. With BIC the result is not good, Akaike gives good results in reference to the means, and K2 shows good results in non-parametric tests.

For future research, it is important to include the costs of wrong classifications in the problem, since a false positive is not the same as a false negative. If the cost of a false negative was considered better than that of a false positive, it could be detected that more students would drop out, although the number of students at risk of abandoning would increase.

References

1. Acid, S., De Campos, L., Castellano, J.: Learning Bayesian network classifiers: searching in a space of partially directed acyclic graphs. Mach. Learn. **59**(3), 213–235 (2005)
2. Akaike, H.: A new look at the statistical model identification. IEEE Trans. Autom. Control **19**, 716–723 (1974)
3. Cheng, J., Russell, G.: Comparing Bayesian network classifiers. In: Proceedings of the Fifteenth Conference on Uncertainty in Artificial Intelligence, pp. 101–108. Morgan Kaufmann Publishers Inc. (1999)
4. Cooper, G., Herskovits, E.: A Bayesian method for the induction of probabilistic networks from data. Mach. Learn. **9**(4), 309–347 (1992)
5. Elvira, C.: Elvira: an environment for probabilistic graphical models. In: Gámez, J., Salmerón, A. (eds.) Proceedings of the 1st European Workshop on Probabilistic Graphical Models, pp. 222–230 (2002)
6. Felgaer, P., Britos, P., Sicre, J., Servetto, A., García-Martínez, R., Perichinsky, G.: Optimización de redes bayesianas basada en técnicas de aprendizaje por instrucción. In: Proceedings del VIII Congreso Argentino de Ciencias de la Computación, vol. 1687 (2003)
7. Friedman, N., Michal, L., Iftach, N., Dana, P.: Using Bayesian networks to analyze expression data. Comput. Biol. **7**(3–4), 601–620 (2000)
8. García, F.: Modelos Bayesianos para la clasificación supervisada: aplicaciones al análisis de datos de expresión genética, Tesis Doctoral, Universidad de Granada (2009)
9. García-Martínez, R., Borrajo, D.: An integrated approach of learning, planning, and execution. J. Intell. Robot. Syst. **29**(1), 47–78 (2000)
10. Irani, K., Jie, C., Usama, F., Zhaogang, Q.: Applying machine learning to semiconductor manufacturing. iEEE Expert **8**(1), 41–47 (1993)
11. Lichman, M.: UCI machine learning repository. University of California, Irvine, School of Information and Computer Sciences (2013). http://archive.ics.uci.edu/ml
12. Oviedo, B., Moral, S., Puris, A.: A hierarchical clustering method: applications to educational data. Intell. Data Anal. **20**(4), 933–951 (2016)
13. Oviedo Bayas, B.W.: Modelos gráficos probabilisticos aplicados a la predicción del rendimiento en educación (2016)
14. Schwarz, G.: Estimating the dimension of a model. Ann. Stat. **6**(2), 461–464 (1978)
15. Webb, G.I., Pazzani, M.J.: Adjusted probability Naive Bayesian induction. In: Antoniou, G., Slaney, J. (eds.) AI 1998. LNCS, vol. 1502, pp. 285–295. Springer, Heidelberg (1998). https://doi.org/10.1007/BFb0095060

An Overview of Multiple Sequence
Alignment Methods Applied
to Transmembrane Proteins

Cristian Zambrano-Vega[1]([✉])(iD), Byron Oviedo[1](iD), Ronald Villamar-Torres[2](iD),
Miguel Botto-Tobar[3,4](iD), and Marcos Barros-Rodríguez[5](iD)

[1] Facultad de Ciencias de la Ingeniería, Universidad Técnica Estatal de Quevedo,
Quevedo, Ecuador
{czambrano,boviedo}@uteq.edu.ec
[2] Université de Montpellier, Montpellier, France
villamartorresronaldoswaldo@yahoo.es
[3] Eindhoven University of Technology, Eindhoven, The Netherlands
m.a.botto.tobar@tue.nl
[4] Universidad de Guayaquil, Guayaquil, Ecuador
miguel.bottot@ug.edu.ec
[5] Universidad Técnica de Ambato, Ambato, Ecuador
ma-barros@uta.edu.ec

Abstract. Transmembrane proteins (TMPs) have received a great deal
of attention playing a fundamental role in cell biology and are considered to constitute around 30% of proteins at genomic scale. Multiple
Sequence Alignment (MSA) problem has been studied for some years
and researchers have proposed many heuristic and stochastic techniques
tailored for sequences of soluble proteins, considering that there are a few
particular differences that ought to be taken into consideration aligning
TMPs sequences, these techniques are therefore not optimal to align
this special class of proteins. There is a small number of MSA methods
applied specifically to TMPs. In this review, we have summarized the
features, implementations and performance results of three MSA methods applied to TMPs: PRALINE[TM], TM-Coffee and TM-Aligner. These
methods have illustrated impressive advances in the accuracy and computational efforts aligning TMPs sequences.

Keywords: Multiple Sequence Alignment · Transmembrane proteins
Computational bilogy

1 Introduction

Given the biomedical of TMPs and the crevice between the number of illumi-
nated TMPs structures and the number of TMPs groupings, arrangement examination methods are significant. Over the past years, Transmembrane Proteins
(TMPs) or Integral Proteins have taken a extraordinary deal of consideration

© Springer Nature Switzerland AG 2019
M. Botto-Tobar et al. (Eds.): CITT 2018, CCIS 895, pp. 410–419, 2019.
https://doi.org/10.1007/978-3-030-05532-5_30

playing a fundamental role in cell biology and are among the foremost tended to targets of pharmaceutical and life science research. TMPs are non-soluble proteins secured in a cell membrane and containing one or more membrane-spanning sections isolated with intra or extra-cellular domains of variable length [3]. They carry out fundamental capacities in numerous cellular and physiological processes, such as cell-cell recognition, molecular transport and signal transduction. Around 30% of proteins encoded by the mammalian genome are transmembrane proteins [2,28]. TMPs are difficult to study [23] and are well known for their complexities in deciding their structures experimentally. Only 3227 (α: 2848, β: 366) TMP structures are available till date with Protein Data Bank of TMP with the version 2017.06.16 [20]. Given the biomedical significance of TMPs and the huge and developing gap between the solved TMPs structures and the TMPs sequences, sequence analysis methods are very significant.

The special environment of a layer protein compared to a water-soluble protein leads to particular natural weights on their groupings: it is transcendently lipophilic, needs hydrogen-bonding potential, and gives small screening of electrostatic interaction [10]. Be that as it may, to date, as it were a little number of MSA strategies have been proposed particularly for TMPs, or tried utilizing TMPs datasets

Multiple Sequence Alignment (MSA) is the process of aligning more than two biological sequences (Protein, DNA or RNA), has many applications in field of computational biology: protein structure prediction, functional genomics, genomic annotation, gene regulation networks, or homology searches. Most current MSA procedures have been built, and tested, to align homologous soluble proteins. Indeed in spite of that numerous such procedures are still applicable to transmembrane regions, yielding a very lower alignment accuracy than for soluble proteins [11]. There are a few particular differences that ought to be taken into consideration, TM domains have an adjusted amino-acid composition and different conservation patterns as compared to soluble proteins. The unique environment of a TMP compared to a water-soluble protein leads to distinct environmental pressures on their sequences: it is predominantly lipophilic, lacks hydrogen-bonding potential, and provides little screening of electrostatic interaction [10]. However, to date, only a few number of MSA techniques have been proposed expressly for TMPs, or tested using TMPs datasets.

In this paper we present an overview of these few MSA methods applied to TMPs: PRALINE^{TM} [25] and TM-Coffee [3] based on homology extension tested on datasets of TMPs from the BALiBASE v2.0 [1] benchmark, and TM-Aligner [2] based on dynamic programming and Wu-Manber algorithm, tested over the BaliBASE v3.0 reference set 7 of α-helical TMPs proteins [5], Pfam [8] and GPCRDB [16] databases that contains structure based alignment of TMPs.

The content of the paper is structured as follows: the next section presents a formal definition of the MSA problem. Section 3 details the transmembrane substitution rates proposed in literature. An overview of the state-of-the-art of MSA methods applied to TMPs is described in Sect. 4. The benchmarking for TMPs is presented in Sect. 5. Section 6 illustrates a summary of the results presented by the methods described in Sect. 4. And Sect. 7 describes concluding comments and propose some works for our future research.

2   Multiple Sequence Alignment

In this section, we describe a definition of the MSA problem as follows (MSA score functions are maximized):

Definition 1. Σ *represents a finite alphabet set and S a set of k sequences $(s_1, s_2, \ldots, s_k)$ of different length l_1 to l_k with $s_i = s_{i1} s_{i2}, \ldots, s_{il_i} (1 \le i \le k)$, where for DNA sequences, Σ is composed by 4 characters of the nucleotides $\{A, T, G, C\}$ and for protein sequences, Σ is composed of 20 characters of the amino acids $\{A, D, C, F, E, H, G, K, I, M, L, P, N, R, Q, T, S, W, V, W, Y\}$; to find an optimal alignment S' of S, with respects to a scoring function $f(S')$, such that:*

$$S' = (s'_{ij}), \ with \ 1 \le i \le k, 1 \le j \le l, max(l_i) \le l \le \sum_{i=1}^{k} l_i \qquad (1)$$

satisfying:

1. *$s'_{ij} \in \Sigma \cup \{-\}$, where "-" represents the gap;*
2. *each row $s'_i = s'_{i1} s'_{i2}, \ldots, s'_{il} (1 \le i \le k)$ of S' is the same sequence s_i if we remove all the gap characters;*
3. *the length of the all the k sequences are equals;*
4. *S' has no fully gaps columns.*

The complexity of finding an optimal alignment is $O(k2^k L^k)$, where k is the number of sequences and L is the $max\{l_1, l_2, \ldots, l_k\}$ [29].

Figure 1 illustrates on the left a set of four unaligned sequences. Then, an aligned solution (MSA) for these sequences is illustrated on the right, with two columns totally aligned.

```
s1: AGERSLAATLVC          s1: AG------ERSLAA--TLV-C
s2: DNAILAHERLSIJ         s2: DNAILAH-ER-------LSIJ
s3: CNGYLFIEQLNA          s3: CNGYLFI-E---Q----L-NA
s4: FGLVSDVFEARHMQRLN     s4: FGLVSDVFEARH--MQRL--N
```

Fig. 1. On the left unaligned sequences and on the right an aligned solution example.

3   Substitution Rates for TMPs

PAM [6] or BLOSUM [13] are traditional score matrices communly utilized for sequence retrieval and alignment, but are consequently not ideal to align TM domains [12]. Substitution rates for TMPs, S_{ij}, are communly based on the frequency of AA substitutions, q_{ij}, in a set of homologous sequences, as indicated by:

$$S_{ij} = \frac{1}{\lambda} \ln \left(\frac{q_{ij}}{f_i f_j} \right) \qquad (2)$$

where λ represents a constant, and f_i represents the background frequencies of AA [12].

Various substitution matrix have been suggested to take the evolutionary trends particularly to transmembrane domains, such as: JTT [18], PHAT [24], the asymmetric SLIM matrices [22] and the bbTM matrix for transmembrane β-barrels [17].

4   Multiple Sequence Alignment Applied to TMPs

Very few methods have been proposed to perform MSA of TMPs. The initial proposal is presented by Cserzö et al. in [4], describing an algorithm which locates helical TM segments. They demonstrated that corresponding helices in another membrane related protein can be pinpointed just with the location of TM helices of a protein. Evaluating the applicability of their proposal, obtained a good starting point for homology modeling of a G-protein couple receptor (human rhodopsin and bacteriorhodopsin).

The STAM (Simple Transmembrane Alignment Method) method was proposed by Shafrir and Robert in [26] represents a second attempt to improve alignment accuracy by combining two substitution matrices since the frequencies of occurrence of the various AAs differ for TM and water-soluble regions. They identified regions likely to form TM α-helices and apply a higher penalty for insertion/deletions in the TM regions than that of a penalty in the loop region (non-TM regions). To our knowledge STAM is considered as the first software that was specifically targeted at TMPs.

Other study presented by Forrest et al. [10] proposed that the use of a bipartite scheme (composed by BLOSUM62 and PHAT) does not significantly improve MSA of TMPs. Introduce HOMEP, a benchmark data set of homologous membrane protein structures and assess current strategies for homology modeling of TMPs.

And recently, three new MSA software for TMPs have been proposed and represent the main topics in this work: PRALINE[TM], TM-Coffee and TM-Aligner. This methods are described follow:

4.1   PRALINE[TM]

PRALINE[TM] incorpores transmembrane specific information into the previously developed multiple alignment tool PRALINE [14,15]. The strategy includes 3 core functions:

Profile Preprocessing. In the 'preprofile' method, for every sequence a master-slave alignment is created, containing data about neighboring sequences and used in subsequent progressive alignment. These sequence pre-profiles avoid mistakes during the progressive steps and are more informative than single sequences [14, 15].

Bipartite Alignment Scheme. Predicts for every input sequence its TM topology utilizing three different predictors: HMMTOP v2.1 [27], TMHMM v2.0 [21] and Phobius [19]. Theses predictors are installed locally and run independently within the PRALINE^{TM} program. Second, to reliably predicted TM positions, the profile-scoring scheme applies the TM-specific substitution score PHAT, applying the following Eq. 3 to score a pair of profile columns x and y:

$$S(x,y) = \sum_{i=1}^{20} \sum_{j=1}^{20} \alpha_i \beta_j M(i,j) \tag{3}$$

where $M(i,j)$ is the exchange weight for residues i and j provided by the selected substitution matrix M and α_i and β_j are the frequencies with which residues i and j appear in columns x and y, respectively. To ensure conflictingly predicted positions don't contrarily impact the alignment quality, two profile columns are coordinated utilizing the PHAT matrix [24] just in the event that every residue in the column is predicted to be part of a TM region, but profile columns are aligned utilizing the BLOSUM62 matrix by default.

Tree-Based Consistency Iteration. In the tree-based consistency iteration used by PRALINE-TM, every edge of a guide tree is utilized to separate the alignment in 2 subalignments, which are progressively realigned. The recent alignment is held just if an enhanced SOP score (Sum-of-Pairs) is accomplished. This score is computed by the entirety of the substitution values of both the BLOSUM62 and PHAT matrix (depending on the TM topology of the AA pair). One iterative cycle suggests that every edge of the tree is visited once.

4.2   TM-Coffee

Chang *et al.* presents in [3] the TM-Coffee software, a TM version of PSI-Coffee able to align TMPs, while utilizing a decreased reference database for homology extension, demonstrating how it can be adjusted and joined with a consistency based approach to improve the MSA of α-helical TMPs. TM-Coffee is included in the T-Coffee software, and a web version is accessible at: http://tcoffee.crg. cat/tmcoffee. With the aim of assess the performance of TM-Coffee, Chang *et al.* tested their proposal over the reference 7 of BAliBASE v2.0 benchmark [1] that contains alpha-helical transmembrane proteins, and demonstrated a relevant improvement over accurate strategies such as MSAProbs, MAFFT, PRO-MALS, ProbCons, PRALINE^{TM} and Kalign.

Position Specific Iterative PSI/TM-COFFEE WEB-SERVER. A web server version was developed by Floden *et al.* and presented in [9]. This version also allows a rapidly perform of homology extension, using PSI-BLAST searches against a choice of reduced complexity redundant and non-redundant database. Furthermore, using the HMMTOP algorithm outputs topological prediction of TMPs. Login procedure is not required.

4.3 TM-Aligner

TM-Aligner (Transmembrane Membrane proteins - Aligner) [2] is the most recent web-server sequence alignment tool of transmembrane proteins. Use Wu-Manber [30] and dynamic string matching algorithm [7]. The performance of TM-Aligner is assessed over Pfam database, GPCRDB and BaliBASE v3.0 reference set 7 of α-helical TMPs. Has been developed in Perl, C and PHP under a wcb server on Linux operative system. It is free and available at: http://lms.snu.edu.in/TM-Aligner/.

Scoring Scheme. TM-Aligner uses by default the PHAT substitution matrix [24], defines a gap insertion penalty value of eigth and a gap extension penalty value of one. The alignment process is based on dynamic programming. Aligns all regions independently.

TM-Aligner Workflow. Given a set of input unaligned sequences, the TM-Aligner workflow is described as follows:

- Predict TMs domains into the sequences using TMHMM (Transmembrane Hidden Markov Model) [21].
- Classify into different groups the input sequences, based on the TMs segments of each sequence.
- For overall alignment process, a seed alignment is defined using classes with the dominant number of TM sequences.
- Input protein sequences are separated into regions of TM, non-cytoplasmic and cytoplasmic.
- Dynamic programming technique is used to aligned all these regions independently.
- Most similar sequences are aligned using Progressive or tree-based strategy,
- Add less similar sequences to alignment until all sequences are aligned, successively.
- An initial guide-tree is created using UPGMA method, this guide-tree describes sequence relatedness.
- Wu-Manber algorithm is used to stitch the TM domains with non-cytoplasmic and cytoplasmic segments.

5   Benchmarking Transmembrane Alignments

In this section we detail two benchmarks used to assess the alignment accuracy of TMPs effectively, and used by PRALINE^{TM}, TM-Coffee and TM-Aligner.

5.1   BAliBASE

BAliBASE [5] is one of the classical benchmark from the literature. Includes a set of alignments obtained from manual alignment and/or structural databases. Contains a special reference set of TMPs, called Reference set 7 [1], with 8 accurately aligned TMPs families namely 7tm, msl, dtd, acr, photo, ion, Nat and ptga. Contains 435 sequences in total. Have from 2 to 14 TM α-helices per sequence. The core domains are authors-defined, examining the alignment of structurally equivalent residues only. The main goal of BAliBASE is assess the capacity of the strategies to recapitulate these core domains, mostly made of α-helices. Furthermore, contains a program to assess accuracy of the candidate alignments over reference alignments provided by the benchmark, called Baliscore that includes two metrics: Total Column (TC) and Sum-of-Pairs (SP) scores.

5.2   Pfam Database

The Pfam [8] is available at http://pfam.xfam.org, is a large database that contains a set of preserved protein families represented by HMMs (Hidden Markov Models) and MSA. With the aim of accurately identify the gap penalty, length parameter in profile hidden markov model and position-specific AA frequency, seed alignment are based on principal protein sequences. The last version of Pfam 31.0 contains 16712 entries and 604 clans, in this release over 36% of Pfam entries are placed within a clan. All the information for every entry as obtained from UniProt Reference Proteomes.

6   Performance Comparison

In this section, we present a performance comparison between PRALINE[TM], TM-Coffee and TM-Aligner, compared with themselves and other classical alignment methods. Sum-of-Pair (SP) score of BAliBASE and CPU processing time (in seconds) were considered for each protein family of BAliBASE reference set7. All these results were taken from the literature [2,3,25]. Table 1 shows the individual and average SP, bold values are the best score for each set.

In Table 1 we see that TM-Coffee achieves the highest average SP over all eight datasets and the best individual SP score for the 7TM, ACR, DTD and PTGA sets. TM-Aligner and PRALINE[TM] achieves the best individual SP score for the MSL and ION sets, respectively. Furthermore, MAFFT is relatively robust on TM sequences, obtains the best individual SP score for the NAT and PHOTO sets. Table 2 shows the results evaluating the CPU processing time in seconds. These results were taken from [2]. Basharat *et al.* tested individually the tools using single threaded machine with two available cores, including TM-Aligner [2].

Table 1. Comparison between the PRALINE^{TM}, TM-Coffee and TM-Aligner methods and other widely-used multiple alignment tools

Set	ClustalW	Muscle	Mafft	ProbCons	Praline	Promals	Kalign	TM-Aligner	PRALINE^{TM}	TM-Coffee
7TM	0.85	0.84	0.84	0.88	0.82	0.83	0.48	0.82	0.86	**0.88**
ACR	0.91	0.95	0.94	0.94	0.93	0.91	0.92	0.92	0.94	**0.95**
DTD	0.79	0.86	0.84	0.88	0.82	0.85	0.50	0.87	0.86	**0.88**
ION	0.35	0.52	0.51	0.53	0.35	0.50	0.29	0.51	**0.54**	0.54
MSL	0.86	0.87	0.85	0.85	0.81	0.85	0.70	**0.89**	0.87	0.84
NAT	0.63	0.74	**0.77**	0.75	0.72	0.75	0.28	0.75	0.71	0.72
PHOTO	0.89	0.90	**0.93**	0.91	0.92	0.91	0.50	0.92	0.93	0.91
PTGA	0.46	0.55	0.73	0.72	0.40	0.74	0.32	0.70	0.68	**0.74**
AVG	0.72	0.78	0.80	0.81	0.72	0.79	0.50	0.80	0.80	**0.81**

Table 2. Comparison of CPU processing time in seconds of TM-Coffee and TM-Aligner methods and other widely-used multiple alignment tools, PRALINE^{TM} is not included because the standalone version is unavailable [2].

Set	PROMALS	ClustalW	Muscle	Mafft	Kalign	TM-Aligner	TM-Coffee
PTGA	17633	5	28	38	3	17	778
ACR	35622	8	28	35	6	26	1836
MSL	1055	1	3	12	1	3	17
DTD	21885	6	32	44	3	24	1443
PHOTO	3962	1	3	26	1	7	38
ION	18521	4	78	45	6	26	1385
NAT	21055	6	32	54	3	21	602
7TM	35865	19	52	117	6	56	4346
AvG	19450	6	32	46	4	23	1306

7   Conclusions

There is a lot MSA methods proposed in the literature, but to date, there is a small number of MSA methods proposed specifically for TMPs. In this work we have addressed three of the MSA methods applied to TMPs: PRALINE^{TM}, TM-Coffee and TM-Aligner. We have summarized their principal features and illustrated a performance comparison between them and other classical MSA methods evaluating SP score and the CPU processing time over the protein family of BAliBASE reference set-7. TM-Coffee achieves high accuracy results, however TM-aligner is the faster method in terms of CPU processing time (seconds).

The studied methods suggest that 2D structure prediction and dynamic programming (TM-Aligner), bipartite scheme using membrane-specific scoring matrices (PRALINE^{TM}) and homology extension (TM-Coffee) can increase alignment quality for TMPs.

Finally, considering the complexity of the problem, we suggest that the alignment process of TMPs can be tackled with stochastic methods, introducing an alternative technique useful from a biological point of view. Furthermore, with parallel techniques to reduce the execution time.

Acknowledgement. This work has been supported by the 5th convocation of Fondo Competitivo de Investigación Científica y Tecnológica FOCICYT of the Universidad Técnica Estatal de Quevedo from Ecuador.

References

1. Bahr, A., Thompson, J.D., Thierry, J.C., Poch, O.: BAliBASE (benchmark alignment database): enhancements for repeats, transmembrane sequences and circular permutations. Nucleic Acids Res. **29**(1), 323–326 (2001). https://doi.org/10.1093/nar/29.1.323
2. Bhat, B., Ganai, N.A., Andrabi, S.M., Shah, R.A., Singh, A.: TM-Aligner: multiple sequence alignment tool for transmembrane proteins with reduced time and improved accuracy. Sci. Rep. **7**(1), 1–8 (2017). https://doi.org/10.1038/s41598-017-13083-y
3. Chang, J.M., Di Tommaso, P., Taly, J.F., Notredame, C.: Accurate multiple sequence alignment of transmembrane proteins with PSI-Coffee. BMC Bioinform. **13**(4), S1 (2012). https://doi.org/10.1186/1471-2105-13-S4-S1
4. Cserzö, M., Bernassau, J.M., Simon, I., Maigret, B.: New alignment strategy for transmembrane proteins. J. Mol. Biol. **243**(3), 388–396 (1994). https://doi.org/10.1006/jmbi.1994.1666
5. Thompson, J.D., Koehl, P., Ripp, R., Poch, O.: BAliBASE 3.0: latest developments of the multiple sequence alignment benchmark. Proteins: Struct. Funct. Bioinform. **61**(1), 127–136 (2005). https://doi.org/10.1002/prot.20527
6. Dayhoff, M., Schwartz, R., Orcutt, B.C.: A model of evolutionary change in proteins. Atlas Protein Seq. Struct. **5**, 345–352 (1978)
7. Durbin, R., Eddy, S.R., Krogh, A., Mitchison, G.: Biological Sequence Analysis: Probabilistic Models of Proteins and Nucleic Acids. Cambridge University Press, Cambridge (1998)
8. Finn, R.D., et al.: The Pfam protein families database: towards a more sustainable future. Nucleic Acids Res. **44**(D1), D279–D285 (2016). https://doi.org/10.1093/nar/gkv1344
9. Floden, E.W., Tommaso, P.D., Chatzou, M., Magis, C., Notredame, C., Chang, J.M.: PSI/TM-Coffee: a web server for fast and accurate multiple sequence alignments of regular and transmembrane proteins using homology extension on reduced databases. Nucleic Acids Res. **44**(W1), W339–W343 (2016). https://doi.org/10.1093/nar/gkw300
10. Forrest, L.R., Tang, C.L., Honig, B.: On the accuracy of homology modeling and sequence alignment methods applied to membrane proteins. Biophys. J. **91**(2), 508–517 (2006). https://doi.org/10.1529/biophysj.106.082313
11. Frishman, D.: Structural Bioinformatics of Membrane Proteins (2010). https://doi.org/10.1007/978-3-7091-0045-5
12. Frishman, D.: Structural Bioinformatics of Membrane Proteins. Springer, Heidelberg (2010). https://doi.org/10.1007/978-3-7091-0045-5
13. Henikoff, S., Henikoff, J.: Amino acid substitution matrices from protein blocks. Proc. Natl. Acad. Sci. **89**(22), 10915–10919 (1992)

14. Heringa, J.: Two strategies for sequence comparison: profile-preprocessed and secondary structure-induced multiple alignment. Comput. Chem. **23**(3), 341–364 (1999). https://doi.org/10.1016/S0097-8485(99)00012-1

15. Heringa, J.: Local weighting schemes for protein multiple sequence alignment. Comput. Chem. **26**(5), 459–477 (2002). http://www.sciencedirect.com/science/article/pii/S0097848502000086

16. Isberg, V., et al.: GPCRdb: an information system for g protein-coupled receptors. Nucleic Acids Res. **44**(D1), D356–D364 (2016). https://doi.org/10.1093/nar/gkv1178

17. Jimenez-Morales, D., Adamian, L., Liang, J.: Detecting remote homologues using scoring matrices calculated from the estimation of amino acid substitution rates of beta-barrel membrane proteins. In: 2008 30th Annual International Conference of the IEEE Engineering in Medicine and Biology Society, pp. 1347–1350, August 2008. https://doi.org/10.1109/IEMBS.2008.4649414

18. Jones, D., Taylor, W., Thornton, J.: A mutation data matrix for transmembrane proteins. FEBS Lett. **339**(3), 269–275 (1994)

19. Käll, L., Krogh, A., Sonnhammer, E.L.: A combined transmembrane topology and signal peptide prediction method. J. Mol. Biol. **338**(5), 1027–1036 (2004). https://doi.org/10.1016/j.jmb.2004.03.016

20. Kozma, D., Simon, I., Tusnády, G.E.: PDBTM: protein data bank of transmembrane proteins after 8 years. Nucleic Acids Res. **41**(D1), D524–D529 (2013). https://doi.org/10.1093/nar/gks1169

21. Krogh, A., Larsson, B., Von Heijne, G., Sonnhammer, E.L.: Predicting transmembrane protein topology with a hidden Markov model: application to complete genomes1. J. Mol. Biol. **305**(3), 567–580 (2001)

22. Müller, T., Rahmann, S., Rehmsmeier, M.: Non-symmetric score matrices and the detection of homologous transmembrane proteins. Bioinformatics **17**(suppl1), S182–S189 (2001). https://doi.org/10.1093/bioinformatics/17.suppl_1.S182

23. Newby, Z.E., et al.: A general protocol for the crystallization of membrane proteins for x-ray structural investigation. Nat. Protoc. **4**(5), 619 (2009)

24. Ng, P.C., Henikoff, J.G., Henikoff, S.: PHAT: a transmembrane-specific substitution matrix. Bioinformatics **16**(9), 760–766 (2000). https://doi.org/10.1093/bioinformatics/16.9.760

25. Pirovano, W., Feenstra, K.A., Heringa, J.: Praline™: a strategy for improved multiple alignment of transmembrane proteins. Bioinformatics **24**(4), 492–497 (2008). https://doi.org/10.1093/bioinformatics/btm636

26. Shafrir, Y., Guy, H.R.: STAM: simple transmembrane alignment method. Bioinformatics **20**(5), 758–769 (2004). https://doi.org/10.1093/bioinformatics/btg482

27. Tusnády, G.E., Simon, I.: The hmmtop transmembrane topology prediction server. Bioinformatics **17**(9), 849–850 (2001). https://doi.org/10.1093/bioinformatics/17.9.849

28. Wallin, E., Heijne, G.V.: Genome-wide analysis of integral membrane proteins from eubacterial, archaean, and eukaryotic organisms. Protein Sci. **7**(4), 1029–1038 (1998)

29. Wang, L., Jiang, T.: On the complexity of multiple sequence alignment. J. Comput. Biol. **1**, 337–348 (1994)

30. Wu, S., Manber, U.: Fast text searching: allowing errors. Commun. ACM **35**(10), 83–91 (1992)

Detection of Desertion Patterns in University Students Using Data Mining Techniques: A Case Study

Dayana Vila[1], Saúl Cisneros[1], Pedro Granda[1], Cosme Ortega[1],
Miguel Posso-Yépez[2], and Iván García-Santillán[1(✉)]

[1] Department of Software Engineering, Faculty of Applied Sciences,
Universidad Técnica del Norte, Ibarra, Ecuador
{dpvilae, sacisnerosb, pdgranda, mc.ortega,
idgarcia}@utn.edu.ec
[2] Faculty of Education, Science and Technology, Universidad Técnica del Norte,
Ibarra, Ecuador
maposso@utn.edu.ec

Abstract. Student desertion is a phenomenon that affects higher education and academic quality standards. Several causes can lead to this issue, the academic factor being a potential reason. The main objective of this research is to detect dropout patterns in the "Técnica del Norte" University (Ecuador), based on personal and academic historical data, using predictive classification techniques in data mining. The KDD (Knowledge Discovery in Databases) process was used to determine desertion patterns focused on two approaches: (i) Bayesian, and (ii) Decision Trees, both implemented on Weka. The classifiers performance was quantitatively evaluated using the confusion matrix and quality metrics. The results proved that the technique based on decision trees had slightly better performance than the Bayesian approach on the processed data.

Keywords: Student desertion · Pattern discovery · Data mining
KDD · Weka

1 Introduction

1.1 Problem Statement

Student desertion is a phenomenon that refers to the abandonment of education. This can happen due to several reasons, such as: academic, social, economic and psychological situations. Dropping out affects not only students, but also the prestige of the education center [1]. This situation is common within Ecuador's higher education, especially in the lower levels. Eight out of ten students that started public college in the year 2012 continued their studies in 2013, and seven out of ten continued in 2014 [2]. This phenomenon contributes to the waste of limited public resources designated for education, decreasing quality standards, and somehow, both rising unemployment and poverty in the country [3].

© Springer Nature Switzerland AG 2019
M. Botto-Tobar et al. (Eds.): CITT 2018, CCIS 895, pp. 420–429, 2019.
https://doi.org/10.1007/978-3-030-05532-5_31

Early identification of university students who have a greater probability of abandoning their career would help improve the quality indicators in higher education. Applying data mining techniques has had a significant impact in the educational sector in recent years [3, 4]. Having a predictive system able to detect students with a high probability of dropping out and, even more, providing patterns of potential deserters is important to propose and apply preventive action plans to contribute to the improvement of student academic performance and mitigate the adverse effects previously mentioned.

The student welfare department of the "Técnica del Norte" University [5] is the entity in charge of, among other things, helping university students to continue their studies. However, the students most susceptible to dropping out have been detected and reported too late. For this reason, it is necessary to implement a system that allows opportune decision making with the purpose of mitigating this phenomenon, motivating and helping the students to continue with their college studies and life plans. This phenomenon negatively affects, mainly, undergraduates in the lower semesters (up to the fourth level).

A predictive model of pattern detection is proposed in this study, which detects college dropouts in the "Técnica del Norte" University (Ecuador), using the personal and academic data of undergraduate students (bachelor's degree and engineering) from the last 5 years. The data were processed following the KDD process (Knowledge Discovery in Databases) and using Bayesian and decision trees data mining techniques [6]. Identifying patterns considering, as possible desertion factors, the ethnic group, disability level (physical, mental, intellectual or sensory), gender, and place of residence makes up the main contribution in this research. Additionally, this study is performed using free software (Weka), fulfilling the Executive Decree of Ecuador No. 1014 [7]. This regulation disposes to use open source software within computer systems and equipment in the public administration of the Ecuadorian government. This makes up the second contribution in this study.

1.2 Review of Literature

Some existing studies were relevant for this research because they were carried out in the educational field of higher education using, among others, predictive data mining techniques. These studies are listed below:

Lehr et al. [8] used data mining techniques to predict college student retention at Embry-Riddle Aeronautical University (USA). To accomplish this goal, the data of 972 students, enrolled in 2008, were used to create predictive models, taking into account previous preparation of the students, grades in the first year, and personal and financial data. The classification techniques used were: Logistic Regression, Naive Bayes, K-Nearest Neighbors, Random Forest, Multilayer perceptron, and Decision trees. Logistic regression obtained the best results according to the error rate.

Hernández et al. [3] developed a predictive system that detects students with high desertion probabilities and the profile of dropouts in the Information and Communication Technologies Engineering career, using logistic regression, clustering, decision trees and neural networks. The results obtained by using logistic regression were best fitted to the study.

Peralta et al. [9], using data mining techniques and statistic models, identified the most relevant variables which predicted desertion and graduation rates of students in the Temuco Catholic University (Mexico). The original database held 15183 students and 143 variables. They used linear statistic models, such as the *Probit* and *Logit* models, as well as the decision tree technique. The main result obtained was that there is a clear relation among variables that depend on factors such as average and ranking.

Merchan and Duarte [10] performed a predictive model of academic performance based on the academic and demographic data of 932 students in the Computer Science career in the "El Bosque" University (Colombia). J48, PART, and Ridor decision tree algorithms were used. The J48 algorithm proved to be the best, classifying correctly around 78% of new instances.

Zaffar et al. [11] carried out research about the performance of classifiers and feature selection algorithms on a set of student data. The evaluation of the algorithms' effectiveness was performed through precision, recall, and f-measure. The best result was obtained using the Random Forest classifier.

Devasia et al. [1] proposed a web application to extract useful information about students dropping out in higher education. The experiment was carried out using the data of 700 students containing 19 attributes. The Naïve Bayes algorithm was the most precise compared to other methods such as decision trees, neural networks, and logistic regression.

Kotsiantis [4] worked with stored data belonging to the Hellenic Open University (Greece), a distance learning program. The main objective was to predict student grades, which helped the tutors better comprehend the population characteristics.

Mishra et al. [12] used clustering tasks on the data of 84 undergraduate students of psychology in the north of Spain, grouping them into three clusters according to the course final grades. The smallest cluster was the most understood while the two bigger clusters were more difficult to interpret.

Moscoso-Zea et al. [13] designed a data warehouse in an educational scenario, using the methodology proposed by Kimball and Ross [14]. This repository is intended to the knowledge discovery process and indicators analysis of academic performance in future researches.

Next, the research methodology used in this study is presented.

2 Materials and Methods

2.1 The KDD Process

The KDD (Knowledge Discovery in Databases) process was used to determine student desertion patterns and it consists of four phases [6]: (i) data collection; (ii) selection, cleansing and transformation of data; (iii) data mining; and (iv) evaluation and interpretation of the model. This research used personal and academic students data from 37 undergraduate careers of the UTN (25 bachelor's degrees and 12 engineering) from last five years (2013–2017). Each phase of the KDD process used in this study is detailed below.

2.2   Data Collection

The purpose in this stage is to integrate all data into a single repository (data warehouse). The main source of the raw data was the academic database of the UTN, which is stored on an Oracle 11g server, containing 17.882 student records. The data are both qualitative and quantitative in nature.

A part of the database was selected, i.e. 9 tables containing personal and academic data. Thirteen variables were considered in this study: age, ethnicity, nationality, place of origin, place of residence, disability level, gender, marital status, family burdens, study modality, faculty, average grades, and current state. The current state variable (active/inactive; YES/NO) was the class attribute, that is, the qualitative variable used to predict the classification (student desertion). The variables age, average grades and disability level are originally of a quantitative nature, while the rest are qualitative attributes.

Some variables mentioned above are relevant for this research, considering that the UTN is in Zone-1 of Ecuador (made up of the provinces: Imbabura, Carchi, Esmeraldas, and Sucumbíos). This zone has 638.979 men and 634.353 women of the following ethnicities: 60.9% mestizos, 21.7% Afro-Ecuadorians and African descendants, 11.5% indigenous, and 4.3% Caucasian white [15]. Also, 36.878 people (2.9%) of this region have a disability [16]. This research is based on the pattern identification in student desertion considering such variables (ethnicity, disability, gender, and place of residence) as possible dropout factors.

A data warehouse was built from the raw data, using PostgreSQL version 9.4 [17]. To accomplish this step, the data were exported from Oracle to a MS Excel file in *xlsx* format, and then imported into PostgreSQL. This database management system was selected due to it is open source and also its easy connection to the Pentaho Community Suite [18], which is used in the next phase.

2.3   Selection, Cleansing, and Transformation of Data

This phase's goal is to obtain clean data, without null or inconsistent values, allowing a highly reliable student desertion patterns. The data selection, cleansing, and transformation tasks were performed using the Pentaho Community Suite, obtaining a mineable view, that is, a dataset ready for applying data mining techniques [13].

This study used only data from the first four levels, considering that the student desertion phenomenon in the UTN frequently occurs at lower levels. The data transformation converted discrete quantitative variables (age, average grade, and disability level) into ordinal qualitative attributes using the categories indicated in Table 1. The age attribute was divided into three categories: low, medium and high. The low level was considered until the 25 years of age because the undergraduate students finish their career mostly in this period. The medium level up to 40 years because the postgraduate students (master's degree) are common in this age range. The high level is considered more than 40 years because here the students are less frequent. The average grade variable was divided into three categories (low, medium and high) considering the academic regulation in the UTN. The disability level was divided into four categories (slight, moderate, severe and very severe) considering the disability regulation of Ecuador [19].

After cleansing and transforming the data, 12620 instances were obtained, which conform the mineable view. Next, it was exported to a plain text file delimited by commas (*.csv) for the following data mining phase.

Table 1. Categories used in the transformation of quantitative data

Attribute	Category	Interval
Age	Low	≤ 25 years
	Medium	26–40 years
	High	≥ 41 years
Average grade	Low	≤ 7 points
	Medium	8–9 points
	High	9–10 points
Disability level	Slight	30–49%
	Moderate	50–74%
	Severe	75–84%
	Very severe	85–100%

2.4 Data Mining

This phase aims to obtain predictive models representative of the data, using the WEKA software version 3.8 [20]. This software is open source and it contains a wide collection of machine learning algorithms to generate different models.

In this study, the prediction used classification techniques, which consists in finding a pattern in an uncategorized data group and classify it into a predefined set of classes [6]. The classifiers used were the following: (i) decision trees with the RandomTree algorithm, due to the simplicity of its model, easy interpretation, and speed to classify new data [6, 21, 22]; and (ii) Bayesian technique with the Naïve Bayes algorithm, because of its simplicity and high precision in several domains [1, 21].

2.5 Evaluation and Interpretation of the Predictive Model

In this stage, the predictive models' performances were evaluated quantitatively. Subsequently, the best model was used to obtain student desertion patterns. The Cross-validation method (10-fold) was used for evaluating the models. For each classification algorithm, the following quality metrics were used [21, 22]: accuracy, error rate, Kappa coefficient, TP rate, FT rate, precision, recall, F1 score, and ROC area. The interpretation of the best model was carried out with the help of an expert using visualization techniques, which facilitate comprehension and discovery of desertion patterns.

Next, the results obtained in this study are presented.

3 Results and Discussion

3.1 Evaluation of Predictive Models

The overall evaluation of the classification was performed by analyzing a confusion matrix and computing several quality metrics [23], which are shown in Table 2.

Table 2. Overall evaluation metrics for the classifiers used in this study

Classifier	Accuracy	Error rate	Kappa coefficient
RandomTree	97.607%	2.393%	0.2046
Naive Bayes	97.544%	2.456%	0.2189

The classifier with the greatest accuracy and the lowest error rate turned out to be the RandomTree algorithm. Regarding the Kappa coefficient, both classifiers keep a "Fair" strength of agreement, according to the classification proposed by Landis and Kock [24]. The coefficient Kappa indicates whether the results obtained in the confusion matrix are significantly better than those produced in a random classification [25].

Some specific metrics used in the evaluation of the classifiers are shown in Table 3. It is noted that similar values were obtained for both classifiers, except for the ROC area, where it was lower for the RandomTree. This discrepancy RandomTree having greater accuracy but a lower ROC area than Naïve Bayes, may be due to an imbalanced dataset [26, 27], i.e. a disparity in the frequencies of the observed classes. This is detailed later.

Table 3. Specific evaluation metrics for the classifiers used in this study (weighted average).

Classifier	TP rate	FP rate	Precision	Recall	F_1 score	ROC area
RandomTree	0.976	0.839	0.968	0.976	0.970	0.836
Naive Bayes	0.975	0.822	0.967	0.975	0.970	0.925

Table 4 shows the confusion matrices generated by both RandomTree and Naive Bayes algorithms, respectively.

Table 4. Confusion matrices for classification algorithms.

Classifier	TP	FN	FP	TN	Number of instances
RandomTree	41	249	53	12277	12620
Naive Bayes	46	244	66	12264	12620

For the RandomTree classifier, 12318 instances were correctly classified and 3022 incorrectly. The results of the errors are the following:

- This classifier attempted to classify 290 examples of the class status = YES. Of these, 41 instances were correctly classified and 249 incorrectly classified as class status = NO.
- It tried to classify 12330 examples of the class status = NO. Of these, 12277 instances were correctly classified and 53 incorrectly classified as class status = YES.

For the Naive Bayes classifier, 12310 instances were correctly classified and 310 incorrectly. The results of the errors are the following:

- This classifier attempted to classify 290 examples of the class status = YES. Of these, 46 were correctly classified and 244 incorrectly classified as class status = NO.
- It tried to classify 12330 examples of the class status = NO. Of these, 12264 were correctly classified and 66 incorrectly classified as class status = YES.

Notably within the confusion matrices of both classifiers (Table 4), the cases for the number of negative examples NO (12330, 97.7%) is much higher than the positive examples YES (290, 2.3%), i.e. it is dealing with imbalanced dataset as mentioned before, than most supervised learning methods will skew the predicted probabilities, tending to predict the abundant class more often. In this case, the goodness of a classifier is best approximated using the F_1 score metric, which can be interpreted as a weighted average of the precision and recall values [21, 28].

In this way, considering F_1 score metric (Table 3), both classifiers keep similar performances. However, RandomTree provides a set of decision rules (representation equivalent to the decision tree) that facilitates the processing and interpretation of the predictive model [3]. Therefore, it was chosen in this study for pattern discovery in students' desertion. The decision rules generated by this model can be seen online in Appendix 1 from https://bit.ly/2Mmy9a7. In contrast, the Naïve Bayes algorithm does not generate a model but rather it performs the classification just at the requested time.

3.2   Detection of Student Desertion Patterns

After selecting the best predictive model (tree and decision rules), the exploration and interpretation of the tree was completed from the root toward the leaves (class attribute) labeled with status = YES [22]. This led to the following student desertion patterns being identified:

a. Older married women studying arts-related careers with a low average.
b. Older married men residing in Imbabura and maintaining a low average.
c. Younger married mestizo people who study in blended modality and live outside Imbabura.
d. Single, indigenous people, regardless of their sex, do not reside in Imbabura and keep a medium or low average.
e. Women in free union who study in the classroom-based modality with a medium or low average.
f. People of Colombian nationality.
g. Women with moderate disabilities and medicine-related studies.
h. People in free union with studies related to health, art or agricultural sciences.

i. Afro-Ecuadorian people studying engineering.

j. Divorced men studying engineering.

The patterns of student desertion identified above are very useful for the UTN's student welfare department and these will allow to propose action plans to mitigate such phenomenon.

3.3 Discussion

The desertion patterns identified in this study coincide with some results from prior researches. Merchan and Duarte [10] indicated that (i) students in free union are potential deserters, whereas in this work there is a higher desertion correlation with students studying health, art or agricultural sciences. Some commonalities with other works that were used in the discovery of student desertion patterns are the place of origin, average grade, study modality [1, 3], whereas some variables that are not consider in this study are the cumulate average and the ranking [9]. In addition, this study considers the data of students from 37 undergraduate careers of the UTN, unlike other works where a specific career is considered [3, 10].

Some limitations in this study are the following: (i) the problem of detection of student desertion patterns is addressed only from the academic point of view, i.e. based on average grades; and (ii) predictive classification techniques are solely used for this purpose.

Finally, some future works hold this research line are the following: (i) expand the study also considering socioeconomic and psychological data; (ii) generate other predictive models based on logistic regression and neural networks; (iii) include descriptive tasks of data mining as the clustering [3, 12], association, outlier detection; (iv) create and compare specific models for each faculty of the UTN.

4 Conclusions

Detection of student desertion patterns in the university academic field is addressed in this study by using predictive classification tasks based on the decision tree (RandomTree) and Bayesian (Naïve Bayes) approaches. The student data used are personal and academic types from 37 undergraduate careers of the "Técnica del Norte" University (Ecuador), and these are processed following the KDD process (Knowledge Discovery in Databases) and using free software (Weka). The classifiers evaluation is quantitatively analyzed considering quality metrics. The RandomTree algorithm provides, slightly, a better performance than Naive Bayes (Table 2). The interpretation of the best model allows to identify relevant patterns of student desertion (Sect. 3.2), which contributes to propose action plans to mitigate this phenomenon. As future work, it is recommended to consider socio-economic and psychological data and include descriptive tasks of data mining.

Acknowledgment. To the IT department of the "Técnica del Norte" University for allowing access to the raw data of the academic database.

References

1. Devasia, T., Vinushree, T.P., Hegde, V.: Prediction of students performance using Educational Data Mining. In: International Conference on Data Mining and Advanced Computing (SAPIENCE), Ernakulam, pp. 91–95 (2016). https://doi.org/10.1109/sapience. 2016.7684167
2. Senescyt: Rendición de cuantas 2015 (Accountability 2015). Quito-Ecuador (2015). http://www.senescyt.gob.ec/rendicion2015/assets/presentacion-rendicion-de-cuentas.pdf. Accessed 13 Mar 2018
3. Hernández, G., Melendez, R.A., Morales, L.A., Garcia, A., Tecpanecatl, J.L., Algredo, I.: Comparative study of algorithms to predict the desertion in the students at the ITSM-Mexico. IEEE Latin Am. Trans. **14**(11), 4573–4578 (2016). https://doi.org/10.1109/tla.2016. 7795831
4. Kotsiantis, S.B.: Use of machine learning techniques for educational proposes: a decision support system for forecasting students' grades. Artif. Intell. Rev. **37**(4), 331–344 (2012). https://doi.org/10.1007/s10462-011-9234-x
5. UTN: Universidad Técnica del Norte (2018). http://www.utn.edu.ec/. Accessed 22 Apr 2018
6. Lara, J.: Minería de Datos (Data Mining). Madrid, Centro de Estudios Financieros (2014)
7. Subsecretaría de Informática: Decreto Ejecutivo No. 1014 (Executive Decree No. 1014) (2009). http://cti.gobiernoelectronico.gob.ec/ayuda/manual/decreto_1014.pdf. Accessed 22 Apr 2018
8. Lehr, S., Liu, H., Kinglesmith, S., Konyha, A., Robaszewska, N., Medinilla, J.: Use educational data mining to predict undergraduate retention. In: IEEE 16th International Conference on Advanced Learning Technologies (ICALT), Austin, TX, pp. 428–430 (2016). https://doi.org/10.1109/icalt.2016.138
9. Peralta, B., Poblete, T., Caro, L.: Automatic feature selection for desertion and graduation prediction: a chilean case. In: 35th International Conference of the Chilean Computer Science Society (SCCC), Valparaiso, pp. 1–8 (2016). https://doi.org/10.1109/sccc.2016. 7836055
10. Merchan, S.M., Duarte, J.A.: Analysis of data mining techniques for constructing a predictive model for academic performance. IEEE Latin Am. Trans. **14**(6), 2783–2788 (2016). https://doi.org/10.1109/TLA.2016.7555255
11. Zaffar, M., Hashmani, M.A., Savita, K.S.: Performance analysis of feature selection algorithm for educational data mining. In: IEEE Conference on Big Data and Analytics (ICBDA), Kuching, pp. 7–12 (2017). https://doi.org/10.1109/icbdaa.2017.8284099
12. Mishra, A., Bansal, R., Singh, S.N.: Educational data mining and learning analysis. In: 7th International Conference on Cloud Computing, Data Science and Engineering - Confluence, Noida, pp. 491–494 (2017). https://doi.org/10.1109/confluence.2017.7943201
13. Moscoso-Zea, O., Andres-Sampedro, Luján-Mora, S.: Datawarehouse design for educational data mining. In: 15th International Conference on Information Technology Based Higher Education and Training (ITHET), Istanbul, pp. 1–6 (2016). https://doi.org/10.1109/ithet. 2016.7760754
14. Kimball, R., Ross, M.: The Data Warehouse Toolkit. Wiley, Indianapolis (2013)
15. INEC: Ecuador en Cifras (Ecuador in figures) (2010). http://www.ecuadorencifras.gob.ec/ resultados/. Accessed 10 Nov 2018
16. Conadis: Estadística y análisis de datos de personas con discapacidad (Statistics and data analysis of people with disabilities) (2018). http://www.consejodiscapacidades.gob.ec/wp-content/uploads/downloads/2018/03/index.html. Accessed 04 Nov 2018

17. The PostgreSQL Global Development Group: Download PostgreSQL (2018). https://www.postgresql.org/download/. Accessed 04 Sept 2018
18. HITACHI: Hitachi Vantara (2018). http://www.pentaho.com/pentaho-community-edition-5-0-now-available. Accessed 04 May 2018
19. Conadis: Reglamento a la Ley Orgánica de Discapacidades del Ecuador (Regulation to the Organic Law on Disability of Ecuador) (2017). https://www.consejodiscapacidades.gob.ec/wp-content/plugins/download-monitor/download.php?id=19&force=1. Accessed 12 Feb 2017
20. The University of Waikato: Weka 3: Data Mining Software in Java (2018). https://www.cs.waikato.ac.nz/ml/weka/. Accessed 22 Mar 2018
21. Sierra, B.: Aprendizaje automático: conceptos básicos y avanzados (Machine learning: basic and advanced concepts). Prentice-Hall, Madrid (2006)
22. Pajares, G., de la Cruz, J.: Aprendizaje automático: un enfoque práctico (Machine learning: a practical approach). Madrid, Ra-Ma (2010)
23. Castillejo-González, I.L., López-Granados, F., García-Ferrer, A., Peña-Barragán, J.M., Jurado-Expósito, M., Sánchez De La Orden, M., et al.: Object and pixel-based classification for mapping crops and their agri-environmental associated measures in QuickBird images. Comput. Electron. Agric. **68**, 207–215 (2009)
24. Landis, J.R., Kock, G.G.: The measurement of observer agreement for categorical data. Biometrics **33**, 159–174 (1977)
25. Congalton, R.G.: A review of assessing the accuracy of classification of remotely sensed data. Remote Sens. Environ. **37**, 35–46 (1991)
26. Saito, T., Rehmsmeier, M.: The precision-recall plot is more informative than the ROC plot when evaluating binary classifiers on imbalanced datasets. PLoS ONE **10**(3), e0118432 (2015). https://doi.org/10.1371/journal.pone.0118432. Ed. by Brock, G.
27. MathWorks (2018). Mastering Machine Learning. https://es.mathworks.com/campaigns/products/offer/mastering-machine-learning-with-matlab.html
28. Jeni, L.A., Cohn, J.F., De La Torre, F.: Facing imbalanced data–recommendations for the use of performance metrics. In: Humaine Association Conference on Affective Computing and Intelligent Interaction, Geneva, pp. 245–251 (2013). https://doi.org/10.1109/acii.2013.47

An Evolutionary Intelligent Approach
for the LTI Systems Identification
in Continuous Time

Luis Morales[1]([✉]), Oscar Camacho[1], Danilo Chávez[1],
and José Aguilar[2]

[1] Dpto. de Automatización y Control Industrial, Escuela Politécnica Nacional,
Quito, Ecuador
{luis.moralesec,oscar.camacho,
danilo.chavez}@epn.edu.ec
[2] Universidad de Los Andes, Mérida 5101, Venezuela
aguilar@ula.ve

Abstract. Identification and modeling of systems are the first stage for development and design of controllers. For this purpose, as an alternative to conventional modeling approaches we propose using two methods of evolutionary computing: Genetic Algorithms (GA) and Particle Swarm Optimization (PSO to create an algorithm for modeling Linear Time Invariant (LTI) systems of different types. Integral Square Error (ISE) is the objective function to minimize, which is calculated between the outputs of the real system and the model. Unlike other works, the algorithms make a search of the most approximate model based on four of the most common ones found in industrial processes: systems of first order, first order plus time delay, second order and inverse response. The estimated models by our algorithms are compared with the obtained by other analytical and heuristic methods, in order to validate the results of our approach.

Keywords: System modeling · System identification · Genetic algorithms
Particle swarm optimization

1 Introduction

In control systems, identification of invariant models in continuous or discrete time is one of the main steps to be carried out regarding the design of controllers and calibration of parameters. In general, the models can have different structures, depending on the intrinsic characteristics of the process; however, at the level of real applications, complex process approximations can be made to linear and reduced order models (at their operational points). So, there are different methods used to perform the identification of a system, some of them are analytical one, based on principles such as laws of physics, thermodynamics and so on; and the other ones based on experiments, which use particular input signals applied to a system to observe the behavior of the output, and based on it try to determine their respective parameters [1]. This is one of the most common methodologies for the case of reduced order systems. For second order

© Springer Nature Switzerland AG 2019
M. Botto-Tobar et al. (Eds.): CITT 2018, CCIS 895, pp. 430–445, 2019.
https://doi.org/10.1007/978-3-030-05532-5_32

systems, a similar methodology has been developed, however, these analyzes require the measurement of different characteristic parameters of the reaction curve, which is a tedious procedure that takes time [2].

In [3] it is proposed a computer tool that allows the modeling of systems, as mentioned above, using input and output data from the system, in which an analysis of different model estimation methods is done through the toolbox CONTSID (CONtinuous-Time System IDentification). CONTSID uses linear filters, integral methods, modulation functions, among others. However, iterative or recursive methods are not studied, which will be considered in this work. [3–5] are works in which models are estimated by heuristic optimization techniques, such as Genetic Algorithms (GA); nevertheless, they do not consider finding a reduced order model, or they have not been used to model systems with time delay or with inverse response. In works such as [6, 7], the optimization of model parameters is done using Particle Swarm Optimization (PSO) [8]. Both, GA and PSO algorithms, are iterative methods that do not disturb or affect the normal performance of the real plant (since they work offline), so they are very useful for the identification of plant's dynamics using the input and output data of the real system. In these previous works, it is essential to know a priori model from which the parameters will be optimized; however, the algorithms do not have the intelligence to find the simplest model that follows the real system, which is a great disadvantage.

In order to discover these models, this paper proposes an intelligent approach that, unlike works presented in [4–8], looks for the simplest reduced order model that fits a real system, using its input and output data. Thereby, we propose an approach that performs the parameterization of four of the most commonly found models in automatic control focused on industrial processes, these are: first order, first order plus time delay, second order, and inverse response. Our approach makes a search of the most similar model (optimal parameters) to the real system based on the input and output data, starting this search in the simplest model (few variables), until the inverse response model (more variables), with the aim of decreasing the computational cost. Our approach uses GA and PSO, and stops when the objective function, in this case the Integral Square Error "ISE", is lower than the threshold established by the user.

The advantage of our approach is that it reduces the estimation time of the model and does not necessarily require a priori knowledge of the real model. Two intelligent computing techniques have been used to discover the most approximate model, which are compared with the analytical results. The motivation to use PSO and GA, is to perform a comparative analysis of the results obtained in the estimation of the models with each method, as an alternative to conventional modeling approaches.

2   Theoretical Framework

In the field of control systems, it is very important for the design of controllers, to know the dynamic behavior of the plant and its mathematical model. In this section is presented a brief description of the most common system models in control.

2.1 Commonly Models in Control Systems

A classical SISO (single-input, single-output) model of continuous time LTI systems can be represented by Eq. (1).

$$y(s) = G(s)u(s) \tag{1}$$

With:

$$G(s) = \frac{b(s)}{a(s)} = \frac{b_0 + b_1 s + \ldots + b_j s^j}{a_0 + a_1 s + \ldots + a_k s^k} e^{-t_0 s}; k \geq j \tag{2}$$

Where: b_i and a_i are the parameters of the transfer function, and t_0 is the dead time. These parameters are unknown, and must be identified by our intelligent algorithm, $u(s)$ is the input, $y(s)$ is the output of the system, and "s" is the operator d/dt.

The identification of the system is the first step to be considered in the design of a controller, and different methods can be used. Model estimation consists of two stages: the selection of an appropriate model (which can often be complicated), and the estimation of its parameters [6]. Currently, many model structures are known that describe the behavior of different types of systems in a very precise way; therefore, the aim is to determine their respective parameters. The dynamic properties of systems can be approximated by the temporal characteristics of simpler systems. Simple models are understood as those that define their dynamics by linear differential equations of first or second order. Reduced order models are commonly found in the field of industrial process, robotics, etc. In this section are presented the models used in this work.

2.2 First-Order Systems (FO)

The order of a system corresponds to the degree of its characteristic polynomial. The transfer function of a first-order system is:

$$G(s) = \frac{K}{Ts + 1} \tag{3}$$

Where K is the static gain, and T the response time (time constant).

In a first-order system, its parameters can be determined experimentally by means of the observation of the response produced in the system by a step input. The static gain "K" will be the final value of the output signal, and the time constant "T" approximates the time that output reaches about 63% of the value of the stationary gain. Figure 1 shows the characteristic response of a first-order system by a step input.

In real cases, when the value of the input variable is modified, the effect of that change on the dynamic response of the system is not immediately observed, it can take some time for the system to start responding to the effect of the change made (see

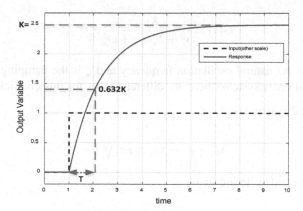

Fig. 1. First-order system response

Fig. 2), which is known as the "first order plus time delay" system (FOPTD). t_0 is the time that system takes to respond. In this case, the transfer function is given by:

$$G(s) = \frac{Ke^{-t_0 s}}{Ts + 1} \tag{4}$$

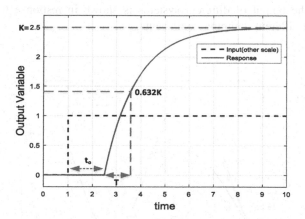

Fig. 2. First-order plus time delay system response

2.3   Second-Order Systems (SO)

The dynamics of a LTI system can be defined by the roots of the denominator. The nature of this expression can be real or complex. If it is real, the response to the input to the step will be defined by the next expression.

$$G(s) = \frac{K\omega_n}{s^2 + 2\xi\omega_n s + \omega_n^2} e^{-t_0 s} \tag{5}$$

Where ω_n is the natural oscillation frequency and ξ is the damping coefficient. For a second order system, there are different cases for this coefficient:

- Underdamped system $0 < \xi < 1$:

$$s_1, s_2 = -\xi\omega_n \pm j\omega_n\sqrt{1 - \xi^2} \tag{6}$$

- Critically damped system $\xi = 1$:

$$s_1, s_2 = -\omega_n \tag{7}$$

- Overdamped system $\xi > 1$:

$$s_1, s_2 = -\xi\omega_n \pm \omega_n\sqrt{\xi^2 - 1}; \tag{8}$$

- Undamped system $\xi = 0$:

$$s_1, s_2 = \pm j\omega_n \tag{9}$$

In Fig. 3, the output of different systems is shown in response to a step input, considering the different damping coefficients.

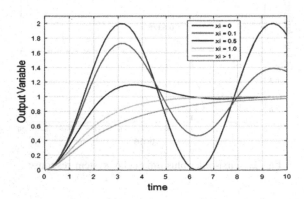

Fig. 3. Second order system response

2.4   Inverse Response Systems (IR)

In these systems, when a step input is applied, the response of the system first decreases until it reaches a minimum, and then begins to "rise" until it reaches the new stationary state, as is shown in Fig. 4. An inverse response system can be represented by:

$$G(s) = \frac{K(-T_3 s + 1)}{(T_1 s + 1)(T_2 s + 1)} \tag{10}$$

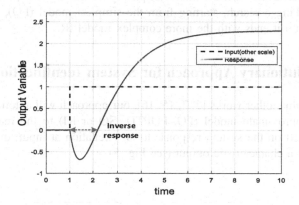

Fig. 4. Inverse response system

These models can be understood as the interaction of slow and fast dynamics, and can be represented as the difference of two systems of first order [9]:

$$G(s) = \frac{K_1}{T_1 s + 1} - \frac{K_2}{T_2 s + 1} \tag{11}$$

With the condition:

$$\frac{T_1}{T_2} > \frac{K_1}{K_2} > 1 \tag{12}$$

2.5   System Identification Problem

The estimation of the aforementioned models can be performed analytically (mathematically), which is well defined in the literature for the case of first and second order systems [1, 9], and for inverse response systems [10], by means of a graphic estimation and calculations that in some cases require a lot of time, and do not guarantee the best possible approximation. Intelligent computing has been used in the field of control systems, both for the identification of systems (estimation) [11, 12], and in the control itself; for example, to determine the optimal parameters of a controller [3].

In this work is proposed the identification of reduced order models based on two well-known techniques of evolutionary computation, such as: GA [13] and PSO [14]. For that, it is necessary to have the input and output data as system information, and based on this, estimate the model closest to the real one.

The algorithms proposed by other authors have the disadvantage that the user must know a priori the type of model, and based on this, it calculates its parameters, which does not guarantee to obtain the most suitable model. Hence, the need for an intelligent approach that approximates the real system to the model of reduced order that most resembles, for example of first order, first order plus time delay, second order, or inverse response, which are the most frequently found in real processes. In our approach is making a search, starting from the simplest model (FO), going through FOPTD, SO, until it ends with the more complex model IR.

3   Our Evolutionary Approach for System Identification

In this paper, unlike other works [5–7, 15, 16], our approach will automatically search for the most approximate model (FO, FOPTD, SO or RI) to the real system. Our approach is based on the system response to an excitation at input, due to that each system type has a characteristic output (see Fig. 5).

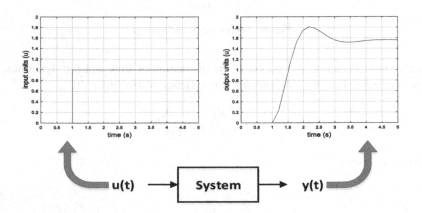

Fig. 5. Schematic of input-output data of a system

The scheme of our proposed approach is shown in Fig. 6. Once the input and output data of the real system has been acquired, one of the algorithms (GA and PSO) is executed, considering an initial structure (in this case, the simplest one, corresponding to a FO model). Once the optimization has been completed, it is verified that the ISE is lower than a given threshold (TH), a value that must be calibrated heuristically, and depends on factors such as, the maximum value of the output, the noise in the data, etc. If the condition is not met, then the model does not correspond to a FO model. So, the algorithm is executed for a FOPDT system estimation. If the ISE at the end of the optimization is below the threshold, then it is determined that the model obtained corresponds to this type of system. However, if this condition is not met, then the same procedure is performed for a SO model and an IR model. In case where it is not found an ISE lower than the threshold in any of the models, the algorithm will give the parameters of the estimated model with the lowest ISE, that is, the model closest to the real one.

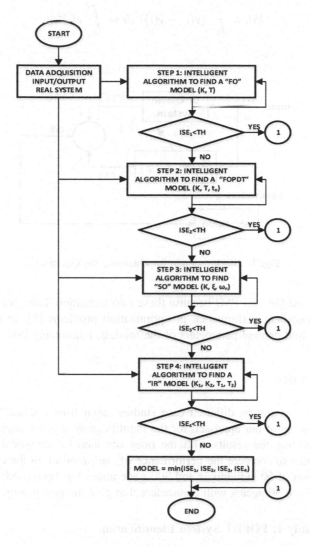

Fig. 6. Block diagram for the proposed algorithm

In this way, the algorithm makes an automatic estimation starting from the simplest model with fewer variables, to the most complex model with more variables. This allows to decrease the search time of the best estimate, since if it finds a good esti-mation represented by the simplest model, then it is not necessary to keep running the algorithm to find other more complex models.

For the identification of the model, our approach minimizes an objective function based on the Integral Square Error (ISE). In Fig. 7 is shown how is obtained this metric, whose mathematical expression is:

$$ISE = \int_0^T (y(t) - \hat{y}(t))^2 dt = \int_0^T e(t)^2 dt \tag{13}$$

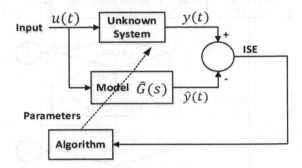

Fig. 7. Block diagram for obtaining the ISE metric

We have used GA and PSO because these two techniques have been well studied and have an excellent performance in optimization problems [8]. In our case, it is appropriate to find optimal parameters of the models, minimizing ISE.

4   Experiments

In this section, we present different case studies taken from different references, to verify the accuracy of our approach for the identification of some simulated and real systems, contrasting the results with the ones obtained by analytical and heuristic methods, in order to compare the performance of our proposal. In the case of GA, an initial population of 50 individuals and 300 generations has been used; in the case of PSO, it starts with 30 agents with parameters that give the best results.

4.1   Case Study 1: FOPDT System Identification

The simulation is performed for the identification of a FOPDT model where there is a random variation of the input (see Fig. 8). The model is easily estimated by our approach in the first stages, determining the parameters shown in the Table 1.

Table 1. Results of the FOPDT system identification

$$G(s) = \frac{-2.47}{3.7s+1}e^{-1.3}$$
$$K = -2.47; \tau = 3.7[s]; t_0 = 1.3[s]$$

Parameters	K	$\tau[s]$	$t_0[s]$	ISE
Real	−2.47	3.70	1.30	
GA	−2.46	3.66	1.28	2.57
Relative error GA	0.40%	1.08%	1.5%	
PSO	−2.46	3.73	1.29	2.34
Relative error PSO	0.40%	0.81%	0.76%	

According to Fig. 8, it is evident that the two algorithms provide values close to the real values; however, PSO is the most accurate, with a lower relative error in all its parameters. It is also observed that estimation is correct, even though the input signal is very variable.

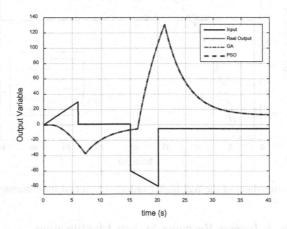

Fig. 8. Comparison of the real FOPDT and the estimated models

4.2 Case Study 2: Higher Order System Identification

Our approach is tested in a higher order system, taken from the example 6.4 presented in [17]. In that work, its approximated models are based on two analytical approaches, which we use to compare them with the results obtained by our proposed. These results are shown in the Table 2.

The results of PSO are the best, followed by the analytical method of Skogestad. In the case of GA, the ISE is not the best because it needs a calibration of its initial parameters (initial population and number of generations) to avoid falling into a local minimum in models of this type; however, its results are better than Taylor Series analytical method, with less time and without the need of mathematical calculations.

Figure 9 shows the response of the real system and of all the estimated models.

Table 2. Results of the higher order system identification

$$G(s) = \frac{1.5(-0.1s+1)}{(5s+1)(3s+1)(0.5s+1)} \ (real \ system)$$

Method	Best estimation	ISE
GA	$G(s) = \frac{1.51}{4.97S+1}e^{-3.13s}$	0.106
PSO	$G(s) = \frac{1.51}{6.89S+1}e^{-2.25s}$	0.025
Analytical 1 (Skogestad)	$G(s) = \frac{1.50}{6.50S+1}e^{-? \cdot 10s}$	0.037
Analytical 2 (Taylor Series)	$G(s) = \frac{1.50}{5.00S+1}e^{-3.60s}$	0.130

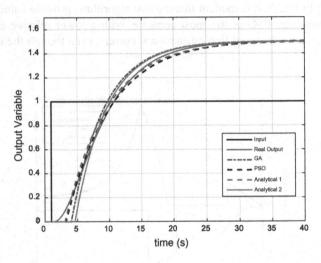

Fig. 9. Comparison of the real higher order system and the estimated models

4.3 Case Study 3: Inverse Response System Identification

For the next test is used the case study presented in [10], where an isothermal continuous stirred tank reactor (CSTR) is considered, from which an analytical model is proposed. In this system, a change of 10% in the manipulated variable (flow through the reactor) occurs, and the response to the output or controlled variable (concentration) is observed, as is shown in the Fig. 10. Results obtained with our approach and analytically, are presented in the Table 3.

In general, PSO and GA propose a very good approximation with respect to the analytical model. This last requires an analytical-graphic analysis considering at least three points of the response curve, and then it performs several mathematical calculations, and a parameter adjustment, which involve a lot of time with respect to the runtime of our approach.

Table 3. Results of the inverse response system identification

Method	Best estimation	ISE
GA	$G(s) = \dfrac{0.78}{0.64s+1} - \dfrac{0.46}{0.24s+1}$	0.0061
PSO	$G(s) = \dfrac{0.95}{0.59s+1} - \dfrac{0.63}{0.27s+1}$	0.0032
Analytical (Balaguer Method)	$G(s) = \dfrac{0.32(-0.35s+1)}{(0.56s+1)(0.31s+1)}$	0.0022

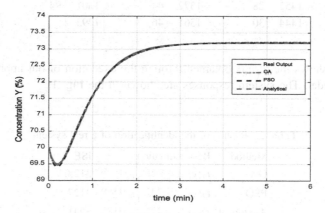

Fig. 10. Comparison of the real inverse response system and the estimated models

4.4   Case Study 4: Identification of a Real System

For this case study, the exercise 10-2 presented in [1] is used, which corresponds to the reactor of the Fig. 11. Once the system is stable at the temperature of 1463 °F, a change of 5% is made in the opening of the fuel valve (input variable with negative step), taking the data (temperature) shown in the Table 4.

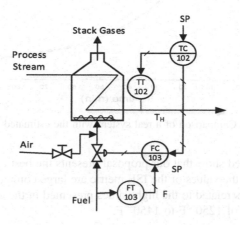

Fig. 11. Schematic of the real process of a heater system (Reactor)

Table 4. Real data of the process of a heater system

Time [min]	T [°F]	Time [min]	T [°F]	Time [min]	T [°F]	Time [min]	T [°F]
0	1463	16	1435	32	1351	48	1287
2	1463	18	1426	34	1341	50	1281
4	1463	20	1415	36	1332	52	1275
6	1463	22	1405	38	1324	54	1275
8	1461	24	1393	40	1316	56	1263
10	1457	26	1382	42	1308	58	1258
12	1452	28	1372	44	1301	94	1235
14	1444	30	1361	46	1293		

Table 5, shows the results obtained through the execution of our approach and an analytical model. The system responses are shown in the Fig. 12.

Table 5. Results of the identification of a real system

Method	Best estimation	ISE
GA	$G(s) = \frac{2.37}{26.02s+1}e^{-13.95s}$	3128
PSO	$G(s) = \frac{2.38}{25.97s+1}e^{-13.95s}$	3127
Analytical	$G(s) = \frac{2.28}{23.25s+1}e^{-14.75s}$	5241

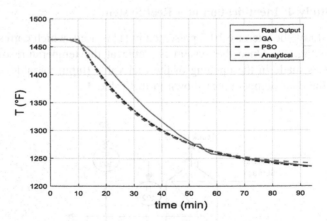

Fig. 12. Comparison of a real system with the estimated models

The results obtained show that our proposal presents the best approximation. It can also be observed that the values of the ISE metric are large compared to the other case studies, because this is related to the high values presented in the output of the system, which is in the order of 1250 °F to 1450 °F.

4.5   Case Study 5: System with Noisy Data

The following experiment is based on the example 6.2 shown in [9]. This is a system with realistic data set for the two stirred-tank heating. The data has noise, which may be due to imperfect mixing, noise in the sensors, among other causes. The estimations of our approach have been compared with the values obtained by means of two analytical strategies presented in [1], which are shown in Table 6.

Table 6. Results of the identification of system with noisy data

Method	Best estimation	ISE
GA	$G(s) = \frac{2.60}{5.55s+1}e^{-4.23s}$	13.95
PSO	$G(s) = \frac{2.74}{7.31s+1}e^{-3.27s}$	13.75
Analytical 1	$G(s) = \frac{2.60}{10.80s+1}e^{-2.40s}$	82.83
Analytical 2	$G(s) = \frac{2.60}{5.90s+1}e^{-3.70s}$	14.03

The PSO algorithm provides the most approximate model, despite the presence of noise in the data (see Fig. 13), showing that the approach performs well, even if a filter has not been placed at the input. One important remark is that our approach determines automatically that the best model is a SO, using GA or PSO.

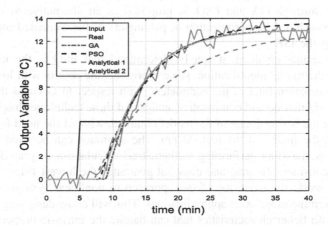

Fig. 13. Comparison of a real system with noisy data and the estimated models

5   Discussion

Based on the results obtained, it is important to differentiate the advantages from the quantitative and qualitative point of view of our approach.

Regarding the quantitative point of view, it can be observed that in most experiments, PSO is the technique that presents the best approximations of the test model, with lower ISE values, even comparing them with analytical models. In the case of inverse response systems, the approximation is quite good, but the Balaguer method [10] has the best estimation; however, it requires mathematical calculations that involve a lot of time.

From the qualitative point of view, it has been possible to observe several advantages with respect to other similar works, such as:

- It is not necessary to know a priori the model to be estimated, because the algorithm automatically finds the reduced order model closest to the real one.
- In the case of data with noise, the algorithm finds the closest model, without the need for additional filters.
- The runtime of the algorithm is low and can be considered as a very good alternative to analytical methods.
- In previous works, we have used genetic programming in identification problems, but the expressions they give are very complex, which are not useful to build later controllers [11, 12]. Our approach based on an optimization problem allows us reusing the classic control models to solve the identification problem.

6 Conclusions

In this paper, an evolutionary intelligent approach for the identification of reduced order models, through GA and PSO, is proposed as an alternative to conventional modeling approaches. The optimization of parameters of the estimated model is done by minimizing the ISE.

From the results obtained, it can be determined that PSO is the most suitable algorithm for the model identification, since it presents the results with lower ISE and reduces the estimation time of the parameters, with respect to GA and the analytical methods. The simulation and comparative analysis of these techniques has been carried out, observing the best estimate of the model obtained, without the need for the user to know a priori the model of the real system. The approach can be used for adaptive control systems, avoiding performing mathematical calculations or graphic estimation that requires considerable time, and does not guarantee the lowest ISE.

As future work, the extension of our approach to nonlinear systems will be considered to determine more exact approximations. This will allow designing more robust controllers, with better characteristics that can handle the intrinsic properties of these systems, which are generally found in real industrial processes. At the same time, the extension of this proposal to discrete models will be of great help, since most systems are measured with digital instruments. This will allow a better modeling of real plants.

References

1. Smith, C., Corripio, A.: Principles and Practice of Automatic Process Control, 3rd edn. Wiley, New York (2006)
2. Johnson, M., Moradi, M.: PID Control - New Identification and Design Methods. Springer, London (2005). https://doi.org/10.1007/1-84628-148-2
3. Kristinsson, K., Dumont, G.A.: System identification and control using genetic algorithms. IEEE Trans. Syst. Man. Cybern. **22**(5), 1033–1046 (1992)
4. Johnson, T., Husbands, P.: System identification using genetic algorithms. In: Parallel Problem Solving from Nature, no. 1, pp. 85–89. Springer, Heidelberg (1991)
5. Zhang, R., Tao, J.: A nonlinear fuzzy neural network modeling approach using an improved genetic algorithm. IEEE Trans. Ind. Electron. **65**(7), 5882–5892 (2018)
6. Alfi, A., Modares, H.: System identification and control using adaptive particle swarm optimization. Appl. Math. Model. **35**(3), 1210–1221 (2011)
7. Dub, M., Stefek, A.: Mechatronics 2013. Springer, Cham (2014)
8. Hassan, R., Cohanim, B., de Weck, O., Venter, G.: A comparison of particle swarm optimization and the genetic algorithm. In: 46th AIAA/ASME/ASCE/AHS/ASC Structures, Structural Dynamics and Materials Conference, no. April, pp. 1–13 (2005)
9. Marlin, T.: Process Control. Design Processes and Control System for Dynamic Performance. McGraw Hill, New York (1995)
10. Balaguer, P., Alfaro, V., Arrieta, O.: Second order inverse response process identification from transient step response. ISA Trans. **50**(2), 231–238 (2011)
11. Aguilar, J., Cerrada, M.: Genetic programming-based approach for system identification. Adv. Fuzzy Syst. Evol. Comput. Artif. Intell. 329–324 (2001)
12. Carabalí, C.A., Tituaña, L., Aguilar, J., Camacho, O., Chavez, D.: Inverse response systems identification using genetic programming. In: Proceedings of the 14th International Conference on Informatics in Control, Automation and Robotics, vol. 1, no. Icinco, pp. 238–245 (2017)
13. Tang, H., Xue, S., Fan, C.: Differential evolution strategy for structural system identification. Comput. Struct. **86**(21–22), 2004–2012 (2008)
14. Venter, G., Sobieszczanski-Sobieski, J.: Particle swarm optimization. AIAA J. **41**(8), 1583–1589 (2003)
15. Aguilar, J.: The evolutionary programming in the identification of discreet events dynamic systems. IEEE Lat. Am. Trans. **5**(5), 301–310 (2007)
16. Garnier, H., Mensler, M., Richard, A.: Continuous-time model identification from sampled data: implementation issues and performance evaluation. Int. J. Control **76**(13), 1337–1357 (2003)
17. Seborg, D., Edgar, T., Mellichamp, D., Doyle, F.: Process Dynamics and Control, 3rd edn. Wiley, New York (2011)

Geographical Information System Based on Artificial Intelligence Techniques

Nayi Sánchez Fleitas[1]([⊠]) [iD], Raúl Comas Rodríguez[2]([⊠]) [iD],
María Matilde García Lorenzo[1] [iD], and Frankz Carrera[2]([⊠]) [iD]

[1] Universidad Central "Marta Abreu" de Las Villas,
50100 Santa Clara, Villa Clara, Cuba
nayi78@gmail.com, mmgarcia@uclv.edu.ec
[2] Universidad Regional Autónoma de los Andes,
Ambato 180101, Tungurahua, Ecuador
raulcomasrodriguez@gmail.com, frankzcarrera@gmail.com

Abstract. The Electrical Union in Cuba develops the Business Management System of the Electrical Union (SIGE) that focuses on the automation of electrical processes. The geographic information systems (SIGOBE) developed don't meet the specific requirements for their generalization due to their limited updating facilities and the small spectrum they cover. The general objective of the research is: to develop the geographic information system of the transmission and distribution processes in the Electric Union, with the use of artificial intelligence techniques, on a deep conceptual scheme of the domain, that responds to the requests of consultation of users as support for decision making. A case-based system on type problem solved was designed, using as an initial case database, the 265 static queries registered in SIGERE. The queries are described by eight data-type predictive traits and three objective traits. The similarity between two cases was determined by the weighted sum of the distance of their traits and the calculation of the distance between traits was done according to its nature. An intelligent real-time queries system was implemented for the SIGOBE, achieving the generation of automatic queries that allow the system to respond to any type of queries in real-time. The experimental study shows the feasibility of the proposal.

Keywords: Geographical information system · Artificial intelligence
Case-based system

1 Introduction

Energy is one of the supports of development in production processes, social progress and technological progress [1, 2]. In this sense, technology has allowed to increase the decisions to make in the energetic production chain. In this environment, the stakeholders need management systems that serve as support for the decision making process, to ensure a more efficient sector [3].

The Electrical Union (UNE, Spanish acronym) in Cuba develops the Business Management System of the Electrical Union (SIGE) for the automation of electrical

M. Botto-Tobar et al. (Eds.): CITT 2018, CCIS 895, pp. 446–461, 2019.
https://doi.org/10.1007/978-3-030-05532-5_33

processes [4]. SIGE is composed of two main subsystems: the Integral System of Network Management (SIGERE) and the Integral Management System of the Electrical Industry Construction Enterprise (SIGECIE).

The functions of SIGERE and SIGECIE are to collect technical, economic and management data to convert them into information. The data collected facilitate and improve the efficiency in the analysis, planning, operation, and control of the distribution and transmission electricity networks. Both systems establish the databases of a Geographic Information System (GIS) of the SIGE.

SIGERE and SIGECIE are considered complex systems because they have 36 modules and a database of: 716 tables, 1303 stored procedures and 74 functions. In addition, other functionalities are in development phase. An average action in the system involves approximately nine tables with different attributes. To carry out a query on a specific topic requires knowledge of the database organization. Despite the number of stored queries, they still do not cover the needs of the customer due to the operational dynamics of the national electro-energy system.

To solve this problem, an analysis of the literature is carried out and a group of experts on the subject is gathered. As a result of the previous analysis is decided:

- Conduct a national tour of all the electric companies and groups of the ECIE for the study of possible solutions.
- Search for information on the subject in the literature.

The geographic information systems developed for the electricity companies in the country do not meet the specific requirements for their generalization due to: their limited updating facilities and the small spectrum they cover. The main limitations found in the analyzed solutions are: fixed queries that are limited, the use of proprietary software and the short validity of the data that are inserted into the map. An investigation is made of existing GIS in the world and the current trends of its development.

Information technologies have evolved towards the construction and implementation of intelligent systems [5–7]. In the 1970s, computerized systems that use knowledge about a domain to arrive at a solution to a problem; and the knowledge and the solution method are separated, are called Knowledge Based Systems (KBS) or Expert Systems (ES). This solution is essentially the same as that obtained by a person experienced in the domain if faced with the same problem.

The general objective of the research is: to develop the geographic information system of the transmission and distribution processes in the Electric Union, with the use of artificial intelligence techniques, on a deep conceptual scheme of the domain that responds to the requests of consultation of users as support for decision making.

2 Analysis of the Methodological Basis

Artificial Intelligence (AI) is the branch of computer science that attempts to reproduce the processes of human intelligence through the use of computers [8]. Within AI, the Expert Systems (ES) or Knowledge Based Systems (KBS) emerges as the field in charge of the study of: the knowledge acquisition, its representation and the generation of inferences about that knowledge. There are different variants to build the KBS based on the representation of knowledge and the method of inference to implement. Among the systems are: Rule Based Systems [9, 10], Frames Based Systems [11], Probability Based Systems [12], Expert Networks [13, 14], and Case-Based Systems or Case-Based Reasoning Systems (CBR) [15–18].

In this sense, CBRs appear as á palliative to the process of knowledge engineering and are based on the premise that: similar problems will have similar solutions [19, 20]. With this principle as the basis, the solution to a problem is retrieved from a memory of solved examples. For each case, the most similar previous experiences that allow finding the new solutions are taken into account [21, 22].

The CBRs need a collection of experiences, called cases, stored in a case database, where each case is usually composed of the description of the problem and the solution applied [23]. Case-based reasoning contributes to progressive learning, so that the domain does not need to be fully represented [24]. The CBRs have three main components: the user interface, the knowledge base and the inference engine [25, 26].

2.1   Case Database

A case contains useful information in a specific context, the problem is to identify the attributes that characterize the context and to detect when two contexts are similar. Kolodner defines that "a case is a contextualized knowledge that represents an experience" and it is described by the values that are assigned predictive and objective traits [27].

To provide the system with a conceptual basis the traits can be organized through ontology. The fundamental role of ontology is to structure and retrieve knowledge, to promote its exchange and communication [28–30]. In addition, relying solely on CBR for distributed and complex applications, can lead to systems being ineffective in knowledge acquisition and indexing [31]. According to Bouhana, et al. [32] use of ontologies in case-based reasoning gives the following benefits:

- It is an easy-to-use tool for case representation.
- Queries are defined using daily terminology.
- It facilitates the assessment of similarity.
- It increases system performance.

A lightweight ontology is provided to the system to give a conceptual basis. In the conceptualization we have the concepts of taxonomy and relations (objects properties). The remaining components of the ontology model (data properties, instances and axioms) aren't developed because the information is already in the database that feeds the system. The ontology was carried out using the Methontology methodology and the Protégé tool [33].

With the ontology the system gives a conceptual basis. Nevertheless, a weakness of the systems proposed is in the dissatisfaction with the queries carried out. If a static inquiry is developed for each problem that arises, the database begins to store a group of scarcely-used queries. In order to solve the problem, the system must be able to generate intelligent queries in real-time, in which the knowledge obtained from previous ones is used.

The success of the Case Based Systems (CBS) is achieved in the knowledge acquisition module because: the basic elements of the problem or domain to be solved are described, and the way to facilitate the representation of the knowledge of the expert is looked [34]. To form the Case Based (BC), systems and subsystems that generate data or information in the knowledge acquisition process must be analyzed.

This domain contains alphanumeric and geographic information. The geographic data correspond to the cartography that can be downloaded from the internet or buy from an enterprise. With the data it obtain the spatial position of the object. The elements of the monolineal are the basic elements of the electrical network that are represented in correspondence with their characteristics in the vectorial scheme, which occupy a position in the geographical space (Table 1).

Table 1. Representation of the network in vectorial scheme.

Points (support points)	Lines (circuit)	Polygons (substation)
Posts	Transmission circuit	Distribution substation
Transformer banks	Subtransmission circuit	Transmission substation
Capacitor banks	Primary circuit	
Generator groups	Secondary circuit	
Disconnectors	Lighting circuit	
Structures		
Lamps		

The data provided by the SIGERE and SIGECIE modules are stored in the database. The database of the SIGERE has 716 tables, 1303 stored procedures and 74 functions; therefore, any query can have a high degree of complexity. For example, a query action, to the transformer module, involves an average of nine tables and approximately 140 attributes. SIGERE and SIGECIE differ in the voltage levels they cover.

A simple query of the SIGOBE (E1), becomes three queries to the system (C1, C2, C3). The steps to perform the development of a query are: 1- (E1) Query entry; 2- (C1) Request of the user; 3- (C2) Query of the database; 4- (C3) Query to the cartographical data; 5- Show C3; 6- Build legend; 7- Locate selection and show the legend.

In the case of a query that has two or more conditions $x_1, x_2, \ldots, x_n$, then $Q(x_1, x_2, \ldots, x_n)$ provides a solution set of S. If the query is decomposed into n simple queries $Q(x_n)$, which provide n solution sets $S_1, S_2, \ldots, S_n$; then, the solution set corresponds to the union, intersection or the Cartesian product of these sets.

$$Q(x_1, x_2, \ldots, x_n) = S \rightarrow Q(x_1) \ op \ Q(x_2) op. \ldots op \ Q(x_n) = S \qquad (1)$$

Where

$Q(x_1, x_2, \ldots, x_n)$: query.

$x_1, x_2, \ldots, x_n$: terms.

op: operator ($\cap / \cup / X$) of the sets resulting from the queries.

S: solution set.

For the research, it's necessary to define a group of experts that provide data and knowledge. In the creation of the group, we work with the methodology proposed by [35], the number of experts needed is calculated using the probabilistic method of the binomial distribution coefficient, an initial list of possible experts is determined and a questionnaire is applied to determine the competence coefficient in correspondence with: years of experience, levels of knowledge and source of acquisition.

To determine the structure of the case, the group of experts brainstorms and determines that each case is composed of eleven fundamental traits: eight predictive traits and three objectives. Figure 1 shows the structure of a case. In the Table 2 identifies the universe of discourse of the predictive and objective traits.

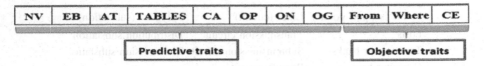

Fig. 1. Cases structure.

Table 2. Universe of discourse of predictive and objective traits

Trait	Possible values	Type
Predictive traits		
NV	Secondary, primary, subtransmission, transmission	Symbolic and single-valued
EB	Posts, transformer banks, capacitor banks, generator groups, disconnectors, structures, lamps, transmission circuit, subtransmission circuit, primary circuit, secondary circuit, lighting circuit, distribution substation, transmission substation	Symbolic and single-valued
AT	Attributes to be returned by the inquiry (code, voltage, name, etc.)	Set
Tables	Tables of the SIGERE involved in the inquiry (accessories, actions, connection, interruptions, line, currentSupplyPrimary, etc....).	Set
CA	Element to compare (attribute being compared)	Symbolic and single-valued
ON	Operator ($\cup$, $\cap$, $\leq$ $\geq$ =, like, etc.)	Symbolic and single-valued
OP	Ontology (descriptive logic) T $\cap$ TP $\cap$ TMon¬SSecon	Ontology
OG	Spatial constraint (descriptive logic)	Ontology
Objective traits		
From	Returns the From of the inquiry to the SIGERE	String
Where	Returns the Where of the inquiry to the SIGERE	String
CE	Returns the GIS inquiry	String

The ON and OG ontological traits are represented by descriptive logic. A possible value of the ON trait would be: T ∩ TPot ∩ TMonophasic ⌐ SSecondary. This range expresses that the element is a monophasic primary transformer without secondary output.

OG works similarly, but their relationship is spatial, an example that refers to the location of an element would be: P ∩ Prov ∩ Muncp. This example expresses that an element belongs to the country (P), to a province (Prov) and to a municipality (Muncp).

As the ontology becomes deeper the element to be consulted fulfills requirements that can be flexible to the user. For one element to be similar to another it doesn't need to be at the same level in the ontology, but it must have gone through the same branch. The degree of importance of each level decreases as one goes deeper in the tree.

In the present investigation for the organization of the CB a hierarchical structure is used because: it favors the system, the access process and the recovery of the most similar cases. To do this, an analysis of the traits is made that allows to discriminate more options in each case.

Sixteen possible structures were tested (Table 3), for which the relationship between: the quality of the generator (percentage of well generated cases) and the complexity of the recuperator (percentage of recovered cases) is established. It was decided that NV was the root of the tree because of the importance of the trait. Additionally, since EB only belongs to one voltage level it does not make sense to put the NV below EB; the number of cases recovered does not change and the three structures contain the EB above the OP. Therefore, the best variant is NV - EB - OP (11), where the highest classification percentage is reached with the lowest percentage of recovered cases.

Table 3. Possible structures were tested.

Heading level	1st level	2nd levels	3rd levels
Without structure (1)	NV (2)	NV - EB (5)	NV - EB - OP (11)
		NV - OP (6)	NV - OP - EB (12)
	EB (3)	EB - NV (7)	EB - NV - OP (13)
		EB - OP (8)	EB - OP - NV (14)
	OP (4)	OP - NV (9)	OP - NV - EB (15)
		OP - EB (10)	OP - EB - NV (16)

Figure 2 shows the hierarchical structure designed, where: NV is the root node; in the second lever EP and in the third level OP, for being discriminative elements. In the leaf nodes there is a subset of cases that represent the examples where the value of NV, EB and OP coincide, which reduces the search of cases in the database, by concentrating on a subset of cases that responds to the values given to the NV, EB and OP. In each case subbase there are 20 cases on average, which increases the speed of the recovery process.

In the present research there are three types of data: symbolic, set y ontologic; for which different distance measurements are used.

- NV, EB, CA and OP traits are symbolic and single-valued type, the distance used is Boolean [36].
- AT and Tables traits are of joint type and use Jaccard distance [37].
- The ON and OG traits represent the general and spatial ontologies and the distance used is Jaro-Winkler [38].

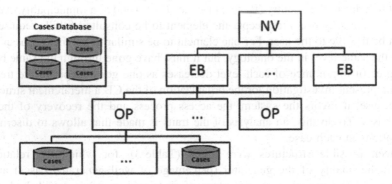

Fig. 2. Cases database structure for the UNE.

The recovery uses local comparison criteria or a local distance that determine the similarity or closeness between values of the same trait and a measure of global dissimilarity, which combines the results of the local criteria of all the predictive traits of the cases to be compared with the new problem.

The global dissimilarity measure used is the one proposed in [39]:

$$DisimGlobal(X, Y) = \left[\sum_{i=0}^{n} w_i * d_i(x_j, y_j) \right] / n \qquad (2)$$

The weights give a level of importance to each trait, the greater the wig the more important the trait. For the calculation of weights we work by means of expert criteria and the AHP method is used [40].

The objective is to recover the most similar k-cases, in a subset of the CB, which contain the cases with the same NV, EB and OP as the problem to be completed.

The correct dimension of the recovered cases was recalculated. Experiments were performed with odd k values from k = 1 to k = 11. As can be seen in Table 4, the results with k = 1 and k = 3 are very similar, but as the value of k increases, the percentage of correctly generated solutions decreases-e. It must be taken into account that the increase in the value of the k complicates the selection process of the initial solution.

Table 4. Possible K.

K	Correct generation	K	Correct generation
1	95.77%	7	89.41%
3	95.23%	9	83.49%
5	92.59%	11	78.83%

The recovered cases are combined together with the new case through the reuse of information. The solution proposal is made through similarity mechanisms that define the proximity or not of the recovered case, with the new one (Fig. 3).

In: P; problem to solve and $BC' = \{bc_1, bc_2, ..., bc_n\}$; sub-set of cases obtain of the sub-base that corresponds to the P case.

Out: Sets of K cases more similar.

$\forall\, bc_j \in BC'$ is calculated the SimGlobal(bc_j, P). Where:

$$SimGlobal(bc_j, P) = \sum_{i=0}^{8} w_i * d_i(bc_{ji}, P_i)/n$$

$$d_i(bc_{ji}, P_i) = \begin{cases} d_i(bc_{ji}, P_i) = \begin{cases} 0 \text{ Si } bc_{ji} == P_i \\ 1 \text{ Si } bc_{ji} \neq P_i \end{cases} & i = 1,2,5,6 \\ d_i(bc_{ji}, P_i) = \dfrac{|bc_{ji} \cap P_i|}{|bc_{ji} \cup P_i|} & i = 3,4 \\ d_i(bc_{ji}, P_i) = \dfrac{1}{3}\left(\dfrac{c}{|bc_{ji}|} + \dfrac{c}{|P_i|} + \dfrac{c - {}^t/_2}{c}\right) & i = 7,8 \end{cases}$$

The most similar K cases are returned with a K=3.

Fig. 3. Recuperator algorithm of k most similar cases.

Based on the transformational analogy, the Algorithm to propose an initial solution is developed. The new case is evaluated and adapted to the conditions on the recovered cases. The pre-set consultations are not necessarily identical to those stored in previous cases. To develop an initial solution, all recovered cases are considered and a combination of the recovered solutions is taken as a starting point.

2.2 Adaptation

The input of the adaptation module is an initial solution of the three objective traits. This module allows to reuse and adapt based on transformational analogy, which implies structural changes in the solution. Transformational adaptation is guided by common sense where the rules were defined and used in the adaptation process. This process is considered a T-space, where the known solution (KS) is going to be transformed with the use of T-operators (Table 5), until it becomes the solution of a new problem.

Table 5. T-operators according to the trait objective

From trait	Where trait	CE trait
Coupling insert	Insertion of restriction	Insertion of restriction
Coupling removal	Removal of restriction	Removal of restriction
Replacing coupling	Substitution in restriction	Substitution in restriction

Each T-operator is defined by a set of rules that perform the operation indicated. These rules perform a chain work that allows inserting, eliminating or replacing part of the solution to adapt it to the needs of the current problem. This work satisfies the restrictions imposed by the experts in domain ontologies and the natural requirements of objective traits. The adaptation module has three stages that are described below.

In stage 1 the review of the three objective trait has an algorithm of 25 rules that allow to check which traits are absent, which are valid and which ones need to adapt.

In stage 2, the set of rules to be applied is chosen according to the adaptation requirements of the previous stage in the following way:

- If there are no requirements, return the initial solution without adapting.
- If there is a requirement for the FROM trait, the set of rules is applied to adapt the FROM trait.
- If there is a requirement for the WHERE trait, the rule set is applied to adapt the WHERE trait.
- If there is a requirement for the CE trait, the set of rules is applied to adapt the CE trait.

In stage 3, a total of 65 adaptation rules are applied. The adaptation rules are divided into subsets by methods 5, 6, 7 and 8.

The methods 5 and 6 contain the set of 24 rules that allow you to adapt the FROM trait. This requirement can be given by:

- The initial result of the trait is absent since the FROM is an empty string or because $\forall Xi \in (Tablas) \mid Xi \notin From$.
- The solution does not contain the correct base table. The rules are responsible for finding the correct base table and replacing it in the initial solution. The replacement of the base table in the solution can lead to the previous one being related to it and replacing it would be a coupling of the new base table with it. The application of rule 7 eliminates this type of coupling.
- $\exists Xi \in (Tablas) \mid Xi \notin From$. In this case there would be no tables in the result, so the solution would be incomplete and it is necessary to add them coupled to the base table.
- $\exists Xi \in (From) \mid Xi \notin Tablas$. In this case, tables would be left over in the result and it is necessary to eliminate the coupling to the base table.
- After the base element is selected, the rest of the missing tables is added.

The method 7 contains the set of 27 rules that allow adapting the Where trait. These rules will be executed when the revision step establishes that the Where trait needs to be adapted. This requirement can be given by:

- The initial result of the Trait is absent because it is an empty string and the case has restrictions.
- The solution does not have the correct OP trait.
- The solution does not have the correct AC trait.
- The solution is not given according to the general ontology of the SIGERE system in the output, phase or type of correct installation.

The method 8 contains the set of 13 rules that allow the CE trait to be adapted. These rules will be executed when the revision step establishes that the CE trait needs to be adapted. This requirement can be given by the absence of any term of the spatial ontology in the query.

Once the adaptation and review of the expert, which confirms that the adaptation is correct, the case will be retained in the base of cases with the aim of enriching it with the solutions of new problems.

The retention is induced from the cases, so it will be necessary to redefine it periodically. The efficiency of the system is affected when the number of cases grows excessively, therefore, it is important to avoid including cases that do not contribute new information to the system.

To carry out the retention of cases, the following steps are followed:

- The degree of information provided by the case to the system is calculated. This degree of information is estimated by the number of T-operators applied between the set of T-operators in the T-space.
- It is considered feasible to retain the case whose degree of information provided is greater than α (represents an information threshold).
- If the case is feasible, it is retained in the corresponding sub-base according to the value of the NV, EB and OP predictive traits, given the calculation of the degree of information provided by an objective trait.

The degree of information provided to the system by the value of an objective trait is calculated as the minimum number of T-operators applied.

3   Results

For the implementation of the CBR, the SICUNE module was developed. The SICUNE module has a national character and is applied in different areas of the electricity companies. This software can be considered as a support system for decision making because it fulfills the following characteristics:

- It's focused on the analysis of the operational data of Cuban electric companies.
- Performs dynamic, flexible and interactive reports, in correspondence with the needs of the decision-making areas in the Cuban electricity companies.
- It presents rapidity in the response time.
- It has availability of historical information, managed in the databases of SIGERE and SIGECIE for more than 15 years.
- It uses in the main areas of knowledge management in the Cuban electricity companies that need graphic modeling.
- Main areas of knowledge management are present in the electricity companies that need graphic modeling.

The incorporation of SICUNE into the SIGOBE increases the spectrum of search requests and provides a group of facilities such as: locating complaints from the population, a failed installation or with abnormal parameters, organizing the route of the cars, visualizing the voltages of the customers on the map, make a study of equipment faults by zones, the optimization of the use and an optimal expansion of the networks, access to the information of a point of the distribution line, the study of electrical losses and certain scales allows to draw the sketch of the new projects with the necessary accuracy.

With the development of ontology, comprehensive access to the database and dynamic queries are achieved, which are fundamental in high demand stages of services due to the speed of the link between alphanumeric and graphic information. The processing of the technical language executed by the system increases the ease and convenience with which requests are made and allows the user ignore the structure of the database. In addition, concepts common in the domain that are not represented in the database are incorporated.

The efficiency is a component of productivity and is related to the use of inputs during the transformation process [41], so it can be evaluated taking into account the computational complexity that indicates the effort that must be made to apply an algorithm and how expensive it is.

In order to validate the investigation in terms of efficiency, the analysis of the computational complexity of the algorithm must be done. The worst case is the complexity of the reasoner without structure, that is to say, if the base of cases had a sequential structure. The computational complexity is calculated as:

$$N * ComplexityDisimGlobal(X, Y) \tag{3}$$

Where:

N: is the number of cases in the base of cases.

Complexity DisimGlobal (X, Y): it is the sum of the complexities of the local dissimilarity functions, in the case of a sum of temporal complexities, the greatest of all the complexities is taken as general complexity. The complexities of the local dissimilarity functions (n_1, n_2) are:

- Jaccard's temporal complexity (n_1) (Used for set type attributes) $O(n)$, where n is equal to the number of elements of the attribute domain. Worst case $n_1 = 90$.
- Temporal Complexity of Jaro (n_2) (Used for ontological traits) $O(m)$, where m is the length of the chain. (AMÓN, 2010). Worst case $n_2 = 25$.

So the complexity of the algorithm would always be an $O(n)$.

Complexity of the reasoner with structure, that is, the hierarchical structure:

$$\frac{N}{12} * ni \tag{4}$$

Where:

N/12: will be the number of average cases recovered.

ni: the greatest of the complexities of local dissimilarity functions.

So it would also be an $O(n)$.

A balance between precision and efficiency is achieved, because the model for data management, which allows smart consultations in the geographic information system for decision making in the transmission and distribution processes in the UNE provides: a good performance of prediction, in a reasonable response time, with low computational complexity.

To test the SICUNE, three departments of an Electric Company, in a province, are selected that use information from different areas of the database and achieve greater coverage in the information contained. The work of these areas is operational and needs the functionality proposed in their daily work: Command post; Engineering department; Customer service.

A study of the exploitation of SIGOBE v1.0 determining their approximate use (Table 6).

Table 6. Queries to SIGOBE v1.0.

Queries	Use	Average of monthly consultations
Command post	See the monolineales Analyze the limits of freeways complaints	100
Engineering department	Analysis of the study area Transformer inquiries	25
Customer service area	Customer service State of complaints Status of projects and studies	50

In all three departments, the exploitation of the new version of SIGOBE begins, with the SICUNE module incorporated, for a period of one month for its validation. Table 7 shows the results by area.

Table 7. Results of SICUNE by area.

Queries	Total queries	Correctly classifies	Bad classifies	Retain	Effectiveness
Command post	230	221	9	23	96.08%
Engineering department	189	178	11	40	94.18%
Customer service area	147	140	7	18	95.23%

The engineering area was the least represented in the case based, because the SIGOBE, version 1.0, focused on the Command post, the attention to the complaints of the population and the investment area. However, 94.18% effectiveness is obtained. The percentage of cases solved incorrectly corresponds to the few cases on these areas that were counted at the beginning of its application.

4 Conclusions

- A case-based system on type problem solver was designed, using as an initial case database, the 265 static queries registered in SIGERE. The queries are described by eight data-type predictive traits and three objective traits. The case database responds to a three-level hierarchical organization, which favors the processes of access, recovery and learning of cases.
- Calculation of the distance between traits was done according to its nature. It was determined that the best results in the study case are: for the traits of nominal type, the Boolean distance; for traits of set type, the Jaccard distance and the ontologies were treated as strings using the Jaro Winkler distance.
- The case retention stage is in preliminary phase, since the current size of the case database does not presuppose reissues of cases, because it is still medium-sized.
- An intelligent real-time queries system is implemented for the UNE (SICUNE), achieving the generation of automatic queries that allow the system to respond to any type of queries in real time.
- The experimental study shows the feasibility of the proposal. The CBS obtains an effectiveness of 94.18%, where 539 searches of the total number of consultations were correctly classified. In the study 81 new cases were retained for a total of 301 in the case base. The percentage of cases solved incorrectly corresponds to the few cases on these areas that were counted at the beginning of its application.
- It's necessaries to develop the axioms of the ontology for the data management of the processes of transmission and distribution of the UNE.
- Extend the SIG to the Generation process of the Electric Union including: Thermal Generation, Distributed Generation and Renewable Energy Sources Management.
- The study of possible applications of the model for data management in other branches of knowledge.

References

1. Mónica Andrea Arango, A., Santiago Arroyave, O.: Análisis de combustibles fósiles en el mercado de generación de energía eléctrica en Colombia: un contraste entre modelos de volatilidad. Revista de Métodos Cuantitativos para la Economía y la Empresa (22), 190–215 (2016)
2. Castillo, Y., Castrillón Gutiérrez, M., Vanegas Chamorro, M., Valencia, G., Villicaña, E.: Rol de las Fuentes No Convencionales de Energía en el sector eléctrico colombiano. Prospectiva 13(1), 39–51 (2015)
3. Garcia, M.L.: Modelos de predicción de demanda eléctrica utilizando técnicas de inteligencia artificial. Aplicación al mercado eléctrico español. Universidad Miguel Hernández de Elche (2016)
4. Fernández Álvarez, R.: Informatización de la Gestión de las Redes Eléctricas, Tesis Doctoral, Facultad de Ingeniería Eléctrica. Universidad Central "Marta Abreu" de Las Villas, Santa Clara (2011)

5. Gondres Torné, I., Rodríguez León, N., Lajes Choy, S.E., del Castillo Serpa, A.: El aprendizaje bajo incertidumbre aplicado al mantenimiento de interruptores de potencia. Ingeniería Energética **XXXV**(2), 149–158 (2014)
6. Martínez, M., Santana, E., Beliz, N.: Análisis de los paradigmas de inteligencia artificial, para un modelo inteligente de gestión de la energía eléctrica. Revista de Iniciación Científica **3**(1), 77–84 (2017)
7. Rueda Calier, F., Rodríguez Suárez, A., Castellanos Granados, H.C.: Desarrollo y tendencias de la inteligencia artificial. Revista Matices Tecnológicos, 4 (2013)
8. Russell, S.J., Norvig, P.: Artificial Intelligence. A Modern Approach. Prentice Hall, Englewood Cliffs (1995)
9. Guerrero, O.E.G., Osorio, J.J.R., Gauta, T.L.A.: Implementación de una estrategia de control difuso para aumentar la producción de crudo en pozo petrolero. Revista Colombiana de Tecnologías de Avanzada (RCTA) **1**(27), 98–103 (2017)
10. Rey, H.C., Ricaurte, J.A.B., Pérez, A.G.: Sistema experto para la selección de personal desarrollador de software. Ingenio Magno **4**(1), 75–81 (2014)
11. Zhang, Y., Luo, X., Zhang, H., Sutherland, J.W.: A knowledge representation for unit manufacturing processes. Int. J. Adv. Manuf. Technol. **73**(5–8), 1011–1031 (2014)
12. Marling, C., Shubrook, J., Schwartz, F.: Case-based decision support for patients with type 1 diabetes on insulin pump therapy. In: Althoff, K.-D., Bergmann, R., Minor, M., Hanft, A. (eds.) ECCBR 2008. LNCS (LNAI), vol. 5239, pp. 325–339. Springer, Heidelberg (2008). https://doi.org/10.1007/978-3-540-85502-6_22
13. Amin, H.H., Deabes, W., Bouazza, K.: Clustering of user activities based on adaptive threshold spiking neural networks. In: 2017 Ninth International Conference on Ubiquitous and Future Networks (ICUFN), pp. 1–6. IEEE, Milan (2017)
14. Platon, R., Dehkordi, V.R., Martel, J.: Hourly prediction of a building's electricity consumption using case-based reasoning, artificial neural networks and principal component analysis. Energy Build. **92**, 10–18 (2015)
15. Cocea, M., Magoulas, G.: Design and evaluation of a case-based system for modelling exploratory learning behaviour of math generalisation. IEEE Trans. Learn. Technol. **14**(8), 1–14 (2017)
16. Garcia Lorenzo, M.M., Bello Pérez, R.E.: A model and its different applications to case-based reasoning. Knowl.-Based Syst. **9**(7), 465–473 (1996)
17. González Benítez, N.: Sistema Experto basado en casos para el diagnóstico de la Fasciola hepática en el ganado bovino. REDVET. Revista Electrónica de Veterinaria **17**(12), 1–11 (2016)
18. Gutiérrez Martínez, I., Bello Pérez, R.E.: Making decision in case-based systems using probabilities and rough sets. Knowl.-Based Syst. **16**(4), 205–213 (2003)
19. Gillespie, K., Gupta, K.M., Drinkwater, M.: Case-based object placement planning. In: Lamontagne, L., Plaza, E. (eds.) ICCBR 2014. LNCS (LNAI), vol. 8765, pp. 170–184. Springer, Cham (2014). https://doi.org/10.1007/978-3-319-11209-1_13
20. Leung, K., Choy, K., Tam, M., Lam, C., Lee, C., Cheng, S.W.: A hybrid RFID case-based system for handling air cargo storage location assignment operations in distribution centers. In: 2017 Ninth International Conference on Ubiquitous and Future Networks (ICUFN), pp. 1859–1868. IEEE, Portland (2017)
21. de la Rosa Turbides, T.E.: Razonamiento basado en casos aplicado a la planificación heurística. Tesis Doctoral, Departamento de Informática, Universidad Carlos III, Madrid, España (2010)

22. Moreno Laverde, R., Joyanes Aguilar, L., Giraldo Marín, L.M., Duque Méndez, N.D., Tabares Morales, V.: Modelo para personalización de actividades educativas aprovechando la técnica de Razonamiento basado en Casos (RbC). Campus Virtuales **4**(1), 118–127 (2015)

23. Chazara, P., Negny, S., Montastruc, L.: Flexible knowledge representation and new similarity measure: application on case based reasoning for waste treatment. Expert Syst. Appl. **58**, 143–154 (2016)

24. Fitzgerald, T., McGreggor, K., Akgun, B., Thomaz, A., Goel, A.: Visual case retrieval for interpreting skill demonstrations. In: Hüllermeier, E., Minor, M, (eds.) ICCBR 2015. LNCS (LNAI), vol. 9343, pp. 119–133. Springer, Cham (2015). https://doi.org/10.1007/978-3-319-24586-7_9

25. Aamodt, A., Plaza, E.: Case-based reasoning: foundational issues, methodological variations, and system approaches. AI Commun. **7**(1), 39–59 (1994)

26. Cordero Morales, D., Ruiz Constanten, Y., Torres Rubio, Y.: Sistema de Razonamiento Basado en Casos para la identificación de riesgos de software. Revista Cubana de Ciencias Informáticas **7**(2), 222–239 (2013)

27. Kolodner, J.: Case-Based Reasoning. Morgan Kaufmann Publishers, San Mateo (1993)

28. Myrgioti, E., Bassiliades, N., Miliou, A.: Bridging the HASM: an OWL ontology for modeling the information pathways in haptic interfaces software. Expert Syst. Appl. **40**(4), 1358–1371 (2013)

29. Valaski, J., Malucelli, A., Reinehr, S.: Ontologies application in organizational learning: a literature review. Expert Syst. Appl. **39**(8), 7555–7561 (2012)

30. Wimmer, H., Rada, R.: Good versus bad knowledge: ontology guided evolutionary algorithms. Expert Syst. Appl. **42**(21), 8039–8051 (2015)

31. Akmal, S., Shih, L.-H., Batres, R.: Ontology-based similarity for product information retrieval. Comput. Ind. **65**(1), 91–107 (2014)

32. Bouhana, A., Zidi, A., Fekih, A., Chabchoub, H., Abed, M.: An ontology-based CBR approach for personalized itinerary search systems for sustainable urban freight transport. Expert Syst. Appl. **42**(7), 3724–3741 (2015)

33. Sánchez Fleitas, N., Comas Rodríguez, R., García Lorenzo, M.M., Riverol Quesada, A.: Modelo de manejo de datos, con el uso de inteligencia artificial, para un sistema de información geográfica en el sector energético. Enfoque UTE **7**(3), 95–109 (2016)

34. Montoya Quintero, D.M.: Modelo para la extracción de conocimiento de un experto humano en un sistema basado en conocimientos usando razonamiento basado en casos. Tesis Doctoral, Facultad de Minas, Departamento de Ciencias de la Computación y de la decisión, Universidad Nacional de Colombia, Medellin, Colombia (2015)

35. Comas Rodríguez, R.: Integración de herramientas de control de gestión para el alineamiento estratégico en el sistema empresarial cubano. Aplicación en empresas de Sancti Spiritus. Doctor en Ciencias Técnicas, Departamento de Ingeniería Industrial, Universidad De Matanzas "Camilo Cienfuegos" (2013)

36. Althoff, K.-D., Auriol, E., Barletta, R., Manago, M.: Review of Industrial Case-Based Reasoning Tools. A1 Intelligence, Oxford, USA (1995)

37. González Castellanos, M.: Extensión de algoritmos representativos del aprendizaje automático al trabajo con datos tipo conjunto. Tesis de Maestría, Departamento de Ciencias de la Computación, Universidad Central "Marta Abreu" de Las Villas, Santa Clara, Villa Clara, Cuba (2010)

38. Winkler, W.E.: Using the EM Algorithm for Weight Computation in the Fellegi-Sunter Model of Record Linkage. Bureau of the Census Statistical Resarch Division, Washington D.C., USA (2000)

39. Skjermo, J., Dah, E., Opland, R., Aamodt, A., Kofod-Petersen, A., Gustavsson, E., et al.: Case-based reasoning for alpine road operation support. In: 23rd ITS World Congress, Paper number EU-TP0079, Melbourne, Australia (2016)
40. Navarro Ferrer, D.G., Delgado, T., Martín, G., Jaimez, E.: An approach of a data-driven spatial decision support system to manage the effects of climate change on agriculture. In: 28th EnviroInfo 2014 Conference, BIS-Verlag, Oldenburg, Germany (2014)
41. González, C.A.S., Araque, D.P.: ¿ Entendemos realmente los conceptos entorno a la productividad?. Revista San Gregorio (17), 90–95 (2017)

Classification Models Applied to Uncertain Data

Yandry Quiroz[1](✉), Willian Zamora[1](✉), Alex Santamaria-Philco[1,2](✉),
Elsa Vera[1](✉), and Patricia Quiroz-Palma[1,2](✉)

[1] Universidad Laica Eloy Alfaro de Manabi, Manta, Ecuador
yandry.quiroz@gmail.com, {willian.zamora,alex.santamaria,
elsa.vera,patricia.quiroz}@live.uleam.edu.ec
[2] Universitat Politecnica de Valencia, Valencia, Spain
{asantamaria,patquipa}@dsic.upv.es

Abstract. In the field of learning models, the quality directly depends
on the training data. That is the reason why data preparation is one
of the stages in the knowledge extraction process where more time is
invested. In fact, the most common scenario consists in a training created under perfect conditions. However, the situation is often entirely
different during the model deployment phase, since, in the real world,
data usually contain noise, there may be missing or incorrect values, or
even be uncertain, in the sense that we do not know their exact value, but
have an approximate knowledge of its value. In this paper, we will study
how to apply the learning models to uncertain data. Specifically, we will
focus on classification problems in which uncertainty is only present in
numerical attributes and present a new approach to apply classification
learned models. Experimental results show that the accuracy achieved
by our methods improve the case of having maximum uncertainty.

Random Forest has a 3.60% control of uncertainty when its maximum
value is achieved. Also, there is a higher level of degradation of 5.59%
and 9.60% for both Decision Trees and Naive Bayes.

Keywords: Learning models · Classification models
Random Forest · Decision trees · Naive Bayes

1 Introduction

Nowadays, technological advances allow the generation and storage of large volumes of data making widespread use of computer tools that allow for the adequate extraction of the knowledge contained in the information. This fact has
transformed data analysis, orienting itself towards specific specialized techniques,
which are encompassed under the name of data mining [17,19].

Data mining uses automatic learning (Machine Learning) and aims to use
data and past experiences to solve a problem. For this purpose, a learning process
is carried out on a set of data, whose class is already known (training set), thus
allowing to generate a model based on relationships, patterns or rules, to classify

© Springer Nature Switzerland AG 2019
M. Botto-Tobar et al. (Eds.): CITT 2018, CCIS 895, pp. 462–475, 2019.
https://doi.org/10.1007/978-3-030-05532-5_34

new elements. The quality of data is vital since the correct analysis depends on it to obtain useful information. To this end, the filtering and cleaning of the data take a fundamental role in the analysis. Being the analysis one of the tasks that more effort requires when building data mining models, it is necessary to adopt productive strategies to make correct decisions [17].

The main problem that we find in the analysis stage is that data is not in the proper format and pattern since there are large volumes of data that have anomalous values. The anomalous values may have been generated by several factors such as uncalibrated sensors, contradictory information because the data come from different sources of information, data that contain noise or have missing values, technical or human errors, and failures in devices [19], among others.

In this paper, we are going to focus on the issue of missing values by trying to detect and treat them before the training and then to make a decision about how they will be resolved, since many learning techniques are sensitive to the absence of values. In effect, the missing value is an example of maximum uncertainty where its value is completely not known, but often we have more knowledge about them, so having a degree of uncertainty in the data. For example, in the field of medicine, the age of a patient can be determined when it is not known, and it is possible to estimate that it ranges between 20 and 30 years because the patient is young. Likewise, there may be the case of employee salaries expressed in intervals, data taken with sensors which have a degree of error that is determined by the characteristics.

In this context, the objective of this research is to define a new approach to apply learned models with *clean and without uncertainty* data, to uncertain data during the test stage. We have used two different classifications methods: one that makes use of the class labels predicted by the model that is, using classifiers of the so-called *crisp* [8] and a second one using the probabilities to belong to each class predicted by a *soft* classifier [14]. Moreover, we evaluated these two methods experimentally using various generation techniques of the classifiers and several data sets. In particular, the Decision tree (AD) [16], Random Forest (RF) [20] and Naive Bayes (NB) [1] algorithms have been used, to evaluate the accuracy over uncertain data.

This paper is organized as follows: Sect. 2 reviews the state of the art on this topic. In Sect. 3, we detailed the different phases to apply classification models to data that contain uncertainty. Then, in Sect. 4, we make a detailed procedure to generate uncertainty, data source, and used tools. In Sect. 5 we present the experimental results obtained to validate the proposal. Finally, Sect. 6 presents our conclusions, and future works are discussed.

2 Related Works

Several research works have developed different techniques to deal with the problem of missing values [2,4,11,13]. The goal of these techniques is that the data is complete in almost *perfect conditions* to obtain quality knowledge. One of the simplest ways to resolve the issue of missing values is the elimination of these instances, the drawback of this technique is that if many instances have missing values they can lose a lot of information degrading the expected knowledge of the data.

In [15], the authors describe an alternative way to treat information, filling in missing values with some value, this can be done through the imputation technique that often involves processes and methods. It is essential to choose an imputation method according to the characteristics of the dataset to minimize noise and bias in them.

In [3], a technique to obtain a complete sample is proposed. This technique replaces each of the missing values with the average of the observed data for that variable. This presents the disadvantage that modifies the distribution of the variable by artificially reducing its variance. It is considered a simple technique to estimate these values.

On the other hand, [7,9] describe a more sophisticated way of estimating a value by means of predicting it from other examples. Using any predictive technique of machine learning (classification or regression) [9], the variable is estimated as objective and remaining variables are used as predictors of the used technique. More specific techniques can be used, such as determining sex from the name. Also, it is possible to segment the tuples by the values that are available, obtain different models for each segment and then combine them. Another valid option may be to modify the data quality policy and wait until the missing data is available.

As it has been shown, there are several works developed to clean the data in the learning phase to generate optimal models. However, no model has been proposed to evaluate whether it applies to learning models with clean data. In this paper, we propose an approach how to apply data mining techniques to data that contain uncertainty and present a methodology that describes the steps to follow to address these problems.

3   Methodology

In this section, we perform an adaptation to the particular context of this study of the *Design Science Research Methodology (DSRM)* [10] which specifies the analysis, design, and experimentation.

3.1   Analysis

In this phase, we propose the definition of three sub-stages: (i) generation of instances, (ii) application of the classifier, and the combination of predictions. Figure 1 shows this sub-stages. Below we present details of these sub-stages.

- **Generation of instances:** It consists of generating N instances from this one that presents uncertainty, these will be obtained based on covering values in the interval. Therefore the classifier is applied to those N instances, and then all the possible predictions are combined to be able to grant a single prediction to the instance.

- **Application of the classifier:** Once the N instances have been generated, and it must be taken into account that the value that the *variable* attribute will bring, which will be each of the profits made within the interval. After this, the application of the classifiers is carried out. We propose for this research work the use of two types of classifiers for the prediction of instances. Below we detail these.
  - *Crisp* classifiers, this type of classifiers when executed results in a class label [8].
  - *Soft* classifiers, when executed, the probability of belonging to each class is obtained as a result [14].
- **Combination of predictions:** A method is defined to carry out the combinations of the predictions obtained by the classifiers *Crisp* and *Soft*, made up of three of the following three activities: [21]
  - **Approximation of majority vote:** To make the combination of the results obtained by the *Crisp* classifiers, the majority vote approach is used, which consists in taking as the prediction of the instance the one that is repeated for each class the most.
  - **Approximation of a likelihood of belonging:** The following approximation that allows obtaining a prediction, is the probability of belonging to the class. It is used to combine the results obtained by the *Soft* classifiers. In which the probability sum of each type class is realized, and the one that is greater is received as a prediction.
  - **Generation of uncertainty:** To be able to evaluate the proposed approaches experimentally, it is necessary to have test data that presents uncertainty in numerical attributes expressed in intervals, it is recommended to generate this uncertainty artificially.

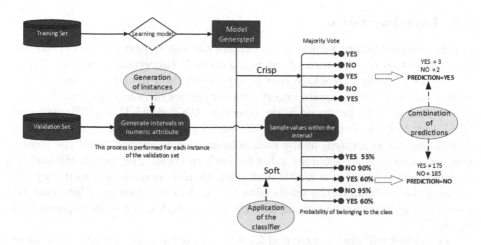

Fig. 1. Analysis sub-stages

3.2   Design

In this phase, we proposed the definition of two sub-stages: the establishment of classification models and the determination of the evaluation measure:

- **Classification models:** The application of the following classification techniques is defined: Decision trees (AD), Naive Bayes (NB) and Random Forest (RF).
- **Measure of evaluation:** To determine the accuracy of the classifiers, the *Accuracy* metric is used. This makes use of the confusion matrix which is a table of order 2 (Fig. 2) which shows the number of correct and incorrect predictions made by the model compared to the actual classifications in the test data. To do this, the rows represent the current classes of an instance, and the columns represent the predicted or estimated classes.

		Prediction	
		C_p	C_N
Real Class	C_p	TP: True positive	FN: False negative
	C_N	FP: False positive	TN: True negative

Fig. 2. Confusion matrix

3.3   Experimentation

For the demonstration, we proceed to explain the way to perform the experimentation based on the variation of the parameters U (uncertainty) and N. Where U is defined as the percentage that is applied to the calculated average of the training set and that generate uncertainty for the set of validation, and N is the values that must be produced in the intervals. We defined $U = (10\%, 20\%$ and $30\%)$ and $N = (5, 7, 9, 11, 13$ and $15)$, and for each value of U the values of N this one are generated, finally each combination is applied to all the validation set, obtaining an accuracy value for each of them. The model will also be executed when its value is known and when there is maximum uncertainty. To perform the evaluation, the values obtained within the generated intervals are sampled. Figure 3 shows an example of the process to follow for the experimental results.

The model will also be executed for when its value is known and when there is maximum uncertainty. The experimentation scenarios that are defined are:

- **Known values (zero uncertainty):** This process would be a normal execution process where your training and test data are under the same conditions. That is to say, the numerical attribute does not present uncertainty, and its value is known. This is being the first result of *Accuracy* in the experiment.
- **Uncertainty ranges:** In this process, it shows degrees of uncertainty based on the established U percentage. This is where the phases defined in the analysis will be applied. Also, the degree of uncertainty in the attribute will present variations and should proceed to sample N values within them. Subsequently, an *Accuracy* value will be obtained for each parameter combination.
- **Maximum uncertainty:** This third scenario occurs when the value of the attribute is not known, having maximum uncertainty.

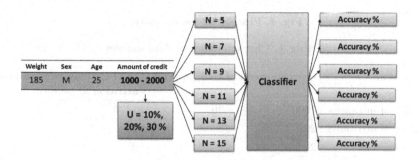

Fig. 3. Process for the evaluation

4   Data Source and Tool

Once the phase of our methodology has been described, we consider appropriate to describe the process for the generation of uncertainty. This consists of taking the numerical attribute of the training data set in which uncertainty will be generated and calculating the average of its values. To this end, we have used percentages U of the calculated average and this value will be added and subtracted to the known value that we have in the validation set, making sure that no negative values are generated, with this we can represent the uncertainty based on intervals, where U it must be increased to have a greater degree of uncertainty present. For the experiment, U varies by 10%, 20%, 30%. Figure 4 shows the followed process. In each instance of the validation set, uncertainty levels have been created in the numerical attribute "Amount of credit", following the example in the first instance, where the value of the attribute is 3400, the intervals are generated based on the percentage U. When $U = 10\%$ the interval is defined by (3120–3680), $U = 20\%$ (2841–3959) and $U = 30\%$ (2561–4239) repeating this process for all instances of the set of validation. With this process, the attribute "Amount of credit" presents intervals with uniform ranges

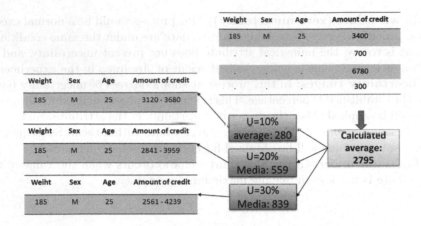

Fig. 4. Process for the evaluation

Table 1. Characteristics of data sources.

Description	German credit	Credit approval	IBM HR analytics employee attrition & performance
Number of instances	1000	690	1470
Number of attributes	20	15	34
Group number	2	2	2
Repository	UCI	UCI	Kaggle
Abbreviation	G. Credit	C. Approval	IBM HR

of amplitude, and it will be the way to proceed to generate uncertainty in the different data sets that are applied for the experiment.

For the application of the classification algorithms, three data-sets were used, which were obtained from the repository of the UCI Machine Learning Repository (University California Irvine) [5] and the Kaggle Repository [6]. The characteristics of the datasets are summarized in Table 1 and their full descriptions can be found in [5,6,18]. The R language [12] and its R Studio interface have been used to validate, process and show our analysis. Table 2 shows the main packages used in the experiments.

5   Experimental Results

In this section we validate our proposal in two scenarios, the first one shows an analysis about the impact of increasing the uncertainty in the data for each model used and we graphically show the results of the precision with the degree of uncertainty of the n generated values. In the second one, the results of the degradation of the classification are presented. For each of the proposed scenarios we have made 20 repetitions, applying the processes described above, and we

Table 2. Description of the packages used.

Package	Description
Rpart	Used to apply the model of Decision Tree
RandomForest	Used to apply the model Random Forest
e1071 (Naive Bayes)	Used to apply the model Naive Bayes
Runif	This function generates values of uniform distribution in an interval
Ggplot2	A data visualization package for the statistical

Table 3. Overall results of the accuracy of each classification model.

Algorithm		Decision tree		Random Forest		Naive Bayes	
Model		Probability	M. vote	Probability	M. vote	Probability	M. vote
U = 0		**84.04**	**84.04**	**84.95**	**84.95**	**80.53**	**80.53**
U = 10%	N = 5	83.07	83.10	84.20	84.2	79.81	79.81
	N = 9	83.13	83.15	84.31	84.33	79.79	79.79
	N = 15	83.28	83.24	84.36	84.54	79.83	79.83
U = 20%	N = 5	82.95	82.96	83.97	84.01	79.65	79.65
	N = 9	82.96	82.90	83.97	83.99	79.71	79.70
	N = 15	83.13	83.05	84.11	84.13	79.70	79.70
U=30%	N = 5	82.55	82.55	83.07	83.71	79.63	79.63
	N = 9	82.87	82.89	83.90	83.94	79.61	79.61
	N = 15	82.75	82.74	83.84	83.84	79.63	79.62
U = Max		**78.45**	**78.45**	**81.35**	**81.35**	**70.93**	**70.93**

calculated the average of their results, avoiding variability, obtaining more stable results for analysis. Concerning the maximum uncertainty occurs when the value of the attribute is not known. The results obtained are detailed below.

5.1 Analysis of Model Prediction

Table 3 shows a summary of the results obtained by varying the different models and levels of uncertainty. In general, we find that by increasing data uncertainty, the classifiers lose accuracy. All the classifiers have a similar behaviour for the three techniques. It has also been possible to determine that Random Forest is the classifier that has obtained the highest accuracy within the experimental phase, followed by Decision trees, and finally Naive Bayes, when there is a typical scenario where the data has no uncertainty.

Analysis of Accuracy for Decision Tree (AD). Figure 5 shows the overall results of the decision tree model, varying its uncertainty. In general, we find that the model that gives the most significant benefit is the probability. In particular, in Fig. 5(a), it is observed that when N = 15 the probability model obtain the high-accuracy value of 83.28% review concerning the majority vote model. In Fig. 5(c) similar performance is observed. Finally, in Fig. 5(c) the results are more similar among their approaches, with an improvement when N = 9 for the majority vote with a value of 82.89%.

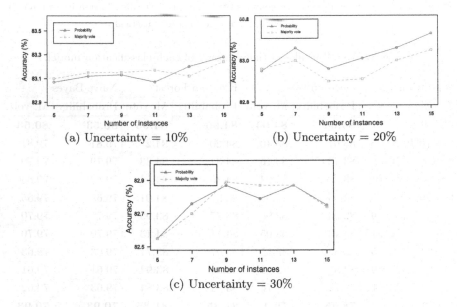

(a) Uncertainty = 10%

(b) Uncertainty = 20%

(c) Uncertainty = 30%

Fig. 5. Analysis of precision model using the AD and varying the uncertainty.

Analysis of Accuracy for Random Forest. Figure 5 shows the results of the Random Forest model. In general, we can see that there are some differences between algorithm of the majority vote-based model has better performance with respect to the probabilistic one. In particular Fig. 5(a) and (b), better results are obtained with the majority vote approach having its highest value when $N = 15$ with 84.54%. Figure 5(c) when $I = 30\%$ the results are more similar among their approximations, with an improvement when $N = 11$ for a majority vote model with value of 83.97%.

Analysis of Accuracy for Naive Bayes. Figure 7 shows the results for the NB model. In general, we can see that the results present similar results schemes. In particular in Fig. 7(a) its predictions are equal for both the majority vote model and the probability model is having its highest point when $N = 11$ with 79.84%. In Fig. 7(b) there is a small difference between the results of their approximations, but they get their best performance when $N = 13$ for the probability

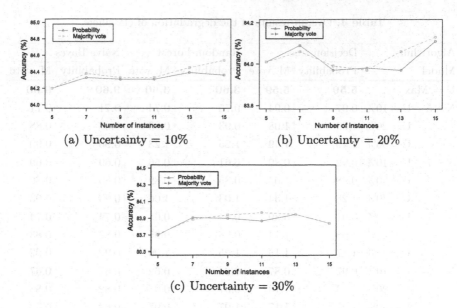

(a) Uncertainty = 10%   (b) Uncertainty = 20%

(c) Uncertainty = 30%

Fig. 6. Analysis of precision model using the RF and varying the uncertainty.

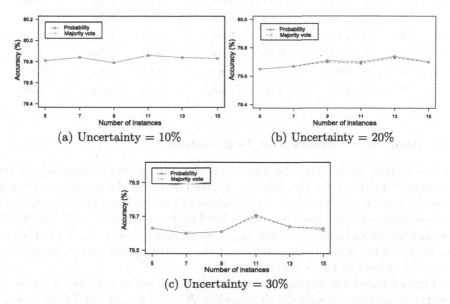

(a) Uncertainty = 10%   (b) Uncertainty = 20%

(c) Uncertainty = 30%

Fig. 7. Analysis of precision model using the NV and varying the uncertainty.

of belonging with a 79.74%. Finally, Fig. 7(c) their results in the approximations are very similar, but the probability models of belonging stand out when $N = 11$ with 79.71%. Therefore, a probabilistic method, the variation of their approximations are seen in a very similar (Fig. 6).

Table 4. Overall results of the degradation of classifiers.

Algorithm		Decision tree		Random Forest		Naive Bayes	
Model		Probability	M. vote	Probability	M. vote	Probability	M. vote
U = Max		**5.59**	**5.59**	**3.60**	**3.60**	**9.60**	**9.60**
N = 5	U = 10%	0.97	0.94	0.75	0.74	0.71	0.71
	U = 20%	1.09	1.08	0.93	0.93	0.88	0.88
	U = 30%	1.49	1.49	1.25	1.23	0.90	0.00
N = 7	U = 10%	0.92	0.89	0.61	0.56	0.69	0.69
	U = 20%	0.98	1.04	0.85	0.89	0.86	0.86
	U = 30%	1.28	1.34	1.03	1.06	0.93	0.93
N = 9	U = 10%	0.91	0.89	0.64	0.61	0.74	0.74
	U = 20%	1.08	1.14	0.98	0.95	0.82	0.83
	U = 30%	1.17	1.15	1.05	1.00	0.92	0.92
N = 11	U = 10%	0.97	0.87	0.64	0.62	0.67	0.67
	U = 20%	1.03	1.13	0.97	0.97	0.82	0.83
	U = 30%	1.25	1.17	1.07	0.97	0.82	0.83
N = 13	U = 10%	1.25	1.17	1.07	0.97	0.82	0.83
	U = 20%	0.98	1.04	0.98	0.88	0.79	0.80
	U = 30%	1.17	1.17	0.99	0.99	0.88	0.88
N = 15	U = 10%	0.76	0.80	0.59	0.40	0.70	0.70
	U = 20%	0.91	0.99	0.83	0.81	0.82	0.82
	U = 30%	1.29	1.30	1.10	1.10	0.89	0.90

5.2   Analysis of Classification Degradation

In this section, we analyze the impact on the degradation of accuracy as the uncertainty increases for the different N generated data. In particular, we find that the Random Forest has a 3.60% control of uncertainty when its maximum value is achieved. Also, there is a higher level of degradation of 5.59% and 9.60% for both Decision Trees and Naive Bayes algorithm respectively. Table 4 shows the results of the accuracy degradation of the models applied as the uncertainty increases for each of the N generated value.

Figure 8 shows the degradation of the classification models based on the N generated instances specifically shown when $N = (5, 9,$ and $15)$. In general, we find that as there is an increase in instances the value accuracy losses tend to slightly decrease. On the other hand, when uncertainty increases, the accuracy tend to increase. In particular, Fig. 8(a), (b), y (c) show that Naive Bayes in most cases i.e., $U = 10\%$, and $U = 20\%$, and $U = 30\%$, one of the is techniques that less tolerance degradation has because its prediction controls uncertainty better when it is minimal. Finally, Fig. 8 (c) shows that the Random Forest Algorithm

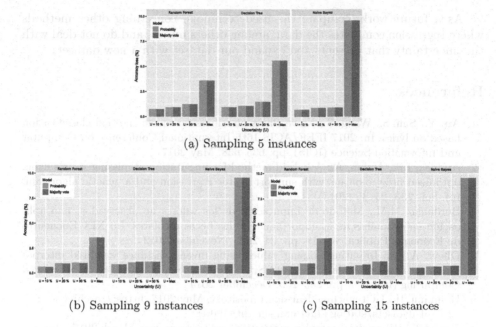

(a) Sampling 5 instances

(b) Sampling 9 instances   (c) Sampling 15 instances

Fig. 8. Degradation of classification models for different sampling

presents the best performance when the majority vote method is applied close to an uncertainty level of 10%.

6   Conclusions and Future Work

In this paper, we proposed a novel approach to dealing with classification problems when you have uncertain data. In particular, we use two models of probabilistic and non-probabilistic classification, and for each of these, we evaluate their performance using three known classification algorithms. In particular, precision in prediction and degradation was evaluated when percentages of known uncertainties are applied.

Experimental results show that the accuracy achieved by our methods improves remarkably the case of having a maximum uncertainty that is the usual situation of dealing with this problem nowadays. Likewise, it was evidenced that the accuracy of the classifiers is affected by the degree of uncertainty present in the data increases.

Also, very similar performance has been detected for the three used algorithms, with Random Forest being the algorithm that obtained the best performance. Concerning the used approaches, different performance was evidenced depending on the learning used technique, with the majority vote being the one that achieved the best results.

As a future work, compare the used technique concerning other methods where regression completes the data, among others means, and do not deal with the uncertainty that presents and expand our dataset with a new dataset.

References

1. An, Y., Sun, S., Wang, S.: Naive Bayes classifiers for music emotion classification based on lyrics. In: 2017 IEEE/ACIS 16th International Conference on Computer and Information Science (ICIS), pp. 635–638, May 2017
2. Aydilek, I.B., Arslan, A.: A hybrid method for imputation of missing values using optimized fuzzy c-means with support vector regression and a genetic algorithm. Inf. Sci. **233**, 25–35 (2013)
3. Bordalejo, M.M.: Método de imputación de los valores no observados. una aplicación en el análisis de la importancia de las becas escolares. In: XIX Encuentro de Economía Pública, vol. 19, pp. 24–2985, November 2012
4. Dhevi, A.T.S.: Imputing missing values using inverse distance weighted interpolation for time series data. In: 2014 Sixth International Conference on Advanced Computing (ICoAC), pp. 255–259, December 2014
5. Hofmann, H.: UCI machine learning repository, May 2017. https://archive.ics.uci.edu/ml/datasets/statlog+(german+credit+data)
6. IBM: IBM HR analytics employee attrition and performance, March 2017. https://www.kaggle.com/pavansubhasht/ibm-hr-analytics-attrition-dataset
7. López, C.P., González, D.S.: Data Mining. Ra-Ma, Paracuellos de Jarama (2006)
8. Nadali, A., Kakhky, E.N., Nosratabadi, H.E.: Evaluating the success level of data mining projects based on CRISP-DM methodology by a fuzzy expert system. In: 2011 3rd International Conference on Electronics Computer Technology, v. 6, pp. 161–165, April 2011
9. Hernndez Orallo, J., Ramírez, M., Ferri, C.: Introducción a la Minería de Datos. Pearson, London (2004)
10. Peffers, K., Tuunanen, T., Rothenberger, M.A., Chatterjee, S.: A design science research methodology for information systems research. J. Manag. Inf. Syst. **24**(3), 45–77 (2007)
11. Pratama, I., Permanasari, A.E., Ardiyanto, I., Indrayani, R.: A review of missing values handling methods on time-series data. In: 2016 International Conference on Information Technology Systems and Innovation (ICITSI), pp. 1–6, October 2016
12. R-Foundation: R project. https://www.r-project.org. Accessed 01 Nov. 2015
13. Rahman, M.G., Islam, M.Z.: *kDMI*: a novel method for missing values imputation using two levels of horizontal partitioning in a data set. In: Motoda, H., Wu, Z., Cao, L., Zaiane, O., Yao, M., Wang, W. (eds.) ADMA 2013. LNCS (LNAI), vol. 8347, pp. 250–263. Springer, Heidelberg (2013). https://doi.org/10.1007/978-3-642-53917-6_23
14. Sharma, R., Garg, P.K., Dwivedi, R.K.: A literature survey for fuzzy based soft classification techniques and uncertainty estimation. In: 2016 International Conference System Modeling Advancement in Research Trends (SMART), pp. 71–75, November 2016
15. Sobrevilla, K.L.M.D., Quiñones, A.G., Lopez, K.V.S., Azaña, V.T.: Daily weather forecast in Tiwi, Albay, Philippines using artificial neural network with missing values imputation. In: 2016 IEEE Region 10 Conference (TENCON), pp. 2981–2985 (2016)

16. Sutton-Charani, N., Destercke, S., Denoeux, T.: Learning decision trees from uncertain data with an evidential EM approach. In: 2013 12th International Conference on Machine Learning and Applications, vol. 1, pp. 111–116, December 2013
17. Swapna, S., Niranjan, P., Srinivas, B., Swapna, R.: Data cleaning for data quality. In: 2016 3rd International Conference on Computing for Sustainable Global Development (INDIACom), pp. 344–348, March 2016
18. UCI: UCI machine learning repository. http://archive.ics.uci.edu/ml/datasets/credit+approval, 05 2017
19. Wu, S.-F., Chang, C.-Y., Lee, S.-J.: Time series forecasting with missing values. In: 2015 1st International Conference on Industrial Networks and Intelligent Systems (INISCom), pp. 151–156, March 2015
20. Xu, X., Chen, W.: Implementation and performance optimization of dynamic random forest. In: 2017 International Conference on Cyber-Enabled Distributed Computing and Knowledge Discovery (CyberC), pp. 283–289, October 2017
21. Hernández Orallo, J., Hervás Martínez, C.: Evaluacion sensible a la distribucion y el coste. http://slideplayer.es/slide/2312433/

Data Scientist: A Systematic Review of the Literature

Marcos Antonio Espinoza Mina[1,2(✉)]
and Doris Del Pilar Gallegos Barzola[3]

[1] Universidad Ecotec, Samborondón, Ecuador
mespinoza@ecotec.edu.ec
[2] Universidad Agraria del Ecuador, Guayaquil, Ecuador
mespinoza@uagraria.edu.ec
[3] MADO S.A., Guayaquil, Ecuador
doris@ecuaportales.com

Abstract. The commercial activities of services and production have accumulated plenty of data throughout the years, hence today's necessity of a professional agent to interpret data, generates information in order to produce valuable results and conclusions. The scope of the current article is to present a systematic review of the literature which main goal was to spot the work and career profile of the so called Data Scientist; realizing that, as a new work field, there are not concretely defined profiles, although knowledge areas are indeed defined, as well as characteristics that are needed to be counted, apart from some technologies that can serve as supporting means for the labor these new technicians do in the IT (Information Technology) area.

Keywords: Data scientist · Work profile · Career profile

1 Introduction

The Data Scientist turns into the type of professional that when facing huge data bases - which in major part have no specific goal - applies their knowledge in numerical areas such as: programming, math and statistics, in order to compile, extract and process the contained relevant information; to then explore and analyze multiple source data, too great in occasions, known as big data, with too different formats at times.

Moreover, the Data Scientist must have a strong business vision to enable them to extract and transmit recommendations to the representatives of a company. On top of that, this professional should provide useful insights and decision-making support; the professionals must be capable of understanding the business issues and framing the appropriate analytical solutions. The necessary business knowledge professionals ranges from general familiarity with the areas of accounting, finance, management, marketing, logistics, and operation management, to the domain knowledge required in specific [1].

Exceptional communication skills are required by a Data Scientist due to the necessity of explaining the process involved in the data analysis in terms of working precision, problem solving and experience on analysis and data cross- verification like

M. Botto-Tobar et al. (Eds.): CITT 2018, CCIS 895, pp. 476–487, 2019.
https://doi.org/10.1007/978-3-030-05532-5_35

SQL, among others. Their work is minimally supervised, for which it is compulsory to have planning and organizing skills, collaborative approach to share ideas and find solutions.

It is known, that the data set may be originated from any type of device and electronic technology media such as: cell phones, social media, medical data, web sites, among others. Data that, significantly affects the current research processes in many fields like: neuro-marketing, biologic science, health, social science and counting.

Activities related to: big data, data mining, machine learning and business intelligence have been studied by many researchers, however, few have been the works carried out that consolidate technical know-how and expertise on professionals who handle and use these tools. Therefore, not much is found on their professional profile and hardly anything on their working profile; or systematic reviews on related works of such profiles. This article seeks to know the career or work profile of a Data Scientist. Jaramillo [2], it indicates the differences between work and career profile. The career profile is delimited by a set of skills and knowledge that determine the professional practice and satisfy the work environment demands. For this reason, their tuition must be a fusion of a set of knowledge with the development of capacities and skills related to the area so that they provide a solid base, both theoretic and practical which allow their application to distinctive domains. The work profile corresponds to both, the charge-function-responsibility as well as the attitude, abilities and skill components required for the professional performance. Consequently, the work profile is made in parts: academic formation, working experience, and charge competences, since such profiles are made by business needs, and these respectively are fundamental in the eligibility of the professional individual; starting from the provable skills to the achieved goals.

2 Limitations of the Current Literature

Regardless of having identified some performance areas for the Data Scientist with certain profiles for such professional, the validity of each conclusion reached by the authors of this field's literature are difficult to evaluate, for being too many the fields in which it is currently performing. For instance, specific [3], unfortunately, data scientist with the analytical and software engineering skills to analyze these large data sets have been hard to come by; only recently have software companies started to develop competencies in software-oriented data analytics.

Additionally, [4] implies as suggested in the literature, skills requirements re-search should be conducted periodically to help information systems educators in redesigning curricula or courses that would better prepare future Data Scientists.

The goal of this study was to have a systematic review of the updated literature in which aspects of the Data Scientist profile are examined, for which there was an attempt to borrow from other works developed in this subject, but until the date when the information survey was done of the present study, other systematic reviews were not found that specifically examine the abilities and competences related to the professional and working profile of the Data Scientist.

3 Systematic Review

3.1 Generality

This section describes the followed process to make the systematic literature review using the reliable methodology of Kitchenham [5]. The basic goal of this reviewing system is to compile and evaluate all the investigations available related to an intended inquiry, wherefore achieving impartial, auditable and repeatable results. The systematic review presented by Kitchenham is aligned to the PICO process (Problem, Intervention, Comparison and Outcome), this framework was developed to facilitate the formulation of clinical queries [6]. Hence, it was configured to get a more efficiently scope, that allows getting to know the Data Scientist profile.

The execution of the systematic review allows identifying, evaluating and analyzing all the signifying studies concerning a research enquiry, theme area or interest phenomena. Some of the advantages provided by a systematic review are: the summary evidences about a specific technology and the existing gap identification in the current investigation which, likewise, allows establishing future investigations. The systematic reviews follow a defined research strategy which analysis unity makes part of the original preliminary studies, from which are meant to answer an investigation query clearly formulated through a systematic and explicit process. The systematic reviews synthesize the results of preliminary investigations through strategies that limit the bias and random error.

3.2 Definition of the Research Question

The characteristics and requirements that a Data Scientist must comply with, and are expected to be known, will be obtained through the formulated query: Is there a defined work and career profile for a Data Scientist?

As the key words used were: data scientist, work profile, career profile and technology.

The presented investigation query reported the following results:

- Which are the knowledge areas a Data Scientist must have access to?
- Which work and career characteristics must a data scientist count with?
- Which technological tools support a Data Scientist job?

3.3 Sources Selection

In this section, the query sources in which queries of the studies regarding the theme were made will be identified. The following pointers were considered:

- Digital versions of articles, magazines and documented conferences were queried about Data Scientist using the established keywords.
- The chosen bibliographic sources had to count with a search engine that allows executing advanced search queries.
- The studies had to be written in English.

With the selection criteria exposed, a study query was made in the digital research libraries: EBSCO host (EBS), IEEE Xplore (IEEEX) and ERIC. The approach was made based on the vast access and coverage in areas like technology, social and human sciences besides accessibility to complete revised works makes it an easy task.

The digital sources present more relevant investigation works, however it was added as bibliographic references to the web sites of companies and organizations that offer software in general to help in a Data Scientist job.

It is important to highlight that there were also made Science Direct and Springer data base searches, but such did not generate acceptable results previously defined in the search strategies; the few related articles in Science Direct required payment to gain total access to their content, and in Springer the articles were not found in English, and the book chapters were excluded.

3.4   Search Strategies

- A series of terms and key words were chosen to reply the query: is there a defined work and career profile for a Data Scientist? And therefore, obtaining the expected results.
- The searching strategy was based on the words "data scientist profile" and "data scientist".
- The structured research chain was: "data scientist" OR "data scientist profile".
- The chains were applied to: title and summary. When the summary matched with the research object, the article was obtained and reviewed in its totality.
- The research language used for the publications was English.
- Publications temporality, since 2014. It allows getting to know the current needs of the labor market that presents a more targeted training and entrepreneurial vision, avoiding outdated information.

3.5   Inclusion and Exclusion Criteria

Defined inclusion criteria:

- Articles published since 2014. It was made this way, since higher education standards are in increasing demand; organizations and markets change quickly in short periods of time, the charge pro-files keep evolving; for which it is needed people capable of acquiring tuition and continuously learning. For this reason, any published article before this year could be considered obsolete.
- Conferences, magazines and international workshops articles.
- When an article is duplicated in the digital libraries only one is selected.

Exclusion criteria:

- Articles which content are not related to a Data Scientist or their profile.
- Works content in slides or books.
- Published works outside the specified range.
- Grey literature.

3.6   Extraction of Information and Review of Works

This step allowed identifying relevant documents related to the objectives of a systematic review and to the reach of the investigation query. The main difficulty to achieve this objective was that the terms used in the query led to excessively wide results. For instance, the word "data" is widely used in many types of publications, and therefore a big quantity of files appeared in the first results obtained using the defined research chain.

For the extraction and reviewing processes of the investigation, were chosen those works that their quality was assumed to be granted by the evaluation made by the same bibliographic sources where they were obtained, because the platforms generate their results ranked by relevance. For the digest, only the works related to the query are taken into consideration.

Most documents were obtained through the completion of query based on the research chain in "any field" or "complete text". In this first phase, a big quantity of investigation documents were obtained, however such results were not the most pertinent because they consisted on comments, letters and duplicated works that not only were limited to query the Data Scientist profiles, but they expanded in contents far from the objective, see Table 1.

The database keywords used were: "data scientist" and "profile data scientist"; together with search strings: "data scientist" in fields "title" and "summary" and "profile of data scientist" in field "Full Text".

The second phase, based in the query chain in fields selected by "title" and by "summary", allowed eliminating some useless results, but that was not enough to satisfy the investigation, see Table 1. Finally, to obtain the definite list of preliminary studies, a chain query based review was made with fields selected by "title" and "summary", as well as selecting only the academic articles, see Table 2.

Table 1. Chain and additional options to queries by source.

Phase	Inclusion criteria	Found articles		
		EBS	IEEEX	ERIC
Based on query chain in any field		1543	722	16
Based on query chain in selected fields	● Data scientist in options "title" and "summary" and "profile of data scientist" in the option "any field"	197	31	16
Based on query chain in selected fields	● All the query terms with full text ● Additional filter within academic publications	13	31	13

4   Results of the Review

Selected studies and mainly reviewed are displayed in Table 2, with data that allows a quick information comparison among each other. They are presented in alphabetic order by title and it does not determine the importance level regarding the objectives of this work.

Table 2. Summary of articles with the knowledge area detail, characteristics and tools that support a data scientist.

Work	Approximation of knowledge areas for a DS	Characteristics of a DS	Supporting technological tools of a DS	DS requiring area
[7]	Scientific, investigative, IT	Leaders, communicative, Thinking skills	Data base	Academic
[8]	Basic math, statistics, communication, IT, data base	Researchers, communicative	Data base	Journalism, IT
[9]	IT, research		Data base IT systems	IT
[10]	Educative, scientific, economic and IT	Researchers, Data interpretation, Communicative	Data base, teaching method	Academic
[11]	Statistics, math, data analysis, scientific knowledge	Statistic, programmer, info graphic designer and narrator	Data base	IT
[12]	Statistics, data mining and engineering skills	Domain experience, knowhow, skills and attributes	Data base	Labor, IT and Academic
[13]	Biology, IT	Developer, researcher	Software, Data base	Medicine
[14]	Computer science, matrixes, calculus		Bi- dimensional matrix algorithm, storage technique	IT
[15]	Scientific, IT, data base		GIDNA and CDM	IT and Data base
[16]	Biology, IT		Data base	Medicine
[17]	Math, probability, statistics, predictive analysis, uncertainty model, Information sciences			Medicine
[18]	IT, Scientific		Overflow, cloud applications, data crowd sourcing	IT
[19]	Educative, IT, data base	To know the business, science and technologic skills, communication skills	Software Hadoopecosystem	Academic
[20]	Educative, investigation, IT and data base	Administrator, quantitative researcher		Academic
[21]	Programming, statistics	Leader, decision-making	R Framework, java,.net	IT

(continued)

Table 2. (*continued*)

Work	Approximation of knowledge areas for a DS	Characteristics of a DS	Supporting technological tools of a DS	DS requiring area
[22]	Statistics, IT	Information analysis	PINQ (McSherry, SIGMOD 2009)	Statistics, math
[23]	Statistics, IT	Information analysis	Data base, applications, technologic tools	Statistics and IT
[24]	IT, Data base	Sharing knowledge	Data base	IT
[25]	IT research	Data consultant, researcher	Data base, Data library	Academic
[26]	Educative, IT and Data base	Formative	Data base	Academic
[27]	Data engineering, statistics, scientist, communicator	Domain expert, team captain	Data base	Academic
[28]	Statistics, business world, IT	Data segmentation, problem forecasting, development	Software TRANE, web site KAGGLE	IT

In the selected articles it was found that the Data Scientist must possess knowledge in many fields weighting more on the IT area, which would allow them to perform better with all the stored information in the data base, so they can use it orderly with quick access. Then, exact sciences knowledge is highlighted as of math and statistics, which are needed for formulation of hypothesis, using a suitable methodology and knowledge systematization. Additionally, a Data Scientist must know about communication and engineering in general. The necessity of this knowledge can be illustrated after reading Treadwell, Ross, Lee and Lowenstein article [8], where it is indicated that in the journalistic newsroom their personnel needs the skills in math and statistics as well as software tools inclusion, programming language like Python, Ruby, PHP or Perl to discover new information.

Zhai, Jocz, and Tan [7] point out that teachers with a positive attitude -from moderate to strong- towards implementation of scientific research teachings, create a pedagogic focus that deepens the learning of scientific concepts, which improves the self-regulation and develops thought skills of higher order that helps forging better leaders; a most required characteristic of a Data Scientist. Communicative and researcher are other of their very important ones.

Many technologies, among the algorithms and presented models, have been developed within the chosen articles that seek to support the data scientist work. Big data bases are studied as well as diverse programs for in-formation extraction; those are the already created software packages or new algorithms, developed by professionals in each area, as it is the case of Trane which was proposed by Schreck and Veera-machaneni [28]. That can be applied to any set of variables in time. Users can connect their data and wait for the software to synthesize forecasting problems. It also interacts with general usage tools like Hadoop, which is a framework open source for the saving and processing big quantities of any type of data fast. Additional help models are presented such as G-DINA (Generalized DINA Model Frame-work) and CDM (Cognitive Diagnosis Modeling). It is additionally evidenced in the review that definitively data bases play an important role because they possess large saved information and therefore this generates the function of a Data Scientist.

It was found that many of the studies are oriented to give support to the academic area, because it is an enormous interest for educational institutions accurately determining the career profile of a Data Scientist, making even its projection and necessity that of fields different from IT, such is the case of nursery, journalism and agronomy. For instance, as Gold et al. indicate [10] students, such as those of agronomy can examine data to explain why the snow depth quickly diminishes in the early summer.

The performance of the Data Scientist is support by a variety of software and applications which make their job trustful and effective. Below, there is a review of five of them, being the last three, free of charge:

- DataRobot, is a platform that allows the production of any model with only a few code lines, making the validation of the model for every modeled technique, scientifically selecting the hyper parameters and options that optimize the performance of their models; this technology is prized [29].
- SubjectiveSystems, it permits to turn the data in the maximum value of the results, helping in everything, from optimizing the way of data acquisition, to designing and implementing panels, integrations and applications based on scalable data. To gain access to this technology it must be paid [30].
- GraphLab-Create 2.1 It allows the developers and Data Scientist apply automatic learning to build products from last generation data. This is a cost free tool, ideal for students [31].
- IPython, is a tool for parallel and interactive IT that is widely used in scientific IT. It is a cost free software [32].
- KNIME Analytics Platform, an open solution that leads to innovation based on data, helping discovering the hidden potential in data, quickly to implement, easy to escalate and intuitive learning. It has more than 2000 modules, hundreds of ready to execute examples, a wide range of integrated tools and the widest variety of available advanced algorithms [33].

5 Discussion

At the beginning, setting for search results was just for studies and no article with this type of systematic review and scope was found. But, after determining there was a shortage in works that make systematic review and orient the establishment on the profile of the Data Scientist, a mapping study was made being the following discussion content about its results.

It was defined that the main objective was to identify if the work and career profile defined for a Data Scientist exists, and after checking the preliminary articles it was found that eight of them, show how many educative institutions and higher education centers are involved in the process to define a study plan adequate for this profession, because even without a third level degree anyone can do activities related to this work. Some academic institutions are opting for identifying and evaluating the work profile requested by private and state companies to define their study plan. Educating and training Data Scientist specialists requires a new model, which reflects by design the whole lifecycle of data, and is aligned by construction with the target research and industry domains context and technologies [12].

It is pointed out in the majority of the articles that the IT, math and statistics areas are the academic bases which the Data Scientist must count with; for this the business area must be added because they must understand about administration, projects, budgets, among other fields, which turn them into multidisciplinary professionals, a role not easily assumed by any human being. Data Scientist, bridges the gap between the programming and implementation of data science, the theory of data science, and the business implications of data. They can take a business problem and translate it to a data question, create predictive models to answer the question, and tell a story about the findings [34].

The characteristics and skills that a Data Scientist must possess are varied, predominating leadership, research and communication, which are the key for the development of their activity, being commercially or industrially. They must have an open and creative mind, being organized since they need to interact with different type of people to comply with assigned activities, dealing some days with operatives and other with directive and management to make them know the information found after analyzing great data bases, which generates great value and competitive advantages.

In the review it is intended to find out about the tools that give support to the Data Scientist and several new algorithms were found, specifically created for a necessity. In other cases, exhausting analysis is made of software tools results already developed and of general use. The most remarkable aspect in the investigation reviewed is the studies about the diverse data base proposed and the way in which the information is extracted. Many Data Scientists compete even on Kaggle, which is a platform for the forecasting modeled and analysis competences, to find better model to present in a logical manner this big quantity of information imbedded in them.

The Forbes magazine [35] points out that Data Scientists lead the group of the best Jobs in the US. This is due to companies in need of someone capable of analyzing dirty dataset, and applies simple statistic tools to ungrounded patterns. Many more technology companies are compiling copious quantity of data, but few managers or executives are capacitated in the IT code needed to compile all that in a report. This provides an advantage to Data Scientist in a world that appeals more to data for decision making.

6 Conclusions and Further Research

The objective of this paper is to make a systematic review of the mapping of the Data Scientist profile and it was made following the Kitchenham [5] model. After running the literature review, the first conclusion points out the existence of a tendency of few articles published where the work profile and the career profile of a Data Scientist is established. Universities and education centers are seeking to make an adequate study plan, since (DS) it is anew profession, an academic program, adapted and updated to the new social circumstances, has not been established yet, in such a way that tuition level does not deteriorate, many of the reviewed articles have enabled clear the air terms in this matter.

In the evaluated articles it is rendered clearly that a Data Scientist must have solid knowledge in IT, math, and statistics. However, when it comes to business and administration knowhow, it is not defined how far the knowledge should be since, private industry and companies represent the higher demand for these type of professionals, it is expected being literate in finance, investment, production or human recourses.

The personal traits of a Data Scientist are very well defined, such as leadership, communication savvy and research, in order to achieve their goals in the data analysis and being able to explicitly communicate results; they must have many skills for accurate decision making and to forecast any type of problems.

Currently there is a lot of technology available to the Data Scientist, even algorithms are still being developed to ease up their job, which can be well applied if such an individual complies with all the appointed requirements; it is the only way they have to enclose the identification processes, capture, processing, analysis and data visualization.

Although the comparative analysis shows that there are studies in which knowledge areas of the Data Scientist are made known, as well as their abilities. No studies were found that emphasize about their work or career profile. This way it is shown that achieving a profile for this profession is still to be realized, to avoid premature obsolesce, with which it is expected to define the academic guidelines required for a groundbreaking profession, and as seen by many considered a new staple profession.

In the future it is expected to be able to execute an investigation that allows realizing an adequate division of the professional field of the Data Scientist, determining their participation levels in the labor market in order to define adequate profiles. Additionally, it is intended to carry on an investigation and a systematic review of the literature that includes more digital libraries.

References

1. Chen, H., Chiang, R.H., Storey, V.C.: Business intelligence and analytics: from big data to big impact. MIS Q. **36**(4), 1165–1188 (2012)
2. Jaramillo, O.: Pertinencia del perfil de los profesionales de la información con las demandas del mercado laboral. Revista Interamericana de Bibliotecología. **38** (2015). https://doi.org/ 10.17533/udea.rib.v38n2a03
3. Kim, M., Zimmermann, T., DeLine, R., Begel, A.: The emerging role of data scientists on software development teams, pp. 96–107. ACM Press (2016). https://doi.org/10.1145/ 2884781.2884783. http://dl.acm.org/citation.cfm?doid=2884781.2884783
4. Ecleo, J.J., Galido, A.: Surveying LinkedIn profiles of data scientists: the case of the Philippines. Procedia Comput. Sci. **124**, 53–60 (2017). https://doi.org/10.1016/j.procs.2017. 12.129

5. Kitchenham, B.: Procedures for performing systematic reviews. **33** (2004)
6. Huang, X., Lin, J.: Evaluation of PICO as a knowledge representation for clinical questions: In: Proceeding of the Annual Symposium oh the American Medical Informatics Association. AMIA Press (2006). http://users.umiacs.umd.edu/~jimmylin/publications/Huang_etal_AMIA2006.pdf
7. Zhai, J., Jocz, J.A., Tan, A.-L.: 'Am I Like a Scientist?': primary children's images of doing science in school. Int. J. Sci. Educ. **36**, 553–576 (2014) https://doi.org/10.1080/09500693.2013.791958
8. Treadwell, G., Ross, T., Lee, A., Lowenstein, J.K.: A numbers game: two case studies in teaching data journalism. Journal. Mass Commun. Educ. **71**, 297–308 (2016). https://doi.org/10.1177/1077695816665215
9. Younge, A.J.: Architectural principles and experimentation of distributed high performance virtual clusters. **24** (2017)
10. Gold, A.U., et al.: Arctic climate connections curriculum: a model for bringing authentic data into the classroom. J. Geosci. Educ. **63**, 185–197 (2015). https://doi.org/10.5408/14-030.1
11. Fuller, M.: BIG DATA: new science, new challenges, new dialogical opportunities: Zygon. Zygon® **50**, 569–582 (2015). https://doi.org/10.1111/zygo.12187
12. Manieri, A., et al.: Data science professional uncovered: how the EDISON project will contribute to a widely accepted profile for Data Scientists (2015)
13. Seo, D., Lee, M.-H., Yu, S.: Development of network analysis and visualization system for KEGG pathways. Symmetry **7**, 1275–1288 (2015). https://doi.org/10.3390/sym7031275
14. Shaikh, M.A.H., Omar, M.T., Azharul Hasan, K.M.: Efficient index computation for array based structured data. In: Efficient Index Computation for Array Based Structured Data, pp. 101–105. IEEE (2015). http://ieeexplore.ieee.org/document/7391930/. Accessed 18 May 2018
15. Rupp, A.A., van Rijn, P.W.: GDINA and CDM packages in R. Meas.: Interdiscipl. Res. Perspect. **16**, 71–77 (2018). https://doi.org/10.1080/15366367.2018.1437243
16. Webb, S.J., et al.: Guidelines and best practices for electrophysiological data collection, analysis and reporting in autism. J. Autism Dev. Disord. **45**, 425–443 (2015). https://doi.org/10.1007/s10803-013-1916-6
17. Brennan, P.F., Bakken, S.: Nursing needs big data and big data needs nursing: nursing needs big data. J. Nurs. Scholarsh. **47**, 477–484 (2015). https://doi.org/10.1111/jnu.12159
18. Tudoran, R., Costan, A., Antoniu, G.: OverFlow: multi-site aware big data management for scientific workflows on clouds. IEEE Trans. Cloud Comput. **4**, 76–89 (2016). https://doi.org/10.1109/TCC.2015.2440254
19. Asamoah, D.A., Sharda, R., Hassan Zadeh, A., Kalgotra, P.: Preparing a data scientist: a pedagogic experience in designing a big data analytics course: preparing a data scientist. Decis. Sci. J. Innov. Educ. **15**, 161–190 (2017). https://doi.org/10.1111/dsji.12125
20. Bowers, A.J.: Quantitative research methods training in education leadership and administration preparation programs as disciplined inquiry for building school improvement capacity. J. Res. Leadersh. Educ. **12**, 72–96 (2017). https://doi.org/10.1177/1942775116659462
21. Malviya, A., Udhani, A., Soni, S.: R-tool: data analytic framework for big data. In: R-Tool: Data Analytic Framework for Big Data, pp. 1–5. IEEE (2016). http://ieeexplore.ieee.org/document/7570960/. Accessed 18 May 2018
22. Ebadi, H., Antignac, T., Sands, D.: Sampling and partitioning for differential privacy. In: Sampling and Partitioning for Differential Privacy, pp. 664–673. IEEE (2016). http://ieeexplore.ieee.org/document/7906954/. Accessed 18 May 2018

23. Rojas, J.A.R., Beth Kery, M., Rosenthal, S., Dey, A.: Sampling techniques to improve big data exploration. Sampling Techniques to Improve Big Data Exploration, pp. 26–35. IEEE (2017). http://ieeexplore.ieee.org/document/8231848/. Accessed 18 May 2018
24. Gehl, R.W.: Sharing, knowledge management and big data: a partial genealogy of the data scientist (2015)
25. Kim, S., Choi, M.-S.: Study on data center and data librarian role for reuse of research data. In: Study on Data Center and Data Librarian Role for Reuse of Research Data, pp. 303–308. IEEE (2016). http://ieeexplore.ieee.org/document/7440517/. Accessed 18 May 2018
26. Eybers, S., Hattingh, M.: Teaching data science to post graduate students: a preliminary study using a « F-L-I-P » class room approach (2016)
27. Baškarada, S., Koronios, A.: Unicorn data scientist: the rarest of breeds. Program **51**, 65–74 (2017). https://doi.org/10.1108/PROG-07-2016-0053
28. Schreck, B., Veeramachaneni, K.: What would a data scientist ask? Automatically formulating and solving predictive problems. In: What Would a Data Scientist Ask? Automatically Formulating and Solving Predictive Problems, pp. 440–451. IEEE (2016). http://ieeexplore.ieee.org/document/7796930/. Accessed 19 May 2018
29. Data robot: Beneficios para los científicos de datos. https://www.datarobot.com/data-scientists/. Accessed 19 May 2018
30. SubjectivesSystems: Convertimos DATA en VENTAJA. https://www.subjectivesystems.com/. Accessed 19 May 2018
31. Turi create intelligence: GraphLab-Create. https://pypi.org/project/GraphLab-Create/. Accessed 19 May 2018
32. Ipython: Ipython interactive computing. http://ipython.org/index.html. Accessed 19 May 2018
33. KNIME: KNIME Analytics Platform. https://www.knime.com/knime-analytics-platform. Accessed 19 May 2018
34. Saltz, J.S., Grady, N.W.: The ambiguity of data science team roles and the need for a data science workforce framework, pp. 2355–2361. IEEE (2017). http://ieeexplore.ieee.org/document/8258190/. Accessed 19 May 2018
35. Forbes: Report: Why « Data Scientist » is the Best Job to Pursue in 2016. https://www.forbes.com/sites/gregoryferenstein/2016/01/20/report-why-data-scientist-is-the-best-job-to-pursue-in-2016/#13caba13a526

Fault-Tolerant Model Based on Fuzzy Control for Mobile Devices

Diego Vallejo-Huanga[1,2,3](✉), Julio Proaño[1], Paulina Morillo[1], and Holger Ortega[1]

[1] IDEIAGEOCA Research Group, Universidad Politécnica Salesiana, Quito, Ecuador
{dvallejoh,jproanoo,pmorillo,hortega}@ups.edu.ec
[2] Department of Mathematics, Universidad San Francisco de Quito, Quito, Ecuador
dvallejoh@asig.com.ec
[3] Department of Physics and Mathematics, Universidad de las Américas,
Quito, Ecuador
diego.vallejo.huanga@udla.edu.ec

Abstract. Nowadays, mobile devices incorporate many sensors to monitor operational parameters, so that possible failures in the systems can be detected and prevented. Therefore, failure detection has become crucial to ensure the automation of certain applications, such as, health monitoring or unmanned aerial vehicles. On the other side, fuzzy models perfectly fit when the input-output relationships use categorical values and they are not deterministic. However, find a feasible model is not a trivial task due to the interaction of many variables at time. In this work, we propose a fault detection model based on fuzzy logic to early detect potential fault in mobile devices. Our approach considers the interaction of four variables, all of them could be measured from sensors of the device. As a proof of concept, we have tested our model in a simulated scenario with random values taken from all the possible combinations of the input fuzzy sets. The mapping into the fuzzy output called, *risk of fault*, shows accordance with the expected values in literature. Finally, results show that our model can distinguish four levels of failure risk and it is able to be implemented in a production environment.

Keywords: Fuzzy logic · Fault tolerance · Mobile devices

1 Introduction

On many occasions, and due to different circumstances, it is difficult for researchers to obtain data that is reliable and with which they can make decisions and find a solution to a specific problem. Sometimes the researchers do not have a Data Acquisition System (DAQ) [1] that allows them to measure an electrical or physical phenomenon such as voltage, current, temperature, pressure or sound. In addition, important factors must be taken into account, such as costs associated with the DAQ, response times of the external measuring elements, elicitation, etc. Also, in mobile computing, the efficient utilization of the

© Springer Nature Switzerland AG 2019
M. Botto-Tobar et al. (Eds.): CITT 2018, CCIS 895, pp. 488–499, 2019.
https://doi.org/10.1007/978-3-030-05532-5_36

information gained from the sensors embedded in the devices, is not a trivial task [22].

A control system is a set of components or mechanisms responsible for managing and regulating the behavior of another system, in order to reduce the probabilities of failure and obtain the theoretically true results [12]. In [36] a fault is defined as any erroneous state of a system's hardware or software. Currently, control systems focused on fault detection are widely used in different industrial processes, due to their performance and reduced operating costs [6]. When some part of the system fails, a fault-tolerant design enables the system to continue its intended operation, at a reduced level, rather than failing completely [20].

One possibility to deal with fault-tolerant control systems could be a system based on machine learning. However, one of the hardest problems to solve in machine learning is getting the right data in the right format. When this information is not available, it is impossible to use a system to train a model to detect faults in its operation. A possible solution is the use of a fuzzy control that, through a set of heuristic rules, where the linguistic variables of the inputs and outputs are represented by fuzzy sets, allows determining a possible failure in a system.

Although fuzzy control was initially introduced as a model-free control design method based on the knowledge of a human operator, current research is almost exclusively devoted to model-based fuzzy control methods that can guarantee stability and robustness in different kinds of systems [33].

In the environment of mobile systems due to high mobility, network connectivity is often lost or degraded. In addition, mobile environments are also usually characterized by their limited resource availability, low bandwidth, frequent disconnection and higher interference [31].

Our paper describes a scheme in which a fuzzy model is used to unify criteria considered critical for the proper operation of a mobile device. The model is implemented as an interpreter of a set of rules expressed as fuzzy conditional statements. Our new fault-tolerant model, based on a fuzzy controller, takes into account four factors at once, for the detection of a possible failure in the system: battery charge level, CPU utilization, battery temperature and response time.

This paper is organized as follows. Section 2 presents the previous work related to fuzzy controllers and fault-tolerant systems. The formalization of the new architecture and the holistic methodology proposed are described in Sect. 3. Section 4 includes simulation results and experiments for the validation of the proposed scheme. Finally, concluding remarks and future work are presented in Sect. 5.

2   Related Work

Fuzzy Logic Control (FLC) was introduced for the first time in the middle of the 60s by Zaden [43], since then a number of improvements and applications of FLC systems have appeared [38]. Fuzzy control systems have been used especially in industrial processes, because the input-output relationships are not deterministic and are feasible to model using categorical values [16], it also has been extensively used as an alternative to manipulate and describe complex systems when traditional control methods do not provide viable solutions [23]. For that reason, FLC system is introduced in many applications from different areas such as: power systems [34], qualitative modeling [37], pattern recognition [3], finance [7], medicine [28], among others [13]. Most recent works show the use of FLC systems to solve problems in the field of mechanical-robotic systems: [4,17,29], for all of these cases a greater efficiency than with traditional control systems is obtained.

On the other hand, the purpose of fault tolerance is to increase the dependability of a system [31] and for that it is necessary to use different mechanisms and techniques that allow the system to continue working. An adequate taxonomy, of fault tolerance techniques, is exposed in [9], where the authors define three categories: redundancy techniques, load balancing strategies and fault tolerance policies.

Failure detection systems have limitations when the control variables cannot be explicitly defined, in these cases, the use of a fuzzy controller facilitates and improves the design of the entire system. Despite the use of FLC is extended in different applications, as mentioned above, there are few examples in the literature of the use of fuzzy controllers in fault-tolerant systems, for instance, in [5] the authors define a fuzzy load balancer for adaptive fault tolerance management in cloud platforms, in such a way that, when an anomaly has been detected, the algorithm directs the system to apply a fault rejuvenation mechanism to an anomalously behaving virtual machine. Article [26], proposes an adaptive fuzzy fault-tolerant control approach for a class of non-triangular structure nonlinear systems, which contain immeasurable states and unknown actuator faults. In this paper, FLCs are used to approximate unknown nonlinear functions, and a fuzzy state observer is designed to estimate immeasurable states. Other studies on fault-tolerant systems, with the use of fuzzy control, can be observed in: [11,19,24,39,44]. It is important to mention that none of them is focused on mobile systems.

3   Methodology

Our fault-tolerant model based on fuzzy control has a preventive and non-corrective nature, and is designed to alert the system in case there is a high failure risk, when the fuzzy membership value so determines. In addition, it is especially constructed for the control of faults in mobile devices.

Due to the accelerated and incremental development of information technologies around the world, the sales of smartphones and smart mobile devices have increased rapidly and exponentially [8]. Smartphones allow multimedia reproduction, Internet access and communication capabilities, but, the growing functionality of smartphones requires more power to support operation throughout the day. Processing power, location systems, sensors and embedded applications decrease the duration of the battery charge [14]. The typical battery capacity of smartphones today is barely above 1500 [mA] [10] and this is an important limitation because mobile devices frequently are used in tasks, to solve problems in industry and engineering. Hence, *battery charge level* reflects the remaining battery and how long it will take to discharge or charge, and for this reason this parameter is very important to determine the correct functioning of a mobile system.

Another parameter, of vital importance in the correct functioning of a mobile device, and one that is closely related to the previous one, is the *battery temperature*. A-priori, the battery temperature for a mobile device depends on its manufacturing materials, but in a generic way, the scientific literature has shown that certain thresholds can be established for all of them.

CPU utilization is considered as a key metric in the performance of mobile systems, it is denoted by the amount of time a CPU is busy in performing a task during a specific interval and is reported as a percentage. CPU anomalies appear if its utilization goes beyond a certain threshold for a sustained period of time [5].

In computing, *response time* is defined as the total amount of time it takes to respond to a request for service [21]. In the environment of mobile systems, response time can be affected by changes in processing time and latency which occur due to changes in hardware resources or utilization.

Therefore, we consider these four parameters: battery charge level, CPU utilization, battery temperature and response time as crisp inputs, for our fuzzy control model for fault-tolerant systems. Figure 1 shows the model used, consisting of four inputs and a single output.

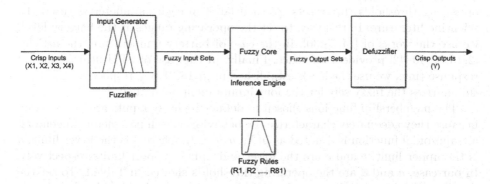

Fig. 1. Block diagram of the fuzzy controller

In fuzzy logic, a linguistic value is a categorical value associated with a fuzzy set, and it is described in natural language. For our model we have considered that all parameters can take three operating states, which have been defined by the following linguistic values (labels): optimum, normal and poor. We do not use the typical low-medium-high scale, because both the *high* label and the *low*

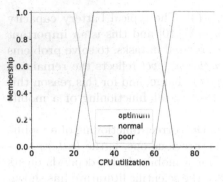

Fig. 2. CPU utilization

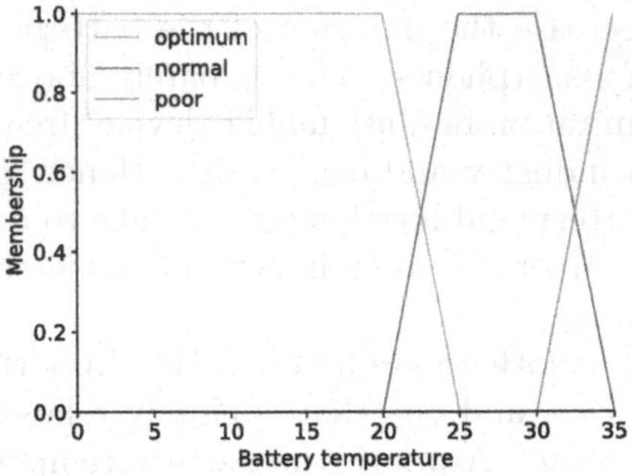

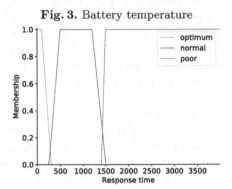

Fig. 3. Battery temperature

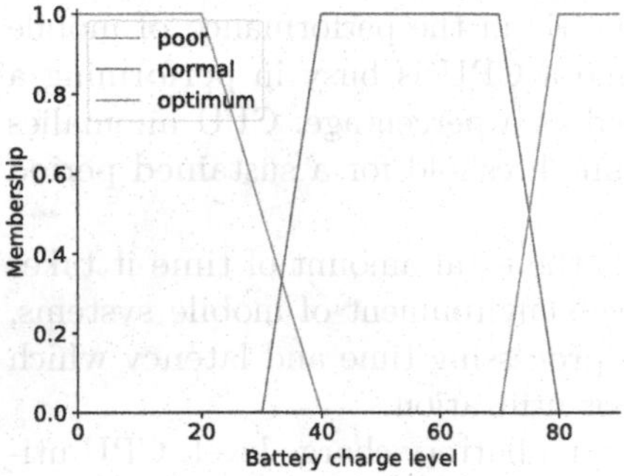

Fig. 4. Battery charge level

Fig. 5. Response time

label contain values that lead to failures in our system. Thus, to determine the operating thresholds (fuzzy sets) of each label in each parameter we used the scientific literature. In this way, to set the operating ranges at the battery level, we use the works of [14, 25, 30]. In the case of battery temperature, the articles [2, 15, 32, 40–42] provide a reference. Finally, in the case of CPU utilization and response time, we use the levels established in [5, 18, 21, 35], respectively. Table 1 summarizes the fuzzy sets for the four inputs mentioned above.

The membership functions chosen to define the fuzzy inputs are trapezoidal, because they adequately characterize the behavior of each parameter. In general, a trapezoidal function is denoted as $\mu(X_i, a, b, c, d)$, where a is the lower limit, d is the upper limit, b and c are the lower and upper support limits respectively. In our case, a and d are the operating thresholds showed in Table 1. To set the function of the intermediate label (normal) b and c are calculated by the empiric criteria of $\pm 10\%$ of a or b. To set the functions of the extreme category (poor or optimum), if the category is the lower: a and b take the same value, otherwise if the category is the upper: c and d are equal. The inputs are represented as membership functions like show Figs. 2, 3, 4, 5.

Usually, the fuzzy controller is constructed of control rules which are ambiguously described by conventional controller strategies and expert knowledge and because its structure theory is not well established yet [27]. Hence, in this fuzzy

Table 1. Operating range of fuzzy inputs

Input	Optimum	Normal	Poor
Battery charge level [%]	70–100	30–80	0–40
Battery temperature [°C]	0–25	20–35	30–40
CPU utilization [%]	0–30	20–70	60–100
Response time [ms]	0–300	250–1500	1400–4000

controller design we take into account all possible combinations that can generate the inputs, in this way, to calculate the number of fuzzy rules we raise the number of categorical values of each input to the number of inputs, obtaining 3^4 rules given by the inputs.

We define the output as the risk of having a failure counting the number of *poor* values that we obtain in the inputs. This number is a discrete random variable Y, which follows a binomial distribution:

$$P\left(Y = k\right) = \binom{4}{k}p^k(1-p)^{k-1} \qquad 0 \le p \le 1 \tag{1}$$

where: Y define our fuzzy output set, k can take values between 0 and 4 and p is the probability that a parameter has a *poor* value and is equal to 1/3. Thus, we establish four new categories for the output: *low, very-low, high* and *very-high*, based on the probability distribution shown in Table 2.

Table 2. Probability distribution of the fuzzy output

Y	P(Y)	Output (failure risk)
0	0.1975	Very-low
1	0.3951	Low
2	0.3963	High
>3	0.1111	Very-high

The method used for inference is known as Mamdani's minimum inference (R_M) whose definition is in Expression 2, where $\mu_y(x)$ is the membership function of the output set y.

$$min(\mu, \mu_y(x)), \forall x \tag{2}$$

For the defuzzification process we use the centroid method described in Eq. 3.

$$y^* = \frac{\int \mu_c(y)y\,dy}{\int \mu_c(y)\,dy} \tag{3}$$

The merit of such a controller is discussed in the light of the results obtained in Sect. 4.

4 Experiments

In this section we test the model presented in Sect. 3 using a simulation tool developed in Python 2.7. In particular, the core of the simulator is based on the scikit-fuzzy package[1]. This package contains a collection of fuzzy logic algorithms that allows to develop scientific tools in Python. The source code used for the simulations is available at https://github.com/dlevalhu/fuzzy-logic-simulation-CITT2018.

The hardware used for developing and testing comprises an Intel Core i7 server composed of 8 Gb of memory and running Ubuntu 16.04 LTS operating system. The total time for running the simulation is approximately 3.06 s.

Before showing the results, the simulator setup is described.

4.1 Simulation Setup

In summary, the simulator receives a vector that contains a level for each parameter: battery charge level, battery temperature, CPU utilization and response time. The range of each level is shown in Table 1. These values are sent to the fuzzy core module. This module calculates the fuzzy output based on the fuzzy rules defined by the probabilities (see Table 2). Finally, to obtain the risk of failure, the defuzzification process transforms the fuzzy value intro a crisp value using Mamdani's inference model. The possible levels of risk are tagged as *low*, *very-low*, *high* and *very-high*.

In order to test each possible output as the level of the risk, we generate a vector that contains each input parameter and we observe the output. This input vector was randomly generated. On the other side, the risk of failure directly depends on the quantity of the input parameters that are set in *poor* level. So, for example, to evaluate the *low* risk scenario, the input vector does not contain any parameter within *poor* level. It means that the risk of having a fault is *low*.

Following this criteria and for testing the *low* risk we set only one input parameter in *poor* level at time, while the rest of parameters are kept in *normal* level. Next, to test the next risk level *high*, we group two by two input parameters and set them in *poor* level. Finally, to test the *very-high* risk of having a failure we set three and even four of input parameters in *poor* level. The results obtained can be seen in Sect. 4.2.

4.2 Simulation Results

A brief of the most relevant results of the simulations are discussed in this section.

The simulation results are divided into four scenarios according to the risk of having a risk of failure such as *low*, *very-low*, *high* and *very-high*. All these results are shown in Table 3.

---

[1] https://media.readthedocs.org/pdf/scikit-fuzzy/stable/scikit-fuzzy.pdf.

Table 3. Results of the simulations

	1	2	3	4	1	2	3	4
	Very-low scenarios				Low scenarios			
Battery temperature [°C]	23	31	22	21	33	37	38	36
Battery charge level [%]	74	77	62	55	67	37	54	41
Response time [ms]	776	591	576	472	600	1226	1369	396
CPU utilization [%]	35	42	43	34	64	38	60	62
Failure-risk	11	20	12	11	45	48	40	46
	High scenarios				Very-high scenarios			
Battery temperature [°C]	37	34	33	38	22	37	30	39
Battery charge level [%]	6	16	39	63	29	1	10	69
Response time (ms)	1102	3402	3598	3391	3011	499	2825	1979
CPU utilization [%]	66	32	69	67	96	· 93	86	83
Failure-risk	75	82	70	78	92	91	90	91

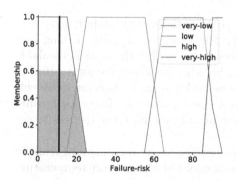

Fig. 6. Case very-low risk   **Fig. 7.** Case low risk

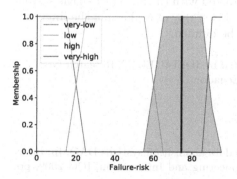
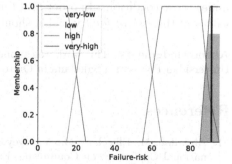

Fig. 8. Case high risk   **Fig. 9.** Case very-high risk

Table 3 shows the values generated when testing all of the possible risk failure scenarios. In all the scenarios, four vectors were generated (cases). It is worth to notice that the output for *very-low* risk is around 10–20%. It means that the risk of having a failure is *very-low*. For the next scenario the output value is around 40–50%. It shows that the percentage of having a failure-risk is *low*. In contrast, for the other 2 scenarios, *high* and *very-high*, the risk of having a failure is around 70–90% which means a *high* risk of having a failure. All the simulations were performed four times and the results show the best values obtained.

Figures 6, 7, 8 and 9 show an example of the failure's risk depend on the level of the input (case). For example in Fig. 6 the percentage of failure' risk is 10% while for low risk it is round 40% as is shown in Fig. 7. In contrast, for the high risk case the percentage is 70% while for the very-high risk it is around 90% (see Figs. 8 and 9). All of these values corresponds with the expected in the literature.

5   Conclusions and Future Work

The simulations run with all the possible combinations of the input fuzzy sets yielded results that are in accordance with the expected outputs. Taking into account that we only use four crisp inputs results show that the model is scalable for more variables and embedded devices. So, this work represents a proof of concept that shows our model can be implemented in a production environment.

The obtained result shows that a control system based on fuzzy logic could be implemented in real devices to give coherent outputs, for these devices to act accordingly in order to prevent fault.

Future works in this respect should be focused on the development of realistic scenarios, with the input data taken from sensors of charge and temperature installed in the device, and the parameters CPU utilization and response time given by the software itself. This data, after undergoing the fuzzy-logic process, would produce an output that can be contrasted with the real state of the system under those conditions. In order to attain this, a way of evaluating the linguistic values of the *risk of fault* variable should be defined.

Acknowledgments. This work was supported by IDEIAGEOCA Research Group of Universidad Politécnica Salesiana in Quito, Ecuador.

References

1. Abdallah, M., Elkeelany, O.: A survey on data acquisition systems DAQ. In: International Conference on Computing, Engineering and Information, ICC 2009, pp. 240–243 (2009)
2. Aghaee, N., Peng, Z., Eles, P.: Adaptive temperature-aware SoC test scheduling considering process variation. In: IEEE 14th Euromicro Conference on Digital System Design (DSD), pp. 197–204 (2011)

3. Ajiboye, A.B., Weir, R.F.: A heuristic fuzzy logic approach to EMG pattern recognition for multifunctional prosthesis control. IEEE Trans. Neural Syst. Rehabil. Eng. **13**(3), 280–291 (2005)
4. Akmal, M.A., Jamin, N.F., Ghani, N.A.: Fuzzy logic controller for two wheeled EV3 LEGO robot. In: 2017 IEEE Conference on Systems, Process and Control (ICSPC) (2017)
5. Arabnejad, H., Pahl, C., Estrada, G., Samir, A., Fowley, F.: A fuzzy load balancer for adaptive fault tolerance management in cloud platforms. In: De Paoli, F., Schulte, S., Broch Johnsen, E. (eds.) ESOCC 2017. LNCS, vol. 10465, pp. 109–124. Springer, Cham (2017). https://doi.org/10.1007/978-3-319-67262-5_9
6. Blanke, M., et al.: Fault-tolerant control systems - a holistic view. Control Eng. Pract. **5**(5), 693–702 (1997)
7. Bojadziev, G.: Fuzzy Logic for Business, Finance, and Management. World Scientific, Singapore (2007)
8. Buennemeyer, T.K., Nelson, T.M., Clagett, L.M., Dunning, J.P., Marchany, R.C., Tront, J.G.: Mobile device profiling and intrusion detection using smart batteries. In: Proceedings in the 41th Hawaii International Conference on System Sciences (2008)
9. Cheraghlou, M.N., Khadem-Zadeh, A., Haghparast, M.: A survey of fault tolerance architecture in cloud computing. J. Netw. Comput. Appl. **61**, 81–92 (2016)
10. Corey, G.P.: Nine ways to murder your battery (these are only some of the ways). In: Battcon (2010)
11. Diao, Y., Passino, K.M.: Stable fault-tolerant adaptive fuzzy/neural control for a turbine engine. IEEE Trans. Control Syst. Technol. **9**(3), 494–509 (2001)
12. Dorf, R.C., Bishop, R.H.: Modern Control Systems. Pearson Education, London (2011)
13. Feng, G.: A survey on analysis and design of model-based fuzzy control systems. IEEE Trans. Fuzzy syst. **14**(5), 676–697 (2006)
14. Ferreira, D., Dey, A.K., Kostakos, V.: Understanding human-smartphone concerns: a study of battery life. In: Lyons, K., Hightower, J., Huang, E.M. (eds.) Pervasive 2011. LNCS, vol. 6696, pp. 19–33. Springer, Heidelberg (2011). https://doi.org/10.1007/978-3-642-21726-5_2
15. Gao, L., Liu, S., Dougal, R.A.: Dynamic lithium-ion battery model for system simulation. IEEE Trans. Compon. Packag. Technol. **25**(3), 495–505 (2002)
16. Gaurav, A.K., Kaur, A.: Comparison between conventional PID and fuzzy logic controller for liquid flow control: performance evaluation of fuzzy logic and PID controller by using MATLAB/Simulink. Int. J. Innov. Technol. Explor. Eng. (IJITEE) **1**(1), 84–88 (2012)
17. Gdaim, S., Mtibaa, A., Mimouni, M.F.: Design and experimental implementation of DTC of an induction machine based on fuzzy logic control on FPGA. IEEE Trans. Fuzzy Syst. **23**(3), 644–655 (2015)
18. Hamad, H., Saad, R., Abed, R.: Performance evaluation of RESTful web services for mobile devices. Int. Arab J. e-Technol. **1**(3), 72–78 (2010)
19. Jiang, B., et al.: Adaptive fault-tolerant tracking control of near-space vehicle using Takagi-Sugeno fuzzy models. IEEE Trans. Fuzzy Syst. **18**(5), 1000–1007 (2010)
20. Johnson, B.W.: Fault-tolerant microprocessor-based systems. IEEE Micro **4**(6), 6–21 (1984)
21. Joseph, M., Pandya, P.: Finding response times in a real-time system. Comput. J. **29**(5), 390–395 (1986)

22. Korpipää, P., Mäntyjärvi, J.: An ontology for mobile device sensor-based context awareness. In: Blackburn, P., Ghidini, C., Turner, R.M., Giunchiglia, F. (eds.) CONTEXT 2003. LNCS (LNAI), vol. 2680, pp. 451–458. Springer, Heidelberg (2003). https://doi.org/10.1007/3-540-44958-2_37

23. Koshiyama, A.S., Vellasco, M.M.B.R., Tanschei, R.: GPFIS-control: a genetic fuzzy system for control tasks. J. Artif. Intell. Soft Comput. Res. 4(3), 167–179 (2014)

24. Kwong, W.A., et al.: Expert supervision of fuzzy learning systems for fault tolerant aircraft control. Proc. IEEE 83(3), 466–483 (1995)

25. Lee, J., Chon, Y., Cha, H.: Evaluating battery aging on mobile devices. In: Proceedings of the 52nd Annual Design Automation Conference, p. 135. ACM (2015)

26. Li, Y., Ma, Z., Tong, S.: Adaptive fuzzy fault-tolerant control of non-triangular structure nonlinear systems with error-constraint. IEEE Trans. Fuzzy Syst. 26, 2062–2074 (2017)

27. Maeda, M., Murakami, S.: A self-tuning fuzzy controller. Fuzzy Sets Syst. 51(1), 29–40 (1992)

28. Mahfouf, M., Abbod, M.F., Linkens, D.A.: A survey of fuzzy logic monitoring and control utilisation in medicine. Artif. Intell. Med. 21(1-3), 27–42 (2001)

29. Pena, M., et al.: Fuzzy logic for omni directional mobile platform control displacement using FPGA and Bluetooth. IEEE Latin Am. Trans. 13(6), 1907–1914 (2015)

30. Petricca, M., Shin, D., Bocca, A., Macii, A., Macii, E., Poncino, M.: An automated framework for generating variable-accuracy battery models from datasheet information. In: 2013 IEEE International Symposium on Low Power Electronics and Design (ISLPED), pp. 365–370 (2013)

31. Saha, G.K.: Fault management in mobile computing. Ubiquity 2003(October), 1 (2003)

32. Sahin, O., Coskun, A.K.: On the impacts of greedy thermal management in mobile devices. IEEE Embed. Syst. Lett. 7(2), 55–58 (2015)

33. Sala, A., Guerra, T.M., Babuska, R.: Perspectives of fuzzy systems and control. Fuzzy Sets Syst. 156, 432–444 (2005)

34. Sa-ngawong, N., Ngamroo, I.: Intelligent photovoltaic farms for robust frequency stabilization in multi-area interconnected power system based on PSO-based optimal Sugeno fuzzy logic control. Renew. Energy 74, 555–567 (2015)

35. Satyanarayanan, M., et al.: The case for VM-based cloudlets in mobile computing. IEEE Pervasive Comput. 8(4), 14–23 (2009)

36. Siewiorek, D.P., Swarz, R.S.: The Theory and Practice of Reliable System Design. Digital Press, Belford (1982)

37. Sugeno, M., Yasukawa, T.: A fuzzy-logic-based approach to qualitative modeling. IEEE Trans. Fuzzy Syst. 1(1), 7 (1993)

38. Takagi, T., Sugeno, M.: Fuzzy identification of systems and its applications to modeling and control. Read. Fuzzy Sets Intell. Syst. SMC−15(1), 387–403 (1993)

39. Tong, S., Huo, B., Li, Y.: Observer-based adaptive decentralized fuzzy fault-tolerant control of nonlinear large-scale systems with actuator failures. IEEE Trans. Fuzzy Syst. 22(1), 1–15 (2014)

40. Xie, Q., et al.: Dynamic thermal management in mobile devices considering the thermal coupling between battery and application processor. In: IEEE/ACM International Conference on Computer-Aided Design (ICCAD), pp. 242–247 (2013)

41. Yeo, I., Kim, E.J.: Temperature-aware scheduler based on thermal behavior grouping in multicore systems. In: Design, Automation and Test in Europe Conference and Exhibition, DATE 2009, pp. 946–951. IEEE (2009)

42. Yeo, I., Liu, C.C., Kim, E.J.: Predictive dynamic thermal management for multi-core systems. In: Proceedings of the 45th Annual Design Automation Conference, pp. 734–739. ACM (2008)
43. Zadeh, L.A.: Fuzzy Sets. Fuzzy Logic, And Fuzzy Systems: Selected Papers, pp. 394–432. World Scientific, Singapore (1996)
44. Zhang, K., Jiang, B., Staroswiecki, M.: Dynamic output feedback-fault tolerant controller design for Takagi-Sugeno fuzzy systems with actuator faults. IEEE Trans. Fuzzy Syst. **18**(1), 194–201 (2010)

Monitoring for the Evaluation Process On-Line Prototype Based on OpenFace Algorithm

Omar Ruiz-Vivanco$^{(\boxtimes)}$, Alexandra Gonzalez-Eras , Jorge Cordero ,
and Luis Barba-Guaman

Universidad Técnica Particular de Loja, Loja, Ecuador
oaruiz@utpl.edu.ec

Abstract. This project was designed to present a prototype of facial authentication system that allows for the recognition of students who are using an online platform to take final evaluations in our Distance Learning Program, with the purpose of detecting fraud and identity theft. It uses the OpenFace algorithm based on neural networks, taking input from two-dimensional images of the student from time to time during the participation on the exam. We present a system for face recognition using an image database of faces in classroom setting to demonstrate the improvement using this OpenFace algorithm for the preprocessing approach. The preliminary results indicate a high accuracy in the recognition of students, in terms of brightness, size and quality of the image of the face.

Keywords: Computational intelligence · Computer vision
Face authentication · Neural networks · OpenFace algorithm

1 Introduction

In recent years the artificial vision techniques have been applied for collecting, processing and analysis of information obtained through digital images, giving capabilities to computational systems to make decisions in the real world, based on the information provided by the processing of images from a capture device [1,14], which are subsequently used in the process of the facial recognition. In identification problems, the input to the system is an unknown face and the system will return a particular identity from a database of known individuals, with a high degree of accuracy. The system needs to confirm or reject the identity of the face.

In higher education institutions, facial recognition systems can be used for many purposes. They can identify students, grant access to specific events and register participation in a variety of activities. Regarding the online assessment processes, automatic facial recognition algorithms are used to verify the student's identity and to detect an unusual behavior of the students during the evaluation. The use of facial authentication within the education system, provides the

M. Botto-Tobar et al. (Eds.): CITT 2018, CCIS 895, pp. 500–509, 2019.
https://doi.org/10.1007/978-3-030-05532-5_37

possibility to verify that there is no fraud while the students carry out with the activities that complement the learning process [10,15].

This article presents the implementation of a student authentication and identification smart system which can perform online identifications, designed with the purpose of increasing accuracy of participants, in addition to generating reports for the authorities, teachers and decision-making processes among others. The system uses OpenFace recognition algorithm to verify the identity of the student and detect anomalous events during the evaluation process.

The main goal is to develop a prototype for the authentication of students before and during the on-line evaluation, through facial recognition. In order to fulfill this objective, we first have made the state-of-art of facial recognition [3,6], to know which methods and techniques have been implemented, especially those which have used open source approach. The System is configured to identify, monitor the student continuously and generate reports of student recognition during the development of the on-line evaluation.

The article is organized as follows. Section 2 illustrates the structure of Open-Face tools. Section 3 presents the methodology used in the development of the prototype, as well as the strategy for validating its operation. Section 4 presents the experiments carried out to validate the prototype and the results obtained. Finally, the conclusion and future work are presented in Sect. 5.

2 Related Works

There are various models proposing solutions to problems of reconnaissance and surveillance. In [8] is presented a system for the remote transmission of digital data and satellite location from fixed or mobile terminals with urban surveillance cameras for facial recognition, gun shots detectors, capture of public safety personnel and person. As well Alonso, [2] uses facial recognition for advertising. In other works, systems control the registration and automated confirmation of identity, [4,13]. All of these are used a collection of two-dimensional images of individuals and algorithms based on neural networks as is the case of OpenFace, to perform facial recognition and comparison [9], such as indexing of images [5].

Some companies have developed tools for facial recognition such as OpenFace. OpenFace is an open source facial behavior analysis toolkit. In [6] described the tool in detail. Based on the computer vision algorithms, this software allows to detect facial points, estimate the pose of the head, facial recognition and an estimate of the gaze. For instance, Fig. 1 describes facial landmark detection, head pose and eye gaze estimation, facial action unit recognition. The outputs from all of these systems (indicated by red) can be saved to disk or sent over a network [6].

In [7] presents the results of the experimentation by averaging the accuracy of ten experiments. The OpenFace results are obtained by the euclidean distance to the square on the pairs and label the pairs under a threshold as the same person and above the threshold as different people. Figure 2 shows the OpenFace ROC curve comparing with other techniques.

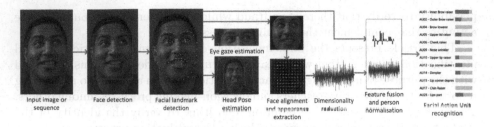

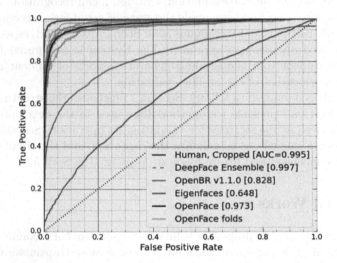

Fig. 1. OpenFace facial behavior analysis pipeline (Color figure online)

Fig. 2. ROC curve on the LFW benchmark with area under the curve (AUC) values.

In the educational context, there are proposals using facial recognition models for the tracking of person [15,16], others in which algorithms validate the identity of the student during an examination conducted in person and others who have taken this concept of evaluation toward the on-line assessments, using as input devices such as is the case of the webcams [17]. Our proposal is directed precisely to the recognition of students who perform tests remotely, from their home and using their personal computer and webcam. The imaging is performed each time during the test and considers the reduction of the images for their treatment. In the following section the methodology used in the present work is explained.

3 Methodology

This section describes the components used for the implementation and validation of the student authentication prototype, corresponding to the development and validation of the prototype. The solution involves the use of a facial recognition tool from great acceptance such as OpenFace [5].

3.1   Development of the Prototype

The architecture of the prototype considers the design paradigm Model-View-Controller (MVC), giving emphasis on the re-use, connectivity and extensibility of components; In addition, the Django development platform is chosen because it facilitates the integration of the facial recognition algorithms in the prototype [11, 12].

Given the nature of the prototype, the use of the agile SCRUM methodology is considered, since it allows the proper management of the development of the components, by means of 6 sprints: Sprint 1, the investigation of tools for the recognition of faces and to propose the scheme of database; Sprint 2, the registration of students in the system. Sprint 3, student registration and monitoring (photo capture). Sprint 4, the functions of the administration panel; Sprint 5, "penface" library adaptation for recognition training and evaluation, Sprint 6, report generation process and validation of results.

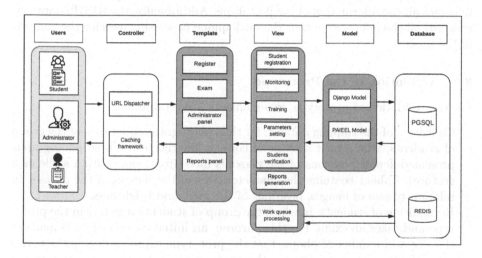

Fig. 3. Surveillance prototype architecture

Figure 3 describes the functionality of the prototype, which includes the following elements:

Users: The presence of 3 users, student, which is the one that enters the system to take a test, the administrator, who is in charge of managing the process of recognition of the student and the teacher, who analyzes the reports generated by the prototype.

Controller: Where is the URL Dispatcher, responsible for managing the requests of users to the views and filtering the URLs of the different templates and pages cached (Caching Framework).

Templates and Views: The templates and views of the prototype can be grouped into 4 large instances: Register, where the student's information is entered, as well as the collection of initial photos that constitute the training base of the algorithm; Exam, where the student selects the test he must perform; Administration panel, where the face training options are located as well as modification of parameters for the capture of photos; Reports panel, where reports of recognition of each exam given by registered students are presented. Additionally, there is the work queue processing, which manages the queue of images that must be analyzed by the facial recognition algorithm.

Model and Database: In the model there are two schemes: The Dyango model, which contains the entities that the prototype uses of the Dyango platform for handling authentication processes; and, the PAIEEL model that contains all the entities of the prototype such as: teacher, student, subject, exam, among the most important. These two models converge in the PGSQL database, which manages all the information of the prototype. Additionally, the REDIS database contains all the information that the work queue processing uses for the analysis of the images.

3.2 Validation of the Prototype

For the validation of prototype, two moments are established:

- Collection of the training dataset: for this, photographs are taken of the group of students, who signed a letter of consent for the test. These photographs present different positions of the person's face (front, side, with a smile or a gesture). Table 1 contains the characteristics of the images of the dataset in relation to size of images, positions of the face, and brightness.
- Recognition of students: in which the group of students registers in the prototype and takes an exam. For this purpose, an initial configuration is made of the size and number of photos that the prototype captures during the entire exam. The prototype compares the photographs taken against the training dataset. Finally, the prototype generates a report with the precision value assigned to each photograph, during the recognition process.

The following section explains the experiments that were carried out to validate the prototype and presents the results obtained during the experimentation process.

4   Experiment and Results

The process begins with the entry of the access credentials for the different types of existing users, student, administrator and teacher. The entry of the database of images of each student is a student user task, where the system to start capturing faces requests through voice prompts to switch between the different poses, storing the images with the identifier for the user.

Table 1. Description of variables.

Variables	Description
Size of images	700 × 500 pixels
Positions of the face	1. Looking straight at the camera
	2. Look slightly to the right
	3. Look slightly to the left
	4. Face look with smile
	5. Look with a gesture
Brightness	Artificial light
	Natural light

The administrator user performs two activities, first, the initial configuration, in terms of the size and number of photos that are acquired during the monitoring process; and secondly, the process of analyzing the photographs by comparing these photographs against the base of reference photographs, by means of the OpenFace algorithm.

The system is responsible for monitoring the assessment, every certain period of time as was configured, and according to the duration of the capture images event from the device in which the student has entered to give the test. The OpenFace algorithm analyzes each captured event (photographs) individually. Facial recognition is processed on the server at the end of the exam. The report is prepared with the consolidation of all events.

In the first moment of experimentation, *collection of the training dataset*, we use the size of the images in 700 × 500 pixels, taking into account the scenarios, the first with natural light and the second with artificial light, both made in the computer lab with laptops with a Lenovo ThinkPad L450 with a 720p webcam resolution. A group of 25 students registered in the facial recognition software and the image capture process were requested, allowing the software of the computer camera by means of the explicit will, and then start the assistant that indicated by voice instructions the positions in which the student must be in front of the camera to capture images, these positions are: "Looking straight at the camera", "Look slightly to the right", "Look slightly to the left", "Face look with smile" and "Look with a gesture".

Six image bases are created to train the facial recognition algorithm as shown in Table 2.

With the obtaining of the base of images and its subsequent training, the next step consists of the facial recognition of the student by means of the capture of the image with the web camera of the computer in real time, while it is rendering the evaluation. This test is applied to the 25 students in the normal classroom and is replicated for each image base.

In the second moment of experimentation, *recognition of students*, the software is configured to analyze three image sizes, so there are three different exper-

Table 2. Base of images.

Base of images	Type of light	Images for each pose (x5)	Images for each student (x25)	Total images
1	Natural	4	20	500
2	Artificial	4	20	500
3	Natural	10	50	1250
4	Artificial	10	50	1250
5	Natural	20	100	2500
6	Artificial	20	100	2500

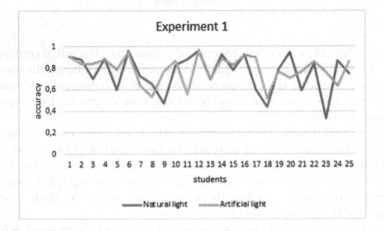

Fig. 4. Experiment 1 with 100 images of each student in size 175 × 125 pixels

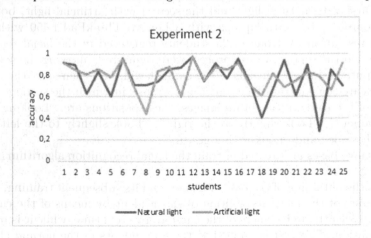

Fig. 5. Experiment 2 with 100 images of each student in size 350 × 250 pixels

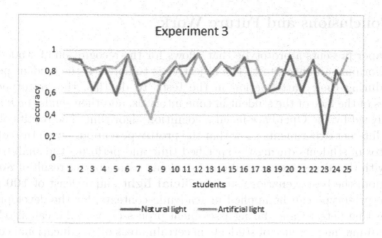

Fig. 6. Experiment 3 with 100 images of each student in size 700 × 500 pixels

Table 3. Experimentation results.

	5 images, each pose		10 images, each pose		20 images, each pose	
	25 images		50 images		100 images	
	Natural light	*Artificial light*	*Natural light*	*Artificial light*	*Natural light*	*Artificial light*
Experiment 1	0,5004	0,4908	0,6404	0,6484	0,758	0,7864
Experiment 2	0,4976	0,4872	0,6508	0,6444	0,7664	0,7892
Experiment 3	0,5004	0,4992	0,6404	0,6576	0,7584	0,8040

iments. Experiment 1: 175 × 125 pixels, Fig. 4; Experiment 2: 350 × 250 pixels, Fig. 5 and Experiment 3: 700 × 500 pixels, Fig. 6, this in the Table 3, which shows the average results of the total of 25 students, the quantity of the photographs does directly affect the results obtained by the algorithm, that is, the more photos are used during the analysis, the algorithm presents higher recognition with the intention of obtaining the best possible prediction.

The results shown in Figs. 4, 5 and 6, were made with the training bases 5 and 6, Table 2, for the 25 students with 100 training images for each one and in the two natural and artificial light scenarios.

As it is observed values, which maintains a closeness for both the scenarios of natural light, as of artificial light (for the case of 100 images in the three experiments). Regarding the pose (position) of the student's face in the photos, the results show that the poses configured in the prototype are sufficient enough to obtain high results in the recognition of the students.

In addition, it is important to note that the size of the photos directly influences the recognition of the student, that is, that the algorithm obtains better results when the photographs have a greater number of pixels (Experiment 3: 700 × 500 pixels). Table 3 shows the trend of the values reached in Experiment 3, where it is observed that the scenario (natural or artificial light) directly influences the increase or decrease of the recognition value of the student, favoring the artificial light stage.

5   Conclusions and Future Work

This paper presents a prototype that allows for the recognition of students who are performing an online test. The objective is to detect if the student performs fraud during their participation in the test. To do this, the prototype takes pictures of the face of the student in time intervals, and then sends the images to be analyzed by the OpenFace facial recognition algorithm. The results obtained in the different experiments show that the prototype complies with the collection of photos of students during the specified time and performs the analysis of the same with the respective recognition of students with a better result of **80.4%** in prediction, the best scenarios using **artificial light** and at least of **100** photos.

The prototype can be applied in academic contexts, for the development of systems that detect fraud during assessment processes, as well it can also be used to determine the presence of students in certain areas of an educational complex. The flexibility of the developed prototype allows its application to other contexts relating to surveillance, recognition of people and identity theft.

The face recognition method works well and with good light conditions has an excellent result. However, when the classroom has poor conditions or absolute darkness this strategy fails. As well as the lighting conditions, the problem with face alignment in extreme conditions will be a specific challenge as a future extension to this work.

References

1. Ahonen, T., Hadid, A., Pietikäinen, M.: Face recognition with local binary patterns. In: Pajdla, T., Matas, J. (eds.) ECCV 2004. LNCS, vol. 3021, pp. 469–481. Springer, Heidelberg (2004). https://doi.org/10.1007/978-3-540-24670-1_36
2. Alonso, J.: Procedimiento para la obtención de publicidad personalizada a partir de reconocimiento facial (2008)
3. Amos, B., Ludwiczuk, B., Satyanarayanan, M.: OpenFace: a general-purpose face recognition library with mobile applications. CMU School of Computer Science (2016)
4. Andrew, J., Marius, D.: Sistema de imágenes faciales para registro y confirmación automatizada de identidad (2001)
5. Angell, J.: Indexación automatizada asistida de forma manual de imágenes usando reconocimiento facial (2006)
6. Baltrušaitis, T., Robinson, P., Morency, L.-P.: OpenFace: an open source facial behavior analysis toolkit. In: 2016 IEEE Winter Conference on Applications of Computer Vision (WACV), pp. 1–10 (2016)
7. Brandon, A., Bartosz, L., Mahadev, S.: OpenFace: a general-purpose face recognition library with mobile applications, pp. 1–20. CMU School of Computer Science (2016)
8. Castillo, P.: Sistemas de transmisión de datos en forma remota y digital y localización satelital desde terminales móviles o fijas con cámaras de vigilancia urbana para reconocimiento facial, detector de disparos, captura de personal de seguridad pública y persona (2006)

9. Donald, M.: Un método y/o sistema para realizar reconocimiento y comparación facial en forma automática usando múltiples imágenes faciales bidimensionales descompuestas de una imagen facial tridimensional captada (2003)
10. Galbally, J., Marcel, S., Fierrez, J.: Biometric antispoofing methods: a survey in face recognition. IEEE Access **2**, 1530–1552 (2014)
11. Holovaty, A., Kaplan-Moss, J.: El Libro de Django. l'ınea. Citado En Junio de 2015. Disponible En: Django-Book. Mkaufmann. Com. Ar (2007)
12. Jafri, R., Arabnia, H.R.: A survey of face recognition techniques. JIPS **5**(2), 41–68 (2009)
13. Kittler, J.: Personal identity authenticatication process and system (2000)
14. Posada, J., et al.: Visual computing as a key enabling technology for industrie 4.0 and industrial internet. IEEE Comput. Graphics Appl. **35**(2), 26–40 (2015)
15. Ramu, T., Arivoli, T.: A framework of secure biometric based online exam authentication: an alternative to traditional exam. Int. J. Sci. Eng. Res. **4**(11), 52–60 (2013)
16. McKenna, S.J., Jabri, S., Duric, Z., Rosenfeld, A., Wechsler, H.: Tracking groups of people. Comput. Vis. Image Underst. **80**(1), 42–56 (2000)
17. Zhenming, Y., Liang, Z., Guohua, Z.: A novel web-based online examination system for computer science education. In: FIE, pp. S3F7-S3F10. IEEE (2003)

Application of Data Mining for the Detection of Variables that Cause University Desertion

X. Palacios-Pacheco[1] , W. Villegas-Ch[2](✉) ,
and Sergio Luján-Mora[3]

[1] Universidad Internacional del Ecuador, Quito, Ecuador
xpalacio@uide.edu.ec
[2] Universidad de Las Américas, Quito, Ecuador
william.villegas@udla.edu.ec
[3] Universidad de Alicante, Alicante, Spain
sergio.lujan@ua.es

Abstract. College desertion is one of the problems currently addressed by most higher education institutions throughout Latin America. From different investigations, it is known that a large percentage of students do not complete their studies, with the consequent social cost associated with this phenomenon. Some countries have begun to design deep improvement processes to increase retention in the first years of university studies. The process considered for the improvement of the desertion is through the data mining, the use of its algorithms allows discovering patterns in the students that help to explain this effect. The algorithms also identify the independent variables that influence the desertion and analyze them according to a level of depth previously established by the interested parties. The purpose of this study is to determine a model that explains the desertion of undergraduate students at the university and design actions that tend towards the decrease of the desertion.

Keywords: Data mining · Desertion · Data analysis · Weka

1 Introduction

Higher education institutions are currently subject to evaluation processes by government entities as well as international agencies that are responsible for the assurance of academic quality. The main factors that are referenced in the evaluation processes are the abandonment of studies known as desertion, repetition and academic effectiveness [12]. The World Bank and UNESCO indicate that desertion at the level of university education reaches a percentage of around 40% in Latin America and the Caribbean [1]. For universities, it has become a very complex task to detect the possible causes of desertion. These causes until a few years ago were based on factors such as the lack of prior information about the career and the student's difficulty in adapting to a university environment. Currently, the studies carried out on the subject include new variables that can be analyzed and seek to answer the percentages of influence they have on the student to drop their studies. The discovery of these variables is the main concern of the

© Springer Nature Switzerland AG 2019
M. Botto-Tobar et al. (Eds.): CITT 2018, CCIS 895, pp. 510–520, 2019.
https://doi.org/10.1007/978-3-030-05532-5_38

university authorities who question the reason for the high dropout rates and the low percentage of graduates that affect the academic effectiveness of an institution [10].

Previous work on the subject analyzed the desertion considering statistical models and tools, measuring economic and academic factors, its main calculation is segmented to whether the student enrolled or not in the next period [9]. This document establishes a model adaptable to the new demands of the evaluation of academic quality, with the use of information and communication technologies allowing more effective decision-making. This process is possible by integrating several data mining tools into the analysis, which will be responsible for evaluating the psychosocial variables and environmental variables of the students and which are usually stored in large university data repositories.

The collection and systematic evaluation of the data allow identifying similarities, defining opportunities and problems that contribute to learning. The analysis of educational data is a means to achieve a specific objective and improve decision-making based on objective data resulting from field research. The factors that intervene in the university dropout allow determining trends and patterns that identify potential problems in the target population [12].

Considering the need to treat the phenomenon of desertion to design actions that tend to decrease, this study aims to determine a method that explains and identifies the factors that influence the university dropout [9]. This work is structured in six sections, the second section gives an account of the review of previous works that have been carried out around the study variables; the third section analyzes and selects the data used in the study; the fourth section provides the description of the method for the analysis of the information and the characterization of the variables; The fifth section is an analysis of the results obtained and the final section discloses the conclusions.

2 Previous Studies

The review of previous studies mostly refers to the desertion of university students; these develop based on two main sociological theories: the model of student integration and the model of student attrition. The first model explains that, given the rest, a greater degree of student integration in the academic and social environment contributes to a greater degree of institutional commitment and this directly affects the student's decision to stay or defect. The second model attributes greater relative importance to factors external to the institution [2]. In many cases, an integrated model is proposed that emphasizes the sociological and psychological processes of student persistence behavior in the university.

Other works perform systematic reviews of several works based on these models using different methodologies. Research shows that students who tend to have lower academic grades on average and parents with less education and lower income are those who leave their studies more frequently [3, 11]. It is also estimated that students with a higher level of interaction with teachers and with other students are less likely to drop out, but it is very possible that such interaction is a function of many of the factors that influence the probability of dropping out. According to the studies, it is established that the dropout is greater in the first and second year of the university career.

The identification of the groups, deserters, and graduates, and the calculation of the probability of belonging to one or another set, given certain characteristics, allow the design of permanent policies, thus maximizing the resources available in the universities. However, previous works address the problem of desertion or graduation under a static method. That is, they only investigate if the event occurs or not, but they do not know what factors this fact depends on. These works conclude that the probability of finishing the degree is not constant throughout the academic life of a student. All these factors can be analyzed from a linear regression model that finds that the academic resources and the attendance pattern are the common factors in the dropout or in the academic effectiveness [4].

The analysis shows that students who prolong their stay at the university are those who have a lower income when they start their studies or are more likely to drop out. Building a trend, three groups of students with a higher risk of abandonment were found. These groups are students who work and are married; students who work and live with their parents; students who work, live alone and come from other areas. Conversely, students who do not work characterize the group that has less risk of abandonment, and their parents pay for their studies. The databases where the searches were carried out are presented in Table 1 as well as the search strings of each database.

Table 1. Bibliographic databases and search strings

Source	Terms of search	Scope of the search
Springer link	'Data mining applied to education and student desertion'	Only articles in English; published since 2015–2018
Web of science	(Data mining applied to education or student desertion)	Refined By: Years of publication: (2018 Or 2017 Or 2016 Or 2015) And types of documents: (Article)
ACM digital library	{(+educational +data +mining student desertion)}	{publicationYear:{gte:2015, lte:2018}}, {owners.owner = HOSTED}
IEEE digital library (Xplore)	((educational data mining) OR student abandonment)	Only articles in English; published since 2015–2018
Scopus	Educational data mining AND e-learning AND student abandonment	Only articles in English; published since 2015–2018

3 Selection of Data

In this research, we used the data of the university that participates in this work specifically in a modality of distance study. In principle, this choice was mainly due to the availability of information provided by the university. Access was obtained to the data on the socioeconomic characteristics of the students that are collected in the student registration systems [3]. There was also data on the approved or unapproved subjects, the regularized subjects, and the percentage of the grade obtained. These data are important to be able to carry out the academic follow-up of the students and detect their condition of deserter, graduate or student who continues their studies. We worked with the cohort of new entrants in 2013; a cohort is defined as the group of students that enroll in a university career in a given year. The advantage, unlike working with the whole group of students at any given time, is to track a group of students who are in the same initial conditions and face the same academic and social aspect. According to the data collected from the different systems, the total number of people registered in the distance education modality was 3,207 students in all the cohorts until the year 2017. The sample considered for this study is the 2013 cohort composed of 208 students. Table 2 shows the current distribution of students by degree as part of the distance education model.

Table 2. Number of students per career of the modality of distance education

Career	Number of students
Commercial engineer	405
Accounting and auditing	2,010
International finances	69
Marketing	242
International business	344
Communication	137

In the internal analysis of retention handled by the institution, the data shown in Fig. 1 is presented, which details the number of students in relation to time. The consideration is made through the analysis of similar periods in each year. This indicates that during 2013, 435 new students entered the two regular school periods. Of these 435, for the following academic period, only 256 students were enrolled, that is, from the first semester of study to the second semester of that group of participants, only 58.85% continued their studies and there was a 41.15% dropout. For the third semester of the 435 new ones, there were only 202 students, that is, the desire for the first year of study was 53.56%. It is important to bear in mind that the highest

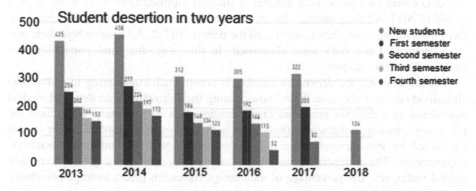

Fig. 1. Student retention report for the period 2013–2016.

percentage of wear is from the first to the second semester. The figures range from 435 to 256 in the 2013 cohort, in the 2014 cohort they go from 458 to 277, in the 2015 cohort they go from 312 to 186. The data for the fourth-semester dropout can be obtained from the students who entered the cohort. 2016. The students of the 2017 cohort do not present final data since the year 2018 is not yet closed for analysis.

3.1 Definition of the Problem

The general objective of this paper is to detect the factors that directly influence the dropout and when this event or an associated one is likely to occur, such as graduating or changing careers. The analysis aims to establish parameters that allow the making of referential decisions regarding dropout and the time that this process takes. The model allows describing the behavior of data in a determined time or the duration from a well-defined origin until the occurrence of some event; this model is based on the "analysis of historical events". This model has several advantages with respect to classical techniques such as the estimation of "classical" logit models, regression or discriminant analysis [5]. The latter is of a static nature, while the duration analysis captures temporality and the variation of circumstances over time.

The central concept of a duration model is not the probability that an event will occur, for example, the probability that an individual will abandon their studies in the fourth year. The analysis also addresses the conditional probability of this happening, for example, the probability that the student will leave in the fourth year since he has been studying for three years. Based on the aforementioned, the analysis of what is done with the use of data mining algorithms that most cases are included in tools such as Microsoft SQL, R, Weka, etc. In this work, one of these tools is used to analyze the data and obtain the expected results for decision-making.

4   Method

This work corresponds to an explanatory investigation of a longitudinal type and of an experimental nature. We work with census data from a university in Ecuador delivered by the admission department, the academic record and the virtual classroom system. The data correspond to the total number of students enrolled from 2013 to the second period of 2017. All the students who entered the 2013 cohort were analyzed, observing them from the semester they entered until the period 2017-2. All cases where there was inconsistency of the data were eliminated. In this way, the final population was composed of 208 students.

For the analysis, the dependent variable is constructed, considering in active state all individuals who continue their studies during the following semester. The student considered as a deserter presented characteristics such as voluntary withdrawal the following semester, withdrew without prior notice, changed to another career or was eliminated by the university due to non-compliance with the minimum academic requirements. The independent variables available for this investigation were age, marital status, sex, the percentage of the average education grade, average percentage of grades per semester.

To analyze the population composed of 208 students and the variables described, the method of analyzing historical events allows for its study in terms of the unit of time considered for observation. This method seeks to identify which variables are those that influence whether the said break occurs or not, controlling for a given unit of time. In this case, the unit of time chosen is the academic period of the university, because it corresponds to the minimum existing time to measure the permanence of a student in the university. For example, a student who has been observed in six semesters in a row constitutes six units of observation.

To construct a model that identifies the most impact on the occurrence of the attrition event, the data were analyzed by means of a linear regression, controlling for the year of admission and school period. In this way, a predictive multivariate model for student desertion was generated, with which it is possible to assign a probability of desertion to the students, thus providing a tool to take measures that reduce the university dropout rate [13]. In another phase of the analysis, the J48 algorithm is applied to the data, which performs a search of the factors that influence desertion with the use of decision trees [7].

4.1 Data Cleaning

The data required for the analysis can be found in several repositories, including learning management systems (LMS); due to their nature as raw data, they need to go through a cleanup [8, 14]. The advantage of a prior preparation of the data is that a smaller data set is generated to improve the efficiency of the data analysis process. The reduction of data is an important factor that is carried out through the selection of characteristics, sampling or selection of instances, discretization, etc. The cleanup provides quality data that derive patterns and rules that will give confidence to the process of data extraction. The system in this way can easily recover incomplete information, eliminate outliers, resolve conflicts, etc.

The 2013 cohort has a database of 2,030 records, after cleaning and processing the data, 306 records were eliminated. Deletion generally occurs in registers that have blank or null fields in the same way records with inconsistent information, erroneous information, etc. After this process, the database has 1,724 records in which the necessary data mining algorithms will be applied to obtain results. The fields in which the different cleaning stages were applied can be observed in Table 3. In this table, the origin of the data is handled and if they are accessible or not.

4.2 Data Mining Application

In Table 4, several of the data mining algorithms that can be used to obtain knowledge about a given event are listed. All these algorithms are included in the Weka tool [6]. The process goes from the loading of the data that in this work has been done from a .csv file. For the classification, the application of the algorithm done J48 is an open source algorithm where a tree is generated considering the independent variables exposed in the database [7]. When applying the data mining method, it is important to consider the confidence factor for pruning, which influences the size and capacity of the

Table 3. Data fields considered for the cleaning stage

Field name	Origin	Accessible
Cohort	Database	Yes
StudentID	Database	Yes
DateBiStudent	Database	Yes
AgeIngress	Database	Yes
Job	Database	Yes
PercentageNoteCollege	Database	Yes
Enrolled	Database	Yes
Coursestaken	Database	Yes
Matterstaken	Database	Yes
Approvedsubjects	Database	Yes
Approved1E	Database	Yes
Approved2E	Database	Yes
Approved3E	Database	Yes
Stay	Database	Yes
CurrentStatusInSchool	Database	Yes
GraduatedCareer	Database	Yes
School	Database	Yes
Faculty	Database	Yes
College	Database	Yes
YearStart	Database	Yes
Period	Database	Yes
Schoolterm	Database	Yes

tree. For each pruning operation, the probability of error that is allowed to the hypothesis that the worsening is significant is defined.

5 Analysis of Results

The analysis was done in relation to the student's status at the university where he can take five states that are active, passive, candidate to graduate, graduated and retired. The confusion matrix detailed in Table 5 indicates that the complete sample was classified in the mentioned groups, presents the values of the diagonal that are correct, and the rest are errors.

Table 6 shows the stratified cross-validation where all the values of the correct instances and the incorrect ones are indicated, in the same way, the values of the absolute value are displayed. The percentages and values that are established within, the analyzes are within the ideal parameters to take the data as valid and that the results have a high degree of certainty.

The decision tree is observed in Table 7, the detail indicates the variables that directly influence the university dropout. The first analysis is done in the variable of

Table 4. Data mining algorithms applied to different tasks

Tasks	Algorithm
Predict a discrete attribute • Identify students from a list of subjects as students with good or bad perspectives • Classify the evolution of students and explore related factors	Decision tree algorithm Naive Bayes algorithm Cluster algorithm Neural network algorithm
Predict a continuous attribute • Predict the grades of a student next year • Predict the students that visit the LMS based on historical and seasonal trends provided	Decision tree algorithm Time series algorithm Linear regression algorithm
Predict a sequence • Perform a clickstream analysis of a university website • Capture and analyse sequences of activities during student visits	Algorithm of sequence clusters
Search for groups of common elements in transactions • Suggest additional activities to students	Association algorithm Decision tree algorithm
Search groups of similar items • Analyse users through search patterns • Identify activities with similar usage characteristics	Cluster algorithm Algorithm of sequence clusters

Table 5. Decision tree generated in Weka

Confusion matrix

A	b	c	d	e	<- classified as
29	10	0	0	3	| a = Active
7	45	0	0	4	| b = Passive
0	0	12	0	0	| c = Candidate to graduate
1	0	0	0	0	| d = Graduated
3	3	0	0	2	| e = Retired

Table 6. Cross-validation stratified

Summary

Correctly classified instances	88	74%
Incorrectly classified instances	31	26%
Kappa statistic	0.5909	
Mean absolute error	0.1194	
Root mean squared error	0.2993	
Relative absolute error	46%	
Root relative squared error	84%	
Total Number of Instances	119	

Table 7. Variables detected by the decision tree

J48 pruned tree
GraduatedCareer = NO
| enrollment <= 8
| | Itremains = NO
| | | Approved2M <= 1
| | | | AgeIngress <= 20
| | | | | Approved1M <= 10: Passive (4.0)
| | | | | Approved1M > 10: Active (2.0)
| | | | AgeIngress > 20: Passive (39.0/1.0)
| | | Approved2M > 1
| | | | S4 <= 55
| | | | | MattersTaken <= 17
| | | | | | enrollment <= 3: Passive (2.92/1.0)
| | | | | | enrollment > 3: Retired (2.0)
| | | | | MattersTaken > 17: Active (3.15/0.38)
| | | | S4 > 55: Passive (12.92/3.85)
| | Itremains = YES
| | | enrollment <= 6: Passive (3.0/1.0)
| | | enrollment > 6: Active (2.0)
| | Itremains = Graduates: Passive (0.0)
| enrollment > 8
| | S4 <= 60
| | | MattersTaken <= 38: Active (2.0/1.0)
| | | MattersTaken > 38: Retired (2.0)
| | S4 > 60: Active (32.0/2.0)
GraduatedCareer = SI: Graduate (12.0)
Number of Leaves: 14
Size of the tree: 26

graduates by career. In the case that they are not graduates, it evaluates them in the case of students who have a number less than or equal to eight enrollments. This factor determines that the analysis focuses on students who are in courses under the fourth year. The next branch integrates the permanence variable that is branched into three additional branches where it evaluates the number of enrollments, especially those who have done second in the case that they have completed at least a few repetitions, assessing the age of entry. For students less than or equal to 20 years, an analysis is made of the number of first enrollments if they are less than or equal to 10, we have four students who have dropped out of school. This is an analysis that covers only one branch of the tree executed in the data-mining model. Another consideration is that there is a group of students who drop out of their studies when they have taken up to 17 subjects, which implies that they attend the fourth semester and their average grade of the semester is lower than 55/100 and has made at least one-third enrollment in one of the subjects.

6 Conclusions

This work includes new concepts that can be considered as a component that helps to improve education with information and communication technologies. What has been sought during this development is to qualify the different platforms according to the needs of a particular educational institution that considers, as the main base, the multiple sources of data. In this work, a data mining method is applied that analyses student data to discover the factors that directly influence university dropout. The analysis shows how the data that most universities do not use maintain information that can respond to problems such as university dropout or academic effectiveness.

In the process of developing this work, several clarifications were obtained about the use of data mining in university systems. In the first place, we can point out that the impulse given today to education has led to the creation of modalities that allow the student to manage the convergence between work and activities. In these education modalities, it is essential to look for methods that allow the evaluation of the variables that help to make decisions. The actions that can be taken vary according to the focus of each institution and the measurement parameters that are handled by government agencies that deal with academic control. Among these actions, we have the segmentation by groups that present the same patterns that allow us to offer a personalized education. Another type of action to take regarding the desertion can be based on the data obtained from a data mining analysis that would allow us to apply corrective measures to reduce these indices.

With the results obtained from the analysis, we can implement measures that strengthen the processes through which students generate knowledge. Another measure that can be used is the identification of groups that have similar needs so that we can apply methods that help students to better understand the subjects they are studying.

The use of data mining on educational platforms every day has a greater depth. However, it is important that the evaluation environment go beyond a single repository. It is important that all the sensors or systems that surround the student are combined into one, so that the trends, problems or help that each student requires can be detected in a timely manner before this influences the abandonment of their studies.

The use of intelligent data has the ability to analyse these systems in depth and establish patterns that tell us how to improve the learning outcomes of a specific student. For the time being, a test has been carried out on the operation of intelligent information using the Weka tool. The results obtained are in the validation stage.

References

1. Ferreyra, M., Avitabile, C., Botero Álvarez, J. Haimovich Paz, F. Urzúa, S.: At a Crossroads: Higher Education in Latin America and the Caribbean. Directions in Development—Human Development. World Bank, Washington, DC. World Bank (2017)
2. Cabrera, F., Amaury, N., Castañeda, M.: College persistence. J. High. Educ., 123–139 (2016)
3. Giovagnoli, P.: Determinants in university desertion and graduation: an application using duration models. Económica 51(1–2), 59–90 (2005)

4. Romero, C., Ventura, S.: Educational data mining: a review of the state of the art. IEEE Trans. Syst. Man Cybern. Part C (Appl. Rev.) **40**(6), 601–618 (2010)
5. Dutt, F., Ismail, M.A., Herawan, T.: A systematic review on educational data mining. IEEE Access **5**, 15991–16005 (2017)
6. Hall, M., Frank, E., Holmes, G., Pfahringer, B., Reutemann, P., Witten, I.H.: The WEKA data mining software: an update. ACM SIGKDD Explor. Newsl. **11**(1), 10–18 (2009)
7. Pandey, P., Prabhakar, R.: An analysis of machine learning techniques (J48 & AdaBoost) for classification. In: 1st India International Conference on Information Processing (IICIP), pp. 1–6 (2016)
8. Villegas-Ch, W., Luján-Mora, S.: Systematic review of evidence on data mining applied to LMS platforms for improving e-learning. In: International Technology, Education and Development Conference (INTED), pp. 6537–6545 (2017)
9. Hernandez Gonzalez, A.G., Melendez Armenta, R.A., Morales Rosales, L.A., Garcia Barrientos, A., Tecpanecatl Xihuitl, J.L., Algredo, I.: Comparative study of algorithms to predict the desertion in the students at the ITSM-Mexico. IEEE Lat. Am. Trans. **14**(11), 4573–4578 (2016)
10. Peralta, B., Poblete, T., Caro, L.: Automatic feature selection for desertion and graduation prediction: a chilean case. In: 35th International Conference of the Chilean Computer Science Society (SCCC), Valparaiso, pp. 1–8 (2016)
11. Gama, J.A., et al.: Quantitative models and software architecture, facing student desertion and permanence. In: Proceedings of IEEE International Conference on Teaching, Assessment and Learning for Engineering (TALE), Bali, pp. 604–611 (2013)
12. Mayra, A., Mauricio, D.: Factors to predict dropout at the universities: a case of study in Ecuador. In: IEEE Global Engineering Education Conference (EDUCON), Tenerife, Islas Canarias, Spain, pp. 1238–1242 (2018)
13. Merchan Rubiano, S.M., Duarte Garcia, J.A.: Analysis of data mining techniques for constructing a predictive model for academic performance. IEEE Lat. Am. Trans. **14**(6), 2783–2788 (2016)
14. Villegas-Ch, W., Luján-Mora, S.: Analysis of data mining techniques applied to LMS for personalized education. In: World Engineering Education Conference (EDUNINE), pp. 85–89. IEEE (2017)

Mobile Biometric Authentication by Face Recognition for Attendance Management Software

Cristian Zambrano-Vega[1]([✉])(iD), Byron Oviedo[1](iD), Jorge Chiquito Mindiola[1](iD),
Jacob Reyes Baque[1](iD), and Oscar Moncayo Carreño[2](iD)

[1] Facultad de Ciencias de la Ingeniería, Universidad Técnica Estatal de Quevedo,
Quevedo, Los Ríos, Ecuador
{czambrano,boviedo,jorgeamin.chiquito,jacobnbaq.reyes}@uteq.edu.ec
[2] Facultad de Ciencias Empresariales, Universidad Técnica Estatal de Quevedo,
Quevedo, Los Ríos, Ecuador
omoncayo@uteq.edu.ec

Abstract. In this paper we present bioFACE, a novel mobile application for the biometric authentication by face recognition of the users of the attendance management software provided by the Human Resources department of the State Technical University of Quevedo. This application converts the smartphones in a biometric device that allows register the workday entries and workday exits from any place inside of the university campus. The user-location is validated by the GPS coordinates using the Android Geofence API and the biometric authentication of the users (employees and professors) is carried out by face recognition performed by Microsoft Face API features.

Keywords: Mobile biometric authentication · Face recognition
Mobile smart applications

1 Introduction

Mobile devices are rapidly becoming a key computing platform, transforming how people access business and personal information. The rich set of input sensors on mobile devices, including cameras, microphones, touch screens, and GPS, enable sophisticated multimedia interactions. Biometric authentication methods using these sensors could offer a natural alternative to password schemes, since the sensors are familiar and already used for a variety of mobile tasks [11].

An increasing attention is given to a new application field of face detection and recognition dealing with mobile phones. This attention is not due to some blind chance but it grew with several practical needs [5,8]. Since more and more mobile phones provide wireless access to the Internet and high computational performance, is then possible to perform a mobile biometric authentication by face recognition.

© Springer Nature Switzerland AG 2019
M. Botto-Tobar et al. (Eds.): CITT 2018, CCIS 895, pp. 521–530, 2019.
https://doi.org/10.1007/978-3-030-05532-5_39

Biometric time and attendance system has brought more precise system to measure group or individual's activities and attendance as well. Biometric attendance machine captures your unique biological/physical feature such as your hand or fingerprint, iris pattern, face and sometimes even your voice as a record for identity verification and allows you to perform something that you are authorized to do.

In this paper we present bioFace, a novel mobile application for biometric authentication by face recognition of the users of the attendance management software provided by the Human Resources department of the State Technical University of Quevedo (UTEQ). The employees and professors in the UTEQ must to register many workdays during all day, workday entries and workday exits. In some cases the biometric devices are not close to their classrooms or offices, it causes that they forget to register their workdays, wrong workdays registrations and that, finally, it becomes a difficult task to perform by the large distance between both places. With the aim of improve the registration process we have developed this application to allow the smartphones become biometric devices connected through JSON WebServices to the attendance management software of the UTEQ, avoiding large crowds in rush hours moments, especially. The biometric authentication by face recognition was implemented using the Microsoft Face API features [3] and the user-location is validated by the Android Geofences API [1].

The rest of this paper is organized as follows: First, the Biometrics definitions are described in Sect. 2. In Sects. 3 and 4 we detail the specification of the APIs to Face Recognition (Microsoft Face API) and GeoLocation (Android Geofencing), respectively. The features, threats and Benefits of our proposal bioFACE are detailed in Sect. 5 and finally, Sect. 6 outlines some concluding remarks and suggest some lines of future work.

2   Biometrics Definitions

Biometrics are unmistakable, quantifiable qualities that are utilized to distinguish us. These identifiers are sorted as physical or social attributes, related the shape of particular body regions or an example of conduct. Physical biometrics incorporate facial structure and shape, fingerprints, iris designs, hand geometry, even the form of your ear. Behavioral biometrics allude to how we swipe, how we write, our gait, our fingers on a touchscreen, or how we sing or speak [12].

2.1   Face Recognition

Facial recognition is an important research area since the 1970's [7]. Given a figure/image with numerous faces, facial recognition ordinarily first run facial detection to disconnect the faces. All faces are preprocessed and then a low-dimensional representation (or embedding) is constructed. A low-dimensional representation is imperative for productive classification [6]. The fomr of the face is a exceptionally particular physical characteristic. Utilizing computer vision methods, the structure and the shape of the face can be identified, with specific "landmark" highlights, including the positions of the eyes, nose, mouth and jaw. The latest work in facial recognition identify a low-dimensional face representation based on ratios of distances, angles and regions [4]. Present high-performance facial recognition methods are based on CNN Convolutional Neural Networks. Google's FaceNet [9] and Facebook's DeepFace [10] systems provide the best performance. In any case, these methods are trained with huge datasets of social media images bigger than accessible datasets for research [4].

3   Microsoft Face API (FKA 'Project Oxford')

Microsoft Face API (Application Program Interface) is a cloud-based service, part of Microsoft's Cognitive Services Platform, that provides advanced techniques to perform facial detection with attributes and facial recognition.

3.1   Face Detection

This API can detects one or more faces in an input image and mark them with rectangles, furthermore provides facial attributes of that faces, like: Emotion, Age, Smile, Gender Facial Hair and Pose together with 27 points of interest for every face within the image. The tested image can be provided by URL or by an uploaded binary file. One example of the result is illustrated by Fig. 1 [3].

Fig. 1. Face detection example with face attributes details

3.2   Facial Recognition

Facial recognition is broadly utilized in numerous scenarios considering natural user interface, security, robotics, image content analysis and management and mobile apps. Facial-Recognition enables four facial recognition methods: face grouping, face verification, person identification and finding similar faces. To perform the facial recognition in our application we have have used the features of the Face-Identify API.

Face-Identify API. This API identifies persons detecting faces registered on the person database called *PersonGroup* and *LargePersonGroup*. These databases can register up to one millon persons and ten hundred objects, and every person object can have associated 248 faces. When a face identification is requested, Face-Identify API calculates similarities between the request face and each face registered on the person database, the databased is identified by a provided *personGroupId* or *largePersonGroupId*, this similarities are in percentage. Then, return a candidate person based on the best similarity confidence rank. One example of the use of this API can be found at [2] and is illustrated by Fig. 2.

(a) A PersonGroup with 3 people   (b) Identification of Bill and Clare in an image

Fig. 2. Face recognition example using the Face-Identify API [2]

4   Geofencing

Geofencing is a android-service based on locations, that sends a notification to an android-phone who enter or exit a defined geographic area. For example, when a child leaves a specified area, this service can notify to the parents, also human resource department can monitoring employees working in special locations. Location of interest are marked by geographic coordinates: latitude and longitude. A radius must to be adjusted to define the proximity for the location. All these parameters define a geofence, creating a fence or a circular area around the location of interest [1]. Figure 3 illustrates an example of geofencing on Android.

In Android, for every geofence definied, you can request to Location Play Services, send you entrance and exit events, or specify a duration within the geofence area to wait, or dwell, before triggering an event. Specifying an expiration duration (milliseconds), we can limit the duration of any geofence in our application [1].

Fig. 3. Geofencing on android example at Quevedo State Technical University.

5   BioFace

BioFace is a mobile application for the control of biometric assistance from mobile devices that uses facial recognition as an authentication measure and the geographic coordinates of the GPS (Global Positioning System) as a validation of the location of employees and professors in their respective dependencies or classrooms. BioFace has a previous storage of the company's employees: personal and biometric (face) data and the GPS coordinates of the geographical location of the company.

The principal features, threats and benefits are described to follow:

5.1   Features

- Biometric authentication of employees through facial recognition.
- Validate the company's rank in real-time geographic location.
- Report of the attendance record of employees with: Day, Time, Date, and compatibility level of the authenticated face.
- Administrator profile to save basic data of the employees of the company.
- Compatible with Android operating systems.
- Interoperability with attendance management systems. Synchronize the registration through jSON Web Services.

5.2   Benefits

- Fast registration of the workday starts and workday exists of your working day from your same work location.

- Avoid long crowds in the place where the control of attendance Rush hours entry or exit of the majority of employees.
- Ideal in companies where work offices are very distant from the biometric devices.
- Reduce costs by purchasing several assistance control equipment, maybe none is necessary.
- The physical characteristics of a face are much more difficult to counterfeit.
- Reasonable prices, flexible licensing and free customer support.

5.3   Threats

- There are third-party applications that manage to modify the actual geographical location of GPS of mobile devices, but their operation requires technical knowledge such as: activate ROOT mode, activate developer options or apply location changes.
- Low internet connection.
- Facial recognition also requires updates to maintain accuracy, while fingerprints, for example, never need it, age affects our appearance, so, as we get older, the images will have to be updated regularly to ensure that the data is accurate

5.4   How It Works

We detail the flowchart of the application:

1. First, we must create a person group foreach career o group of employees, with an specified: personGroupId, name, and user-provided userData. After

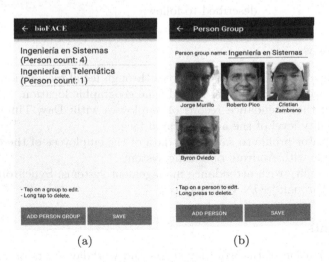

(a)   (b)

Fig. 4. Creating Person Groups foreach dependency or career. (a) List of careers or dependencies and (b) List of professors of one career (group).

creation, we have to add persons (employees or professors) into each group, taking the face images and saving it into the employee personal data, then train the PersonGroups to get ready for Face - Identify (Fig. 4).

2. The first time that the application is executed, request to user assign the permissions to access of: internet, camera, media storage and geolocation (Fig. 5).

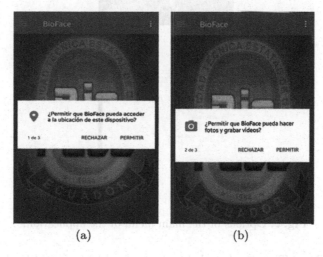

(a)   (b)

Fig. 5. Permissions requests: (a) GPS geolocation permissions request, (b) Camera permissions request.

3. Login User: All the employees and professors must login to the system using their identification card number, so that the application identifies and recognize their registered dependency or faculty (Fig. 6).

Fig. 6. User login.

4. Main Interface: This is the interface of the application. Among the options are: the function to register the start and end of work, configuration of the personal information and a report with the registers (Fig. 7).

Fig. 7. Options of the main menu of the application.

5. Personal Data: The user (employees or professors) can modify their personal data, including: Name, E-mail and registered career (Fig. 8).
6. Register the workday entry or workday exit: When a user requests register its start or end of the workday, first, the application validates that he is inside the university campus, then the camera is opened for the biometric

Fig. 8. Personal data setting.

authentication of the employee and captures the face as an image. The facial recognition is carried out with the help of the Face API. Once confirmed that the face corresponds to the person who registers, the application registers the event to the system sending by JSON Web Service the personal data: EmployeeID or ProfessorID, Date and Time and GPS coordinates (Fig. 9).

Fig. 9. Register the workday start or workday exit.

7. Reports: the application shows a report with all the registrations performed by user, the fields are: Date, Time and the confidence percentage with which the facial recognition was performed (Fig. 10).

REPORTE

# de Registro	1
Fecha	2018/01/30
Hora	23:12
Confianza	0.88733
# de Registro	2
Fecha	2018/02/02
Hora	00:32
Confianza	0.77107
# de Registro	3
Fecha	2018/02/08
Hora	21:42
Confianza	0.92118
# de Registro	4
Fecha	2018/02/08

Fig. 10. Report of the registrations.

6   Conclusions

The mobile application bioFACE represent a faster and more efficient method to register the workdays of the UTEQ employees and professors. BioFACE converts the smartphone to biometric devices allowing register the workday starts and the workday exists being at any place inside of the university campus. Banks or any commercial enterprise can deploy bioFACE to enhance their attendance management software, making workdays registration more secure and more convenient for their customers and employees.

As future work we have considered add information about the work schedules to create reminders for the professors, and we will implement machine learning algorithms (deep neural networks) embedded in the same application avoiding the requirement of internet access to use the Microsoft Face APIs.

References

1. Android Geofences (2018). https://developer.android.com/training/location/geofencing. Accessed 20 May 2018
2. Identify faces in images (2018). https://docs.microsoft.com/en-us/azure/cognitive-services/face/face-api-how-to-topics/howtoidentifyfacesinimage. Accessed 20 May 2018
3. Microsoft-Face-API (2018). https://docs.microsoft.com/en-us/azure/cognitive-services/face/overview. Accessed 20 May 2018
4. Amos, B., Ludwiczuk, B., Satyanarayanan, M.: Openface: a general-purpose face recognition library with mobile applications. CMU School of Computer Science (2016)
5. Hadid, A., Heikkila, J., Silvén, O., Pietikainen, M.: Face and eye detection for person authentication in mobile phones. In: First ACM/IEEE International Conference on Distributed Smart Cameras, ICDSC 2007, pp. 101–108. IEEE (2007)
6. Jebara, T.S.: 3D pose estimation and normalization for face recognition. Centre for Intelligent Machines. McGill University (1995)
7. Kanade, T.: Picture Processing System by Computer Complex and Recognition of Human Faces (1974)
8. Liu, H., Xie, X., Ma, W.Y., Zhang, H.J.: Automatic browsing of large pictures on mobile devices. In: Multimedia 2003, pp. 148–155. ACM, New York (2003). https://doi.org/10.1145/957013.957045
9. Schroff, F., Kalenichenko, D., Philbin, J.: Facenet: a unified embedding for face recognition and clustering. In: Proceedings of the IEEE Conference on Computer Vision and Pattern Recognition, pp. 815–823 (2015)
10. Taigman, Y., Yang, M., Ranzato, M., Wolf, L.: Deepface: closing the gap to human-level performance in face verification, pp. 1701–1708 (2014)
11. Trewin, S., Swart, C., Koved, L., Martino, J., Singh, K., Ben-David, S.: Biometric authentication on a mobile device: a study of user effort, error and task disruption, ACSAC 2012, pp. 159–168. ACM, New York (2012). https://doi.org/10.1145/2420950.2420976
12. Veridium: Biometrics Definitions (2018). https://www.veridiumid.com/biometrics/. Accessed 20 May 2018

Computer Aided Diagnosis
of Gastrointestinal Diseases Based
on Iridology

Enrique V. Carrera$^{(\boxtimes)}$ and Jennifer Maya

Departamento de Eléctrica y Electrónica, Universidad de las Fuerzas Armadas ESPE,
Sangolquí 171103, Ecuador
{evcarrera,jemaya}@espe.edu.ec

Abstract. Gastrointestinal diseases are important causes of mortality and expenses around the world. Since conventional methods for diagnosing gastrointestinal problems are expensive and invasive, alternative medicine techniques emerge as a possibility for helping physicians in this type of diagnosis. Hence, this work proposes a computer aided diagnosis system based on iridology for early detection of gastrointestinal diseases. The proposed system employs image processing and machine learning algorithms to identify gastrointestinal disorders in iris images. The evaluation of the system uses 100 iris images showing a maximum accuracy of 96% and a predictive capacity of 99%. This work shows that alternative medicine techniques have potential for diagnosing problems associated to gastrointestinal disorders.

Keywords: Gastrointestinal diseases · Iridology techniques
Image processing · Machine learning

1   Introduction

Gastrointestinal diseases are important causes of mortality and expenses around the world. There are about 60–70 million people affected by digestive diseases only in the United States [4], generating direct medical expenses of around $100 billion. Conventional methods for diagnosing gastrointestinal diseases are sophisticated and expensive [14]. In fact, some methods like colonoscopies and biopsies are invasive and discourage the participation of patients in prophylactic screenings of gastrointestinal disorders.

It is then important to create new diagnostic methods that could be fast, cheap, and non-invasive in order to help preventing gastrointestinal diseases in the population. An available alternative is to verify the effectiveness of unconventional medicine techniques such as iridology [6,8,9]. Iridology is an ancient technique oriented to identify possible alterations in people's health according to some characteristics presented in the iris.

Since digital image processing and machine learning algorithms have had many successful applications in the last years [1,2,11], this work proposes to

© Springer Nature Switzerland AG 2019
M. Botto-Tobar et al. (Eds.): CITT 2018, CCIS 895, pp. 531–541, 2019.
https://doi.org/10.1007/978-3-030-05532-5_40

create a computer aided diagnosis (CADx) system based on iridology to identify gastrointestinal diseases. The basic idea of this proposal is to recognize iris alterations associated to problems in the gastrointestinal tract, converting it to our CADx system in an automatic preventive diagnosis tool.

The implemented system was evaluated with 100 iris images. Twelve features were extracted from every image to classify them as healthy or sick using supervised learning algorithms. Four machine learning algorithms were used obtaining up to 96% of accuracy and 99% of predictive capacity.

The rest of this paper is organized as follows. Section 2 introduces iridology and its relation with gastrointestinal diseases. Section 3 presents the computer aided diagnosis system designed for detecting gastrointestinal diseases. The main results and their implications are analyzed in Sect. 4. Finally, Sect. 5 concludes this paper.

2   Iridology and Gastrintestinal Diseases

Iridology is the analysis of health based on examination of the iris of the eye. Although iridology is not widely used as a scientific tool for healthcare professionals, it has been used as a supplementary source to help the diagnosis of medical conditions [8]. The basic idea of this alternative medicine technique is to detect the conditions of the body and its organs by noting irregularities of the pigmentation in the iris [9]. Figure 1 shows the Jensen chart used by iridologists to associate specific diseases to iris changes [6].

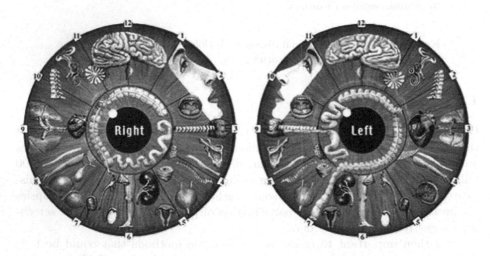

Fig. 1. The Jensen chart used by iridologists.

We can see in Fig. 1 that the region of interest, in the case of gastrointestinal diseases, is the area around the pupil. That area has an approximated width of a third/quater of the whole iris width. Thus, our CADx system will be focused in that particular region of the iris.

3   Computer Aided Diagnosis System

In order to diagnose gastrointestinal diseases based on the image processing of the iris, we have designed the CADx system shown in Fig. 2. Even though iris images can be taken by any high-resolution camera, an external database of images is used to train the supervised classifier. Each image is evidently preprocessed before extracting significant features that can be used by the classifier to identify the existence or not of gastrointestinal diseases.

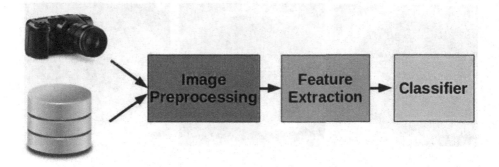

Fig. 2. Computer aided diagnosis system for gastrointestinal diseases.

The proposed system was implemented entirely in Python 2.7 with OpenCV-Python 3.3 [7,12] and Sklearn 0.19 [3] for the image processing and pattern recognition tasks, respectively. The implemented system was executed in a computer running Windows 10 Pro (64 bits) with an Intel Core i7 (2.6–3.2 GHz) processor and 8 GB of RAM.

3.1   Image Database

Although there are several public iris databases, this work is based on the database created by Iriso [5]. The Iriso database includes 77 high-definition iris images with different illumination levels. Some examples of those images are shown in Fig. 3. Every image is stored in JPG format with a resolution of 4608 × 3456 pixels.

In order to determine the robustness of the proposed system, a set of 23 new locally-obtained iris images was added to the Iriso database. These new images have different resolutions being the lowest one 640 × 480. In the rest of this work, we will refer to this new database as the *extended database*.

Since iris databases do not provide information about the gastrointestinal condition of the people to whom the images belong, we have requested the help of an expert iridologist (Dr. Telmo De la Torre) to label each image as healthy or sick. In the original database were detected 15 people out of 77 as sick (*i.e.*, 19% of the images). In the extended database the number of sick people increases to 33 out of 100.

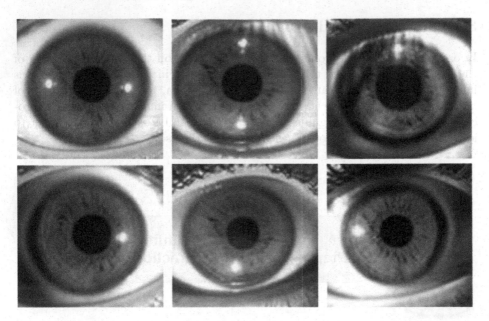

Fig. 3. Typical examples of iris images available in the Iriso database.

3.2   Image Preprocessing

The preprocessing of the iris images includes the four stages shown in Fig. 4. All images are first resized to a 640 × 480 resolution, allowing the system to work with different image inputs. Additionally, the usage of small images speeds up the time required to diagnose every image. For instance, images as big as 4608 × 3456 can take almost 12 min to finish the preprocessing and feature extraction stages. After resizing the images to 640 × 480, the preprocessing and feature extraction stages take around 0.3 s.

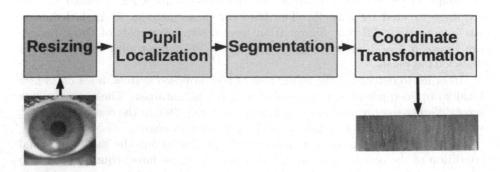

Fig. 4. Image preprocessing of iris images before feature extraction.

Pupil Localization. After the resizing of the images, an iris detection technique proposed by Wildes [13] is applied to each image with some minor changes. While the original technique is based on the Canny border detection algorithm and the Hough transform [2], our work replaces the border detection algorithm by a simple gray-scale transformation of the original full-color image. Normally, the classical border detection algorithm produces too many boundaries in this kind of images, while the gray-scale representation is enough to localize the eye pupil.

On the gray-scale image, the Hough transform is used to localize the pupil. The Hough transform requires as parameters the minimum and maximum radius of the pupil (*i.e.*, 30 and 66 pixels in the resized images), and the minimum distance among centers (*i.e.*, any value greater than 640 pixels, since there is just one pupil in every image).

Considering that the area of interest in the Jensen chart is the region of the iris closest to the pupil, it is not necessary to identify the external border (*i.e.*, the border between the iris and the sclera). Instead, we choose a set of pixels of width L around the pupil as showed in Fig. 5. Note that in the resized databases, the average radius of the pupil is 49 pixels, while the average width of the iris is 122 pixels. Thus, the choice of an optimum value for L is not an easy task and it will be studied further in Sect. 4.

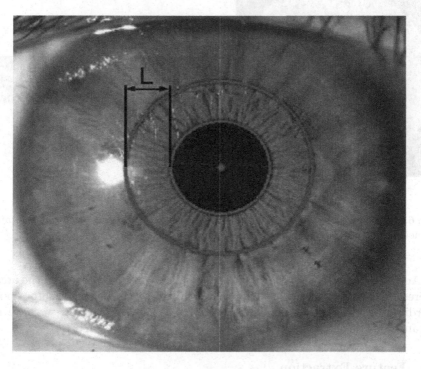

Fig. 5. Localization of the pupil and selection of the area of interest depending on the parameter L. (Color figure online)

Segmentation and Coordinate Transformation. Once we have the center and radius of the pupil, and the external radius of the area of interest, we can extract the region of the iris to be analyzed. This is done through a simple binary mask [2].

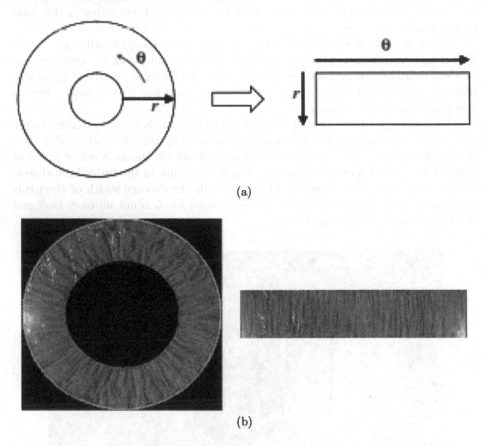

(a)

(b)

Fig. 6. Rectangular to polar coordinate transformation: (a) conceptual representation, (b) actual outcome.

Additionally, in order to create an homogeneous representation of the area of interest, the rectangular-coordinate representation is transformed into a polar-coordinate representation as shown in Fig. 6 [1,12]. As a result, we have new rectangular images of fixed dimensions.

3.3 Feature Extraction

The original images are not always good inputs for most machine learning algorithms. We usually need to extract a set of features that help to discriminate

the gastrointestinal condition of each person to whom the iris image belongs
[11]. Thus, we have extracted a set of twelve valid features using the color channels (*i.e.*, RGB components) and the gray-scale transformation of each polar-
coordinate representation:

- Average color of the iris in each RGB component.
- Standard deviation of the color in each RGB component.
- Minimum color intensity in each RGB component.
- Affectation level of the iris according to the range of gray-scale values shown
  in Table 1 [10].
- Density of anomalies in the gray-scale image according to its average color and
  standard deviation. The assumed distribution of gray-scale values is shown
  in Fig. 7.
- Presence or not of the absorption ring (*i.e.*, the existence of values equal to
  0—black color).

Table 1. Identification of affectations according to gray-scale ranges.

Affectation	Markings	Gray-scale
Acute	White	201–255
Subacute	Light gray	151–200
Chronic	Dark gray	101–150
Degenerative	Black	0–100

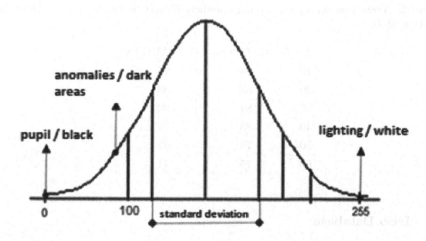

Fig. 7. Distribution of gray-scale values in iris images and the identification of
anomalies.

3.4 Classifier

The twelve features described in the previous subsection are presented to several machine learning algorithms, namely: nearest neighbors (k-NN), decision tree (DT), neural network (NN), and support vector machine (SVM) [11]. All these algorithms were evaluated in order to define the best classifier. For the evaluation of the mentioned classifiers, a k-fold cross validation mechanism [15] was also used in all the tests.

4 Results

The main results for the Iriso database (77 images) and the extended database (100 images) are presented in this section. But first, we analyze the influence of the parameter L in the performance of the machine learning algorithms.

4.1 Parameter L

In order to define the best value of L, we have trained 4 classifiers based on different machine learning algorithms. The algorithms utilized in this analysis are k-NN, DT, NN, and SVM. Since the goal of this first evaluation is to define the best value of L, we have computed the average accuracy and average predictive capacity (*i.e.*, the area under the curve—AUC) of these 4 classifiers. Table 2 summarizes the performance results for different values of L. As you can see, the best result is obtained with L around 30 pixels. This value will be used in all the following evaluations.

Table 2. Average accuracy and average predictive capacity of the four classifiers as a function of L.

L (pixels)	Accuracy (%)	AUC (%)
10	78	75
20	88	83
30	89	90
40	83	80
50	78	72
60	75	71

4.2 Iriso Database

Considering the 77 images from the original Iriso database, the 4 classifiers mentioned previously presented the performance results shown in Table 3. We can see that SVM presents the best performance for accuracy, sensibility, specificity,

Table 3. Performance of the machine learning classifiers for the Iriso database.

Classifier	Accuracy	Sensibility	Specificity	AUC
k-NN	82%	7%	100%	64%
DT	95%	87%	97%	91%
NN	91%	67%	97%	98%
SVM	96%	87%	98%	99%

and predictive capacity. SVM is followed closely by the DT and NN classifiers, in that order.

In favor of analyzing more in detail the SVM performance, we can check the confusion matrix of this classifier (Table 4). Although the existing unbalance between healthy and sick people (*i.e.*, 62 vs. 15), we have only 3 misclassified images. However, the sensibility is reduced to 87% because of the 2 false negatives in 15 people originally diagnosed with gastrointestinal problems.

Table 4. Confusion matrix for the SVM classifier and the Iriso database.

Actual class	Predicted class	
	Sick	Healthy
Sick	13	2
Healthy	1	61

4.3   Extended Image Database

A more challenging task is detecting gastrointestinal disorders in our extended database where images of different quality were included. An advantage of the extended database is a slightly more balanced number of positive and negative gastrointestinal diagnosis (*i.e.*, 33 vs. 67). Thus, the performance results for the 4 classifiers with 100 iris images are presented in Table 5. Again, SVM shows the best performance for accuracy, sensibility, and predictive capacity.

Table 5. Performance of the machine learning classifiers for the extended database.

Classifier	Accuracy	Sensibility	Specificity	AUC
k-NN	85%	81%	86%	89%
DT	92%	76%	100%	88%
NN	83%	67%	91%	89%
SVM	94%	88%	97%	92%

Table 6 also shows the confusion matrix of the SVM classifier for the 100 images in the extended database. We can see that 6 misclassified images reduce the overall accuracy to 94%, although the sensibility increases to almost 88%.

Table 6. Confusion matrix for the SVM classifier and the extended database.

Actual class	Predicted class	
	Sick	Healthy
Sick	29	4
Healthy	2	65

All the previous classifiers were tuned for maximum accuracy. In the case of DT, the splitting criteria uses entropy instead of the Gini-index. In addition, seven splits based on 6 features were enough to stabilize the accuracy results with just 10 nodes. In the case of k-NN, $k = 4$ neighbors produces the best performance. Finally, SVM was evaluated with 3 kernels: linear, polynomial and Gaussian [11]. The best results were obtained with the Gaussian kernel, using just 5 extracted features: average red color, anomaly density and standard deviation of all RGB components.

5 Conclusions

This work proposes a computer aided diagnosis system based on iridology for early detection of gastrointestinal diseases. The proposed system is based on image processing and machine learning algorithms, and presents good results of accuracy and predictive capacity. The study presented in this paper shows that alternative medicine techniques have the potential to solve problems related to diagnose diseases like gastrointestinal disorders in a fast, cheap and non-invasive way. We are studying the possibility of extent this work to other type of diseases in order to offer simple and effective computer aided diagnosis systems that can help to take care of people's health in places without access to physicians or clinical infrastructure.

Acknowledgments. Authors would like to thank Dr. Telmo De la Torre for helping us to diagnose gastrointestinal diseases in the iris images used in this work. This work was partially supported by the Universidad de las Fuerzas Armadas ESPE under Research Grant 2015-PIC-004.

References

1. Daugman, J.: How iris recognition works. In: The Essential Guide to Image Processing, pp. 715–739. Elsevier (2009)
2. Gonzalez, R.C., Eddins, S.L.: Digital Image Processing Using Matlab (2017)

3. Haroon, D.: Python Machine Learning Case Studies: Five Case Studies for the Data Scientist, vol. 1. Apress, New York City (2017)
4. National Institutes of Health and US Department of Health and Human Services: Opportunities and challenges in digestive diseases research: recommendations of the national commission on digestive diseases. National Institutes of Health, Bethesda, MD (2009)
5. Iriso: Iriso camera, July 2015. https://sites.google.com/view/irisocamera
6. Jensen, B.: Iridology Simplified. Book Publishing Company, Summertown (2012)
7. Laganière, R.: OpenCV Computer Vision Application Programming Cookbook, vol. 2. Packt Publishing Ltd, Birmingham (2014)
8. Mangalam, J.S.S., Deepa, S.: Analysis of iridology using Zhang-Suen's algorithm. Int. J. Adv. Res. Comput. Sci. **8**(3), 1233–1237 (2017). https://doi.org/10.26483/ijarcs.v8i3.4084
9. Samant, P., Agarwal, R.: Diagnosis of diabetes using computer methods: soft computing methods for diabetes detection using iris. Power **651**, 63915 (2017)
10. Sivasankar, K., Sujaritha, M., Pasupathi, P., Muthukumar, S.: FCM based iris image analysis for tissue imbalance stage identification. In: Emerging Trends in Science, Engineering and Technology, pp. 210–215. IEEE (2012)
11. Theodoridis, S., Pikrakis, A., Koutroumbas, K., Cavouras, D.: Introduction to Pattern Recognition: A Matlab Approach. Academic Press, Cambridge (2010)
12. Van der Walt, S., et al.: Scikit-image: image processing in Python. PeerJ **2**, e453 (2014)
13. Wildes, R.P.: Iris recognition: an emerging biometric technology. Proc. IEEE **85**(9), 1348–1363 (1997)
14. Wilson, A.D.: Recent applications of electronic-nose technologies for the noninvasive early diagnosis of gastrointestinal diseases. In: Multidisciplinary Digital Publishing Institute Proceedings, vol. 2, p. 147 (2017)
15. Wong, T.T.: Performance evaluation of classification algorithms by k-fold and leave-one-out cross validation. Pattern Recognit. **48**(9), 2839–2846 (2015)

Method for the Automated Generation of a Forest Non Forest Map with LANDSAT 8 Imagery by Using Artificial Neural Networks and the Identification of Pure Class Pixels

Juan-Carlos Tituana, Cindy-Pamela Lopez$^{(\boxtimes)}$ (iD), and Sang Guun Yoo (iD)

Facultad de Ingeniería de Sistemas, Escuela Politécnica Nacional, Quito, Ecuador
{juan.tituana,cindy.lopez,sang.yoo}@epn.edu.ec

Abstract. In this work, a methodology for the automated classification of Landsat 8 images from the integration of Artificial Neural Networks and the identification of pixels of pure classes is presented. The exercise carried out in this research by using the SEPAL platform, allowed to obtain a mosaic L8 of the study area, fully preprocessed and calibrated, and it was generated automatically in a short period of time. This result represents a significant advance in terms of preprocessing capacity that currently exists for the management of satellite data compared to the state of the area a decade ago. This relevant advance has been possible due to the use of artificial neural networks and the cross-correlation coefficient of the pixels of the Landsat 8 satellite platform images. Their use and differentiation of areas in remote sensing of wooded, agricultural and water areas are discussed.

Keywords: Artificial neural networks · Forest non-forest map
Cross correlation coefficient · LANDSAT 8 imagery

1 Introduction

Remote sensing has become in one of the mainly applied techniques for Earth Observation [1]. Satellite remote sensing has shown great advantages relates with (i) capability for sensing the earth surface and its atmosphere from a wide range of the electromagnetic spectrum, (ii) feasibility to build a time series of satellite data with regular measurements since 70's until nowadays, and (iii) provides information for huge surface dimensions almost simultaneously. Regardless of this clear advantages, an agreement about good practices for the classification of satellite images to obtain a thematic cartography of the surface cover is still a challenge. In this study, a automated methodology for LANDSAT 8 imagery classification is presented in order to generate a forest non forest (FNF) map by using artificial neural networks and the identification of pure pixels by mean

© Springer Nature Switzerland AG 2019
M. Botto-Tobar et al. (Eds.): CITT 2018, CCIS 895, pp. 542–552, 2019.
https://doi.org/10.1007/978-3-030-05532-5_41

of the cross correlation coefficient principle, in order to facilitate the training process of the neural net.

Most of researcher agree that supervised classification approaches work better than unsupervised ones [2], however it is time consuming and human bias could be introduced during the procedure, especially when using optical images not properly corrected. By the other side, the quality of the unsupervised classification is quite depending of the methodological approach used. Some of this approaches try to emulate the human knowledge strengths of supervised method by using artificial intelligence techniques as training data generation strategy in unsupervised methods [3].

Artificial Neural Networks (ANNs) is one of the most known techniques for developing Machine Learning (ML) based classifier algorithms, due mainly to the facility it provides to build from scratch autonomous algorithms for making decision. ANNs has been used for satellite images classification for more than three decades, and it has shown satisfactory results when is compared with know methods, such as Maximum likelihood [4].Some relevant applications of ANNs for LANDSAT 8 imagery includes general thematic classification [5,6], clouds detection [7], land use and coverage [8–10], multitemporal analysis [11], spectral moisture analysis [12,13], biodiversity [14], change detection [15], radiometric normalization [16], inversion methods [17,18], pattern recognition [19], and segmentation [20].

A successful implementation of an ANNs based algorithm requires of two important elements: (i) the training data generation/selection procedure, and (ii) the training strategy. This research deals with the data generation step, in order to propose an methodological framework to pruning and automated selection of elements to build the dataset for the training procedure of ANNs. For the training strategy step see [21]. When classifying LANDSAT images using ANNs, a region of interest (ROI) must be generated to be used as data input for training the net. The challenge with this method is the difficulty related with the ROI selection, in others words, is hard to be confident about the set of pixel to be selected, also the number of pixels to be considered in order to conform the dataset.

With the aim of improve the selection process of pixels to build a training dataset automatically, in this study is applied the cross correlation coefficient in order to propose a pure pixel detection algorithm to filter pairs of pixels that belong to the same class, and be able to take only pure pixels. To avoid selecting pixels high cross-correlated, the pixels with a coefficient higher than 0.95 will be disregarded from the dataset list, and the list will be conformed with pixels that have a cross-correlation values smaller than that. The Eq. 1 shows the cross correlation coefficient computation ρ_{nm}, between the pixels n and m, where i is an specific spectral band, and N is the total number of bands that conform the scene.

$$\rho_{nm} = \frac{\sum_{i=0}^{N} n_i * m_i}{\sqrt{\sum_{i=1}^{N} n_i^2 * \sum_{i=1}^{N} m_i^2}} \tag{1}$$

In Table 1 are listed all the bands of LANDSAT 8 platform. The mosaic to be used in this research will be conformed by the bands 2, 3, 4, 5, 6 and 7. Hence in the Eq. 1, N will be equal to 6, and i will take values from 1 to 6.

Table 1. LANDSAT 8 bands

Id	Band	Frequency (μ)	Resolution (m)	Sensor
1	Coust	0.43–0.45 m	30	OLI
2	Blue	0.450–0.51	30	OLI
3	Green	0.53–0.59	30	OLI
4	Red	0.64–0.67	30	OLI
5	Near-Infrared (NIR)	0.85–0.88	30	OLI
6	SWIR 1	1.57–1.65	30	OLI
7	SWIR 2	2.11–2.29	30	OLI
8	Panchromatic (PAN)	0.50–0.68	15	OLI
9	Cirrus	1.36–1.38	30	OLI
10	TIRS 1	10.6–11.19	100	TIRS
11	TIRS2	11.5–12.51	100	TIRS

In order to assess the performance of this method for training ANNs, a FNF map will be built and validated. The building stage involve, (i) the generation of a 6 band LANDSAT 8 mosaic, (ii) a preliminary FNF map will be generated in order to produce training data, (iii) construction of a 7 band mosaic including a FNF class, (iv) implementation of the cross correlation coefficient to select the training dataset from the 7 band mosaic, (v) training of the ANNs classifier, (vi) Classification of the 6 band mosaic using the ANNs algorithm, (vii) validation of the FNF map.

1.1 Study Area

In the Frame of the Program Reducing Emissions from Deforestation and Forest Degradation (REDD), Ecuador have reported the decreasing of the deforestation annual rate as consequence of implementation of suitable practices for forest conservation [22]. In the context of this research, it is interesting to generate a FNF map in where there is a significant deforestation activity because the non forest class is harder to detect accurately. Nueva Loja is a developing city that belongs to the province of Sucumbios-Ecuador and has a very interesting deforestation pattern. For this reason, Nueva Loja have been selected in order to elaborate a FNF map in order to assess the performance of the proposed method. In Fig. 1 is shown the city of Nueva Loja, where it is important to mention that the main covers are conformed by forest, water bodies, agriculture, and urban zone. Nueva Loja has a population close to 50000, expansion and the city borders, which are mostly forest cover, are exposed to a constant pressure for expansion.

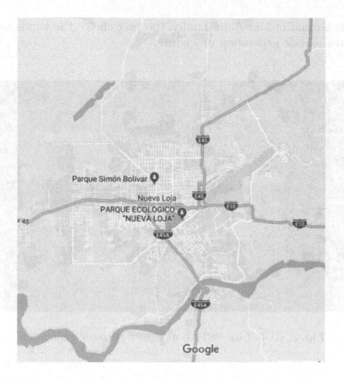

Fig. 1. City of Nueva Loja. Area of Interest (AOI) of the research

2 Proposed Method

The aim of this study, is the assessment of the cross correlation coefficient as a tool to generate automatically training data for an ANN to classify FNF from LANDSAT 8 imagery. Consequently, in order to reach this task, the necessaries steps are: (i) building of a mosaic for the AOI integrated by bands from 2 to 7 of LANDSAT 8, (ii) Generation of a FNF classification to be used as training data for the ANNs, (iii) Adding the FNF class as a band into the LANDSAT 8 mosaic, (iv) Implementation of the pure class pixel detection technique to generate the training data for the ANNs, (v) elaboration of the FNF map of AOI using the ANNs algorithm, (vi) accuracy estimation of the FNF map.

2.1 LANDSAT 8 Mosaic Building

The building of the LANDSAT 8 mosaic was carried out by using the System for earth observations, data access, processing & analysis for land monitoring (SEPAL) [23] of The Food and Agriculture Organization of United Nations (FAO). In the Fig. 2, is shown the graphical user interface (GUI) of the SEPAL module for mosaic generation. In order to generate a mosaic from SEPAL, the user has to include parameters related with the target date, AOI, and also making some decisions about applying a snow or cloud mask, or implementing a radiometric normalization. Additionally, the user choice the bands to be down-loaded in the mosaic generation procedure.

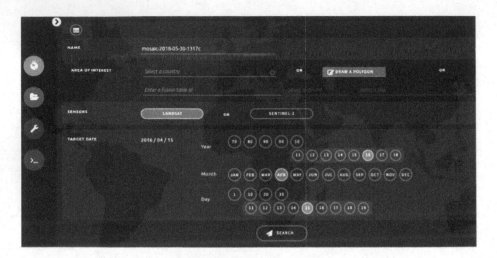

Fig. 2. GUI of the SEPAL module for mosaic generation

2.2 FNF Map for Training Data Generation

A preliminary FNF map was generated in order to get training data for the construction of the ANNs based algorithm. It was possible by making a training dataset using the Collect Earth Online (CEO) module from SEPAL. This dataset was used as input in the classification module of SEPAL. The output of this step was a FNF map to train the ANNs.

2.3 Pure Class Pixel Detection Technique

The pure class pixel detection is an approach aimed to build a training dataset by listing only representative pixels from the classes that conform the scene. To do this, the cross correlation coefficient, shown in Eq. 1, was implemented to disregard pairs of pixels with coefficient higher than 0.95. This focus helps to avoid the listing of pixels cross correlated. The list conformed at the end, will be used as input to train the neural network.

2.4 ANNs Training

The ANNs was trained following the recommendations of [21]. The training data was conformed by a layer-stack created from the fusion of the LANDSAT 8 mosaic and the FNF class map generated from SEPAL. The traing algorithm selected was the L-BFGS method, and it was implemented from a C++ script integrating both ALGLIB and OPENNN libraries. The ANN architecture design involved a input layer with 6 neurons, a first hidden layer with 10 neurons, a second hidden layer with 5 neurons, and an output layer with one neuron. The resultant ANNs is able to classified between Forest and Non Forest class when a six band pixel is provided as input.

2.5   FNF Map Generation

The LANDSAT 8 mosaic was provided as input into the ANNs algorithm to generate the FNF map. The method to generate this FNF map, is a combination of supervised and unsupervised focuses by mean of the training of a artificial neural network.

2.6   Accuracy Estimation of the FNF Map

The accuracy estimation of the FNF map was accomplished by completing two steps: (i) the FNF map was used as input in the stratified area estimator design os SEPAL to generate a random sampling design to create a validation dataset. Using the CEO module, the validation data set was created by sampling 905 points with satellite imagery from Google Earth Engine (GEE) and DigitalGlobe Basement (DGB). (ii) Once the validation dataset was created, it was used in the stratified area estimator analysis to calculate the accuracy of the FNF map.

3   Results and Discussion

The first result obtained in this work was the LANDSAT 8 mosaic for the AOI. In Fig. 3, the brown and dark orange tonalities belong to forest cover, green pixels are agriculture zones, dark blue is for water bodies, and turquoise color for urban cover. This mosaic generated on the SEPAL platform was automatically corrected in atmospheric and radiometric anomalies. Additionally it was cloud masked, and a process of radiometric normalization was carried out. The mosaic of the Fig. 3 was used in combination with training data from CEO to build the FNF map of Fig. 4. This FNF map was classified from LANDSAT 8 mosaic random forest who is already implemented on SEPAL. Once the FNF map was generated, it was added to the LANDSAT 8 mosaic to get a 7 bands mosaic to train the artificial neural network. Figure 4 shows the overall scenario of forest cover inside and around city of Nueva Loja.

The main feature of the forest cover in Fig. 4 is the high level of fragmentation. Most of the forest cover have been penetrated, and is quite strange identify a continuous pattern of forest cover. Agriculture activity seens to be the bigger factor of pressure for the deforestation activities. In second place, the expansion of the urban zone shows an impact on the deforestation rate. In Fig. 5, the FNF map generated with the artificial neural network is shown. It looks more continuos patterns about the forest cover, and a better identification of water bodies is also distinguishable. In a general point of view, both maps looks congruent.

Fig. 3. LANDSAT 8 Mosaic. The view was created using a NIR, SWIR1, and RED RGB composition (Color figure online)

Fig. 4. FNF map generated from SEPAL to train the ANNs. Green pixels belong to forest cover, and whites to non forest cover. (Color figure online)

Table 2. Stratified sampling design resume. Class 1 is No-Forest cover, class 2 is for Fores cover, and 3 for No-data

Map class	Proportional	Adjusted	Final	Total pixelss
1	191	172	172	165420
2	708	636	636	611846
3	8	100	100	7369

Fig. 5. FNF map generated from the ANNs Algorithm. Green pixels belong to forest cover, and whites to non forest cover. (Color figure online)

Using the FNF map of the Fig. 5, a sampling design for the accuracy estimation of the classification output have been proposed. The size of the FNF class map is 867 x 905, what means 784635 pixels. However, the sampling design can be observed on Table 2. For forest and non forest classes the sampling size was about 0.103% of the universe, for the No data class the sampling was 1.357%. The sampling to complete the validation data was performed using CEO, and it was conformed by 905 sampling points. The sampling points were classified as forest or non forest class taking as reference LANDSAT collections from GEE and high resolution imagery from DGB.

The validation dataset was combined with the FNF map to estimate the accuracy of the classification map. The results about the accuracy of the map are shown in Fig. 6.

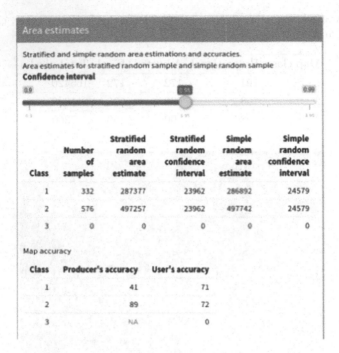

Fig. 6. Results for the estimation of accuracy for the FNF map derived from the neural network algorithm.

The accuracy of producer shows a high kappa value for the forest class (class 2) of 0.89, but a lower value for the non forest class. This results suggests that an improvement of the selection od data training for the neural network is needed. In the case of accuracy of the user, both results were moderately high.

4   Conclusion

In this research, a novel methodology for generation automated of training data for artificial neural network have been proposed. The results obtained from the validation process confirmed that the automatic training of neural network, by using the cross correlation coefficient to detect pure pixels is feasible and promising. It is important also to mention that the use of the SEPAL platform for the downloading of LANDSAT imagery was really helpful. Some of the main advantages to highlight is the facility to generate mosaic and composites with customized parametrization, and also the possibility for processing big data in a high performance computer remotely.

The accuracy obtained by the neural network was satisfactory for the forest class, however for the non forest class there is a need to improve the data training selection in order to get higher kappa values for this class. The automatic training of the neural network by using the pure class pixel detection technique demonstrated a relevant decrease on time for the training process. The artificial neural network was trained using the L-BFGS algorithm, who showed a good generalization and performance in the application. It is important to highlight that testing of another training algorithm was of the out of the scope of this research, it is feasible to increase the accuracy of the results reported by trying with other training algorithm.

The exercise done in this work, was oriented to show the possibility of improvement the neural network training process by using cross-correlation coefficient. for this reason, Forest and Non-Forest were the only two classes selected to make a simple classification. Further research could be oriented to assess the possibility of classify subclasses from forest and non-forest cover, in order to improve the thematic classification in the context al land cover use.

References

1. Belward, A.S., Skøien, J.O.: Who launched what, when and why; trends in global land-cover observation capacity from civilian earth observation satellites. ISPRS J. Photogram. Remote Sens. **103**, 115–128 (2015)
2. Hasmadi, M., Pakhriazad, H.Z., Shahrin, M.F.: Evaluating supervised and unsupervised techniques for land cover mapping using remote sensing data. Geogr.-Malays. J. Soc. Space **5**(1), 1–10 (2017)
3. Lary, D.J., Alavi, A.H., Gandomi, A.H., Walker, A.L.: Machine learning in geosciences and remote sensing. Geosci. Front. **7**(1), 3–10 (2016)
4. Bischof, H., Schneider, W., Pinz, A.J.: Multispectral classification of LANDSAT-images using neural networks. IEEE Trans. Geosci. Remote Sens. **30**(5), 482–490 (1992)
5. Kamata, S.-I., Eason, R.O., Perez, A., Kawaguchi, E.: A neural network classifier for LANDSAT image data. In: Proceedings 11th IAPR International Conference on Pattern Recognition, 1992, Conference B: Pattern Recognition Methodology and Systems, vol. II, pp. 573–576 (1992)
6. Salahova, S.: Remote sensing and GIS application for carth observation on the base of the neural networks in aerospace image classification. In: 2007 3rd International Conference on Recent Advances in Space Technologies RAST 2007, pp. 275–278 (2007)
7. Lee, J., Weger, R.C., Sengupta, S.K., Welch, R.M.: A neural network approach to cloud classification. IEEE Trans. Geosci. Remote Sens. **28**(5), 846–855 (1990)
8. Gao, Y., Zhang, W., Wang, J., Liu, C.: LULC classification of LANDSAT- 7 ETM+ image from rugged terrain using TC, CA and SOFM neural network. In: 2007 IEEE International Geoscience and Remote Sensing Symposium IGARSS 2007, pp. 3490–3493 (2007)
9. Mas, J.-F.: An articial neural networks approach to map land use/cover using Landsat imagery and incillary data. In: 2003 Proceedings of IEEE International Geoscience and Remote Sensing Symposium 2003 IGARSS 2003, vol. 6, pp. 3498–3500 (2003)
10. Paola, J.D., Schowengerdt, R.A.: A detailed comparison of backpropagation neural network and maximum-likelihood classifiers for urban land use classification. IEEE Trans. Geosci. Remote Sens. **33**(4), 981–996 (1995)

11. Chae, H.S., Kim, S.J., Ryu, J.A.: A classfication of multitemporal LANDSAT TM data using principal component analysis and artificial neural network. In:1997 IEEE International Geoscience and Remote Sensing, IGARSS 1997, vol. 1, pp. 517–520. Remote Sensing-A Scientific Vision for Sustainable Development (1997)
12. Lee, S., Lathrop, R.G.: Subpixel analysis of Landsat ETM/sup+/using self-organizing map (SOM) neural networks for urban land cover characterization. IEEE Trans. Geosci. Remote Sens. **44**(6), 1642–1654 (2006)
13. Yoshida, T., Omatu, S.: A remotely sensed data separation method with neural networks. In: IEEE 2001 International Geoscience and Remote Sensing Symposium, IGARSS 2001, vol. 7, pp. 3300–3302 (2001)
14. Foody, G.A., Cutler, M.E.: Remote sensing of biodiversity: using neural networks to estimate the diversity and composition of a Bornean tropical rainforest from landsat TM data. In: 2002 IEEE International Geoscience and Remote Sensing Symposium, IGARSS 2002, vol. 1, pp. 497–499 (2002)
15. Feldberg, I., Netanyahu, N.S., Shoshany, M.: A neural network-based technique for change detection of linear features and its application to a Mediterranean region. In: 2002 IEEE International Geoscience and Remote Sensing Symposium, IGARSS 2002, vol 2, pp. 1195–1197 (2002)
16. Velloso, M.L.F., de Souza, F.J., Simoes, M.: Improved radiometric normalization for land cover change detection: an automated relative correction with artificial neural network. In: 2002 IEEE International Geoscience and Remote Sensing Symposium, IGARSS 2002, vol. 6, pp. 3435–3437 (2002)
17. Fang, H., Liang, S.: Retrieving leaf area index with a neural network method: simulation and validation. IEEE Trans. Geosci. Remote. Sens. **41**(9), 2052–2062 (2003)
18. Zhao, D., Zhang, W., Shijin, X.: A neural network algorithm to retrieve near surface air temperature from landsat ETM+ imagery over the Hanjiang River Basin, China. In: IEEE International Geoscience and Remote Sensing Symposium, IGARSS 2007, pp. 1705–1708 (2007)
19. Neagoe, V., Strugaru, G: A concurrent neural network model for pattern recognition in multispectral satellite imagery. In: World Automation Congress, WAC 2008, pp. 1–6 (2008)
20. Solaiman, B., Mouchot, M.C., Koffi, R.K: Multispectral LANDSAT images segmentation using neural networks and multi-experts approach. In: International Geoscience and Remote Sensing Symposium, IGARSS 1994, vol. 4, pp. 2109–2111. Surface and Atmospheric Remote Sensing: Technologies, Data Analysis and Interpretation (1994)
21. Munoz, E.A., Di Paola, F., Lanfri, M.A.: Advances on rain rate retrieval from satellite platforms using artificial neural networks. IEEE Lat. Am. Trans. **13**(10), 3179–3186 (2015)
22. Ministerio del Ambiente del Ecuador: Estadísticos de Patrimonio Natural, Publicaciones del MAE (2015)
23. Sepal-FAO.: System for earth observations, data access, processing & analysis for land monitoring (2018). https://sepal.io/. Accessed 30 May 2018

A Computer Aided Diagnosis System for Skin Cancer Detection

Enrique V. Carrera$^{(\boxtimes)}$ and David Ron-Domínguez

Departamento de Eléctrica y Electrónica, Universidad de las Fuerzas Armadas ESPE,
Sangolquí 171103, Ecuador
{evcarrera,dvron}@espe.edu.ec

Abstract. Melanoma is the deadliest form of skin cancer, accounting for about 75% of deaths related to this type of disease. Fortunately, melanoma early detection can increase the survival rate of victims considering that melanoma skin cancer is often visible to patients and physicians. However, recommended self-examinations or physician-directed exams are not significantly reducing melanoma deadly cases due to the absence of knowledge of the patients or the lack of access to well-trained physicians. Based on that, this paper proposes a computer aided diagnosis system that detects melanoma skin cancer using dermatoscopy images, image processing techniques, and machine learning algorithms. Our main goal is to create a cheap, relatively accurate, and easy-to-use system available as an initial procedure to detect melanomas. The evaluation of the designed system using 748 dermatoscopy images shows sensitivities around 98%, when a simple feature-extraction stage is applied and a classifier based on support vector machines is utilized.

Keywords: Melanoma · Skin cancer · Digital image processing
Machine learning

1 Introduction

Melanoma is by far the deadliest form of skin cancer, accounting for about 75% of deaths related to this disease [11]. In consequence, melanoma skin cancer is a major public health concern since this disease is currently the sixth most common cancer in the US and the number one in adults between 25 and 29 years old [13].

Early detection of melanoma skin cancer can significantly reduce both morbidity and mortality, since the risk of dying from this disease is directly associated to the amount of time that it has been growing ignored. Thus, melanoma early detection can increase the survival rate of victims considering that this type of cancer is often visible to both patients and physicians [10]. In fact, the most common recommendation to early detection of melanoma skin cancer is to perform patient self-examinations and physician-directed exams.

© Springer Nature Switzerland AG 2019
M. Botto-Tobar et al. (Eds.): CITT 2018, CCIS 895, pp. 553–563, 2019.
https://doi.org/10.1007/978-3-030-05532-5_42

However, recommended self-examinations or physician-directed exams are not significantly reducing melanoma deadly cases due to the absence of knowledge of the patients or the lack of access to well-trained physicians. Because of that, this work proposes a computer aided diagnosis (CADx) system that detects melanoma skin cancer using dermatoscopy images, image processing techniques, and machine learning algorithms. The main goal of this work is to create a cheap, relatively accurate, and easy to-use system available as an initial procedure to detect melanomas. The proposed CADx system is not intended to be a replacement for the procedures carried out by physicians, but a first diagnosis tool for people that do not feel capable of performing a self-examination or do not have direct access to a physician.

The designed CADx system was trained with 748 dermatoscopy images using a 10-fold cross-validation. The system starts extracting 28 features from the original images and uses both support vector machines (SVM) and decision trees (DT) to classify the presence or not of melanoma skin cancer. Results are very promising in the sense that a sensibility of 98% is achieved with a SVM. DT algorithms were not as good as SVM, but DT results are more balanced. In addition, a scheme for automatic segmentation of the pigmented areas of the skin in the dermatoscopy images was proposed.

The rest of this paper is organized as follows. Section 2 describes the most relevant information about melanoma skin cancer. Section 3 presents the design of our computer aided diagnosis system. The main results and their implications are analyzed in Sect. 4. Finally, Sect. 5 concludes this paper.

2   Melanoma Skin Cancer

Moles, brown spots and growths on the skin are usually harmless. However, ultraviolet radiation can lead skin cells to multiply rapidly and uncontrollably, forming malignant tumors. These tumors, called melanomas, when begin in the cells that give to the skin its color, often resemble moles, and anyone who has more than 100 moles is at greater risk for melanoma.

The first signs appear in one or more atypical moles, being important to look for the ABCDE signs of melanoma [10]:

- Asymmetry: Asymmetrical moles are a warning sign for melanoma, since benign moles are normally symmetrical.
- Border: Benign moles has smooth and even borders, unlike melanomas that have uneven, scalloped or notched borders.
- Color: Most benign moles are all one color, while having a variety of colors is a warning signal.
- Diameter: Benign moles usually have a smaller diameter (*i.e.*, less than 6 mm) than malignant ones.
- Evolving: Commonly, benign moles look the same over time. When a mole starts to evolve or change in any way, the patient must be alert.

Dermatoscopy techniques have been developed to improve the diagnostic of melanoma. Dermatoscopy is a recent noninvasive technique of visual inspection that both magnifies the skin and eliminates surface reflection in order to increase the clarity of the spots. Nevertheless, automatic recognition of melanoma from dermatoscopy images is still a difficult task as it has several challenges. In fact, diagnostic accuracy with dermatoscopy is just around 75–84% [4].

3 Computer Aided Diagnosis System

The computer aided diagnosis system designed in this work to detect melanoma skin cancer is described in Fig. 1. Even though dermatoscopy images can be taken by any digital dermatoscope, an external database of images is used to train the supervised classifier. Basically, every dermatoscopy image is segmented to isolate the pigmented region of the skin before extracting significant features that can be used by the classifiers to identify melanoma skin cancer.

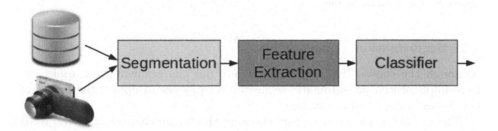

Fig. 1. Computer aided diagnosis system for skin cancer detection.

3.1 Image Database

The database used in this study was obtained from the International Society for Digital Imaging of the Skin and its ISIC project [4]. ISIC (International Skin Imaging Collaboration: Melanoma Project) has developed an open source public access archive designed to facilitate the application of digital skin imaging in order to help reducing melanoma mortality. The 'Skin Lesion Analysis Towards Melanoma Detection' database was selected because its good image resolution and the existence of segmentation masks [9]. Some examples of images and their masks in the ISIC database are presented in Fig. 2.

The selected database has 2000 full-color images, where 374 of them correspond to melanoma skin cancer and the other ones are benign nevus or non-cancerous tumors. In order to balance the number of examples used by each classifier, we only used the 374 melanoma images and other 374 randomly selected images from the benign nevus. Thus, our image database is a partial set of the ISIC database containing only 748 dermatoscopy images.

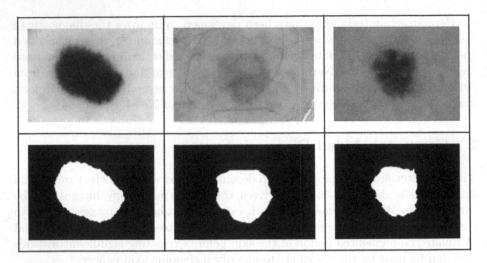

Fig. 2. Examples of dermatoscopy images and their segmentation masks in the ISIC database (Color figure online).

3.2   Segmentation

Although the chosen ISIC database already has the segmentation masks, we have implemented an automatic segmentation process to obtain the masks of new images entered to the system.

The segmentation process start choosing the image channel (*i.e.*, the RGB component) with higher entropy. Using only the image channel with higher entropy, a histogram equalization operation is applied to improve the image contrast [1]. After that, a dilatation operation is employed to remove small hairs or imperfections of the skin. The obtained gray-scale image is then binarized according to an optimal threshold which is searched interactively. At the end, external borders and holes are removed eliminating discontinuities in the different regions of the mask [8].

Regardless of whether the segmentation mask is part of the chosen database or the segmentation mask is computed through the procedure described above, the mask is multiplied by the original image in order to isolate just the pigmented region of the skin.

3.3   Feature Extraction

The features extracted from the segmented image are: asymmetry, border quality, texture parameters, and blue-white veil.

- In the case of asymmetry, the distance between the centroid of the mask and the weighted centroid of the segmented image is given as a resulting feature. While the computation of the centroid considers equal weight for all the pixels, the weighted centroid use the pixel intensities in the segmented

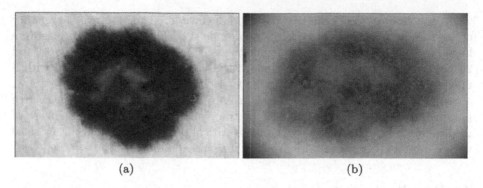

(a)   (b)

Fig. 3. Different types of edges: (a) a well-defined edge with a Jaccard index of 0.32 (b) a fuzzy edge with a Jaccard index of 0.97 (Color figure online).

image as their corresponding weights. In addition, the number of times that the diametrically opposite distances to the centroid are quite different every 15° is returned.

- The border quality is defined by the uniformity of the edges around the pigmented region of the skin, and it could be basically well defined or fuzzy. The metric in this case is the Jaccard index between the RGB components binarized, segmented according to the mask, and eroded. This value is normally maximized when the edges are irregular, uneven or ill-defined. Figure 3 shows examples of well defined and fuzzy edges with their corresponding Jaccard indexes [2].

- In the case of texture parameters, we work with the gray-scale representation of the original image and its three RGB components separately. Each one of the four matrices is segmented according to the mask and six operations are applied on them: average, standard deviation, smoothness, third-order momentum, homogeneity, and entropy [5,7]. Note that the final result of each operation is computed using only the pixels inside the mask.

- Finally, the blue-white veil parameter returns the relation between the blue-white veil area and the total segmented area. For that, the segmented red and blue components are binarized to show those pixels with intensities between 80 and 170. The intersection of these two areas is the set of pixels corresponding to the blue-white veil.

All the features mentioned above are normalized prior to be presented to the classifiers. The type of normalization used in all the cases is z-score [14].

3.4   Classifiers

In order to classify the 28 features described in the previous section, we used two different machine learning classifiers: support vector machines (SVM) and decision trees (DT) [3].

In the case of SVM, the free parameters considered to improve the quality of the results were the type of kernel and scale [12]. The evaluated kernels were lineal, polynomial, and Gaussian, while the scale was evaluated between 0.1 and 20 in steps of 0.1. On the other hand, the DT classifier was evaluated with a maximum of 100 branches and pruning to avoid over-training.

All the classifiers use k-fold as a cross-validation technique, and the free parameters were optimized for both accuracy and sensibility [3]. In the case of medical applications, sensibility is a more critical parameter than accuracy since we are interested in avoid false negative diagnoses mainly.

4   Results

The computer aided diagnosis system described in the previous section was implemented in Matlab R2015a [6] and executed in a computer running Windows 7 (64 bits) with an Intel Core i5 (2.53 GHz) processor and 8 GB of RAM. The time required for the segmentation and feature extraction of the 748 dermatoscopy images is around 43 min.

4.1   Image Segmentation

As mentioned in Sect. 3, although the database already has hand-made masks for the dermatoscopy images, we have proposed a segmentation algorithm to extract the pigmented area of the skin [8]. In order to evaluate the quality of our proposed method, the Jaccard index [2] between the provided mask and the new generated mask is used. Note that the Jaccard index provides the ratio intersection over union, and it is a metric for similarity.

Figure 4 shows an example image, its mask provided by the database, and the new mask computed by our method. We can see a good matching among the two masks and the Jaccard index in this case is 0.9. However, not all the segmentations are good enough, and the average Jaccard index for all the 748 images is only 0.6. The main reason for this low average value is that some pigmented areas are quite irregular and can include holes in their final representation. An example of such a case is the image shown in Fig. 5, where considerable sets of internal pixels have the same color as the surrounding skin.

4.2   Classification Results

Using the 28 features (i.e., asymmetry—2, border quality—1, texture—24, and blue-white veil—1), the masks provided by the database, and the SVM algorithm as classifier, the confusion matrix for the sensibility-optimized model is the one presented in Table 1. Note that for all the results presented in this paper, performance results belong to a k-fold cross-validation with $k = 10$. As you can see in the table, the sensibility is 98%, but the accuracy is just 63%. However, this type of systems is able to avoid false negatives with high precision.

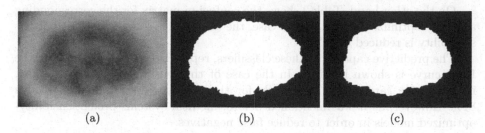

(a)   (b)   (c)

Fig. 4. Comparison of segmentation results: (a) original image, (b) database mask, and (c) result of proposed segmentation.

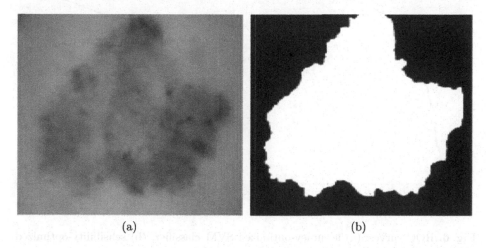

(a)   (b)

Fig. 5. A difficult image to segment: (a) original image, and (b) database mask. (Color figure online)

Table 1. Confusion matrix for the sensibility-optimized SVM classifier with 28 features.

Actual class	Predicted class	
	Healthy	Melanoma
Healthy	244	130
Melanoma	7	367

Table 2. Confusion matrix for the accuracy-optimized SVM classifier with 28 features.

Actual class	Predicted class	
	Healthy	Melanoma
Healthy	346	28
Melanoma	47	327

On the other hand, Table 2 shows the confusion matrix for the corresponding accuracy-optimized model. In this case, the accuracy is as high as 87%, but the sensibility is reduced to 93%.

The predictive capacity of these classifiers, represented by the area under the ROC curve is shown in Fig. 6. In the case of the sensibility-optimized model, its predictive capacity is 75%, while for the accuracy-optimized model, it is 81%. However, as it was mentioned before, medical systems prefer sensibility-optimized models in order to reduce false negatives.

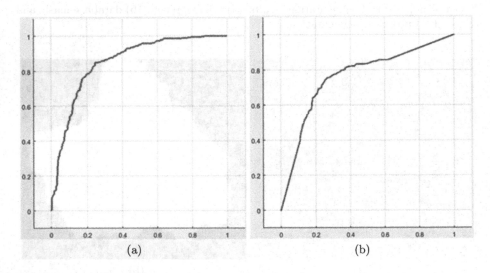

(a)   (b)

Fig. 6. ROC curves: (a) accuracy-optimized SVM classifier, (b) sensibility-optimized SVM classifier.

When a DT algorithms was used as classifier, results are more balanced between the sensibility and accuracy-optimized systems. Table 3 shows the confusion matrix for the sensibility-optimized DT model. In this case, the sensibility is only 86% with an accuracy of 73%.

Table 3. Confusion matrix for the sensibility-optimized DT classifier with 28 features.

Actual class	Predicted class	
	Healthy	Melanoma
Healthy	320	54
Melanoma	52	322

On the other hand, the accuracy-optimized DT model presents the confusion matrix shown in Table 4. In this case, the accuracy is 74% while the sensibility is 83%.

Table 4. Confusion matrix for the accuracy-optimized DT classifier with 28 features.

Actual class	Predicted class	
	Healthy	Melanoma
Healthy	337	37
Melanoma	63	311

The predictive capacity of these classifiers is shown in Fig. 7 as the area under the ROC curve. In the case of the sensibility-optimized DT model, its predictive capacity is 73%, while for the accuracy-optimized DT model is 75%.

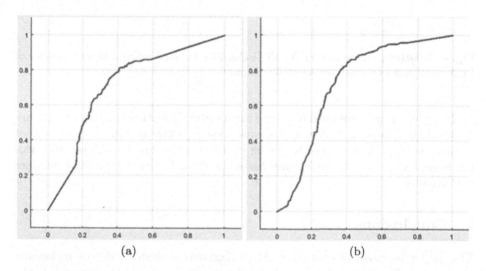

(a)   (b)

Fig. 7. ROC curves: (a) accuracy-optimized DT classifier, (b) sensibility-optimized DT classifier.

Hence, we can conclude that SVM is a much better classifier in terms of sensibility, since the values of this parameter can be as high as 98%.

4.3   Dimensionality Reduction

In order to optimize the execution time of the classifiers reducing the number of features used by these models, a principal component analysis (PCA) technique was applied to reduce the number of parameters employed as inputs to each model. We prove that 8 PCA coefficients produce better performance results in terms of accuracy. In particular, Fig. 8 shows the relative performance (y axis) of the SVM classifier when different number of PCA coefficients (x axis) are selected.

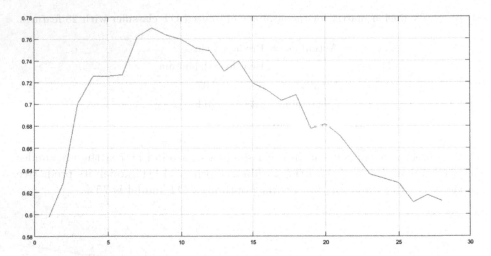

Fig. 8. Relative performance of the SVM classifier (y axis) when different number of PCA coefficients (y axis) are selected as input.

In addition, we have tried to reduce the number of features eliminating redundant values. However, 28 features always present better results that any subset of those values. In other words, the 28 characteristics can be reduced to 8 values using PCA, but all the features has some contribution to the final classifier performance.

5   Conclusions

This paper proposes a computer aided diagnosis system to detect melanoma skin cancer. The performance results of the system in terms of accuracy is in the range of previous related works [4]. However, the sensibility of our proposal is able to reach 98%, avoiding a significant number of false negatives diagnoses. In addition, we have proposed an automatic segmentation scheme that eliminates the need of working with databases that provide masks for the different moles, spots or growths. Thus, this work proves that is possible to create a cheap, relatively accurate, and easy-to-use system that detects automatically melanoma skin cancer with high sensibility.

As future works we are planning to prove other dermatoscopy databases, to improve our basic segmentation process, to refine the current extracted features, and to evaluate new machine learning techniques (*e.g.*, deep learning).

Acknowledgment. This work was partially supported by the Universidad de las Fuerzas Armadas ESPE under Research Grant 2015-PIC-004.

References

1. Andrade, F., Carrera, E.V.: Supervised evaluation of seed-based interactive image segmentation algorithms. In: 2015 20th Symposium on Signal Processing, Images and Computer Vision (STSIVA), pp. 1–7. IEEE (2015)
2. Berman, M., Rannen Triki, A., Blaschko, M.B.: The lovász-softmax loss: a tractable surrogate for the optimization of the intersection-over-union measure in neural networks, pp. 4413–4421 (2018)
3. Chen, C.H.: Handbook of Pattern Recognition and Computer Vision. World Scientific, Singapore (2015)
4. Codella, N.C., et al.: Skin lesion analysis toward melanoma detection: a challenge at the 2017 international symposium on biomedical imaging (ISBI), hosted by the international skin imaging collaboration (ISIC). In: 15th International Symposium on Biomedical Imaging (ISBI 2018), pp. 168–172. IEEE (2018)
5. Gonzalez, R.C.: Digital Image Processing. Prentice Hall, Upper Saddle River (2016)
6. Gonzalez, R.C., Woods, R.E., Eddins, S.L.: Digital Image Processing Using Matlab. Dorling Kindersley Publishing, Noida (2017)
7. Haralick, R.M., Shanmugam, K., et al.: Textural features for image classification. IEEE Trans. Syst., Man, Cybern. **6**, 610–621 (1973)
8. Khan, M.W.: A survey: image segmentation techniques. Int. J. Futur. Comput. Commun. **3**(2), 89 (2014)
9. Li, Y., Shen, L.: Skin lesion analysis towards melanoma detection using deep learning network. Sensors **18**(2), 556 (2018)
10. Robinson, J.K., Turrisi, R.: Skills training to learn discrimination of ABCDE criteria by those at risk of developing melanoma. Arch. Dermatol. **142**(4), 447–452 (2006)
11. Rogers, H.W., et al.: Incidence estimate of nonmelanoma skin cancer in the united states, 2006. Arch. Dermatol. **146**(3), 283–287 (2010)
12. Rojo-Alvarez, J.L., Muñoz-Marí, J., Camps-Valls, G., Martínez-Ramón, M.: Digital Signal Processing with Kernel Methods. Wiley-IEEE, Hoboken (2018)
13. Siegel, R.L., Miller, K.D., Jemal, A.: Cancer statistics, 2016. CA: Cancer J. Clin. **66**(1), 7–30 (2016)
14. Witten, I.H., Frank, E., Hall, M.A., Pal, C.J.: Data Mining: Practical Machine Learning Tools and Techniques. Morgan Kaufmann, Burlington (2016)

Modeling 911 Emergency Events in Cuenca-Ecuador Using Geo-Spatial Data

Pablo Robles[✉], Andrés Tello, Miguel Zúñiga Prieto,
and Lizandro Solano-Quinde

Universidad de Cuenca, Cuenca, Ecuador
{pablo.robles,andres.tello,miguel.zunigap,lizandro.solano}@ucuenca.edu.ec

Abstract. We present several techniques for modeling emergency events using data from 911 emergency calls in the city of Cuenca-Ecuador. We apply three types of models. First, we use a probabilistic description of events using Gaussian kernels based on both, regular segmentation and mixture models, to represent the spatial distribution of occurrences. Second, we verify the qualitative relation of the clusters obtained with our kernel model with respect to the geo-political organization of the city. Finally, we develop an emergency model using a large dataset corresponding to the period January 1st 2015 through December 31st 2016 and test various data mining algorithms for prediction purposes. We verify the usefulness of our approach experimentally.

Keywords: 911 calls · Emergency calls · Kernel models · GMM

1 Introduction

Predicting emergencies is a relatively unexplored problem that has important applications for decision makers in areas of civil security and urban planning. The objective is to identify optimal solutions for timely and cost-effective assignment of resources, creation and maintenance of infrastructure, and contingency planning. In Ecuador, the ECU-911[1] is the largest system for monitoring emergencies, which coordinates the solution of incidents through call-centers and dispatchers. The tasks of ECU-911 agents facilitate the deployment and support from various institutions such as, National Police, Public Health Ministry, Social Security Office, Army, Fire Departments, National Secretary of Risk Management, and Transit Commission. These interactions enable a logistic control for the solution of problems as soon as they are detected or reported.

However, to this day there is no manner to optimize the work of ECU-911. This optimization could improve the pre-assignment and deployment of resources, according to the level of incidences, the type of event, the geo-spatial, and the historical data.

---

[1] http://www.ecu911.gob.ec.

© Springer Nature Switzerland AG 2019
M. Botto-Tobar et al. (Eds.): CITT 2018, CCIS 895, pp. 564–577, 2019.
https://doi.org/10.1007/978-3-030-05532-5_43

Predicting an incidence facilitates planning and resource allocation. Several approaches use temporal, spatial, and demographics data to create prediction models of different types of events. The work of Chandrasekar et al. [4] analyzes crime data from the city of San Francisco to classify types of crime based on time of occurrence and location. The authors suggest that, instead of classifying crime events into very specific classes, grouping events into larger categories allows to find patterns in the data. Bappee et al. [2] use machine learning to find the relationship between criminal activity and geographical regions. They use spatial information from open street map data, and crime hotspots based on density clustering algorithms as features to train classifiers of different types of crime. Other approaches focus on predicting traffic incidences. The work of Yuan et al. [16] uses a dataset of vehicle crashes from 2006 to 2013, in the state of Iowa, USA, as well as various weather attributes with one hour of granularity to create prediction models. An interesting approach to detect traffic accidents is shown in [14]. This work uses machine learning algorithms trained with location information from smart-phones at vehicles not involved in the incident to detect traffic accidents.

In this paper, we introduce mathematical models to describe the distribution of events in time and in geo-space using ECU-911 data. Although demographics provide valuable information for prediction models, previous studies that include demographics are focused on cities or regions within the United States where conditions, life standards, and customs differ significantly from those in Ecuador. Therefore, in this initial approach, we use only spatiotemporal data. We focus on the case of the city of Cuenca and consider three types of events: *Civil Security*, *Transit*, and *Hospital and Health Services*. We propose several models and compare the performance of these models against a baseline approach.

The remainder of this paper is organized as follows. Section 2 describes previous work in this field. In Sect. 3 we introduce our proposed models based on geo-spatial data. Section 4 discusses the experiments to evaluate our models and the obtained results. Finally, Sect. 6 presents the conclusions and some directions for future work.

2   Related Work

Predicting emergency events, as registered through 911 calls in various cities in the world, is a complex and relatively new problem. Such predictions are important for decision making that would optimize costs and response-times, as well as resource allocation and creation/maintenance of new infrastructure. City planning and maintaining the overall security of a city can benefit from research in this area. Many researchers [5–8,11,13,15] have shown the importance of this problem and have provided valuable insights on how to model emergencies. These models are highly dependent on specific information and are applicable to specific datasets. However, in the case of Ecuador, and more specifically of the city of Cuenca, there are not publicly available datasets with the structure required by these models. It is important to notice some insights from the current literature on modeling emergencies. The work of [6] not only implemented a system for the analysis of historical information of event-reponses for the Coast Guard of USA but also analyzed the potential risk associated to seek and rescue operations. The authors of [10] created an analytic and visual model for the study of spatial-temporal correlations among various datasets. For this purpose, their model separates the correlations using several levels of aggregation. However, there are big challenges with emergency modeling, which include, the way the information is represented [7], the user interaction with the system, the representation of multiple datasets, and prediction [9].

Another goal associated for developing models of emergency events is to provide interactive tools [8] for both common and specialized users that may include decision makers. The objective of these software tools is to increase the level of awareness in a specific scenario. These tools provide users with a set of interactive options for analysis and detection of trends, patterns, and anomalies, and also provide options for evaluating risks associated to criminal, vehicular, or civil incidents, depending on the location and the time of the event.

In addition to the problems related to descriptive modeling, predicting emergencies is an even more complex problem where external information is usually necessary. The work of [11] is an example of predictive model that uses exogenous variables of incidents reported in Chicago between 2001 and 2014. Their results show that in addition to factors such as time of the year, weekends, and holidays, that are generally expected to have higher relations with criminal activity, exogenous variables, such as the temperature of the city at certain times of the day affect the behavior of people and can help to improve predictions, independently of the time of the year. The work of [12] also introduced a model of emergency events. This analytic-visual work provides with a tool to help decision makers to assign resources. The tool provides options for selecting the level of geo-spatial and temporal resolution for predictions and it uses *Seasonal Trend Decomposition based on LOESS* (STL) [1]. STL can be applied to spatial-temporal data to predict events based on correlations using regression. The work in [12] can also be used to estimate correlation among adjacent regions. It has been successfully applied to criminal, traffic, and civil datasets.

Among these, the works that are closer to ours are [6,7]. Although [6] provides with a tool for cluster analysis, the prediction of events and detection of anomalies, the study is applied to a large complex city that has little, if any, resemblance to the activities in a city like Cuenca-Ecuador. Also, the size, origin, and nature of the datasets are different. On the other hand, although [7] is a predictive model of emergencies, this prediction is based on work activities of the population, i.e., number of jobs, businesses, etc., as well as the level of education, i.e., number of graduates, of the people per zones. However, this type of information is not available for predicting events for Cuenca.

In summary, the current literature contains important work for modeling and predicting emergencies. However, some of these models are applicable to specific geographic and demographic scenarios and are dependent on external data that are not available to the study emergencies in Cuenca.

3   Modeling Emergencies with Geo-Spatial Data

In this Section we propose methods based on Gaussian kernels to model emergency events. A bivariate-Gaussian kernel density function has the form:

$$f(\mathbf{x}) = \sum_{i=1}^{N_C} \frac{1}{N_C} f_i(\mathbf{x})$$

where the function $f_i(\mathbf{x}) = \frac{1}{2\pi\sqrt{|\Sigma_i|}} e^{-\frac{1}{2}(\mathbf{x}-\mu_i)^T \Sigma_i^{-1}(\mathbf{x}-\mu_i)}$ is the i-th component of the kernel and N_C is the number of components of the kernel. In order to identify the adequate construction for these components, two sub-types of kernel models for geo-spatial emergency data are proposed in this paper: a homogeneous model and a heterogeneous model.

3.1   Homogeneous Model

The first sub-type of kernel model is a homogeneous model. In this work the geographic area of interest is divided into homogeneous, regular, squared-cells of equal size. Then each component of the kernel is assigned to one cell in the grid. As it is discussed later, cells of one squared meter are considered in the analysis of this work.

Result: μ, Σ
minLat= -2.9, minLon= -79.05, maxLat= -2.85, maxLon= -78.92;
gridsize = 5*0.00089;
cells = divideInGrid (minLat, maxLat, minLon, maxLon, gridsize, data);
for *cell-i in cells* **do**
$\quad \mu_i \leftarrow$ mean(data points in cell-i);
$\quad \Sigma_i \leftarrow$ covariance(data points in cell-i);
end

Algorithm 1. Homogeneous Gaussian-Kernel Algorithm

In a traditional Gaussian mixture model, the data is divided in sub-regions or components and each sub-region is assigned to a normal bivariate distribution. The parameters of each sub-region's distribution are estimated such that the sub-regions could overlap. Each component has a different weight in the final density function, depending on the number of elements of the component. These parameters are estimated using random partitions or groups of data points. To simplify the estimation, the geo-spatial data is divided in a grid such that the components are predefined in the mixture, i.e. each component is bivariate normal. Overlaps are avoided to prevent reusing data. Thus, each cell has a bivariate normal distribution associated.

Algorithm 1 creates partitions of equal size using the geo-spatial indices of each data point and considers all the event locations within each cell. It is worth noticing that certain cells cannot be modeled with a normal distribution. In such scenarios we merge the content of that cell with the adjacent cell. Finally, the weight of each component in the kernel, that can be thought of as the probability of each component in the kernel, is proportional to the number of events in each cell.

Figure 1 shows the density as due to the homogeneous kernel. This particular plot corresponds to the type of events *transit* and *mobility*. This homogeneous kernel could also be used as a mixture model where each component correspond to a cell in the grid.

3.2   Heterogenous Model

The second sub-type of kernel model is a heterogeneous model. This kernel is built on the basis of a traditional Gaussian mixture model. In other words, the components are estimated based on clusters obtained from the Gaussian mixture model. In this case, the cells are overlapping, have different sizes, and are not necessarily squared but rectangular. As in the previous case, each cell is associated to a component of the kernel, which is then built with the parameters estimated for each component of the Gaussian mixture model. Algorithm 2 creates partitions using the clusters estimated from a Gaussian mixture model fitted to the data. As in the previous model, the cells that cannot be modeled with a normal distribution are simply not used for that component of the kernel or joined with an adjacent or overlapping cell. Finally, the weight of each cell in the mixture is proportional to the probability of each component.

Result: μ, Σ
minLat= -2.9, minLon= -79.05, maxLat= -2.85, maxLon= -78.92;
gridsize = 5*0.00089;
cells = divideInGrid (minLat, maxLat, minLon, maxLon, gridsize, data);
continue = True;
while *continue* **do**
    cells = computeGaussianMixtureModel(minLat, maxLat, minLon, maxLon, gridsize,datos);
    continue = False;
    if *GMM is not stable* **then**
        | continue = True;
    end
    for *cell-i* **in** *cells* **do**
        | $\mu_i \leftarrow$ mean(datos in cell-i);
        | $\Sigma_i \leftarrow$ covariance(datos in cell-i);
    end
    if *parameters μ, Σ are not computed* **then**
        | continue = True;
    end
end

Algorithm 2. Homogeneous Gaussian-Kernel Algorithm

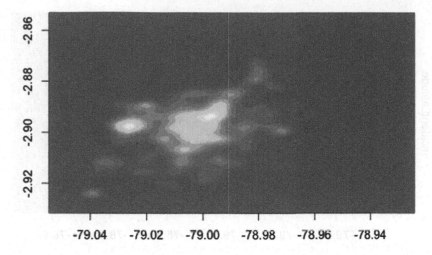

Fig. 1. Model with regular and equally sized kernel components

Figure 2 shows the density obtained with the heterogeneous kernel for the case of incidences *transit and mobility*. Notice that although the details of the components are slightly different, the overall shape as well as the most representative modes of the distribution are similar to the previous case of homogeneous kernel. An advantage of the heterogeneous kernel is that it uses fewer cells and could be computationally convenient. However, this convenience comes at the expense of lower details and possibly stability.

3.3 Global Temporal Models

In order to integrate the temporal information to the spatial information, this section describes several machine-learning algorithms that predict a set of event types. Specifically, this work considers decision trees, random forests, and regression analysis. Because of the spatiotemporal nature of the variables studied in this paper, the type of prediction models developed need to deal with the continuous nature of the location information and the temporal information. This analysis complements the spatial information obtained from the kernel models described in the previous subsections. As it is discussed later in the section devoted to the experiments, we consider three types of events associated to 911 calls: health-management, civil security, and transit events. The following is a description of the algorithms we selected.

Decision Tree Learning. The advantage of using a decision tree algorithm is that they provide a human-readable description of the interactions among variables which may include variables of different nature than spatiotemporal. Specifically, the C4.5 algorithm is considered in the present analysis. This algorithm builds a tree as by partitioning a set of features S using the *information*

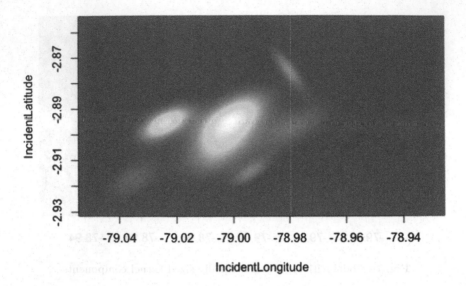

Fig. 2. Model with random kernel components

gain as a metric. In particular, it minimizes the total entropy of the subsets $\{S_i\}$ where $S_i \in S$ are obtained from the partition. Another heuristic to partition the set S is to consider the *default gain ratio*. More precisely, the information gain is calculated as the difference of the entropy of the data before the partition minus the entropy of the partitions when using a specific feature a for such partitioning.

Random Forests. A random forest is an ensemble learning algorithm. This means that the estimation is done over a finite set of sub-models, which in this case are trees. The objective of the random forest algorithm is to create a number of tree-models (in the case of the present analysis we used 20) and then combine the prediction using certain specific voting schema. We use the Breiman and Cutler algorithm that uses the Gini gain during partition of the nodes of each tree instead of the information gain.

Logistic Regression. Finally, the third type of algorithm we consider is the logistic regression model. Since we consider three types of events: health-management, civil security, and transit events, we define the following triple-model for classification.

$$y_i = \alpha + x_1\beta_1 + x_2\beta_2 + x_3\beta_3$$

where $i = 1, 2, 3$ represent the log-regression for each of the three types of events of our interest. Each variable x corresponds to the attributes *longitude, latitude* and *time*. The parameters were estimated for each type of event using mean squares. The thresholds used for discriminating the type of event for each type of event were: for health-management events we used a threshold of 0.2, for civil security events 0.5, and for transit events 0.3.

4 Experiments

4.1 Data Preprocessing

In this work, we use two years of data provided by the ECU-911 that belong to the period between January 1, 2015 and December 31, 2016. The data include the records of reported events which were verified to be an incident. Fake calls were filtered out from the dataset. After some exploratory analysis, we found the data presented common anomalies of formatting and content: outliers, duplicates, missing values, and dispatcher typographical mistakes.

The formatting issues found in most of the categorical attributes of the emergency dataset include inconsistent capitalization, and unnecessary whitespace characters. For example, the attribute *Province* contains values such as "azuay", "Azuay", or "AZUAY". The attribute Region contains values such as "sur", "Sur", or "SUR". Notice that, besides inconsistent capitalization, the latter example, also has trailing white-space characters. Even though these errors are easy-to-solve issues, they are time-consuming to detect and repair. Another common problem are the fields with date and time data types. In our emergency dataset the field that contains the date when the event was reported shows several format inconsistencies. It has three different formats, e.g., dd-mmm-yy, dd/mm/yy and dd/mmm/yyyy. To solve this issue we transform all the values to the standard format dd/mm/yyyy. In addition, fields with time data types such as Incident Time Duration (TDI, spanish acronym) or Call Duration Time (TDL, spanish acronym) contains values expressed in milliseconds or expressed in the format HH:MM:SS (hours, minutes, seconds). We transformed all these values to the format HH:MM:SS. Two common problems with data content encountered in the dataset are null and erroneous values. For instance, time data fields with negative values, or dates with the value 01/01/1900, which represents the initial value of the system's date.

Initially, we did not consider operating system compatibility issues, which might hinder cleaning tasks. However, since the data was generated on Microsoft Windows and processed in a Linux computer, we need to deal with the differences in file conventions between both operating systems [3]. One of the main differences is how a date is calculated. For instance a Microsoft Excel for a specific OS configuration may compute a date by using January 1, 1900 as a starting date, while in Linux the starting date is December 30, 1899. The data provided by the ECU-911 was store in .xlsx files so we had to take special care for datetime fields expressed in milliseconds.

Finally, the last cleaning task was removing duplicates. Our dataset included several records for one reported event. This included the whole sequence of records associated to one event from the time it was reported to the moment when it was closed. In this work we use the frequency of events within a delimited geographic zone. For our experiments we only needed one record for each event, hence we deleted duplicates of events with the same field *IncidentNumber* that happened in the same date.

4.2 Models Setup

The region we used for evaluation is the squared-area enclosed by coordinates: $minLat = -2.931543$, $minLon = -79.054440$, $maxLat = -2.853047$, $maxLon = -78.92402$ and consider a grid size of $5 * 0.00089$, which is roughly speaking about one meter in length.

We consider the events that fall in the categories: *Civil Security*, *Transit*, and *Hospital and Health Services*.

As briefly mentioned before, for the random forest the number of trees used were 20. For logistic regression, since there are three models y_i, we used different thresholds to discriminate the events. The thresholds used were: for health-management events we used a threshold of 0.2, for civil security events 0.5, and for transit events 0.3.

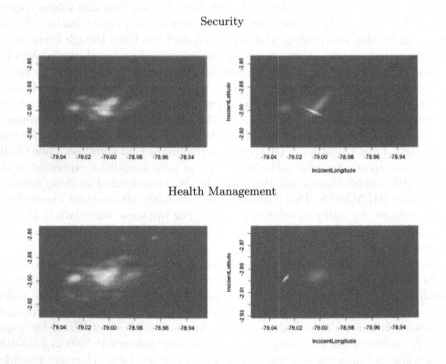

Fig. 3. Model with random kernel components. Security and health management

4.3 Results

We applied the models described in Sect. 3. For this purpose we implemented Algorithms 1 and 2 and studied the dataset *ECU-911 emergency calls* described in the Subsect. 4.1. We studied three types of incidents: transit or transportation events (e.g. accidents), civil security, and health related events. The results of modeling transit events through the Algorithms 1 and 2 are shown in Figs. 1 and 2. We discussed these results in Sect. 3. Additionally, the results of modeling both security and health-management events through the Algorithms 1 and 2 are shown in Fig. 3.

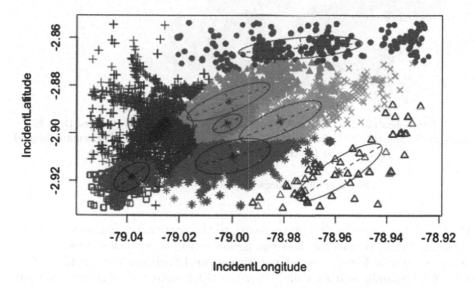

Fig. 4. Segmentation of Cuenca based on the heterogeneous model

The left side of Fig. 3 shows the density as due to the homogeneous kernel. The top-left element shows the case of citizen *security* events and the bottom left plot shows the density of *health-management* events. The homogeneous kernel provides a more fine-grained detail of the variable interactions than the heterogeneous model. The right sub-plots of Fig. 3 show the density obtained with the heterogeneous kernel for the case of incidences *security* and *health-management* events. Contrary to what happened with the case of *transit* events the details of the components for the heterogeneous model are different than the homogeneous models, even although the main distribution modes of both distributions are captured by the heterogeneous models, the details of variable interactions are largely lost in the heterogeneous model. Thus, even though the heterogeneous kernel uses fewer cells the details lost in this approach make the heterogeneous model less suitable than the homogeneous model for the case of *health* and *security* events.

We also performed a qualitative assessment of the quality of the components of the heterogeneous model. For this purpose we consider the Gaussian mixture model clusters defined by each component of the heterogeneous model. The partition of events is shown in Fig. 4, which shows a clustering of Cuenca. This

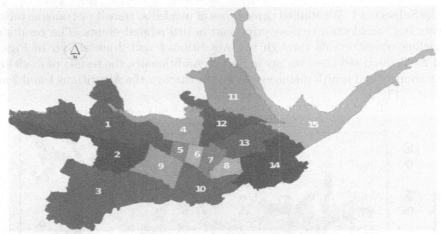

1. San Sebastián 2. El Batán 3. Yanuncay 4. Bellavista 5. Gil Ramírez D. 6. El
Sagrario 7. San Blás 8. Cañaribamba 9. Sucre 10. Huayna Cápac 11. Hermano Miguel
12. El Vecino 13. Totoracocha 14. Monay 15. Machángara

Fig. 5. Political organization of Cuenca-Ecuador

clustering has some qualitative similarity to the partition of parishes in Cuenca
shown in Fig. 5. We merged these two figures in Fig. 6. As shown there, the most
sparse cluster of Fig. 4 is associated with a rural parish in the outskirts of the
city (Chilcapamba and El Valle). Parishes Gil Ramírez, El Sagrario, and part
of Sucre (i.e., 5, 6, and part of 9) are clustered in the same area, which roughly
speaking corresponds to Downtown Cuenca. Totoracocha an Machángara (i.e.,
13 and 15) are grouped in the same cluster. Bellavista an El Vecino (4 and 12) are
grouped in the same cluster, while the Northern parishes and Western parishes
of Cuenca are grouped in separated clusters.

Predictive Results. It is worth mentioning that one of the objectives of the
predictive analysis was to identify spatiotemporal relations in the dataset that
could help identifying certain types of events that the ECU-911 could use for
assessment and planning. We considered the accuracy of the alternative models:
decision tree, random forest, and logistic regression. The results are shown in
Tables 1 and 2.

Parameter Estimation for the Models. For *Decision Tree Learning* The C4.5
tree used in this analysis was trained using the RWeka library. For *Random
Forests* we used 20 trees and default parameters of the randomForest library. For
Logistic Regression we simply trained three models and combined them during
classification (test) by selecting the label with largest likelihood. We used a 80-20
partition proportion for the train and test sets and consider the temporal order,
i.e. we used 80% past events to classify 20% future events. The partition of the
data is stratified per month.

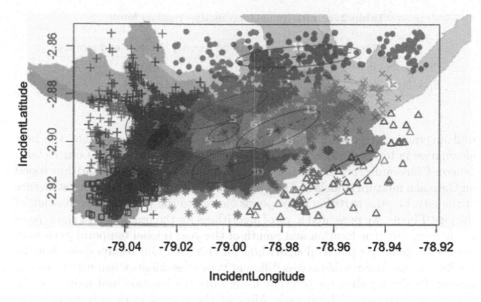

Fig. 6. Segmentation of Cuenca based on the heterogeneous model

Table 1 shows that decision tree is the best performing model to identify the month an event is more likely to happen. Random forest is the most stable model with the best performance across different event-types. Random forest is also the best performing model for health events and security events. However, logistic regression performs the best for transit events. Because random forest is the most stable model we further analyze the performance of this model by studying the specificity and sensitivity of this model as shown in Table 2.

Table 1. Accuracy per model

Decision tree	0.5883
Random forest	0.5144
Logistic regression	0.5104

5   Discussion

In this article we presented the results of applying kernel methods and Gaussian mixture models to the study of emergencies in the city of Cuenca-Ecuador. There are three types of algorithms that we evaluated. First, we presented descriptive spatial models that use kernel density estimation with Gaussian kernel. The choice of a Gaussian kernel is due to previous evident that suggests it performs

Table 2. Sensitivity and specificity - random forest

	Health-management	Citizens security	Transit and mobility
Sensitivity	0.3864	0.8576	0.10507
Specificity	0.8384	0.3750	0.98254

well in practice (see, for instance, [12]). Our observation shows that the best alternative in terms of smoothness of the density obtained is to use our HeterogeneousGaussianKernel. Second, we presented a segmentation algorithm based on Gaussian mixture models and showed that it conveys the qualitative structure of the city, i.e., the partition corresponds closely to the political organization of the city. Finally, we presented a set of algorithms for the prediction of the type of event using only the location and month of the year (global temporal patterns). We used popular yet powerful algorithms for this task. Our results show that the predictions are more stable across different type of incidents when using random forests. Predicting the type of event using only the location and month of the year is an extremely difficult task. Most of the related work only predict the occurrence of emergencies. Ours is the first analysis of this type. In the future we will explore using additional features to try to find alternative solutions to this problem that may provide further improvements.

6   Conclusion

In this paper we presented a set of models for the analysis of 911 events. We introduced two kernel methods based on both homogeneous and heterogeneous partitions of geo-spatial data associated to the emergency calls. The homogeneous model provides more fine-grained details of the variable interactions. The heterogeneous model provides a representation that uses fewer cells but may not be as thorough as the homogeneous model. However, the heterogeneous model also provides us with a tool that is computationally convenient and allows us to perform spatial segmentation as needed. We also provided an analysis of possible temporal predictions where we consider a set of algorithms for classification of temporal data partitioned per month. The predictive analysis identified spatiotemporal relations in the dataset that could help predicting certain types of events for the ECU-911. This can help with assessment and planning tasks. The present work is intended to achieve this goal.

Acknowledgements. This article is part of the project "Análisis predictivo de la ocurrencia de eventos de emergencia en la provincia del Azuay", winner of the"XV Concurso Universitario de Proyectos de Investigación" funded by the Dirección de Investigación de la Universidad de Cuenca. The authors also thank the Servicio Integrado de Seguridad ECU911 - Zona 6 for their collaboration and data provided.

References

1. Cleveland, R.B., Cleveland, W.S., McRae, J.E., Terpenning, I.: STL: a seasonal-trend decomposition procedure based on loess. J. Off. Stat. **6**, 3–33 (1990)
2. Bappee, F.K., Junior, A.S., Matwin, S.: Predicting crime using spatial features. CoRR abs/1803.04474 (2018). http://arxiv.org/abs/1803.04474
3. Cady, F.: The Data Science Handbook. Wiley, Hoboken (2017)
4. Chandrasekar, A., Raj, A.S., Kumar, P.: Crime prediction and classification in San Francisco city
5. Chirigati, F., Doraiswamy, H., Damoulas, T., Freire, J.: Data polygamy: the many-many relationships among urban spatio-temporal data sets. In: Proceedings of the 2016 International Conference on Management of Data, SIGMOD 2016, pp. 1011–1025. ACM, New York (2016). https://doi.org/10.1145/2882903.2915245
6. Chohlas-Wood, A., Merali, A., Reed, W.R., Damoulas, T.: Mining 911 calls in New York city: temporal patterns, detection, and forecasting. In: AAAI Workshop: AI for Cities (2015)
7. Cramer, D., Brown, A.A., Hu, G.: Predicting 911 calls using spatial analysis. In: Lee, R. (ed.) Software Engineering Research, Management and Applications 2011, pp. 15–26. Springer, Heidelberg (2012). https://doi.org/10.1007/978-3-642-23202-2_2
8. Kim, S.Y., Maciejewski, R., Malik, A., Jang, Y., Ebert, D.S., Isenberg, T.: Bristle maps: a multivariate abstraction technique for geovisualization. IEEE Trans. Vis. Comput. Graph. **19**(9), 1438–1454 (2013). https://doi.org/10.1109/TVCG.2013.66
9. Malik, A., Maciejewski, R., Collins, T.F., Ebert, D.S.: Visual analytics law enforcement toolkit. In: 2010 IEEE International Conference on Technologies for Homeland Security (HST), pp. 222–228 (2010)
10. Malik, A., Maciejewski, R., Elmqvist, N., Jang, Y., Ebert, D.S., Huang, W.: A correlativeanalysis process in a visual analytics environment. In: 2012 IEEE Conference on Visual Analytics Science and Technology (VAST), pp. 33–42 (2012)
11. Malik, A., Maciejewski, R., Maule, B., Ebert, D.S.: A visual analytics process for maritime resource allocation and risk assessment. In: 2011 IEEE Conference on Visual Analytics Science and Technology (VAST), pp. 221–230 (2011)
12. Malik, A., Maciejewski, R., Towers, S., McCullough, S., Ebert, D.: Proactive spatiotemporal resource allocation and predictive visual analytics for community policing and law enforcement. IEEE Trans. Vis. Comput. Graph. **20**, 1863–1872 (2014)
13. Razip, A.M., et al.: A mobile visual analytics approach for law enforcement situation awareness. In: 2014 IEEE Pacific Visualization Symposium, pp. 169–176 (2014)
14. Thomas, R.W., Vidal, J.M.: Toward detecting accidents with already available passive traffic information. In: 2017 IEEE 7th Annual Computing and Communication Workshop and Conference (CCWC), pp. 1–4, January 2017. https://doi.org/10.1109/CCWC.2017.7868428
15. Towers, S., Chen, S., Malik, A., Ebert, D.: Factors influencing temporal patterns in crime in a large American city; a predictive analytics perspective. SSRN (2016)
16. Yuan, Z., Zhou, X., Yang, T., Tamerius, J., Mantilla, R.: Predicting traffic accidents through heterogeneous urban data: a case study. In: UrbComp-2017 (2017)

Optimization of the Network of Urban Solid Waste Containers: A Case Study

Israel D. Herrera-Granda[1], Wilson G. Imbaquingo-Usiña[1],
Leandro L. Lorente-Leyva[1(✉)], Erick P. Herrera-Granda[2],
Diego H. Peluffo-Ordóñez[3,5], and Diego G. Rossit[4]

[1] Facultad de Ingeniería en Ciencias Aplicadas, Universidad Técnica del Norte,
Av. 17 de Julio, 5-21, y Gral. José María Cordova, Ibarra, Ecuador
{idherrera,wgimbaquingo,lllorente}@utn.edu.ec
[2] Mechanical Engineering School, National Polytechnic School,
Av. Ladrón de Guevara E11-253, Quito, Ecuador
erick.herrera@epn.edu.ec
[3] Escuela de Ciencias Matemáticas y Tecnología Informática,
Yachay Tech, Hacienda San José s/n, San Miguel de Urcuquí, Ecuador
dpeluffo@yachaytech.edu.ec
[4] Departamento de Ingeniería, Universidad Nacional del Sur (UNS)-CONICET,
Av. Alem 1253, 8000 Bahía Blanca, Argentina
diego.rossit@uns.edu.ar
[5] Corporación Universitaria Autónoma de Nariño, Pasto, Colombia

Abstract. This paper presents the results of the optimization of the urban solid waste container network in the urban sector of the Ibarra City, Ecuador by the implementation of an optimization model, which consists of a multi-objective mixed integer programming model which has been successfully used in the context of recycling in past studies. This model was modified so that possible locations of the containers at each corner of the blocks containing the constructed buildings were considered. As well, a restriction to count the containers to be installed was added. Furthermore, to add robustness to the model, it was also considered the filling of the container based on the density of the deposited waste and the model objective functions – being, a weighted sum of the cost of the installation of the network along with the average walking distance between users and the assigned containers. The outputs of the model are the total number of containers and a map with the optimal locations of municipal solid waste containers for Ibarra city. The model was implemented in GAMS platform wherein parameters can be permanently revised so that the results may be updated in case of variations of the initial conditions.

Keywords: Optimization · Collection network · Reverse logistics
Urban solid waste · Facility Location Problem · NP-hard

1 Introduction

At the global and local levels, one of the most important aspects to guarantee health and quality of life for urban populations is the adequate access to solid waste collection systems [1, 2]. Several programs have been designed in search of a sustainability

© Springer Nature Switzerland AG 2019
M. Botto-Tobar et al. (Eds.): CITT 2018, CCIS 895, pp. 578–589, 2019.
https://doi.org/10.1007/978-3-030-05532-5_44

among population growth, caused environmental impact, and mortality rates reduction –mainly, in urban settlements. Most of such programs consider the importance of ensuring equitable access to municipal solid waste (MSW) collection services [3–6].

The world's major cities invest a large part of their resources in their municipal solid waste collection systems, but –in contrast- developing countries have fewer resources, and therefore they are prone to seek for alternatives to boost their expenses efficiency [5, 7]. Notwithstanding, such alternatives entail a high joint commitment from all the parties: institutions responsible for the waste management, and the general population producing wastes.

In Ecuador, the aforementioned issues cause high concern among the scientific community and the local governments. Despite existing several regulations and legislation to provide guidelines for the proper MSW management, there is no an enough funding support for improving projects, nor an adequate access to training to whom are willing to developing solutions to this kind of problems [2, 8] (Fig. 1).

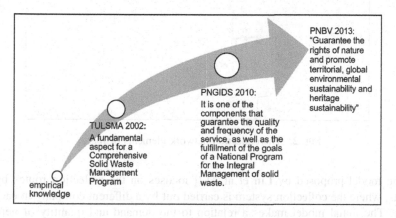

Fig. 1. Legal framework for the MSW management in Ecuador

One of the key aspects for the optimization of the MSW collection service in a human settlement is the adequate design of the collection network, which should consider the population typical aspects to be attended through a characterization study, an uprising of the processes of collection and a costs study in collection operations [9].

This research presents as a case study the Ibarra city with 121616 inhabitants, on which a characterization study that allowed to detect a demographic growth in the population of this city was developed, and led to the expansion of the urbanized area. It was also possible to show that not all urban sectors benefit equitably from the current MSW collection service, which leads to the emergence of micro-wastes in sidewalks, reducing the life quality of the inhabitants and increasing the environmental impact [10, 11].

The lifting of the collection process showed the operation of the MSW collection network. The collection is carried out essentially on containers installed at certain points of the town. There is a deposit for the collecting vehicles (depot), a transfer station which includes a waste separator plant for the recyclable materials recovery (EHU), and a final landfill to which the unusable waste (disposal) is shipped, as shown in Fig. 2.

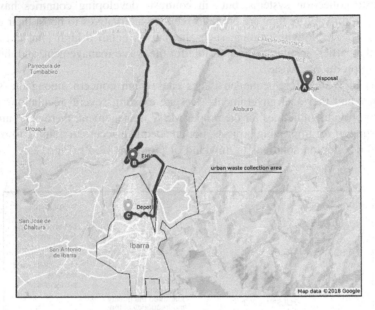

Fig. 2. The collection network elements of Ibarra.

The model proposed by Lin et al. [12] focuses on the collection routes by sub-regions, where the collection system is carried out by a different company in each sub-region. The initial model makes a relation to the demand and quantity of generated waste with the objective of reducing the cost of the collection service and the investment risk, That model allowed the creation of equitable districts in terms of the area, but such a model does not consider important variables such as generation rates and number of inhabitants in each zone. The improved re-district model was used to avoid unfair competition between the companies that provide collection services.

In 2014, Di Felice [9] proposes a method to determine the points in which the MSW accumulates in urban territories, and to determine the quantity of necessary containers in relation to the waste generated by the inhabitants. The position of the containers is established taking into account the distance to the inhabitant's houses. The model consider spatial and descriptive factors.

The model proposed by García et al. [13] for arc territory design of Eulerian districts, approaches the redistricting problem for the execution of the routing activities and sectorization, which consists in the division of a road network in a number of explicit sectors to facilitate the distribution of mediation within the region and promote workload balance. This model can be applied to similar operations such as postal delivery, meter reading, road maintenance and even solid waste collection.

Khan et al. [14] present a case study in the city of Dhanbad-India for the allocation of solid waste collection containers in suitable locations, with a uniform distance and a place of easy access for vehicles. Analyzing issues such as population density, container location, road network, waste collection schedules, capacity and trucks characteristic, this analysis presents at the end a reduction of costs that allow to be compared with current practices in the area. To estimate operating expenses, the ArcGIS tool was used to simulate the waste collection scenarios taking into account the travel time and distance simultaneously.

In 2015 Rossit et al. [15], develop a multi-objective model of mixed whole linear programming to optimize the collection of plastic waste in densely populated urban areas. This model is able to determine the optimal location of the containers, minimizing the costs of installation and distances from the inhabitants' houses to these containers. Exploring the frontier of Paretto for the solution of the problem, it also proposes an optimization model based on the capacitated vehicle routing problem (CVRP). This determines the optimal route of waste collection in containers.

The remaining of this paper is structured as follows: Sect. 2 outlines the used optimization model. Section 3 describes the implementation aspects. Section 4 gathers the experimental results. Finally, the concluding remarks are mentioned in Sect. 5.

2   Model to Optimize Container Distribution

A mixed integer programming multi-objective optimization model was implemented to determine the optimum location of the MSW containers in the Ibarra city. The objective is to focus simultaneously on minimize the cost of investment in such containers and the average distance that users from a generator or housing must travel to an assigned container.

2.1   Assumptions

In regard to indexes, we consider $i \in I$ that represents the potential amount of MSW generators within the urban area of the Ibarra city, while the indexes $j \in J$ represents the number of possible locations of urban solid waste containers.

In regard to binary variables, we have K_{ij} that takes value 1 if the i generator deposits its residue in the j container and 0 otherwise. Also the variable, L_j that takes value 1 if a container is installed at the j location and take a value of 0 if not.

Moreover, we consider an external variable that in the end will help us to post the total number of containers to be installed.

The parameters used are, $distance_{i,j}$ that represents the distance between the i generator and the j location; $installation\_cost$ provides the cost of obtaining and installing an MSW container; $rate$ is the amount of waste produced daily by a i generator; $container\_capacity$ is the maximum capacity that supports a container of urban solid waste; $max\_distance1$ is the maximum distance that is willing to travel the generator to deposit the residue in a container.

Minimization Indicator: With this indicator, the cost of acquiring and installing a container is optimized efficiently and jointly, and in turn, reduces the distance between a generator and a container, that is to say, this must be the minimum that is willing to walk a person to place their waste in a container.

Satisfaction Indicator: Is the maximum satisfaction that the client who manages the model, at the time of handling the model and adjust it to the needs of the company that is why, the model is in a free version for the modification of variables that are changeable with the passage of time or according to the economic need.

2.2   Objective Function

The objective function of the F problem can be declared in Eqs. (1, 2 and 3), which is aimed at simultaneously minimizing two target functions, which makes it a multi-objective function.

$$F = F(fc; fd) \tag{1}$$

Being f_c the objective function that minimizes the cost of installing a waste container, while, f_d is the objective function that minimizes the average distance to be traversed by the generator to the container assigned. To do this, each function is presented as follows:

$$f_c = \sum_{j}^{J} (L_j * installation\_cost) \tag{2}$$

$$f_d = \sum_{i,j}^{I,J} (distance_{i,j} * K_{i,j}) \tag{3}$$

2.3   Restrictions

Distance Restriction from Generator to Container
This restriction limits the distance between the generator and the container in which the waste should be deposited. It is not allow to exceed the maximum tolerable distance to which the settlers are willing to move from their home to the container location, as shown in Eq. (4).

$$K_{ij} * distance_{ij} \leq \max\_distance1 \tag{4}$$

Container Maximum Capacity Restriction
This restriction limits the container capacity in the formulation (5), that is, limits the number of generators that can use that container.

$$\sum_{i}^{I} (rate * K_{ij}) * filling\_coef \leq container\_capacity * L_j * SL \tag{5}$$

Where *filling_coef*, is the container filling coefficient that determines the percentage of MSW filling container based on the density of the waste that is deposited in the container. The filling maximum coefficient is given when you can use the container maximum volume with the maximum permissible mass per container.

SL is the service level to be provided considering the collection frequencies, in the present case study it is stipulated to provide a service level of 100% by collecting 7 times a week. However, the SEDESOL [16] specifies that, in the worst case, a waste collection can be carried out twice a week, for that matter it would also be necessary to consider the trips number that will be made by the garbage truck as this coefficient would cause the amount of containers needed to be lifted, as shown in Table 1.

Table 1. Provided service level according to the collection frequency.

Collection frequency	Rate $\left(\frac{kg}{inhab * day}\right)$	Average population per generator	Rate $\left(\frac{kg}{generator * collection}\right)$	Service level - SL (%)
$\frac{7}{7}$	0.685	4	2.74	100
$\frac{7}{3}$			6.39	42.85
$\frac{7}{2}$			9.59	28.57

A Generator Restricting for a Single Container
This restriction establishes a container for a generator, i.e. a generator can deposit its waste in just one container.

$$\sum_{i}^{I} K_{ij} = 1 \tag{6}$$

Restriction to Add the Total Number of Containers to be Installed
With this restriction, you can count the total number of MSW containers that will need to be installed.

$$\sum_{j=1}^{N} L_j = N \tag{7}$$

2.4   Multi-objective Approach

There is a conflict between the objectives considered. The installation of a larger quantity of containers causes an unwanted increase of the investment cost, however, it also reduces the average distance that the users must walk. Otherwise, if the number of available containers is reduced, investment costs will be reduced, however, this increases the average distance that separates users from the respective allocated containers. Clearly, you are dealing with a multi-objective problem in which the best solution will be one that approaches more to the ideal point, according to the Zeleny's axiom [11], according to which one can define the degree of proximity between a k-th (f_k) objective and its ideal value in the feasible region (f_k^*), as follows: $f_k^* - f_k$.

Then the proximity degrees must be defined for different objectives of the problem. Since the different objectives are not measured in the same dimensional units, they can be standardized by means of the following expression (8):

$$h_k = \frac{(f_k^* - f_k)}{(f_k^* - f_{k^*})}; \forall \ h_k \in [0, \ldots, 1] \tag{8}$$

Where h_k represents the proximity degree of the k-th normalized objective and f_{k^*} represents the anti-ideal value of that objective; h_k is bounded between 0 and 1, starting from the ideal value to the anti-ideal value correspondingly. The preferences are then defined w_k which has the decision-making agent of each target. Finally, this approach allows to include the weights w_k that represent the preferences that the decision-making agent has for each target, so the objective function is as follows in Eq. (9):

$$F = \sum_{k}^{K} w_k * h_k \tag{9}$$

Consider that w_c and w_d are the relative weights associated with cost and distance objectives. In terms of the problem under analysis in this work, the general objective function can be defined in the following way:

$$Min \ F = w_c * \frac{f_c^* - f_c}{f_c^* - f_{c^*}} + w_d * \frac{f_d^* - f_d}{f_d^* - f_d}; \forall \ \{w_c + w_d = 1\} \tag{10}$$

$$where \begin{cases} f_c = \sum_{j}^{J} (L_j * installation\_cost) \\ f_d = \sum_{ij}^{IJ} (distance_{ij} * K_{ij}) \end{cases}$$

3 Implementation of the Optimization Model

3.1 Guidelines for the Implementation

The methodology used has been separated into three central axes which are the information collection through the analysis of similar studies, analysis or diagnosis of the information where the basic elements will be designed, for example, the cartography construction of the city, design and programming of the mathematical model, and finally, a proposal that would arise from the analysis of the variables analyzed during the period of execution, as shown in Fig. 3.

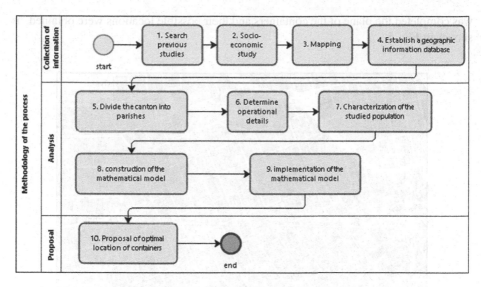

Fig. 3. Diagram flow of the methodologies used.

3.2 Home Buildings Mapping

As a starting point for the implementation, the map facilitated by the Government of Ibarra city was used, which consists of the urban sector of the Ibarra city differentiating with nodes the properties built or generators and the unbuilt, as shown in Fig. 4.

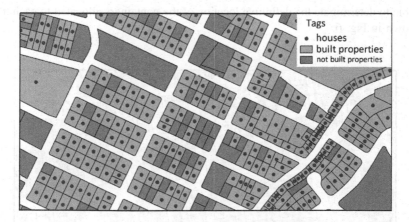

Fig. 4. Buildings or generators - *i*.

Possible Container Locations Mapping

For the implementation of the proposed model, it was determined that it could be placed as possible locations of the containers to each of the blocks of the Ibarra city, inspired especially in the Khan's work [14], the possible container locations were made at each of the corners of the block with properties built in the city [17]. Once this work was completed the plane of the containers and their possible locations were obtained, as shown in Fig. 5.

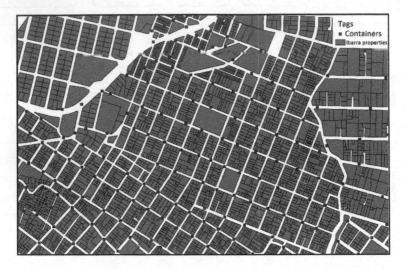

Fig. 5. Possible containers locations - *j*.

In order to obtain the matrix of distances between buildings - *i* and the possible locations of the containers - *j*, the software QGIS version 1.7.4 was used. However, it is important to have a systematic codification of each one of them, so that later it is possible to determinate the definitive location of the containers allocated to each house, as shown in Fig. 6.

Fig. 6. Coding buildings - *i* and possible container locations - *j*.

As a result, matrixes from each of the parishes of the city were obtained, which will be used later in the GAMS software optimization that contains the model to optimize the distribution of containers previously reviewed.

3.3 Model Execution to Optimize Container Distribution

Because the present problem can be understood within the Facility Location Problem, which is a NP-hard problem, initially it was tried to solve the model of optimization for the whole city in the same execution (30404 houses generating waste and 3023 possible locations of the containers). The global solution could not be obtained by restriction issues in the GAMS software license, however, it was decided to run the same model on two different computers for smaller instances, in this case, for each of the urban parishes that compose the city.

4   Results and Discussion

The model was applied in the different parishes of the city, each one of these are densely populated, considering a daily collection of the waste and, therefore, the rate of daily generation was used. In relation to generators, an average number of inhabitants per household is taken into account. A container capacity of 1.1 m^3 or 510 kg was considered and the cost of buying and installing a container was estimated at $570. The maximum tolerance distance that the settlers are willing to take to deposit their residue was considered at 100 m, as recommended in the work of Alonso et al. in 2016 [18].

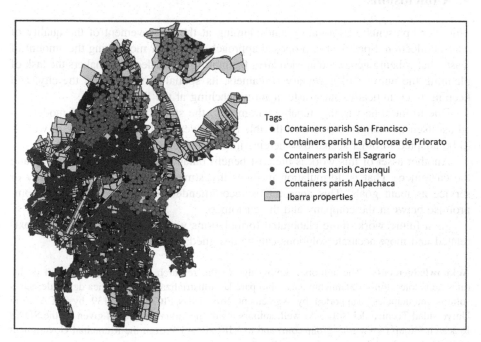

Fig. 7. Final map with the waste containers location for Ibarra city.

We consider a generation rate of 2.74 kg/generator and a filling coefficient of 0.55. The models were solved using the IBM ILOG CPLEX resolution software in a GAMS 24.9.4 version environment, in a computer with an Intel® Core™ i7-4790m CPU @ 3.60 GHz processor with a 64bits operating system and a 6.00 GB RAM installed memory. As a better solution, the optimum for this case is shown in Fig. 7, which involves the installment of 1541 waste containers.

For each parish was considered a number of generators of urban solid waste, as well as the possible locations of the containers of solid waste and through the application of this model was obtained as best solution, the optimum, and for each case the respective computational analysis, as showed in Table 2.

Table 2. Computational results

Parish	Number of generators - i	Number of inhabitants	Possible locations - j	Optimal solution - N	Computational analysis time
El Sagrario	5082	20328	410	192	5 min and 3 s
San Francisco	8919	35676	999	454	23 min and 44 s
Caranqui	8577	34308	908	532	17 min and 4 s
Alpachaca	3871	15484	262	133	7 min and 36 s
La Dolorosa de Priorato	3962	15848	444	230	1 min and 30 s

5 Conclusions

This work presents a exploratory study aiming at the improvement of the quality of waste collection. Specifically, proposed approach allows for monitoring the amount of waste that is being generated at each area, facilitating to the decision-makers the task of planning the number of necessary containers, its spatial distribution in the city, and keeping track indicators the waste quantity reaching at the landfill.

Due to the time-varying, tunable parameters, the studied mathematical model can adjust itself to changes -being then flexible to any eventuality that may arise as well as to be adapted to other scenarios wherein similar problems can be formulated.

Another asset of this work is the cost-benefit balancing for both the company and the customers. That is, formulation includes investments cost but also the quality of service as main goals. This approach is recommended to maintain a suitable compromise between the company and the customers.

As a future work, more elaborated formulations will be explored so that context-related and more accurate solutions can be designed.

Acknowledgements. The authors acknowledge to the research project "Optimización de las rutas de recolección y tratamiento anaerobio para la industrialización energética de los desechos sólidos municipales" supported by Agreement Nro. UTN-FICA-2016-1139 by FICA from Universidad Técnica del Norte. As well, authors thank the valuable support given by the SDAS Research Group (www.sdas-group.com) and to VIRSAP – EP from the Municipal Government of Ibarra City, Ecuador.

References

1. Wilson, D., et al.: Global Waste Management Outlook 2015, 1st edn. United Nations Environment Programme, Austria (2015)
2. SENPLADES: Plan nacional de desarrollo 2017–2021. Toda una Vida, Senplades, pp. 1–148 (2017)
3. Kinobe, J.R., Bosona, T., Gebresenbet, G., Niwagaba, C.B., Vinnerås, B.: Optimization of waste collection and disposal in Kampala city. Habitat Int. **49**, 126–137 (2015)
4. Sakurai, K.: Diseño de las Rutas de Recolección de Residuos Sólidos. Div. Protección la Salud Ambient. Cent. Panam. Ing. Sanit. y Ciencias del Ambient, pp. 32–34 (1980)
5. Scheinberg, A., Wilson, D.C., Rodic, L.: Solid waste management in the world's cities water and sanitation in the world's cities. UN HABITAT, vol. 3, no. 2005, Washington, D.C. (2010)
6. Herrera-Granda, I.D., et al.: Optimization of the university transportation by contraction hierarchies method and clustering algorithms. In: de Cos Juez, F., et al. (eds.) HAIS 2018. LNCS, vol. 10870, pp. 95–107. Springer, Cham (2018). https://doi.org/10.1007/978-3-319-92639-1_9
7. OPS: Informe de la evaluación Regional del Manejo de Residuos Sólidos de America Latina y el Caribe (2010)
8. Ministerio del ambiente de Ecuador: Programa PNGIDS Ecuador (2017)
9. Di Felice, P.: Integration of spatial and descriptive information to solve the urban waste accumulation problem. Procedia - Soc. Behav. Sci. **147**, 182–188 (2014)
10. INEC: Base de Datos-Censo de Población y Vivienda 2001. Instituto Nacional de Estadística y Censos (2001)
11. Bonfanti, F.A.: La incorrecta gestión de los residuos Sólidos Urbanos y su incidencia en la calidad de vida de la población de Resistencia. Univ. Nac. del Nord. Comun. Científicas y Tecnológicas. Argentina (2004)
12. Lin, H.Y., Kao, J.J.: Subregion districting analysis for municipal solid waste collection privatization. J. Air Waste Manag. Assoc. **58**(1), 104–111 (2008)
13. García-Ayala, G., González-Velarde, J.L., Ríos-Mercado, R.Z., Fernández, E.: A novel model for arc territory design: promoting Eulerian districts. Int. Trans. Oper. Res. **23**(3), 433–458 (2016). https://doi.org/10.1111/itor.12219
14. Khan, D., Samadder, S.: Allocation of solid waste collection bins and route optimization using geographical information system: a case study of Dhanbad City, India. Waste Manag. Res. **34**, 666–676 (2016)
15. Rossit, D., Broz, D., Rossit, D., Frutos, M., Tohmé, F.: Modelado de una red urbana de recolección de residuos plásticos en base a optimización multi-objetivo. In: XXVIII Encuentro Nacional de Docentes en Investigación Operativa (2015)
16. SEDESOL: Manual Técnico sobre generación, recolección y transferencia de Residuos Sólidos Municipales, pp. 1–139 (2009)
17. Lorente-Leyva, L.L., et al.: Developments on solutions of the normalized-cut-clustering problem without eigenvectors. In: Huang, T., Lv, J., Sun, C., Tuzikov, A. (eds.) ISNN 2018. LNCS, vol. 10878, pp. 318–328. Springer, Cham (2018). https://doi.org/10.1007/978-3-319-92537-0_37
18. Alonso, A.B.: Localización óptima de contenedores de residuos sólidos urbanos en alcalá de henares/optimal location of solid waste containers in alcalá de henares. M+A Rev. Electrónica Medioambiente **17**(1), 1–23 (2016). https://doi.org/10.5209/MARE.53155

Inductive Machine Learning with Image Processing for Objects Detection of a Robotic Arm with Raspberry PI

Mao Queen Garzón Quiroz[1,2]([email]) [in]

[1] Universidad Católica de Santiago de Guayaquil,
Av. Carlos J. Arosemana Km 1 1/2, Guayaquil, Ecuador
mao.garzon@cu.ucsg.edu.ec
[2] Facultad de ingeniería industrial, Universidad de Guayaquil,
Cdla. Universitaria "Salvador Allende", Guayaquil, Ecuador
mao.garzonq@ug.edu.ec
http://www.ucsg.edu.ec/

Abstract. *Goals.* The present study was designed to build a prototyping and develop algorithms that allow the detection, classification, and movement of objects of a robotic arm of 4 DOF with the following technologies: ArmUno arm structure, Raspberry Pi 3 B+, PiCam 2.1, driver PCA9685 for servomotors, Opencv3, and python. Another goal was to measure the effectiveness of prediction and classification of objects photographed by the robotic arm, using machine learning with the KNN classifier method.

Methodology. The generation of a dataset of 800 photographic images was proposed, in 4 categories: volumetric geometric shapes conformed by 200 images each one of them. With this, processing techniques were applied to the image captured by the camera to detect the object in the image: Grayscale filtering, Gaussian filtering, and threshold.

Then, the characteristics of the object were obtained through the first two invariant moments of HU, and finally, the machine learning method KNN was applied to predict, that the image captured by the robotic arm belongs or not to a certain category. In this way, the robotic arm decides to move the object or not.

Results. According to the plot of the obtained data described in the results section; the level of correct answers increases markedly by using the techniques described above. The prediction and classification using KNN were remarkable, For all the tests carried out The average effectiveness of KNN method was 95.42%. Once the scripts were integrated, the operation of the robotic arm was satisfactory.

Keywords: Opencv3 · Python · Machine learning · KNN · Robotics Raspberry Pi

M. Botto-Tobar et al. (Eds.): CITT 2018, CCIS 895, pp. 590–604, 2019.
https://doi.org/10.1007/978-3-030-05532-5_45

1 Intoduction

The following research deals with an analysis of the algorithms necessary for the optimal processing and classification of images captured by a camera integrated into a robotic arm of 4 DOF (Degree of Freedom), with the aim of being able to detect and select objects through artificial mink by computer and, also applying the machine learning methodology with the purpose of predicting percentage to which category the geometric image captured by the camera belongs.

The main problem that surrounds the present study, is to determine if the Raspberry Pi platform has the capacity to control, manipulate and process images, and at the same time grant the ability to select and move geometric objects to a robotic arm of 4 DOF (Degree of Freedom), also using the KNN classifier method as machine learning methodology.

For which, the KNN classifier method and image processing are used to clean, equalize and detect objects within the photographic image, which is taken by the PiCam 2.1 built into the Raspberry Pi 3 model B [2], device robotic arm driver. The PiCam has a resolution of $2,592 \times 1,944$ pixels (approximately represents 5 megapixels), but for this project the configuration of 640×480 pixels was used, for reasons of standardization of the study.

The mechanism used is the following: First, the robotic arm takes a picture with the PiCam 2.1 mentioned above, the same one that passes through several methods for image processing. Then, the characteristics of the object are obtained through the first two invariant moments of HU, and finally, the KNN method is applied to predict that the image captured by the robotic arm belongs to a specific category (Geometric Shape Categorized).

Regarding the robotic arms, are very versatile and can be used for a series of applications in real life. The design of a robotic arm depends on the number of parameters among which the Degree of Freedom (DOF) is the most basic. Each DOF is a joint on which it can be bent or rotated; this project uses 4 DOF. The DOF number will be the number of actuators of the robotic arm [15].

Robotic arms are used for their ability to perform tasks very similar to a human, wrapped by several characteristics such as dexterity, flexibility, space saving, less complexity of tools and gripping devices. The robotic arm of this study has a clamp as a gripper, see Fig. 3 [13,14].

Besides, robotic arms are very flexible for their design and configuration even in 3D virtual environments.

Another important aspect is to define the movement of the robot, the proposed approach allows the automatic generation of robot movements, requesting a small number of critical positions, for example, the location of grabbing the piece, avoiding instructing positions to avoid collisions with accessories, see Table 1 [13,14].

The start and rotation positions of each DOF are fixed for this investigation; this is because the robotic arm is static, the same would happen in industrial conditions, that is, a robotic arm that selects objects in a band, it would be located in a fixed position.

By including sensors and internet connection, the robotic arms can even be operated remotely. There is a wide range of applications such as: in medicine for human operations or training of new surgeons, in the academy for the teaching of physics, in primary sciences as motivators for small students, and in the industry all in assembly lines [13,14,16].

This project intends to use Raspberry Pi as a control platform and to determine an introduction with machine learning and image processing, to create a prototype of a robotic arm that can detect objects with a high predictive level.

2   Prototype Construction

2.1   Control of Devices with Raspberry Pi

For the control of the robotic arm, Raspberry Pi was used (Figs. 1 and 2), in recent years this reduced plate computer (SBC) has motivated research in colleges and universities not only in Europe, but throughout the world, has a small size which favors mobility, has the characteristics of a standard computer, that is, has USB ports, a micro-SD that is used as a hard disk at low cost has a memory of 1 GB, and its ARM Cortex A53 processors run to 1.2 GHz 64-bits [11].

Fig. 1. Raspberry Pi B+ 3 (source: Raspberry Pi Foundation) [1,11]

The current project uses the Raspberry Pi 3 Model B+ (Fig. 1). One of the most favorable aspects of the Raspberry [2], is that it has 40 pins of connection and interactivity with external hardware to the devices, as shown in Fig. 2, in the particular case of this project, these pins served to control the 4 servo motors (DOF) of the robotic arm, plus an advantageous feature of the Raspberry is that it has an operating system, among the most used, are Raspbian (Stretch with Desktop April-2018 used in this project), Ubuntu Mate, Windows 10 IOT, Openelec, OSMC, among others.

In this way, you can load some platforms and applications to the Raspberry device, for this research project, the following software packages were installed: Python 3.6, OpenCV 3, and the following drivers: Python SMBus (I2C), Adafruit PCA9685 [11].

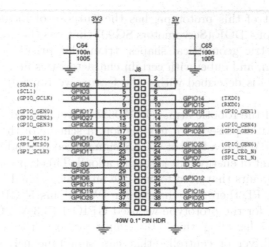

Fig. 2. Raspberry Pi GPIO model 3 (source: Raspberry Pi Foundation) [1,11]

2.2 Raspberry Pi for Robotics, Advantages

Starting from the fact that Raspberry in all its models is an SBC (Single Board Computer), that is to say, it is a miniature computer, it has all the elementary and essential characteristics of a machine, and also its GPIO (Fig. 2), allows interaction with other hardware, constructed or embedded.

From the above, it can be mentioned that it is a computer with a great ability to add functionality to other hardware, this allows, for example, adding sensors, servomotors, among other modules to this device, that is why, and that the Raspberry PI is one of the leaders of the mini-open source computer market, for which reason it was chosen as the base platform for this research project [1,5,11].

One of the most flexible and secure features is its ability to run on various operating systems, such as those of the Linux family: Raspbian, Ubuntu Mate, PIdora, Minibian, ArchLinux ARM, Openelec, among others. These platforms favor the loading of packages that facilitate the development and support to work in various applications on Raspberry PI [11].

It should also be noted that its low power consumption, full performance model B consumes 330 ma, this is full capacity including video playback and internet connection, low consumption favors the creation of portable applications with built-in rechargeable batteries. For this research, we used python, OpenCV 3, libraries that were installed on the device under the Raspbian operating system [5].

2.3 Robotic Arm Movement with PWM on Raspberry Pi

Within the applications or uses of robotics most used, are the robotic arms, these can be applied in different instances and contexts of the life of the human being.

The development of this prototype, has the purpose of introducing a robotic arm application of 4 DOF (Servomotors SG90) that has the ability to detect the following volumetric geometrical shapes: triangular prism, pentagonal prism, rectangular prism, and cube; with certain characteristics and colors, the ability to recognize ways is described within the feature vector and image processing section below.

For control of the robotic arm, a PCA9685 driver is used, which works correctly with PWM or pulse width modulation, a scheme of the type of signal is shown in Fig. 4. PWM is a type of voltage signal used to send information or to modify the amount of energy that is sent to a load. This type of signals is widely used in digital circuits that need to emulate an analog signal [6,11].

In Raspberry PI, there is a channel for PWM, this is GPIO 18 (Not used for this project), for the prototype we used GPIO 1 (3.3 V), GPIO 2 for data, and GPIO 3 clock handling, this is the configuration of the Raspberry Pi with PCA9685, this driver or controller that can simultaneously handle up to 16 channels.

The motors used in the robotic arm are SG90 servomotors. This type of motor is controlled by the Raspberry PI and maneuvers the position through PWM pulses. The servos, short form to call them, have a nominal control voltage between 4.8 and 7.2 V with an electric current between 0.2 and 5 A. The value of the voltage rating will depend on how many servos will be connected at the same time. The servomotors, present an angular movement between 0° and 180° normally, If a more extensive range is desired in the position, a continuous rotating servo is required. On the contrary, these motors are controlled by speed, the servomotors that are controlled by their position [3,7,8].

The servos can be analog or digital, although most are analog, like the ones used (DOF) in the robotic arm. The digital servomotors are more precise and tend to be of better quality and with longer service life. They can also operate at higher frequencies (on the order of 300 Hz), but they can work correctly for simple, low-power applications. The servos only run at a frequency of 50 Hz and have a low power consumption [3,4,11].

To use the PCA9685 driver, the Adafruit driver was used for 16 channels; however the robotic arm is 4 DOF, so only 4 of the 16 channels were used. For the robotic arm, we worked with the channels 0,1,2,3 of the PCA9685; It is worth mentioning that the Adafruit controller needs 3 V power, the same ones that are charged through the 3.3V GPIO Output Pin [3,4,11].

Modulation Amplitude Strategy. By working with the PCA9685 driver, the optimal use of the Raspberry GPIOs is guaranteed, since we will only occupy two pins, all thanks to the fact that the PCA9685 uses the I2C protocol, which also ensures that several devices are connected through a serial bus of data like teachers, and a bi-directional communication takes place in the case of our project, but at the same time if more connected devices are demanded also it could be implemented.

Fig. 3. ArmUno arm structure with Raspberry Pi of this project

With the PCA9685 and the I2C protocol, pulses can be generated through software, so the following Table 1 is implemented with Python and the Adafruit Library for PCA9685, explains the pulses used for each servomotor, the angular limits and the name that was used with these within the robotic arm controller script.

Table 1. Servomotors values of the project

Name	Programming name	Angular limits []	Pulse limits	Canal at PCA9685
Rotation	RotationArm	[0,180]	[140,550	0
Up down right	UpDown1	[80,120]	[220,350]	1
Up down left	UpDown2	[90,160]	[300,450]	2
Pincers	OpenClosePincers	[0,150]	[140,300]	3

3   Vector of Features and Image Processing

As mentioned in the introduction to the present study, the images are captured at a resolution of 640 × 480 pixels at 32 bits of color by the Picam 2.1 installed in the Raspberry Pi driver device. For the application of the robotic arm, geometric objects are detected and classified.

For the processing of the images, the color space of the image is changed to grayscale. To eliminate the noise and soften the image a Gaussian filter function (GaussianBlur) is used. Then, thresholding is applied to segment the image and obtain the object to be identified. The thresholding returns a binary image, where the pixels with value '1' represent the object and the pixels with value '0' the background.

To obtain the characteristics that identify each geometric object the invariant moments of Hu were used, which are seven invariant descriptors that quantify the shape of an object. The first two moments of Hu are obtained, and with these descriptors, the vector of characteristics that serves as an input for the classification of the objects is formed by the KNN classification method of the nearest neighbor [9,10].

3.1   Conversion of BGR Color Struct to Grayscale in OpenCV

OpenCV has an information structure to manipulate the pixels of an image when loading the picture, it is structured according to coordinates where the pixels that make up the image itself, in this way, when loading a color image in BGR it would have the following matrix:

$$\mathcal{I}_{m,n} = \begin{bmatrix} a_{1_1} a_{1_2} a_{1_3} \cdots \\ a_{2_1} a_{2_2} a_{2_3} \cdots \\ a_{3_1} a_{3_2} a_{3_3} \cdots \\ a_{i_j} a_{i_j} a_{i_j} \cdots \end{bmatrix}$$

OpenCV has an information structure to manipulate the pixels of an image when loading the picture each element of the matrix has a particular value. If it is a BGR image, the element $a_{1_1} = [B, G, R]$ [12], that is, that coordinate would contain a triad of values to represent a pixel of color, that is B represents the blue channel, G the green, and R the red. When converting the image captured by the PiCam 2.1 to grayscale format, instead, each pixel is represented by a unique value between 0 and 255 (0 represents black and 255 white). The implementation with OpenCV is as follows:

```
$imagegray = cv2.cvtColor(imagen, cv2.COLOR_BGR2GRAY)$
```

3.2   Smoothing

The next step is to apply the Gaussian Blur function to eliminate the noise and soften the edges. This function allows the elimination of high-frequency noise by convolving the image with a Gaussian kernel. The kernel is a square matrix, which must be odd. A kernel of size $[5 \times 5]$ and a standard deviation of 1 is applied for the x-axis, and for the y-axis, as shown in the implementation with Python and Opencv [9]. The mathematical application of the Gaussian kernel will be as follows: Since H_1 is the coordinate matrix of the image captured by the PiCam 2.1 and H2 the transpose of the said matrix and Sigma with 1, the K kernel is defined by:

$$K = \varrho^{(-(H12+H22)/(2*2))}$$

$$KNORMAL = K_{i,j} / \sum K$$

For the Kernel (K) standardization, the scale of the data is basically standardized, as shown in the KNORMAL equation, each Kernel element given by Ki, j is divided for the sum of all the elements given by K, in this way each part of K is normalized. Next, the implementation with python and OpenCV with the same mathematical base is shown:

$imageblur = cv2.GaussianBlur(imagegray, (5, 5), 1, 1)$

3.3   Thresholding

For the identification of geometric objects, it is necessary to separate the pixels that interest us from others. This separation is based on the variation of the intensity between the object pixels and the background pixels. A comparison of each pixel with the established threshold is made. In this way, a binary image is obtained, where the pixels that are in the range of the threshold take the value of 1 representing the object and the remaining pixels take the value of 0. According to the tests carried out, the threshold value was determined in 87 [10].

```
ret,thr = cv2.threshold(imageblur, 87, 255, cv2.THRESH_BINARY)
```

3.4   Feature Extraction (Hu Moments)

After processing the image, we obtain the characteristics that will allow us to differentiate and classify each object. To obtain these characteristics, the first two invariant moments Hu were used. The moments enable quantifying the characteristic shape of an object using the way in which the pixels of the object are distributed on the plane of an image.

The moments of Hu are invariant to the geometric transformations that the object can undergo (translation, rotation, and scaling); that is, very similar values are obtained for objects of the same type and at the same time they are discriminant since different values are obtained according to the type of object [12].

The moments of Hu are calculated based on the geometric moments of the object. The geometric moments of the order $(p+q)$ are calculated in the following way:

$$m_{p,q} = \sum_x \sum_y x^p y^q I(x, y)$$

where $I(x, y)$ is a pixel of the object with coordinates (x, y). From these moments we can obtain the second order normalized central moments:

$$\mu_{p,q} = \mu_{p,q}/\mu_{00}^{1+(p+q)/2}$$

Based on $\mu_{p,q}$ Hu, he obtained the seven invariant moments, the first two being:

$$\theta_1 = n_{20} + n_{02}$$

$$\theta_2 = (n_{20} + n_{02})^2 + 4n_{11}^2$$

In OpenCV two functions are used: cv2.moments with which the moments of the object are obtained and cv2.HuMoments that is applied to the moments of the object.

```
momentosHu = cv2.HuMoments(cv2.moments(thr))
for i in range(len(momentos)):
    for j in range(len(momentos[i])):
        if i == 0:
            Hu1 = momentos[i][j]
        elif i == 1:
            Hu2 = momentos[i][j]
```

Image captured   Gray scale image   Applied GaussianBlur filter   Applied threshold

Fig. 4. Application of filters to the image captured by the PiCam 2.1

4   Construction of Data Training

The test dataset was made taking different photographs of the objects to be classified. The pictures were taken with the PiCam 2.1 at a resolution of 640×480 pixels with 32 bits of color. Each type of object has the same dimensions and different colors. The photographs taken were taken with natural light and artificial light generating some kinds of shade. The dataset consists of 800 elements, having 200 items for each type of object.

In the construction of the data training, the images of the dataset are processed, and each object is characterized by a vector that contains the characteristics that identify it, called pattern, which is associated to a class tag that identifies it among the different classes of objects. For this investigation, each object is represented by a vector of two characteristics (Hu1 and Hu2) and is associated with one of the four object classes: 1 = triangular prism, 2 = pentagonal prism, 3 = rectangular prism, 4 = cube. For training and testing the KNN method, the dataset was divided: 70% (760 images) for training and 30% (240 images) for the test.

For standardization of image processing, the resolution was used 640×480, with an optimal resolution, it was also decided to use natural lighting, inside the laboratory where the experiments were processed artificial light did not provide the necessary conditions, to assemble a dataset with good results when applying both the processing techniques and the KNN.

Under this context, in the first instance, the color histogram used, to obtain one of the characteristics that would form part of the vector of parameters for the data training, standardization of the size of images. Therefore the expected results were not obtained, these processing techniques were left aside, they consumed a lot of processing time in the Raspberry Pi, and the KNN did not reflect the best predictions.

On the other hand, the background chosen to capture the photographic images of the robotic arm was the white color, although some trials were done with a black background, but did not provide the necessary conditions to improve the results in the image processing to build the dataset and the KNN, it is also included, that the shadow that is projected with artificial and natural light also affects the result in the vector of characteristics.

To reduce overfitting, photographs were taken with different color scales to vary the intensity and add a shadow factor to obtain results closer to the real world. For schemes of use of the robotic arm in industrial applications or factories, the brightness levels should be adjusted. Improve the camera resolution to obtain clearer results, in this way the algorithm used for image processing would work optimally.

5   Classification Method (KNN) and Inductive Learning

Inductive Learning allows creating models of concepts from generalizing simple examples, primarily derived from the search for common patterns that somehow explain the cases, in other words with inductive learning you get general conclusions of specific information. Inductive reasoning, on the other hand, allows you to make statements based on the evidence you have collected so far, a scientific experiment for example. However, the evidence is not the same as a fact: the solid proof of something that is only suggested, albeit strongly, that it is a fact in itself [10].

The KNN classifier method is based on the fact that a new sample is classified according to the class of the closest neighbors of the training pattern. The recognition of objects is done by comparing the object to be classified with a reference sample of each type of object; assigning him the class of his closest neighbors. The algorithm makes this assignment according to the nearest K neighbors using the Euclidean distance between each of the samples [10].

The learning process in this project consists in storing in a vector the characteristics of the training set together with the class label associated to each sample forming the training data (data training), the tests carried out applying this methodology will be shown in the next section. o select the optimal k value; a test process was carried out in several instances, as shown in Fig. 5, the best result was with k = 3.

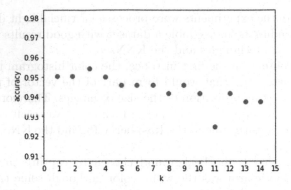

Fig. 5. Accuracy of K value

6   Results

For all tests, it was determined that the optimal number of neighbors was determined, k = 3, as explained in the previous section on Classification method KNN. Then the test was carried out with 240 images of the different types of objects to be classified (53 triangular prisms, 67 pentagonal prisms, 66 rectangular prisms and 54 cubes).

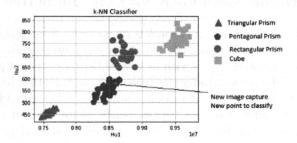

Fig. 6. Pentagonal prism test

In the test plotted in Fig. 6, which represents the trial with the pentagonal prism, that is, in front of the robotic arm, the volumetric geometric figure is placed, and this is captured with the PiCam, the photograph captured by the robotic arm falls on the nearest neighbor [2.2.2.], whose values represent precisely the category Pentagonal Prism, with a Euclidean distance of 1.3566319e-14 for each of the neighbors with slight variations. Of the 67 data to classify as a pentagonal prism, it ranked 8 as a rectangular prism and scored 59, having a precision of 88%, Table 2 (Classification Report) details the results.

On the other hand, in the test plotted in Fig. 7, which represents the test with the rectangular prism, the photograph captured by the robotic arm falls on the

Table 2. KNN Classification Report

Geometric objects	Precision	Recall	F1-score	Support
Triangular prims	1.00	1.00	1.00	53
Pentagonal prims	0.95	0.88	0.91	67
Rectangular prims	0.89	0.95	0.92	54
Cube	1.00	1.00	1.00	27
Avg./Total	**0.96**	**0.95**	**0.95**	**240**

nearest neighbors [3.3.3.], whose values represent exactly the Pentagonal Prism category, with values for the Euclidean distance of $[0.0000000e + 000.0000000e + 002.7098367e - 13]$ for each of the close neighbors. The Euclidean distance, is the distance calculated between two points within a Euclidean space, obtained from the Pythagorean theorem. [9] the 66 data to classify as a rectangular prism, it classified 3 as a pentagonal prism and scored 63, obtaining a precision of 95%, Table 2 (Classification Report) details the results.

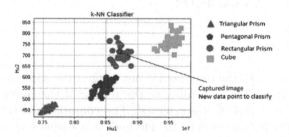

Fig. 7. Rectangular prism test

Finally, the test plotted in Fig. 8, which represents the test with the cube, the photograph captured by the robotic arm falls on the nearest neighbors given by [4.4.4.], whose values represent exactly the Pentagonal Prism category, with values for the Euclidean distance of $[0.0000000e + 001.2050940e - 156.5864266e - 14]$ for each of the close neighbors.

The confusion matrix is a square matrix whose order is the number of classes. The real classes are presented in the columns, while the categories assigned by the classifier are shown in the rows [10].

The description of the confusion matrix for KNN is as follows: 53 true positives for triangular prism, for pentagonal prism 59 true positives and 3 false positives were obtained, while for rectangular prism 63 true positives and 8 false positives were collected and for the cube, the true positives were 54.

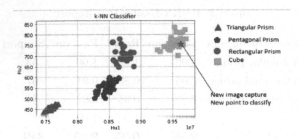

Fig. 8. Cube test

$$\textbf{KNN Confusion Matrix} = \begin{bmatrix} 53 & 0 & 0 & 0 \\ 0 & 59 & 8 & 0 \\ 0 & 3 & 63 & 0 \\ 0 & 0 & 0 & 54 \end{bmatrix}$$

For the KNN test, the respective matrix confusion and the classification report shown in Table 2 are shown. For all the tests carried out The **average effectiveness** of KNN was 95.42%

7   Discussion

The results achieved by the tests carried out suggest the acceptable performance of the robotic arm. First, according to the results of the confusion matrix, an average accuracy of 95.42% was achieved. The confusion matrix presents information on the prediction made by the method. It is a square matrix whose order is the number of classes. The real classes are shown in the columns, while the categories assigned by the classifier are presented in the rows, see Table 2.

For trained data, the robotic arm can take classification and movement activities with a greater than 89% accuracy for the case of the rectangular prism, but in the case of the cube, and the triangular prism is 100% accurate (see Table 2). On the other hand, for the processing of 800 images of the dataset and form the vector of characteristics, which is the input of the data training and data test, it takes 32 s in the Raspberry Pi 3 B+, previously an experiment was performed with a datasets of 400 images, earning a time of 20 s. For the final examinations, the dataset was left with 800 illustrations, whose construction was specified in the construction section of the data training.

After this initial process, the robotic arm takes two seconds to take the picture, do the image processing and classify it, which is a good time of action for the Raspberry Pi. For an industrial robotic arm, it may not be a good time, but we should consider better hardware features and the use of better deep learning methods for future tests.

8   Conclusions

By applying these techniques and the machine learning methods, it was demonstrated that the optimal use of the Raspberry Pi as a controller. On the one hand, worked controlling the movements of the robot arm, its ability to contain software solutions empower prototypes, the handling of 4 servomotors with PCA9685, high-level coding was carried out using Python, due to the Adafruit library as an interface between Python and Raspberry Pi.

In the same way, Raspberry Pi worked at a high level with the processing of the images necessary for the data training characteristics vector, approximately 32 s to capture and process each image, an excellent process time. This led to an appropriate construction of the data formation, and to very good executions of the presented method.

The reliability of the results was determined by the confusion matrix, and the sci-kit learn classification report, where the magnitude of the application of the KNN method was predicted.

It is estimated that the use of more efficient algorithms in classification will be used for future works, such as neural networks, all of this to improve the productivity and automatic learning of the robotic arm. One of the objectives of this research project is to introduce in the medium term the use of robotic arms for industrial applications and education.

References

1. Sharma, J., et al.: IOP Conference Series: Materials Science and Engineering, vol. 263, p. 052049 (2017)
2. Anandhalli, M., Baligar, V.P.: A novel approach in real-time vehicle detection and tracking using Raspberry Pi. Alexandria Eng. J. **57**, 1597–1607 (2017). https://doi.org/10.1016/j.aej.2017.06.008. ISSN 1110-0168
3. Vazquez Navarro, D.: Control of a robotic arm using an Omega 2+ module. Thesis, Universitat Politècnica de Catalunya (2018)
4. Rahman, M.F., Patterson, D., Cheok, A., Betz, R.: 30 - motor drives. In: Rashid, M.H. (ed.) Power Electronics Handbook, 4th edn, pp. 945–1021. Butterworth-Heinemann, Oxford (2018). https://doi.org/10.1016/B978-0-12-811407-0.00034-9. ISBN 978-0-12-811407-0
5. Perumal, V.S.A., Baskaran, K., Rai, S.K.: Implementation of effective and low-cost building monitoring system (BMS) using Raspberry PI. Energy Proc. **143**, 179–185 (2017). https://doi.org/10.1016/j.egypro.2017.12.668. ISSN 1876-6102
6. Soriano, A., Marn, L., Valls, M., Valera, A., Albertos, P.: Low cost platform for automatic control education based on open hardware. IFAC Proc. Vol. **47**(3), 9044–9050 (2014). https://doi.org/10.3182/20140824-6-ZA-1003.01909. ISSN 1474-6670
7. Di Piazza, M.C., Pucci, M.: Techniques for efficiency improvement in PWM motor drives. Electr. Power Syst. Res. **136**, 270–280 (2016). ISSN 0378-7796
8. Soriano, A., Marin, L., Valles, M., Valera, A., Albertos, P.: Low cost platform for automatic control education based on open hardware. IFAC Proc. Vol. **47**(3), 9044–9050 (2014). ISSN 1474-6670, ISBN 9783902823625
9. Beyeler, M.: Machine Learning for OpenCV. Intelligent Image Processing with Python, 1st edn. Packt Publishing, Birmingham (2017). ISBN 978-1-78398-028-4

10. Muller, A.C., Guido, S.: Introduction to Machine Learning with Python, Kindle edn. O'Reilly Media, Sebastopol (2017). ISBN 978-1-449-36941-5
11. Monk, S.: Raspberry Pi CookBook, 2nd edn. O'Reilly Media, Sebastopol (2016). ISBN 978-1-491-93910-9
12. Yoon, D.C., Mol, A., Benn, D.K., Benavides, E.: Digital radio-graphic image processing and analysis. Dent. Clin. North Am. **62**(3), 341–359 (2018). https://doi.org/10.1016/j.cden.2018.03.001. ISSN 0011-8532, ISBN 9780323610766
13. Tlach, V., Kuric, I., Kumicakova, D., Rengevic, A.: Possibilities of a robotic end of arm tooling control within the software platform ROS. Proc. Eng. **192**, 875–880 (2017). https://doi.org/10.1016/j.proeng.2017.06.151. 12th International Scientific Conference of Young Scientists on Sustainable, Modern and Safe Transport. ISSN 1877-7058
14. Makris, S., et al.: Dual arm robot in cooperation with humans for flexible assembly. CIRP Ann. **66**(1), 13–16 (2017). https://doi.org/10.1016/j.cirp.2017.04.097. ISSN 0007-8506
15. Sunny, T.D., Aparna, T., Neethu, P., Venkateswaran, J., Vishnupriya, V., Vyas, P.S.: Robotic arm with brain. Computer interfacing. Proc. Technol. **24**, 1089–1096 (2016). https://doi.org/10.1016/j.protcy.2016.05.241. International Conference on Emerging Trends in Engineering, Science and Technology, ICETEST 2015. ISSN 2212-0173
16. Kadir, W.M.H.W., Samin, R.E., Ibrahim, B.S.K.: Internet controlled robotic arm. Proc. Eng. **41**, 1065–1071 (2012). https://doi.org/10.1016/j.proeng.2012.07.284. International Symposium on Robotics and Intelligent Sensors, IRIS 2012. ISSN 1877-7058

Dynamic Difficulty Adjustment
for a Memory Game

Vladimir Araujo(✉), Alejandra Gonzalez, and Diego Mendez

Pontificia Universidad Javeriana, Carrera 7 No. 40 - 62, Bogota, Colombia
{vladimir.araujo,agonzalez,diego-mendez}@javeriana.edu.co

Abstract. Working memory is an important function for human cognition, it is related to some skills, such as remembering information or developing a mental calculation. Several games have been developed to train the working memory. Nevertheless, sometimes the game does not adjust adequate to users. Consequently, they end up bored by the game and leave it. This article presents a system of dynamic adjustment of the difficulty for a working memory training game, which allows generating customized levels so that the users obtain a better performance during the training of the memory. The proposed system was tested with young people, the results show that the training performance was better in comparison with a classic game and provide a better game experience to the users.

Keywords: ANFIS · DDA · Fuzzy · Machine learning
Memory game · N-back · Working memory training

1 Introduction

The video games industry has ventured into different genres, formats, and orientations that are not limited to entertainment. On this scope, cognitive games, meaning videogames oriented to improve cognitive skills (memory, motor skills, decision-making, etc.), such as Brain Age [12], Cogmed [4], Lumosity [7]. For instance, Working Memory (WM) refers to the ability to store and manipulate information for short periods of time, and it is involved in cognitively demanding activities such as academic studies or professional work [3]. It was shown that it is possible to improve WM through its training [8], the improvement also helps other cognitive systems like fluid intelligence.

Sometimes, the player's experience is a critical parameter that determines the progress of the user inside a memory game. If the purpose of a memory game is to improve the cognitive skills of a user, it is important avoid frustration, anxiety, or boredom [5]. Games of different genres use the technology known as Dynamic Difficulty Adjustment (DDA), in order to give a customizable game experience. However, a DDA approach has not applied to memory games or WM training.

This paper analyses the incorporation of DDA to a video game prototype designed to develop working memory skills. It focuses on examining the data

© Springer Nature Switzerland AG 2019
M. Botto-Tobar et al. (Eds.): CITT 2018, CCIS 895, pp. 605–616, 2019.
https://doi.org/10.1007/978-3-030-05532-5_46

provided by the comparison of users performance on college students who played video games with and without DDA.

The remainder of this paper is organized as follows: Sect. 2 shows a brief review of the related work; Sect. 3 introduces the proposed game; Sect. 4 shows the methodology; Sect. 5 analyzes the experiments and results; and Sect. 6 synthetizes the mains conclusions of the project.

2   Related Work

2.1   Working Memory and Games

WM is a human cognitive system that is responsible for temporarily holding information for processing. Past researches reveal that WM is related to academic performance [6], feelings of euphoria and reward [11], among others; also in [8], authors prove that it is possible to improve the fluid intelligence (Gf) through the WM training. Gf refers to the ability of a person to adapt and face new situations in an agile way, without prior learning. For these reasons many games have been developed as a tool to improve memory capacity.

A popular method used for working memory training is N-back task, in which a subject receives a sequence of stimuli, which can be perceived through his or her senses. The user has to remember the stimulus that was shown 'N' steps before but also remember the new stimulus. The 'N' value will increase, which means the person needs to remember more and more stimuli as the game progresses.

In [5], the authors show a review of different techniques for memory training, and N-back is presented as a positive one due to its effectiveness in children up to older adults. Additionally, in [2] a game based on N-back with a kinesthetic modality is shown; they implemented a computer-based game with external devices so that the user can make physical movements during the game. Furthermore, action video games with N-back task were used to evaluate memory abilities [10]; results show that short-term visual memory was enhanced.

2.2   DDA Systems

Dynamic Difficulty Adjustment consists in changing parameters, scenarios or behavior of computer games. The aim is to keep the game level adapted to the performance of the user, avoiding frustration because the games are too hard or boredom because the game is too easy. This is possible by applying algorithms with artificial intelligence approaches [1].

A modified version of the famous video game Super Mario Bros was used on [13]. Researchers collected statistical information from 327 players to train a multi-layer perceptron. This neural network provides new parameters to generate customized levels. Super Mario was improved in [15], in this case, a genetic algorithm was developed to automatically generate levels for the gamers; this approach uses less memory than reinforcement learning.

Fuzzy approaches also were used. In [14], an adaptive neuro-fuzzy inference system (ANFIS) was used in order to balance a shooting game. The authors collected features such as received damage and killed enemies to train the network. They obtained better results in the training error than with a neural network.

In [9], a DDA in Tetris game is presented. Researchers created clusters from previous game traces to capture different playing styles. The system provides dynamic help to the player choosing Tetris pieces. They report improvements in terms of game experience.

The fuzzy approach mentioned was used to implement a DDA with the purpose of adjusting the memory training game according to the progress of the user. In addition, there is no background evidence of a game based on the N-back task with DDA.

3   Proposed System

Some training memory games sometimes tend to generate boredom or frustration among the players, which may compromise the effectiveness of the learning process. Therefore, a memory training game with DDA based on N-back task is proposed to give a customized experience during the training process in comparison with a normal game. The aim is also to increase performance during memory training.

3.1   Classic Game

A game without DDA (classic game) was built on MATLAB 2015a, it was based on the N-back task with visual stimuli. Figure 1 shows an example of the process on which a sequence of stimuli (numbers) and the correct answers according to the level of N-back are presented.

To clarify the process of the N-back task, level 1-back is explained. In this example, a number 2 is presented, there should not be an answer in this turn. Then a number 4 is displayed and the user must respond with the number 2 as correct. The next number presented is 3 and the player must respond with a number 4. The process continues in the same way for several iterations.

In general, the game starts displaying a sequence of random numbers from 1 to 4, and each one is displayed for 3 s on the screen. Then the user must respond within 5 s with the numeric keypad depending on the N-back level. Next, a new random number is displayed and immediately the user must give a response again. This process continues until the level is completed.

The game shows 15 stimuli every level before the first sequence. It always starts on the 1-back level and only allows to level up when all the answers are correct. There is no maximum limit level and there is no maximum time to finish each level.

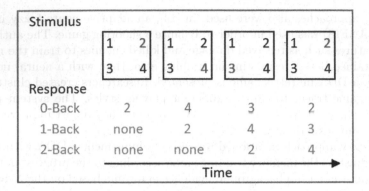

Fig. 1. Diagram of N-back task.

3.2 Game with DDA

Data obtained from the classic game was used to train an ANFIS structure as a DDA system. The classic game interface was used with the proposed DDA, which adjusts some parameters at each level depending on the user performance during the last level. The DDA takes the parameters of the last level played by the user in order to adjust a new one.

The mentioned parameters and details of the DDA are explained in the following sections.

4 Methodology

4.1 Feature Selection

After testing some memory games based on the N-back task, it was possible to detect two important features that are involved in the training process. One of them is the response time, it is the time that a user delays to give an answer after seeing a new stimulus. Second, the rate of positive answers is the percentage of correct responses during a level.

Having chosen the features of these games, the classic game was used to collect data to train the DDA system. The dataset was obtained with 300 instances of college students.

Other characteristics were considered, such as the record of players in the game, the final level reached, the number of stimuli and the time played. They will be taken into account in future work.

4.2 Adaptive Neuro Fuzzy Inference System for Dynamic Difficulty Adjustment

For this study, it was decided to use the ANFIS model because it combines the advantages of both fuzzy inference systems and artificial neural networks.

The ANFIS has some advantages such as capturing the nonlinear structure of a process, adaptation capability, and rapid learning capacity. These features are appreciated in this application.

An ANFIS model with the zero-order sugeno-type inference was implemented. Figure 2 shows the final architecture of the proposed ANFIS, and its characteristics are described below.

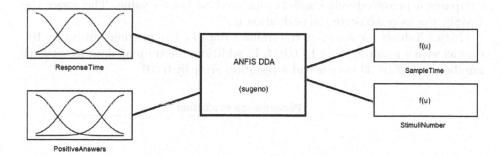

Fig. 2. ANFIS DDA structure

Inputs. Two inputs were previously selected for this system.

- *Response time input*: This input is obtained by calculating the average time response of each level. This value is in the range of 0 to 5 s.
- *Positive answers input*: This input is obtained by calculating the percentage of positive responses at each level. This value is in the range of 0 to 100 percent.

Outputs. Two outputs are also proposed. These variables are some modifiable parameters in the game, which could help the user to perform in a better way.

- *Sample time*: This output represents the time by which the stimulus appears. It has three states: High Time (HT) with 3 s, Middle Time (MT) with 2 s and Low Time (LT) with 1 s.
- *Stimuli number*: This output is the number of stimuli that will be displayed during a level. It has three states, Few Stimuli (FS) with 9 units, Normal Stimuli (NS) with 12 units and Many Stimuli (MS) with 15 units. Because the output of ANFIS is between 1 and 3; the actual value is calculated with the following equation.

$$StimuliNumber = 3 * Output + 6 \qquad (1)$$

Training of ANFIS. 90% of the instances of the data set was used as training data and the rest as testing data. The scaled conjugate gradient (SCG) algorithm was used as the optimization method for training the network. Because of MATLAB does not allow MIMO (Multiple inputs multiple outputs) structures, it was necessary to create an ANFIS structure per output.

The performance evaluation was assessed using root mean square error (RMSE), which measures how much error there is between two data sets. It compares a predicted value and an observed or known value. The lower the RMSE, the more accurate the evaluation is.

Figure 3 shows the results of the training data for Sample time output by 100 epochs with a resulting error by 0.074. In addition, the training data for Stimuli number output by 30 epochs had a resulting error by 0.607.

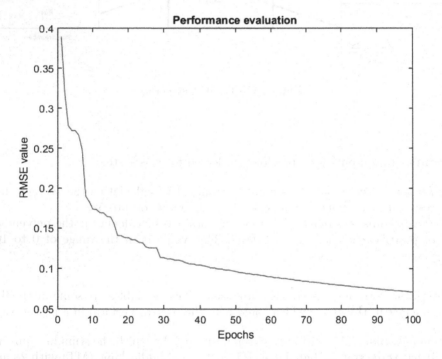

Fig. 3. Training data result in normal for the output "Sample Time"

Resulting Membership Functions. The membership functions resulting from each input are drawn as follows.

On the one hand, Figs. 4 and 5 show the resulting membership functions for the "Sample Time" output. In both figures is possible to see one membership function neglected. For Fig. 4, Mf3 overlap the rest of the functions, because it has the bigger range. For Fig. 5, the same effect has occurred but with Mf1. In both cases, these rules carry an important weight in order to get the final result.

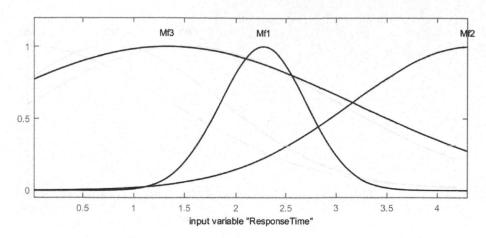

Fig. 4. The membership functions of the input "Response Time" for the output "Sample Time".

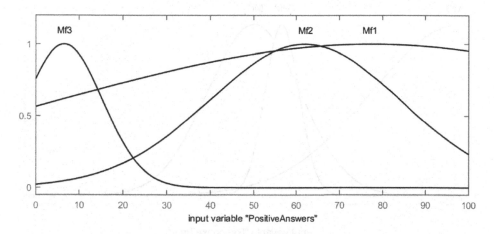

Fig. 5. The membership functions of the input "Positive Answers" for the output "Sample Time".

On the other hand, Figs. 7 and 6 show the resulting membership functions for the "Stimuli Number" output. In these fuzzy sets, it is possible to see a similar effect to that of before. For Fig. 7, Mf1 and Mf2 overlap and when the input is between 4 and 5, the rules don't be activated. For Fig. 6, the three functions have been adjusted to overlap, in this case, the rules act when the input is greater than 50.

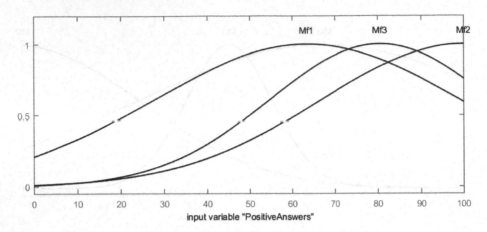

Fig. 6. The membership functions of the input "Positive Response" for the output "Stimuli Number".

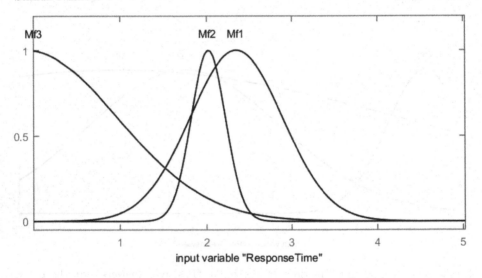

Fig. 7. The membership functions of the input "Response Time" for the output "Stimuli Number".

5   Experiments and Results

Due to the type of game, the experiment involves analyzing the performance of the N-back level achieved by users for some days with the two memory games developed. In addition, a survey was conducted to compare the user's gaming experience.

5.1 Experimental Setup

A group of college students was exposed to the classic game (control group), and another to the proposed game with DDA (training group). Their ages were between 17 and 22, the detailed characteristics of each group are shown in the Table 1.

Table 1. Characteristics of the trained and control groups

	N-back training (n = 12)	
	Training group (n = 6)	Control group (n = 6)
Average age	20,75	20,33
Gender	50% Female	50% Female
Average years of education	15,5	14.83

The 12 students were divided into two groups with gender criteria, which means that each group had 50% women and 50% men. They were not aware of the difference between the two games due to the similar interface used in the two games. The requirement was that they play and try to reach the highest possible N-back level in order to improve their WM capacity.

The training was performed for 15 sessions (15 days), each one was about 20 to 30 min in which the user could play various N-back levels. The user cannot play more than once per day in this experiment. This setup was based on [8], which shows that improved memory capacity can be obtained from day 14.

5.2 Memory Training Results

To evaluate memory training, the performance of the N-back level reached by the users was used.

Figure 8 shows a boxplot of the results collected from both groups in the experiment. It presents relevant information such as extreme values, quartiles, median and mean.

The N-back average level (color-filled circle) is usually used for analyzing the progress of WM training. On one hand, users of the classic game reached a maximum average of around 4-back. On the other, DDA game users reached around 6-back. Therefore, it is possible to appreciate that the proposed game provides a better performance in comparison with the classic game during N-back training. Consequently, with the purpose of verifying this hypothesis, a statistical analysis was performed.

A mixed repeated measure ANOVA was conducted with methods used (classic game, game with DDA) as between-subject and training time (weeks 1–3) as within-subject factor. The training data of the users were added to a t-score distribution and the weekly WM performance was on average 5 days. The purpose was to find out how performance is changed using the developed games.

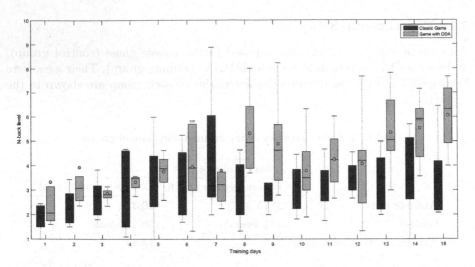

Fig. 8. Boxplot of the N-back level reached by the training and control groups for 15 days.

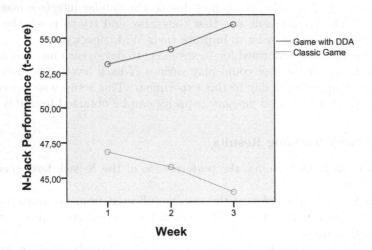

Fig. 9. Mean WM performance across 3 weeks.

Results show that N-back performance during 3 weeks differs to using classic game or game with DDA $(F(2,20) = 0.33; p > 0.05; \eta^2 = 0.03)$. But in general, there is a relevant effect due to the method used in N-back performance regardless of the time $(F(1,10) = 6.99; p < 0.05; \eta^2 = 0.41)$.

In addition, Fig. 9 shows the graph of marginal means of N-back performance, which represents the comparison of between-subjects factor. The users who used the classic game started out with below-average performance, while students who used the game with DDA started out with above-average performance. In both cases, performance continued that trend in the coming weeks.

5.3 Survey Results

In order to analyze the game experience, three important questions were inquired in the survey, which was answered by all users of both games.

The first question was: "How difficult is the game at the beginning?". Computer users indicated at 16.67% that it was easy, but DDA game users indicated 50%. These results could be related to the implemented DDA system that tries to balance the levels according to the user.

The second question was: "How immersed were you during the activity?". In this question, people had to choose a rating from 1 to 3, where 3 was a higher level of immersion. Users of the game with DDA had a mean of 2, while the computer-based game users had a mean of 1.83.

The third question was: "Do you consider that the system has helped to improve your memory?". In this case, computer users say yes at 50%, but DDA game users reached 66.67%. It is a fact that N-back task is responsible for these results, and in both cases, improvement in WM should be achieved.

The survey revealed that the game with DDA implemented had slightly better results during the training process related to the user point of view.

6 Conclusion

With this work, it was demonstrated that it is possible to implement a memory game with DDA, which uses a machine learning approach. This methodology allows giving users a customized game, consequently, obtaining a higher performance than using a classic game.

Statistical analysis showed that there is a significant effect on N-back level performance depending on the game used. A higher level was obtained with the game with DDA. In Addition, according to the opinion of the users of the surveys conducted. A better gaming experience was achieved during the process. These results may be related to the work of the DDA system, which adapts the game parameters according to the user.

The addition of DDA technology in games allows the development of customized and interesting games, as a result of this, users could generate engagement to the game, and that is really necessary to get positive results in this type of games.

For future work, it is possible to use the player's record to adjust some other parameters of the game. It could allow obtaining better results than this study, related to performance and game experience.

References

1. Andrade, G., Ramalho, G., Santana, H., Corruble, V.: Automatic computer game balancing: a reinforcement learning approach. In: Proceedings of the Fourth International Joint Conference on Autonomous Agents and Multiagent Systems, AAMAS 2005, pp. 1111–1112. ACM, New York (2005). https://doi.org/10.1145/1082473.1082648

2. Bouker, J., Scarlatos, A.: Investigating the impact on fluid intelligence by playing N-Back games with a kinesthetic modality. In: 2013 10th International Conference and Expo on Emerging Technologies for a Smarter World (CEWIT), pp. 1–3, October 2013. https://doi.org/10.1109/CEWIT.2013.6713747

3. Brehmer, Y., Westerberg, H., Bckman, L.: Working-memory training in younger and older adults: training gains, transfer, and maintenance. Front. Hum. Neurosci. **6**, 63 (2012). https://doi.org/10.3389/fnhum.2012.00063

4. Chacko, A., et al.: A randomized clinical trial of Cogmed Working Memory Training in school-age children with ADHD: a replication in a diverse sample using a control condition. J. Child Psychol. Psychiatry Allied Discipl. **55**(3), 247–255 (2014). https://doi.org/10.1111/jcpp.12146

5. Deveau, J., Jaeggi, S.M., Zordan, V., Phung, C., Seitz, A.R.: How to build better memory training games. Front. Syst. Neurosci. **8**, 243 (2015). https://doi.org/10.3389/fnsys.2014.00243

6. Gutirrez-Martnez, Ramos, M.: La memoria operativa como capacidad predictora del rendimiento escolar. Estudio de adaptacin de una medida de memoria operativa para nios y adolescentes. Psicol. Educ. **20**(1), 1–10 (2014)

7. Hardy, J.L., et al.: Enhancing cognitive abilities with comprehensive training: a large, online, randomized, active-controlled trial. PLoS ONE **10**(9) (2015). https://doi.org/10.1371/journal.pone.0134467

8. Jaeggi, S., Buschkuehl, M., Jonides, J., Perrig, W.: Improving fluid intelligence with training on working memory. PNAS **105**(19), 6829–6833 (2008)

9. Lora, D., Sánchez-Ruiz-Granados, A.A., González-Calero, P.A., Gómez-Martín, M.A.: Dynamic difficulty adjustment in tetris. In: FLAIRS Conference (2016)

10. McDermott, A.F., Bavelier, D., Green, C.S.: Memory abilities in action video game players. Comput. Hum. Behav. **34**, 69–78 (2014). https://doi.org/10.1016/j.chb.2014.01.018

11. McNab, F., et al.: Changes in cortical dopamine D1 receptor binding associated with cognitive training. Science **323**(5915), 800–802 (2009). https://doi.org/10.1126/science.1166102

12. Nouchi, R., et al.: Brain training game improves executive functions and processing speed in the elderly: a randomized controlled trial. PloS One **7**(1), e29676 (2012). https://doi.org/10.1371/journal.pone.0029676

13. Shaker, N., Yannakakis, G., Togelius, J.: Towards automatic personalized content generation for platform games. In: Proceedings of the Sixth AAAI Conference on Artificial Intelligence and Interactive Digital Entertainment, AIIDE 2010, Stanford, California, USA, pp. 63–68. AAAI Press (2010)

14. Sutanto, K., Suharjito, D.: Dynamic difficulty adjustment in game based on type of player with ANFIS method. J. Theor. Appl. Inf. Technol. **65**(1), 254–260 (2014)

15. Watcharasatharpornpong, N., Kotrajaras, V.: Automatic level difficulty adjustment in platform games using genetic algorithm based methodology. In: International Conference and Industry Symposium on Computer Games, May 2009

Machine Learning Methods for Classifying Mammographic Regions Using the Wavelet Transform and Radiomic Texture Features

Jaider Stiven Rincón[1] , Andrés E. Castro-Ospina[1] , Fabián R. Narváez[2] ,
and Gloria M. Díaz[1](✉)

[1] Grupo de Investigación Automática, Electrónica y Ciencias Computacionales,
Instituto Tecnológico Metropolitano, Medellín, Colombia
jaiderrincon204297@correo.itm.edu.co,
{andrescastro,gloriadiaz}@itm.edu.co
[2] Grupo de Investigación en Bioingeniería y Biomecatrónica - GIByB,
Universidad Politécnica Salesiana, Quito, Ecuador
fnarvaeze@ups.edu.ec

Abstract. Automatic detection and classification of lesions in mammography remains one of the most important and challenging problems in the development of computer-aided diagnosis systems. Several machine learning approaches have been proposed for supporting the detection and classification of mammographic findings, and are used as computational tools during different diagnosis process by the radiologists. However, the effectiveness of these approaches depends on the accuracy of the feature representation and classification techniques. In this paper, a radiomic strategy based on texture features is explored for identifying abnormalities in mammographies. For doing that, a complete study of five feature extraction approaches, ten selection methods, and five classification models was carried out for identifying findings contained in regions of interest extracted from mammography. The proposed strategy starts with a region extraction process. Some square regions of interest (ROI) were manually extracted from the Mammographic Image Analysis Society (miniMIAS) database. Then, each ROI was decomposed into different resolution levels by using a Wavelet transform approach, and a set of radiomic features based on texture information was computed. Finally, feature selection algorithms and machine learning models were applied to decide whether the ROI undergoing analysis contains or not a mammographic abnormality. The obtained results showed that radiomic texture descriptors extracted from wavelet detail coefficients improved the performance obtained by radiomic features extracted from the original image.

Keywords: Breast cancer · ROI classification
Machine learning methods · Radiomics

G.M. Díaz—This work was supported by Colciencias (RFC 740-2017) and the Instituto Tecnológico Metropolitano.

© Springer Nature Switzerland AG 2019
M. Botto-Tobar et al. (Eds.): CITT 2018, CCIS 895, pp. 617–629, 2019.
https://doi.org/10.1007/978-3-030-05532-5_47

1 Introduction

Breast cancer is the most common cancer in women worldwide and is considered the second leading of cancer death in that population [14]. According to the World Health Organization (WHO), in 2012, more than 1.6 million of new cases of breast cancer and 522,000 of breast cancer deaths were reported in worldwide [14]. However, it is well known that breast cancer can have a positive prognosis if it is diagnosed in early stages and an appropriate treatment is carried out. Therefore, the increase of sensitivity of breast cancer screening is still one of the most challenging research problems.

Currently, mammography is considered the best method for breast cancer screening in worldwide. However, a considerable variability interpretation inter and intra-observer have been reported [8]. In order to reduce this variability, several advanced image analysis methods have been proposed to describe different radiographic properties of lesions contained into regions of interest. In this way, multiresolution texture analysis had proved higher accuracies for identifying breast abnormalities [10]. Moreover, some authors had shown that standard feature descriptors extracted from decomposed images could improve the classification task. Jona et al. [6] used a hybrid of both Particle Swarm Optimization (PSO) and Genetic Algorithm (GA) techniques, called Genetic Swarm Optimization (GSO), to optimize a set of features extracted from the gray level co-occurrence matrix for classifying breast tissue as normal or abnormal. Results reported an accuracy of 0.94 using a Support Vector Machine (SVM) learning model. Görgel et al. [4] proposed to use the Spherical Wavelet Transform (SWT) and a SVM classifier, obtaining an accuracy of 0.96 and 0.935 in the normal-abnormal and benign-malignant classification, respectively. Beura et al. [1] proposed a feature extraction method by using two dimensional DWT and gray-level co-occurrence matrix (GLCM) approaches. They combined both, t-test and F-test feature selection methods with a neural network to classify breast tissue as normal-abnormal and benign-malignant. The reported results shown an accuracy between 0.942 and 0.988, respectively.

On the other hand, in the last years, the *"radiomic feature"* concept has been introduced as the high-throughput extraction of large amounts of image features from radiographic images [3,12], which are processed by conventional machine learning techniques to identify or predicting cancer progression. Alike to classical machine learning methods, the radiomic workflow includes both stages, an extraction-selection of image features and make-decision process by using learning models, respectively. Because of large number of available methods, an optimal selection is required, as was demonstrated by Parmar et al. [12], who carried out a study of several feature selection and classification methods from radiomic features for survival prediction of patients with lung cancer.

In this paper, a comprehensive study of radiomic texture features for detecting breast abnormalities contained into mammographic regions of interest is presented. This study aims to determine the effect of applying different feature extraction, feature selection and classification models on a radiomic-based decision scheme. As proposed in [1], a DWT-based multiresolution analysis along with radiomic texture features was applied. Thus, five feature extraction approaches were evaluated, in four of them, images were decomposed into different resolution levels by using a Wavelet transform, and a set of radiomic features based on texture information was computed. The fifth descriptor resulted by the concatenation of radiomic features computed from the original RoI image. In addition, ten feature selection methods and five classification models, chosen from state-of-the-art, were evaluated.

The rest of this paper is organized as follows: in the Sect. 2, feature extraction, selection and classification models used in this study are introduced. Section 3 presents the obtained results by evaluating the different proposed techniques. Finally, in Sect. 4, some conclusions and future works are discussed.

2 Materials and Methods

An overview of the proposed evaluation scheme is shown in Fig. 1. The proposed radiomic-based classification approach is composed of three main stages: feature extraction, feature selection, and classification. In this work, the effect of using the most relevant state-of-the-art feature extraction, selection, and classification techniques was evaluated for defining if a Region of Interest (ROI) contains or not a mammographic abnormality. Firstly, five different texture descriptors were used in the feature extraction stage for describing the visual content of the ROI. Then, ten feature selection approaches were evaluated for choosing a subset of relevant features. In this stage, four subsets named 10, 20, 50 and 100 most relevant features were assessed. Finally, the performance of five machine learning algorithms for classifying ROIs between normal and abnormal was evaluated by using a 10-fold cross-validation strategy.

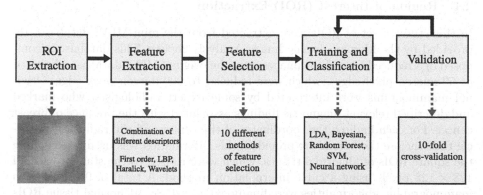

Fig. 1. Block diagram of the proposed scheme for evaluating different feature extraction, feature selection and machine learning models in the classification of mammographic ROIs.

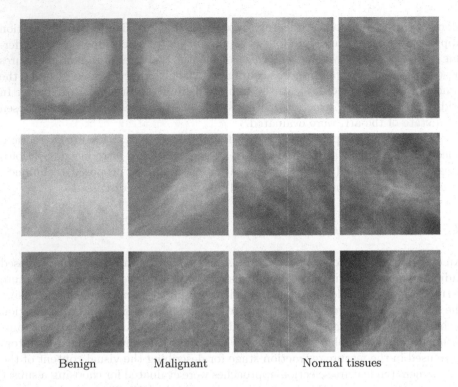

Benign   Malignant   Normal tissues

Fig. 2. ROI examples from the dataset used for evaluation. Six abnormalities, including three benign and six malignant findings, are shown in the two first columns. Six portions of normal tissues are shown in the last two columns.

2.1   Region of Interest (ROI) Extraction

In this study, a set of ROIs were extracted from the mini-MIAS database [16] provided by the Mammographic Image Analysis Society. This database is composed of a reduced type of the images from the original MIAS database (digitized at 50-micron pixel edge), which were reduced to 200-micron pixel edge. Original mammograms were interpreted by some expert radiologists, who marked and described relevant diagnostic findings associated with the presence of breast cancer. For each finding, the coordinates of the center and the radius of the circle that enclose the lesions are provided, this information was used for cropping the square ROIs of abnormal tissues, which were resized to the standard size of 128 × 128 pixels using a cubic interpolation method. A total of 91 ROIs with mammographic abnormalities were finally extracted. So, 91 normal tissue ROIs were also extracted from the images labeled as normal tissue, but a random pixel was selected as the center, and a radius of 64 pixels was applied; taking care of not to include background portions into ROIs containing findings. Regions with calcification were not taken into account. Figure 2 shows examples of some ROIs of the dataset used for evaluation.

2.2   Feature Extraction

As described above, the feature extraction stage allowed to evaluate the effect of using different texture descriptors for representing the visual content of the ROI. Following the proposal of [1], images are initially processed using a multiresolution decomposition based on the Discrete Wavelet Transform (DWT), which represent the original image by four coefficients named approximation and detail at horizontal, vertical and diagonal directions. Then, texture descriptors are computed from the detail coefficients, allowing to obtain a more complex representation of the image texture. In this study, original images were decomposed four times using the family of Haar wavelet, and three texture descriptors, i.e., first-order statistical moments, gray level co-occurrence matrix and local binary patterns (LBPs), were implemented. Thus, five feature extraction methods were evaluated, three of them, obtained by the extraction of the three texture descriptors from the detail wavelet coefficients along four resolutions; one more, named Wavelet-Radiomic, which corresponds to the concatenation of the previous three; and the last one, which is obtained by the extraction and concatenation of the features obtained by the three feature extraction models from the original image (Radiomic features).

First-Order Statistical Measures. These metrics, computed on the image histogram, describes the global intensity distribution of the pixels in an image. In this case, the 13 first-order features, i.e., energy, entropy, kurtosis, mean, mean deviation, median, root mean square, skewness, standard deviation, uniformity, variance, middle histogram, and suavity, are computed from the detail wavelet coefficients.

Haralick Features. These are the 13 second order statistics derivated from the GLCM proposed for Haralick [5], i.e., angular second moment, contrast, correlation, sum of squares, variance, inverse difference moment, sum average, sum entropy, entropy, difference variance, difference entropy, and information measures of correlation 1 and 2. As GLCM describe the distribution of co-occurring pixel values in a specified distance d and directions θ, the four main directions $0°$, $45°$, $90°$ and $135°$ and a distance d of 1 were used.

Uniform Local Binary Patterns (LBP). Local binary patterns are a texture descriptor that encodes the relationship between the intensity of the central pixel and the intensity of the surrounding pixels. In this work, the uniform LBP operator was used, which is a variation of LBP that significantly reduce the feature vector dimension selecting only the patterns with at most two circular 0–1 and 1–0 transitions [11].

2.3   Feature Selection

The dimension of the feature vector obtained using the combination of different feature estimation methods is high, which could lead these approaches to underlie the curse of dimensionality. This problem is addressed by the implementation of appropriate feature selection approaches. Several feature selection methods have been proposed in the literature. In this work, we decided to evaluate the performance of 10 feature selection methods (summarized in Table 1), which are implemented in the scikit-feature repository, provided by the Arizona University (http://featureselection.asu.edu). Theoretical and implementation details of these techniques can be found in [9].

Table 1. Feature selection methods used in the evaluation

Feature selection method name	Acronym
Fisher Score	FSCR
Relief	RELF
Gini-index	GINI
Joint mutual information	JMI
Conditional infomax feature extraction	CIFE
Double input symmetric relevance	DISR
Mutual information maximization	MIM
Conditional mutual information maximization	CMIM
Interaction capping	ICAP
Minimum redundancy maximum relevance	MRMR

2.4 Classification Models

Different supervised classification models have been proposed to identify abnormalities in medical imaging [2]. In this work, five of the most well known and accurate models were evaluated, namely, Support Vector Machine (SVM), Multilayer Perceptron neural network (MLPC), Random Forest (RF), Bayesian model (BY), and Linear Discriminant Analysis (LDA). All of them were implemented using the scikit-learn Python library [13]. Main parameters settings for each method are summarized below.

Support Vector Machine (SVM). An SVM with radial basis function (RBF) was used because of its well-known performance in mammography classification tasks [15, 17]. For each case, the bandwidth (γ) was calculated as the mean of the distance matrix of data, while the regularization parameter (C) was obtained by an exhaustive search, varying it between 1 and 100, with increment steps of 0.1. The best parameter was found to $C = 56$, which was finally used for the comparison.

Multilayer Perceptron (MLPC). A Multilayer Perceptron neural network trained with the back-propagation algorithm was used. The network architecture was heuristically defined by an exhaustive search. To the end, this was provided with 5 hidden layers and 30 nodes for each layer. The activation function RELU, the Adam solver, and a learning rate of 0.001 were used. Additionally, the maximum number of iterations was set to 1000.

Random Forest (RF). To make sure of the classification convergence in the training model, a large number of decision trees was considered in the Random Forest model. An exhaustive search was carried out, varying between 1 and 10000 decision trees, searching for a trade-off between the performance and the execution time. After the search, the number of decision trees was set to 1000.

Bayesian Model (BY). It is a classification method based on the naive Bayesian classifier, in which the likelihood of the features is assumed to be Gaussian. In this case, the parameters σ_y and μ_y were estimated automatically by the algorithm implemented in the scikit-learn library, using maximum likelihood [13]. The a-priori class probabilities were adjusted according to the data.

Linear Discriminant Analysis (LDA). Linear discriminant analysis classification was performed using the LDA classifier provided by scikit-learn, which provides several solvers to use. In this case, the singular value decomposition (SVD) was selected as solver.

3   Experimental Results

Performance evaluation was carried out using the well-known 10–fold cross-validation strategy. Because both normal and abnormal classes are balanced, the average classification accuracy was used for comparison. Comparative charts are presented in the Figs. 3, 4, 5, with feature selection methods in the x-axis, accuracy in the y-axis, and feature extraction methods represented by the different curves in each chart. Four charts were generated per classifier, which corresponds to the 10, 20, 50 and 100 most relevant features selected by each selection approach. The effect of varying the three learning components, i.e., feature extraction, feature selection and classification models, will be discussed below.

3.1   Overall Performance

Best performance was reported by different learning models. Thus, the SVM classifier reports an overall accuracy of 0.96 ± 0.04 using the 50 and the 100 features extracted with the Wavelet-Radiomic approach and selected by Fisher score and Gini-index. The same result was reported by the SVM classification model, using features selected from those generated by the Wavelet-Haralick feature extractor. In both cases, 20 features selected by the CIFE approach, and 50 features selected by Fisher score and Gini-index methods were used.

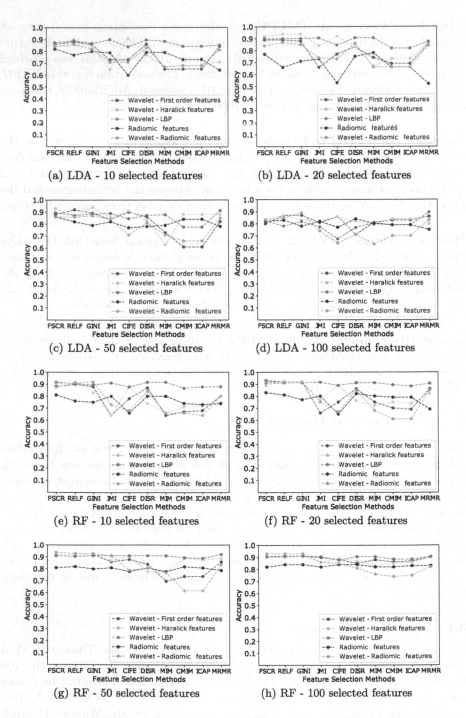

Fig. 3. Accuracy of LDA and Random forest (RF) classifiers for different feature extraction and selection methods

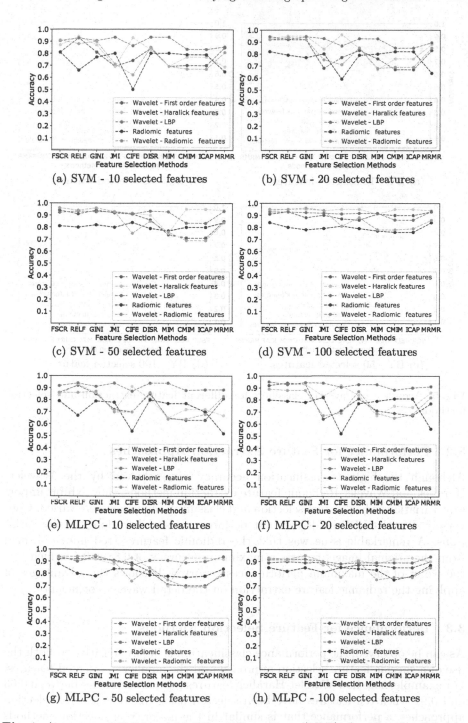

Fig. 4. Accuracy of SVM and Multilayer Perceptron (MLP) classifiers for different feature extraction and selection methods

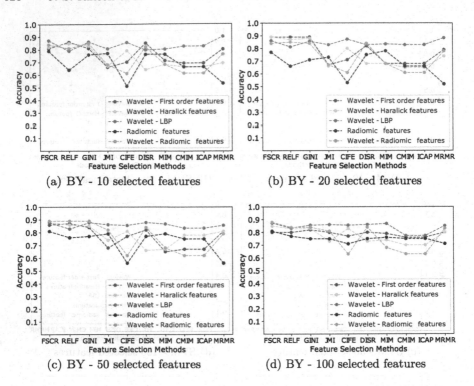

(a) BY - 10 selected features   (b) BY - 20 selected features

(c) BY - 50 selected features   (d) BY - 100 selected features

Fig. 5. Accuracy of Bayesian classifiers for different feature extraction and selection methods.

3.2 Performance for Feature Extraction Approaches

Although the highest classification accuracy was achieved by the Wavelet-Haralick and Wavelet-Radiomic feature extraction methods, they exhibit important variations when feature selection and classification models were varied. Conversely, Wavelet-LBP holds the best performance stability along all the variations. A remarkable issue was that the radiomic features (red line) obtained from the original image, reports a maximum accuracy of 0.88 ± 0.7, which was the worst of the maximum performances reported. It shows the advantages of applying the radiomic feature extraction on the detail wavelet coefficients.

3.3 Performance for Feature Selection Methods

As can be observed, the performance classification is highly sensitive to both the use of a specific feature selection approach and the number of selected features. For example, note how Wavelet-Haralick features reports accuracies between 0.63 and 0.91 when ten features have been selected using different feature selection approaches, a performance that is similar in the majority of selection methods evaluated. Particularly, CIFE approach exhibits the larger variabilities, generating the best and worst subset of features. Even so, Fisher score, Relief and

Gini-index methods maintain a similar performance for all feature extraction and classification models, a reason why they are considered the most stable approaches. In this item, it is relevant to note that the use of a larger number of selected features improves the performance stability, especially for the RF and MLPC learning models.

3.4   Performance for Classification Models

From the results reported in the Figs. 3, 4, 5 it is not evident the effect of classification models in overall performances. Thus, there is not a learning model that outperforms others in all cases. The Table 2 presents the best performance reported by each evaluated classifier. Additionally, the feature extraction and selection methods, and the number of selected features are reported for each case. SVM reports the best performances for two feature extraction methods, selecting 20, 50 and 100 features, and using different selection models. However, no significant differences are found with MLPC, RF and LDA models. Only, Bayesian classifier obtains a significantly lower performance.

Table 2. Best performances for each classification model

Classification model	Feature extaction	Feature selection	Best accuracy
LDA	Wavelet-Haralick	Relief (20 features)	0.94 ± 0.03
	Wavelet-Haralick	Gini index (20–50 features)	0.94 ± 0.05
Bayes	Wavelet-LBP	MRMR (10 features)	0.90 ± 0.06
RF	Wavelet-Radiomic	Fisher (20 features)	0.94 ± 0.05
SVM	Wavelet-Haralick	CIFE (20 features)/Gini index (50 features)	0.96 ± 0.04
	Wavelet-Radiomic	Fisher - Gini index (50–100 features)	0.96 ± 0.04
MLPC	Wavelet-Radiomic	Gini index (50–100 features)	0.95 ± 0.04
	Wavelet-Haralick	Fisher (20 features)	0.95 ± 0.04
	Wavelet-LBP	Fisher (20 features)	0.95 ± 0.04

4   Conclusions and Future Work

In this paper, a comprehensive study of the effect of varying the main components of the machine learning framework in the identification of abnormalities in mammographic regions was presented. Different feature extraction, feature selection, and classification models were evaluated using the well-known public miniMIAS database. Experimental results showed that an appropriate selection of machine learning methods determine the classification performance, even when a large number of features is initially extracted.

In the feature extraction stage, the advantage of extracting radiomic texture features from detail wavelet coefficients was evidenced. Suggesting that the extraction of a large number of features is not enough to improve the learning models as it is presented by the Radiomics framework [7]. Moreover, although LBP did not achieve the best results, its performance was the most stable. On the other hand, the feature selection stage was the most determining component, i.e., the classification performance varied markedly depending on the selection method used. Additionally, the number of selected features was also fundamental. In this case, although the best performance was obtained with small subset of features, most of the machine learning models were most stable when a larger number of features were used. Finally, with respect to the classification models, these result less relevant if feature extraction and selection are properly selected.

In the future work, a similar evaluation in the classification of the breast abnormalities should be performed. A task that requires a large number of samples per abnormality, then, other databases should be used. Additionally, other aspects such as preprocessing techniques must be also assessed. From those evaluations, we intend to develop a system to support the diagnosis of breast cancer based on mammography, which takes advantages of the radiomics features and the state-of-the-art learning algorithms. Additionally, a comparison between classification models based on radiomic features and the most recent deep learning models will be performed. For doing so, a large set of images is required, which must contain both normal and abnormal regions.

References

1. Beura, S., Majhi, B., Dash, R.: Mammogram classification using two dimensional discrete wavelet transform and gray-level co-occurrence matrix for detection of breast cancer. Neurocomputing **154**, 1–14 (2015). https://doi.org/10.1016/j.neucom.2014.12.032
2. Erickson, B.J., Korfiatis, P., Akkus, Z., Kline, T.L.: Machine learning for medical imaging. Radiographics **37**(2), 505–515 (2017)
3. Gillies, R.J., Kinahan, P.E., Hricak, H.: Radiomics: images are more than pictures, they are data. Radiology **278**(2), 563–577 (2015)
4. Görgel, P., Sertbas, A., Ucan, O.N.: Mammographical mass detection and classification using local seed region growing-spherical wavelet transform (LSRG-SWT) hybrid scheme. Comput. Biol. Med. **43**(6), 765–774 (2013). https://doi.org/10.1016/j.compbiomed.2013.03.008
5. Haralick, R., Shanmugan, K., Dinstein, I.: Textural features for image classification (1973). https://doi.org/10.1109/TSMC.1973.4309314
6. Jona, J.B.: A hybrid swarm optimization approach for feature set reduction in digital mammograms. WSEAS Trans. Inf. Sci. Appl. **9**(11), 340–349 (2012)
7. Lambin, P., et al.: Radiomics: extracting more information from medical images using advanced feature analysis. Eur. J. Cancer **48**(4), 441–446 (2012)

8. Lee, A.Y., et al.: Inter-reader variability in the use of bi-rads descriptors for suspicious findings on diagnostic mammography: a multi-institution study of 10 academic radiologists. Acad. Radiol. **24**(1), 60–66 (2017)
9. Li, J., et al.: Feature selection: a data perspective (2016). https://doi.org/10.1145/3136625
10. Narváez, F., Díaz, G., Poveda, C., Romero, E.: An automatic BI-RADS description of mammographic masses by fusing multiresolution features. Expert. Syst. Appl. **74**, 82–95 (2017)
11. Ojala, T., Pietikainen, M., Harwood, D.: Performance evaluation of texture measures with classification based on Kullback discrimination of distributions. In: Proceedings of 12th International Conference on Pattern Recognition, vol. 1, pp. 582–585 (1994). https://doi.org/10.1109/ICPR.1994.576366
12. Parmar, C., Grossmann, P., Bussink, J., Lambin, P., Aerts, H.J.: Machine learning methods for quantitative radiomic biomarkers. Sci. Rep. **5**, 1–11 (2015). https://doi.org/10.1038/srep13087
13. Pedregosa, F., et al.: Scikit-learn: machine learning in Python. J. Mach. Learn. Res. **12**, 2825–2830 (2011)
14. Stewart, B.W., Wild, C.P.: World cancer report 2014 (2014)
15. Subashini, T.S., Ramalingam, V., Palanivel, S.: Automated assessment of breast tissue density in digital mammograms. Comput. Vis. Image Underst. **114**(1), 33–43 (2010). https://doi.org/10.1016/j.cviu.2009.09.009
16. Suckling, J., et al.: The mammographic image analysis society digital mammogram database. In: Experta Medica, International Congress Series, vol. 1069, pp. 375–378, January 1994
17. Wang, D., Shi, L., Heng, P.A.: Automatic detection of breast cancers in mammograms using structured support vector machines. Neurocomputing **72**(13–15), 3296–3302 (2009). https://doi.org/10.1016/j.neucom.2009.02.015

Balanced Scorecard as Evaluation Tool with Sterilization Processes by Using Fuzzy Logic

Lorenzo J. Cevallos-Torres[1]([✉]), Miguel Botto-Tobar[1,2],
Jefferson Nuñez-Gaibor[1], David Cardenas-Giler[1],
Alexandra Wilches-Medina[1], and Joffre León-Acurio[3]

[1] Universidad de Guayaquil, Guayaquil, Ecuador
{lorenzo.cevallost, miguel.bottot, jefferson.nenezg,
david.cardenasg, alexandra.wilchesm}@ug.edu.ec
[2] Eindhoven University of Technology, Eindhoven, The Netherlands
[3] Universidad Técnica de Babahoyo, Babahoyo, Ecuador

Abstract. The sterilization plants, in the different public hospitals in Guayaquil city, are responsible for the manipulation and handling of surgical instruments. However, the lack of adequate control of these materials due to the possible failure to comply with the norms and procedures, can generate both in patients and in the persons who manipulate the surgical instruments, a certain uncertainty degree, therefore we conducted an analysis based on an organizational use management tool, which measures the performance of the company, as the Balanced Scorecard (BSC), so that this tool can integrate techniques to reduce the uncertainty and to be able to treat the inaccurate data as if they were true through fuzzy logic (FL), guaranteeing the performance and contributing to the optimal decision making, determined by the experts.

Keywords: Surgical instruments · Sterilization · Balanced Scorecard
Fuzzy logic · Mamdani method · Membership function

1 Introduction

Balanced Scorecard (BSC) has proven to be a handy tool for strategic management because it is based on the definition of strategic objectives, indicators, and strategic initiatives, establishing the relationships between cause and effect through a strategic map, and this is possible thanks to the fact that the BSC is based on four perspectives bases of an organization: financial, clients, internal processes and learning-growth [5, 7, 18].

In both public and private hospitals, the BSC has obtained very satisfactory results, one of its advantages, is that it helps to advance towards its objectives and goals, covering all areas of the organization [11]. By focusing on this research in the field of health, it is essential to ensure that the four fundamental perspectives contained in the BSC referred to in the preceding paragraph are addressed and simultaneously guaranteeing possible results; explicitly focusing on the sterilization department [8, 19, 24].

© Springer Nature Switzerland AG 2019
M. Botto-Tobar et al. (Eds.): CITT 2018, CCIS 895, pp. 630–643, 2019.
https://doi.org/10.1007/978-3-030-05532-5_48

On the other hand, surgical hygiene is a fundamental role of the sterilization departments, since they must comply with the guidelines that guarantee the cleanliness of each one of the surgical instruments that are used in invasive surgeries [22]. For this reason, the process of disinfection and antisepsis is necessary for any intervention; in the absence of adequate cleaning of the surgical material, an atmosphere of uncertainty is created giving the opportunity to apply tools such as fuzzy logic, in this way that they improve the treatment of the subjective data and this is due to the risk that these instruments have because they can cause the partial or total death of patients [4, 10, 24, 26].

Fuzzy systems have been shown to have a high capacity to solve complex decision-making problems involving the management of vague, uncertain or ambiguous information [9, 25, 33]. They have been used as a structure of representation and processing of vague or uncertain knowledge based on the concepts of fuzzy sets, linguistic rules of the If-then form, as well as this kind of systems incorporates a system of fuzzy reasoning (approximate reasoning system) based on fuzzy logic, whereby such systems have achieved successful applications in the medicine area [20].

On the basis of the exposed in the above paragraph, we can indicate that fuzzy logic helps linguistic comprehension; allowing the computer to handle a human response of imprecise behavior, being these methodologies beneficial for the sterilization departments to handle key indicators, allowing to measure performance, contributing the verification of processes to obtain a concrete result under uncertainty [25, 34].

Finally, this research aims to conduct an analysis based on an organizational use management tool, which measures the performance of the sterilization department, as is Balanced Scorecard (BSC), in such a way this tool can integrate techniques to reduce uncertainty and be able to treat inaccurate data as whether they were true through fuzzy logic (FL) obtaining a surgical instrument suitable for use and preventing contamination risk.

The Importance of Sterilization Plants

The sterilization plant, as a support center in both public or private hospitals, is subject to different norms and laws which guarantee the safety of patients and the quality of health care. The safety and effectiveness of the sterilization process must be affirmed through the control of the variety of procedures and the validation of operations [1, 3, 10, 21].

On the other hand, the sterilization plants are considered as the most important areas where all materials are controlled, classified and processed to be used in each surgical intervention [14, 29]; its main objective is to avoid the generation of infections, where all pathogenic and non-pathogenic microorganisms present in the equipment, instruments, and materials are destroyed by making a disinfection, preparation, conditioning, and sterilization indispensable for the provision of medical services [12, 35]; this representation is shown in Fig. 1.

In the scenario of Fig. 1, we observe the process of sterilization classified by colors, where:

Red

1. Pre-wash: It is the cleaning given in the operating room, before delivery to the plant.
2. Washing and disinfecting: It is proceeding in the department, doing a thorough cleaning.

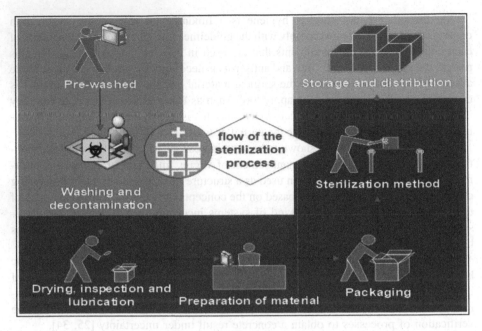

Fig. 1. Sterilization process.

Blue Color

3. Drying, inspection and lubricating: At this point, the excellent material is verified and treated.
4. Preparation of the material: Where the instrument is classified according to the procedure.
5. Packaging: The material assigned to the sterilization method is used.
6. Sterilization method: The starred or autoclave machine is used.

Green

7. Storage and Distribution: Finally, we proceed to store or deliver.

2   Balance Scorecard

Balanced Scorecard model was initially developed by Kaplan and Norton in the year 1992, as a mechanism to complement traditional financial indicators that provide a partial and incomplete view of business performance. The development of the model transcended including operational efficiency measures such as customer performance, learning and business growth. To design the company's strategy and include management indicators in the priority areas, the use of Balanced Scorecard can lead to better business decisions, by adding to the financial indicators, future performance indexes [11].

Díaz-Curbelo and Marrero-Delgado stated about the idea that through vision and strategy giving raise specific challenges that must necessarily be individual for each organization, and by implementing policies implies an improvement in services, acquiring equipment or merely stop performing some function that hinders the process [11].

Before this, we seek to follow up these processes to take the actions that lead to the main indicators that are the value added for the correct functioning of the company [28, 32].

This tool is based and developed around four fundamental perspectives:

- Financial Perspective
- Customer Perspective
- Internal processes Perspective
- Training and growth perspective.

Figure 2 depicts the relationship that exists in the management level according to the indicators found in this study; it clearly shows the integration of the processes evaluated by the model BSC.

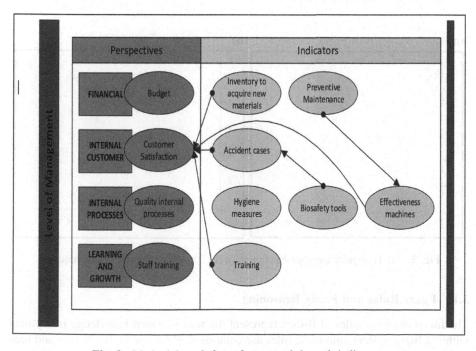

Fig. 2. Methodology balanced scorecard through indicators.

3 Fuzzy Set Theory and Fuzzy Logic

The fuzzy set theory developed by Zadeh [37], it is an extension of the conventional boolean logic, which restricts us to the rigid sets defined as true and false with their respective degrees of membership, 0 and 1. It is very common to meet with linguistic terms that cannot be defined appropriately using classical logic, such as: "does not become young", "very young", "not so young", "young to dry", "not young anymore" and "no longer young", these expressions have an ambiguous meaning and are perceived differently by each individual, since they lack a criterion of a degree of membership precise, however they are linguistic terms frequently used in everyday life.

The fuzzy sets are defined through a continuous degree of membership and in turn, they are characterized by having a function of membership (characteristic), which is responsible for assigning to each object a degree of membership within a range of 0 and 1 [2], such sets are used to define the language terms as stated above. There are different types of membership functions used to represent these sets, such as triangular function, trapezoidal, Gaussian, Sigmoidal, etc. [31]. Membership functions allow us to represent a fuzzy set graphically. On the x - axis (abscissas), which represents the discourse universe, while on the y-axis (ordinates) represent the degrees of membership in a closed interval of [0.1] (Fig. 3).

(a)   **(b)**

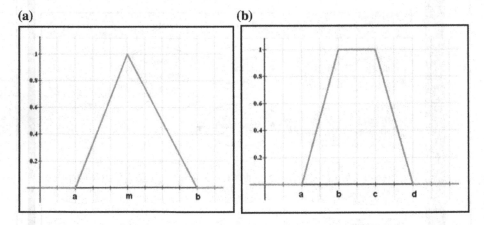

Fig. 3. (a) Triangular membership function; (b) Trapezoidal membership function.

3.1 Fuzzy Rules and Fuzzy Reasoning

The fuzzy inference rules of If-then represent the way in which knowledge is captured within a fuzzy system, and these rules are composed of two parts, the If part and then part also referred to as the antecedent and the considerable part [36].

A diffuse rule of the form If-then with two linguistic variables as input in the antecedent part, and a linguistic variable as output in the significant part, it assumes the following form:

if x_1 is A and x_2 is B **then**
    y is C
end if

Where x_1 is an element that belongs to linguistic variable $X1 (x_1 \in X1)$, and x_2 is an element that belongs to the linguistic variable $X2 (x_2 \in X2)$; **A** is a linguistic term defined by a fuzzy set in the linguistic variable $X1$; **B** is a linguistic term defined by a fuzzy set in the linguistic variable $X2$, and it is an element that belongs to the linguistic variable $Y (y \in Y)$, and **C** is a linguistic term defined by a fuzzy set in the linguistic variable Y [16]. The conclusion is obtained from the rules of fuzzy sets.

3.2   Application of Fuzzy Logic Using BSC Indicators

For this research is intended to obtain an existing relationship between the management level and the different indicators that were given as a result in the process map (BSC), to reduce the incidence of uncertainty in the processes of decision making [15]; these indicators can be seen in Fig. 2. For a better understanding, it will work specifying the perspective Quality Internal Processes, and their respective indicators such as hygiene measures, bio-safety tools and machine effectiveness which corresponding to Fig. 4.

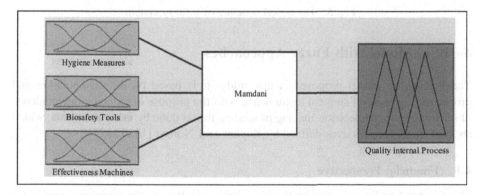

Fig. 4. Fuzzy inference system in the perspective quality internal processes

3.3   Fuzzy Inference System of Mamdani Type and De-diffusion

Inference systems have been used as a structure of representation and processing of vague or uncertain knowledge, and it is essential to be clear that these systems are based on the concepts of fuzzy sets, linguistic rules of the If-then form and a fuzzy reasoning system based on fuzzy logic. On the other hand, diffuse inference systems contain three stages [23, 30]:

– *Diffusion*: It consists in transforming the input values in the antecedent part of the system into fuzzy values with a membership degree between 0 and 1.

- *The fuzzy rules base*: It stores the knowledge in a set of rules of the form If <antecedent> then <consequent>.
- *De-diffusion*: It consists in the transformation of fuzzy values obtained from utilizing actions of the system into rigid values so that the output value of the system is obtained. We can use many methods that help us to make the transformation of the linguistic variables, as is Mamdani method (Fig. 5), this method was initially developed by Mamdani-Assilan [6], as a control system for a steam engine by using a combination of linguistic rules obtained from expert operators in the area of knowledge.

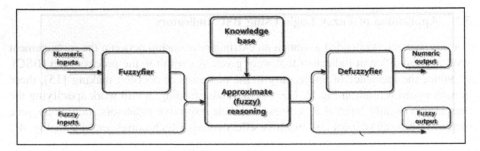

Fig. 5. The typical structure of a fuzzy system

4   BSC Model with Fuzzy Approaches

The BSC-fuzzy model proposed in this study, it is based on the manipulation and proper management of surgical instruments, with the purpose of reducing the incidence of uncertainty in the decision-making processes, this is done by using indicators, which are part of the perspectives defined by Kaplan and Norton [13, 17, 27].

4.1   Financial Perspective

The financial indicators present the economic stability of the company, and these criteria can vary according to system level and the life of the company. According to several studies we have the first indicator measured by the *Inventory of new materials*, which serves as a useful resource to request changes in equipment, and the second indicator is *Preventive maintenance indispensable*, this serves as a measure to preserve the product life; the two indicators prioritize the economy of the organization limited to *Budget*.

4.2   Customer Perspective

This perspective defines specific objectives regarding the different elements of the value proposition; thus, they are key indicators to create or maintain the image that the customer has the product or the company and their satisfaction. In this perspective it was determined as a key indicator *case of accidentalness*, this indicator directly influences the satisfaction of the internal customer who is collaborators in the sterilization plants.

4.3 Intern Process Perspective

It is based on history, as the traditional approach, however, it looks for new processes, with which the two objectives can be achieved. The indicators related to this perspective: hygiene measures, bio-safety tools, and machine effectiveness; these indicators seek to incorporate innovative processes that allow the value creation.

4.4 Training and Growth Perspective

This perspective identifies the assets with which the company counts and which it must build to learn and improve in the short, medium or long term, by considering the three main sources: capacity and competence of people, information systems, and culture-climate-motivation. By using the indicator *Training* as an academic factor, it is expected that the knowledge of the collaborator is unified.

Figure 6 depicts the relationships of indicators in BSC perspectives, in relation to the organizational performance and management level that the company is looking for from the processes evaluated in the model.

5 Fuzzy Study of BSC Model

To solve the problem, a fuzzy inference system was designed, in which each variable from Fig. 6 were modeled into a linguistic variable. As linguistic valuations are estimation that can be obtained by consulting experts. It was allowed for each linguistic label to be assigned numerical values, represented adequately with fuzzy triangular numbers. Linguistic terms were determined as high, medium and low, by forming the membership function included in the ranks [0.6, 1, 4], [0.1, 0.5, 0.9], [−0.4, 0, 0.4], respectively, by being these that provide an output, which is detailed in Table 1.

5.1 Control Rules

Showing in detail the indicators involved, it was possible to define 81 semantic rules applied to the relationships that exist between the indicators in Table 1, and the variable Quality of Internal Process, this process is illustrated in Table 2. To define the base rules of a fuzzy driver, the following array is considered.

In the same way that in the previous process, to obtain a fuzzy value, the calculation must be made by using the method of the centroid, which according to the parameters given to trapezoidal type membership function referenced the management level, which is defined by the categories with their respective classification low [0 0 0.2 0.4], medium [0.2 0.5 0.8] and high [0.6 0.8 1 1].

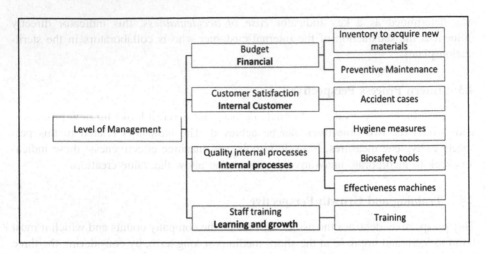

Fig. 6. Methodology of the study model.

Table 1. Fuzzy study from BSC model.

Indicator	High	Medium	Low
Inventory to acquire new materials	[0.6 1 1.4]	[0.1 0.5 0.9]	[−0.4 0 0.4]
Preventive maintenance	[0.6 1 1.0]	[0.2 0.5 0.8]	[0 0 0.4]
Accident cases	[0.6 1 1.4]	[0.1 0.5 0.9]	[−0.4 0 0.4]
Hygiene measures	[0.6 1 1.4]	[0.1 0.5 0.9]	[−0.4 0 0.4]
Biosafety tools	[0.6 1 1.4]	[0.1 0.5 0.9]	[−0.4 0 0.4]
Effectiveness machine	[0.6 1 1.4]	[0.1 0.5 0.9]	[−0.4 0 0.4]

5.2 Study of Application and Integration Methods

For the integration of the model, it has been considered the contribution generated by using fuzzy logic altogether with Balance Scorecard contributions. Table 3 shows each one of the indicators with the information extracted through surveys directed to the experimented personal in the sterilization area.

Table 2. Linguistic rules from quality internal process.

Hygiene measures	Biosafety tools	Effectiveness machine	Quality internal process
Fairly important	Inappropriate	Moderately required	Bad
Very important	Inappropriate	Moderately required	Bad
Less important	Totally suitable	Moderately required	Regular

Table 3. Application of fuzzy method to indicators.

Perspectives	Indicator	Value
Budget area sterilization	Inventory to acquire new material	60.50%
	Preventive maintenance	68.40%
Customer satisfaction	Accident cases	50.00%
	Hygiene measures	94.70%
Quality processes	Biosafety tools	48.80%
	Effectiveness machine	55.70%
Training of staff	Training	36.80%

6 Results

As a result of this study by using Mamdami type, we have that *management level* variable with a percentage of 59.30%, which represents a qualitative value *medium*. The result obtained from the analysis of the four perspectives: Budget, Internal Customer Satisfaction, Quality of Internal Processes and Staff Training; giving as resulted 54.40% in Financial Perspective; 49.60% in satisfaction perspective Internal client; 71.30% in perspective internal processes, and 46.90% in perspective learning and growth (See Table 4).

Table 4. Results of the indicators' management.

Perspectives	Value
Budget area sterilization	54.40%
Customer satisfaction	49.60%
Quality processes	71.30%
Training of staff	46.90%

We can see from all perspectives; training and learning perspective has the least percentage of evidence, this implies that this perspective causes greater uncertainty in the staff working at the sterilization plant of HUG, which could verify the validity of application BSC with FL.

The development of this study resulted in a data valorization that was obtained through the application of FL and BSC, which led for getting the precise percentage of the management level carried out by sterilization plant in public hospitals in Guayaquil city. As far as fuzzy logic could be established that its application led to fade any uncertainty existing in the persons working in that area on possible contamination in surgical instruments after the sterilization process, these results were obtained through surveys aimed at experts in such area, determining which variables can be influenced in the key indicators.

The fuzzy system for the analysis of the variables was developed using Matlab. This tool provides various prototypes of reasoning, depending on the input linguistic models, the mechanisms of inference and knowledge bases, where the variables that compose the fuzzy sets are established, fuzzy rules are created and provide a set of diffusion and de-diffusion methods. Figure 7 shows part of fuzzy set rules type If-then defined in the fuzzy system. In this work, 81 rules of this type were defined, and Mamdani type system was chosen for analysis.

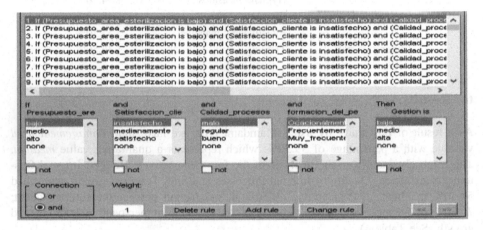

Fig. 7. Fuzzy rules defined in Matlab.

Figure 8 depicts the different values that take the output variable, management level value, from fuzzy inference system; method was chosen in de-diffusion to determine the most representative value of this variable is the centroid or center of mass, resulting from the values determined to the input variables to the system.

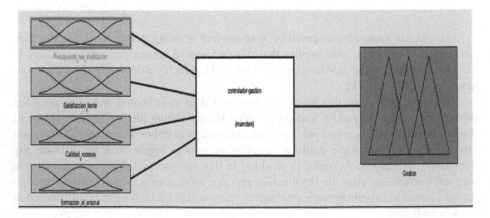

Fig. 8. Fuzzy system proposed in Matlab.

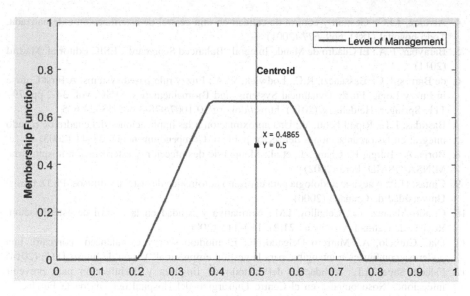

Fig. 9. Output variable - management level.

7 Conclusions

Based on the evaluation of the sterilization processes of the surgical instruments, a fuzzy balanced Scorecard was obtained allowing to visualize the behavior of the fuzzy controllers of each stage of BSC obtaining, as a result, membership functions.

The Balanced Scorecard and fuzzy Logic together are tools that allow creating an uncertainty model, allowing to analyze the execution of strategies of the processes that are valuable for organization managers.

The data extraction was carried out through surveys directed to experts, with the aim of obtaining linguistic variables of qualitative type, and thus to be able to relate them with the input variables that are part of this study, to achieve reducing complex situations that are subject to uncertainties, in many cases ambiguous, which usually arise in areas of public health.

We have noted the BSC not only focuses on a single perspective however it depends on the performance of the rest of perspectives, as they directly influence to achieve a common goal (Fig. 9).

References

1. Acosta-Gnass, S.I.: Manual de esterilización para centros de salud. Pan American Health Org. (2008)
2. Aguado, C.G.: Estudio de la sensibilidad de las funciones de pertenencia, en problemas de optimizacion con restricciones imprecisas. Ph.D. thesis, Universidad de Granada (1990)
3. Aguiar, B.C., Soares, E., da Silva, A.C.: Evolución de la central de material y esterilizacion: historia, actualidad y perspectivas de la enfermerÍa. Enfermería Glob. **8**(1) (2009)

4. Álvarez, J.J.C.: Gestion y control de calidad en una central de esterilización externalizada. Todo hospital (181), 669–677 (2001)
5. Baraybar, F.A.: El Cuadro de Mando Integral "Balanced Scorecard". ESIC Editorial, Madrid (2011)
6. de Barros, L.C., Bassanezi, R.C., Lodwick, W.A.: Fuzzy rule-based systems. A First Course in Fuzzy Logic, Fuzzy Dynamical Systems, and Biomathematics. SFSC, vol. 347, pp. 79–111. Springer, Heidelberg (2017). https://doi.org/10.1007/978-3-662-53324-6_5
7. Bastidas, E.L., Ripoll Feliu, V.: Una aproximación a las implicaciones del cuadro de mando integral en las organizaciones del sector público. Compendium 6(11), 23–41 (2003)
8. Borja, A., Burga, P., Chang, J., et al.: Manual de desinfección y esterilización hospitalaria. MINSA-USAID, Perú (2002)
9. Cintas, H.P.: Nueva metodología para el diseño automático de sistemas difusos. Ph.D. thesis, Universidad de Granada (2000)
10. Criado-Álvarez, J.J., Ceballos, I.M.: Normativa y calidad en la central de esterilizacion. Revista de Calidad Asistencial 21(2), 110–115 (2006)
11. Díaz Curbelo, A., Marrero Delgado, F.: El modelo scor y el balanced scorecard: una poderosa combinación intangible para la gestión empresarial. Visión de futuro 18(1) (2014)
12. Falcon Supe, A.L.: Validación del método de limpieza y desinfección para prevenir infecciones Nosocomiales en el Centro Quirúrgico del Hospital del Día de la Fundación Internacional Buen Samaritano Paul Martel. B.S. thesis, Escuela Superior Politécnica de Chimborazo (2015)
13. Fernández, A.: El balanced scorecard. Revista de antiguos alumnos del IESE 81(2001)
14. Gaona, C., Humercinda, E.: Técnica de preparación de instrumental a esterilizar. B.S. thesis (2009)
15. Gómez, M., Bosque, J.: Aplicación de análisis de incertidumbre como método de validacion y control del riesgo en la toma de decisiones. GeoFocus. Revista Internacional de Ciencia y Tecnología de la Información Geográfica (4), 179–208 (2004)
16. Jang, J.S.R., Sun, C.T., Mizutani, E.: Neuro-fuzzy and soft computing; a computational approach to learning and machine intelligence (1997)
17. Kaplan, R.S., Norton, D.P.: Linking the balanced scorecard to strategy. Calif. Manag. Rev. 39(1), 53–79 (1996)
18. Kaplan, R.S., Robert, N.P.D.K.S., Davenport, T.H., Kaplan, R.S., Norton, D.P.: The Strategy-Focused Organization: How Balanced Scorecard Companies Thrive in the New Business Environment. Harvard Business Press, Boston (2001)
19. Larrea Noroña, J.J.: Plan estratégico con Balanced Scorecard para el Hospital del IESS de Latacunga. B.S. thesis, LATACUNGA/ESPE/2008 (2008)
20. Lazzari, L., Machado, E., Pérez, R.: Los conjuntos borrosos: una introducción. Cuadernos del CIMBAGE (2) (2012)
21. López Rodríguez, S.G.: Calidad y seguridad en los procesos de esterilización. Ph.D. thesis, Universidad Autónoma de Nuevo León (2010)
22. Luzardo Silveira, E.M., Mendoza, D.G., González Castilla, R., Adames Isalgue, S.: Efectividad de la cirugía mínimamente invasiva en un hospital universitario de Santiago de Cuba. MediSan 17(11), 7079–7085 (2013)
23. Mamdani, E.H., Assilian, S.: An experiment in linguistic synthesis with a fuzzy logic controller. Int. J. Man-Mach. Stud. 7(1), 1–13 (1975)
24. Méndez Hernandez, M.: Algunos aspectos relacionados con los riesgos en una central de esterilización. Revista Cubana de Enfermería 20(1), 1 (2004)
25. Moreno Velo, F.J.: Un entorno de desarrollo para sistemas de inferencia complejos basados en logica difusa (2013)

26. Muley Montesinos, M.: Seguridad del paciente en el bloque quirúrgico. Una perspectiva enfermera (2013)
27. Nogueira Rivera, D., Medina León, A., Hernández Pérez, G., Nogueira Rivera, C., Hernandez Nariño, A.: Control de gestión y cuadro de mando integral: énfasis en la perspectiva financiera-aplicación en una empresa de servicios de informática. Revista de Administração-RAUSP **44**(3) (2009)
28. Pacheco, J.C., Castañeda, W., Caicedo, C.H.: Indicadores integrales de gestión, Bogot (2002)
29. Paredes Maldonado, M.F.: Análisis de la eficacia de los procesos de desinfección y esterilización del instrumental quirúrgico en el servicio de central de esterilización del Hospital Alfredo Noboa Montenegro de la Ciudad de Guaranda de marzo–mayo 2012. B.S. thesis, Uniandes (2012)
30. Pérez, R.A.M.: Sistemas de inferencia basados en lógica borrosa: Fundamentos y caso de estudio. Revista de investigación de Sistemas e Informática **7**(1), 91–104 (2010)
31. Piñero, P.Y., Arco, L., García, M.M., Acevedo, L.: Algoritmos genéticos en la construccion de funciones de pertenencia borrosas. Inteligencia Artificial. Revista Iberoamericana de Inteligencia Artificial **7**(18) (2003)
32. Rios Giraldo, R.M.: Seguimiento, medición, análisis y mejora en los sistemas de gestion: enfoque bajo indicadores de gestión y balanced scorecard. Bogotá: Icontec 47–96 (2010)
33. Saldaña, R., Fernando, J., García Flores, R.: Toma de decisiones mediante técnicas de razonamiento incierto. Ingenierías **8**(28), 32–42 (2005)
34. Soto Medellín, J.S.: Sistema de control difuso para unidades de cuidado intensivo (UCI). B. S. thesis (2014)
35. Toledo, C., Elizabeth, J.: Procesos de preparación, almacenamiento y distribución del material quirúrgico para garantizar la esterilidad en el servicio de central de esterilización del Hospital del Instituto Ecuatoriano de Seguridad Social Santo Domingo de Los Tsachilas. Master's thesis (2016)
36. Vazquez, F., Gibert, K.: Generación automática de reglas difusas en dominios poco estructurados con variables numéricas (2001)
37. Zadeh, L.A.: Fuzzy sets. Inf. Control **8**(3), 338–353 (1965). https://doi.org/10.1016/S0019-9958(65)90241-X. http://www.sciencedirect.com/science/article/pii/S001999586590241X

An Approach to the Detection of Post-seismic Structural Damage Based on Image Segmentation Methods

Lorenzo J. Cevallos-Torres[1(✉)], Diana Minda Gilces[1],
Alfonso Guijarro-Rodriguez[1], Ronald Barriga-Diaz[1],
Maikel Leyva-Vazquez[1], and Miguel Botto-Tobar[1,2]

[1] Universidad de Guayaquil, Guayaquil, Ecuador
{lorenzo.cevallost,diana.mindag,alfonso.guijarror,
ronald.barrigad,maikel.leyvav,
miguel.bottot}@ug.edu.ec
[2] Eindhoven University of Technology, Eindhoven, The Netherlands
m.a.botto.tobar@tue.nl

Abstract. Crack detection is critical in ensuring basic structural security, however manual identification of cracks is time-consuming and is subject to the judgments of reviewers. This research presents a crack detection technique based on image processing. The digital image processing is divided into different phases and each of them follow techniques that improve the quality of the images. In the segmentation phase, images traits need to be highlighted. This document portrays the image segmentation of a set of digital photographs of cracks and crevices of the different structures of the buildings of the faculties of the University of Guayaquil. In this study, a function is developed using the computational tool, Matlab, to obtain results by submitting the images to the different segmentation techniques applied during the investigation, for which methods are proposed such as: The Canny transform, The Sobel Operator and the Prewitt Transform. With the obtained results, crack measurement is applied based on the manual selection of pixels in order to generate damage assessment.

Keywords: Image segmentation · Image processing · Cracks · Fissures
Earthquake

1 Introduction

Every now and then telluric events of different magnitudes take place around the world, causing minor or severe damage to the structures of buildings. Over time, several forms, methodologies and procedures have appeared to approach the reconstruction of these structures and respond satisfactorily in the presence of possible future seismic events [1–3].

Among the different issues that this kind of natural phenomenon can cause there exists: presence of cracks, crevices or the complete collapse of the building. For this reason, damages originated in the structures are considered one of the main problems that a building can suffer; this is due to the great impact that an earthquake has worldwide.

© Springer Nature Switzerland AG 2019
M. Botto-Tobar et al. (Eds.): CITT 2018, CCIS 895, pp. 644–658, 2019.
https://doi.org/10.1007/978-3-030-05532-5_49

This research aims to contribute to the knowledge and evaluation of the damages caused by the magnitude 7.8 earthquake that occurred in the coastal zone of Ecuador, in terms of loss of life, housing and especially the structural damage suffered by the different buildings of the University of Guayaquil (UG). The results arise from the integration of information sources of different nature and are presented in disaggregated form with the purpose of complementing existing information as a support to the decision making for the experts [6–9]. It is important to note that this type of records are useful to identify the vulnerabilities of the buildings and the degree of risk that they represent to the human resource who work in the educational institution (authorities, administrative personnel, service personnel, teachers and students), to efficiently plan the use of contingency measures in the advent of this type of natural phenomenon [6, 10, 11].

The purpose of this document is to study the seismic vulnerability of the buildings of the UG through image segmentation; a technique that has managed to characterize a series of problems caused by natural phenomena. This paper, as well as it related work, has allowed the study of the different segmentation techniques which provide mea-surable results to enhance decision making. Among the techniques to be tested, the following are proposed: Prewitt Operator, Sobel Operator, Canny Edge Detection, Mean Filter, and the Gaussian filter.

Based on the foregoing, a curve of maximum accelerations is identified for the earthquake under study and then compared to a curve resulting from the prediction of 13 attenuation curves with respect to distance. The attenuation laws which are closer to the recorded accelerations are identified, as well as the most conservative curves, the relative error and the ranges in which they are more efficient. To fulfill the project's objective, a study of the image segmentation techniques is carried out through the use of the MATLAB tool as a computer support for decision making.

2   General Earthquake Information

2.1   Seismic History of the Region

The 2016 Ecuador earthquake was a seismic movement that occurred at 6:58 p.m. PT on April 16, 2016, with the epicenter between the Pedernales and Cojimíes parishes of the Pedernales district, in the Ecuadorian province of Manabí. With a magnitude of 7.8. Mw, it constitutes the strongest earthquake felt in the country. The most affected areas are the provinces of Manabí, Esmeraldas, Santa Elena, Guayas, Santo Domingo and Los Ríos, which were declared by the Government in an "emergency state". The most affected province was Manabí; one of its cantons, Pedernales (55,000 inhabitants), has been declared a "disaster zone", with limited access.

An earthquake is considered by experts as a shaking of the ground that occurs due to the collision of tectonic plates and the release of energy in the course of a sudden reorganization of materials of the earth's crust to overcome the state of mechanical equilibrium [1], these have a place of underground origin called hypocenter which is that zone to the interior of the Earth where the fracture or rupture of the rocks begins, those that propagate by means of seismic waves (Table 1).

Table 1. Types of seismic waves

Seismic wave type	Description
Longitudinal or Primary waves	First to arrive at seismic stations. Vibrate a particle in the longitudinal direction, which means that they stress the soil through alternate expansion and compression in the direction of the wave propagation. Their velocity of propagation is between 8 and 13 km/s. and are characterized by traveling through liquid bodies as solids
Secondary waves	Recorded by measuring instruments in second place, their propagation speed goes from 4 km/s to 8 km/s. These waves differ from primaries in that they only travel through solid bodies
Surface waves	They spread from the epicenter to 3.5 km/s in the form of waves similar to those generated on the surface of the sea

In Fig. 1 it is possible to observe that, the trajectory described by the particles in the medium as the wave propagates is retrograde elliptical and occurs in the propagation plane of the wave. An analogy to these waves are those which occur on the surface of water.

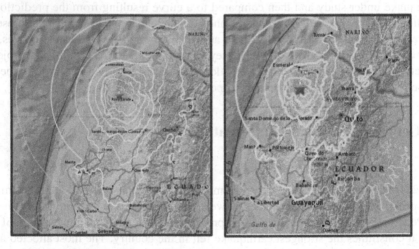

Fig. 1. Graph representing the trajectory that particles in the medium describe when the wave propagates.

Currently, an earthquake can be measured according to its magnitude and intensity. The magnitude is the term used to refer to the power of the earthquake and is expressed in the Richter seismological scale which is an arbitrary logarithmic scale that assigns a number to quantify the energy released in an earthquake, as shown in the Table 2. The effects of the earthquake are classified according to the magnitude of the earthquake.

Table 2. Magnitudes on the Richter scale

Magnitude	Earthquake effects
Less than 3.5	Generally not felt, but registered
3.5–5.4	Usually felt, but only causes minor damage
5.5–6.0	Causes light damage to buildings
6.1–6.9	Can cause severe damage in heavily populated areas
7.0–7.9	Major earthquake: causes serious damage
8 or higher	Great earthquake: completely destroys nearby populations

2.2 Rapid Damage Assessment and General Building Characteristics

The assessment of structural damage is an essential part of the recovery process. Expert staff, such as engineers and architects, must examine all the buildings within the affected area to assess damage, safety and usability. They also need to identify buildings that require emergency strengthening to provide reliable data to the authorities, and plan new relief, rehabilitation and safety measures.

As a consequence of the seismic crisis in Ecuador, which began on April 16, 2016 with an earthquake of 7.8 Mw, the National Secretariat of Higher Education, Science, Technology and Innovation (SENESCYT), together with the risk management secretariat, reported that After the examination of 59 universities, there is one in Ecuador that has had medium impact: the "Eloy Alfaro de Manabí" Lay University (ULEAM) and two low impact: the Technical University of Manabí and the Luis Vargas University Torres de Esmeraldas, these institutions of higher education present affectations in their facilities, it is worth noting that the University of Guayaquil, some of their buildings have cracks in the walls of their faculties.

The intensity is directly related to the visible effects left by the earthquake and to express it we use the Modified Mercalli Intensity Scale which is a scale of 12 points, written in Roman numerals, developed to assess the intensity of earthquakes through of the effects and damages caused to different structures as described in Table 3.

Table 3. Modified Mercalli intensity scale

Degrees	Description
I Imperceptible	Almost imperceptible to people
II Scarcely felt	Felt only by some people at rest, particularly those located on the upper floors of buildings. Objects tend to oscillate
III Weak	Felt by some people inside buildings, especially on high floors. Many do not recognize it as an earthquake. Stopped cars move slightly; the sensation is similar to the passing of a small truck
IV Largely observed	Felt by most people inside buildings, but by few people outdoors during the day. Disturbance in ceramics, doors and windows may awake some people during the night. Walls make noise. Detained cars move with more energy. The sensation is similar to the passing of a large truck

(continued)

Table 3. (*continued*)

Degrees	Description
V Strong	Shaking felt by everyone and some pieces of crockery or glass windows break; few cases of flattening cracking; unstable objects fall. Disturbances are observed in trees, poles and other tall objects
VI Slightly damaging	Shaking felt by everyone. Some heavy furniture change their location. The shake causes minor damage, especially in homes made of light materials
VII Damaging	It is difficult for people to stand still. Damaged furniture. Insignificant damage to structures of good design and construction. Light to moderate damage to ordinary, well-built structures. Significant damage to poorly constructed structures. Damaged masonry. Perceived by people in moving vehicles
VIII Heavily damaging	Minor damage to specialized structures. Considerable damage to ordinary, well-built structures. Severe damage to poorly constructed structures. Masonry seriously damaged or destroyed. Furniture completely torn away from its place. Probability of collapses
IX Destructive	Generalized panic. Significant damage to specialized structures and walls outside of lead. Large damages in important buildings, with partial collapses. Buildings displaced outside their bases
X Very destructive	Some well-constructed wooden structures are destroyed. Most masonry structures and frames destroyed with their bases. Bent rails
XI Devastating	Few masonry structures, if any, remain standing. Bridges destroyed. Rails curved to a large extent
XII Completely devastating	Total destruction with few survivors. Objects fly through the air. Levels and perspectives are distorted. It is impossible for people to stand still

3 Digital Images Analysis

The digital analysis of images is composed of five phases, for the purpose of this study the first three stages are selected and are explained below:

The first phase is image acquisition. This phase includes the use of instruments such as digital cameras or scanners which have an image sensor that converts the light beams into electrical pulses that subsequently, depending on the given treatment, will become a digital image.

The next stage is preprocessing. In this phase algorithms dedicated to image adjustment are applied to decrease the noise present in the image and enhance features of interest such as edges.

Following preprocessing is the segmentation phase, considered as one of the most fundamental processes, which aims to divide an image into parts that have a strong correlation with objects or areas of the real world contained in the image [6] this phase is usually used to identify objects or other relevant information in digital images.

3.1 Methodology Development

The process begins with the capture of the image using a camera of 18.1 MP controlled manually by a person, which will have to take into account the following rules at the moment of taking the photo:

- The camera must be horizontal. The use of a tripod is recommended.
- The distance of the camera with respect to the anomaly must be given by the full view of a 30 cm ruler arranged vertically.
- The image should not be overexposed or very bleak. The values of the histogram should be centered within the range 0.52–0.70.
- Seek a uniform illumination of the area to photograph, to avoid the use of flash, depending on the surface, it may act as a mirror reflecting much of the light emitted by the camera back to the goal. The pictures stored on the camera's SD memory are transferred to the computer which requires the Matlab program installed and the function developed in this research preloaded.
- The FisuCrackMeter function in its first lines of code verifies the installation of the toolbox that is dedicated to the analysis of images. due to the fact that part of the functions used in the present investigation are associated with it, then we proceed to specify the Directory automatically taking into account the location of the function FisuCrackMeter, once that task the following code instruction set will allow the user to display a pop-up window where you must choose the captured image.
- The first box that will be displayed is the representation of the original photograph, the second will contain the histogram of the picture so the original image was converted to HSV color space **(Hue = Hue   Saturation = Saturation Value = Brightness)** using the rgb2hsv function, the resulting conversion was it stored in a variable called "" which was obtained the values of channel 3 equivalent to lighting to then be used as a parameter in the function histogram() which will show the histogram generated by the obtained values.

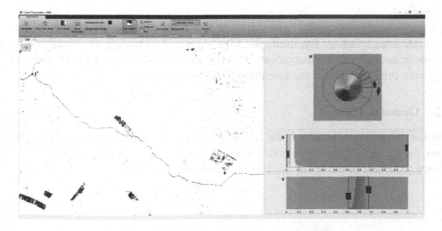

Fig. 2. GUI color threshold (Color figure online)

- In the next step a pre-installed Matlab app named color threshold is used. This app allows the identification of the range of values with the greatest number of pixels. To suit the development of this research, the focus is set on the lighting in the HSV color space. A series of 12 photographs of fissures and cracks were under observation in order to reach the conclusion of defining the range of 0.52–0.70. A pattern in their lighting histogram was found, which directly responds to the recommendations mentioned earlier in this document, at the moment of the capture (Fig. 2).

4 Image Pre-processing Techniques

4.1 Mean Filter

The operation of the median filter lies in inspecting each of the pixels for which the image is formed and replace it with the average of neighboring pixels. It can be implemented to perform anti-aliasing image since it is considered one of simpler filters. Easy and intuitive, it can operate using convolution through a mask determined support the reduction of variations in intensity between the neighboring pixels (Fig. 3).

Code	Result
BinaryImage = imbinarize(equalImage, *'adaptive'*, *'Foreground-Polarity'*, *'dark'*, *'Sensi tivity'*, 0.0001); FilteredImage = imfilter (BinaryImage, fspecial (*'average'*)); imshow(BinaryImage);	

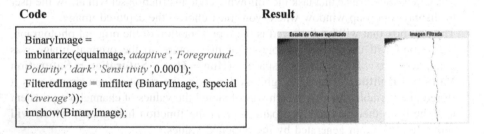

Fig. 3. Mean filter

Analysis

Change is barely noticeable, however using this filter allows noise reduction through moderate image fading. By itself, the filter does not constitute an advantage to the improvement of rift segmentation; nevertheless accompanied by other filters, it improves the definition of the line prior to the segmentation.

4.2 Gaussian Filter

The Gaussian filter is similar to the mean filter, the difference is that is uses a different mask for its application, its objective is to reduce the distortion of an image. This filter allows reduction of the noise level of an input signal (Fig. 4).

Code

Result

```
BinaryImage =
imbinarize(equalImage,'adaptive','Foreground-
Polarity','dark','Sensi tivity',0.0001);
FilteredImage = imfilter (BinaryImage, fspecial
('gaussian'));
imshow(BinaryImage);
```

Fig. 4. Gaussian filter

Analysis

The Gaussian filter in the preprocessing phase aims to enhance the horizontal lines in the image, in the N graphic. It is possible to observe the slight improvement of the line reflected in a small increase in its extension, keeping the direction and thickness of the original image. The presence of this feature is very important especially when analyzing images containing fissures in the horizontal direction, resulting in a more refined image segmentation phase.

4.3   Median Filter

This filter is used when you have an image with a random noise, applying this filter aims to standardize the pixels that have different intensities within a neighborhood of pixels. The median filter allows the assignment of the median value to each point in the image. This is, it generates a new image, in which pixels have been generated after the median calculation of the total set of pixels that compose the original image.

Code

Result

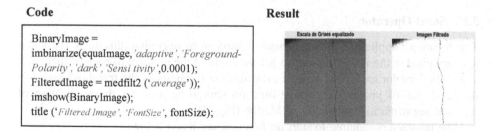

```
BinaryImage =
imbinarize(equalImage,'adaptive','Foreground-
Polarity','dark','Sensi tivity',0.0001);
FilteredImage = medfilt2 ('average'));
imshow(BinaryImage);
title ('Filtered Image','FontSize', fontSize);
```

Fig. 5. Median filter

Analysis

As seen in Fig. 5, at a first glance the variation is hard to detect. However the application of this filter, significantly improves the union of pixels that form a line which translates into a better input for the segmentation process of segmenting avoiding dashed lines.

5 Image Segmentation Techniques

Digital Image Processing, features techniques which facilitate the identification of patterns that help improve the quality of the images among them are those considered in points 4.1, 4.2 and 4.3. Prior to the application of these techniques, a binary mask should be generated to highlight anomalies present in the wall. To do so, a range of values was established based on the image lighting in the histograms; the range covers values from 0.520 to 0.700. These values were established based on the pattern of the histogram of 15 different images captured on the premises of the Faculty of Mathematics and Physical Sciences at the University of Guayaquil (UG) (Fig. 6).

Code   Result

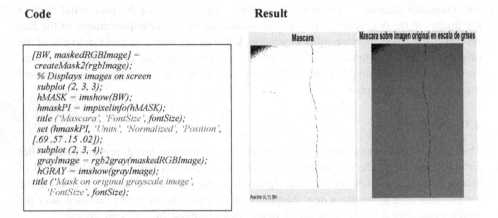

```
[BW, maskedRGBImage] =
  createMask2(rgbImage);
  % Displays images on screen
  subplot (2, 3, 3);
  hMASK = imshow(BW);
  hmaskPI = impixelinfo(hMASK);
  title ('Mascara', 'FontSize', fontSize);
  set (hmaskPI, 'Units', 'Normalized', 'Position',
  [.69 .57 .15 .02]);
  subplot (2, 3, 4);
  grayImage = rgb2gray(maskedRGBImage);
  hGRAY = imshow(grayImage);
title ('Mask on original grayscale image',
  'FontSize', fontSize);
```

Fig. 6. Mask generated based on values established for the thresholding

5.1 Sobel Operator

This technique applies a 3 × 3 dimensional mask in its operation; this mask is applied to every pixel in the image in order to get the value of the gradient of each of them, the value obtained for each pixel will be evaluated on the basis of the threshold preset to the in service of process. The Edge function should be used for the application of different segmentation techniques in Matlab (Fig. 7).

The parameters required to start up function are listed below:

1. The first parameter is dedicated to the entrance of the variable that stores the image in grayscale.
2. The second parameter allows the user to specify through a string type variable the technique to apply for the image segmentation, in this case should the word 'sobel' should be input.
3. The third parameter is optional; it allows the user to specify the threshold for the chosen technique. Edges with a lower value than the minimum value set in the threshold are ignored.

Code   Result

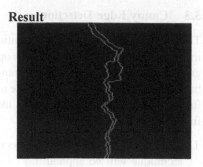

```
imagen1 = bwmorph (imagenFiltrada,
'remove',100);
  Edge1f = bwmorph (imagen1, 'clean');
  Edge1f=edge (Edge1f,'Sobel', 0.25);
imshow(Edge1f);
```

Fig. 7. Segmentation using the Sobel operator

5.2 Prewitt Transform

This technique works similarly to the Sobel technique with the difference that the coefficients in this technique does not focus on pixels that are found near the center of the mask. It is characterized by having a better detection of horizontal and vertical edges. The edge function should be used to apply this technique. The parameters used to start up function are (Fig. 8):

1. The first parameter is dedicated to input of the variable that stores the image's grayscale.
2. The second parameter allows the user to specify through a string variable the technique to apply for the segmentation of the image in this case the word 'prewitt' should be typed.
3. The third parameter is optional; it allows the user to specify the threshold for the chosen technique. Edges with a lower value than the minimum value set in the threshold are ignored.

Code   Result

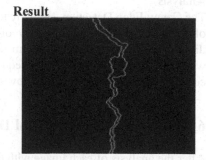

```
imagen1 = bwmorph (imagenFiltrada,
'remove',100);
  Edge1f = bwmorph (imagen1, 'clean');
  Edge1f=edge (Edge1f,'Prewitt', 0.25);
```

Fig. 8. Segmentation using Prewitt transform

Analysis

Although the result at first sight may seem very similar; when zooming in to a specific area of the image, it is easy to detect dashed lines on outgoing edges of the corners, altering the original morphology of the fissure, thus avoiding later correct measurement.

5.3   Canny Edge Detection

This works by applying a convolution using a Gaussian Filter aiming to soften the image, on the result of the previous operation is undone - identify pixels where there is greater variation product of the transition from pixels belonging to an object on a background, as final step is a double moral standards to eliminate false edges. The edge function should be used to apply this technique. The parameters to use to start up function are (Fig. 9):

1. The first parameter is used to specify the variable that stores the images in which the technique will be applied.
2. The second parameter allows the user to specify through a string variable the technique to apply for the segmentation of the image in this case the word 'canny' should be typed.

Code   **Result**

```
imagen1 = bwmorph (imagenFiltrada,
'remove',100);
   Edge1f = bwmorph (imagen1, 'clean');
   Edge1f=edge (Edge1f, 'Canny', 0.25);
```

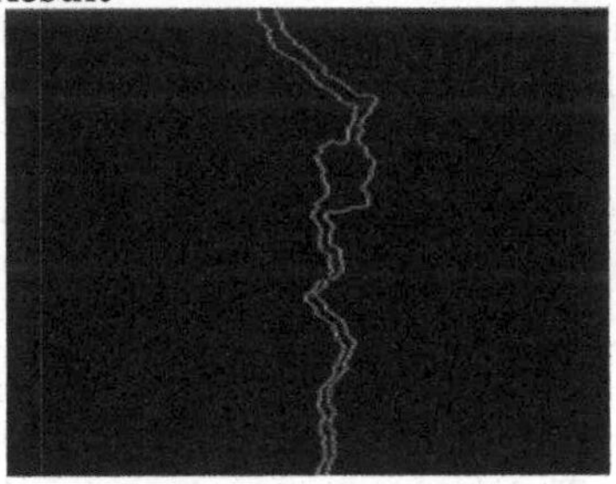

Fig. 9. Segmentation through Canny Edge detection

Analysis

The Canny Edge Detection, similarly to the Sobel Transform, generates a segmentation of great quality by the continuity of the lines marked on the edge with the only difference that the Canny transform delimits the edge with a distance I knew-inside which generates Sobel in tr subsequent attachments leads to the disappearance of certain regions of the rift for the low accuracy of the location of the edge.

6   Results of the Structural Damage Level

After the analysis of each image with each algorithm applied to it, the level of damage that the structure has undergone is identified. Depending on whether the structure presents a fissure or a crack, the level damage is determined based on Table 4, which describes the evaluation of post-seismic structural damage in buildings.

Table 4. Damage level – in between floors

Damage level	Observations
None/Very slight	Certain cracks of width lower than 0.2 mm, almost imperceptible on the surface
Minor	Cracking perceptible to the naked eye, with widths between 0.2 mm and 1.0 mm above the surface
Moderate	Cracks with widths between 1.0 and 2.0 mm on the surface, incipient loss of the coating
Strong	Significant cracking, loss of the coating on the surface
Severe	Degradation and crushing of material, severe cracking

Code:

```
function assessment = masonry (distance)
     if distance < 0.2
            assessment = ' Very Light';
     else if distance >= 0.2 && distance < 1.0
            assessment = 'Leve';
     else if distance > 1.0 && distance < 3.0
            assessment = ' strong';
        else
           assessment = 'Severe';
        end
     end
   end.
```

Data for the evaluation are as follows:
< 0.2 = Very Slight
>= 0.2 = Minor
> 1.0 y < 3.0 = Strong
> 3.0 = Severe

```
function assessment = tapia(distance)
     if distance < 0.4
            assessment = ' Very Light';
     else if distance >= 0.4 && distance < 2.0
            assessment = 'Leve';
      else if distance >= 2.0 && distance < 4.0
            assessment = ' strong';
        else
           assessment = 'Severe';
        end
     end
   end.
```

```
function assessment = mezzanines (distance)
     if distance < 0.2
            assessment = ' Very Light';
     else if distance >= 0.2 && distance < 1.0
            assessment = 'Leve';
      else if distance >= 1.0 && distance < 2.0
            assessment = ' strong';
        else
           assessment = 'Severe';
        end, end, end.
```

Once the code is executed and the image to be processed is selected, the last step is to select the area for the respective assessment as described below:

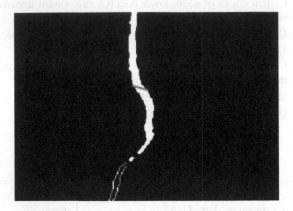

Fig. 10. Selection of affected area for assessment

Once the area has been selected and the type of material is chosen, it is possible to visualize the crack distance, as well as its equivalence in pixels and finally the evaluation of the structure, as shown in the Fig. 10, according to the results of the Table 5.

Table 5. Assesment of affected area

Tipe	Result
Material	Mansory
Distance	1.5 mm
Equivalence	20.8 pixeles
Valuation	Strong

7   Conclusions

The use of image segmentation techniques, as a tool for decision-making, will serve as a support to the work made by experts in this case, civil engineers. However, this digital image analysis, is also very useful for those who wish to know the status of the different buildings, through evaluation of the digital measurement of the fissures or cracks.

Having compared the different segmentation techniques applied in this research which were: Sobel Operator, Canny Edge Detection and the Prewitt Transform, allowed us to conclude based on results, the technique that provided the best assessment is the Canny Edge Detection, since its application in MATLAB, allowed us to present a better performance when connecting the pixels that form part of the cracks and crevices, this aids at the time of applying the function to fill enclosed areas, enhancing in a much better way the line formed by the crevice and the fissure.

MATLAB is a very versatile tool that helps the segmentation process of through the application of different techniques or methods of image segmentation such as: watershed transform, canny edge detection, sobel operator, k-means and top-hat. This is the reason we used this tool since its versatility helped to achieve the expected results for each of the techniques described during the investigation.

References

1. Blanco, M.: Criterios fundamentales para el diseño sismorresistente. Revista de la Facultad de Ingeniería Universidad Central de Venezuela **27**(3), 071–084 (2012)
2. Cevallos-Torres, L.J., et al.: Evaluation of vulnerability and seismic risk parameters through a fuzzy logic approach. In: Valencia-García, R., Lagos-Ortiz, K., Alcaraz-Mármol, G., Del Cioppo, J., Vera-Lucio, N., Bucaram-Leverone, M. (eds.) International Conference on Technologies and Innovation. CCIS, vol. 749, pp. 113–130. Springer, Cham (2017). https://doi.org/10.1007/978-3-319-67283-0_9
3. Soto, A.D.G., et al.: Estimación del peligro sísmico debido a sismos interplaca e inslab y sus implicaciones en el diseño sísmico. Ingeniería sísmica **86**, 27–54 (2012)
4. Gómez-Martínez, F., et al.: Comportamiento de los edificios de HA con tabiquería durante el sismo de Lorca de 2011: Aplicación del método FAST. In: Informes de la Construcción, vol. 67, no. 537, pp. 1–14 [e065] (2015). https://doi.org/10.3989/ic.12.110
5. Barbat, A.H., et al.: Evaluación probabilista del riesgo sísmico de estructuras con base en la degradación de rigidez. Revista Internacional de Métodos Numéricos para calculo y diseño en Ingeniería **32**(1), 39–47 (2016)
6. Cardona, O.D.: La necesidad de repensar de manera holística los conceptos de vulnerabilidad y riesgo (2002)
7. Cárdenas, P., Aníbal, H.: Desarrollos metodológicos y aplicaciones hacia el cálculo de la peligrosidad sísmica en el Ecuador Continental y estudio de riesgo sísmico en la ciudad de Quito (2016)
8. Moncayo Theurer, M.: Terremotos mayores a 6.5 en escala Richter ocurridos en Ecuador desde 1900 hasta 1970. Ingeniería Revista Académica de la Facultad de Ingeniería Universidad Autónoma de Yucatán **21**(2), 55–64 (2017)
9. Moncayo Theurer, M., et al.: Análisis sobre la recurrencia de terremotos severos en Ecuador. Prisma Tecnológico **8**(1), 12–17 (2017)
10. Bonachea Pico, J.: Desarrollo, aplicación y validación de procedimientos y modelos para la evaluación de amenazas, vulnerabilidad y riesgo debidos a procesos geomorfológicos. Universidad de Cantabria (2006)
11. Zobin, V.M., Ventura Ramírez, J.F.: Vulnerabilidad sísmica de edificios residenciales y pronóstico de daños en caso de sismos fuertes en la ciudad de Colima. Geos **19**(3), 152–158 (1999)
12. Caicedo Caicedo, C., et al.: Vulnerabilidad sísmica de edificios. Centre Internacional de Mètodes Numèrics en Enginyeria (CIMNE) (1994)
13. Herrera, D.M., Rincón, M., Sarria, H.: Un refinamiento del método de canny usando multirresolución. Boletín de Matemáticas **15**(2), 92 (2008)
14. Falconí, R.A., García, E., Villamarín, J.: Leyes de atenuación para sismos corticales y de subducción para el Ecuador. Revista **13**(1), 1–18 (2010)
15. Bak, P., Tang, C.: Earthquakes as a self-organized critical phenomenon. J. Geophys. Res.: Solid Earth **94**(B11), 15635–15637 (1989)

16. Hancock, J., Bommer, J.J.: A state-of-knowledge review of the influence of strong-motion duration on structural damage. Earthq. Spectra **22**(3), 827–845 (2006)
17. Doocy, S., et al.: The human impact of earthquakes: a historical review of events 1980-2009 and systematic literature review. PLoS Currents **5** (2013)
18. Ye, L., et al.: The 16 April 2016, M w 7.8 (M s 7.5) Ecuador earthquake: a quasi-repeat of the 1942 M s 7.5 earthquake and partial re-rupture of the 1906 M s 8.6 Colombia–Ecuador earthquake. Earth Planet. Sci. Lett. **454**, 248–258 (2016)
19. Ellingwood, B.R.: Earthquake risk assessment of building structures. Reliab. Eng. Syst. Saf **74**(3), 251–262 (2001)

Application of Genetic Algorithms in Software Engineering: A Systematic Literature Review

Pablo F. Ordoñez-Ordoñez[1,2](✉) [iD], Milton Quizhpe[1],
Oscar M. Cumbicus-Pineda[1,3] [iD], Valeria Herrera Salazar[1] [iD],
and Roberth Figueroa-Diaz[1] [iD]

[1] Facultad de Energía, CIS, Universidad Nacional de Loja,
Ave. Pío Jaramillo Alvarado, La Argelia, Loja, Ecuador
pfordonez@unl.edu.ec
[2] ETSI Sistemas Informáticos, Universidad Politécnica de Madrid,
Calle Alan Turing s/n, 28031 Madrid, Spain
[3] Departamento de Ciencias de la Computación e Inteligencia Artificial,
Universidad del País Vasco, Leioa, Spain

Abstract. Software engineering was born from the need to establish an adequate and efficient methodology for the development of the software, not using appropriate methods in the software produces a large number of errors, today on Software has evolved drastically and is considered as a discipline that has its own principles and requirements to obtain more structured solutions with planning, development and culmination. The genetic algorithms present an alternative to solve problems of optimization in the software engineering, therefore in this work a systematic literature review (SLR) of the application and technologies was carried out of the genetic algorithms in it. The results are presented based on 127 initial documents which, after passing through a review protocol, were reduced to 20 chords to the research topic, where it was indicated that the greatest application is in the tests of software.

Keywords: Optimization · Software engineering
Genetic algorithms · Genetic programming · Evolutionary algorithms

1 Introduction

Software Engineering is an application of the systematic and disciplined approach to the design, development, operation and maintenance of software [31], the detection of software vulnerabilities is a critical step to ensure the quality and security of the software [28] however, software testing is a time-consuming and costly task, consuming almost 50% of the resources for the development of the system software [27,29]. Automated software testing is better than manual testing, however, very few test data generation tools are currently available commercially [6].

© Springer Nature Switzerland AG 2019
M. Botto-Tobar et al. (Eds.): CITT 2018, CCIS 895, pp. 659–670, 2019.
https://doi.org/10.1007/978-3-030-05532-5_50

Genetic algorithms (GA) are formed from the evolutionary algorithms conceived by John Holland in the United States well known during the late sixties [7], these have been widely used in software engineering as a method of optimization [13]. Consequently, this research focuses on the technology and application of genetic algorithms in the problems of software engineering.

This systematic review is based on the protocol proposed by [16,17,22]: According to the information that exists on the application of genetic algorithms in software engineering, it was targeted: "Specify the most recent research about the applications of genetic algorithms in software engineering" as a guide for this review. Taking into account that in the phases of software development a greater optimization and resources are needed, the following research questions (RQ) have been determined:

- **RQ1:** What problem does the genetic algorithm solve in software engineering?
- **RQ2:** What application and technology do genetic algorithms have in Software Engineering?

In Sect. 2, the SLR is executed, the result of which is described in Table 2. On the basis of these results, Sect. 3 presents the most notable details and the synthesis argued and discussed in the 20 primary studies and Sect. 4 concludes as research questions the consequences of the review, and specific lines of research for the future.

2   Review Protocol Development

2.1   Research Identification

The criterion for the choice of search sources was based on web accessibility and the inclusion of search engines that allow to carry out advanced queries, in this way the following were used: ACM [2], IEEE library [1], SCOPUS Library [11] and RRAAE [23].

For the choice of keywords it was considered: research questions and keywords of previously reviewed articles: optimization, software engineering, genetic algorithms, genetic programming, evolutionary algorithms, requirements and testing.

Searches were performed using logical operators: (AND) and (OR) and the following inclusion criteria were considered for the search:

- Take as relevant current publications since 2012.
- Search results in the area of science and computation.
- Documents in Spanish and English language.
- Search the Abstract of the article for keywords.

The Table 1 correspond to the search chains in the different bibliographic sources.

Table 1. Bibliographic sources and search strings.

Digital library ACM:
(+genetic +algorithms +software +engineering +software +requirements)   (+genetic +algorithms +software +requirements)   (+genetic +algorithms +software +testing)   (+optimization +computer +systems +genetic +algorithms)
Digital library IEEE:
(("Abstract" :software engineering) AND "Abstract" :genetic algorithms))   (("Abstract" :evolutionary algorithms,) AND "Abstract" :software requirements)   (("Abstract" :genetic algorithms) AND "Abstract" :software requirements)
Digital library scopus:
(TITLE-ABS-KEY (optimization software engineering) AND TITLE-ABS-KEY (genetic algorithms)) AND PUBYEAR > 2012 AND (LIMIT-TO (SUBJAREA, "COMP"))   (TITLE-ABS-KEY (genetic algorithms) AND TITLE-ABS-KEY (software requirements) AND TITLE-ABS-KEY (software design)) AND PUBYEAR > 2012 AND PUBYEAR < 2017 AND (LIMIT-TO (SUBJAREA, "COMP")   (TITLE-ABS-KEY (genetic algorithms) AND TITLE-ABS-KEY (web software) OR TITLE-ABS-KEY (software patron)) AND PUBYEAR > 2012 AND (LIMIT-TO (SUB-JAREA, "COMP")   (TITLE-ABS-KEY (genetic algorithms) AND TITLE-ABS-KEY (engineering phase of the software development)) AND PUBYEAR > 2012
Digital library RRAE:
(Todos los Campos:ingenieria de software y Todos los Campos:algoritmos geneticos)   (Todos los Campos:algoritmos geneticos y Todos los Campos:pruebas de software))   ((Todos los Campos:diseño de software y Todos los Campos:algoritmos geneticos))

2.2 Selection of Primary Studies

Once the results were obtained with the searched questions, the criterion that will be followed in the execution of the review for the selection and evaluation of primary studies was described. The results of the search that have not been relevant to the stated objective have been discarded taking into account the following exclusion criteria:

- Studies that do not contain information that helps answer RQ1 and/or RQ2 research questions.
- In the summary and content there is no information about the application of the algorithms in software engineering.
- Work that is poorly structured and unclear.
- The conclusion must have relevant information for the investigation.

2.3 Data Extraction

The Table 2 presents the relevant information for each of the selected articles (S01...S20) according to the search by pointing out elements such as: (RQ1) Problem that genetic algorithms solve in software engineering and (RQ2) Application and technology of genetic algorithms in software engineering.

Table 2. Data extraction from the primary studies.

ID-Ref.	Article	Problem-solution	Application-technology
S01-[32]	Minimizing test suites in software product lines using weight-based genetic algorithms	The redundant test cases in the software production lines	Application of genetic algorithms (gas) based on weight to minimize the set of tests
S02-[8]	Cost-priority cognizant regression testing	The redundant cases in the regression tests	Genetic algorithms have been used to optimize the prioritization of test
S03-[25]	UML modeling of load optimization for distributed computer systems based on genetic algorithm	The allocation of resources in distributed systems	Implementation of the genetic algorithms to optimize the waiting time in the allocation of resources you are in distributed systems
S04-[5]	Improved heuristics for solving OCL constraints using search algorithms	Limitations in UML models	Improve the existing heuristic to solve OCL restrictions. Using search algorithms
S05-[15]	Critical components testing using hybrid genetic algorithm	The critical test components	Optimization based on hybrid genetic algorithms
S06-[20]	Development of a framework for test case prioritization using genetic algorithm	The prioritization of test cases in the maintenance phase	Framework for prioritization of test cases using genetic algorithms
S07-[26]	Random or genetic algorithm search for object-oriented test suite generation	Unit test in object-oriented classes	Genetic algorithm in unit tests
S08-[3]	Minimizing feature model inconsistencies in software product lines	Selection of features for the configuration of a product	Optimization of the process of selection of the characteristics by genetic algorithms
S09-[31]	A dynamic approach for retrieval of software components using genetic algorithm	Software reuse	Recovery through the use of genetic algorithms
S10-[19]	Component-based software system test case prioritization with genetic algorithm decoding technique using Java platform	Regression tests	Software test prioritization framework based on component
S11-[4]	Optimization of soft cost estimation using genetic algorithm for NASA software projects	Cost estimation with COCOMO model	Adjustment of the parameters of the COCOMO coefficients using genetic algorithms

(continued)

Table 2. (*continued*)

ID-Ref.	Article	Problem-solution	Application-technology
S12-[30]	Software quality assurance for object-oriented systems using meta-heuristic search techniques	Quality of software for object-oriented systems	Use of search techniques for software optimization of fault prediction
S13-[14]	A novel approach for test case generation from UML activity diagram	Tests based on models	Application of genetic algorithms for the generation of test cases
S14-[10]	A novel strategy for automatic test data generation using soft computing technique	Generation of automatic test data	AG-based heuristics for automatic generation of test sets
S15-[33]	Prioritization of test scenarios using hybrid genetic algorithm based on UML activity diagram	The scenarios of test cases	Prioritization of test scenarios using hybrid genetic algorithm
S16-[21]	Efficient parallel evolutionary algorithms for deadline-constrained scheduling in project management	Estimation of times in the planning of software development projects	Parallel evolutionary algorithms to solve the problem term of programming with limitations in the management of projects
S17-[12]	Automatic generation of basis test paths using variable length genetic algorithm	Destination route tests	Genetic algorithm for the generation of test trajectories
S18-[24]	Retrieving sequence diagrams using genetic algorithm	Software reuse	Genetic algorithm for the determination of the similarity of the graphic representations of the sequence diagrams
S19-[9]	Methods for cost estimation in software project management	Bad estimation of costs in the management of software projects	Estimation of costs in the management of software projects using genetic algorithms
S20-[18]	Predicting project effort intelligently in early stages by applying genetic algorithms with neural networks	Estimation of effort in the management of software projects	Estimation models for software projects using neural networks and genetic algorithms

2.4   Data Synthesis

Once the primary studies have been determined, it can be observed that in the present review, 127 have been taken into account for the analysis, of which the

primary ones were considered, 20 of which the following synthesis is illustrated
(Table 3):

Table 3. Summary of reviewed studies.

Sources	Studies	Relevants	Selected
ACM	616	27	8
IEEE	245	40	5
SCOPUS	450	60	7
RRAAE	0	0	0
Totals	1311	127	20

In Fig. 1, the incidence of the studies that have been analyzed is shown, in this
table it is shown that only one of them S01 [32] has maintained a very significant
influence and takes as a direct reference for another 13 studies. S15 and S16 show
that the impact that has been obtained has been medium since they have been
taken into account more than 4 times and in the rest of the studies the impact
they have shown has been low since they have only been considered in less than
4 studies and in three cases S08, S09 and S13 the incidence has been null since
they have not been considered for other references.

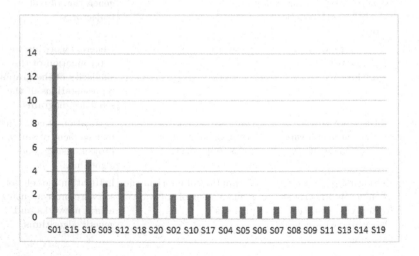

Fig. 1. Synthesis by impact

Figure 2 shows the direct participation of the authors in the different studies
that were analyzed, they are the most prominent, as you can see the authors
have not collaborated in another study different from the one mentioned in each

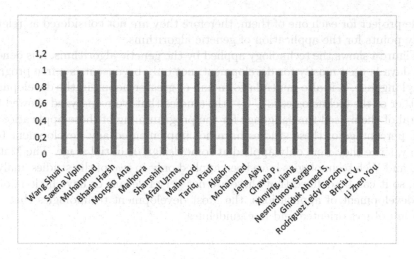

Fig. 2. Synthesis by author.

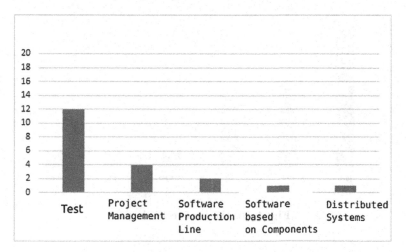

Fig. 3. Synthesis of the AG applications.

one of the sections. Taking into account the results shown, it can be concluded that the topics are related and the results obtained are as desired, so it has not been considered feasible to carry out a second study to corroborate the data obtained in it.

Figure 3 shows clearly that the main application is in the testing phase of a project, and these can be regressive, initial or terminal. It is also shown that these algorithms can be applied in the management of projects, which helps to optimize the overall level of the project as indicated by 4 of the studies, regarding the Production, Distributed Systems and Software Engineering based on components, only the application of these algorithms has been tested in a single project for each one of them, therefore they are not considered as relevant study points for the application of genetic algorithms.

Figure 4 shows the technology applied by the genetic algorithms, it is denoted that Java is used mostly for development, not only because it is a free programming language, it is also multiplatform and of greater boom. in the development. Another of the technologies is C++, the studies that were analyzed showed that several of them used this language for the programming of these applications. A large percentage of these studies have not implemented any development technology, since they were only applied at some design or initial stage. The Matlab, OLC and Web technologies have been applied only in two of the studies analyzed each, so it can be defined that these are not very relevant or have little boom in the development of applications, the Most development technologies that were used are object oriented and free guidelines.

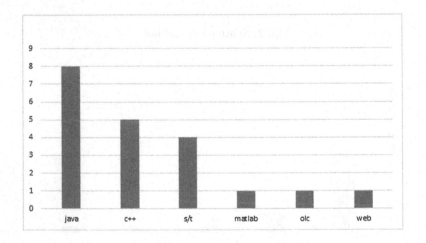

Fig. 4. Synthesis of technology.

3   Discussion

S01 and S08 agree that the test in the Software Product Lines can be minimized appropriately using genetic algorithms since the total number of test cases is reduced, improving its efficiency.

S02, S14 and S17 propose to the Genealogical Algorithms as a solution for the automatic generation of tests, since the software development process invests at least 50% of the total cost in the testing process. software.

S03, S04, S13, S15 and S18 agree that the benefits of software reuse multiply if carried out in the early stages of software development. Sequence diagrams are commonly used to model the functionality of software systems in the early stages of the software development life cycle.

In S05, S06 and S10 they emphasize that the cases of prioritization tests is an essential task that reduces the test effort in the maintenance phase to a considerable degree. These articles propose a framework for the prioritization of test cases using a tool based on a genetic algorithm, developed in the Java language.

S07 and S12 agree that the identification of faults in the very early phase of life cycle software development is very necessary. This helps software developers focus more on quality assurance, use the workforce in the right perspective, and reduce the cost of debugging software development in particular.

S11, S16, S19 and S20 agree that the deadline, limited programming in project management, is a problem of optimization with greater relevance in software engineering and other real-life situations. they are responsible for the planning of the activities that must be completed before the specified dates to resolve the programming period with limitations in the management of projects. The genetic algorithms have been designed to calculate precise solutions in the times of reduced execution.

4   Conclusion and Future Work

Regarding the technology used, it is noted that the highest percentage of studies carried out are based on Java, a programming language for free and object-oriented guidelines, which is used at all levels of programming. n. On the other hand a large number of the works: S04, S13, S115, S18, S19, were still in stages of study and many of these have been made in their development process in UML or in its initial phases.

There are primary studies S02, S03, S06, S07, S10, S12 that are specific and offer a clear answer on the problems that the application of General Algorithms has solved. Likewise, the application of these algorithms allowed the optimization of several of the stages in the development of the Software Engineering, in addition to the technologies in which a software can be executed. Genetic algorithm are not limited or do not show restrictions on those that currently exist. Based on the primary studies S02, S04, S09, S11, S15 analyzed there are several scopes in the application of genetic algorithms in the Software development, most of these are shown in the design and testing stages, which mainly streamlines the control of programming errors and optimizes the time and costs that are generally the stages in the which concentrates most of the effort and budget of a project.

Finally, the applications of genetic algorithms are of greater height according to their timeline, denoting a great use in initial stages or tests, since the results that have been obtained in each of these have clearly shown that in all they have achieved the optimization of processes, which demonstrates the improvement of the cost-time-effort ratio. However, the need for applications in the software life cycle is present, when this process is caused by frameworks and agile methodologies that involve great interaction with the user.

References

1. IEEE Xplore Digital Library. https://ieeexplore.ieee.org/Xplore/home.jsp
2. ACM: The ACM Digital Library. https://www.acm.org/
3. Afzal, U., Mahmood, T., Rauf, I., Shaikh, Z.A.: Minimizing feature model inconsistencies in software product lines. In: Proceedings of the 17th IEEE International Multi-Topic Conference Collaborative and Sustainable Development of Technologies, IEEE INMIC 2014, pp. 137–142 (2015). httpoi//doi.org/10.1109/INMIC.2014.7097326
4. Algabri, M., Saeed, F., Mathkour, H., Tagoug, N.: Optimization of soft cost estimation using genetic algorithm for NASA software projects. In: 2015 5th National Symposium on Information Technology: Towards New Smart World, pp. 1–4 (2015). https://doi.org/10.1109/NSITNSW.2015.7176416, http://ieeexplore.ieee.org/lpdocs/epic03/wrapper.htm?arnumber=7176416
5. Ali, S., Iqbal, M.Z., Arcuri, A.: Improved heuristics for solving OCL constraints using search algorithms. In: 16th Genetic and Evolutionary Computation Conference, GECCO 2014, pp. 1231–1238 (2014). https://doi.org/10.1145/2576768.2598308
6. Alzabidi, M., Kumar, A.: Automatic software structural testing by using evolutionary algorithms for test data generations. J. Comput. Sci. 9(4), 390–395 (2009). http://paper.ijcsns.org/07_book/200904/20090453.pdf
7. Baccichetti, F., Bordin, F., Carlassare, F.: λ-Prophage induction byfurocoumarin photosensitization. Experientia 35(2), 183–184 (1979). https://doi.org/10.1007/BF01920603. http://www.gbv.de/dms/ilmenau/toc/01600020X.PDF
8. Bhasin, H.: Cost-priority cognizant regression testing. ACM SIGSOFT Softw. Eng. Notes 39(3), 1–7 (2014). https://doi.org/10.1145/2597716.2597722
9. Briciu, C.V., Filip, I., Indries, I.I.: Methods for cost estimation in software project management. In: IOP Conference Series: Materials Science and Engineering, vol. 106, no. 1 (2016). https://doi.org/10.1088/1757-899X/106/1/012008, http://www.scopus.com/inward/record.url?eid=2-s2.0-84960154391&partnerID=tZOtx3y1
10. Chawla, P., Chana, I., Rana, A.: A novel strategy for automatic test data generation using soft computing technique. Front. Comput. Sci. 9(3), 346–363 (2015). https://doi.org/10.1007/s11704-014-3496-9. http://www.scopus.com/inward/record.url?eid=2-s2.0-84938208965&partnerID=40&md5=6b7065f7903d0a046c17613f79b6ecd1
11. Elsevier B.V.: Scopus. https://www.scopus.com/home.uri
12. Ghiduk, A.S.: Automatic generation of basis test paths using variable length genetic algorithm. Inf. Process. Lett. 114(6), 304–316 (2014). https://doi.org/10.1016/j.ipl.2014.01.009
13. Hsinyi, J.: Can the genetic algorithm be a good tool for software engineering searching problems? In: Proceedings of the International Conference on Computer Software and Applications, vol. 2, pp. 362–364 (2006). https://doi.org/10.1109/COMPSAC.2006.123
14. Jena, A.K., Swain, S.K., Mohapatra, D.P.: A novel approach for test case generation from UML activity diagram. In: 2014 International Conference on Issues Challenges in Intelligent Computing Techniques, pp. 621–629 (2014). https://doi.org/10.1109/ICICICT.2014.6781352, http://www.scopus.com/inward/record.url?eid=2-s2.0-84899098078&partnerID=tZOtx3y1

15. Jeya Mala, D., Sabari Nathan, K., Balamurugan, S.: Critical components testing using hybrid genetic algorithm. ACM SIGSOFT Softw. Eng. Notes **38**(5), 1 (2013). https://doi.org/10.1145/2507288.2507309. http://dl.acm.org/citation.cfm?doid=2507288.2507309

16. Kitchenham, B.: Procedures for performing systematic reviews. Keele University, Keele, UK 33(TR/SE-0401), 28 (2004). https://doi.org/10.1109/METRIC.2004. 1357885

17. Kitchenham, B., et al.: Systematic literature reviews in software engineering: a tertiary study. Inf. Softw. Technol. **52**(8), 792–805 (2010). https://doi.org/10.1016/ j.infsof.2010.03.006

18. Li, Z.Y.: Predicting project effort intelligently in early stages by applying genetic algorithms with neural networks. Appl. Mech. Mater. **513–517**, 2035–2040 (2014). https://doi.org/10.4028/www.scientific.net/AMM.513-517.2035

19. Mahajan, S., Joshi, S.D., Khanaa, V.: Component-based software system test case prioritization with genetic algorithm decoding technique using Java platform. In: 2015 International Conference on Computing Communication Control and Automation, pp. 847–851 (2015). https://doi.org/10.1109/ICCUBEA.2015. 169, http://ieeexplore.ieee.org/lpdocs/epic03/wrapper.htm?arnumber=7155967

20. Malhotra, R., Tiwari, D.: Development of a framework for test case prioritization using genetic algorithm. ACM SIGSOFT Softw. Eng. Notes **38**(3), 1 (2013). https://doi.org/10.1145/2464526.2464536. http://dl.acm.org/citation.cfm?doid=2464526.2464536

21. Nesmachnow, S.: Efficient parallel evolutionary algorithms for deadline-constrained scheduling in project management. Int. J. Innov. Comput. Appl. **7**(1), 34–49 (2016). https://doi.org/10.1504/IJICA.2016.075468

22. Pino, F., García, F., Piattini, M.: Revisión sistemática de mejora de procesos software en micro, pequeñas y medianas empresas. Rev. Espanola Innovación Calid. e Ing. del Softw. REICIS **2**(1), 6–23 (2006). http://redalyc.uaemex.mx/pdf/922/92220103.pdf

23. RRAAE: Red de Repositorio de Acceso Abierto del Ecuador. http://www.rraae. org.ec/

24. Salami, H.O., Ahmed, M.: Retrieving sequence diagrams using genetic algorithm, pp. 324–330. IEEE Computer Society (2014). https://doi.org/10.1109/JCSSE. 2014.6841889

25. Saxena, V., Arora, D., Mishra, N.: UML modeling of load optimization for distributed computer systems based on genetic algorithm. SIGSOFT Softw. Eng. Notes **38**(1), 1–7 (2013). https://doi.org/10.1145/2413038.2413043

26. Shamshiri, S., Rojas, J.M., Fraser, G., Mcminn, P., Court, R.: Random or genetic algorithm search for object-oriented test suite generation? In: Proceedings of the 2015 Annual Conference on Genetic and Evolutionary Computation, pp. 1367–1374 (2015). https://doi.org/10.1145/2739480.2754696, http://dl.acm.org/ citation.cfm?id=2754696

27. Sharma, C., Sabharwal, S., Sibal, R.: A survey on software testing techniques using genetic algorithm. Int. J. Comput. Sci. Issues **10**(1), 381–393 (2013). https://arxiv.org/ftp/arxiv/papers/1411/1411.1154.pdf

28. Shuai, B., Li, M., Li, H., Zhang, Q., Tang, C.: Software vulnerability detection using genetic algorithm and dynamic taint analysis. In: 2013 Proceedings of the 3rd International Conference on Consumer Electronics, Communications and Networks, CECNet 2013, pp. 589–593 (2013). https://doi.org/10.1109/CECNet.2013. 6703400, http://ieeexplore.ieee.org/xpl/articleDetails.jsp?arnumber=6703400

29. Sommerville, I.: Software engineering (2010). https://doi.org/10.1111/j.1365-2362.
2005.01463.x
30. Suresh, Y.: Software quality assurance for object-oriented systems using meta-
heuristic search techniques, pp. 441–448 (2015)
31. Vodithala, S.: A dynamic approach for retrieval of software components using genetic algorithm. http://ieeexplore.ieee.org/xpl/articleDetails.jsp?
arnumber=7339085
32. Wang, S., Ali, S., Gotheb, A.: Minimizing test suites in software product lines using
weight-based genetic algorithms. In: Proceeding of the Fifteenth Annual Conference on Genetic and Evolutionary Computation, pp. 1493–1500 (2013). https://
doi.org/10.1145/2463372.2463545
33. Wang, X., Jiang, X., Shi, H.: Prioritization of test scenarios using hybrid genetic
algorithm based on UML activity diagram, pp. 854–857. IEEE Computer Society,
November 2015. https://doi.org/10.1109/ICSESS.2015.7339189

Automatic Categorization of Tweets on the Political Electoral Theme Using Supervised Classification Algorithms

Oscar M. Cumbicus-Pineda[1,4]([✉]) [iD], Pablo F. Ordoñez-Ordoñez[1,2] [iD],
Lisset A. Neyra-Romero[3,4] [iD], and Roberth Figueroa-Diaz[1] [iD]

[1] Facultad de Energía, CIS, Universidad Nacional de Loja,
Ave. Pío Jaramillo Alvarado, La Argelia, Loja, Ecuador
oscar.cumbicus@unl.edu.ec
[2] ETSI Sistemas Informáticos, Universidad Politécnica de Madrid,
Calle Alan Turing s/n 28031, Madrid, Spain
[3] Departamento de Ciencias de la Computación y Electrónica,
Universidad Técnica Particular de Loja, Loja, Ecuador
[4] Departamento de Ciencias de la Computación e Inteligencia Artificial,
Universidad del País Vasco, Leioa, Spain

Abstract. The increase and use of social networks to share content
and opinions with different characters allows to have a large volume of
information. Twitter, is just one of the most used social networks and has
been selected for this study; the users of this network they become not
only passive actors of reception and consumption of information, they
are also generators of contents. Tweets analysis requires a systematic
process for collecting, processing and classification, which is why this
article determines the best Classifier categories: positive, negative and
neutral public opinion corresponding electoral political issues. For this,
a total of 745 tweets collected in Spanish from the main accounts of
media, political figures and political organizations of Ecuador. These
tweets were preprocessed, transformed and the results indicated that the
vector support machines (SMO) with a sensitivity error rate (RECALL)
of 0.8% proved to be the best. Likewise, the algorithm Syntetic Minority
Over-Sampling Technique was used (SMOTE) to balance classes and
increase capacity predictive of the models excluding the decision trees
for the categorization of this type of tweets.

Keywords: Supervised classification · Categorization of tweets
Algorithms · SMOTE · Twitter and politics

1 Introduction

Today, the role of social networks on the Internet is indisputable, since its impact
on political, economic and social life, allowed transform the dynamics to communicate and acquire information [6]. Twitter is currently one of the major players

© Springer Nature Switzerland AG 2019
M. Botto-Tobar et al. (Eds.): CITT 2018, CCIS 895, pp. 671–682, 2019.
https://doi.org/10.1007/978-3-030-05532-5_51

in the global network. This communication platform has established, based on popularity, a new form of communication: the microblogging. After more than 8 years of use and more of 500 million users, Twitter has become an essential platform for the follow-up, diffusion and coordination of events of diverse nature and importance [13].

The use of social media and in particular, the microblogging Twitter have transformed the communication routinely politics. In social networks communication new modes including public discussion of politic issues have emerged. Messages, controlled by powerful gatekeepers in traditional media, now flowing freely in a passive medium in which callers are the citizens themselves and messages are diversified [15].

A representative democracy of educated citizens, requires a form of communication in which those may move its opinion to the rulers in reaction to politics applied or intend to implement. ICTs create the spaces for a different politics communication, in which all citizens, politics leaders, journalists and other influential can intervene on an equal footing. Interaction is the key to the new process proposed communication social media [15].

The National Electoral Council of Ecuador Republic (CNE), is the highest body of suffrage. Its functions are to organize, manage, monitor and guarantee transparent and effective electoral processes, organize processes referendum, referendum or revocation of authority, keep a permanent record of politics organizations and ensure the transparent election development [5].

The National Electoral Council has defined objectives and strategic axes corresponding to the achievement of the constitutional principles of quality and efficiency in the public service. It is therefore important to identify the positioning of the institution within the State and taking into account the objective "To increase the effectiveness and institutional efficiency to provide quality services" and strategic axes "Institutional Strengthening" measurements are made in social networks institutional image. The CNE has 24 provincial branches, one for each province to devolve electoral services throughout the country.

The mission of the National Electoral Council is to strengthen democracy in Ecuador, guaranteeing the rights of politic Organization technical citizen, promoting the exercise of democracy and exerting community rectory, planning, adjustments makes 'on and control mechanisms direct and representative democracy [5].

On February 18, 2016, one year after the elections, the CNE approved the electoral schedule in which the first electoral round would take place on February 19, 2017, where the new president and the Vice President of Ecuador would be elected for the period 2017–2021; The election of five representatives to the Andean Parliament and 137 Assemblymen for the same period, as well as a popular referendum on the opinion of Ecuadorians on the subject of public officials who have accounts, would also be held and companies in tax havens.

12,816,698 voters were authorized throughout Ecuador to participate in this electoral process, which also involved 7 national parties, 9 national movements and 54 provincial political movements, giving a total of 70 political organizations.

Eight binomials were presented for the dignity of president and vice president; because none of the presidential binomials participating in this electoral process get the vote to be elected in a single round, a second round of elections had to be carried out with the two most voted presidential binomials. This new electoral process was held on April 2, 2017, winning the presidential binomial of Lenin Moreno and Jorge Glas representatives of the Alianza PAIS movement, with a vote equal to 51.16% of the universe of suffragists. This research work focuses on the categorization of tweets collected mainly from media accounts, political figures and political organizations through the delegation communication team. Electoral provincial of Loja; the tweets were collected from those accounts to those who made publications related to the National Electoral Council, tweets that were classified into three categories (classes) called: positive, negative and neutral; which were defined a priory in each Tweet.

The importance of this work lies in finding the best model for the automatic categorization of tweets [10], applying supervised classification algorithms; This will significantly minimize the current work done by the communication area of the electoral provincial delegation of Loja.

2   Methodology

The development of this research work was based on the data mining process; the method and strategy used are shown in the flow chart in Fig. 1.

A set of 745 tweets were collected to be the independent variable; the dependent variable was the result of the analysis of the publications that were related to the National Electoral Council of Ecuador and that were categorized into three classes that were: positive, neutral and negative. The next step was to transform the data set to ARFF format, which is the format that Weka software reads; Afterwards, we proceeded to obtain the Bag Of Words using the filter called "StringToWordVector" [4].

Models based on Naive Bayes, Logistic Regression, SMO, IBK, Decision Table, J48 and Random Forest were built to perform the classification [12]. To address the class imbalance in the data, the synthetic technique on minority sampling (SMOTE) was used [7]. The models were validated by the cross-validation technique (10-fold-CV). To compare the performance of each classifier, the results of their performance measures were analyzed, which included: accuracy, precision, recall, the Matthews MCC Correlation Coefficient and the ROC Area [2].

More detailed information on these steps is given in the following subsections.

2.1   Phase 1: Recollection of Tweets

The data collected for this study were taken from accounts tweets during the pre-electoral and electoral period of the general elections to elect the new President

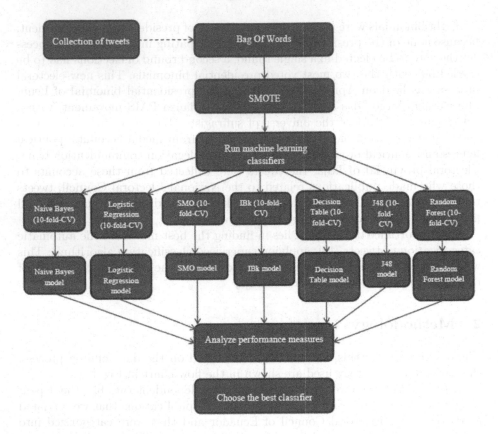

Fig. 1. Configuration of methodology

of Ecuador made allusions to the work carried out by the National Electoral Council.

The information is currently collected manually by the staff of the communication area of this institution in the province of Loja and is entered in an excel file in which the published tweet classification is recorded assigning one of the following three Categories: positive, negative or neutral.

Once the file was obtained, we proceeded to purge the data; first, columns that were considered unnecessary were deleted leaving only two columns containing the tweet and the category.

As a second step, all the links or hyperlinks to web pages that could exist were removed from the tweets, considering that this information does not influence the categorization of the tweet and could worsen the work of the classifiers.

Once this file was refined, the transformation to ARFF format was carried out, with two attributes: the tweet and the class that could be positive, negative or neutral.

2.2   Phase 2: Obtaining Bag of Words

Once we have obtained the ARFF file, we load it in the weka software using the explorer interface and to obtain the bag-of-words [3] we apply the filter "StringToWordVector"; this filter transforms string attributes into word vectors, that is, creates an attribute for each word that encodes the presence or count of words within the string.

This filter is applied to obtain words that are repeated sometimes and that are directly related to the classes. The bag-of-words obtained has a total of 3259 attributes and 745 instances.

2.3   Phase 3: Balancing Classes with SMOTE

One set of data is unbalanced if the classes are not represented more or less the same. This is true in our case studies since 465 tweets were classified as neutral, 114 as positive and 166 as negative.

If the imbalance is not corrected it can lead to very low recall levels and the precision to measure the performance of the classifier. To balance the data set, therefore, we apply the SMOTE approach, one of the most used strategies in the system learning community, to deal with unbalanced classes in classification problems.

This technique over-shows the minority class by creating synthetic examples instead of oversampling with replacement. It is administered by taking each sample of the minority class and introducing synthetic examples along the linear segments by joining any of the nearest k neighbors of the nearest minority class k. Depending on the number of samples required, nearest k neighbors are selected at random.

SMOTE has been used successfully to balance classes of classification problems with data from a social network. Here, for our case when applying 3 iterations of SMOTE to the set of tweets, the results were: 465 tweets for the neutral class, 456 for the positive class and 332 for the negative class, giving a total of 1253 instances.

2.4   Phase 4: Execution of the Classifiers

Once the database was balanced, models were built applying six classifiers Naive Bayes, Logistic Regression, SMO, IBk, Decision Table and Random Forest, with the aim of reaching the highest percentage of success in the classification of tweets in the three classes defined a priory [8].

To avoid overflowing, the models generated by the originally named classifiers were validated using the k-fold cross-validation technique (in our study we used 10-fold-CV). This technique randomly divides the original sample into 10 "folds" or sub-samples. One of the nine sub-samples is used to test the model, while the remaining nine are used for the algorithm training process. This process is repeated 10 times for each of the sub-samples of k. Thus, the 10 results are obtained which are then averaged to evaluate the performance of the classifier.

3 Results

3.1 Evaluation

The classifiers were evaluated using the standard accuracy, precision, recall and the area under the ROC curve suggested for small data sets Table 1. They were also evaluated with the correlation coefficient Matthews (MCC), which is often used to measure performance with unbalanced databases.

Table 1. Performance to evaluate the classifiers [11]

Performance measure	Formula
Accuracy	$\frac{TP+TN}{TP+FP+FN+TN}$
Precision	$\frac{TP}{TP+FP}$
Recall	$\frac{TP}{TP+FN}$
MCC	$\frac{TP.TN-FP.FN}{\sqrt{(TP+FP)(TP+FN)(FP+TN)(FN+TN)}}$
ROC area	$\frac{1}{2}(\frac{TP}{TP+FN} + \frac{TN}{TN+FP})$

Table 2, shows the values of the performance measures for each of the applied classifiers without using the SMOTE class balancing, where it can be seen that the model with SMO [14] is the one with the highest average scores. For accuracy and recall, while Logistic Regression has the highest precision and MCC coefficient; Random Forest obtains the best ROC Curve.

In Table 3, we can see the percentage of global success of the classifiers applied to the database without SMOTE, where the vector support machines obtained the best result with 70.06%.

Table 4, shows the values of the performance measures for each of the classifiers applied, taking into account that previously realize the rolling of classes with SMOTE, where it can be observed that the model with SMO is the one with the highest average scores for accuracy, recall and MCC, while Logistic Regression has the highest precision and Random Forest obtains the best ROC Curve.

Regarding the global percentage of hits Table 5, the model that had the highest percentage of success was the vector support machine (SMO) [1], followed very closely by the Logistic Regression algorithm, which also obtained a good percentage of successes, while the decision tables were the ones that obtained the lowest percentage of success.

4 Discussion

Without using SMOTE, the classifiers deliver the worst results Table 6. We will analyze these results taking the measurement of recall performance or in Spanish

Table 2. Measures performance of classifiers without SMOTE

Category	Naive Bayes	Logistic	SMO	IBk	Decision table	J48	Random forest
Accuracy							
Neutral	0.671	0.748	0.841	0.634	0.946	0.858	0.981
Positive	0.307	0.491	0.254	0.482	0.000	0.088	0.114
Negative	0.735	0.590	0.614	0.084	0.373	0.416	0.217
(Avg.)	0.630	0.674	0.701	0.489	0.674	0.642	0.678
Precision							
Neutral	0.776	0.819	0.745	0.756	0.680	0.695	0.667
Positive	0.255	0.303	0.326	0.165	0.000	0.192	0.591
Negative	0.592	0.726	0.779	0.667	0.689	0.580	0.923
(Avg.)	0.655	0.719	0.688	0.646	0.578	0.592	0.712
Recall							
Neutral	0.671	0.748	0.841	0.634	0.946	0.858	0.981
Positive	0.307	0.491	0.254	0.482	0.000	0.088	0.114
Negative	0.735	0.590	0.614	0.084	0.373	0.416	0.217
(Avg.)	0.630	0.674	0.701	0.489	0.674	0.642	0.678
MCC							
Neutral	0.340	0.463	0.385	0.286	0.297	0.268	0.294
Positive	0.135	0.239	0.177	0.029	−0.044	0.030	0.212
Negative	0.549	0.569	0.617	0.182	0.415	0.374	0.396
(Avg.)	0.355	0.452	0.405	0.224	0.271	0.255	0.304
ROC area							
Neutral	0.755	0.790	0.679	0.663	0.636	0.648	0.800
Positive	0.656	0.677	0.621	0.530	0.472	0.526	0.687
Negative	0.877	0.887	0.822	0.594	0.736	0.735	0.906
(Avg.)	0.767	0.794	0.702	0.627	0.633	0.649	0.807

Table 3. Percentage of overall success of classifiers without applying SMOTE

Classification algorithms	Percentage hit
Naive Bayes	62.95%
Logistic	67.38%
SMO	70.06%
IBk	48.86%
Decision table	67.38%
J48	64.16%
Random forest	67.78%

Table 4. Performance measures of classifiers using SMOTE

Category	Naive Bayes	Logistic	SMO	IBk	Decision table	J48	Random forest
Accuracy							
Neutral	0.776	0.794	0.811	0.254	0.927	0.811	0.972
Positive	0.783	0.976	0.98	0.989	0.656	0.772	0.871
Negative	0.889	0.979	0.958	0.946	0.307	0.729	0.768
(Avg.)	0.808	0.909	0.911	0.704	0.664	0.775	0.881
Precision							
Neutral	0.752	0.963	0.945	0.959	0.567	0.699	0.77
Positive	0.913	0.846	0.873	0.564	0.857	0.850	0.973
Negative	0.772	0.945	0.93	0.952	0.708	0.807	0.988
(Avg.)	0.816	0.916	0.915	0.813	0.71	0.783	0.902
Recall							
Neutral	0.776	0.794	0.811	0.254	0.927	0.811	0.972
Positive	0.783	0.976	0.98	0.989	0.656	0.772	0.871
Negative	0.889	0.979	0.958	0.946	0.307	0.729	0.768
(Avg.)	0.808	0.909	0.911	0.705	0.664	0.775	0.881
MCC							
Neutral	0.621	0.814	0.812	0.402	0.504	0.591	0.775
Positive	0.769	0.852	0.88	0.552	0.636	0.710	0.88
Negative	0.761	0.948	0.923	0.93	0.362	0.689	0.835
(Avg.)	0.712	0.863	0.866	0.596	0.514	0.660	0.829
ROC area							
Neutral	0.883	0.967	0.888	0.625	0.825	0.846	0.968
Positive	0.932	0.97	0.953	0.779	0.831	0.885	0.985
Negative	0.939	0.996	0.977	0.966	0.744	0.885	0.993
(Avg.)	0.916	0.976	0.935	0.771	0.806	0.870	0.981

Table 5. Percentage of global accuracy of classifiers using SMOTE

Classification algorithms	Percentage hit
Naive Bayes	80.84%
Logistic	90.90%
SMO	91.14%
IBk	70.47%
Decision table	66.40%
J48	77.49%
Random forest	88.10%

Table 6. Recall results in database without using SMOTE

Categoría	Naive Bayes	Logistic	SMO	IBk	Decision table	J48	Random forest
Recall							
Neutral	0.671	0.748	0.841	0.634	0.946	0.858	0.981
Positive	0.307	0.491	0.254	0.482	0.00	0.088	0.114
Negative	0.735	0.59	0.614	0.084	0.373	0.416	0.217

sensitivity (it refers to the fraction of examples of the class of the whole set that are classified correctly), as the basis for this analysis.

By having 465 tweets classified as neutral, 114 as positive and 166 as negative, the classifiers have an easy bias towards the majority class, that is, the error rate of the classifier is not representative of how well the task performs. For example, if we observe the Recall of the SMO classifier in Table 5, the algorithm classifies 84.1% of samples as Neutral class, 25.4% of samples as Positive class and 61.4% as negative class; Even though there is a high percentage of classifications of the neutral class, this does not mean that it is a good classifier, because contrary it had a 75.6% error in the classification of the samples of the positive class. "But what happens when applying 3 iterations of SMOTE to the database and obtaining 465 samples for the neutral class, 456 for the positive class and 332 for the negative class giving a total of 1253 instances and applying the classifiers".

It happens that the percentages of success increase with respect to the application of these algorithms to the database, now for example in this case Naive Bayes reaches 80.84%, SMO obtains 91.14%.

Table 7. Recall results in database using SMOTE

Category	Naive Bayes	Logistic	SMO	IBk	Decision table	J48	Random forest
Recall							
Neutral	0.776	0.794	0.811	0.254	0.927	0.811	0.972
Positive	0.783	0.976	0.98	0.989	0.656	0.772	0.871
Negative	0.889	0.979	0.958	0.946	0.307	0.729	0.768

As can be observed in Table 7 when balancing the classes with the application of SMOTE, the recall for the positive and negative classes improves at the cost of assuming a worse recall of the neutral; For example, if we observe the recall of the SMO classifier, 81.1% of samples are classified as neutral class, 98% of samples as of positive class and 95.8% of samples as negative class; that is, the error rate of the classifier is representative of how well it performs its task.

With the Knowledge Flow interface of weka [9] Fig. 2, the ROC curves of the application of the SMO classifier were obtained both in the database without applying SMOTE Fig. 3, and in the application of the algorithm to the database applying three iterations of SMOTE Fig. 4. The graphs of the ROC curves were made for the neutral, positive and negative class in each case.

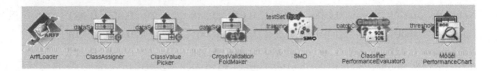

ArffLoader   ClassAssigner   ClassValue   CrossValidation   SMO   Classifier   Model
                               Picker   FoldMaker   PerformanceEvaluator3   PerformanceChart

Fig. 2. Configuration of the Knowledge Flow interface in weka to obtain ROC curves

As shown in Fig. 3 Negative class has improved ROC curve Positive class and Neutral, having a significant difference in area under the curve, these results are obtained by applying the SMO algorithm on the basis of unbalanced data without applying SMOTE. Figure 4 shows the ROC curves having applied the vector support machines to the database balanced with SMOTE, here the area under the curves of the Positive and Negative classes are similar and the difference with the ROC curve of the Neutral class is not significant.

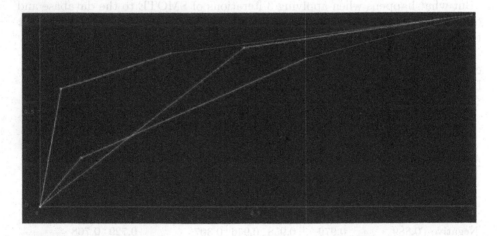

Fig. 3. SMO ROC curve without applying SMOTE

If we compare Figs. 3 and 4, we can see that the ROC curves improve in Fig. 4 with respect to Fig. 3, since these are the curves of the classes neutral, positive and negative result of the application of the algorithms to the database that was balanced with SMOTE; we can also observe that the curves in Fig. 4 have a cut-off point close to 1, thus Verify that applying SMOTE to the database not only improves the overall percentage of success but also improves each of the performance measures for each of the classes and does not bias these measures for the majority class.

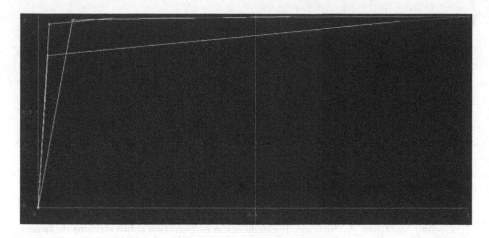

Fig. 4. ROC curve using SMO SMOTE

5 Conclusion and Future Work

5.1 Conclusion

It has been identified that Vector Support Machines and Logistic Regression, have proved to be the most suitable models for this classification problem, and could be implemented in the categorization of politics trendy tweets.

We can exclude the Decision Tables for the categorization of tweets, considering that they were the ones with the lowest percentage of global success obtained in the present study.

The results show that the models generated by the Linear Regression present low levels of error in the results of the classification, a signal that SMOTE combined with LR helps to increase the predictive capacity of the models of the classes.

5.2 Future Work

From the reviewed bibliography it was observed that there are several research studies that include the normalization of tweets, so that the problem posed above could be improved by adding a process of normalization before to treat the tweets.

Another improvement that can be added to the developed model is the automatic collection of tweets, using APIs for this collection and thus increasing the number of tweets in the database.

A future work that can be done is to add new categories to be predicted, such as: Informative, Very Positive, Very Negative. In this case, it would be necessary to take into account the intensification and attenuation strategies existing in grammar. Perhaps adding as attributes the retweet number of a message or the number of hashtags it contains can help the classifier.

References

1. Blanco-Hermida Sanz, E.-J.: Algoritmos de clustering y aprendizaje automático aplicados a twitter (2016)
2. Buill Vilches, J., Grau Sala, R., Vallbé, J.J.: Clasificación automática de textos y explotación bi (2014)
3. Calvo Vilares, D.: Análisis de contenidos en Twitter: clasificación demensajes e identificación de la tendencia política de los usuarios. B.S. thesis (2014)
4. Cámara, E.M., Cumbreras, M.Á.G., Valdivia, M.T.M., López, L.A.U.: Sinai en tass 2012. Procesamiento del lenguaje natural **50**, 53–60 (2013)
5. CNE: Certificación ISO/TS 17582:2014 ISO 9001:2008 Objetivo y Desafío de la Institucionalidad Electoral. Consejo Nacional Electoral, 1st Edn. (2016)
6. Gálvez-Pérez, J.R., et al.: Sistema automático para la clasificación de la opinión pública generada en twitter. Res. Comput. Sci. **95**, 23–36 (2015)
7. Godino Martínez, A.: Sistema de clasificación automática sobre streams de tweets. Master's thesis (2014)
8. González Rubio, C.: Clasificación automática de texto para el seguimiento de campañas electorales en redes sociales. B.S. thesis (2015)
9. Lage García, L.: Herramienta para el análisis de la opinión en tweets periodísticos (2014)
10. Martis, M., Alfaro, R.: Clasificación automática de la intención del usuario en mensajes de twitter. In: I Workshop en procesamiento automatizado de textos y Corpora, Viña del Sausalito (2012)
11. Masías, V.H., Valle, M., Morselli, C., Crespo, F., Vargas, A., Laengle, S.: Modeling verdict outcomes using social network measures: the watergate and caviar network cases. PloS One **11**(1) (2016)
12. Neyra Romero, L.A.: Categorización automática de respuestas aplicando algoritmos de clasificación supervisada al análisis de las contestaciones de estudiantes a una serie de preguntas tipo test (2016)
13. Amaya de la Peña, I.: Presencia en twitter de los candidatos a las elecciones madrileñas de 2015 (2015)
14. Pla, F., Hurtado, L.F.: Elirf-upv en tass-2013: Análisis de sentimientos en twitter. In: XXIX Congreso de la Sociedad Española para el Procesamiento del Lenguaje Natural (SEPLN 2013), pp. 220–227. TASS(2013)
15. Sánchez, M.M., Damas, S.H.: Cómo puede contribuir twitter a una comunicación política más avanzada. Arbor **191**(774), 257 (2015)

e-Government and e-Participation

Citizen Participation in the Use of the IRS Portal that Electronic Government Brings in the City of Milagro

Oscar Bermeo-Almeida(✉) ⓘ, Mario Cardenas-Rodriguez ⓘ,
Ivan Ramirez-Sánchez ⓘ, Enrique Ferruzola-Gómez ⓘ,
and William Bazán-Vera ⓘ

Computer Science Department, Faculty of Agricultural Sciences,
Agrarian University of Ecuador, Av. 25 de Julio y Pio Jaramillo,
P.O. Box 09-04-100, Guayaquil, Ecuador
{obermeo,mcardenas,iramirez,eferruzola,
wbazan}@uagraria.edu.ec

Abstract. The purpose of this article is to analyze the importance of using the electronic government portal for the collection of taxes and their involvement in the city of Milagro. At present, the use of technological tools for process of control has allowed several activities to be carried out in such a way that the citizens does not have to go the government offices.

In the review of literatures, important concepts related to the e-government plan, the use of ICTs in the government of Milagro and e-government in Milagro and its surroundings were researched, the methodology used for the data collection was the survey, the same one that allowed obtaining quantitative and statistical information to carry out a detailed analysis of the use of ICTs in local government.

The results obtained from the researched detail the services offered by the Internal Revenue Service (IRS) in the city of Milagro, as well as the utility that the web page provides to citizens.

It is important to establish that this work was carried out with the purpose of determining the degree of impact in terms of the participation of the people in the use that is given to the IRS portal of the electronic government, it is possible to conclude that previously there had not been carried out a similar study, because people did not have knowledge and showed little interest in the inclusion of institutional portals that dynamically help to generate processes saving time for users.

Keywords: Electronic government · Web portal · Municipality
Taxes

1 Introduction

E-government today has become something of vital importance for the development of the country, according to the Inter-American Agency for Cooperation and Development that considers that the Electronic Government: "is the use of ICTs by government

M. Botto-Tobar et al. (Eds.): CITT 2018, CCIS 895, pp. 685–696, 2019.
https://doi.org/10.1007/978-3-030-05532-5_52

organizations, to provide an improvement in services and information provided to citizens, raising the level of efficiency and effectiveness of public management for transparency in the public sector" [1]. Also based on a research that was conducted at the University of Malaga in Spain [2] they indicated that: "Electronic Government is associated with the use of ICTs, where the way in which governments manage and execute their internal processes is changed, and it expands the possibility of giving improvement and increase of communication channels towards citizenship". In addition, what is intended according to the research in the Electronic Government National Plan, 2016 [3] that seeks to improve the way of relating to the four main actors such as: the Government, citizens, the productive sector and public servants, to eliminate the different barriers of communication and reinforcing relationships and links through the use of technology in this globalized world. Through the use of the different technological tools offered by the electronic government, which favors in such a way that the citizens have a greater intervention with the different Government Institutions in Internet, to obtain benefits in the Public Administration, counting on the support and immediate solution of their services, promoting the saving of time and money, for the economic development of Ecuador.

This is why, in the present research, the participation of citizens of Milagro with respect to the use of the IRS citizen portal will be announced, where the method of data collection will show the impact that the use of this portal has on citizens, in this way we present the analysis, the arguments, conclusions and recommendations regarding the subject that will be mentioned below.

2 Literature Review

The use of Information and Communication Technologies (ICTs), from now on ICTs, radically changes the way governments administer and execute their internal processes [2] allowing better communication with citizens. In addition, contribute to the economic, social, cultural growth and modernization of the State [4].

According to Danziger and Andersen (2002), they mention the potential of ICTs as an instrument that enables communication and participation among the different political actors, helping to improve public participation in the Government process, obtained from Vargas [5].

Likewise, ICTs contribute to reducing costs, benefiting public entities, so that entities can be focused on speed, comfort, available information, achieving efficiency and effectiveness of the service provided to citizens.

The United Nations defines e-government as "the incorporation and use of ICTs, such as wide area networks, the Internet and mobile computing, by the government for the provision of information and public services for citizens" (United Nations, 2016) [4, 6, 7], classifying it into 4 evolutionary levels according to their level of maturity, which will allow to complete the process of enrichment of civic life (Fig. 1):

E-government refers to the use of ICTs, in particular the use of Internet, as a tool to achieve better governance [4, 8].

ICTs make it possible to access a higher level of information and have the potential to reduce the access that exists to the use of information among different social agents.

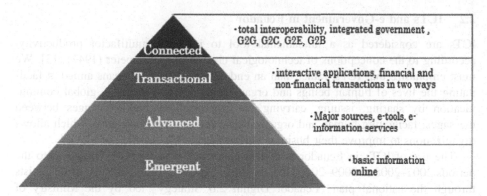

Fig. 1. Stages of evolution of e-government according to the United Nations Organization. Source: National Electronic Government Plan [3]

"E-Government has become a term used to refer to the use of ICTs applications in the public sector" [5].

2.1 Electronic Government Plan

Electronic Government involves the rational, coherent and precise use of ICTs in the context of a State vision seeking "consistency with good public administration and management practices, promoting the governance of relations between the State and the various social actors" [9].

The Electronic Government Plan mentions this as a living instrument that is continuously enriching, for which the involvement, commitment and participation of all citizens is crucial, facilitating the completion of procedures [10] since they can be done electronically and that only in the exceptions does the citizen have to go personally [9].

This plan in Ecuador is divided into three sections that are: Close Government for the services that public entities provide to citizens, reducing queues and time. The Open Government is all the information that the State makes available to the citizen for decision making, generating a participatory and transparent democracy. And the efficient and effective Government is oriented to improve, speed up, reduce, simplify and optimize the administrative processes for the services of the citizens, reducing the attention times, costs.

In the Capital of the Republic, a "Design, development and implementation project of the Electronic Government [11] models and strategies for an open, close, efficient and effective management of the Public Administration was started in 2014 in order to be finish by December 2016", with this project it is intended that Ecuador will not be left behind in comparison to other countries that are located in a good position.

Not only Ecuador is promoting the implementation of E-Government, several countries have this very useful tool as for example Bolivia, that is making use of ICT's in the Government, the Municipality of La Paz made a system of municipal procedures that began to work on May 2, 2002, it had to go through stages of creation and development using digital electronics that help to systematize the procedures that citizens need to do and at the same time seek transparency [12], efficiency and effectiveness.

2.2   ICTs and e-Government in Ecuador

ICTs are considered as a fundamental tool to intensify multifactor productivity, according to the conceptions of technological change of Schumpeter (1947) [13]. We must emphasize that ICTs, rather than an end or a benefit, is a means aimed at facilitating the lives of human beings and organizations. ICTs generate a global communication by sharing, issuing, carrying out conversations and exchanges between messages, facilitating human and organizational relational performance, which allows organizations to improve their business performance.

The use of ICTs in Ecuador is increasing in recent years [14], compared to the periods 2007–2008 al 2009–2010 [15], this is due to the institutional support that exists through the national plan "Ecuador Digital 2.0 Strategy" led by the Ministry of Telecommunications and Information Society (MINTEL).

The current management carried out in the City of Milagro and its surroundings has developed several municipal policies where it is intended to implement a model of public administration, using ICTS, and having as a strategic objective the relationship between the local government and the citizen carrying out an information strategy [16].

2.3   The Electronic Government and the Society of Milagro and Its Surroundings

"E-government for Ecuador not only modernizes the State and introduces the country into democracy 2.0, but it also implies the challenge of consolidating the democracy we want, and this implies, not only using technology but also creating new spaces of government and democratic participation" [9].

The National Plan for Electronic Government (2014–2017) informs us that "E-Government introduces ICTs to improve the way of relating to the actors, making reference to society and to the various interactions that each one performs, detailed below:

Citizens: It is the important part in the management of the Government.
Government: Administers the stipulations of the constitution, making use of ICTs.
Productive Sector: Organizes and develops production processes, planning, financing of services, through interactions with the Government.
Public servants: It refers to the human talent that operates the E-Government. Each of these actors contribute to the City of Milagro to know the various services it provides. For example, on the web page http://www.milagro.gob.ec/ we can keep ourselves informed of each of the activities that are performed, as the rights and obligations of citizens, another web page in which we can obtain information about the processes that take place in our city is http://educacion.gob.ec/, links, portal of citizen procedures, where a list containing 16 procedures that can be done in the Decentralized Autonomous Government will be displayed (Fig. 2).

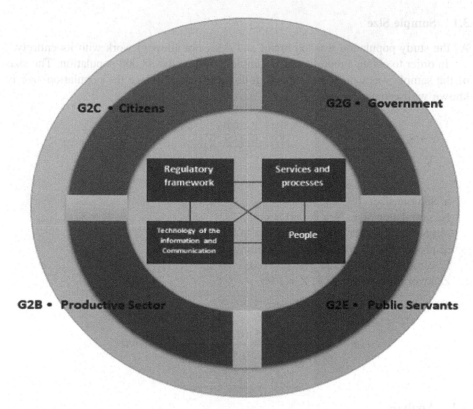

Fig. 2. Interaction of the pillars of e-government.   Source: National Plan for Electronic Government 2014–2017

3   Methodology

The data collection tool chosen was the survey, which allowed us to obtain quantitative and statistical data for a better analysis about methodology: Citizen Participation in the use of the IRS Citizen Portal that attracts Electronic Government in the City of Milagro.

For the execution and obtaining of information it is used a quantitative analysis, with a sampling of snowball through formulation of surveys, where some individuals that meet the characteristics are located, which lead to others, and these to others, and so on until getting the proposed sample.

For the analysis, the citizens of the city of Milagro was selected as a sample. The proposed survey was conducted to 100 people who helped answer the 10 questions online.

The results obtained through the civic participation of Milagro citizens are shown below.

3.1   Sample Size

As the study population was too broad and does not allow to work with its entirety.

In order to obtain a representative sample based on the 88,000 population. The size of the sample was calculated with the following formula since the population size is known with certainty

$$n = \frac{Npq}{\frac{(N-1)E^2}{Z^2} + pq}$$

n: sample size.
N: population size, N = 88000 people,
p: probability of an event happening, p = 0.5
q: probability of an event not happening, q = 0.5
E: error, it is considered 5%; E = 0.05
Z: level of trust, for 95%, Z = 1.96

Sample for the citizens in Milagro

$$n = \frac{88000(0.5)(0.5)}{\frac{(88000-1)0.05^2}{1.96^2} + (0.5*0.5)} = 383 \; people$$

3.2   Analysis

According to the question made to the citizens of Milagro, about the knowledge that they have *about the services offered by the Citizen Portal of the IRS through the Electronic Government*, the same one that seeks to analyze the knowledge *about the services of the Citizen Portal of the IRS* that the citizens have. It was carried out in the City of Milagro with 100 people and showed the following results: 3% of the respondents stated that they know a lot about the IRS citizen portal, while 7% knows pretty much, on the other hand, 23% reveals that they know about this citizen portal on a regular basis, while the 45% knows little, and 22% does not know anything on this topic.

To know what services people would like to find in the IRS Citizen Portal on the Internet, the respective question was asked to the citizens of Milagro, delivered the following results that 36% of the respondents wish to find the online consultation service, 14% preferred the online consultation service, while 21% would like to find the document verification in the IRS Portal, the next result with 29% of visitors who agreed to enter the IRS Citizen Portal and others did not comment.

By asking the question if the Citizen Portal of the IRS of the Electronic Government has been used, in which it has carried out some type of Procedures, Requests or Online Services, its purpose is: to analyze the use that is given in the IRS Citizen Portal, in which the following results were obtained: where 5% said that they use a lot of citizen portals to do some type of procedure, requests or services online, 7% said that they use it some of the time, on the other hand 19% do it in a regular manner. On the other hand, a considerable 42% use it a little and 27% mention that IRS citizen portal is not used at all.

The main objective of question four is to analyze the frequency of visits in the IRS citizen portal that is offered through the e-government system. Obtaining that: 5% visit the IRS citizen's website a lot, 6% visit it some of the time, 23% visit it regularly, while a considerable 51% do it very little, providing a final result with 15% that don't do anything with the IRS citizen portal through e-government.

9% of citizens said that the IRS citizen portal is easy to access, 15% claimed that access to the portal is easy, 43% mentioned that access is very regular, while 25% stated that little, providing a final result with 8% that access is not easy. The main objective of this section is to analyze the accessibility of citizens in the Information of the IRS Citizen Portal, by asking the question: *Do you consider that the service provided by the IRS Citizen Portal regarding the use of information is easy to access?*

Have you consulted online in the IRS Citizen Portal to find out about a topic of your interest? The sixth question of the survey where the following results were obtained: it was noted that 6% have made a lot of online consultations, an 8% have done a lot of consulting, 26% do it regularly, while 33% do so little and 30% don't consult online with the IRS Citizen Portal of any kind. The main objective is to analyze if the citizen has made interesting consultations in the IRS Citizen Portal.

In question seven, are you aware of the security measures that the IRS Citizen Portal offers regarding the protection of your personal data? Of the 100 respondents, the results were as follows: 9% are very aware of the security of your data entered in the IRS portal, 9% are quite aware, 16% are regularly updated, while 29% are a little aware and a large percentage with 37% know nothing about the security of their data in the portal. Obtaining the main objective: to analyze if citizens know about the protection of data in the IRS Citizen Portal.

Do you agree that the service provided by the IRS Citizen Portal helps in saving time and money as it does not have to personally attend the entity to request information about any procedure or consultation? In question eight, they asked in the survey, the following result was obtained: 23% expressed that the use of this portal helps a lot in saving time and money, 12% said that most of the time, 18% mentioned that regular, while 22% mentioned that little is saved and 31% think that it doesn't help anything in terms of saving time when requesting information about a procedure or consultation in the IRS Citizen Portal. The results demonstrate the stated objective: to know the opinion of the citizenship about whether the IRS portal helps a lot in saving time and money.

To know the participation of the citizens regarding the use of the IRS Citizen Portal through technology, it was asked if it is favorable for you to continue using the SRI Citizen Portal for better participation with the citizens and the Government using technology. Obtaining that 21% inclined that, if it is necessary to use more of this portal since it is very favorable, instead 39% said they used it some of the time, on the other hand, 18% mentioned that it favors it in a regular way, while 14% mentioned that it is unfavorable and 8% considered that the use of the IRS Citizen Portal is not favorable. The main objective was to know the participation of citizens with respect to the use of the IRS Citizen Portal through technology.

Do you consider that the use of Technologies through e-government contributes to the development of the City of Milagro? Whose objective is to analyze if the electronic government contributes to the development of the City.

In this last question, the citizens of Milagro mentioned the following: 35% said that the use of technologies contributes a lot to the development of the City, 37% said it was used most of the time, 13% mentioned that was used on a regular basis, while the 12% mentioned that the contribution is low and 3% think that the implementation of technologies through Electronic Government is not favorable.

4 Results and Discussion

4.1 Services Offered by the IRS for the Citizen of Milagro

Given the results of the survey conducted on the citizens of Milagro, it was noted that they were unaware of the services offered by the IRS Portal, where they only considered more relevant, that only line inquiries could be made, but the Director of the IRS Leonardo Orlando, through the WEB Portal, makes available more than 56 services on the Internet, among which stand out: "the issuance of tax documents, bank account records for automatic debits, special discounts for vehicle taxes, online shift requests" [17], as well as the application of smartphones through the mobile IRS, among other innovative services available for the Citizens of Milagro.

Compared to the Country of Peru, where Victor Shiguiyama Superintendent of the National Superintendence of Tax Administration (SUNAT) makes available on the web portal, which also offers the public 26 services online, in: "where they highlight Online queries, Simplified statements, Electronic payment, Consults of shipment status among others" [18]. This suggests that both Government Institutions continue to work to provide better management in online processes.

It is clear that the Citizens of Milagro and the other cities, parishes, provinces and the rest of the country can make use of the different services that can be done in the IRS Citizen Portal for their respective purposes.

4.2 Usefulness of the IRS Web Portal for the Citizens of Milagro

The results issued by Milagros Citizens indicate that they do not use the IRS portal for any type of service because they may not consider that: *"to use the services of the Web Portal, it is necessary to have an identification and access code to enter the system, and to be able to receive tax benefits through online management"* [17]. That is, for the citizens of Milagro before making use of these services, they must be registered in the IRS System to be able to receive all the tax benefits, and thus carry out any procedure, request or online management.

Therefore, according to studies of the report of the International Tax Organization carried out by Noti, (2010) [19], it indicates that the countries that adopt it are: "Argentina, Bolivia, Peru, Colombia, Chile, United States, among others, also they have Systems for the entrance to their Web Portal", so that citizens can make use of the services, by means of the Identification and access key and to carry out the tax administrations.

4.3   Data Protection in the Citizen Portal of the IRS-SII

In addition, in the results issued by the citizens of Milagro, a very low percentage was noted in terms of the lack of knowledge about the security measures that must be taken for the Protection of Data in the IRS Web Portal, therefore, the terms of use of the portal stipulate that, the information that we issue to the IRS system, *"is protected from access by third parties with SSL certifications (Secure Socket Layer), reimbursed through the protection of the Regulations as stipulated by the National Constitution of Ecuador in order to maintain the confidentiality of its users"* [20].

In Chile, more emphasis is being given, through the Internal Revenue Service (SII), where they focus on protecting and ensuring the information that users issue on their Web Portal, where *"they have implemented the SSL system that encrypts the information, so that it is impossible to decipher through the network, helping to better control the protection of personal data"*.

Now it is clear to us that the information that is issued by the IRS Portal is protected so that other people cannot use it for another purpose, always taking into account the regulations and laws in accordance with the Constitution of Ecuador with regard to Protection of Personal Data.

4.4   Electronic Government Plan in Ecuador and Uruguay

Through the National Electronic Government Plan, 2016 [3] its main objective is *"to improve the way of relating to the four main actors (the Government, citizens, the productive sector and public servants), to eliminate the different barriers of communication and reinforcing relationships and links through the use of technology in this globalized world, obtaining a close, open, efficient and effective electronic government"*, for which they are working to improve the management in the public administration, and to be able to use the different technological tools that the electronic government brings, to speed up the managements and to promote the saving of the time and money, when doing it over the internet. Ecuador, according to the World Ranking of Electronic Government of 2016, is in position 74 of the 193 countries in which the Electronic Government is being implemented.

In the same way, other South American countries are promoting the Electronic Government, one of them, which leads in South America is Uruguay, positioning itself in the 34th place according to the World Ranking of Electronic Government, where the organism for the implementation of the electronic government in Uruguay(AGESIC) has established among its main objectives: *"a modern, effective and efficient public administration, digital by default, a close, quality and homogeneous citizen attention throughout the public administration, the good use of information technologies, extending the limits of the State"* [21], in which a lot of work is being done to contribute to the development of the country, making most of the use of new technologies offered by the Electronic Government to Citizens.

Furthermore, to collaborate with our country, in which Milagro citizens are part of it, what the Internal Revenue Service is doing according to the alignment of the National Plan for Good Living (PNBV) is *"Strengthening the progressivity and efficiency of the tax system"* in accordance with the National Plan for Good Living, 2017.

That is to say that what is intended is to be able to extend a greater participation by the Citizens, thus increasing the tax contribution, so that processes can be optimized and tax spending can be reduced with each one of its internet services.

4.5   Electronic Government and the Contribution for the City of Milagro

In this last part, where the Citizen of Milagro responded that it would contribute in a great way in the development of the City so that they continue using the technological tools, therefore, studies carried out by the Citizen Channel in Quito indicate that the IRS "since February 24, 2012, the date on which the new electronic billing scheme began, until now, 2,670,141,991 electronic vouchers have been issued. This has made it possible to avoid cutting 347,118 trees by not requiring paper bills" [22], which would greatly help the development and economy of the City of Milagro, and environmental conservation.

We conclude our analysis indicating that the different Public Institutions of the Government, work with the same approach of giving an effective service for the public administration to the Citizens, by means of the employment of the different technological tools that the electronic government brings, because encouraging the culture 'zero paperwork', which will also provide economic benefits for both our city and the rest of the country.

To the citizens of Milagro, it is necessary to inform them more about all the benefits that e-Government brings, so that there may be a greater participation in helping the government in the development and improvement of the Economy of the Country.

5   Conclusions and Recommendations

5.1   Conclusions

E-government is a fundamental tool for the development of Ecuador, because it is allowing to form a link with the different actors such as: government and civil society, through ICTs. The citizen portal of the IRS has made available different services for tax management through the Internet, providing benefits to the citizens at any time.

According to the analysis made from the data obtained in the survey, it was found that the use of the services provided by the Institutional Portals of this State dependency to the citizens helps people in such a way that processes can be streamlined, fast and effective way, thus encouraging the saving of time and money.

The IRS being an Institution that offers services to the citizens through its Web Portal, is driven to reduce the use of physical documents, thus increasing digital documents, to help in the conservation and preservation of the environment.

It is also expected that the socialization of this study will promote the use of electronic government in other government entities that could provide this service virtually, as is the case of judicial registration inquiries, municipal procedures, among others.

The terms and policies regarding the protection of data held by the Government Citizen Portals are governed by the Electronic Commerce and Data Messages Act and other related regulations, all protected by the National Constitution of Ecuador to guarantee integrity, confidentiality and availability of the data that citizens have access to.

5.2 Recommendations

The Government should make people aware, about the different services offered by citizen portals on the Internet, for the benefit of citizens.

Raise awareness among citizens to use technological means so that they can carry out any online management, through the different services offered by citizen government portals.

The Internal Revenue Service should promote, through training by the use of the different media, the services offered on the web for better citizen participation, thus helping to increase the rate of electronic government in Ecuador.

The government institutions should provide training to citizens in order to make them aware of laws, regulations and articles, which allow the citizen to feel a backup with respect to the security of personal information, which is issued to each one of the government's public institutions that offers its services through the Internet.

Encourage the citizens of Milagro through seminars, training, etc., to save paper and reduce the percentage of the use of physical documents by electronic ones, for the conservation of the environment.

References

1. AICD: OEA, Gobierno Electrónico en las ORGANIZACIONES DE ESTADOS AMERICANOS, pp. 25–28 (2006)
2. de Armas Urquiza, R., de Armas Suárez, A.: Fases y Dimensiones del Gobierno Electrónico (2011). http://www.eumed.net/rev/cccss/13/auas.htm
3. E. Plan Nacional Gobierno Electrónico: Objetivos y Estrategias, Lineamientos PNBV (2016). https://www.gobiernoelectronico.gob.ec/wp-content/uploads/downloads/2016/12/Plan-Gobierno-Electro%CC%81nico-2017.pdf
4. Barragán-Martínez, X., Guevara-Viejó, F.: El gobierno electrónico en Ecuador, vol. 9, no. 19, pp. 110–127 (2016)
5. Vargas Díaz, C.D.: El Gobierno Electrónico o e-Gobierno, vol. 11, no. 1 (2011)
6. Diéguez, G., Gasparín, J.M., Sánchez, J., Schejtman, L.: Escenarios y perspectivas del gobierno electrónico en América Latina y el Caribe, CIPPEC (2015)
7. CEPAL: Modelo multi-dimensional de medición del gobierno electrónico para América Latina y el Caribe, Colección Documentos de Proyectos. Naciones Unidas-CEPAL (2007)
8. OCDE: Utilización de las TIC en el sector público (2003)
9. Secretaría Nacional de la Administración Pública: Plan Nacional de Gobierno Electrónico 2017. http://www.administracionpublica.gob.ec/
10. Castillo, C.: La simplificación de trámites ciudadanos Ecuador. El Ecuador sostenible y las Tics, pp. 45–55 (2016)
11. Arias Zambrano, J.W., Laica Guzmán, S.E.: Análisis de la Implementación del Gobierno Electrónico en Ecuador, Politécnica del Litoral, pp. 20–29 (2015)
12. Rodríguez, G.S.: Gobierno Electrónico: Hacia la modernización y transparencia de la gestión pública, REVISTA DE DERECHO. UNIVERSIDAD DEL NORTE, vol. 21, pp. 1–23 (2011)

13. S.J.A.: The creative response in economic history. J. Econ. Hist. **7**, 149–159
14. CAF: Sector TIC ECUADOR (2013)
15. Calderón Contreras, A.: Situación de la Educación Rural en Ecuador (2015)
16. Brys, C.: Plan estratégico para el Gobierno Electrónico de la Provincia de Misiones. Argentina, Editorial Universitaria de Misiones (2014)
17. Orlando, L.: GOBIERNO ELECTRÓNICO Y SUS INCIDENCIAS (2016). www.sri.gob.ec
18. Sunat, P.: Términos de uso del portal web (2017). http://www.sunat.gob.pe/
19. Noti, F.: INFORME ORGANISMOS TRIBUTARIOS INTERNACIONALES (2010). http://www.noticiasfiscais.com.br/2006/03/29/organismos-tributarios-internacionales/
20. SRI: Términos Generales de Uso del Portal WEB Ecuador (2017). http://www.sri.gob.ec/web/guest/home
21. Agesic, U.: AGESIC (2017). https://www.agesic.gub.uy/innovaportal/v/33/1/agesic/que-es-agesic.html?idPadre=19
22. El Ciudadano, E.: Medio oficial de la revolución ciudadana (2017). http://www.elciudadano.gob.ec/116898/
23. Sii, C.: Servicio de Impuestos Internos (2017). https://zeus.sii.cl/admin/pagina_segura.html
24. Administración Pública del Ecuador: Gobierno Electrónico en la Administración Pública (2015). http://www.administracionpublica.gob.ec/wp-content/uploads/downloads/2016/04/Gobierno-Electronico-23-12-2015.pdf. (Último acceso: 25 enero 2017)
25. ONU: Definición Gobierno Electrónico (1986). http://www.un.org/es/index.html
26. Mariano Gálvez, G.: Gobierno Electrónico (2016). https://amcohorte1.files.wordpress.com/2016/02/mc3b3dulo-a-unidad-1.pdf. (Último acceso: 6 febrero 2017)
27. Jorge Troya, F.: Sucesos del Gobierno Electrónico (2015). https://www.registrocivil.gob.ec/?p=4848. (Último acceso: 19 enero 2017)
28. Nacimba, A.: Ranking Países que implementan Gobierno Electrónico (2016). http://www.elciudadano.gob.ec/ecuador-avanza-en-el-ranking-de-gobierno-electronico/
29. E. Servicio de Rentas Internas, Servicios Oficiales Portal SRI (2017).http://www.sri.gob.ec/web/guest/detalle?idnoticia=392&marquesina=1. (Último acceso: 28 enero 2017)
30. Sancho Royo, D.: Gobierno electrónico y participación. Factores de éxito para su desarrollo Reforma y Democracia, Reforma y Democracia, Revista del CLAD, pp. 25–100 (2002)

Analysis of e-Government Strategy Implementation in Ecuador

Galo Enrique Valverde Landívar[✉]

Universidad Politécnica Salesiana, Campus Guayaquil, Guayaquil, Ecuador
gvalverde@ups.edu.ec

Abstract. E-Government is a comprehensive process of improvement of State management, the following is an analysis of the inclusion of the strategy, and the roles that have played the political sector, Academy, civil society, and development achieved on the implementation in the public sector within the planning of Ecuador, with a comparison of successful models in Latin America, to determine how necessary is the change of management and the transformations of the State in the construction of an organizational model to achieve its full operation.

Keywords: State · Strategy · e-Government

1 Introduction

The unique and ever-changing nature of the internet not only enables individuals to exercise their right of opinion and expression but also form part of their human rights and promotes the progress of society as a whole. Unlike other media, the accessibility of internet allows anyone in the world to disseminate their ideas.

However, not all people have access to this technology. The General Assembly of the United Nations in June 2011 stated: *"Governments should strive.... for making the Internet widely available, accessible and affordable for all (...)"* Ensure universal access to the internet should be a priority of all Governments"; and *"the internet as a means to exercise the right to freedom of expression only can serve these purposes if States assume their commitment to develop effective policies to achieve universal access"*.

While the UN declared access to internet as a human right, and also as a means to exercise the right to freedom of expression, in Ecuador according to 2013 census, the 65% of Ecuadorians have access to Internet, and for 2011 it drew 37 over 100 free expression on the internet. It is clear that it's necessary to shorten the "digital divide"[1], most democratizing the access and use of the Internet.

The Internet is one of the technological tools that are necessary for the implementation of e-Government, through this technology, processes and transactions in a more optimal and transparent manner helping citizens to carry a greater control over the State's economy, also special public management to avoid and fight corruption, but not

---

[1] Digital divide: Gap between social groups with regard to access and the use of information and communication technologies.

© Springer Nature Switzerland AG 2019
M. Botto-Tobar et al. (Eds.): CITT 2018, CCIS 895, pp. 697–706, 2019.
https://doi.org/10.1007/978-3-030-05532-5_53

everyone has connection and access to a community or citizenship to integrate into the new model of management, it is necessary to answer these questions: Why do you want to be connected? How will you use this technology? How will its appropriation become a tool for development? How will you train people? To enhance E-Government in our midst strategies of training promoting citizen participation should be designed [1].

The political powers, business management and mass media rest on scientific and technological pillars. The life of the ordinary citizen is also greatly influenced by these advances. The promotion of social technological studies, from the 60's should be understood as a response to the social and intellectual challenges that have become evident in the second half of the 20th century.

The reform of the State is the implementation of changes that embrace various dimensions, which are related to public institutions, the political system, governmental organizations running public policies and State relations with the market and civil society. *"The process of reform of the State produces a redefinition of their relations with society (of the State); It is an eminently political process, through which you are configuring the relations of power in societies"* [2].

On the other hand, the modernization of the State relates to the process of adopting measures that would seek to achieve the values of modernity, suitable to public management. The *"... Modernity is, fundamentally, human progress, on a human scale, with positive results for all human beings"*, then the modernization would be an instrument by means of which leads to the State of modernity, where *"... everything is modern or is the central component of social reality"* [3].

The modernization of public management its understood as the incorporation of new approaches of business nature, such as Benchmarking, reengineering, Outsourcing, whose purpose was to overcome the bureaucratic administration that characterized the countries least developed [4].

E-Government is much more than just technology; It is the possibility that provide IT[2] resources to encourage the Government to reach more citizens by providing information, spaces for interaction and participation for collective discussion to increase citizen participation.

Sancho [5] defines elements that characterize "good governance": democratic legitimacy characterized by its ability to respond to the demands and expectations of citizens, respect for laws, transparency in public affairs, political and public managers responsible for their actions against citizens and greater participation and involvement of citizens in public affairs.

Under these concepts, what has been done by the Ecuadorian Government in regards to e-Government is part of the modernization of the State. Today, more and more habitants of Ecuador register on the Internet, with faster broadband connections and increased use of smartphones. It's also seen increasingly on line the need to express their personal views on many topics in social media platforms more popular such as Facebook, Twitter, YouTube, as well as discussion blogs and forums for public and private companies [6].

---

[2] IT: Information Technologies.

National Electronic Government Plan driven by the National Secretariat of Public Administration (SNAP) in Ecuador is based on efforts and awareness-raising for the citizen participation. The Government intends to expand and strengthen the efforts and experiment with new ways to harness the wisdom and resources of the citizens. In addition, the technology community (public and private companies) aims to facilitate and promote dialogue among these groups, through the use of virtual platforms for participation and class instances as working groups, workshops and seminars.

Another issue to consider is the use of free Software, which is becoming more encouraged in the countries of Latin America since it represents a step forward for the sovereignty of these countries, allowing the use of the four freedoms that free Software provides. Its philosophy is based on the collaborative work of a community of software development that enables an application, based on the concept that knowledge is free and should be shared with an articulated and evolutionary work.

The four freedoms concern:

1. Freedom to run the program as you wish.
2. Freedom to study the program source code and make the changes that are required according to the needs of the end user.
3. Freedom to distribute the program to others, i.e. to create exact copies of the program and distribute them free of charge or with the freedom to sell the development. These two options are allowed by the community.
4. Freedom to contribute to the community. Make copies of the modified versions and distribute them to others.

2   Referential Framework

The concept of citizen has to evolve according to the development of society and the "times signs", not just "our interpretation of reality". The companies are facing a process of symbiosis and hegemony of concepts such as "Big Data", "Expert systems", "Virtual reality" and "Artificial Intelligence". It is also important to remember that what characterizes novelty is that we have a technological system that revolutionizes the forms of information processing and communication and transforms the way we live and communicate between us. Internet requires one much larger cultural and educational level of user development. Therefore, the true gap in relation to the use of the internet is the oldest gap of humanity: culture and education. "Those more educated in the era of the internet increase their capacity for action on the society and themselves" [7].

Authentic human development has a moral character and assumes full respect for the person that is integral maintaining the nature and context of each being and their social relations therefore the concept of modern citizen to make them active and participatory should embrace the complexity of all these aspects. We are now facing a "dumbing down the subject" and "numerical disruption" in this new society with a (virtual) disarranged reality that removes room for critical thinking.

This new "social complexity" manifests itself mainly in a restructuring accelerated labor market, in the expansion and diversification of educational demand and the differentiation of the structure of the education system. Each of these orientations may describe elements or perspectives, positive or negative, but in either case, it is directed towards the realization of a structure of the subject and society. While the Latin American University gives greater importance to applied research, not only on the financial issue, but because you are looking for the development of the region, in the academic world they have begun to appreciate in the same terms as basic research.

It is important to remember that "what characterizes this new? is that we have a technological system that revolutionizes the forms of information processing and communication and transforms the way we live and communicate between us..." Those more educated in the era of the internet increasing its capacity for action on the society and themselves [7].

The framework of Good Living National Plan (PNBV) of Ecuador establishes a national long-term strategy, which seeks to diversify the productive matrix. On the other hand, the National Plan of Development 2013–2017 sets the strategy for the reduction of poverty, to support and facilitate these two great national interests, where the State should improve their management and the quality of its services, in which the use of the information technology and communications (TIC) becomes a key factor.

In the National Plan of e-Government of Ecuador: "*Article 1.-e-Government-the implementation of e-Government in the public administration Central, institutional and depending on the Executive function, which consists in the use of the information and communication technologies by the entities to transform relations with citizens, government agencies and private companies in order to improve the quality of government services to citizens, promote the interaction with private enterprises, strengthen citizen participation through access to information and Government services efficient and effective and contribute to transparency, participation and cooperation of citizens*" [8].

Related to this strategy, the broad legal framework, regulatory and instructional officers that are in force in Ecuador, are:

- Electronic commerce, electronic signatures and data messages Law
- National Plan of e-Government 2014–2017
- General of the Organic Law of transparency and access to the information[3]
- Executive Decree 1014 regulation standards and free Open Software
- Executive Decree 1384 and rules of interoperability
- Executive Decree No 867 of electronic signature
- Executive Decree 149, E-governance and simplification of procedures
- Agreement 166, Information Security Scheme
- WEB accessibility (NTE INEN-ISO/IEC 40500)
- Agreement of Constitution and Operation of e-Government Observatory
- Agreement for dissemination of knowledge public, free and/or open
- Standardization WEB sites Normative
- Open Data Normative
- Software public regulation Normative
- Hot Spots Normative
- Quality Regulation Normative
- Technical Normative of Services Management

---

[3] LOTAIP Regulation: Executive Decree N° 2471, Official Register N° 507 of January 19 of 2005.

- IT Government Normative
- Cloud Standards Use Normative
- Digital Unique Identity Normative
- Content of training Regulations Normative
- Citizen Participation Mechanisms Normative
- One-stop Usability Regulatory Normative

Likewise, in April 2008, the President of Ecuador, signed the Decree 1014 which Free Software happens to be a State policy, to be adopted by all entities. The President stated *"this way the guidelines of the Government, which sets policy for the Central Administration the use of free Software in all of its instances are met"*. Under this Free Software Decree allows access to the source code and improve applications. Which is a greater computer security, free access to data and programs, savings in the licensing cost, and the employment generation for our Ecuadorian professionals, as well as frees us from software tools dependence produced by big transnational.

3 Methods

The growth that has had access to the internet in Ecuador in recent years, thanks to the applied State policies are significant at the regional level; 32.8% of all households nationwide have internet access, 10.3 points more than four years ago, in the urban area growth is 9.6 points, while in rural areas of 8.9 points [9].

It is important the analysis of all web portals within this strategy, enabling to carry out all the administrative procedures, such as: public procurement, document management (Quipux), taxes and electronic invoice (SRI), loans and medical appointments (IESS), municipal instances (payment of taxes), inter institutional public e-mailing service (Zimbra), etc. in search of a guaranteed higher level of availability, reliability, and usability.

It also verifies the existence of Management by Results (GPR) website, with detailed WHAT? and very detailed rates, as well as training courses for citizens and public employees, for a real monitoring of the implementation of this public policies and appropriate assessment and accountability for those responsible.

The possibility of obtaining technological tools that can be modified and adapted without restrictions and that are also free of payment of licensing represents an opportunity to lower costs that represent the use of proprietary systems. In addition, by having access to the source code of the operating systems you can learn in depth the behavior of computer programs in order to alter its functioning and to make adaptations to the particular needs.

Increasingly the countries concerned to adopt technologies of free software in public administration institutions since it represents the opportunity to have equitable access to technologies of information and communication and the opportunity to promote the technological development.

In the case of Brazil, it became world reference for being the first government carried out a massive deployment of free software in public administration. Free software is within strategic e-Government projects and is a strategic option for the Federal Government to reduce costs, increase competition, create employment and develop the knowledge and intelligence of the country.

4 Results

Based on the Decree 1014 "Use of Free Software", it is important to note that the website of the Public Procurement System (SERCOP) was built entirely with free software tools and developed by professional 100% Ecuadorian, showing the possibilities and technological capabilities committed to the progress of the country.

Is presented a comparisons (See Table 1) of the administrative systems and it solutions used for public procurement portals (references) from Chile, Peru and Ecuador, highlighting the important differences in the handling of the issue.

Table 1. Comparative public procurement between Chile, Peru and Ecuador Portals

Country	Characteristic	Benefit	Drawback
chile compra	Portal **http://www.chilecompra.cl/** related information to bind to the buyers (State entities), providers with training providers (PYMES). Very focused and Agile for a person concerned.	Specialized web pages: Mercadopublico tender's platform analyzes business opportunities, buyers, and planning stock Chileproveedores, register them and their training. Comprassustentables.CL, room improvements in procurement processes	Maintenance and update
SERCE OSCE	Portal http://www2.seace.gob.pe/ have information related to purchases that are State entities, providing information - training providers. The order that has been raised does not provide the information that one wants to.	www.osce.gob.pe for the registration, monitoring, training of consultants, executors of works and suppliers of goods and services of the State.	Incorporate the established procedures, provide security, privacy and registration criteria in the design of web pages. Administration, maintenance and upgrade of IT in charge of services and interoperability between them. Adaptation of services so that transactions can be carried out from anywhere in the country.
Compras	Portal http://portal.compraspublicas.gob.ec/incop/ It has all the information related to purchases of all public entities. It has a user-centered agile distribution, whether this vendor or contractor	It is governed by the SERCOP (public procurement Undersecretary) and sections associated with suppliers, contracting entities and certification of competencies. It requires an electronic certification for transactions and is under constant review.	Failure to integrate mechanisms of digital or electronic invoice and interoperation with other systems

5 Discussion

In Ecuador there have been achieved great advances in the implementation of e-Government in some State institutions, processes that are possible through a change in the conception of the State model. The democratization of information and the impact of ICT in recent years, show that they have ceased to be an exclusive and luxury, service to gradually become a tool needed as a priority within the society.

Entire organization seeks efficiency in their management, and in the case of e-Government, this should be positioned as a bridge between the State (governmental institutions) and society (citizens), that helps to break down barriers of bureaucracy and the public workers fulfil their vocation of the service and commitment to citizenship.

To the extent that those spaces are strengthen decreases the distance between the State and the citizens, creating a new concept among the Government-Citizen. It could be said that applying fully the phases of e-Government, we could have more efficiency, transparency, and participation that are the foundations for improved governance.

E-Government is often part of a more comprehensive reform process of the State. It is not an end per se? but an essential tool for the treatment of the information that the State manages and produces, depending on Government decisions. E-Government plays a fundamental role in which are involved many countries in the region today.

The main aspects of the modernization of public management are defined around five axes [10]:

5. **User.** The modernization of public management raised to establish public institutions a clearly customer-oriented management style, to create a culture of citizens, not subjects.
6. **Public official.** In addition, the modernization process started would pose as one of its essential aspects to dignify the public functions and put them at the service of users. The core was that public servants feel not mere employees but that they felt as public servants with a clear vocation of service.
7. **Results-oriented management.** Management, the modernization of the public administration was a new type of management oriented to the achievement of results, flexible, responsible and appropriate use of scarce public resources.
8. **Effective and efficient use of resources.** The current situation in the State would require a public sector where the actions of managers and public servants is within the good use of resources, which would increase efficiency levels involved in public policies and institutional operation of the State.
9. **Strengthening of public ethics.** Without a doubt, an aspect of particular relevance says relationship with the public servant's behavior in exercise and performance of his charges. The ethics of the public service must always look towards the interest of the citizens. Its strengthening is associated with the common good, and its consolidation is a matter of State.

Key actors in the implementation of this strategy of e-Government are the leaders in e-government policies and technologies of the information of the public and private institutions (CIO). The feedback on the progress on an ongoing basis, at the time that will facilitate the dissemination and implementation of initiatives within their organizations to e-Government.

In the case of Ecuador, we are developing an intense Plan for the implementation of e-Government. The most recent covers a time period from 2014 to 2017. It's one of the best plans, in terms of the detail that has in its planning, whereas the cost for the implementation thereof featured a great diagnosis prior to the implementation in Ecuador, as well as the potential opportunities and challenges in the country.

However, as they stand out in the work, the lack of a National Plan until very recently has made some administrations to initiate its implementation alone. They are now with the hard work of coordinating new strategies for the implementation of the Plan. This, moreover, has made highlighted the lack of interoperability between public institutions, as well as specific training for those responsible. Finally, it is essential to involve the citizen and bridging the digital divide.

One of the main actions that can be adopted for the coordination of the different sectors is to enable both virtual and physical communication channels that the debate and the immediate involvement of those involved in the implementation.

In addition, should an ambitious plan bring the necessary technology to all regions devoid? Thus reducing the digital divide and actions could be undertaken from the institutions to train citizens in the use of TIC and its benefits for participation in public affairs.

In terms of constraints, it is very difficult that citizens become involved to 100% in the participation and collaboration work initiated by the institutions, so the tasks of marketing and education are fundamental.

The issue of the use of Free Software in the public administration, is one of the most explored to date. The experiences of the region to larger scale have been held in government areas.

This breaks the paradigm of eternal technological dependence that have proprietary software, which is required, not just pay the fee for use of a license, but that any adaptation of the application depends on the maintenance agreement signed with the provider, because proprietary software providers reserve knowledge of the architecture and features of the programs offered.

6 Conclusions

It is important to highlight the growth that the access to internet in Ecuador has had in recent years, thanks to the applied State policies. It's time to integrate services for bridging the digital divide with vision of State and appropriate solutions with professionals trained for this new reality pictures.

However, there is a difference between the performance between these portals and the different public institutions, where they are ones with positive results in management and others with opportunities for significant improvement in these aspects.

E-Government provides for a participatory community and officials, multi-sectoral approach with different governmental bodies O agencies? and conformation of multidisciplinary teams in the development of its different phases and processes.

It is necessary for e-government initiatives to promote public services and information to citizens through ICTs. The idea is that citizens can interact with Government and public entities by any means that provides you access, anywhere, all the time. The main benefit of this relationship model is that it has tools and mechanisms that allow to strengthen the powers of the servants and public servants.

Ecuador seeks a change of the productive matrix; that, in practice, extends to a great quality problem projecting, mainly from within the organizations out, focusing on aspects such as the relationships with customers or external bodies, decision making management and productivity.

The most important and which characterizes the strategy of e-Government is measurement of the participation of citizens in all its phases, as well as transparency.

In the analysis found, moreover, that it is necessary to formalize a scheme of Government of ICTs that allow establish, align, formalize, strengthen and implement in a coordinated manner, the actions related to information technologies, based on the COBIT model.

On the other hand, the absence of a culture of information assets and corporate data was found as weakness. This, added to a decentralized system of information security.

Each country and Government presents different levels of focus in the implementation of e-government programmers; however, should remember that information technologies have to adapt to international standards in its application and use.

Among other issues to be considered are the interoperability of all administrative levels and all public services falling within its competence, and data portals and their compliance with all the requirements of open data (Open Data).

Also, there should be a plan for regional interoperability of e-Government whose determinants must come from acting in the common environment restrictions identified in the study of the experiences of e-governance and interoperability in the countries of Latin America and Caribbean. This requires unified languages and manages common metadata, using international standards.

There is a shallow level in the conceptualization of the model of the information society, and their relationship and connection with other government bodies.

It is still required the management of change and transformations of the State in the construction of an organizational model and full functioning of e-Government, provide:

- Integration and interaction between the different ministries and Government agencies
- Standards and common standards availability
- Management model that includes best practices, actions and citizen services.

The equipment have the Mission of efficiently manage all the technology that is available, aiming to provide quality services to all the users and clients both internal and external; for this you need the selection and adoption of best practices for technology management (ITIL and COBIT) integral to the entire public sector for the creation of value, and in search of continuous improvement that permit to guarantee the continuity, availability, and quality of the service.

We must also consider in an alternate study all of these dependencies between systems, and the level of direct interaction with the users, to raise collateral and transversal aspects as risks of security at all levels, and environmental factors, as determining elements of certain projects within this new model of management.

To promote the objectives of "Buen Vivir" (Good Living or welfare) in Ecuador, the current circumstances require us to take advantage of all technology resources available to provide development opportunities to all citizens, since the social advancement of a country depends on the talent that each one can contribute from their workstations.

It is necessary that public companies make a rethinking of their roles and services, on the basis of a portfolio of them, and arrive to become real instruments to local and national economic development.

It obliges to a change of organizational culture, putting aside interests of power, to support synergies and develop support processes to prepare for smart grid technology, which means to reorganize and upgrade the network, improve collection and management of technical information, enabling the analysis of the operation, and the standardization of systems within the public sector.

References

1. CONFERENCE 2016, LNCS, vol. 9999, pp. 1–13. Springer, Heidelberg (2016)
2. Mejia, A.: E-Government a nivel del país, Ingenius Núm. 3, pp. 73–76 (2008)
3. Fleury, S.: Reforma del estado: del proyecto liberal a una agenda social, Instituciones y Desarrollo No 14–15, pp. 81–121, (2003)
4. Ramirez, L.: Política y modernización del estado en Chile: 1990–1996. Instituto de Ciencia Política de la Universidad de Chile, Santiago de Chile (1997)
5. Molina, K.D.: Síntesis del proceso de modernización del estado en Chile (1994–2003), Documentos de Apoyo Docente no. 6, p. 34 (2006)
6. Royo, S.: Gobernar en la era del conocimiento: nuevas oportunidades, viejos peligros, The Role oh Humanity in the Information Age: An Ibero-American Perspective, pp. 1–13 (2002)
7. Rivero, B.A.y.M.: Experiencias andinas de gobierno electrónico, FLACSO-Sede Ecuador, p. 131 (2007)
8. Secretaria Nacional de Administración Pública, Plan Nacional de Gobierno Electrónico Ecuador 2014–2017. SNAP, Quito (2014)
9. INEC: Encuesta Nacional de Empleo Desempleo y Subempleo – ENEMDU (2012–2015). INEC, Quito (2016)
10. Orellana, P.: Contra la Burocracia, Apuntes de clases de la asignatura Ciencia de la Administración, p. 131 (2003)

Author Index

Printed in the United States
by Bookmasters

Printed in the United States
By Bookmasters